THE HIDDEN PLACES OF

ENGLAND

By Peter Long

© Travel Publishing Ltd.

Published by: Travel Publishing Ltd, 64-66 Ebrington Street, Plymouth, Devon PL4 9AQ

ISBN13 9781904434733

© Travel Publishing Ltd

First published 1998, second edition 2000, third edition 2002, fourth edition 2004, fifth edition 2006, sixth edition 2008

Printing by: Ashford Colour Press, Gosport

Maps by: ©Maps in Minutes ™ (2008) All rights reserved. ©Collins Bartholomews 2008 All rights reserved.

Editor: Peter Long

Cover Design: Lines and Words, Aldermaston

Cover Photograph: Scotney Castle, nr Lamberhurst, Kent
© www.picturesofbritain.co.uk

Text Photographs: © www.picturesofbritain.co.uk
and © Bob Brooks, Weston super Mare
www.britainhistoricsites.co.uk

Foreword

This is the 6th edition of the *Hidden Places of England* which has been fully updated. In this respect we would like to thank the Tourist Information Centres in England for helping us update the editorial content. The guide is packed with information on many interesting places to visit within each county. You will find comprehensive details of places of interest as well as advertisers of places to stay, eat and drink included under each village, town or city which are cross referenced to more detailed information in a separate, easy-to-use section to the rear of the guide.

The *Hidden Places* series is a collection of easy to use local and national travel guides taking you on a relaxed but informative tour of Britain and Ireland. Our books contain a wealth of interesting information on the history, the countryside, the towns and villages and the more established places of interest. But they also promote the more secluded and little known visitor attractions and places to stay, eat and drink many of which are easy to miss unless you know exactly where you are going.

We include hotels, inns, restaurants, public houses, teashops, various types of accommodation, historic houses, museums, gardens, and many other attractions all of which are comprehensively indexed. Most places are accompanied by an attractive photograph and are easily located by using the map at the beginning of each chapter. We do not award merit marks or rankings but concentrate on describing the more interesting, unusual or unique features of each place with the aim of making the reader's stay in the local area an enjoyable and stimulating experience.

Whether you are visiting England for business or pleasure or are a local inhabitant, we do hope that you enjoy reading and using this book. We are always interested in what readers think of places covered (or not covered) in our guides so please do not hesitate to use the reader reaction form provided to give us your considered comments. We also welcome any general comments which will help us improve the guides themselves.

Finally if you are planning to visit any other corner of the British Isles we would like to refer you to the order form for other *Hidden Places* titles to be found at the rear of the book and to the Travel Publishing website at www.travelpublishing.co.uk

Travel Publishing

Did you know that you can also search our website for details of thousands of places to see, stay, eat or drink throughout Britain and Ireland? Our site has become increasingly popular and now receives over 160,000 hits per day. Try it!

website: www.travelpublishing.co.uk

Location Map

Contents

GEOGRAPHICAL AREAS:

ADVERTISEMENTS:

INDEXES AND LISTS:

Bedfordshire

The often overlooked county of Bedfordshire is one of charming typically English villages and small market towns surrounded by a rich rural landscape. Despite their modern appearance, the towns of Luton and Dunstable, in the south of the county, have their roots firmly in the past and it was at Dunstable that Archbishop Cranmer held court in 1533 to dissolve the marriage of Henry VIII and Catherine of Aragon.

The county town of Bedford also has a long history and has strong associations with John Bunyan, who was born nearby. The county is littered with stately homes and old country houses, including the splendid Houghton House, which is widely believed to be the inspiration for the House Beautiful in *Pilgrim's Progress*, and magnificent Woburn Abbey, the seat of the Dukes of Bedford, which is famous for its superb art collection and its Wild Animal Kingdom and Leisure Park. The Abbey is certainly one of the county's finest attractions, but Bedfordshire is also home to Whipsnade Wild Animal Park, the largest centre of conservation in Europe, and the headquarters of the Royal Society for the Protection of Birds (RSPB).

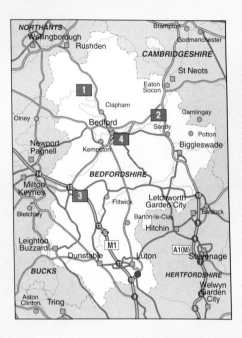

1 THE SUN INN

Felmersham

A pretty-as-a-picture thatched inn that attracts a wide cross-section of locals, walkers, cyclists, tourists and motorists. A new restaurant is in the offing.

 see page 365

2 THE SALUTATION

Blunham

New tenants have brought the good times back to a fine old inn serving a wide choice of drinks and favourite pub dishes.

 see page 366

BEDFORD

Bedford was already a thriving market place before the Norman Conquest but it is for its association with John Bunyan that the town is best known. Born in Elstow, just to the south, Bunyan went into the same trade as his father, a tinsmith, and during the Civil War he was drafted into the Parliamentarian Army. In the 1650s he met John Gifford, the then pastor of the Independent Congregation, and it was their lengthy discussions that led to Bunyan's conversion; he was baptised by Gifford in a backwater leading off the Great Ouse. It was while preaching in the villages of Bedfordshire that Bunyan came into conflict with authority and he served two terms at the County Gaol. During his imprisonment, between 1660-72 he wrote many of his works including his most famous, *Pilgrim's Progress*.

Following his release in 1672, he was elected pastor of the Independent Congregation and built a meeting house that was finally completed in 1707. The church seen today dates from 1849 and now houses the **Bunyan Museum**.

For a greater insight into the history of the town and surrounding area the Bedford Museum is well worth a visit, as is the adjoining **Cecil Higgins Art Gallery** with its internationally renowned collection.

Immediately southeast of Bedford is the village of **Cardington**, home of the Whitbread family of brewing fame. The skyline is dominated by the two giant green hangars that were built to house the airships, including the R100 and R101, which were once thought to be the future of flying. The **Church of St Mary** contains the Whitbread family vault, and across the road from the church is the tomb of the victims of the R101 disaster. The airship crashed in France in 1930; one of those on borad was the Minister for Air, Lord Thomson.

It was from the airfield at Twinwood, near Bedford, in December 1944 that Glen Miller took off in a transport plane to give a concert in Paris. No sign of the plane or its occupants has ever been found.

AROUND BEDFORD

BIGGLESWADE

9½ miles SE of Bedford on the A6001

Biggleswade was the home of Dan Albone, the inventor of the modern bicycle and designer of the first practical tandem and a ladies

God, Gold and Kings Exhibition, Bedford Museum

Swiss Garden, Biggleswade

3 THE ROSE & CROWN

Ridgmont

A charming 300-year-old inn with a warm greeting for all the family, well-kept beers, classic pub dishes, a function room and field for tents and caravans.

 see page 367

4 THE CARPENTERS ARMS & SUNFLOWER RESTAURANT

Cranfield

An attractive village pub with a particularly friendly ambience and a good choice of drinks and classic pub dishes.

 see page 367

cycle with a low crossbar and a skirt guard. He developed a racing cycle, which in 1888 set speed and endurance records with the doughty CP Mills in the saddle. He was also responsible for the Ivel Agricultural Tractor, forerunner of the modern tractor.

To the west of Biggleswade lies **Old Warden**, an enchanting village which was developed in the early 19th century by Sir Robert Ongley who also created the **Swiss Garden**, a romantic fantasy with a tiny thatched Swiss style cottage and arches of creepers. In the grounds of this Jacobean style mansion house, is the fantastic Shuttleworth Collection of historic aircraft.

North of Biggleswade is the headquarters of the **Royal Society for the Protection of Birds**, The Lodge, which is also home to a nature reserve of open heath, woodland and formal gardens.

LUTON

18 miles S of Bedford on the A6

The largest town in Bedfordshire and perhaps best known for its Airport and Vauxhall cars, Luton first prospered in the 17th century on the strength of its straw plaiting and hat making industries. The **Stockwood Craft Museum and Gardens**, housed in a Georgian stable block, provides the opportunity to step back in time; also here is the **Mossman Collection** of over 60 horse-drawn vehicles.

Close by is the magnificent

3

Leighton Buzzard Railway

Park in 1694 and the parkland, landscaped by Capability Brown, is now the **Ampthill Deer Park**. To the east lies **Maulden Woods**, an area of mixed woodland and open meadows with muntjac deer and badgers, while, just to the north is **Houghton House**, reputed to have been the inspiration for the House Beautiful in *Pilgrim's Progress*.

A little further afield is Silsoe and Wrest Park, whose gardens are a living history of English gardening from 1700-1850.

house of **Luton Hoo**, which now houses a superb art collection. Its parkland was landscaped by Capability Brown. To the west of Luton lies **Dunstable**, an important centre in Roman Britain and a busy market town for around 1,000 years. Close by, at **Whipsnade**, is the **Tree Cathedral** (National Trust), where, after World War I, trees were planted in the shape of a cathedral complete with nave, transepts and chancel. **Whipsnade Wild Animal Park** is the country home of the Zoological Society of London and one of Europe's largest wildlife conservation centres.

AMPTHILL

7½ miles SW of Bedford off the A507

A historic town that was a great favourite with Henry VIII but its castle was replaced by Ampthill

LEIGHTON BUZZARD

17½ miles SW of Bedford on the A4012

A prosperous market town where visitors can take a steam train journey on the **Leighton Buzzard Railway** on tracks laid in 1919 to carry sand from the local quarries. The town lies at one end of the Greensand Ridge Walk, which extends for some 40 miles across Bedfordshire to Gamlingay, Cambridgeshire.

WOBURN

12 miles SW of Bedford on the A4012

This originally Saxon hamlet is best known as the home of **Woburn Abbey**, the seat of the Dukes of Bedford. Along with the fantastic art collection and superb furniture in the house, Woburn has an antiques centre and a deer park that is also home to the **Wild Animal Kingdom and Leisure Park**.

Berkshire

The eastern region of the Royal County of Berkshire has been graced for over 900 years by the royal presence at Windsor. The Castle is a magnificent royal residence and Windsor Great Park is what remains of an ancient royal hunting ground. The River Thames, too, plays a part in forming the landscape here, as well as acting as the county border between Oxfordshire, and there are many delightful riverside towns and villages to explore. To the west, at the ancient town of Reading, the county's other principle river, the Kennet, joins the Thames, closely accompanied by the Kennet and Avon Canal. Further westwards is the prosperous old wool town of Newbury, to the north of which are the Berkshire Downs, a rolling area of grassland that contains many prehistoric remains and is also a training ground for racehorses.

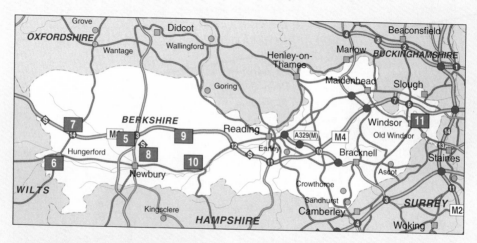

5 THE WINTERBOURNE ARMS

Winterbourne Arms, nr Newbury

An atmospheric village pub with award-winning tradional and contempory meals and snacks

 see page 368

6 THE DOWNGATE

Hungerford

Real ales, home cooking and great company in a classic country pub.

 see page 368

7 THE PHEASANT INN HOTEL

Shefford Woodlands, nr Hungerford

An inn of great charm and character and a magnet for racing folk, with great food, great drinks and great company.

 see page 369

NEWBURY

A prosperous wool town in the Middle Ages, evidence of which can be seen in the splendid 'wool' **Church of St Nicholas** built in the 16th century. The town will be forever linked with the legend of Jack o' Newbury, a wool merchant who was asked to raise two horsemen with footmen for Henry VIII's campaign against the Scots. Jack raised 50 of each and led them himself, but they only got as far as Buckinghamshire before news of the victory at Flodden reached them and they returned home. Two centuries later, Newbury became a busy coaching stop on the route between London and Bath and in 1810 came the opening of the **Kennet and Avon Canal**. Newbury Lock, built in 1796, was the first lock to be built along the canal and is also the only lock to have lever-operated ground paddles.

Back in the town centre and housed in a 17th century cloth hall is **Newbury Museum**, which, among its many displays, tells the story of the two battles fought nearby during the Civil War.

To the north lies **Donnington**, home to 18th century **Grove House**, the childhood home of Beau Brummel, and to **Donnington Castle**, of which only the imposing twin-towered gatehouse survives.

AROUND NEWBURY

HUNGERFORD

8½ miles W of Newbury on the A338

The town's heyday came in the 18th century, when the turnpike road from London to Bath was built, and the good times continued with the opening of the **Kennet and Avon Canal**. Several of the old coaching inns have survived and it was in 1688 at the Bear Hotel that a meeting took place between William of Orange and representatives of James II that culminated in the end of the House of Stuart and James's flight to France.

LAMBOURN

11½ miles NW of Newbury on the B4000

Situated up on the Berkshire Downs, this village is best known

Donnington Castle

as a centre for the training of racehorses. The Lambourn Trainer's Association organises guided tours of the village's famous stables and also trips up to the gallops to see the horses going through their paces.

To the north of the village are the **Lambourn Seven Barrows**, one of the most impressive Bronze Age burial sites in the country.

EAST ILSLEY

8½ miles N of Newbury on the A34

Along with its neighbour, **West Ilsley**, the village is associated with racehorses that use the gallops on the downs as their training grounds.

COMBE

7½ miles SW of Newbury off the A343

This isolated hamlet is overlooked by **Walbury Hill** which, at 974 feet, is the highest point in Berkshire. A popular place with walkers, it has an Iron Age hill fort on the summit, from where there are superb panoramic views. Close to the hill lies **Combe Gibbet**, one of the last public hanging places in the country.

To the north of Combe is **Inkpen Common**, a Site of Special Scientific Interest where, along with the heath and woodland, a wet valley bog and pond have been created in an old clay pit.

READING

The town grew up around its Abbey, which was founded in 1121 by Henry I and became one of the most important religious houses in

Reading Abbey

the country. Reading is also one of only a handful of towns where kings of England have been laid to rest - Henry I was buried in the Abbey, and a plaque marks the approximate spot.

Adjacent to the ruins of **Reading Abbey** is **Reading Prison**, where Oscar Wilde was incarcerated and where he wrote *De Profundis*. His confinement inspired him to compose the epic poem *The Ballad of Reading Gaol* while in exile in Paris in 1898.

With the building of roads and the opening of the canal, Reading really began to boom and to become linked with great names such as Sutton Seeds, Huntley & Palmer biscuits and the brewing industry. **Reading Museum** tells the story of the town from its earliest beginnings. Situated on the banks of the River Kennet and housed in a range of canal buildings, **Blake's Lock Museum** concerns itself with the life of the town in the 19th and early 20th century.

Near Hampstead Norreys on the B4009, is Wyld Court Rainforest, a fascinating World Land Trust conservation centre where visitors can walk through several indoor tropical rainforests viewing a unique collection of spectacular and rare plants along with rainforest animals.

8   THE CASTLE INN

Cold Ash, nr Thatcham

Well-kept ales and great home cooking brings the crowds to this delightful country inn.

 see page 370

9   THE POT KILN

Frilsham, nr Yattendon

One of the finest dining pubs in the county, with a super menu of British and European inspiration – game a seasonal speciality.

 see page 370

10   THE SIX BELLS

Beenham, nr Reading

Exotic and traditional décor in a popular pub in picturesque surroundings. Bar and restaurant menus, 4 rooms for B&B.

 see page 371

AROUND READING

ALDERMASTON

9 miles SW of Reading on the A340

It was in this tranquil village that in 1840 the William Pear was first propagated by schoolmaster John Staid; it was first known as the Aldermaston pear, and a cutting of the plant is believed to have been taken to Australia, where it is now called the Bartlett pear. The lovely **Church of St Mary** provides the atmospheric setting for the York Mystery Cycle, 14th century nativity plays that are performed here each year.

Close to the village there is a delightful walk along the Kennet and Avon Canal to **Aldermaston Wharf**, a beautifully restored 18th century building that houses the **Kennet and Avon Canal Visitor Centre**.

PANGBOURNE

4½ miles NW of Reading on the A329

Situated at the confluence of the Rivers Pang and Thames, the town grew up in the late 19th and early 20th centuries as a fashionable place to reside, and the numerous attractive villas that have survived include a row of ornate Victorian houses known as the Seven Deadly Sins. It was to Pangbourne and **Church Cottage** that the author Kenneth Graham retired and wrote *The Wind in the Willows*, based on the original bedtime stories he invented for his son. An elegant iron bridge links the town with **Whitchurch**, on the opposite bank of the River Thames; it was at Whitchurch Lock that the characters in Jerome K Jerome's *Three Men in a Boat* abandoned their craft after a series of mishaps and returned to London.

SONNING

3½ miles NE of Reading off the A4

An attractive little village on the banks of the River Thames, this was once home to a palace belonging to the Bishops of Salisbury. Behind the wall of the old palace is Deanery Gardens, a well-hidden house built to the design of Lutyens. To the southeast, on the site of Woodley Airfield, is the **Museum of Berkshire Aviation**, which chronicles the history of this once thriving centre of the aircraft industry.

WARGRAVE

6½ miles NE of Reading on the A321

The peace of this charming riverside village was shattered in 1914 when suffragettes burnt down the church in protest that the vicar refused to remove the word 'obey' from the marriage service. In the churchyard stands the **Hannen Mausoleum**, a splendid family monument designed by Lutyens in 1906.

The nearby **Druid's Temple** stands in the garden of **Temple Combe**, close to a house designed by the architect Frank Lloyd Wright. The only house of his in England, it was built in 1958 on an elaborate U-shaped design, and its many unusual features include suede-panelled interior walls.

COOKHAM

14 miles NE of Reading on the A4094

This small town on the River Thames was the birthplace of Sir Stanley Spencer, who used it as the setting for many of his paintings. The **Stanley Spencer Gallery**, housed in a converted Victorian chapel, has a permanent exhibition of his work. He was born here, spent most of his life here, and is buried in the churchyard of Holy Trinity.

BRACKNELL

10 miles SE of Reading on the A322

It was designated a New Town in 1948, but Bracknell dates back to the 10th century when the community stood at the junction of two major routes through Windsor Forest.

What now remains of the great royal hunting ground of Windsor Forest (also called Bracknell Forest) lies to the south and in this vast area of parks and nature reserves is the **Lookout Discovery Park**, an interactive science centre that brings to life the mysteries of both science and nature.

SANDHURST

11 miles SE of Reading on the A3095

The town is the home of the **Royal Military Academy**, the training place for army officers for almost a century, and the academy's Staff College Museum tells the history of officer training from its inception to the present day.

WINDSOR

The largest castle in the country and a royal residence for over 900 years, **Windsor Castle** was built by William the Conqueror in the late 11th century as one of a chain of defences on the approaches into London. Down the centuries several monarchs have added to the Norman structure, most notably Henry VIII, Charles II and George

Windsor Castle

9

FROGMORE HOUSE

Windsor

Frogmore House has been a royal retreat since the 18th century and is today used by the Royal Family for private entertaining.

 see page 371

IV. Various parts of the Castle are open to the public, including 16 state apartments that house a remarkable collection of furniture, porcelain and armour. Also here is **Queen Mary's Dolls' House**, which was designed by Lutyens and has both electric lights and running water. In November 1992, a massive fire swept through the northeast corner of the castle but, after much restoration, the affected rooms, including **St George's Hall**, are now once again open to the public.

Frogmore House, a modest early 18th century manor house standing in Home Park, has acted as a second, more relaxed royal residence than the nearby castle. In the **Royal Mausoleum** Queen Victoria is buried beside her beloved husband Prince Albert. The Castle and its environs are the final resting place of many other monarchs and royalty.

The charming town grew up beneath the walls of the castle and there is plenty here to interest the visitor. Windsor is the home of the Household Cavalry, at Combermere Barracks, and here there is the superb **Household Cavalry Museum**. To the south of the town lies **Windsor Great Park**, the remains of the extensive royal hunting forest.

AROUND WINDSOR

ETON

1 mile N of Windsor on the A355

Situated just across the River Thames from Windsor, the town has grown up around **Eton College**, the famous public school that was founded in 1440 by Henry VI and was originally intended for the education of 70 poor and worthy scholars.

ASCOT

6 miles SW of Windsor on the A329

This was a small village until 1711 when Queen Anne moved the original Windsor race meeting here and founded the world famous **Ascot Racecourse**.

Buckinghamshire

South Buckinghamshire, with the River Thames as its southern county boundary, lies almost entirely within the Chiltern Hills and is a charming and delightful area that has, over the years inspired many writers and artists, including Milton, Shakespeare and Roald Dahl. Though many of the towns and villages here have histories going back well before the Norman Conquest, the influence of London is never far away and several have been linked with the capital for many years by the Metropolitan Railway. The links with London have also seen many famous and wealthy people make their homes here and, tucked away in the rolling countryside, can be found two fabulous former residences of the Rothschild family, Waddesdon Manor and Mentmore Towers. Buckinghamshire is also home to the country retreat of the Prime Minister, Chequers. The north of the county is dominated by the New Town of Milton Keynes.

11

Hellfire Caves, West Wycombe

HIGH WYCOMBE

The largest town in Buckinghamshire and originally an old Chilterns Gap market town, High Wycombe is traditionally known for its manufacture of chairs and, in particular, the Windsor design. Several old buildings survive today, including the Little Market House of 1761, and what is now the **Wycombe Local History and Chair Museum**.

Just to the north of the town lies **Hughenden Manor**, which was bought by Benjamin Disraeli shortly after the publication of his novel *Tancred* and was his home until his death in 1881. Today, the remodelled 18th century house displays an interesting collection of memorabilia of Disraeli's life; the great Victorian Prime Minister lies buried in the estate church.

To the west of Wycombe lies the charming estate village of **West Wycombe** and **West Wycombe Park**, the home of the Dashwood family until the 1930s. The house dates from the early 18th century, and the grounds and parkland, landscaped by a pupil of Capability Brown, contain temples and an artificial lake shaped like a swan. Hewn out of the nearby hillside are **West Wycombe Caves**, which were created by Sir Francis Dashwood, Baron le Despencer, Chancellor of the Exchequer from 1762 to 1763, who employed his estate workers on the task after a series of failed harvests. Along with his passion for remodelling old buildings, Sir Francis had a racier side to his character and was a founder member of the **Hellfire Club**, a group of rakes who engaged in highly colourful activities.

AROUND HIGH WYCOMBE

PRINCES RISBOROUGH

7½ miles NW of High Wycombe on the A4010

Once home to a palace belonging to the Black Prince, the eldest son of Edward III, this attractive place has a host of 17th and 18th century cottages. Nearby is **Princes**

Forestry Commission, Wendover Woods

13 THE PLOUGH INN

Hyde Heath, nr Amersham

A popular country dining pub with expanded space for enjoying an interesting choice of excellent home cooking.

see page 372

14 THE BELL

Chartridge, nr Chesham

A charming village pub offering warm and genuine hospitality, real ales and a tempting choice of cooked-to-order dishes.

see page 372

15 THE KINGS ARMS

Chesham

The warmest of welcomes precedes a good choice of food and drink in a pleasant inn closed to the town centre.

see page 373

Risborough Manor House (National Trust), which is an early example of a redbrick building – it dates from 1670.

One of the most famous residences in the country lies at nearby **Great Kimble**: the 16th century mansion, **Chequers**, has been the country house of the British Prime Minister since 1920.

GREAT MISSENDEN
5 miles N of High Wycombe on the A4128

This attractive village is home to the early 15th century **Old Court House**, one of only two court houses in the Chiltern Hundreds, and the home of Roald Dahl, the author of much loved children's books. His grave is in the churchyard of St Peter and St Paul.

WENDOVER
9½ miles N of High Wycombe on the B4009

A delightful old market town situated in a gap in the Chiltern Hills, Wendover has several half-timbered, thatched houses and cottages, the best example of which are **Anne Boleyn's Cottages**. Close by, on the edge of the Chiltern escarpment, lie **Wendover Woods**, created for recreational pursuits as well as for conservation and timber production by the Forestry Commission.

AMERSHAM
6 miles NE of High Wycombe on the A404

The town's main street has a good mix of fine old buildings, notably the 17th century Market Hall and **Amersham Museum**, housed in part of a medieval hall.

Amersham was a staging post for coaches and many of the old inns remain, including the **Crown Hotel** that many will recognise from the film *Four Weddings and a Funeral*.

To the east of Amersham is the picturesque village of **Chenies** and the fascinating 15th century **Chenies Manor House**. Originally the home of the Earls of Bedford (before they moved to

13

16 THE BOOT & SLIPPER

Amersham

A large, comfortable inn with a long-hours menu of snacks and main meals and a fine choice of cask ales and wines.

see page 373

17 THE ELEPHANT & CASTLE

Old Amersham

A splendid old coaching inn serving a fine range of food and drink in a warm, inviting ambience.

see page 374

The Palladian mansion that John Penn built in Stoke Poges is now the clubhouse of Stoke Park Golf Club, known to James Bond fans as the place where Bond met Auric Golfinger and where Oddjob deftly removed the head of one of the statues that stand outside the clubhouse.

Woburn), the house was built by the architect who enlarged Hampton Court for Henry VIII.

CHALFONT ST GILES

7 miles E of High Wycombe off the A413

The most famous building in this typical English village is the 16th century **Milton's Cottage**, where the poet stayed in 1665 to escape the plague in London. Though he only lived here a short time, the blind poet wrote *Paradise Lost* and began *Paradise Regained* before moving back to London. The cottage and its garden are now a museum dedicated to the poet. A fascinating place in the nearby **Newland Park** is the **Chiltern Open Air Museum**, dedicated to rescuing vernacular architecture.

BEACONSFIELD

5 miles SE of High Wycombe on the A40

The old part of this town is known for its literary connections: the 17th century poet Edmund Waller was a resident (and is buried in the churchyard of St Mary and All Saints), and GK Chesterton, the poet Robert Frost and the children's author Enid Blyton all made Beaconsfield their home. Here, too, is **Bekonscot**, a rural model village which was created by Roland Callingham, a London accountant, in the 1920s and 30s. It was apparently the inspiration for Noddy's Toytown – Enid Blyton lived in a house called Green Hedges, a model of which can be seen in Bekonscot.

To the southeast lies **Stoke Poges**, whose churchyard provided Thomas Gray with the inspiration to write his much-loved *Elegy Written in a Country Churchyard*. The poet is buried in the church; to the east stands the massive **Gray Monument**, built in 1799 by John Penn, grandson of William Penn, founder of Pennsylvania.

Just south of Beaconsfield lie **Burnham Beeches**, an area that has long been a place of leisure and relaxation for Londoners.

MARLOW

4 miles S of High Wycombe on the A4155

An attractive commuter town on the banks of the River Thames. It was at a riverside pub, the Two Brewers, that Jerome K Jerome wrote his masterpiece *Three Men in a Boat*. Today, Marlow is probably best known for its annual June Regatta.

To the west lies the much-filmed village of **Hambleden**, which was given to the National Trust by the family of the bookseller WH Smith (later Viscount Hambleden).

MILTON KEYNES

One of the town's most notable buildings is **Christ Church**, built in the style of Christopher Wren, which is the first purpose-built ecumenical church in Britain. The rural heritage of the villages that are now incorporated into its suburbs has not been forgotten and the **Museum of Industry and Rural Life** has a large collection of industrial, domestic and agricultural bygones; in the Exhibition Gallery, displays of art, crafts and local history can be seen.

AROUND MILTON KEYNES

OLNEY

8 miles N of Milton Keynes on the A509

This pretty town on the banks of the River Ouse is associated with William Cowper, reformed slave-trader, preacher and hymn-writer, who lived here between 1768 and 1786; his house is now the **Cowper and Newton Museum**, which not only concentrates on Cowper's life and work but also houses a nationally important Lace Collection.

BLETCHLEY

3 miles SE of Milton Keynes on the A5

Now virtually a suburb of Milton Keynes, Bletchley is famous as the home of **Bletchley Park**, the Victorian mansion that housed the country's wartime code breakers.

MENTMORE

12 miles SE of Milton Keynes off the B488

The village is home to the first of the Rothschild mansions, **Mentmore Towers**, which was built for Baron Meyer Amschel de Rothschild in the mid 19th century. A splendid building in the Elizabethan style and a superb example of grandiose Victorian extravagance, the house was sold in the 1970s and is now the headquarters of the University of Natural Law. To the southeast lies **Ivinghoe Beacon**, an Iron Age hill

Bletchley Park

fort which provides a wonderful viewpoint on the edge of the Chiltern Hills. The Beacon is at one end of Britain's oldest road, the **Ridgeway National Trail** - the other end is at the World Heritage site of Avebury in Wiltshire.

AYLESBURY

16 miles S of Milton Keynes on the A418

The county town of Buckinghamshire since the 18th century, this ancient town sheltered by the Chiltern Hills is famous for its Aylesbury ducks. The old part of the town (now a conservation area) is centred on the market square and here, amongst the sleepy lanes, is the **King's Head Inn** where Henry VIII is said to have wooed Anne Boleyn.

During the Civil War, Aylesbury was a base for both Cromwell and the King, depending on how well the conflict was progressing and, nearby, at Holman's Bridge, Prince Rupert suffered a crushing defeat.

18 THE CLIFDEN ARMS

Worminghall

A quintessential English country inn, with a welcome for all the family, well-kept ales and a good selection of freshly prepared dishes.

see page 375

At Boarstall, close to the village of Brill, are two interesting NationalTrust properties. Boarstall Duck Decoy is a rare working example of an ingenious contraption for catching ducks that was common in the 17th century. Boarstall Tower is a superb moated gatehouse and the only part that remains of Boarstall House, which was built in 1312.

Housed in a splendid Georgian building, the **County Museum** has an excellent section on Louis XVIII of France, who lived at Hartwell House during his years of exile.

To the northwest, near the village of **Waddesdon**, is another of the county's magnificent country houses, **Waddesdon Manor**, built between 1874 and 1889 for Baron Ferdinand de Rothschild in the style of a French Renaissance château. The house contains one of the best collections of 18th century French decorative arts in the world. Close by, at **Quainton**, is the **Buckinghamshire Railway Centre**, a working museum with one of the largest collections of steam and diesel locomotives in the country.

MIDDLE CLAYDON
11 miles SW of Milton Keynes off the A413

Close to the village lies 17th century **Claydon House**, best remembered for its associations with Florence Nightingale who stayed here for long periods, especially during her old age (her sister had married into the Verney family, who owned the house). 'Florrie's Lorry', the carriage used by Florence in the Crimea, is one of the many fascinating exhibits on display.

BUCKINGHAM
10 miles W of Milton Keynes on the A413

Dating back to Saxon times, Buckingham was a prosperous place in the Middle Ages, though few old buildings survived a disastrous fire in 1725. As a consequence many of the buildings here are Georgian and the **Old Gaol Museum** is a fine example of mid 18th century architecture. One building that did survive the flames is **Buckingham Chantry Chapel**, built in 1475 on the site of a Norman building. A more recent addition to this delightful market town is the **University of Buckingham**, granted its charter in 1983.

To the north of Buckingham lies **Stowe School**, a leading public school that occupies an 18th century mansion that was once the home of the Dukes of Buckingham. The grounds of the house, **Stowe Landscape Gardens**, were created in the 18th century by Earl Temple and his nephew and they remain one of the most original and finest landscape gardens in Europe.

Cambridgeshire

The southeast of the county is dominated by the county town, Cambridge, one of the leading academic centres of the world and a place that needs plenty of time to explore. The surrounding countryside is fairly flat and ideal for walking or cycling; it contains a surprising variety of habitats along with stately homes and windmills - a particular feature of East Anglia.

Extending over much of the county from The Wash are the flat fields of The Fens that contain some of the richest soil in England. Here, too, villages and small towns such as Ely were originally island settlements in the days when this was a misty landscape of marshes and bogs. The massive project of draining this land has spanned the centuries, starting with the Romans, who were the first to construct embankments and drains to lessen the frequency of flooding. Throughout the Middle Ages large areas of marsh and bog were reclaimed, and after the Civil War, the New Bedford River was cut to provide more drainage. First windmills and then steam and finally electric pumping engines have been used to remove the water from the fields. The Fens offer unlimited opportunities for exploration on foot, by car, by bicycle or by boat.

The old county of Huntingdonshire lies at the heartland of the rural heritage of Cambridgeshire and the former county town, Huntingdon, is famous as the birthplace and home of Oliver Cromwell. Places associated with the great Parliamentarian abound but there are also many ancient market towns and villages to discover along with numerous nature reserves and prehistoric sites. Cambridgeshire was the favourite shire of Rupert Brooke, and Grantchester his favourite place in the shire.

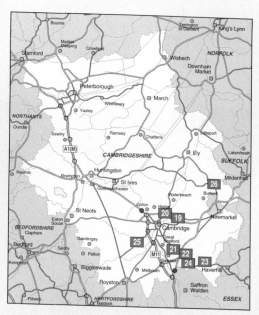

CAMBRIDGE

One of the world's leading university cities, Cambridge was an important market town centuries before the scholars arrived, as it stood at the point where the forest met the fenlands, at the lowest fording point of the River Cam. The oldest college is **Peterhouse**, founded by the Bishop of Ely in 1284, and in the next century Clare, Pembroke, Gonville and Caius, Trinity Hall and Corpus Christi followed.

The colleges reflect a variety of architectural styles but the grandest and most beautiful is undoubtedly King's College. Among the many university and college buildings to explore there are some that simply should not be missed, including **King's College Chapel**, with its glorious stained glass and Rubens' *Adoration of the Magi*; **Pepys Library** in Magdalene College; and Trinity's wonderful **Great Court**. By tradition, students attempt to run round the Court in the time it takes the great clock to strike 12. This tradition was immortalised in the film *Chariots of Fire*, though the sequence in the film was actually filmed at Eton College.

A trip by punt along the Backs of the River Cam gives a unique view to many of the colleges and the waterway also passes under six bridges including the **Bridge of Sighs** and the extraordinary **Mathematical Bridge**.

Apart from the colleges, Cambridge has plenty of other grand buildings and some of the country's leading museums, including the **Fitzwilliam Museum**, renowned for its art collection and ancient world antiquities. One of the city's greatest treasures is the **University Library**, one of the world's greatest research libraries, with six million books, a million maps and 350,000 manuscripts. For many, the most interesting place to visit is the **Botanic Gardens**, not really a museum, but a wonderful collection of plants (over 8,000 plant species) that rivals the gardens at Kew and Edinburgh. The Gardens were opened in 1846 by Professor John Henslow, teacher and mentor of Charles Darwin.

- *Hobson Street, which runs between Sidney Sussex and Christ's Colleges, remembers the 16th century notable Thomas Hobson, benefactor and sometime Mayor of Cambridge. He was also a carrier, hiring out horses, but his customers could only choose the horse that happened to be standing next to the stable door, giving rise to the expression Hobson's Choice - i.e. no choice at all.*

Cambridge Botanic Gardens

18

Fitzwilliam Museum, Cambridge

Among the city's many fine churches is the **Church of the Holy Sepulchre**, always known as the Round Church, one of only four surviving round churches in England.

The village of **Grantchester**, where Rupert Brooke lived for two happy years at The Orchard, can be reached by a pleasant walk from the city or a leisurely punt along the River Cam. The village was immortalised in Brooke's words:

"Stands the church clock at 3 And is there honey still for tea?"

The Orchard, first planted in 1868, became a tea garden by chance when a group of Cambridge students asked the owner if she could serve tea under the trees rather than on the front lawn. So started a tradition that continues to this day.

AROUND CAMBRIDGE

LODE
6 miles NE of Cambridge off the B1102

This attractive and peaceful village

is home to **Anglesey Abbey**, an early 17th century mansion house that was built on the site of an Augustinian priory. It holds Lord Fairhaven's magnificent collection of paintings, furnishings, tapestries and clocks, and its garden is a charming place for a peaceful stroll. To the south is the village of **Bottisham**, whose Holy Trinity Church was described by John Betjeman as 'perhaps the best in the county'.

Further afield, to the north, is **Denny Abbey**, which was founded in the 12th century by the Benedictine order but has also been the home of the Knights Templar, Franciscan nuns and the Countess of Pembroke. After the Dissolution of the Monasteries the abbey became a farmhouse and is

19 THE WHITE SWAN

Stow cum Quy

A lovely Grade II listed pub with a convivial little bar, four real ales and classic pub dishes.

🍴 see page 376

20 THE PLOUGH

Green End, Fen Ditton

A stylish modern riverside pub serving real ales, Continental lagers, excellent wines and a mix of traditional and modern dishes.

🍴 see page 377

Anglesey Abbey, Lode

19

21 THE GEORGE INN
AT BABRAHAM

Babraham

Only the best will do at this outstanding inn, where well-kept ales and superb cooking have established a wide-ranging reputation.

 see page 378

22 THE PEAR TREE

Hildersham

A very friendly and civilised village pub serving hearty home-cooked dishes. Two B&B rooms in a converted cottage.

 see page 379

23 THE OLD RED LION

Horseheath, nr Haverhill

A wide cross-section of visitors come here to enjoy well-kept ales and an interesting choice of food, and to take an overnight or longer stay in the roadhouse-style B&B rooms.

 see page 380

now home to the **Farmland Museum**.

BURWELL

10 miles NE of Cambridge on the B1102

A sad sight in the churchyard of St Mary's is a gravestone that marks the burial place of some 78 people of Burwell who all died in a barn fire while watching a travelling Punch and Judy Show. The **Devil's Dyke**, thought to have been built to keep out Danish invaders, runs through Burwell on its route from Reach to Woolditton.

To the southwest of Burwell lies **Swaffham Prior** where there are two churches in the same graveyard and two fine old windmills, one of which, an 1850 tower mill, has been restored and still produces flour.

DUXFORD

8 miles S of Cambridge off the A505

To the west of the village lies **Duxford Aviation Museum**, now

part of the Imperial War Museum, with an outstanding collection of over 150 historic aircraft.

Between Duxford and Cambridge, close to Stapleford, there is some great walking, in parkland, where there are traces of an Iron Age hill fort, and on Magog Downs. To the west, near the village of **Shepreth**, is the **Shepreth L Moor Nature Reserve**, an important area of wet meadowland that is home to birds and many rare plants.

ARRINGTON

10 miles SW of Cambridge off the A1198

This village is home to the spectacular **Wimpole Hall**, one of the best examples of an 18th century country mansion in England. The lovely interiors contain fine collections of furniture and paintings, while the magnificent, formal gardens include a Victorian parterre and a rose garden.

Duxford Aviation Museum

20

MADINGLEY

2 miles W of Cambridge off the A1303

Madingley is home to one of the most peaceful and evocative places in the region, the **American Cemetery**. A place of pilgrimage for the families of American service men who operated from the many wartime bases in the county, the cemetery commemorates 3,800 dead and 5,000 missing in action in World War II.

ELY

The jewel in the crown of the Fens, the city owes its existence to St Etheldreda, Queen of Northumbria, who founded a monastery on the Isle of Ely in AD 673. However, it was not until 1081 that work on the present **Cathedral** began and it was completed more than a century later. The most outstanding feature is the Octagon, built to replace the original Norman tower that collapsed in 1322, but there are many other delights, including the 14th century Lady Chapel, the Prior's Door and St Ovin's Cross, the only piece of Saxon stonework in the building. Ely's Tourist Information Centre is housed in a pretty black and white timbered building that is the only known surviving house, apart from Hampton Court, where Cromwell and his family are known to have lived. Etheldreda was also known as St Awdrey, and an annual fair was held in her memory. The cheap jewellery and lace sold at the fair

St Etheldreda, Ely Cathedral

were known as St Awdrey's Lace, later corrupted to Tawdry, a word now applied to anything cheap and showy.

AROUND ELY

SOHAM

5½ miles SE of Ely off the A142

Downfield Windmill was built in 1726 as a smock mill and then rebuilt as a tower mill in 1890 after it had been destroyed by gales. To the southwest lies **Wicken Fen**, the oldest nature reserve in the country, famous for its rich variety of plant, insect and bird life. It is also home to Highland cattle and the wild Konik ponies. Wicken Windmill is an impressive smock mill restored to full working order.

24 THE DOG & DUCK

Linton

A charming thatched pub with Greene King ales, an across-the-board choice of food and a pretty riverside garden.

see page 381

25 THE HARE & HOUNDS

Harlton

A cosy little village pub that attracts locals and visitors with well-kept Charles Wells ales and a good variety of home-cooked food.

see page 381

26 QUEENSBERRY

Fordham

A very quiet, comfortable Bed & Breakfast house noted for its excellent breakfasts.

see page 382

21

Stretham Old Engine Pumping Station, nr Haddenham

HADDENHAM

6 miles SW of Ely on the A1123

At 120 feet above sea level, Haddenham is the highest village in the Fens and, not surprisingly, it too has a windmill – **Haddenham Great Mill** which was built in 1803, has four sails and three sets of grinding stones. Last worked commercially in 1946, it was restored in the 1990s.

To the north, at Sutton, is a great family attraction, the **Mepal Outdoor Centre** that includes a children's play park, an adventure play area and boats for hire. Providing a unique insight into Fenland history and industrial archaeology, the **Stretham Old Engine**, at Stretham, is a fine example of a land drainage steam engine.

SOMERSHAM

11 miles W of Ely on the B1050

Once the site of a palace for the Bishops of Ely, Somersham is now home to the **Raptor Foundation** where owls and other birds of prey find refuge. This is a very popular attraction, with regular flying and falconry displays.

MARCH

13 miles NW of Ely on the B1101

This settlement once occupied the second largest island in the great level of the Fens, and as the land was drained March grew as a trading and religious centre and, later, as a market town and hub of the railway. The **March and District Museum** tells the story of the people and history of the town and surrounding area. **St Wendreda's** uniquely dedicated church in March was described by John Betjeman as "worth cycling 40 miles into a headwind to see." Its roof, adorned with over 100 carved angels, is certainly a stirring sight.

WISBECH

19 miles NW of Ely on the A1101

This town also lies at the centre of a thriving agricultural region and the 18th century saw many fine buildings constructed along the river. The finest of these is undoubtedly **Peckover House**, built in 1722 and bought at the end of the 18th century by Jonathan Peckover, a member of the Quaker banking family. Behind its elegant façade are charming panelled rooms and ornate plaster decorations.

The town was the birthplace in 1838 of Octavia Hill, co-founder of the National Trust, and the house in which she was born is now the **Octavia Hill Museum** where her work is commemorated.

The **Wisbech and Fenland Museum** is one of the oldest purpose-built museums in the country, and its numerous displays include the manuscript of Charles Dickens' *Great Expectations* and Napoleon's Sèvres breakfast set captured at Waterloo.

HUNTINGDON

First settled by the Romans and the former county town of Huntingdonshire, Huntingdon was the birthplace, in 1599, of Oliver Cromwell. He attended Huntingdon Grammar School, where Samuel Pepys was also a pupil, before becoming the MP for Huntingdon in the Parliament of 1629. His school is now the **Cromwell Museum** and it houses the only public collection relating specifically to him. Opposite the museum stands **All Saints' Church**, which contains the Cromwell burial vault. On the Market Square, the 16th century Falcon Inn was Cromwell's headquarters during the Civil War.

Cowper House, with its impressive early 18th century frontage, was the home of the poet William Cowper from 1765 to 1767, and a former coaching inn, The George Hotel, is reputed to have been used by the highwayman Dick Turpin.

At nearby Hemingford Abbots stands **Hemingford Grey**, a manor that is one of the oldest continuously inhabited houses in England – it was built in around 1130.

Peckover House and Gardens

A footpath leads from the famous Chinese Bridge (1827) to **Port Holme Meadow**, one of the largest meadows in England and the site of Roman remains as well as being home to a huge diversity of botanical and bird species.

AROUND HUNTINGDON

RAMSEY

7 miles N of Huntingdon on the B1040

It was in this pleasant market town in AD 969 that Earl Ailwyn founded **Ramsey Abbey**, which by the 12th century had become one of the most important in England. However, after the Dissolution the Abbey and its lands were sold to Sir Richard Williams, great-grandfather of Oliver Cromwell. Most of the buildings were demolished and, in 1938, the house was converted for use as a school – which it remains today.

•

Linked to Huntingdon by a 14th century bridge across the River Ouse, Godmanchester was a Roman settlement and has continued in importance down the centuries. There are several grand houses here including Island Hall, a mid 18th century mansion that was built for John Jackson, the Receiver General for Huntingdon.

•

Housed in an 18th century farm building and several barns is the **Ramsey Rural Museum**, where the exhibits include restored farm and traditional craftsmen's equipment.

To the southwest of Ramsey lie the scattered village of Upwood and **Woodwalton Fen Nature Reserve**.

WHITTLESEY

15 miles N of Huntingdon on the A605

This market town, where brick-making was a local industry, was the birthplace of the writer LP Hartley, author of *The Go-Between*, and of the soldier Sir Harry Smith, a hero of many 19th century Indian campaigns. The highlight of the year here is the ancient **Straw Bear Procession** when a man clad in a suit of straw dances through streets during a four-day January festival.

To the southeast lies **Flag Fen Bronze Age Excavation**, comprising massive 3,000-year-old timbers that were part of a major settlement and have been preserved in the peaty ground. A Roman road, re-creations of a Bronze Age settlement, a museum of artefacts and rare breed animals can also be seen here.

To the north is **Thorney Abbey**, though what stands today is only a small part of this once great Benedictine Abbey.

ST IVES

4 miles E of Huntingdon on the A1123

Oliver Cromwell lived in St Ives in the 1630s and a statue of him stands on Market Hill – the statue was erected here in 1901 after it was rejected by Huntingdon. Other notable townsfolk include Sir Clive Sinclair, who developed his pocket calculators in the town, and the Victorian rower John Goldie, whose name is remembered by the second Cambridge boat.

ST NEOTS

8½ miles SW of Huntingdon on the B1428

The first bridge over the River Great Ouse was built in 1180 in the town, which takes its name from the Cornish saint whose remains were interred in the priory before the Norman Conquest. The priory was demolished with the Dissolution of the Monasteries and in the early 17th century the old bridge was replaced by a stone one which became the scene of a battle during the Civil War.

Flag Fen Bronze Age Excavation

GRAFHAM

5 miles SW of Huntingdon off the B661

Created in the 1960s as a reservoir, **Grafham Water** offers a wide range of sports facilities in its 1,500 acres. The area is a Site of Special Scientific Interest, and a nature reserve at the western edge is run jointly by Anglian Water and the Wildlife Trust.

To the west lies Kimbolton, a place with plenty of history and several interesting buildings, including **Kimbolton Castle** where parts of the original Tudor building can still be seen.

The gatehouse at the Castle was added by Robert Adam in 1764. Henry VIII's first wife Catherine of Aragon spent the last 18 months of her life imprisoned here and died here in 1536. She is buried in Peterborough Cathedral.

Nene Valley Railway, Peterborough

PETERBOROUGH

Cambridgeshire's second city, Peterborough has a long and interesting history that dates back to the Bronze Age. In 1967 it was designated a New Town, and modern development and expansion have increased its facilities without, thankfully, destroying its historic heart. Henry VIII elevated the 12th century church to a **Cathedral** and his first wife Catherine of Aragon is buried here as, for a while, was Mary, Queen of Scots after her execution at Fotheringhay. Railway enthusiasts are in their element here with the twin attractions of **Railworld**, a hands-on exhibition dealing with modern rail travel, and the wonderful **Nene Valley Railway**, which operates between the city and its Museum at Wansford. Close by is the **Thorpe Meadows Sculpture Park**, one of several open spaces in and around the city.

Also on the outskirts of the city are **Longthorpe Tower**, part of a fortified manor house which is graced by some very fine 14th century domestic wall paintings, and **Peakirk Waterfowl Gardens**, home to hundreds of birds.

Cheshire

There are many aspects to Cheshire: the rural landscape of the Cheshire Plains, the textile towns in the east, the ancient salt towns and the grand stately homes. Chester, the prosperous county town, was first established by the Romans, who built a fort here to protect against invasions from Wales. Salt had been mined in Cheshire long before the Romans arrived but the particular need for brine for the fledgling chemical manufacturers along the River Mersey saw a great increase in activity. Further east is the famous silk town of Macclesfield, while Styal was created as a model village for one of the first cotton mills in the area, Quarry Bank Mill. Cheshire is also home to some of the country's grandest country houses, including Tatton Park, Arley Hall, Tabley Hall and Dunham Massey Hall.

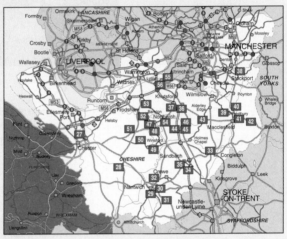

CHESTER

It was in AD 70 that the famous 20th Legion, the Valeria Victrix, established its headquarters and took full advantage of Chester's strategic position on the River Dee, close to the Welsh border. During this period the **City Walls** were first built; today they remain the most complete in the country and provide an excellent 2-mile walk as well as fine views of the River Dee, Chester's glorious buildings and the Welsh mountains in the distance. At one point, the wall runs alongside St John Street, which was in Roman times the main thoroughfare between the fortress and the **Amphitheatre**, the largest such construction to be uncovered in Britain and one that was capable of seating 7,000 spectators.

The Normans began the construction of what is now **Chester Cathedral**, a majestic building of weathered pink stone on a site that has been a place of worship for 1,000 years. It was originally an abbey – one of the very few to survive Henry VIII's closure of the monasteries in the 1540s – and the cloisters are regarded as the finest in England. It was at Chester Cathedral, in 1742, that George Frederick Handel personally conducted rehearsals for his oratorio *The Messiah* before its first performance in Dublin.

During the Civil War Chester supported the Royalist cause but it was while watching from the city's walls that Charles I saw his troops heavily defeated at nearby Rowton Moor. Chester has many museums telling the city's story from Roman times through the dark days of the Civil War to the present day. Visitors can also enjoy a unique shopping experience – two-tiered galleries of reconstructed medieval shops under covered walkways known as **The Rows**.

The city has some ancient sporting links: **Chester Regatta** hosts the oldest rowing races in the world, and **Chester Races** are held

The Rows, Chester

27

27 CHESTER ZOO

Chester

Chester Zoo is the UK's number one charity zoo, with over 7000 animals and 400 different species

 see page 382

28 BEESTON CASTLE

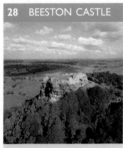

Beeston, nr Tarporley

Standing majestically on a sheer rocky crag, Beeston has perhaps the most stunning views of any castle in England.

 see page 383

on the oldest Racecourse in the country, the Roodeye. Finally, no visit to Chester is complete without a trip to **Chester Zoo**, at Upton-by-Chester on the city's northern outskirts, and where, surrounded by landscaped gardens, over 5,000 animals from 500 different species can be seen in near natural enclosures. A mile-long overhead railway provides a splendid bird's-eye view of the animals.

AROUND CHESTER

ASHTON

6½ miles E of Chester on the B5393

Maintained by the Forestry Commission since the early 1900s, **Delamere Forest**, once a hunting ground for royalty and the nobility, lies just a couple of miles northeast of Ashton and although it is an excellent place for walking and picnicking it remains a working forest of some 4,000 acres.

TARPORLEY

9 miles E of Chester off the A49

At the time when most of the surrounding area was part of Delamere Forest, Tarporley was the headquarters of the forest wardens (the verderers) who meted out rough justice to offenders of the forest laws from their own courts. One such court was at Utkinton, just north of the town, and in an old farmhouse is the trunk of an ancient forest tree with its roots still in the ground. When the court was in session, the wardens placed the Hunting Horn of Delamere – their symbol of authority – on the tree.

BEESTON

9½ miles SE of Chester off the A49

Rising some 500 feet from the Cheshire Plain, the craggy cliff of **Beeston Hill** is one of the most dramatic sights in the county and it is made all the more impressive by the ruins of **Beeston Castle** (the 'Castle of the Rock') on the summit. Although it was built in around 1220, the castle did not see military action until the Civil War when a Royalist captain and just eight musketeers captured the fortress and its garrison of 60 soldiers – without even firing a shot! Later, Cromwell ordered the castle to be partially destroyed but it is still very imposing with walls 30 feet thick and a well 366 feet deep. An exhibition tells the 4,000-year story of the site.

Seen clearly from the top of Beeston Hill is another of Cheshire's fortifications, **Peckforton Castle**. Further south again from Beeston is another marvellous mock medieval construction, **Cholmondeley Castle**, built in the early 19th century and particularly noted for its gardens.

FARNDON

7 miles S of Chester off the B5130

During the Civil War, Farndon's strategic position, between Royalist North Wales and Parliamentarian Cheshire, along with its bridge, led to many skirmishes and these events are depicted in the stained glass windows of the parish church.

Farndon's most famous son,

the cartographer John Speed, was born in the village in 1542. Speed followed his father's trade as a tailor, married, had 18 children and was nearly 50 before he began to devote his time to researching and producing his beautifully drawn maps.

NESTON

10 miles NW of Chester on the B5135

Right up until the early 19th century, Neston was the most significant town on **The Wirral**, the once desolate and wind swept peninsula that, following the rise of shipbuilding and other industries in the 19th century, has not only become a desirable place to live but has also been justifiably dubbed the 'Leisure Peninsula' by tourism officials.

After Neston became useless as a port, maritime traffic moved along the Dee estuary to **Parkgate** and, as the new gateway to Ireland, this still attractive village saw some notable visitors: John Wesley preached here while waiting for favourable winds to take him to Ireland, Handel landed here after conducting his first performance of *The Messiah* in Dublin, and Turner came here to sketch the panoramic views across the estuary of the Flintshire hills.

To the east of Neston, centrally placed between the Dee and Mersey estuaries, is the village of **Willaston**, the home of **Hadlow Road Station**. Although a train

has not run through here since 1962, the station, along with its signal box and ticket office, has been restored to appear as it would have done in the early 1950s. This is one of the more intriguing features of the Wirral Way, a nature reserve and walk that follows the track bed of the old railway between Hooton and West Kirkby. On the Mersey side of the Wirral peninsula lies **Eastham Woods Country Park**, an area of woodland that is home to all three species of native woodpecker.

Further up the Mersey lies **Ellesmere Port**, situated at the point where the Shropshire Union Canal meets the River Mersey. The canal basin is now home to the **Boat Museum**, where the world's largest collection of historic narrow boats and barges has been assembled. Towards the top of The Wirral Peninsula, **Birkenhead** was a tiny, insignificant village until in 1824 William Laird set up a shipbuilding firm. It became

One of the Wirral's major attractions is Ness Botanic Gardens, just to the southeast of Neston and situated on the banks of the Dee Estuary. Now run by the University of Liverpool as an Environmental and Horticultural Research Station, the 64-acre gardens have been planned to provide magnificent displays all year round.

Boat Museum, Ellesmere Port

Nantwich

Family-run and family-friendly inn serving ales from its own brewery and a good choice of snacks and meals.

 see page 383

Willaston, nr Nantwich

An attractive, inviting village inn open lunchtime and evening for well-kept ales and popular pub dishes.

 see page 383

Wybunbury, nr Crewe

Five real ales, food for all tastes and appetites and comfortable en suite accommodation in a grand old country hostelry.

  see page 384

Birkenhead Park

Cammell Laird, one of the busiest and most successful shipyards in the world. The **Wirrall Museum** tells the story of the shipyard.

The Birkenhead Heritage Trail takes in tram rides, an Edwardian street scene display, historic warships, a German U-Boat and a pumping station that was used to extract water from the Mersey railway tunnel.

Port Sunlight is a model village created in 1888 by William Heskleth Lever, later the 1st Viscount Leverhulme, for workers in his soap factory. It was named after his most famous product, Sunlight Soap. The **Lady Lever Art Gallery** is home to a marvellous collection of pre-Raphaelite paintings by Millais, Rossetti and Ford Madox Brown, portraits by Gainsborough and Reynolds and landscapes by Turner and Constable. Birkenhead is the birthplace of the actresses Glenda Jackson and Patricia Routledge.

NANTWICH

This attractive market town surrounded by the rich dairy farmlands of south Cheshire was once second only in importance in the county to Chester, its prosperity built on the mining of salt.

The most disastrous event in Nantwich's long history was its great fire in 1583 that saw some 600 thatched and timber-framed buildings destroyed. The most striking building to survive the fire, probably because it was surrounded by a moat, is the lovely black and white house in Hospital Street that is known as **Churche's Mansion** after the merchant, Richard Churche, who built it in 1577. The upper floor has been furnished in the Elizabethan style and is open to the public during the summer. Another building spared from the fire is the town's impressive 14th century church that is often called the **Cathedral of South Cheshire**.

During the Civil War Nantwich supported Cromwell's Parliamentarian army and, after several weeks of fighting, the Royalist forces were finally defeated on 25th January 1644 and the townspeople celebrated the victory by wearing sprigs of holly in their hair. There are records of the Civil War in the **Nantwich Museum**, which also contains exhibitions on the town's long history and its salt, dairy and cheese-making industries.

A few miles south of Nantwich, just off the A530 Whitchurch road, stands **Hack Green Secret Bunker**. Built as a centre of regional government in the case of a nuclear war, it was declassified in 1993 and has since become a major visitor attraction.

AROUND NANTWICH

CREWE

4 miles NE of Nantwich on the A534

Crewe is very much a product of the railway age and it was only

when the Grand Junction Railway arrived here in 1837 and, five years later, moved all its construction and repair workshops to this site that the town was founded. The **Railway Age Museum** offers a fascinating insight into Crewe's place in railway history.

CONGLETON

14½ miles NE of Nantwich on the A534

In the foothills of the Pennines, the land around Congleton has been inhabited since the Stone Age and the remains of a 5,000-year-old chambered tomb, known as **The Bridestones**, can be seen beside the road running eastwards from the town towards Leek. In Elizabethan times, the people of the town had such a passion for bear baiting that it became known locally as the Bear Town, and Congleton was the very last town in England to outlaw this cruel practice.

The town developed as an important textile centre during the

 32 THE ROYAL OAK

Worleston, nr Nantwich

A stylish, spacious, sociable village inn open every lunchtime and evening for a good choice of food and drink.

see page 385

33 YE OLDE WHITE LION

Congleton

Warm hospitality, well-kept ales and a good choice of honest pub food ensures that this splendid old inn does a roaring trade.

 see page 386

Little Moreton Hall, Astbury

31

34 LOCK 57

Hassall Green, Sandbach

Superb cooking in a marvellous café/brasserie by a lock on the Trent & Mersey Canal.

see page 387

35 THE MARKET TAVERN

Sandbach

A distinguished old inn with a fine reputation for hospitality, food and ales.

see page 388

36 THE COURTYARD COFFEE HOUSE

Knutsford

The finest in hospitality and cooking, with the unique bonus of a museum of antique bicycles.

 see page 389

18th century with many of its mills involved in silk manufacturing, cotton spinning and ribbon weaving. In Mill Green, near the River Dane, part of the very first silk mill to operate here still stands.

Just a couple of miles south of Congleton lies the pretty village of **Astbury** set around a triangular village green. Black and white half-timbered houses have almost become a symbol for the county of Cheshire and one of the most stunning examples of all is **Little Moreton Hall**, the 'wibbly wobbly' house that provided the memorable location for the television adaptation of *Moll Flanders*.

Further south again lies the famous folly, **Mow Cop**, which was built by Randle Wilbraham in the 18th century on his Rode Hall estate to enhance the view from his house. This mock ruin stands on a rocky hill, some 1,100 feet above sea level and, from its summit, on a clear day, there are magnificent views across the Pennines to the northeast, Cheshire to the west, and northwards to Alderley Edge.

SANDBACH

8½ miles NE of Nantwich on the A534

The handsome market square of this former important coaching town is dominated by its two famous stone crosses. Although only the superbly carved shafts have survived, the crosses were created sometime in the 9th century and the striking scenes they depict are believed to represent the conversion of Mercia to Christianity during the reign of King Penda.

KNUTSFORD

The Knutsford of the 19th century that Elizabeth Gaskell wrote about so vividly has expanded a great deal, but its centre still evokes the

Tabley House, nr Knutsford

intimacy of a small Victorian town with its narrow streets and cobbled alleyways. More recent is the **Gaskell Memorial Tower**, a tall blank-walled building that was erected in her memory by entrepreneur and glove manufacturer Richard Harding Watt in 1907.

It was back in 1262 that Edward I granted the town a charter and the **Knutsford Heritage Centre**, housed in a timber-framed 17th century former smithy, is an ideal place to discover more of the town's long history.

Close by is an unusual exhibition, the **Penny Farthing Museum**. These curious machines were in fashion for just 20 years before the last model was manufactured in 1892, and the collection here includes a replica of the famous 'Starley Giant' with a front wheel that is seven feet in diameter!

Just north of Knutsford is **Tatton Park**, a historic country estate that is centred on a magnificent Georgian mansion. A short walk from the grand house is **Home Farm**, the heart of the estate, where there are the old estate offices and many original farm animal breeds to be seen. Surrounding the mansion is a vast deer park that has a history stretching back to 8000 BC when the deer here were hunted for meat and clothing.

Another grand Georgian mansion, **Tabley House**, lies to the west of Knutsford. Designed by John Carr for the 1st Lord de

Tabley in 1761, the house today is home to a wonderful collection of English paintings, including works by Turner, Reynolds and Opie, that were put together by Lord Tabley and his son, who were the founders of London's National Gallery.

To the south of Knutsford is the charming Cheshire village of **Lower Peover** and the delightful old coaching inn the **Bells of Peover**, which flies not only the Union Flag but also the American Stars and Stripes to commemorate the visit made here by General Patton and Eisenhower during World War II. For a time, in those dark days, General Patton lived at nearby Peover Hall.

37 CRANFORD CAFÉ & SANDWICH BAR

Knutsford

Daytime delights include an amazing variety of sandwiches, snacks and sweet delights to eat in or take away.

see page 389

Quarry Bank Mill, Styal

38 THE DUKE OF YORK

Romiley

Six real ales and a wide-ranging Mediterranean-inspired menu attract a loyal band of regulars and plenty of passing trade.

see page 391

39 THE LEGH ARMS

Prestbury Village

One of the finest inns in the county, with exceptional standards of food and accommodation.

 see page 390

40 THE SPINNERS ARMS

Bollington

Real ales and snacks in the popular Spinners Arms. Nearby fellow pub the Robin Hood Inn offers good food and drink and quality B&B rooms.

 see page 391

34

AROUND KNUTSFORD

WILMSLOW

6 miles NE of Knutsford on the A538

Just to the north of the bustling commuter town of Wilmslow and surrounded by the 150-acre **Styal Country Park** is **Quarry Bank Mill**, a grand old building dating from 1784 that was one of the first generation of cotton mills. Visitors can follow the history of the mill through a series of museum displays, see weaving and spinning demonstrations and discover what life was like for the children who lived at the Apprentice House. Also within the park is the delightful factory village of **Styal**, which was established by the mill's original owner, Samuel Greg, a philanthropist and pioneer of the factory system.

To the south of Wilmslow lies the long wooded escarpment, **Alderley Edge**, nearly two miles long, that rises to 600 feet and culminates in sandy crags overlooking the Cheshire Plain. Walkers can roam through the woods along the many footpaths, one of which leads to **Hare Hill Gardens**, whose Victorian grounds include fine woodland and a walled garden themed in blue, white and

White Nancy, Bollington

yellow flowers.

STALYBRIDGE

6 miles E of Manchester on the A57

Set beside the River Tame and with the North Pennine Moors stretching for miles to the east, Stalybridge was one of the earliest cotton towns. One of the cotton workers' most prominent leaders was the Rev Joseph Rayner Stephens, and a granite obelisk in his memory stands in the town's Stamford Park.

BOLLINGTON

11 miles E of Knutsford on the B5091

A striking feature of this former cotton town is the splendid 20-

arched viaduct that once carried the railway over the River Dean and which today is part of the **Middlewood Way**, a 10-mile country trail that follows a scenic, traffic-free route from Macclesfield to Marple. Just as remarkable as the viaduct is **White Nancy**, a round stone tower that stands on the 900 feet summit of **Kerridge Hill**; it was built to commemorate the Battle of Waterloo.

MACCLESFIELD

11 miles SE of Knutsford on the A523

The town nestles below the High Peak, and it was on this rock that Edward I and Queen Eleanor

West Park Museum, Macclesfield

founded a church. Reached via a gruelling flight of 108 steps, the **Church of St Michael and All Angels** was extended in the 1890s, but its early core remains, including the Legh Chapel that was built in 1422 to receive the body of Piers Legh, who had fought at Agincourt and died at the Siege of Meaux.

It was in Macclesfield in 1743 that Charles Roe built the first silk mill beside the River Bollin. The industry flourished and, 150 years later, it had become known as the Silk Town. Several excellent museums tell the story of the town's connection with silk. On the northwestern edge of the town is the **West Park Museum**, whose exhibits include a collection of Egyptian antiquities and a gallery devoted to the work of Charles Tunnicliffe.

To the east of the town centre runs the **Macclesfield Canal**, one of the highest waterways in England, that was opened in 1831 and which links with the Trent and Mersey and the Peak Forest canals. Between Macclesfield and Congleton, the canal descends over 100 feet in a spectacular series of 12 locks before crossing the River Dane by Thomas Telford's handsome iron viaduct. Another unusual feature of this superbly engineered canal are the two 'roving bridges' south of Congleton that swing from one bank to the other, where

41 THE RISING SUN INN

Rainow, nr Macclesfield

A lovely old coaching inn serving a selection of home-made traditional and modern dishes.

see page 392

42 THE CAT & FIDDLE

Macclesfield Forest

A dramatic setting, outstanding hospitality and super home cooking have made this one of the best-known and best-loved pubs in the region.

see page 393

43 THE EGERTON ARMS

Chelford

Patrons come from all over the region to enjoy excellent hospitality, food and drink in a charming village inn.

see page 394

35

44 THE THREE GREYHOUNDS

Allostock, nr Knutsford

A popular village pub - a very friendly and welcoming village inn with a great choice of home cooking for all tastes and appetites.

 see page 395

45 THE COTTAGE RESTAURANT & LODGE

Allostock, nr Knutsford

A charming country hostelry serving a selection of outstanding traditional and modern dishes. Twelve spacious, comprehensively equipped en suite bedrooms.

 see page 396

46 THE DROVERS ARMS

Allostock, nr Knutsford

A comfortable and convivial pub open all day for a wide range of excellent food and drink.

 see page 397

Jodrell Bank, Lower Withington

the towpath changes sides, and enable horses to cross over without having to unhitch the towrope.

Close to the village of Warren, a couple of miles southwest of Macclesfield, is the black and white half-timbered **Gawsworth Hall** that was built in 1480 by the Fitton family. The celebrated beauty Mary Fitton is believed to be the 'Dark Lady' of Shakespeare's sonnets. Gawsworth's famous open-air theatre stages a summer programme that ranges from Shakespeare to Gilbert and Sullivan opera.

LOWER WITHINGTON
6½ miles SE of Knutsford on the B5392

To the northwest of this village, and visible from miles around, is the huge white dish of the world famous **Jodrell Bank** radio telescope that first came into service in 1957. The **Science Centre** here (long may it last!) offers visitors a wonderful array of hands-on exhibits, and a superb 35-acre **Arboretum** is planted with 2,500 species of trees and shrubs. It houses the National Collections of Sorbus and Malus.

NORTHWICH
7 miles SW of Knutsford on the A559

Although salt production in Cheshire began even before the Roman occupation, its extraction and processing at Northwich began on a major scale in 1670 when rock salt was discovered in nearby Marston. Its extraction from the Keuper marl of the Cheshire Plain has had some spectacular side effects – in Elizabethan times, John Leland recorded that a hill at Combermere suddenly disappeared into underground workings! Northwich later became notorious for the number of its buildings leaning at crazy angles due to the subsidence - the White Lion Inn lies a complete storey lower than its original height.

Cheshire's and Northwich's

Nantwich Salt Museum

long involvement with salt is vividly recorded at the **Salt Museum** which is housed in what used to be the Northwich Workhouse, a handsome Georgian building designed by the architect of Arley Hall.

To the north of the town is one of the most impressive feats of engineering of the canal age and one of the country's most fascinating attractions – the **Anderton Boat Lift**, constructed in 1875 to transfer boats from the Trent and Mersey Canal to the Weaver Navigation 50 feet below. It was designed by Edward Leader Williams, the engineer behind the

Anderton Boat Lift, Northwich

50 THE PLOUGH INN

Whitegate

Real gem of a "hidden place" pub, serving superb food and real ales; spacious beer garden.

 see page 400

51 THE FOREST VIEW

Oakmere

Fine old traditional inn serving superb home-made food and real ales; beer garden and play area.

 see page 400

52 THE STANLEY ARMS HOTEL

Anderton

Canalside inn serving excellent choice of home-made food, plus 3 real ales

 see page 401

Marbury Country Park

Manchester Ship Canal, and is now fully restored; two barges could enter the lift's upper tanks, two the lower, and, by pumping water out of the lower tank, the boats exchanged places and canals. A six-mile circular walk visits the Boat Lift, the Lion Salt Works and Great Budworth (Arley hall & Gardens), providing a fascinating insight into the area's industrial heritage and also its rural character.

About a mile north of Anderton, **Marbury Country Park** was formerly part of a large country estate but the area is now managed by Cheshire County Council whose wardens have created a variety of habitats for plants, trees and animals.

In Victorian times, the **Old Salt Mine** at **Marston**, just northeast of Northwich, was a huge tourist attraction: in 1844, the Tsar of Russia sat down to dinner, along with eminent members of the Royal Society, in a huge cavern that was lit by 10,000 lamps. The village is home to the **Lion Salt Works Museum**, where volunteers keep alive the only surviving open-pan saltworks in the country.

GREAT BUDWORTH

6 miles W of Knutsford off the A559

To the north of this village of attractive old cottages lies another of Cheshire's great estates, **Arley Hall** and Gardens, where visitors can find one of its grandest houses in perfect harmony with one of the county's finest gardens. Along with the sumptuous stately home that had all the latest state-of-the-art innovations, the conservationist Squire Egerton-Warburton and his wife masterminded the magnificent gardens; he is credited with creating what is believed to be the first herbaceous border in England.

Arley Hall, Great Budworth

WARRINGTON

Warrington is North Cheshire's largest town – an important industrial centre since Georgian and Victorian times and with substantial buildings of those days to prove it. Its imposing **Town Hall** was built in 1750 in very grand style with windows framed in painfully expensive copper, and elaborately designed entrance gates. A major Victorian contribution to the town is its excellent **Museum and Art Gallery** in Bold Street, one of the earliest municipal museums. The exhibits are remarkably varied: among them are shrunken heads, a unique china teapot collection, a scold's bridle, Egyptian mummies, Roman artefacts and some very fine Victorian watercolours and oils.

The TV presenter Chris Evans was born in Warrington, and the comedian and ukulele player George Formby is buried in the Catholic section of the town cemetery.

AROUND WARRINGTON

WIDNES

6 miles SW of Warrington on the A557

Widnes stands on the north shore of the Mersey, linked to Runcorn by a remarkably elegant road bridge. A popular attraction is Spike Island, which provides a landscaped walk from which the superstructures of ships passing along the Manchester Ship Canal can be seen gliding past.

DARESBURY

5 miles SW of Warrington on the A558

All Saints Church in Daresbury has a unique stained glass window: there are panels depicting a Gryphon and a Cheshire Cat, others show a Mock Turtle, a March Hare and a Mad Hatter. This is of course the **Lewis Carroll Memorial Window**, commemorating the author of *Alice in Wonderland*. Carroll himself is

39

Hollins Green nr Warrington

The **Black Swan** attracts patrons from near and far with outstanding food, fine ales and wines and high-class service.

see page 180

Statham, nr Lymm

New tenants are bringing back the good times to a much-loved local rescued from developers and once again the hub of the community.

 see page 168

---

shown at one side, dressed in clerical garb and kneeling. His father was Vicar of Daresbury when Carroll was born here in 1832 and baptised as Charles Lutwidge Dodgson. The boy enjoyed an apparently idyllic childhood at Daresbury until his father moved to another parish when Charles/Lewis was eleven years old.

RUNCORN

7 miles SW of Warrington on the A557

Runcorn is one of Britain's best known post-war new towns, developed around a much older town bearing the same name. Here, **Norton Priory** is always a delightful and intriguing place for a family outing, whatever the weather. The Augustinian priory was built in 1134 as a retreat for just 12 'black canons', so named because they wore a cape of black woollen cloth over a white linen surplice.

Work by the **Norton Priory Museum Trust** has uncovered the remains of the church, chapter house, cloisters and dormitory, and these finds are informatively explained in an audio-visual presentation. The Museum is open every afternoon, all year; the Gardens, which include a charming walled garden, are open from April to October.

LYMM

4 miles SE of Warrington on the A56

During the stage coach era, Eagle Brow was notorious, a dangerously steep road that dropped precipitously down the hillside into the village of Lymm. To bypass this hazard, a turnpike was built (now the A56), so preserving the heart of this ancient village with its half-timbered houses and well preserved village stocks. **Lymm Dam**, popular with anglers and bird-watchers, is part of a lovely woodland centre which is linked to the surrounding countryside and the canal towpath by a network of footpaths and bridleways.

DUNHAM MASSEY

4 miles E of Lymm on B5160

Dunham Massey Hall and Park (National Trust) has 250 acres of parkland where fallow deer roam freely and noble trees planted in the late 1700s still flourish. A restored water mill is usually in operation every Wednesday, and there are splendid walks in every direction. The Hall, once the home of the Earls of Stamford and Warrington, is a grand Georgian mansion of 1732 that boasts an outstanding collection of furniture, paintings and Huguenot silver. The Hall is open most days from April to October; the Park is open every day.

Cornwall

An isolated beauty that contains some of the most dramatic and spectacular scenery in the country. This is an apt description of Cornwall, a land of strong Celtic heritage and ancestry, a place dotted with monuments such as crosses, holy wells and prehistoric sights and where legends of old, particularly those surrounding King Arthur, still have a strong romantic appeal among the Cornish people and to visitors. Surrounded by rugged coastline, Cornwall has often been referred to as the English Riviera, encompassing pretty little fishing ports, secluded picturesque villages, narrow winding lanes and romantic seafaring traditions. While the northern coastline is dramatic, the southern Cornish coast is one of sheltered coves. Here, too, is one of the country's largest natural harbours, at Falmouth, but many of the fishing villages expanded to manage the exportation of the vast quantities of mineral ore and china clay that were extracted from inland Cornwall. Finally, there is Land's End, the westernmost tip of England, where the granite of Cornwall meets the Atlantic Ocean in a dramatic series of steep cliffs.

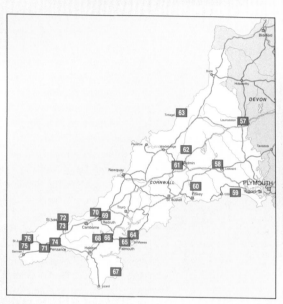

57   THE WHITE HORSE

Launceston

Once a farmhouse, now a popular inn and a magnet for lovers of good country cooking.

 see page 405

LAUNCESTON

Situated on the eastern edge of Bodmin Moor and close to the county border with Devon, it was here, shortly after the Norman Conquest, that William I's half-brother, Robert of Mortain, built the massive **Launceston Castle** overlooking the River Kensey. Although now in ruins, the 12-feet thick walls of the keep and tower can still be seen. Launceston also had a powerful Augustinian priory, founded beside the river in 1136; the main buildings have gone, but its chapel of ease remains.

To the west of the town, the **Launceston Steam Railway** takes visitors on a scenic trip through the beautiful Kensey Valley.

Launceston is also the start of the **Tamar Valley Discovery Trail**, a 30-mile footpath from here to Plymouth that takes in many of the villages that litter the Cornwall-Devon border. At **St Ann's**

Chapel, near Gunnislake, stands the **Tamar Valley Donkey Park**, Cornwall's only donkey sanctuary and home to more than two dozen donkeys and other rescued animals.

AROUND LAUNCESTON

CALSTOCK

12 miles SE of Launceston off the A390

Well known for its splendid views of the Tamar valley, this village was an important river port in the 19th century and its decline came with the construction of the huge Railway Viaduct which carries the picturesque Tamar Valley Line southwards to Plymouth.

Just to the southwest of Calstock is one of the best preserved medieval estates in the West Country – **Cotehele House** (National Trust), built between 1485 and 1624. Along with its Great Tudor Hall, fabulous tapestries and period furniture, the fortified granite house incorporates some charming features such as the secret spy-hole in the Great Hall and a tower clock with a bell but no face or hands. Surrounding the house are, firstly, the grounds, containing exotic and tender plants that thrive in the mild valley climate, and beyond that the estate with its ancient network of pathways that allow exploration of the valley.

The River Tamar runs through the estate and close to an old cider house and mill is **Cotehele Quay**, a busy river port in Victorian times and now home to an outstation of the **National Maritime Museum**,

Launceston Castle

an art and craft gallery and a licensed tea room. The restored Tamar sailing barge *Shamrock* is moored alongside the museum.

SALTASH

17 miles SE of Launceston on the A38

The 'Gateway to Cornwall', here the River Tamar is spanned by two mighty bridges. Designed by Isambard Kingdom Brunel in 1859, the iron-built **Royal Albert Bridge** carries the railway, while alongside is the much more slender **Tamar Bridge**, a suspension road bridge that was opened in 1961. To the south of Saltash lies **Mount Edgcumbe House**, to where the Earls of Edgcumbe moved when they left Cotehele House; it is surrounded by a country park that encompasses a stretch of heritage coast, numerous follies and one of Cornwall's greatest gardens. The southernmost point of the country park takes in **Rame Head**, 400 feet cliffs that guard the entrance into Plymouth Sound. Also on this peninsula is 18th century **Antony House**, home to a wonderful collection of paintings (many by Sir Joshua Reynolds), tapestries and furniture. Surrounding the house are the gardens and grounds landscaped by Humphry Repton.

St Michael's Chapel, Rame Head

LISKEARD

13½ miles SW of Launceston on the B3254

Although it is a small town, Liskeard boasts some grand Victorian public buildings, including the Guildhall and the Public Hall, home to a local museum. In Well Street, lies one of Liskeard's most

curious features – an arched grotto that marks the site of **Pipe Well**, a medieval spring reputed to have curative powers, especially for afflictions of the eye. It is said that the well has never run dry.

Another well lies to the southwest: **St Keyne's Well** is named after the daughter of a Welsh king who settled here in the 5th century.

LOOE

20 miles SW of Launceston on the A387

The tidal harbour at Looe, created by the two rivers the East Looe and West Looe, made this an important fishing and seafaring port and it is still Cornwall's second most important port with fish auctions taking place at East Looe's famous **Banjo Pier**. East Looe is the older

58   THE MARKET INN

St Cleer, nr Liskeard

A lovely old stone inn with a reputation for fine food that extends far beyond the local community.

see page 404

59   THE SWAN COFFEE
SHOP

Downderry, nr Looe

A super little coffee shop serving a day-long selection of home-cooked snacks and meals.

 see page 405

60   THE SHIP INN

Lerryn, nr Lostwithiel

A lovely pub in an idyllic riverside setting, with an exciting menu of home-cooked dishes and a choice of B&B or self-catering accommodation.

 see page 406

part, and housed in the 16th century **Old Guildhall** is the town's Museum.

The South East Cornwall Discovery Centre in West Looe introduces visitors to the wealth of wildlife, plant life and splendid scenery of the region.

To the southwest of Looe is **Polperro**, many people's idea of a typical Cornish fishing village, its steep, narrow streets and alleyways filled with picturesque fisherman's cottages.

Two miles west of Looe, at Murrayton, is the famous **Monkey Sanctuary**, the world's first protected colony of Amazonian woolly monkeys.

FOWEY

24½ miles SW of Launceston on the A3082

A lovely old seafaring town, with steep, narrow streets, Fowey has one of the most beautiful natural harbours along the south coast. The town's **Museum** is an excellent place to discover Fowey's colourful past and its literary connections:

Daphne du Maurier (1907-1989) lived at Gribbin Head and Sir Arthur Quiller-Couch (1863-1944), son of a Cornish doctor, lived for over 50 years at The Haven, on the Esplanade.

Daphne du Maurier's ashes were scattered on the cliffs near her home. Sir Arthur Quiller-Couch ('Q'), who was the Mayor of Fowey in 1937-8, died after being hit by a car; he was buried in the Church of St Fimbarrus.

To the south of Fowey lies **St Catherine's Castle**, part of a chain of fortifications that were built by Henry VIII to protect the harbours along the south coast.

Just up the River Fowey is **Golant** and the Iron Age lookout point of **Castle Dore Earthworks**, while further upstream is **Lostwithiel**, a small market town that was the capital of Cornwall in the 13th century. The strategic crossing point of the River Fowey here is protected by the surprisingly complete remains of 12th century **Restormel Castle**.

BODMIN

19½ miles SW of Launceston on the A389

Situated midway between Cornwall's two coasts and at the junction of two ancient trade routes, Bodmin has always been an important town, and Castle Canyke was built during the Iron Age to defend this important route. To the south is **Lanhydrock House**, one of the most fascinating late 19th century houses in England, surrounded by wonderful formal gardens, woodland and parkland.

Bodinnick Ferry, Fowey

Rough Tor, Bodmin Moor

Bodmin

61 THE BODMIN & WENFORD RAILWAY

A marvellous preserved railway operating a regular timetable of steam-hauled trains, with special events throughout the year.

 see page 407

BOLVENTOR

10½ miles SW of Launceston on the A30

Situated at the heart of **Bodmin Moor**, this scenic village is home to the former coaching inn that was immortalised by Daphne du Maurier in her famous novel, *Jamaica Inn*. Structurally little changed today, Jamaica Inn still welcomes visitors who come here not only seeking refreshment and accommodation but also to discover the secrets of the moors and the life and works of du Maurier.

Bodmin Moor is the smallest of the three great West Country moors; at 1,377 feet, **Brown Willy** is the highest point on the moor, while, just to the northwest, lies **Rough Tor**, the moor's second highest point. Throughout this wild and beautiful moorland there are remains of early occupiers, including Bronze Age hut circles and field enclosures and Iron Age hill forts.

To the south of Bolventor is the mysterious natural tarn, **Dozmary Pool**, a place that is strongly linked with the legend of King Arthur and said by some to be the place where the Lady of the Lake received the dying King's sword, Excalibur.

To the southeast lies the one-time mining village of **Minions**, and close by are the impressive **Bronze Age Hurlers Stone Circle** and **Trethevy Quoit**, an impressive enclosed chamber tomb that originally formed the core of a vast earthwork mound.

BUDE

15 miles NW of Launceston off the A39

A traditional seaside resort with sweeping expanses of sand, rock pools and Atlantic breakers, Bude has also developed into a popular surfing centre. Completed in 1820, the **Bude Canal** was an ambitious project that aimed to connect the Atlantic with the English Channel via the River Tamar. However, the

62 THE BLISLAND INN

Blisland, nr Bodmin

A magnet for real ale connoisseurs (with an annual beer festival) and lovers of good home cooking.

see page 408

45

The history of Bude and its canal can be explored in the Bude-Stratton Museum, which stands on the canal side near the sea lock in the Canal Company's former smithy.

63 TINTAGEL CASTLE

Tintagel

For over 800 years the tale has been told that **Tintagel Castle** was the birthplace of King Arthur

 see page 409

only stretch to be finished was that between Bude and Launceston and it is now the Bude Canal Trail footpath.

Close to the canal's entrance stands **Bude Castle**, designed by the local 19th century physician and brilliant inventor, Sir Goldsworthy Gurney. What makes this building (now an office) particularly interesting is that it is thought to have been the first building in Britain to be constructed on sand. To celebrate the new millennium, Carole Vincent and Anthony Fanshawe designed the **Bude Light 2000**, the first large-scale public sculpture to combine coloured concrete with fibre optic lighting. To the south of Bude is one of the most dramatic places along this stretch of coastline, **Crackington Haven**, a tiny port overlooked by towering 400 feet cliffs.

TINTAGEL

17 miles W of Launceston on the B3263

Tintagel Castle, set on a wild and windswept headland, is forever linked with the legend of King Arthur, and the village naturally owes much of its popularity to its Arthurian connections; one of its many interesting attractions on this theme is King Arthur's **Great Hall**.

Also worth seeing here is the weather-beaten **Old Post Office**, a 14th century manor house that became a Post Office in the 19th century. Purchased by the National Trust in 1903 for £100, the building still has its original stone-paved medieval hall and ancient fireplace along with the ground floor office of the postmistress.

To the south lies the most famous slate quarry in Cornwall, **Delabole Slate Quarry**.

TRURO

The administrative and ecclesiastical centre of Cornwall, this elegant small city was once a fashionable place to rival Bath. The foundation stone of **Truro Cathedral** was laid

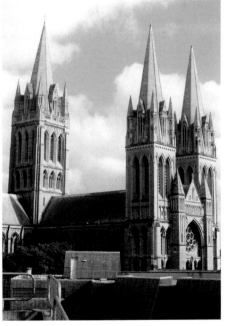

Truro Cathedral

in 1880 and this splendid Early English style building, with its celebrated Victorian stained glass window, was finally completed in 1910. To the northeast lies **Probus**, a large village that is home to the 'really useful garden' – **Probus Gardens**. Here, too, is **Trewithen House and Gardens**, which were laid out in the early 20th century.

AROUND TRURO

NEWQUAY
10 miles N of Truro on the A392

Huer's Hut, Newquay

A traditional English seaside resort, with all the usual trappings, Newquay also has a long history and for centuries was an important pilchard fishing village. On the Towan Headland stands a **Huer's Hut** from where the Huer would scan the sea looking for shoals of pilchards and, once spotted, he would cry 'hevva' to alert the awaiting fishing crews. Today, its beautiful rocky coastline and acres of golden sands have seen it develop into a popular seaside resort famous throughout the world for its surfing.

Inland are the imposing engine house and chimney stack of **East Wheal Rose** mine, Cornwall's richest lead mine, and close by is the delightful small Elizabeth manor house, **Trerice**, which is also home to a Mower Museum.

PADSTOW
19½ miles NE of Truro on the A389

It was here that the Welsh missionary St Petroc landed in the 6th century and founded a Celtic Minster. Beginning at the door of the town's 13th century parish **Church of St Petroc**, the Saints Way is a middle-distance footpath that follows the route that was taken by travellers and pilgrims crossing Cornwall on their way from Brittany to Ireland.

Although the River Camel silted up in the 19th century, the Harbour remains the town's focal point and here are many of Padstow's older buildings, including **Raleigh Cottage**, where Sir Walter Raleigh lived while he was Warden of Cornwall, and the tiny Harbour Cottage. The harbour is also home to the **Shipwreck Museum**.

On the other side of the Camel Estuary are the small resorts of **Polzeath** and **New Polzeath** and a beautiful coastal path that takes in the cliffs and farmland of Pentire Point and Rumps Point.

The **Church of St Enodoc** is a Norman building that has, on several occasions, been virtually submerged by windblown sand. The beautiful churchyard contains

*It was on the cliffs above Polzeath that Laurence Binyon wrote his ode **For the Fallen**, the words of which are better known than the name of their author:*

*"They shall not grow old,
as we that are left grow old:
Age shall not weary them,
nor the years condemn.
At the going down of the sun
and in the morning
We will remember them."*

To the southeast of St Austell lies Charlestown, a small fishing village that developed into a harbour for exporting china clay. Close to the docks is the Charlestown Shipwreck, Rescue and Heritage Centre which offers an insight into the town's history, local shipwrecks and the various devices that have been developed over the years for rescuing and recovering those in peril at sea.

the graves of many shipwrecked mariners and that of the poet Sir John Betjeman, who is buried here along with his parents. Betjeman spent many of his childhood holidays in the villages and coves around the Camel Estuary, and his affection for the local people and places was the inspiration for many of his works. The church is reached across a golf course that is regarded as one of the most scenic links courses in the country.

WADEBRIDGE

20 miles NE of Truro on the A39

Standing at the historic lowest bridging point on the River Camel, this ancient port and busy market town is now a popular holiday centre. The town is also home to the **Bridge on Wool**, which was constructed on bridge piers that were sunk on foundation of woolsacks; the bridge still carries the main road that links the town's two ancient parishes. The town's former railway station is now home to the **John Betjeman Centre**.

ST AUSTELL

12½ miles NE of Truro on the A390

When William Cookworthy discovered large deposits of kaolin, or china clay, in 1748, this old market town, a centre of tin and copper mining, was transformed. Over the years, the waste material from the clay pits to the north and west of the town has been piled up into conical spoil heaps that have led to the area being nicknamed the Cornish Alps. More recently, action has been taken to soften the countryside and the heaps and disused pits have been landscaped with planting, undulating footpaths and nature trails.

In the heart of the Cornish Alps lies **Wheal Martyn**, an old clay works that is now home to the **Wheal Martyn China Clay Museum**. To the northeast, in the heart of the china clay area, lies the wonderful **Eden Project**, an ambitious undertaking that aims to "promote the understanding and responsible management of the vital relationship between plants, people and resources."

MEVAGISSEY

11½ miles E of Truro on the B3273

The largest fishing village in St Austell Bay. Housed in a harbour building dating from 1745 are the **Mevagissey Folk Museum**, the World of Model Railway Exhibition and The Aquarium. In the 1750s, when John Wesley first came to Mevagissey to preach, he was greeted with a barrage of rotten eggs and old fish and had to be

Wheal Martyn China Clay Museum, nr St Austell

rescued from the crowd and taken to safety. In return for their hospitality, Wesley gave his hosts James and Mary Lelean his silver shoe buckles.

To the northwest of Mevagissey lie the famous **Lost Gardens of Heligan**, one of the country's most interesting gardens that was originally laid out in 1780 but lay undisturbed for 70 years before being rediscovered in 1990. Today, this beautiful and intriguing place is once again attracting visitors from all over the world.

ST MAWES

7½ miles S of Truro on the A3078

This charming town in the shelter of Carrick Roads is dominated by its artillery fort, **St Mawes Castle**, which was built in the 1540s as part of Henry VIII's coastal defences.

FALMOUTH

8 miles SW of Truro on the A39

A spectacular deep-water anchorage that is the world's third largest

natural harbour, Falmouth lies in Britain's Western Approaches and guards the entrance into **Carrick Roads**. Standing on a 200 feet promontory overlooking the entrance to Carrick Roads, Henry VIII's **Pendennis Castle** is one of Cornwall's great fortresses and, along with St Mawes Castle, it has protected Britain's shores from attack ever since its construction.

Falmouth's nautical and notorious past is revealed at the **National Maritime Museum Cornwall**.

To the north lies **Feock**, one of the prettiest small villages in Cornwall and to the south lies **Restronguet Point**. It was from **Tolverne**, just north of Feock, that Allied troops left for the Normandy coast during the D-day landings and on the shingle beach the remains of the concrete honeycombed mattresses can still be seen. Close by lies the estate of **Trelissick**, a privately owned 18th century house that is surrounded by

64   THE VICTORY INN

St Mawes

A traditional public house looking down on the harbour, a great setting for enjoying a drink and a meal. Also two rooms for B&B.

 see page 409

65   THE FOUR WINDS INN

Falmouth

A popular inn standing in its own grounds, with a fine reputation for its excellent home cooking.

see page 410

National Maritime Museum, Falmouth

66   THE HALFWAY HOUSE

Penryn

A popular and sociable public house with a menu of home-cooked dishes that really does cater for all appetites.

 see page 410

67   THE WHITE HART

St Keverne, Helston

A friendly, relaxing village inn serving super food lunchtime and evening. Three rooms for B&B guests.

 see page 410

marvellous gardens and parkland that offer wonderful views over Carrick Roads.

HELFORD

12½ miles SW of Truro off the B3293

A picture postcard village on the southern banks of the Helford estuary, Helford was once the haunt of smugglers, but today it is a popular sailing centre. From the village, the five-mile **Helford River Walk** takes in several isolated hamlets and a 200-year-old fig tree that grows in the churchyard at **Manaccan**.

On the northern banks of the River Helford are two glorious gardens: **Glendurgan Garden**, created in the 1820s, and **Trebah Garden** that has often been called the 'garden of dreams'.

LIZARD

22 miles SW of Truro on the A3038

The most southerly village in mainland Britain, Lizard is a place of craft shops, cafés and art galleries that lends its name to the **Lizard Peninsula**, an area that is physically separate from mainland Cornwall. The Lizard is known for its unique serpentine rock, a green mineral that became fashionable in the 19th century after Queen Victoria visited Cornwall and ordered many items made from the stone for

her house, Osborne, on the Isle of Wight.

To the south of the village lies **Lizard Point**, the tip of the peninsula, whose three sides are lashed by waves whatever the season.

To the northwest of Lizard, close to Mullion, is the popular sandy beach of **Poldhu Cove**, from where in 1901 Guglielmo Marconi transmitted the first wireless message from the clifftops and across the Atlantic. A granite column commemorates the event. A couple of miles inland, on **Goonhilly Downs**, is a monument to the very latest in telecommunications – the **Earth Satellite Station**.

Goonhilly Downs Earth Station

HELSTON

15 miles SW of Truro on the A394

Dating back to Roman times, this ancient stannary town also developed as a port but, today, it is best known for the famous **Festival of the Furry**, or Flora Dance, a colourful festival of music and dance with ancient pagan connections.

On the nearest Saturday to St Michael's Day (May 8th) the Flora Dance Festival is celebrated with dances led by the Helston Town Band; in the principal dances the participants wear top hat, tails and dress gowns.

Among the town's surprising number of Georgian, Regency and Victorian buildings are the **Helston Folk Museum** and 16th century Angel House, the former town house of the Godolphin family.

To the northwest lie **Trevarno Estate and Gardens**, and close by is the **Poldark Mine Heritage Complex**, with its underground tour of tunnels and the famous 18th century Poldark village.

To the east of the town is another interesting family attraction, **Flambards**, which is based around a faithful re-creation of a Victorian street. Nearby is the Royal Navy's land and sea rescue headquarters at **Culdrose**, one of the largest and busiest helicopter bases in Europe.

REDRUTH

8½ miles SW of Truro on the A393

This market town owes its past prosperity to its location – at the heart of Cornwall's mining industry – and some pockets of Victorian, Georgian and earlier buildings can still be found. In the 19th century the land around Camborne was the most intensely mined in the world with, in the 1850s, over 300 mines producing some two thirds of the world's copper! With such a history of mining it is not surprising that Camborne is home to the world famous **School of Mining** and its **Geological Museum**.

Immediately south of Redruth lies dramatic **Carn Brea**, a granite hill that rises some 738 feet above sea level and is crowned by a 90 feet monument to Francis Basset, a local benevolent mine and land owner. Nearby is the mysterious **Gwennap Pit**, a round, grass-covered amphitheatre that is thought to have been created by the collapse of a subterranean mine shaft.

To the north, along the coast, lie the two thriving holiday centres of **Porthtowan** and **Portreath**, which, although they developed as a copper mining village and ore exporting port respectively, are now the summer preserve of holidaymakers and surfers.

ST AGNES

8 miles NW of Truro on the B3285

Once known as the source of the finest tin in Cornwall, this old village still retains many of its original miners' cottages while, surrounding the village, are the ruins of old mine workings including the clifftop buildings of

68   THE STAR INN

Porkellis

Outstanding hospitality and super home cooking in a picture postcard village pub.

 see page 411

69   THE STAR INN

Vogue, St Day, Redruth

The hub of the local community, a great place for food, drink, entertainment and good company.

see page 412

70   CLIFF HOUSE

Portreath

A very pleasant small family run B&B in a prime position close to the shore.

see page 412

71 THE TARBERT HOTEL

Penzance

An outstanding small hotel offering the very best in service, comfort and cuisine.

  see page 413

one of Cornwall's best known mines – **Wheal Coates**. The mine operated between 1860 and 1890 and the derelict Engine House is one of the more exceptional landmarks along this stretch of coast. The remains of **Wheal Kitty** provide panoramic views over this once industrial area. The tin production processes is explained on guided tours around **Blue Hills Tin Streams** at nearby **Trevellas**.

Just up the coast lies the holiday resort of **Perranporth** whose Celtic heritage is kept alive during the annual **Lowender Peran Festival** of music and dance.

In the dunes overlooking Penhale Sands, a mile from Perranporth, lies St Piran's Oratory, the oldest Christian church in the UK, burial place of the Saint who is said to have travelled from Ireland to Cornwall on a millstone. His landing place is marked by a Celtic cross.

PENZANCE

Cornwall's only promenade stretches from here to Newlyn, and

other interesting buildings include the exotic **Egyptian House** created from two cottages in the 1830s, and the **Union Hotel**, where the first announcement in mainland England of the victory of Trafalgar and the death of Nelson was made. Penzance's links with the sea are remembered at the **Maritime Museum** and the **Trinity House Lighthouse Centre**.

To the southwest lies **Newlyn**, the largest fish landing port in England. As well as being home to the **Pilchard Works Heritage Museum**, the town is known for its artistic associations: it was here in the late 19th century that the Newlyn School of art was founded.

AROUND PENZANCE

ZENNOR

5½ miles N of Penzance on the B3306

This delightful ancient village shows evidence of Bronze Age settlers and the **Wayside Folk Museum** has numerous exhibits that tell of this region's industrial past. DH Lawrence lived here with his wife Frieda during World War I and it was during his stay here, under police surveillance, that Lawrence wrote *Women in Love*. However, his pacifist tendencies and Frieda's German heritage (her cousin was the flying ace the Red Baron) caused them to be 'moved on' in October 1917. By the porch in the church at Zennor is a memorial to John Davey, who died in 1891, stating that he was the last person to have any great knowledge

Trinity House Lighthouse Centre, Penzance

Chysauster Ancient Village, Zennor

72 BUMBLES TEA ROOM

St Ives

The irresistible allure of home-baked cakes and pastries keeps the customers happy – and the savouries are just as good!

see page 414

of the native Cornish language Kernuack. It is said that he remained familiar with the language by speaking it to his cat. To the southeast of the village lies the Neolithic chamber tomb, **Zennor Quoit** while, close by, is **Chysauster Ancient Village**, a Romano-Cornish village that was built around 2,000 years ago and has one of the oldest identifiable streets in the country.

ST IVES

7 miles NE of Penzance on the A3074

Now one of the most-visited places in the county, this was once one of the most important fishing centres in Cornwall, and locally mined ores and minerals were exported from the harbour (St Ives Museum is housed in a former mine building). St Ives is also home to **Tate St Ives**, dedicated to the work of 20th century painters and sculptures, and the **Barbara Hepworth Sculpture Garden and Museum**, housed in her former studio.

73 TATE ST IVES

St Ives

A superb modern building which houses a unique collection of contemporary and modern art.

see page 416

Barbara Hepworth Sculpture Garden, St Ives

74 MOUNT VIEW HOTEL

Longrock, nr Penzance

A handsome Victorian hotel with comfortable rooms for B&B, a self-catering cottage and top-notch Cornish cooking of top-notch Cornish ingredients.

see page 415

HAYLE

7½ miles NE of Penzance on the B3301

It was here in the early 1800s that the Cornish inventor Richard Trevithick built an early version of the steam locomotive and, a short time later, one of the first railways in the world was constructed here to carry tin and copper from Redruth down to the port.

MARAZION

3 miles E of Penzance off the A394

For centuries the most important settlement around Mount's Bay, this harbour town of fine old inns and residential houses that overlook the sandy beach is now a windsurfing and sailing centre. To the northwest is **Marazion Marsh**, an RSPB reserve with breeding colonies of grey herons and visiting waders and wildfowl.

Situated a third of a mile offshore and connected to Marazion by a cobbled causeway that is exposed at high tide, **St Michael's Mount** rises dramatically out of the waters of Mount's Bay. In the 11th century, Edward the Confessor founded a priory on the mount and these remains are incorporated into the marvellous **St Michael's Mount Castle**.

LAND'S END

9 miles SW of Penzance on the A30

Mainland Britain's most westerly point and one of the country's most famous landmarks, it is here that the granite of Cornwall finally meets the Atlantic Ocean in a series of savage cliffs, reefs and sheer-sided islets. Land's End has been a tourist destination since the early 19th century, and down the years an ever-expanding complex of man-made attractions has been added to the majestic scenery that nature has provided. From this headland can be seen **Longships Lighthouse**, just off shore, and **Wolf Rock Lighthouse**, seven miles away. Just to the southeast, and protected by **Gwennap Head**, is **Porthcurno**, from where in 1870 the first telegraph cable was laid linking Britain with the rest of the world. Housed in a secret underground wartime communications centre is the **Porthcurno Wartime Telegraph Museum**. This interesting village is also home to the marvellous **Minack Theatre**, an open-air amphitheatre cut into the cliff that was founded by Rowena Cade in the 1930s.

St Michael's Mount

Land's End

75 THE KINGS ARMS

St Just

A fine old stone inn open all
day for food and drink.

see page 416

76 THE QUEENS ARMS

Botallack, St Just

A fine country inn open all
day for drinks, with menus
that include super fish
specials. September Beer
Festival. Self-catering cottage
for two.

see page 416

ST JUST

6½ miles NW of Penzance on the A3071

The westernmost town in mainland Britain, St Just was once a thriving mining centre, and the surrounding area is littered with industrial remains. A narrow road leads westwards to **Cape Cornwall**, the only cape in England and, along the way, the road passes the last remains of Cape Cornwall Mine – its tall chimney.

St Just marks the start of the **Tinners' Way**, an ancient trackway between the town and St Ives that follows ancient moorland paths.

To the northeast lies **Pendeen**, where tin has been mined since prehistoric times. The last of 20 or so mines in this area, **Geevor Tin Mine and Heritage Centre** not only preserves the mine but also offers visitors the chance to experience the conditions that miners had to endure underground. Also close by is the mighty **Levant Steam Engine**, housed in a tiny building perched high on the cliffs.

Cumbria

The second largest county in England, Cumbria is much more than the Lake District National Park that lies within its boundaries. It was here that the British Celts managed to preserve their independence from the Saxons and the Norse influence can still be detected in the place names here. The county town, Carlisle, lies to the north, close to the Scottish border and was for centuries a base for English soldiers who planned their attacks on Scotland from here, as well as defending Carlisle from border raids. The Lake District National Park is not only home to England's largest lake, Windermere, but also to the country's highest peak, Scafell Pike. An area of magnificent crags, isolated fells and expanses of water, this dramatic landscape has inspired Wordsworth and many other poets and artists. Of the county's coastline, the Furness Peninsula is probably the most attractive - a place of elegant and small seaside resorts and once an area of great ecclesiastical power.

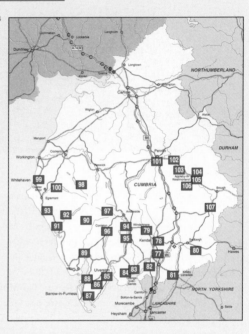

KENDAL

The capital of south Lakeland, Kendal has royal connections: the Parr family lived at **Kendal Castle** until 1483, and it was Catherine Parr, a descendant, who became Henry VIII's last wife. Today, the castle's gaunt ruins stand high on a hill overlooking Kendal. The woollen industry, on which much of the town's prosperity was based, has long since disappeared, but there is one local product that all visitors should try: Kendal Mint Cake, a tasty, very sweet confection, sometimes covered in chocolate, that is cherished by climbers and walkers for its instant infusion of energy.

A number of interesting museums and galleries can be found in Kendal including the **Museum of Lakeland Life and Industry** and the **Abbot Hall Art Gallery** that includes the work of John Ruskin. At the town's Quaker Meeting House, the history of the Quaker Movement is told through a series of 77 panels that combine to form the **Quaker Tapestry Exhibition**.

AROUND KENDAL

RAVENSTONEDALE

14½ miles NE of Kendal off the A685

Known locally as Rissendale, this pretty village, clustered along the banks of Scandal Beck, lies on the edge of the Howgill Fells; its church, built in 1738, is one of the few Georgian churches in Cumbria.

SEDBERGH

9 miles E of Kendal on the A684

Although Sedbergh is in Cumbria it lies within the Yorkshire Dales National Park and the surrounding scenery is typical of the Dales. One spectacular local feature is **Cautley Crag**, a great cliff alongside which tumbles a beautiful narrow waterfall, **Cautley Spout**. Firbank Knott, on nearby Firbank Fell, is considered to be the birthplace of Quakerism as it

77 THE PUNCH BOWL

Barrows Green, Kendal

Loyal locals and visitors to Kendal enjoy a friendly ambience and hearty home cooking at the **Punch Bowl**.

🍴 *see page 417*

78 DICKIE DOODLES

Kendal

Open every evening from 8 till late, **Dickie Doodles** is a magnet for lovers of good music and well-kept beer.

🍴 *see page 418*

79 WILF'S CAFÉ

Staveley, nr Kendal

A splendid café overlooking the River Kent, open all day for fresh, wholesome snacks and meals.

🍴 *see page 417*

57

80 THE GEORGE & DRAGON

Dent, nr Sedbergh

Superb food, beer and accommodation provide everything the visitor could wish for.

 see page 419

81 THE SNOOTY FOX HOTEL

Kirkby Lonsdale

A charming, atmospheric Jacobean inn renowned for its food, beer, wine and accommodation.

 see page 420

82 THE CROSS KEYS HOTEL

Milnthorpe

A friendly, relaxing inn serving well-kept ales and super food. Also top-quality B&B rooms and a self-catering cottage.

 see page 420

58

Devil's Bridge, Kirkby Lonsdale

was here, in 1652, that George Fox gave his great sermon to inspire over a thousand 'seekers' from the whole of the north of England. The **Quaker Meeting House** is the oldest in the north of England.

KIRKBY LONSDALE

11 miles SE of Kendal on the A65

There has been a bridge over the River Lune here for at least 700 years and, for centuries, it has drawn people who come here to experience what John Ruskin described as "one of the loveliest scenes in England." The subject of a painting by JMW Turner, the Devil's Bridge is said to have been built by Satan in just three days.

LEVENS

4½ miles S of Kendal off the A590

To the south of the village and overlooking the Lyth valley is the superb Elizabethan mansion, **Levens Hall**, which was developed from a 14th century pele tower. Best known for its fine furniture

and unique topiary gardens, it also houses a collection of working steam engines.

MILNTHORPE

7½ miles S of Kendal on the A6

Close to this market town on the A6 is the **Lakeland Wildlife Oasis** that, since opening in 1991, has established itself as one of the county's premier attractions.

GRANGE-OVER-SANDS

12 miles SW of Kendal on the B5278

This charming town on the north shore of Morecambe Bay is the starting point of the **Cistercian Way**, an interesting 33-mile long footpath through Furness to Barrow.

To the west of Grange lies **Cartmel**, one of the prettiest villages in Furness, that is dominated by the famous **Cartmel Priory** that was founded by Augustinian canons in 1188. It was dismantled in 1537, and all that is left are the substantial remains of

Holker Hall and Gardens, Grange-over-Sands

the 12th century Gatehouse.

Just to the southwest of Grange lies Cumbria's premier stately home, **Holker Hall**, one of the homes of the Dukes of Devonshire. An intriguing blend of 16th century, Georgian and Victorian architecture, the Hall is surrounded by a large estate that includes a deer park, formal gardens and the **Lakeland Motor Museum**.

NEWBY BRIDGE

10 ½ miles SW of Kendal on the A592

The bridge here crosses the River Leven that runs from the southern tip of Windermere into Morecambe Bay, and visitors to this popular tourist destination can reach the famous lake by taking a steam train on the **Lakeside and Haverthwaite Railway**. Just to the north is Fell Foot Park, delightful landscaped gardens and woodlands that were laid out in the late 19th century.

ULVERSTON

17½ miles SW of Kendal on the A590

Ulverston boasts England's shortest, widest and deepest canal, built by the engineer John Rennie in late 18th century. Crowning a hill to the north of the town centre is the **Barrow Monument,** a 100 feet-high replica of the Eddystone Lighthouse that was erected in 1850 to commemorate the explorer, diplomat and author Sir John Barrow. He served as a Lord of the Admiralty and it was his naval reforms that contributed to England's success in the Napoleonic Wars.

Even more famous was Stanley Jefferson, who was born in Argyle Street on 16 June 1890. Better known as Stan Laurel, he made more than 100 films in a 30-year career with his partner Oliver Hardy, and visitors can learn all about this celebrated duo in the town's **Laurel and Hardy Museum.**

83 THE ROYAL OAK INN

Cartmel

The oldest inn in Cartmel is a magnet for anyone who wants the best in well-kept ales and delicious food – and a warm Cumbrian welcome.

🍴 🛏 *see page 421*

84 UPLANDS COUNTRY HOUSE HOTEL

Cartmel

A lovely location, comfortable accommodation and outstanding food in one of the region's top hotels.

🛏 🍴 *see page 422*

85 THE DEVONSHIRE ARMS

Ulverston

The most sociable of pubs, and a great place to enjoy a drink, a meal and excellent company.

🍴 *see page 421*

59

86 THE DERBY ARMS

Great Urswick, nr Ulverston
A friendly local with traditional beer and four well-appointed rooms for B&B guests.

 see page 423

87 THE CROFTERS

Barrow-in-Furness
A pleasant town inn serving Thwaites ales and home-cooked pub classics.

 see page 423

88 THE BLACK DOG INN

Dalton-in-Furness
A pristine 300-year-old inn with a superb choice of real ales and outstanding food.

see page 425

Dock Museum, Barrow-in-Furness

BARROW-IN-FURNESS

24 miles SW of Kendal on the A590

Right up until the early 1800s, Barrow-in-Furness was just a tiny hamlet but, in just 40 years, it became the largest iron and steel centre in the world and also a major shipbuilding centre. The impressive **Dock Museum** tells the story of the town through a series of audio-visual displays and an interactive film show brings to life the people who made Barrow so successful.

Furness Abbey, a magnificent ruin of red sandstone, is the focal point of south Cumbria's monastic heritage. Another historic building nearby is Dalton Castle, a 14th century pele tower that provided a refuge for the monks of the abbey against Scottish raiders.

To the south of Barrow lies the **Isle of Walney**, a 10-mile long island joined to the peninsula by a bridge from Barrow that is home to two important nature reserves: **North Walney National Nature Reserve**, with a great variety of habitats, including sand dunes, heath, salt marsh and shingle; and **South Walney Nature Reserve**, the largest nesting grounds of herring gulls and lesser black-backed gulls in Europe.

Furness Abbey, Barrow-in-Furness

60

Swinside Stone Circle, Broughton-in-Furness

BROUGHTON-IN-FURNESS

19 miles W of Kendal on the A595

Some of the Lake District's finest scenery lies within easy reach of Broughton. A couple of miles west of the town is **Swinside Circle**, a fine prehistoric stone monument, 60 feet in diameter, while, to the north, in the peaceful hamlet of Broughton Mills, is the **Coleridge Trail**. During his 'circumcursion' of Lakeland in August 1802, the poet stopped to refresh himself at the Blacksmith's Arms here and the inn, built in 1748, has outwardly changed little since his visit.

RAVENGLASS

27 miles W of Kendal on the A595

The town's major attraction is the 15-inch narrow gauge **Ravenglass and Eskdale Railway** that runs for seven miles up the valleys of the Mite and Esk. One of the few settlements on the route of the railway is Eskdale Green and close by are a group of buildings that make up Eskdale Mill where cereals have been ground since 1578 and which is in full working order.

Owned by the Pennington family

Muncaster Castle, Ravenglass

89 THE BLACK COCK INN

Broughton-in-Furness

A much-loved hostelry offering high standards of hospitality, food, drink and accommodation

 see page 424

90 THE WOOLPACK INN & HARDKNOTT BREWERY

Boot, Eskdale

A wonderful hostelry in a remote, beautiful location, with characterful accommodation, terrific food and its own micro-brewery.

 see page 426

91 THE LUTWIDGE ARMS HOTEL

Holmrook

A convivial village hostelry with bar and restaurant menus and 16 well-appointed en suite bedrooms.

 see page 425

92 STRANDS HOTEL AND BREWERY

Nether Wasdale

Premier hotel in scenic location offering quality cuisine, its own micro-brewery ales, and comfortable en suite rooms.

 see page 427

93 THE STANLEY ARMS HOTEL

Calderbridge, Seascale

A former coaching inn with lovely gardens, Thwaites ales, home cooking and 12 en suite bedrooms.

  see page 428

94 THE LAKES HOTEL

Windermere

Two excellent offerings in one: a comfortable, well-appointed B&B hotel and tours by luxury mini-coach.

 see page 428

since 1208, **Muncaster Castle**, just east of Ravenglass, is not only famous for its many treasures - including outstanding collections of tapestry, silver and porcelain - but also for its vast and beautiful grounds, which include an Owl Centre.

A focal point for fishing, beach casting, wind surfing and water skiing, **Seascale**, up the coast from Ravenglass, is one of the most popular seaside villages in Cumbria. Its Victorian wooden jetty was restored to mark the Millennium.

WINDERMERE

8 miles NW of Kendal on the A591

The village was originally called Birthwaite, but when the railway arrived in 1847 the Kendal and Windermere Railway Company named the station after the nearby lake even though it was over a mile away. Within a few yards of Windermere Station (now serving a single-track branch line) is a footpath that leads through woodland to one of the finest viewpoints in Lakeland – Orrest Head.

Just to the north of Windermere is the village of **Troutbeck**, a designated conservation area with attractive old houses and cottages grouped around a number of wells and springs that, until recently, formed the only water supply. The best-known building here is **Townend**, an enchanting example of Cumbrian vernacular architecture.

Now all but merged with Windermere, **Bowness-on-Windermere** is an attractive town right on the edge of the lake; it is from here that most of the lake cruises operate. Along with all the boating activity, the town is also home to the **Windermere**

Cumbrian Mountains across Windermere

Steamboat Museum with its unique collection of Victorian and Edwardian steam launches, some of them still in working order. Just down the road from the museum is the Old Laundry Visitor Centre, the home of The World of Beatrix Potter where there are some fascinating re-creations of this much loved Lakeland author's books.

HAWKSHEAD

11 miles NW of Kendal on the B5285

It was in this charming little village at the head of Esthwaite Water that Beatrix Potter's solicitor husband, William Heelis, had his office; this is now The Beatrix Potter Gallery, which features an exhibition of her original drawings and illustrations along with details of her life. Using the royalties from her first book, *The Tale of Peter Rabbit*, Beatrix Potter purchased Hill Top in the village of Near Sawrey, having fallen in love with the place during a holiday. In accordance with her will, Hill Top has remained just as she would have known it and it is now full of Beatrix Potter memorabilia.

To the southwest of Hawkshead lies Grizedale Forest, acquired by the Forestry Commission in 1934 and famous for its 80 tree sculptures.

CONISTON

14 miles NW of Kendal on the A593

To the south of the once major copper mining centre of Coniston is Coniston Hall, the village's oldest building. But it is the Ruskin

Museum that draws most visitors to the village. Containing many of the famous man's studies, pictures, letters and photographs, as well as his collection of geological specimens, the museum is a fitting tribute to one of its most famous residents.

Coniston Water also has tragic associations with Sir Donald Campbell who, in 1955, had broken the world water speed record here. Some 12 years later, in an attempt to beat his own record, his boat, *Bluebird*, crashed while travelling at 320 miles per hour. In March 2001 his widow was present as the tailfin of the boat was hauled to the surface after 34 years. Campbell's body was recovered later and was buried in the village cemetery on September 12th 2001 - an event overshadowed by the tragic events in New York and Washington the day before.

Today, boats on Coniston Water are limited to 10 miles per hour, an ideal speed for the wonderful old steamship, the *Gondola*, which was built in 1859 and was restored by the National Trust in 1980.

AMBLESIDE

11½ miles NW of Kendal on the A591

The centre of the town is a conservation area and contains the town's most picturesque building. The Bridge House, a tiny cottage perched on a packhorse bridge, is now an information centre, but in the 1850s it was the home of Mr and Mrs Rigg and their six children. Close by, at Adrian Sankey's

95 STORRS HALL HOTEL

Windermere

A luxurious Grade II listed Georgian mansion offering comfortable accomodation set within 17 acres of grounds and woodland.

☒ ▮ *see page 429*

•

Overlooking both the village of Coniston and the lake is the great crumpled hill of the Coniston Old Man and from the summit there are extensive views as far north as Scotland, out to the Isle of Man and, of course, over Lakeland. From here, too, can be seen Brantwood, the home of John Ruskin from 1872 until his death in 1900 that lies on the opposite side of the lake from the town.

•

96 CONISTON GONDOLA

Coniston

The original steam yacht Gondola was first launched in 1859 and now provides a passenger service on Lake Coniston

 see page 431

63

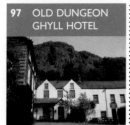

97 OLD DUNGEON GHYLL HOTEL

Great Langdale, nr Ambleside
A perfect base for walkers, climbers and tourists in a dramatic setting at the head of the Great Langdale Valley.

see page 430

Bridge House, Ambleside

Glass Works, visitors can watch glass being made in the traditional way and admire the restored water mill that stands next to the studio. A short walk leads to the **Armitt Museum**, dedicated to the area's history since Roman times and to John Ruskin and Beatrix Potter.

The Homes of Football is an exhibition of football memorabilia that covers the game from the very top level right down to amateur village football. Real sporting activity takes place in the summer in the famous Ambleside Sports, featuring traditional sports such as carriage driving, ferret and pigeon racing, Cumberland and Westmorland wrestling (a bit like sumo but without the rolls of fat), fell racing and hound trailing. The main road leading northwards from the town climbs sharply up to the dramatic **Kirkstone Pass** that is so called because of the rock at the top (almost 1,500 feet above sea level) which looks like a church steeple.

GRASMERE

15 miles NW of Kendal on the A591

With one of the finest settings in all Lakeland, this compact rough-stone village is one of the most popular in the Lake District. Although it is the glorious scenery that draws many here, it is also its associations with Wordsworth, who lived at the tiny **Dove Cottage** from 1799 to 1808; in dire poverty he was obliged to line the walls with newspaper for warmth. Today, this place of pilgrimage has been preserved intact, and next door is an award-winning museum dedicated to the poet's life and works.

Dove Cottage, Grasmere

Grief stricken after the death of their two young children, Mary and William Wordsworth moved from Grasmere to Rydal Mount in 1813, a handsome house overlooking tiny Rydal Water that lies just to the east of the village. The interior of the house has changed little since Wordsworth's day and it contains first editions of his works and personal possessions. The graves of Wordsworth and his sister Dorothy are in **St Oswald's Churchyard**, while a notable occupant of the town cemetery is William Archibald Spooner, sometime Warden of New College, Oxford. He gave his name to Spoonersims and produced gems such as 'You have hissed all my mystery lessons' or 'Yes indeed: the Lord is a shoving leopard'.

KESWICK

The undisputed capital of the Lake District, Keswick has been a magnet for tourists since the mid 1700s and was given a huge lift by the Lakeland poets in the early 19th century. The grandeur of the setting is the biggest draw, but Keswick also offers man-made attractions, including the fascinating **Cumberland Pencil Museum** that draws visitors from near and far and boasts the largest pencil in the world, and the popular Theatre by the Lake that hosts a year-round programme of plays, concerts, exhibitions, readings and talks. Another attraction to pencil in lies east of the town: this is **Castlerigg Stone Circle**, some of whose 38 standing stones are 8 feet high. Close by is the charming village of Threlkeld, the ideal starting point for a number of mountain walks, including an ascent of Blencathra.

Running south from Keswick is **Borrowdale**, home to the extraordinary **Bowder Stone**, a massive cube-shaped boulder weighing almost 2,000 tons that stands precariously on one corner apparently defying gravity.

AROUND KESWICK

POOLEY BRIDGE

12 miles E of Keswick on the B5320

This charming village stands at the northern tip of Ullswater and there are regular cruise departures from here during the season, stopping at Glenridding and Howton. Along the northern shore of the lake is a series of waterfalls that tumble down through a wooded gorge, known collectively by the name of the largest fall, **Aira Force**. The southern end of Ullswater is overshadowed by **Helvellyn** (3,115

Castlerigg Stone Circle, nr Keswick

98 THE FISH HOTEL

Buttermere, nr Cockermouth

Period charm, modern comforts, six real ales and home cooking in a family-run hotel in a glorious setting.

 see page 431

99 THE GEORGIAN HOUSE HOTEL

Whitehaven

A top-quality enterprise combining an elegant town house hotel with an acclaimed restaurant.

 see page 432

100 THE SHEPHERDS ARMS HOTEL

Ennerdale Bridge

Gem of a country house hotel offering en suite rooms, home cooked cuisine and real ales.

  see page 433

feet) and an assault on its summit is best tackled from Glenridding.

It was while walking by Ullswater with his sister Dorothy that William Wordsworth chanced upon a mass of daffodils that inspired him to write the much-loved poem '*I wandered lonely as a cloud*'.

BAMPTON

15 miles SE of Keswick off the A6

To the south of Bampton, lies **Haweswater**, the most easterly of the lakes - actually it's a reservoir, created in the late 1930s to supply the growing needs of industrial Manchester.

BUTTERMERE

8 miles SW of Keswick on the B5289

To many connoisseurs of the Lake District landscape, Buttermere is the most splendid of all the Lakes. The walk around Buttermere gives superb views of the eastern towers of **Fleetwith Pike** and the great fell wall made up of High Crag, High Stile, and Red Pike. Fed by both Buttermere and Loweswater, **Crummock Water** is by far the largest of the three lakes and its attractions can usually be enjoyed in solitude.

WHITEHAVEN

19 miles SW of Keswick on the A595

A handsome Georgian town which by the mid-1700s had become the third largest port in Britain, but the harbour's shallow draught halted further expansion. The harbour is now a conservation area and the Beacon tells the history of the town and its harbour.

To the south lies **St Bees Head**, a red sandstone bluff that forms one of the most dramatic natural features along the entire coast of northwest England. From here the 190-mile **Coast to Coast Walk** starts on its long journey across the Pennines to Robin Hood's Bay in North Yorkshire. **St Bees Head** is now an important nature reserve and the cliffs are crowded with guillemots, razorbills, kittiwakes, gulls, gannets and skuas.

Just inland from Whitehaven is the pretty town of **Egremont**, dominated by its 12th century Castle. Its prosperity was based on its local iron ore, and jewellery made from ore can be bought at the nearby **Florence Mine Heritage Centre**.

BRAITHWAITE

3 miles W of Keswick on the B5292

This small village lies at the foot of the **Whinlatter Pass**, another of Cumbria's dramatic routes, with a summit some 1,043 feet above sea level. The road also runs through **Whinlatter Forest Park**, the only Mountain Forest in England and one of the Forestry Commission's oldest woodlands.

MARYPORT

17 miles NW of Keswick on the A596

Dramatically located on the Solway Firth, Maryport is a charming Cumbrian coastal town rich in interest and maritime history. Some of the first visitors to Maryport were the Romans who built a clifftop fort here, **Alauna**, which is now part of the **Hadrian's Wall World Heritage Site**. The award-winning **Senhouse Roman Museum** tells the story of life in this outpost of the empire.

COCKERMOUTH

10 miles NW of Keswick on the A66

A delightful market town since 1226, Cockermouth was the birthplace in the 1770s of both Fletcher Christian, who was to lead the mutiny on the *Bounty*, and William Wordsworth. The house in which the latter was born is now called **Wordsworth House** and contains a few of the poet's personal possessions.

The town is also home to the unusual **Printing House Museum**, where a wide range of historic presses and printing equipment is on display, of Jennings Brewery and of the excellent **Cumberland Toy & Model Museum**.

BASSENTHWAITE LAKE

4 miles NW of Keswick on the A66

Here's one for the Pub Quiz: Which is the only lake in the Lake District? Answer: Bassenthwaite, because all the others are either Waters or Meres. Only 70 feet deep and with borders rich in vegetation, Bassenthwaite provides an ideal habitat for birds - more than 70 species have been recorded around the lake.

At the northern end of the lake, at Coalbeck Farm, **Trotters World of Animals** is home to

Wordsworth House, Cockermouth

many hundreds of animals - rare breeds, traditional farm favourites, endangered species, birds of prey and reptiles.

On the eastern shore of Bassenthwaite Lake is the secluded **Church of St Bridget & St Bega** which Tennyson had in mind when, in his poem *Morte d'Arthur*, he describes Sir Bedivere carrying the dead King Arthur: "to a chapel in the fields, A broken chancel with a broken cross, That stood on a dark strait of barren land".

CALDBECK

13 miles N of Keswick on the B5299

Caldbeck is closely linked with John Peel, the famous huntsman who died in 1854 after falling from his horse and is buried in the churchyard here. His ornate tombstone is decorated with depictions of hunting horns and his favourite hound.

It was John Peel's great friend and drinking companion John Graves who wrote the words to the song that remembers the huntsman:

•

Rising grandly above Bassenthwaite's eastern shore is Skiddaw, which ever since the Lake District was opened up to tourists by the arrival of the railway in the 19th century has been one of the most popular peaks to climb. Although it rises to some 3,054 feet, the climb is both safe and manageable, and from the summit, on a clear day, there are spectacular views to Scotland in the north, the Isle of Man in the west, the Pennines to the east, and to the south the greater part of the Lake District.

•

101 THE CROWN HOTEL

Eamont Bridge

Former coaching inn serving appetising home-made food and quality en suite accommodation.

 see page 433

102 THE KINGS ARMS HOTEL

Temple Sowerby

300-year-old former coaching inn in peaceful location offering wholesome home-made food and real ales.

 see page 434

103 EDEN VALE INN

Bolton Village

Inviting old village hostelry serving superb food and real ales; also spacious beer garden.

 see page 434

D'ye ken John Peel with his coat so gray?
D'ye ken John Peel at the break of day?
D'ye ken John Peel when he's far away
With his hounds and his horn in the
morning?'
Also buried here are John Peel's wife Mary and their four children. Some 200 years ago Caldbeck was an industrial village, with corn mills, woollen mills, and a paper mill all powered by the fast-flowing 'cold stream' - the **Caldbeck**. **Priest's Mill**, built in 1702 by the Rector of Caldbeck, next to his church, was a stone grinding corn mill, powered by a waterwheel which has now been restored to working order.

ULDALE

11 miles N of Keswick off the A591

To the northeast of Bassenthwaite Lake stretches the area known locally as the 'Land Back of Skidda', a crescent of fells and valleys constituting the most northerly part of the Lake District National Park.

PENRITH

The Saxon capital of the Kingdom of Cumbria, Penrith was sacked several times by the Scots and by the time of the Civil War **Penrith Castle** was in a ruined state. Cromwell's troops destroyed what was left but, today, the ruins remain impressive, standing high above a steep-sided moat. Other buildings in the town include the Town Hall that is the result of a 1905 conversion of two former Adam-style houses, one of which was

known as Wordsworth House as it was the home of the poet's cousin, Captain John Wordsworth.

Rheged Discovery Centre dedicates itself to 2,000 years of Cumbria's history, mystery and magic.

The town of Penrith is dominated by **Beacon Hill Pike**, which stands amidst wooded slopes high above Penrith. The tower was built in 1719 and marks the place where, since 1296, beacons were lit to warn the townsfolk of an impending attack. To the southeast of the town are the substantial remains of Brougham Castle standing on the foundations of a Roman fort.

AROUND PENRITH

LITTLE SALKELD

6 miles NE of Penrith off the A686

Close to the village are **Long Meg and her Daughters**, a most impressive Bronze Age site and second only to Stonehenge in size. There are more than 60 stones in the circle and the tallest, Long Meg, is 15 feet high.

Just to the south, in the village of **Edenhall**, is a Plague Cross that stands where there was once a basin filled with vinegar. This acted as a disinfectant into which plague victims put their money to pay for food from the people of Penrith.

APPLEBY-IN-WESTMORLAND

12 miles SE of Penrith on the B6260

The old county town of

Westmorland, Appleby was originally built by the Norman, Ranulph de Meschines, who set it within a broad loop of the River Eden that protects it on three sides. The fourth side is guarded by Castle Hill: at its foot is 16th century Moot Hall and at its head rises the great Norman keep of Appleby Castle.

Appleby is best known for its **Gypsy Horse Fair**, when hundreds of gypsies flood into the little town with their caravans and horse-drawn carts. The trade, principally in horses, and the trotting races provide a picturesque and colourful spectacle.

KIRKBY STEPHEN

21 miles SE of Penrith on the A685

Surrounded by spectacular scenery, inside the church in this old market town, is the 10th century **Loki Stone**, one of only two such carvings in Europe to have

Lakeland Bird of Prey Centre, Lowther

survived. Loki was a Norse God and presumably Viking settlers brought their belief in Loki to Kirkby Stephen.

LOWTHER

4 miles S of Penrith off the A6

Lowther is the estate village to **Lowther Castle**, a once grand place that is now only a shell. It was clearly once grand, as after one visit Queen Victoria is reputed to have said that she would not return as it was too grand for her. The grounds include the **Lakeland Bird of Prey Centre**, whose aim is to conserve birds of prey through education, breeding and caring for injured or orphaned birds before releasing them back into the wild.

SHAP

10 miles S of Penrith on the A6

In the stage coaching era Shap was an important staging post for the coaches before they tackled the daunting climb up **Shap Fell** to its summit, some 850 feet above sea level. Much earlier, in medieval times, the village was even more significant because of nearby **Shap Abbey**, the last abbey to be consecrated in England (about 1199) and the last to be dissolved, in 1540. The nearby 16th century Keld Chapel was built by the monks of Shap Abbey.

104 THE GOLDEN BALL

Appleby-in-Westmorland

Cosy, friendly town centre pub which is open all day for drinks and great bar food - also rooms for B&B

 see page 435

105 TUFTON ARMS HOTEL

Appleby-in-Westmorland

Outstanding and friendly family-run town centre hotel offering excellent cuisine and quality en suite rooms.

 see page 436

106 THE NEW INN

Hoff

Rural pub in scenic location noted for its real ales, wholesome cooking, and regular live entertainment.

see page 437

69

107 THE PENNINE HOTEL

Kirkby Stephen

Town centre hotel serving appetising home-made food and real ales; regular live entertainment.

 see page 438

•

Located on the northwestern edge of Carlisle, Kingmoor Nature Reserve occupies an area of moorland given to the city in 1352 by Edward III. In 1913, Kingmoor became one of the first bird sanctuaries in England and today provides a peaceful retreat away from the bustle of the city.

•

GREYSTOKE

5 miles W of Penrith on the B5288

According to Edgar Rice Burroughs, **Greystoke Castle** was the ancestral home of Tarzan, Lord of the Apes, a fiction that was perpetuated in the dismal 1984 film Greystoke. Greystoke village itself is a gem, its attractive houses grouped around a trimly maintained village green. Nearby are the stables where Gordon Richards trained his two Grand National winners, Lucius and Hello Dandy.

CARLISLE

Carlisle was a major Roman centre that supported the military base that guarded the western end of Hadrian's Wall, and today the squat outline of 12th century **Carlisle Castle** dominates the skyline of this fascinating city. After the Civil War, Cromwell's troops took the unusual step of rebuilding the Castle rather than demolishing it. Although one of the smallest in England, **Carlisle Cathedral** has many interesting features, including an exquisite east window that is considered to be one of the finest in Europe. It was here that Edward I excommunicated Robert the Bruce, and the bells were rung to welcome Bonnie Prince Charlie in 1745. The award-winning **Tullie House Museum**, close to the cathedral, tells the fascinating story of the

notorious Border Reivers, who occupied the lands from the 14th to the 17th century, with a law - or rather, a lack of it - unto themselves. Their treacherous deeds have also added such words as 'bereave' and 'blackmail' to the English language. The first railway to Carlisle opened as early as 1836 and today it is still an important centre of communications. It is also the northern terminus of the famous **Settle to Carlisle Railway** line, which takes in some of the most dramatic scenery that the north of England has to offer.

AROUND CARLISLE

BEWCASTLE

14 miles NE of Carlisle off the B6318

Now occupied by the ruins of a Norman Castle, a Roman fort once stood here, guarding the crossing

Bewcastle Cross

over Kirk Beck. A more impressive reminder of the past stands in the village churchyard – **Bewcastle Cross**, erected around AD 670 and one of the oldest and finest stone crosses in Europe.

BRAMPTON

8½ miles NE of Carlisle on the A6071

To the east of this delightful little town, nestling in the heart of Irthing Valley, is **Lanercost Priory**, founded in 1166 by Robert de Vaux. An impressive red sandstone ruin set in secluded woodland, the priory suffered greatly in the border raids of the 13th and 14th centuries, one of them led by William Wallace. When the priory closed in 1536 much of its masonry was used for local houses.

South of Brampton are **Gelt Woods**, lying in a deep sandstone ravine carved by the fast-flowing River Gelt, and close by is **Talkin Tarn**, now the focus of a 120-acre country park, which has been a popular place for water sports for over 100 years.

GILSLAND

15 miles NE of Carlisle on the B6318

Located in one of the most picturesque settings along the whole length of Hadrian's Wall and overlooking the River Irthing, **Birdoswald Roman Fort** is one of the best preserved mile-castles along the wall. Set high on a plateau with magnificent views over the surrounding countryside, the early turf wall, built in AD 122, can be seen along with the fort, where

Birdoswald Roman Fort, Gilsland

all the components of the Roman frontier system can still be seen.

WIGTON

10½ miles SW of Carlisle off the A596

The pleasant market town of Wigton has, for centuries, been the centre of the business and social life of the Solway coast and plain, its prosperity being based on the weaving of cotton and linen. In the Market Place is the magnificent Memorial Fountain that was erected in 1872 by the philanthropist George Moore in memory of his wife.

SILLOTH

18½ miles W of Carlisle on the B5300

This charming old port and Victorian seaside resort has a two-mile-long promenade that provides wonderful views of the Solway Firth and the coast of Scotland. A popular attraction is the **Solway Coast Discovery Centre**, where Michael the Monk and Oyk the Oystercatcher guide visitors through 10,000 years of local history.

Derbyshire

Derbyshire was at the forefront of modern thinking at the beginning of the Industrial Revolution, and the chief inheritor of this legacy is the county town of Derby, the home of Rolls-Royce and Royal Crown Derby porcelain. An early landmark of this new age is Richard Arkwright's mill and the associated village at Cromford. Much of the county is dominated by the Peak District National Park, the first of the ten National Parks, whose landscape changes from deep limestone valleys to bleak, desolate moorland. Along with numerous attractive villages and small towns, ancient monuments and caves, the Park is home to two of the finest stately homes not just in Derbyshire but in the whole country – Haddon Hall and Chatsworth.

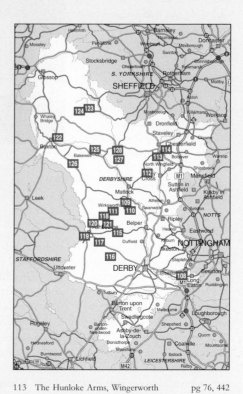

DERBY

This city is famously linked with two names: Rolls-Royce and Royal Crown Derby. When, in 1906, Sir Henry Royce and the Hon CS Rolls joined forces and built the first Rolls-Royce (a Silver Ghost) at Derby, they built much more than just a motor car. From the start they were considered by many to be the best cars in the world, and it was often said that the noisiest moving part in any Rolls-Royce was the dashboard clock! **Derby Industrial Museum** specialises in the history of railway engineering in the city, and also has a fine Rolls-Royce aircraft engine collection.

Guided tours round the **Royal Crown Derby** factory, museum and shop offer an intriguing insight into the high level of skill required to create the delicate flower petals, hand-gild the plates and hand-paint the superb porcelain that is instantly recognisable around the world.

The city's **Cathedral of All Saints** possesses a fine 16th century tower, the second highest Perpendicular tower in England. Its treasures include a beautiful wrought iron screen by Robert Bakewell and the tomb of Bess of Hardwick Hall - Elizabeth Talbot, Countess of Shrewsbury.

One of Derby's most interesting museums is **Pickford House**, situated on the city's finest Georgian street. Built in 1770 by the architect Joseph Pickford as a combined family home and place of work, the house offers an insight into the everyday lives of a middle-class family during the 1830s. The **Derbyshire Constabulary Memorabilia Museum** has a display of uniforms and weapons from the 17th century to the present day.

AROUND DERBY

ILKESTON

8 miles NE of Derby on the A6007

The third largest town in Derbyshire, Ilkeston received its royal charter for a market and fair in 1252 and both have continued to the present day. Once a mining and lace-making centre, its history is told in the **Erewash Museum**.

OCKBROOK

4 miles E of Derby off the A52

In this quiet village, a Moravian Settlement was founded in the mid-18th century when a congregation of the Moravian Church was formed. The Settlement has several fine buildings, including The Manse, built in 1822, and the Moravian Chapel.

• *In 1721 Derby had the first silk mill in the country, located on the banks of the River Derwent. Silk production ended in 1908 and the mill was burnt down in 1910, but the tower was rescued, later to be incorporated into the Derby Industrial Museum.* •

Pickford House, Derby

South of Ockbrook lies the Elvaston Castle estate, home of the Earls of Harrington. The magnificent Gothic castle seen today was finished in the early 19th century and stands in grounds that include Italian, parterre and old English gardens, tree-lined avenues and a large ornamental lake; the most impressive feature is the Golden Gates, erected in 1819 at the southern end of the gardens.

108 THE SHAKESPEARE INN & RESTAURANT

Shardlow

Cheerful family-run inn serving a great choice of unpretentious pub grub.

 see page 439

109 THE RISING SUN

Middleton, nr Matlock

A friendly, unpretentious village pub serving good simple food. Two rooms for B&B.

see page 439

To the north are the ruins of **Dale Abbey**, founded by Augustinian monks in the 13th century. The **Church of All Saints**, at Dale, is surely the only church in England that shares its roof with a farm.

MELBOURNE
6½ miles S of Derby off the B587

Melbourne's most famous son is Thomas Cook, who pioneered personally conducted tours and gave his name to the famous worldwide travel company. In 1841 Thomas Cook organised a trip from Leicester to Loughborough for a temperance rally. 570 passengers each paid one shilling (5p).

The birthplace of the 19th century statesman Lord Melbourne, and also the home of Lady Caroline Lamb, **Melbourne Hall** is another fine building in this area of Derbyshire. The hall is surrounded by beautiful gardens, whose most notable feature is a wrought-iron birdcage pergola built in the early 1700s by Robert Bakewell.

To the south is the large Baroque mansion of **Calke Abbey** that has been dubbed the 'house that time forgot' as, since the death of the owner, Sir Vauncy Harpur-Crewe in 1924, nothing has been altered in the mansion!

REPTON
7 miles SW of Derby off the B5008

Repton, on the banks of the Trent, was established as the capital of the Saxon kingdom of Mercia in the 7th century, and a monastery founded. The parish **Church of St**

Wystan is famous for its chancel and crypt, which claims to be one of the oldest intact Anglo-Saxon buildings in England.

Parts of a 12th century Augustinian priory are incorporated in the buildings of **Repton College**, founded in 1557. Two of its headmasters, Dr Temple and Dr Fisher, went on to become Archbishops of Canterbury. The gatehouse featured in the film *Goodbye Mr Chips*.

MATLOCK

Essentially a Victorian town, Matlock nestles in the lower valley of the River Derwent and is the administrative centre of Derbyshire as well as being a busy tourist centre bordering the Peak District National Park. Matlock once had the steepest gradient tramway in the world: opened in 1893, the tramcars ran until 1927 and the Depot can still be seen at the top of Bank Street. **Peak Rail** is a rebuilt, refurbished and now preserved railway running between Matlock Riverside station to its other terminus Rowsley South.

High up on the hill behind the town is the brooding ruin of **Riber Castle**, built in the 1860s by John Smedley, a local hosiery manufacturer who became interested in the hydropathic qualities of Matlock. He constructed his own gas-producing plant to provide lighting for the lavishly decorated interior of the Castle.

To the south of Matlock lies **Matlock Bath**, which developed into a spa town and by the early 19th century had become a popular summer resort. Many buildings connected with its heyday as a spa can still be visited. Down by the riverbank is the **Peak District Mining Museum** and **Temple Mine** that tells the story of lead mining in the surrounding area from as far back as Roman times.

Heights of Abraham, Matlock Bath

High Tor Grounds, some 400 feet above Matlock, offer spectacular views along with nature trails, and on the opposite side of the valley are the **Heights of Abraham Country Park and Caverns**, featuring steep rocky gorges, vast caverns, fast-running rivers, woodland walks and refreshment areas. A cable car runs from Matlock railway station up to this unique attraction.

To the south of Matlock Bath is **Cromford**, the world famous 'model' village that was developed by Richard Arkwright into one of the first industrial towns. **Cromford Mill** and the associated buildings and attractions are now an International World Heritage Site.

The **High Peak Trail**, which stretches some 17 miles up towards Buxton, starts at Cromford and follows the trackbed of the Cromford and High Peak Railway.

AROUND MATLOCK

CHESTERFIELD

9 miles NE of Matlock on the A61

A friendly, bustling town on the edge of the Peak District National Park, Chesterfield grew up around a market that was established over 800 years ago. The town centre has been conserved for future generations by a far-sighted council, and many buildings have been saved, including the Victorian Market Hall built in 1857. There are also several Tudor buildings in the heart of Chesterfield, most notably the former Peacock Inn that is now home to the **Peacock Heritage Centre**. The town's most famous landmark is the **Crooked Spire of St Mary & All Saints' Church** – the magnificent spire rises to 228 feet and leans over 9 feet from its true centrepoint. The spire has eight sides, but the herringbone pattern

Wirksworth

A sturdy town-centre family-run pub serving wholesome, unpretentious food.

see page 440

111 THE MINERS ARMS

Carsingham, nr Matlock

A popular village inn with old-world décor, a good choice of cask ales and a long list of home-cooked dishes on the chalkboard.

see page 441

112 THE BLACK SWAN

Ashover

Six brews are a magnet for real ale connoisseurs, and cooking based on fresh local produce is another plus.

see page 441

113 THE HUNLOKE ARMS

Wingerworth

A handsome 18th century inn with a fine reputation for food, in a village just off the A61 south of Chesterfield.

🍴 see page 442

114 SOMERSET HOUSE

Calow, Chesterfield

Traditional pub food is served at kind prices in a popular roadside inn.

🍴 see page 442

of the lead slates tricks the eye into seeing 16 sides from the grounds.

Chesterfield owed much of its prosperity during the industrial age to the great railway engineer George Stephenson. His home, Tapton House, lies just outside the town; he retired here and carried out work and experiments in horticulture. His death was announced in one local newspaper under the headline 'Inventor of the straight cucumber dies.' He was buried beneath the communion table in Holy Trinity Church, where he is commemorated by the stained glass in the east window.

BOLSOVER

12½ miles NE of Matlock on the A632

Above the town on a limestone ridge stands **Bolsover Castle**, a fairytale folly built for Sir Charles Cavendish during the early 1600s on the site of a ruined 12th century castle.

AULT HUCKNALL

11 miles NE of Matlock off the A617

Situated on a ridge close to the Nottinghamshire border, this village is home to the magnificent Tudor house, **Hardwick Hall**. Set in rolling parkland, the house, with its glittering tiers of windows and crowned turrets, has the letters ES carved in stone: ES, or Elizabeth of Shrewsbury, is perhaps better known as Bess of Hardwick, who married and survived four husbands. Bess died at Hardwick and was buried in the Cavendish family vault in the Cathedral Church of All Saints in Derby.

Bolsover Castle

National Tramway Museum, Crich

The formal gardens were laid out in the 19th century and the parkland, which overlooks the valley of the Doe Lea, is home to an impressive herd of Longhorn cattle and the ruins of Hardwick Old Hall.

Thomas Hobbs, tutor to the Cavendish family, spent the last years of his life at Hardwick and is buried in the Church of St John the Baptist.

CRICH

6 miles SE of Matlock off the A6

This large village, with its hilltop church and market cross, is the home of the **National Tramway Museum**, which provides a wonderful opportunity to enjoy a tram ride along a re-created Victorian street scene. To the east stand the graceful ruins of the 15th century **Wingfield Manor** that held Mary, Queen of Scots prisoner under the care of the Earl of Shrewsbury on two separate occasions.

RIPLEY

8½ miles SE of Matlock on the A610

Once a typical small market town, Ripley expanded dramatically during the Industrial Revolution, and the town's Butterley Ironworks created the roof for London's St Pancras station. Close to the town is the **Midland Railway Centre** at Butterfield, with steam trains running along a line from Butterley to Riddings.

HEANOR

12 miles SE of Matlock on the A6007

This busy town is centred on its market place where the annual fair is held as well as the twice-weekly market. Away from the bustle of the market are the Memorial Gardens, while to the south is Shipley Country Park, on the estate of the now demolished Shipley Hall.

BELPER

8 miles SE of Matlock on the A517

In 1776, Jedediah Strutt set up one

77

of the earliest water-powered cotton mills here, harnessing the natural power of the River Derwent to run his mills. With the river providing the power and fuel coming from the nearby South Derbyshire coalfield, the valley has a good claim to be one of the cradles of the Industrial Revolution. Belper's industrial heritage is explained at the **Derwent Valley Visitor Centre**.

The Derwent Valley so closely resembled the topography of the Ruhr Valley that the reservoirs were the natural choice for the Lancaster bombers to practise dropping the Bounding Bombs prior to their attack on the Ruhr dams. The Valley was also used for the filming, in 1954, of *The Dam Busters*.

ASHBOURNE

11 miles SW of Matlock on the A515

Originally a small settlement lying on the northern bank of Henmore Brook, Ashbourne boasts many fine examples of 18th century architecture as well as some older buildings, notably the **Gingerbread Shop** that probably dates from the 15th century. Traditional Ashbourne gingerbread is said to be made from a recipe that was acquired from French prisoners of war who were kept in the town during the Napoleonic Wars. Also worthy of a second glance is the Green Man and Black's Head Royal Hotel; the inn sign stretches over the St John's Street and was put up when the Blackamoor Inn joined with the Green Man in 1825. Ashbourne was one of Dr Johnson's favourite places, and he visited the hotel so frequently that he even had his own seat – it's still there.

The area to the north of Ashbourne is dominated by the conical hill of **Thorpe Cloud**, which guards the entrance to

Thorpe Cloud and Dovedale

Dovedale. The steep sides to its valley, the fast-flowing water and the magnificent white rock formations all give Dovedale a special charm. The **Stepping Stones**, a delight for children, are the first point of interest, and further up the dale is the limestone crag known as Dovedale Castle.

BUXTON

At the heart of the Peak District and England's highest market town, Buxton is also a spa town, whose waters are maintained at a constant temperature of 82 degrees F (28 degrees C). **St Anne's Well** still provides water and many people coming to the town make a point of trying the pure, tepid liquid. Among the notable architectural features of the town are The Colonnade, The Crescent, The Devonshire Royal Hospital and the attractive Edwardian **Opera House** that was restored in 1979. Gertrude Lawrence, Gracie Fields and Hermione Gingold all performed here, and on one famous occasion in the 1930s Douglas Fairbanks and Mary Pickford were in the audience to watch the great Russian ballerina Anna Pavlova. **Buxton Museum and Art Gallery** has a fine collection of Ashford Marble and Blue John ornaments, and visitors can explore the Wonders of the Peak through seven time zones. The ancient custom of **Well Dressing** has been a part of Buxton's cultural calendar since the Duke of Devonshire provided the townsfolk with their first public

water supply at Market Place Fountain. From then on, High Buxton Well and St Anne's Well were decorated sporadically, and in 1923, the Town Council set about organising a well-dressing festival and carnival that continues to this day. Every year on the second Wednesday in July, this delightful tradition is enacted.

To the west of the town lies the 1,800 feet **Axe Edge**, from where the panoramic views of Derbyshire are overwhelming; just beyond, at 1,690 feet above sea level, the Cat and Fiddle Inn is the second highest pub in England.

AROUND BUXTON

HAYFIELD

8½ miles N of Buxton on the A624

This small town below the exposed moorland of **Kinder Scout**, the highest point in the Peak District, is a popular centre for exploring the area and offers many amenities for hillwalkers. The town grew up around the textile industry, in this case wool weaving and calico printing, and many of the houses seen today were originally weavers' cottages. Hayfield was the birthplace, in 1914, of the actor Arthur Lowe, Captain Mainwaring in the much-loved TV series *Dads Army*.

GLOSSOP

13 miles N of Buxton on the A624

At the foot of the **Snake Pass**, Glossop displays an interesting mix of styles, the industrial town of the 19th century with its towering

122 THE OLD SUN INN

Buxton

A 400-year-old coaching inn serving six real ales and tasty home-cooked food.

 see page 447

•

Three miles northeast of the town of Hayfield is Kinder Downfall, the highest waterfall in the county, where the River Kinder flows off the edge of Kinder Scout. In very low temperatures Kinder Fall can freeze – a truly breathtaking sight. It is renowned for its 'blow-back' effect: when the wind is fierce, the water is forced back against the rock and appears to run uphill.

•

123 THE WOODROFFE ARMS

Hope

Friendly hosts, traditional English food and comfortable accommodation in a popular village inn.

 see page 448

124 CAUSEWAY HOUSE B&B

Castleton

A superior B&B establishment providing a warm, friendly ambience and great value for money.

 see page 448

Victorian mills contrasting with the 17th century village with its charming old cottages standing in the cobble streets. A little way north, at Hadfield, is the Longdendale Trail, which follows a former railway line and is part of the Trans-Pennine Trail.

PEAK FOREST

5 miles NE of Buxton off the A623

High on the White Peak plateau, Peak Forest takes its name from the fact that it once stood at the centre of the **Royal Forest of the Peak**. The Peak Forest Canal, completed in 1800, followed the valley of the River Goyt and had its terminal basin at Buxworth.

Within walking distance of Peak Forest is the renowned Eldon Hole, considered in legend to be the Devil's own entrance to Hell; thousands of pot-holers can testify to the inaccuracy of the legend that the pit is bottomless.

EDALE

8½ miles NE of Buxton off the A625

Edale marks the start of the Pennine Way, the long-distance footpath inaugurated in 1965 that follows the line of the backbone of Britain for some 270 miles to Kirk Yetholm, just over the Scottish border. Not far from the village is the famous **Jacob's Ladder**, overlooking the river, and nearby are the tumbledown remains of a hill farmer's cottage, the home of Jacob Marshall, who cut the steps into the hillside leading up to Edale Cross.

CASTLETON

8 miles NE of Buxton on the A6187

Situated at the head of the Hope Valley, Castleton is overlooked by the Norman ruins of **Peveril Castle**, the only Norman castle in Derbyshire, and by Mam Tor; to the west, the road runs through the Winnats Pass, a narrow limestone gorge. The hills to the west of Castleton are famous for their caves and the **Blue John Mine and Caverns** are one of Derbyshire's most popular attractions. The huge vases and urns in the village's **Ollerenshaw Collection** are made of the unique Blue John fluorspar.

At the bottom of **Winnats Pass** lies **Speedwell Cavern**, a former lead mine that used boats on an underground canal to ferry the miners and iron ore to and from the rockface; they now ferry visitors. Peak Cavern, reached by a delightful riverside walk, has the widest opening of any cave in Europe.

EYAM

10 miles NE of Buxton off the B6521

This village, pronounced 'Eem', will forever be known as the Plague Village. In 1666, a tailor received a bundle of plague-infected clothing from London. The infection soon spread and the terrified villagers prepared to flee, but the local rector, William Mompesson, persuaded the villagers to stay, and as a result most of the neighbouring villages escaped the disease. Eyam was quarantined for over a year, relying on outside help for supplies of food that were left on the village boundary. Only 83 villagers survived out of 350.

The home of the Wright family for over 300 years, **Eyam Hall** is a wonderful, unspoilt 17th century manor house that is also home to Eyam Hall Crafts Centre.

ASHFORD IN THE WATER

9 miles SE of Buxton off the A6

Developed around a ford that spanned the River Wye, this was once an important crossing place on the ancient Portway; the medieval **Sheepwash Bridge** is one of three bridges in the village and is a favourite with artists. So-called Black Marble, but actually a highly polished grey limestone, was mined nearby and, particularly during the Victorian era, it was fashionable to have decorative items and fire surrounds made from the stone. The founder of the marble works, Henry Watson, is remembered by a tablet in the great limestone **Church of the Holy Trinity**.

Ashford is perhaps most famous for its six beautifully executed well-dressings, which are held annually in early June. Rather than adhering strictly to the custom of depicting scenes from the Bible, the well-dressers of Ashford have pictured such unusual themes as a willow pattern to celebrate the Chinese Year of the Dog.

BAKEWELL

10½ miles SE of Buxton on the A6

The only true town in the Peak District National Park, Bakewell attracts many visitors, some to sample the confection that bears its name. One of the more famous guests at the Rutland Arms Hotel was Jane Austen, who stayed here in 1811; the town and the hotel feature in *Pride and Prejudice*.

Behind Bakewell's large parish church is the lovely **Old House Museum**, housed in a building on Cunningham Place that dates back to 1534 and is thought to be the oldest house in Bakewell. The late 17th century Bath House is one of the few other buildings remaining from the days when Bakewell was a minor spa town.

Bakewell is perhaps best known as the home of the Bakewell Tart (referred to locally as a pudding). A mile to the south of Bakewell stands romantic **Haddon Hall**, thought by many to have been the first fortified house in the country, though the turrets and battlements were put on purely for show. The home of the Dukes of Rutland for over 800 years, the hall has enjoyed a fairly peaceful existence, in part no doubt because it stood empty and neglected for nearly 300 years after 1640, when the family chose Belvoir Castle in Leicestershire as their main home. The 16th century terraced gardens are one of the chief delights and Haddon's splendour and charm have led it to be used as a backdrop to numerous television and film productions including *Jane Eyre*, *Moll Flanders* and *The Prince and the Pauper*.

The gritstone landscape of **Stanton Moor**, which rises to some 1,096 feet, lies to the south

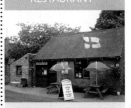

125 THE BULLS HEAD

Ashford-in-the-Water
Small, friendly and welcoming, with a good choice of cask ales and an excellent, imaginative menu.

see page 449

126 THE OLD SMITHY TEA ROOMS & RESTAURANT

Monyash, nr Bakewell
A friendly, cosy tea room and restaurant open all day for drinks, snacks and full meals.

see page 450

127 THE OLD SMITHY

Beeley

A traditional village shop and licensed café in a converted smithy. Super deli food, breakfasts, lunches and snacks.

 see page 451

128 CHATSWORTH HOUSE

Edensor

Chatsworth House, known as the "Palace of the Peak", is without doubt one of the finest of the great houses in Britain.

 see page 450

of Haddon and a Bronze Age stone circle on the moor is known as the Nine Ladies. Legend has it that one Sunday nine women and a fiddler came up onto the moor to dance and, for their act of sacrilege, they were turned to stone. Also in the area is the site of an Iron Age hillfort known as Castle Ring.

Northeast of Bakewell, near Edensor, lies the home of the Dukes of Devonshire, **Chatsworth House**, one of the finest of the great houses of Britain. The origins of the house as a great showpiece must be attributable to the redoubtable Bess of Hardwick, one of whose husbands, Sir William Cavendish, bought the estate in 1549. Over the years, the Cavendish fortunes have continued to pour into Chatsworth, making it an almost unparalleled showcase for art treasures.

The gardens of Chatsworth, which used the talents of Capability Brown and Sir Joseph Paxton, also have some marvellous features, including the Emperor Fountain that dominates the Canal Pond. Sir Joseph Paxton was also responsible for the world's largest glass house – the Great Conservatory, designed at Chatsworth as a model for his Crystal Palace, star of the Great Exhibition of 1851. This extraordinary structure was demolished in 1920.

ARBOR LOW

9 miles SE of Buxton off the A515

This remote Bronze Age stone circle is often referred to as the Stonehenge of the Peaks, and although many of the stones now lie on the ground it is still an impressive sight. There are several stone circles in the Peak District but none offer the same atmosphere as Arbor Low, nor the same splendid views.

LYME PARK

8 miles NE of Buxton off the A6

The ancient estate of Lyme Park was given to Sir Thomas Danyers in 1346 by a grateful King Edward III after a battle at Caen. Danyers then passed the estate to his son-in-law, Sir Piers Legh, and it remained in the family until 1946. Famous for its fantastic Palladian mansion, the work of Venetian architect Giacomo Leoni, the estate includes a late 19th century formal garden and a medieval deer park. The 1,400 acres of moorland, woodland and parkland at Lyme Park include an early-18th century hunting tower, Lyme Cage, so called because it was used to detain poachers. Lyme was Pemberley in the 1995 BBC film *Pride and Prejudice*.

Devon

Known for its enchanting scenery, maritime history and bleak expanse of moorland, Devon, England's third largest county, has plenty to offer the visitor. To the southeast are the old textile towns, including Axminster that lent its name to the most luxurious of carpets, and Honiton, still famed for its lace. Here, too, lies the cathedral city of Exeter, the county capital, which has its roots firmly in Roman times. The south coast is littered with attractive and genteel seaside resorts that are particularly highly regarded for their mild climate while, in the west, is Plymouth, where Sir Francis Drake famously insisted on finishing his game of bowls before leaving to intercept the Spanish Armada. The middle of the county is dominated by Dartmoor National Park, home to the famous prison and a wealth of ancient monuments. Lastly, there is north Devon, with its

spectacular coastline while, just inland, is Tarka country, the area of Devon that was made famous by Henry Williamson in his popular novel.

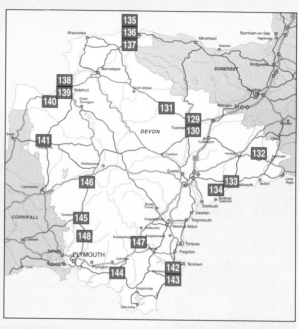

129 THE HALF MOON

Tiverton

With the same owners for 20 years, the **Half Moon** serves excellent home-cooked food from 8.30 to 2.

 see page 452

130 THE MAD HATTERS RESTAURANT

Tiverton

A delightful little restaurant with a daytime menu of excellent home-cooked dishes and Devon cream teas.

 see page 452

131 THE STAG INN

Rackenford, nr Tiverton

Outstanding food, much of it sourced from a local organic farm, brings customers from near and far to a historic country inn.

 see page 453

EXETER

First settled by the Romans, whose spectacular **Roman Bath House**, or Caldarium, was uncovered in the Cathedral Close in the 1970s, it was in the late 11th century that William the Conqueror took control of Exeter. After ordering the construction of **Rougemont Castle**, the gatehouse and tower of which can still be seen, work began on the construction of St Peter's Cathedral, a massive building project that was not completed until 1206. As well as being an ecclesiastical centre, Exeter was also an important port and this is reflected in its dignified 17th century Custom House that now forms the centrepiece of the **Exeter Historic Quayside**. There are some excellent museums in Exeter, and other attractions include the **University Sculpture Walk**, which takes in works by Barbara Hepworth and Henry Moore, and guided tours through Exeter's Underground Passages.

To the northeast of Exeter is the large estate of **Killerton**, which is centred on a grand 18th century mansion set in parkland that contains the Dolbury Iron Age hill fort and the 15th century Marker's Cottage.

AROUND EXETER

CADBURY

8 miles N of Exeter off the A3072

Cadbury Castle is an Iron Age hill fort that claims to have the most extensive views in Devon. To the northeast lies Bickleigh, a charming place of thatched cottages, which is home to Bickleigh Mill, now a craft centre, and, Bickleigh Castle, a moated and fortified late 14th century manor house.

TIVERTON

13 miles N of Exeter on the A396

A strategic point on the River Exe, in 1106, Henry I ordered the building of **Tiverton Castle**,

Exeter Quayside

around which the town began to develop. The castle was later destroyed on Cromwell's orders though the remains are substantial. A few miles north of Tiverton, up the Exe Valley, is **Knightshayes Court**, a striking house that was the home of the Heathcoat-Amory family.

OTTERY ST MARY

12 miles NE of Exeter on the B3177

Cadhay Manor, Ottery St Mary

This small town is justly proud of its magnificent 14th century **Church of St Mary**. The vicar here during the mid 18th century was John Coleridge, whose tenth child, Samuel Taylor, born in 1772, went on to become a celebrated poet.

A mile to the northwest of the town is **Cadhay**, a beautiful manor house that was built in 1550, while close by is **Escot Park and Gardens**, where visitors can see an arboretum and rose garden along with a collection of wildlife.

HONITON

16 miles NE of Exeter on the A30

Once a major stopping place on the great Roman road, Fosse Way, Honiton is best known for the lace that is still sought today. First introduced to east Devon by Flemish immigrants during the reign of Elizabeth I, the lace is still made here and can be bought from local shops and also seen in Allhallows Museum.

AXMINSTER

24 miles NE of Exeter on the A358

This ancient town on the River Axe is famous for the carpets that bear the town's name. The creation of just one carpet took so much time that each one's completion was celebrated by a procession to St Mary's Church – which naturally has its own Axminster carpet. Carpets are still manufactured here and the factory welcomes visitors, while the **Axminster Museum** dedicates some of its exhibition space to the industry.

SEATON

20 miles E of Exeter on the B3174

Once a significant port, Seaton expanded during the Victorian era as wealthy families, looking for sea air, came here and built their villas. The railway line that brought many of the Victorians here has been replaced by the **Seaton Tramway**,

132 THE TUCKERS ARMS

Dalwood, nr Axminster

A truly delightful village hostelry with a fine reputation for quality cuisine and comfortable accommodation

see page 454

133 BROPHY'S

Sidmouth

Excellent home cooked snacks and meals served in a friendly town centre coffee shop restaurant.

see page 452

which links the resort with the ancient town of **Colyton**, three miles inland. From Seaton, the **South West Coast Path** follows the coastline eastwards to Lyme Regis in Dorset. Considered by naturalists as the last and largest wilderness on the southern coast of England, this area of unstable cliffs, wood and scrub is a haven for wildlife.

To the west of Seaton is the picturesque old fishing village of **Beer**, best known for the superb white freestone that can be seen in churches all over Devon as well as in the Tower of London and Westminster Abbey.

SIDMOUTH

13 miles E of Exeter off the A3052

It was here that the future Queen Victoria saw the sea for the first time, brought here by her proud, penniless father, the Duke of Kent. Some 50 years later, Queen Victoria presented a stained glass window to Sidmouth parish church in memory of her father.

Sidmouth Museum provides a very vivid presentation of the Victorian resort along with an interesting collection of local prints, a costume gallery and a display of lace. In 1912, Sir Joseph Lockyer founded the **Norman Lockyer Observatory** for astronomical and meteorological research.

Sedate Sidmouth undergoes a transformation in the first week of August each year when it plays host to the International Folklore, Dance and Song Festival.

BUDLEIGH SALTERTON

11½ miles SE of Exeter on the B3178

A famous Victorian visitor to Budleigh was the celebrated artist Sir John Everett Millais, who stayed here during the summer of 1870 in a curiously shaped house that is known as The Octagon. On the seafront is **Fairlynch Museum**, one of the very few thatched museums in the country.

Just to the north lies **Hayes Barton**, a wonderful E-shaped

Norman Lockyer Observatory

Tudor house that was the birthplace of Sir Walter Raleigh. On the banks of the River Otter stands **Otterton Mill**, a part medieval building, and **Bicton Park Botanical Gardens** that were laid out in the 18th century.

EXMOUTH

9 miles SE of Exeter on the A376

Situated at the mouth of the River Exe, this small fishing village was one of the first seaside resorts in Devon and was dubbed the 'Bath of the West'. On the northern outskirts of the town is one of the most unusual houses in Britain – **A La Ronde** – a unique 16-sided house that was built in the late 18th century on the instructions of two spinster cousins who were inspired by the basilica of the San Vitale at Ravenna. On the opposite bank of the river stands **Powderham Castle**, the home of the Earls of Devon, surrounded by one of the finest parks in the county.

BARNSTAPLE

One of the most attractive buildings here is **Queen Anne's Walk**, a colonnaded arcade that has a statue of Queen Anne on top of its central doorway. Opened in 1708, it was used by the Barnstaple wool merchants who accepted that any verbal bargain they made over the Tome Stone would be legally binding.

Barnstaple is also the northern terminus of the **Tarka Line**, a wonderfully scenic 39-mile route that follows the gentle valleys of the Rivers Yeo and Taw, where Tarka the Otter had his home. Walkers, too, can discover the countryside that inspired the novel by taking the **Tarka Trail**, an unusual figure-of-eight long-distance footpath of some 180 miles that crosses over itself at Barnstaple.

AROUND BARNSTAPLE

MUDDIFORD

3½ miles N of Barnstaple on the B3230

Just to the southwest of this pretty village are **Marwood Hill Gardens** with their collections of rare and unusual trees and shrubs, while to the northeast lies **Arlington Court**, the family home of the Chichesters from 1534 until the last owner, Miss Rosalie Chichester, died in 1949.

COMBE MARTIN

9 miles N of Barnstaple on the A399

A popular seaside resort, with an exceptionally long main street. The village is home to a remarkable

134 BICTON PARK BOTANICAL GARDENS

East Budleigh
Stunning gardens spanning three centuries of horticultural history with several other attractions to make an enjoyable day out..

🏛 see page 455

•

The village of Shirwell, near Muddiford, was the birthplace of the yachtsman Sir Francis Chichester, whose father was the vicar. Sir Francis died in Plymouth after being taken ill on his fourth transatlantic race; he is buried in the churchyard of St Peter, Shirwell.

•

River Taw, Barnstaple

135 MOTHER MELDRUM'S TEA GARDENS

Lynton

A dramatic setting for a popular tea room and garden serving home-cooked snacks and meals from Easter to the end of October.

 see page 456

136 THE GREENHOUSE RESTAURANT

Lynton

A thriving, beautifully appointed café and gastro-wine bar open from 9am to 9.30pm for an impressive selection of food and drink.

 see page 455

137 THE ROCK HOUSE HOTEL

Lynmouth

An unbeatable location by the harbour, with high standards of comfort, service and cuisine

 see page 457

Rosemoor Garden, Great Torrington

architectural curiosity, the 18th century **Pack o' Cards Inn**, which represents a pack of cards with four decks, or floors, 13 rooms and 52 windows.

LYNMOUTH

14 miles NE of Barnstaple on the A39

This pleasant village has benefited from two great enthusiasms, romantic scenery and sea bathing, and both Coleridge and Wordsworth came here on a walking tour in the 1790s, while Shelley visited in 1812. To aid the growing tourist trade the **Lynton-Lynmouth Cliff Railway** opened in 1890, linking the town with its neighbour Lynton, a place of chiefly Victorian architecture. To the west lies the **Valley of the Rock** that RD Blackmore transforms into the Devil's Cheesewring in his novel *Lorna Doone*. To the southwest is one of Exmoor's most spectacular wooded valleys, **Heddon Valley**.

CREDITON

26 miles SE of Barnstaple on the A377

This sleepy market town was, in AD 680, the birthplace of Wynfrith, who went on to become one of only a few Britons to become saints - he adopted the name Boniface. It was nearly 1,200 years before the people of Crediton gave their saint any form of recognition when in 1897 an east window was installed in the town's cathedral-like **Church of the Holy Cross** that depicts scenes from his life.

GREAT TORRINGTON

10 miles SW of Barnstaple on the A386

This hilltop town has several thriving industries, including **Dartington Crystal**, where visitors can see skilled craftsmen blowing and shaping the molten glass.

Just to the south of Great Torrington and occupying a breathtaking location in the Torridge Valley is the Royal Horticultural Society's **Rosemoor**, a wonderful place that includes mature planting in Lady Anne Palmer's magnificent garden and arboretum.

BIDEFORD

8 miles SW of Barnstaple on the A386

This was once Britain's third busiest port, and evidence of this golden age can still be seen around the town in the various opulent merchants' houses that have survived. It was while staying here that Charles Kingsley wrote *Westward Ho!*, the swashbuckling Elizabethan story that is based around the town.

To the north, on the east bank of the River Torridge, are **Tapeley Park Gardens** – some 20 acres of gardens that have been divided into four distinctly different themed areas. Overlooking Bideford Bay is

Westward Ho!, the only place ending with an exclamation mark, which developed into a resort following interest shown in Charles Kingsley's novel. Appledore, three miles north of Bideford, is a delightful old fishing village of narrow winding lanes and sturdy 18th and 19th century fishermen's cottages overlooking the Taw-Torridge estuary.

CLOVELLY

17 miles SW of Barnstaple on the B3237

This unbelievably quaint village, which tumbles down a steep hillside in terraced levels, is many people's idea of the typical Devonshire coastal village. Charles Kingsley lived and attended school here in the 1820s and the **Kingsley Exhibition** explores the novelist's links with the village, while the neighbouring Fisherman's Cottage provides an insight into what life was like in Clovelly at that time.

To the west lie **Hartland Point**, from where there are

Bideford

Sweet and savoury palates are equally well catered for in a friendly town-centre café/restaurant.

see page 458

139 THE SWAN INN

Bideford

Fine food is complemented by excellent, friendly service and a lovely riverside setting.

see page 458

140 THE BELL INN

Parkham, nr Bideford

An atmospheric country inn serving the best of West Country produce on wide-ranging menus.

see page 459

Hartland Point

141 HOLSWORTHY MUSEUM

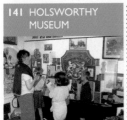

Holsworthy
A small museum with themed displays, offering a fascinating insight into the history of Holsworthy.

🏛 see page 459

breathtaking views, **Hartland Abbey**, which houses a unique exhibition of documents that date back to 1160, and **Hartland Quay**, where a museum records the many shipwrecks that have littered this jagged coastline.

HOLSWORTHY

26 miles SW of Barnstaple on the A388

This old market town lies just four miles from the Cornish border, serving a large area of rural Devon. Each Wednesday, it comes alive with its traditional street market, and in July the town plays host to the three-day long **St Peter's Fair**, an ancient event first held here in 1185. Holsworthy's most striking architectural features are the two Victorian viaducts that once carried the railway line through to Bude. Situated high above the southern outskirts of the town, they now form part of a footpath along the old track bed and it is possible to walk across them. Housed in an 18th century parsonage, the volunteer-run **Holsworthy**

Museum gives visitors an insight into local history and traditions by various themed displays.

BRAUNTON

4 miles NW of Barnstaple on the A361

Claiming to be the largest village in Devon, Braunton is home to one of the few remaining examples of a Saxon open field strip system that is still actively farmed, while in the dunes is the **Braunton Burrows** nature reserve. Just to the northwest lies **Croyde**, renowned for its family-friendly beach, and close by, at Georgeham, is the house which Henry Williamson built and lived in after World War I, and where he wrote his famous novel, *Tarka the Otter*.

ILFRACOMBE

9½ miles NW of Barnstaple on the A361

Ilfracombe developed in direct response to the early 19th century craze for sea bathing and seawater therapies and the **Tunnel Baths** were opened in 1836, by which time a number of elegant residential terraces had been built on the hillside to the south of the old town.

TOTNES

Claiming to be the second oldest borough in England, Totnes, according to local legend, is said to have been founded by a Trojan named Brutus in around 1200 BC; the **Brutus Stone**, in the pavement of the town's main shopping

Capstone Point, Ilfracombe

Brutus Stone, Totnes

street, commemorates this event. The first recorded evidence of the settlement was in the mid 10th century, when King Edgar established a mint here. There was already a Saxon castle here but the remains of **Totnes Castle** are of a once imposing Norman fortification.

Totnes Museum, housed in an Elizabethan building, remembers the town's most famous son, Charles Babbage.

AROUND TOTNES

NEWTON ABBOT

7 miles NE of Totnes on the A381

It was here in 1688, that William, Prince of Orange, was proclaimed King William III and, while here, he stayed at the Jacobean manor house, Ford House, which had played host to Charles I in 1625. The whole character of this attractive town changed in the 1850s when the Great Western Railway made it their centre of locomotive and carriage repair works; it was also the junction for the Moretonhampstead and Torbay branch lines. Newton Abbot racecourse, which stages a number of National Hunt races during the season, is one of the most popular tracks in the southwest.

DAWLISH

14 miles NE of Totnes on the A379

From its earliest days as a seaside resort, Dawlish has attracted many distinguished visitors, including Jane Austen, John Keats and Charles Dickens, who in his novel of the same name had Nicholas Nickleby born near the town. To the northeast of the town is **Dawlish Warren**, a nature reserve that is home to many species of flowering plant, including the rare Jersey Lily.

TEIGNMOUTH

12 miles NE of Totnes on the A379

There are two distinct sides to this town – the popular holiday resort with its fine Regency residences and the working port on the northern bank of the River Teign. Just north of the town lies the **Shaldon Wildlife Trust** breeding centre for rare small mammals, reptiles and exotic birds.

TORQUAY

6 miles E of Totnes on the A379

A genteel and elegant resort that has become known as 'The English Naples', Torquay, which grew up around Torre Abbey that was

To the west of Brixham is Berry Head, noted for stupendous views, rare plants and colonies of sea birds.

142 THE DART ROCK CAFÉ

Dartmouth

A friendly modern eatery serving an excellent variety of dishes based on the very best locally sourced produce.

¶ see page 459

founded in 1195, was the birthplace, in 1890, of Agatha Christie. It was here that she began writing her crime novels while her second husband was away on active service during World War I. One of the town's most popular attractions is the **Agatha Christie Memorial Room** in the Abbot's Tower. Just inland lies **Compton Castle**, a wonderful fortified manor house built between the 14th and 16th centuries.

A more recent attraction is **Living Coasts** on the harbour, a kind of zoo-by-the-sea and a natural habitat for seals, penguins and sea birds.

PAIGNTON

5 miles E of Totnes on the A379

The development of Torquay saw neighbouring Paignton soon become a resort, complete with pier and promenade, that still appeals to families today. Among the main attractions are **Paignton**

Zoo and the **Paignton and Dartmouth Steam Railway** that follows the coastline along the bottom of Tor Bay before travelling through woodland to Kingswear. Here passengers alight and catch a ferry to Dartmouth. Just to the south, at Galmpton, lies **Greenway**, the house to which Dame Agatha Christie moved for the last 30 years of her life.

BRIXHAM

7 miles E of Totnes on the A3022

Brixham was once the most profitable fishing port in the UK and still supports a fishing fleet. The vicar at All Saints Church from 1823 to 1847 was the Rev Henry Lyte, who composed the hymn *Abide With Me*. The bells of the church play the tune every evening.

DARTMOUTH

7 miles SE of Totnes on the A379

One of England's principal ports for centuries, the town also has a long connection with the Royal Navy, the oldest of the British services (the *Mayflower* put in here for repairs before sailing on to Plymouth and on to America). Guarded by **Dartmouth Castle**, built by Edward IV after the War of the Roses, Dartmouth's harbour is home to the handsome 18th century **Custom House**, while its most famous building is the **Britannia Royal Naval College**.

Dartmouth was the home of John (Jack) Russell, the 'sporting parson', a keen fox-hunting man who developed the breed of small terrier that bears his name.

Paignton and Dartmouth Steam Railway

Dartmouth Quayside

143 THE STEAM PACKET INN

Kingswear, Dartmouth

A bright, welcoming inn serving a good choice of home-cooked food lunchtime and evening.

║ see page 459

•

Passengers for Dartmouth arriving by train from Torquay had to take the GWR ferry from Kingsbridge and arrived at what was in effect a railway station, except that it never saw a train nearer than across the River Dart at Kingsbridge.

•

On the opposite bank of the Dart estuary are the impressive remains of **Kingswear Castle** that is a twin to Dartmouth's fortification. A huge chain was strung between the two castles when there was thought to be an added threat of invasion.

SALCOMBE

14 miles SW of Totnes on the A381

Standing at the mouth of the Kingsbridge estuary, this delightful town enjoys one of the most beautiful natural settings in the country. The harbour throngs with pleasure craft, and its old Customs House is home to the **Salcombe Maritime and Local History Museum**.

To the south of the town lies **Overbecks**, a charming house that was built in 1913 and was the home of research chemist Otto Overbeck from 1918 to 1937. The house holds Overbeck's wide-ranging collection, including late 19th century photographs of the area,

local shipbuilding tools, model boats, toys and much more. The beautiful, sheltered garden, with views out over Salcombe estuary, is planted with many rare trees, shrubs and plants, giving it a Mediterranean feel.

KINGSBRIDGE

11 miles SW of Totnes on the A381

At the head of the Kingsbridge estuary, this pretty town is a place of narrow alleys that has retained its Elizabethan market arcade, The Shambles, while its rather modest Victorian town hall has an unusual onion-shaped clock tower that adds a touch of glamour to the building.

For anyone looking to learn more about this area of Devon a visit to the **Cookworthy Museum of Rural Life** is a must. Just offshore and reached by a causeway from **Bigbury on Sea** is **Burgh Island**, which is an island only at high tide. When the tide recedes, it can be reached by walking across the sandbank or by taking an

144 THE EXETER INN

Modbury

An outstanding inn offering the very best in hospitality, well-kept ales, good food and comfortable B&B room

║ ⊨ See page 460

93

Sea Tractor, Bigbury on Sea

145 THE MARKET INN

Tavistock

A cosy, inviting atmosphere and an exceptional choice of home-cooked food in a splendid family-run pub.

 see page 461

exciting ride on the Sea Tractor. The whole of this 28-acre island, complete with its 14th century Pilchard Inn, was bought in 1929 by the eccentric millionaire Archibald Nettlefold, who built a hotel here in extravagant Art Deco style.

Notable guests at the hotel on Burgh Island included Noël Coward, The Duke of Windsor and Mrs Simpson, and Agatha Christie, who set two novels in this atmospheric location.

TAVISTOCK

This handsome old market town grew up around the 10th century **Abbey** and flourished following the discovery of tin on the nearby moors. The town seen today is essentially the creation of the Dukes of Bedford, who acquired the Abbey at the time of the Dissolution and remained there until 1911. While little remains of the Abbey, one of its legacies is the annual **Goose Fair**, a marvellous traditional street fair held in October. Tavistock was also permitted to hold a weekly market that, 900 years later, still takes place every Friday in the **Pannier Market**, one of the finest market buildings in the southwest.

Also on the western side of Tavistock can be found the **Tavistock-Morwellham Canal**, which was built in the early 19th century as the town and surrounding area were experiencing a copper boom. Today, **Morwellham Quay**, just south of the town, has been restored to re-create the busy atmosphere of the 1850s, when half the world's copper came through this tiny hamlet.

AROUND TAVISTOCK

LYDFORD
7½ miles NE of Tavistock off the A386

A royal borough in Saxon times, Lydford's former importance is reflected in its austere stone fortress **Lydford Castle**. To the southwest of the village, the valley of the River Lyd suddenly narrows to form the mile and a half long **Lydford Gorge**, one of Dartmoor's most spectacular natural features. A circular walk around the gorge begins high up before passing through the enchanting riverside scenes, including the thrilling Devil's Cauldron. Further south again is **Brent Tor**, a 1,100 feet volcanic plug that is one of the most striking sights in the whole of Dartmoor. The **Church of St Michael of the Rocks** stands on the top of it. The fourth smallest complete church in England, St Michael's is only 15 feet wide and 37 feet long and has walls only 10 feet high but three feet thick.

OKEHAMPTON

15 miles NE of Tavistock on the B3260

The town occupies a strategic position on the main route to Cornwall, and situated on the top of a wooded hill are the remains of **Okehampton Castle**, the largest medieval castle in Devon. Housed in an ancient mill is the **Museum of Dartmoor Life** while, in the surrounding courtyard, is the **Dartmoor National Park Visitor Centre**. To the south of Okehampton are Dartmoor's greatest peaks, **High Willhays** and **Yes Tor**, which rise to over 2,000 feet.

CHAGFORD

17 miles NE of Tavistock on the B3192

An ancient settlement that was one of Devon's four stannary towns, Chagford today is noted for the numerous ancient monuments that litter the surrounding countryside. Close by, near the pretty village of **Drewsteignton**, are two Iron Age hill forts along with the rather more modern **Castle Drogo**, designed by Sir Edwin Lutyens and built between 1910 and 1930.

PRINCETOWN

6½ miles E of Tavistock on the B3212

Situated at the heart of Dartmoor, some 1,400 feet above sea level, Princetown is the location of one of the country's best-known and most forbidding prisons – **Dartmoor Prison**, which first opened in 1809. Princetown is also home to the National Park's **Moorland Visitor Centre** that contains some excellent and informative displays about the moor. To the west lies **Widecombe in the Moor**, home to a grand old church that has been dubbed the **Cathedral of the Moors** and to a famous September fair. Sir Arthur Conan Doyle stayed in Princetown while gathering material for his most famous story *The Hound of the Baskervilles*. Fox Tor Mire became Grimpen Mire, where Sherlock Holmes lay low at **Grimspound**, the most impressive of all Dartmoor's Bronze Age relics.

BOVEY TRACEY

21 miles E of Tavistock on the B3344

To the north of this small town lies Parke, the former estate of the de Tracey family and now the headquarters of **Dartmoor National Park**; the present house dates from the 1820s and the grounds are home to a Rare Breeds Farm.

To the east of Bovey Tracey lies **Ugbrooke House and Park** that was built in the mid 18th century for the Clifford family and is still their

146 THE FOX & HOUNDS

Bridestowe, nr Okehampton

A friendly, sociable country pub serving a good selection of food and drink. Also a choice of accommodatrion.

see page 463

Powder Mills, Dartmoor

147 THE WHITE HART HOTEL

Buckfastleigh

Originally a coaching inn, now a fine country pub with well-kept ales and super home-cooked food.

 see page 462

148 KNIGHTSTONE TEA ROOMS & RESTAURANT

Yelverton

Morning coffee, afternoon teas, home-made hot and cold meals and traditional Sunday roasts in a delightful tea room/restaurant. Two rooms for B&B.

 see page 463

•

12 miles out in the English Channel from Plymouth lies the famous Eddystone Lighthouse. The present Eddystone Lighthouse is the fourth. The first lighthouse, a timber structure, was swept away in a storm in 1703; a later lighthouse, built in 1759, was dismantled and re-erected on the Hoe, where, as Smeaton's Tower, it is one of the city's most popular visitor attractions.

•

home today. To the northwest is one of Dartmoor's most popular villages, **Lustleigh**, from where there are delightful walks, and Becky Falls Woodland Park.

BUCKFASTLEIGH

17 miles SE of Tavistock on the B3380

A former wool town on the banks of the River Mardle, Buckfastleigh is the western terminus and headquarters of the **South Devon Railway**, whose steam trains continue to make the seven-mile journey through the valley of the River Dart to Totnes. Another popular attraction close to the town is the **Buckfast Butterflies and Dartmoor Otters**, where the exotic butterflies can be seen in a specially designed tropical rain forest environment; the three species of otter include the native British otter.

BUCKLAND MONACHORUM

4 miles S of Tavistock off the A386

Tucked away in a secluded valley above the River Tavy, 13th century **Buckland Abbey** was the last home of Sir Francis Drake, who purchased it from his rival, Sir Richard Grenville.

PLYMOUTH

The most famous part of this historic city is undoubtedly **Plymouth Hoe**, the park and promenade overlooking Plymouth Sound where Sir Francis Drake was playing bowls when he was told of the approaching Spanish Armada. Just offshore, in the waters of the

mouth of the River Tamar, lies **Drake's Island**, an English Alcatraz that was, in medieval times, known as St Nicholas' Island. Plymouth's oldest quarter, the **Barbican**, is today a lively, open area of restaurants, pubs and an innovative small theatre, while close by is The Citadel, a massive fortress that was built by Charles II as a defence against a seaborne invasion. Near here is a reminder that Plymouth was the departure point for the Pilgrim Fathers; the **Mayflower Stone** stands at the point where they boarded their ship (they named their point of landing in America, Plymouth Rock). The names of the ship's company of *The Mayflower* are listed on a board on Island House, and their story is told in the **Plymouth Mayflower Visitor Centre**.

The Mayflower connection is everywhere in Plymouth. Jacka' Bakery, which has claims to be the oldest commercial bakery in the UK, is reputed to have supplied the ship's biscuits for the vessel's voyage to America. Sons of Plymouth include William Bligh (born 1754), Michael Foot (1913), Donald Sinden (1923), Ron Goodwin (1925), David Owen (1938) and Wayne Sleep (1948).

Five miles east of Plymouth, **Plympton** is home to **Saltram House and Park**, a prestigious 18th century mansion surrounded by a large estate near the tidal creek of the Plym estuary. The **Plym Valley Railway** runs from Marsh Mills, Plympton, to the local beauty spot of **Plym Bridge**.

Dorset

Although Dorset is not a large county, it provides an extraordinary variety of attractions. There are the dramatic cliffs of the western coastline and the more gentle harbours and bays to the east, while inland, chalk upland and heathland supports a wealth of bird and plant life. Over the years, many of the little ports have become seaside resorts of which the most famous is Lyme Regis, with its fossils and The Cobb, but the wonderful, natural harbour of Poole continues to be a commercial port. Inland are charming, ancient market towns, many of which have their roots in Roman times and, along with the Georgian elegance of Blandford Forum, there is historic Dorchester, one of the

country's most appealing towns. It was close to the county town that Thomas Hardy was born and many of the towns and villages of the county have featured in the great writer's novels.

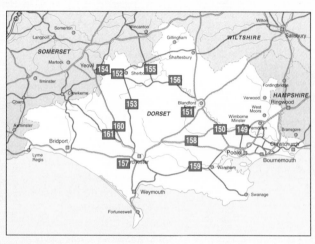

The Thomas Hardy connection is strong throughout Dorset, and Bournemouth is no exception. As Sandbourne, it is mentioned in Tess of the d'Urbevilles and Jude the Obscure.

BOURNEMOUTH

At the end of the 18th century, Bournemouth hardly existed, but once the virtues of its fresh sea air were advertised it began to expand as a resort. It continued to expand during the Victorian age; the splendid pier was built in 1855 and again in 1880 when a theatre was added. Beautiful gardens are a feature of this civilised place, and above the Cliff Gardens is **Shelley Park**, named after Sir Percy Florence Shelley, son of the poet Percy Bysshe Shelley, and sometime lord of the manor of Bournemouth. **Shelley House** is devoted to the life and works of the poet. Shelley's ashes lie in a cemetery in Rome (he drowned off a beach in Italy), but his heart is reputedly buried in the churchyard of the **Church of St Peter**, Bournemouth, along with his wife Mary Wollstonecraft Shelley, author of *Frankenstein*. William Gladstone took his last communion in the church, which is notable for its brilliant Gothic Revival interior and some Pre-Raphaelite stained glass. Among the many other places to visit are the **Rothesay Museum**, mainly nautical but with a collection of 300 vintage typewriters; the **Teddy Bear Museum**; and the **Aviation Museum** at Bournemouth International Airport.

AROUND BOURNEMOUTH

CHRISTCHURCH

5 miles E of Bournemouth on the A35

Situated at the junction of the Rivers Avon and Stour, Christchurch began life as a Saxon village and it was here that, in 1094, Ranulf Flambard began the construction of the magnificent **Christchurch Priory** that has ever since been used as a place of worship. Said to be the longest parish church in England, it is home to **St Michael's Loft Museum**. Christchurch is also home to the most modern of all the country's Scheduled Ancient Monuments – a World War II pillbox and anti-tank obstacles.

SANDBANKS

3½ miles SW of Bournemouth on the B3369

This spit of land, along with Studland to the southwest, almost cuts off Poole harbour from the sea, and it is these two headlands that provide the harbour with its shelter. At the top of the headland lies Compton Acres, a series of themed gardens that are separated

Christchurch

by paths, steps, rock walls and terraces.

POOLE

4 miles W of Bournemouth on the A350

Once the largest settlement in Dorset, Poole has a huge natural harbour and a history that goes back to Roman times. The **Waterfront Museum**, housed in an 18th century warehouse and the adjoining medieval town cellars, tells the 2,000-year story of the port. Poole Pottery made the famous red tiles for London Underground's stations and was the HQ of the US Navy during the Second World War. **Poole Harbour** is the second largest natural harbour in the world (Sydney Harbour is the largest).

Out in Poole harbour are several islands, the largest of which is **Brownsea Island**, where the heath and woodland are home to a wide variety of wildlife and where the Scout movement was born. In August 1907 20 boys came here under the auspices of Lieutenant-general Robert Baden Powell to learn about scouting skills, fair play and good manners. At Sandbanks, by the entrance to the harbour, Marconi established one of the world's first radio stations. One of Poole's most famous sons is the writer John Le Carré, born David Cornwell in 1931.

Just to the north of Poole lies **Upton Country Park**, a large estate of parkland, gardens and meadows that surround a handsome early 19th century manor house.

WIMBORNE MINSTER

7 miles NW of Bournemouth on the A31

A wonderful old market town, Wimborne Minster is dominated by its **Minster**, a glorious Norman building that is the best example of its kind in the county. Close by the Minster is the Priest's House, a 16th century town house that is now home to the **Museum of East Dorset Life**.

Around Wimborne there are several places of interest: to the east, at **Hampreston**, is **Knoll's Garden and Nursery**, a delightful, informal and typically English garden that was planted over 30 years ago, while further east again is **Stapehill**, a 19th century Cistercian nunnery that is now a craft centre and countryside museum.

To the west of Wimborne lies **Kingston Lacy House**, a superb country house containing an outstanding collection of paintings that is set in attractive parkland. Elsewhere on the estate is the Iron Age hill fort of **Badbury Rings** and the 18th century White Mill.

BLANDFORD FORUM

An attractive market town in the Stour valley. The handsome Georgian buildings here were mostly designed by two talented architects, the brothers John and William Bastard, who were charged with rebuilding much of the town after a devastating fire in 1731. To mark the completion of the town's rebuilding in 1760, the **Fire**

149 THE LAUGHING POT TEA ROOMS

Wimborne

The **Laughing Pot Tea Rooms**, among the best in the region, prove that good things often come in small packages.

see page 463

150 THE BLACK HORSE

Sturminster Marshall, nr Wimborne

In an area rich in scenic and historic attractions, the **Black Horse** is an excellent place to stop for a drink and a snack or leisurely meal

see page 464

151 THE CROWN

Winterborne Strickland

A friendly thatched pub with good home cooking and a programme of events and entertainment

see page 465

152 THE PLUME OF FEATHERS

Sherborne

A mellow stone inn across from the Abbey, with four real ales, a menu of pub favourites and comfortable B&B rooms.

see page 465

153 THE HUNTERS MOON

Middlemarsh, nr Sherborne

An outstanding hostelry in every respect – drinks, a very varied choice of food and comfortable en suite accommodation

see page 466

154 THE ROSE & CROWN TRENT

Trent, nr Sherborne

An attractive village setting for a handsome inn with a fine reputation for hospitality, food and drink.

see page 467

100

Monument was erected in front of the church and had a dual purpose – to provide water for fire fighting and for the public to drink.

To the northeast of the town lies **Blandford Camp** and the **Royal Signals Museum**, where there is a wealth of interactive displays on codes and code breakers, animals at war and the SAS.

AROUND BLANDFORD FORUM

SHERBORNE

16½ miles NW of Blandford Forum on the A352

In AD 705, St Aldhelm founded **Sherborne Abbey** as the Mother Cathedral for the whole of the southwest of England and the building that now occupies the site features some of the finest fan vaults in the whole country. Some of the old buildings now house **Sherborne School**, whose alumni include Cecil Day Lewis, the poet

laureate, and the writer John Le Carré, born David Cornwell.

Sherborne School has been used as the setting for at least three major films: *The Guinea Pig* (1948), *Goodbye, Mr Chips* (1969) and *The Browning Version* (1994).

Sherborne's best-known resident was Sir Walter Raleigh, who, while enjoying the favouritism of Elizabeth I, was granted the estate of **Sherborne Old Castle** in 1592. This stark and comfortless residence was not to his taste, so he built a new castle, the splendid **Sherborne Castle**, which remains today one of the grandest of Dorset's country houses.

SHAFTESBURY

10½ miles N of Blandford Forum on the A350

This hilltop town, which stands over 700 feet above sea level, was founded in AD 880 by King Alfred who fortified the settlement here and established a Benedictine abbey for women installing his daughter as the first prioress. Just a hundred

Sherborne Castle and Lake

years later, King Edward, who was murdered at Corfe Castle, was buried at **Shaftesbury Abbey**, which soon became a place of pilgrimage. The nearby **Shaftesbury Abbey Museum** houses many of the finds from the abbey's excavations and state of the art, touch screen displays bring the ancient religious house to life.

The town's most famous sight must be **Gold Hill**, a steep cobbled street, stepped in places and lined with delightful 18th century cottages. Many people who have never visited the town will recognise this thoroughfare as it was made famous through the classic TV advertisement for Hovis bread. The cottage at the top of Gold Hill is home to the **Shaftesbury Museum**. Button-making was once an important cottage industry in the town and some of the products can be seen here including the decorative Dorset Knobs, which share their name with a famous, also locally-made, biscuit.

TOLPUDDLE

9 miles SW of Blandford Forum off the A35

Like so many villages beside the River Piddle, Tolpuddle's name was changed by the Victorians from the original – Tolpiddle. It was here in 1834 that the first trades union was formed when six villagers, in an attempt to escape from grinding poverty, banded together to form the Society of Agricultural Labourers, taking an oath of mutual support. The story of the martyrs is told in the **Tolpuddle Martyrs**

Museum, housed in memorial cottages that were built in 1934 by the TUC.

To the west lies **Athelhampton House**, one of the finest stone-built manor houses in England.

CERNE ABBAS

14½ miles SW of Blandford Forum on the A352

The most famous 'inhabitant' of this pretty village is the **Cerne Abbas Giant**, a colossal figure cut into the chalk hillside. The extraordinary club-brandishing full-frontal Cerne Abbas giant, 180 feet in height, is best viewed from a lay-by on the A352, though according to legend a rather closer and more intimate encounter is required by women who wish to become pregnant.

DORCHESTER

After capturing the Iron Age hill fort of Maiden Castle in around AD 50, the Romans went on to found Durnovaia. The hill fort is one of the biggest in England and nearby is another ancient monument utilised by the Romans, who converted the Neolithic henge monument of Maumbury Rings into an amphitheatre.

As with so many towns in Dorset, Dorchester played host to the infamous Judge Jeffreys and here he sentenced over 70 men to death. Later, in the 1830s, the town was once again the scene of a famous trial, when in the **Old Crown Court** the Tolpuddle Martyrs were sentenced. The Old

Stalbridge

A pleasant village pub with a warm ambience and a fine variety of home-cooked snacks and meals.

❙ *see page 468*

Gold Hill, Child Okeford, nr Blandford Forum

One of the most delightful and attractive country inns you'll ever come across, with outstanding food and drink and very comfortable B&B accommodation

❙ ⊨ *see page 469*

157 THE BREWERS ARMS

Winterborne St Martin, nr Dorchester

A nice pub with nice people and very nice hosts; well-kept ales and a wide range of home-cooked snacks and meals

🍴 see page 470

158 THE DRAX ARMS

Bere Regis, nr Wareham

A lovely traditional Dorset inn with a fine reputation for hospitality and good food.

🍴 see page 471

Crown Court and its cells are now open to the public.

Just to the northeast of the town, lies **Max Gate**, the house that Hardy designed and lived in from 1885 until his death in 1928. Situated on the River Cerne, on the northern outskirts of Dorchester, is the attractive village of **Charminster**, the home of **Wolfeton House**, a splendid medieval and Elizabethan building surrounded by water meadows.

Just to the east of Dorchester is the village of **Stinsford** that appeared as Melstock in Hardy's *Under the Greenwood Tree*. Hardy's heart is buried in the churchyard of the **Church of St Michael**, beside his first wife, and his parents are buried nearby. (Hardy's official funeral was at Westminster Abbey and his ashes were placed in the south transept.) Just beyond the village is **Hardy's Cottage**, where the novelist was born in 1840 and where he continued to live, on and off, until his marriage to Emma Gifford in 1874.

Hardy's Monument on Black Downs to the southwest of Dorchester was erected in memory not of the writer but of Sir Thomas Masterson Hardy, the flag captain of HMS *Victory* at Trafalgar and the man who escorted Nelson's body home.

AROUND DORCHESTER

MORETON

7 miles E of Dorchester off the B3390

Moreton's Gothic **Church of St Nicholas** was wrecked by a Second World War bomb and its glass replaced with superb engraved glass by Laurence Whistler. In the cemetery is the grave of T E Lawrence - Lawrence of Arabia, Arabic scholar, traveller, soldier and man of action. To the northeast of this charming village is **Cloud's Hill**, a tiny redbrick cottage where Lawrence lived after retiring from the RAF in 1935. Lawrence had long been a devotee of Brough Superior motor cycles, calling his first (in 1922) Boanerges. It was in 1935, while riding a later version, which he named George VII, that he clipped the wheel of an errand boy's bicycle and sustained fatal injuries. The King of Iraq and Winston Churchill were among those who attended his burial in the graveyard at Moreton.

To the east of Moreton is **Bovington Camp**, where Lawrence served as a private in the Royal Tank Corps. The camp houses the **Tank Museum**, where the collection of 300 tanks and

Bovington Camp Tank Museum

armoured vehicles starts with Britain's first tank, Little Willie, built in 1915.

CORFE CASTLE

18 miles SE of Dorchester on the A351

This greystone village is dominated by the majestic ruins of **Corfe Castle** high on a hill. An important stronghold that protected the gateway through the Purbeck Hills, the castle was constructed in the years immediately following the Norman Conquest. Now owned by the National Trust, the castle is part of an extensive estate, with a network of footpaths taking in both the coastline and the inland heath, and encompassing important habitats for many rare species, including all six species of British reptile.

SWANAGE

20 miles SE of Dorchester on the A351

This seaside town, complete with its fully restored Victorian pier and its little exhibition, built its early fortune on Purbeck stone. The **King Alfred Column**, on the seafront, records that this was where the king fought and saw off the Danish fleet in AD 877. The column is topped by cannonballs that would, undoubtedly, have been a great help to King Alfred, had they been invented at the time. These particular cannonballs date from the Crimean War.

An attraction not to be missed is the **Swanage Railway**, which uses old Southern Region and BR Standard locomotives to pull trains on a six-mile scenic journey to Norden, just north of Corfe Castle.

To the north of Swanage lies **Studland**, whose fine sandy beach stretches from Handfast Point to South Haven Point and the entrance to Poole Harbour. The heathland behind the beach is a haven for rare birds and is a National Nature Reserve. A footpath leading along the coast takes in **Tilly Whim Caves**, named after the owner, Mr Tilly, who used a whim, or wooden derrick, to load stone into barges for transportation to Swanage.

EAST LULWORTH

12 miles SE of Dorchester on the B3070

This charming little village stands on a minor road that leads down to one of the country's best loved beauty spots, **Lulworth Cove**, an almost perfectly circular bay that is surrounded by towering cliffs. **Lulworth Castle** was built as a hunting lodge in the early 17th century and played host to seven monarchs before a devastating fire in 1929 reduced it to a virtual ruin.

159 KEMPS COUNTRY HOUSE HOTEL

East Stoke, nr Wareham

A superbly converted Victorian rectory offering the very best in food, accommodation, comfort and service.

 see page 472

Lulworth Castle

In 1789 George III came to Weymouth to try out the newly invented bathing machine; the story goes that as he entered the water a band, hidden in an adjacent bathing machine, struck up God Save the King. An unusual painted statue of the King was erected in 1810, and close by is the colourful Jubilee Clock that was put up in 1887 to celebrate Queen Victoria's Golden Jubilee.

On the MoD's Lulworth Range is the deserted village of **Tyneham**, occupied in 1943 when the range had to be expanded for the testing of increasingly powerful weapons.

WEYMOUTH

7 miles S of Dorchester on the A354

Weymouth owed its early prosperity to the woollen trade, but in the late 18th century it also began to develop as a resort.

One of the town's most popular tourist attractions is **Brewers Quay**, with specialist shops and a museum. Not far from Brewers Quay is **Nothe Fort**, which was built as part of the defences of the new naval base that was being established at nearby Portland. The fort is now the home of the **Museum of Coastal Defence**.

ISLE OF PORTLAND

11 miles S of Dorchester on the A354

The Isle of Portland is not, strictly speaking, an island but a peninsula that is joined to the mainland by the amazing **Chesil Beach**, a vast bank of pebbles worn smooth by the sea

that stretches for 18 miles from the island westwards to Abbotsbury. The island's most famous building is **Portland Castle**, constructed by Henry VIII as part of his south coast defence. **Portland Museum** was founded by the birth control pioneer, Marie Stopes, and occupies a pair of thatched cottages.

At the tip of the island, **Portland Bill**, are two lighthouses, the older of which (1788) is now a bird observatory and field centre.

ABBOTSBURY

8 miles SW of Dorchester on the B3157

This delightful village has three main attractions that draw holidaymakers here in their thousands each year – the **Swannery**, the **Sub Tropical Gardens** and the **Tithe Barn Children's Farm**. To the north lie several ancient monuments, among them Kingston Russell Stone Circle, a Bronze Age circle.

BRIDPORT

13½ miles W of Dorchester on the A35

Rope-making was an important industry here, and it also has close links with the non-conformists, with two well-appointed chapels. In the early 18th century Bridport's harbour began to silt up, so the townspeople built a new one at the mouth of the River Britt and called it West Bay.

LYME REGIS

22 miles W of Dorchester on the A3052

In 1588 Sir Francis Drake's fleet fought a small battle with the Spanish Armada in Lyme Bay, and

Abbotsbury Swannery

in 1685 the Duke of Monmouth landed at Lyme Regis and began his unsuccessful rebellion that would lead to the Bloody Assizes of Judge Jeffreys. During the 18th century, Lyme Regis developed into a fashionable seaside resort; the town's most famous landmark is undoubtedly **The Cobb**, which was built in medieval times to protect the harbour. John Fowles set a part of *The French Lieutenant's Woman* on The Cobb, and the film of the book also used the location. Jane Austen stayed in the town writing a part of *Persuasion*, and Henry Fielding is said to have based the character of Sophie in *Tom Jones* on a local girl.

Lyme Regis is particularly famous for the fossils that were first discovered here in the early 19th century and there are fine specimens in **Lyme Regis Museum** and in the **Dinosaurland & Fossil Museum**. The fossil frenzy was fuelled by one Mary Anning, born in 1799, who with her family searched for fossils in the local cliffs and sold them to supplement the income of their carpenter father. The most famous discovery of Mary and her brother Joseph was the fossilised skeleton of an ichthyosaur; it took several years to free it from the cliff, and Mary sold it to the British Museum for £23.

The eight-mile stretch of coast to the east of Lyme Regis includes the highest cliff on the south coast, Golden Cap, and also the **Charmouth Heritage Coast Centre** that aims to further the public's understanding and appreciation of this area's scientific wealth.

BEAMINSTER

14 miles NW of Dorchester on the A3066

As a result of a series of fires, the centre of this ancient market town is largely a handsome collection of 18th and 19th century buildings. However, some older buildings did survive the fires, including the 15th century **Church of St Mary** with its splendid 100 feet tower from which, it is said, a number of citizens were hanged during the Bloody Assizes.

Just to the south of the town lies **Parnham House**, a beautiful Elizabethan mansion enlarged and refurbished by John Nash in the 19th century. Surrounded by glorious gardens, the house is certainly one of Dorset's finest Tudor residencies but, much more recently, in the 1970s, it came into the ownership of John Makepeace and his wife Jennie. Today, this is a showcase for the very best in modern furniture, much of which is created by John and his students at the **John Makepeace Furniture Workshops** that he runs from here. In the gardens, Jennie has created a magical environment with unusual plants, a lake rich in wildlife and a play area for children.

To the southeast of Beaminster, **Mapperton Gardens** surround a fine Jacobean manor house with stable blocks, a dovecote and its own church.

160 THE GREYHOUND INN

Sydling St Nicholas, nr Dorchester

A picturesque village inn with cask ales, an interesting menu of home-cooked dishes and six splendidly appointed bedrooms.

see page 471

161 CHALK & CHEESE

Maiden Newton

The hub of the local community, with well-kept ales and a good variety of favourite pub dishes.

see page 473

County Durham

County Durham is dominated by the marvellous city of Durham and, in particular, the magnificent cathedral that is now a World Heritage Site. The county's prosperity was founded largely on coal mining, and now that the industry has all but disappeared the scars it created are being swept away. County Durham's countryside has always supported an important farming industry, and Central and South Durham still retain a gentle landscape of fields, woodland, streams and country lanes.

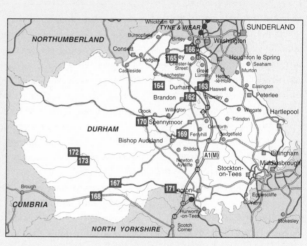

DURHAM CITY

Arriving in Durham by train, the visitor is presented with what must be one of the most breathtaking urban views in Europe. Towering over the tumbling roofs of the city is the magnificent bulk of **Durham Cathedral**, third only to Canterbury and York in ecclesiastical significance but excelling them in architectural splendour. The cathedral owes its origin to the monks of Lindisfarne, who, in AD 875, fled from Viking attacks, taking with them the coffin of St Cuthbert. In AD 980 they finally settled at this easily defended site, where the River Wear makes a wide loop around a rocky outcrop, and they built the White Church, where St Cuthbert's remains were finally laid to rest. The founder of the present cathedral was a Norman, William de St Carileph, Bishop of Durham from 1081 to 1096. He was determined to replace the little church with a building of the scale and style of the splendid new churches he had seen being built in France and in 1093 the foundation stones were laid. The result was the creation of the finest and grandest example of Norman architecture in Europe.

The Cathedral contains the tomb of the Venerable Bede, saint, scholar-monk and Britain's first true historian. Bede spent most of his life in Jarrow, where he died in AD735 and where he was initially buried. His body was later moved to its final resting place in the Cathedral in 1370.

Sharing the same rocky peninsula is **Durham Castle**, whose impregnability ensured that Durham was one of the few towns in Northumbria that was never captured by the Scots through force. The castle is now used as a hall of residence for the students of **Durham University**, which was founded in 1832, making it the third oldest English university, after Oxford and Cambridge.

The rest of Durham reflects the long history of the castle and cathedral it served. There are winding streets, the ancient Market Place, elegant Georgian houses and quiet courts and alleyways, churches, museums, art galleries and heritage centres.

The **Botanic Gardens**, run by the University, feature a large collection of North American trees, including junior-sized giant redwoods, a series of small 'gardens-within-gardens' and walks

162 STONEBRIDGE INN

Durham

Good cooking, value for money and excellent service in a popular pub on the western edge of Durham.

¶ see page 475

163 THE GILESGATE MOOR HOTEL

Durham

Good-value, practical accommodation in a hotel a short drive from the city centre and from J62 of the A1 (M).

🛏 ¶ see page 474

Durham Cathedral

Hartlepool Historic Quay and Museum

164 THE ROYAL OAK HOTEL

Cornsay Colliery

A friendly, unpretentious pub with good honest home cooking and 5 rooms for B&B.

 see page 476

through mature woodland.

On the western outskirts of the city is the site of the Battle of Neville's Cross, fought between the English and the Scots in 1346. The Scots were heavily defeated and their king was taken prisoner.

AROUND DURHAM

HARTLEPOOL

15 miles SE of Durham on the A179

On 16 December, 1914 Hartlepool was the first town in Britain to suffer from enemy action, when it was shelled from German warships lying off the coast. Nowadays it is a thriving shopping centre, with some outstanding tourist attractions, including the **Hartlepool Historic Quay and Museum**. Guided tours are available of HMS *Trincomalee*, Britain's oldest surviving warship, and the PSS *Wingfield Castle*, an old paddle steamer.

One of the more bizarre

stories told in Hartlepool Museum concerns a monkey who was washed ashore on a piece of wreckage during the Napoleonic Wars. Not understanding its gibberish, the citizens decided that the monkey was a French spy and hanged the poor creature.

STOCKTON-ON-TEES

17 miles SE of Durham on the A177

Stockton-on-Tees is famous for being one end of the Stockton to Darlington railway, which opened in 1825 so that coal from the mines of South Durham could have access to the River Tees. Notable natives of Stockton include John Walker, the inventor of the humble friction match, born here in 1781; Thomas Sheraton, the furniture maker and designer, born here in 1751; and Ivy Close, who won Britain's first ever beauty contest in 1908.

DARLINGTON

17½ miles S of Durham on the A167

An ancient market town that was founded in Saxon times, Darlington's greatest claim to fame lies in the role it played, with its neighbour Stockton, in the creation of the world's first commercially successful public railway. The **Darlington Railway Centre and Museum** houses relics of the pioneering Stockton and Darlington Railway, including a replica of Stephenson's Locomotion No 1.

CHESTER-LE-STREET

5½ miles N of Durham on the A167

A busy market town on the River Wear, the town's medieval **Church** of St Mary and St Cuthbert stands on the site of a 9th century cathedral that was established by the monks of Lindisfarne while they stayed here for 113 years before moving to Durham. Waldridge Fell Country Park, southwest of Chester-le-Street, is County Durham's last surviving area of lowland heathland.

To the northeast lies one of the regions most popular attractions, the award-winning North of England Open Air Museum at Beamish. Set in 200 acres of countryside, it illustrates life in the North of England in the late 19th and early 20th centuries by way of a cobbled street full of shops, banks and offices, a colliery village complete with drift mine, an old engine shed, a horse yard and terraced gardens. To the northwest of Beamish is Causey Arch, which claims to be the world's first single-arch railway bridge; it was built in 1726 by coalmine owners to take coal from Tanfield to the River Tyne.

In the old part of Washington, northeast of Chester-le-Street, is Washington Old Hall, the home of the Washington family, ancestors of George Washington, the first American president. The present house was built in around 1623 and the interiors re-create a typical manor house of the 17th century. Also in Washington is the Washington Wildfowl and Wetlands Centre, a conservation area and bird watchers' paradise, and the Glaxo Wellcome Wetland Discovery Centre.

SUNDERLAND

11½ miles NE of Durham on the A690

Sunderland is one of Britain's newer cities: the Church of St Michael and All Angels, the first minster to be created in England since the Reformation, was proclaimed Sunderland Minster in January 1998. To the south of the city centre is the Ryhope Engines Museum, based on a pumping station that supplied the city and surrounding area with water.

On the north side of the Wear, in the suburb of Monkwearmouth, is an important site of early Christianity. Glass was first made in Sunderland in the 7th century at St Peter's Church and the National Glass Centre is close by.

PETERLEE

10½ miles E of Durham on the A1086

Peterlee was established as a New Town in 1948 to re-house the mining families that lived in the colliery villages around Easington and Shotton. It is named after an

165 THE PUNCH BOWL

Craghead

Sociable village inn serving traditional pub snacks and meals. Weekend musical entertainment, 3 rooms for B&B.

🍴 ⊨ *see page 475*

166 THE RED LION

Ouston, nr Chester-le-Street

A popular roadside pub serving a wide variety of home-cooked dishes for all appetites.

🍴 *see page 477*

North of England Open Air Museum at Beamish

167 THE BEACONSFIELD

Barnard Castle

A generous welcome, well-kept ales and wholesome home cooking keep the customers happy at this busy, popular pub.

 see page 477

168 THE ANCIENT UNICORN

Bowes, nr Barnard Castle

A real pub-lover's pub, with cask ales locally sourced food and en suite guest bedrooms.

 see page 478

Bowes Museum, Barnard Castle

outstanding Durham miner and county councillor, Peter Lee, who fought all his life for the well-being of the local community. **Castle Eden Dene National Nature Reserve**, on the south side of the town, is one of the largest woodlands in the North East that has not been planted or extensively altered by man.

BARNARD CASTLE

This old market town derives its name from its Castle, founded in the 12th century by Bernard, son

of Guy de Baliol, one of the knights who fought alongside William I. The town has an especially rich architectural heritage, with handsome houses, cottages, shops and inns dating from the 17th to the 19th centuries and an impressive octagonal Market Cross.

The town is home to the extraordinary **Bowes Museum**, a grand and beautiful building styled on a French château. The fabulous collections on show include paintings by Goya, El Greco, Turner, Boudin and Canaletto, tapestries, ceramics, a wonderful display of toys (the world's first toy train set) and the breathtaking life-size Silver Swan that is an automaton and music box.

AROUND BARNARD CASTLE

BISHOP AUCKLAND

12 miles NE of Barnard Castle on the A688

Auckland Castle, still the official palace of the Bishop of Durham, began as a small 12th century manor house and was added to by successive bishops. The palace grounds contain an ancient herd of red deer. At **Shildon**, three miles south of Bishop Auckland, is Locomotion: The National Railway Museum, whose exhibits include a full-size replica of Timothy Hackworth's *Sans Pareil* of 1829, built for the famous Rainhill Trials on the Liverpool to Manchester railways.

In the small village of **Escomb**, two miles northwest of Bishop Auckland, is one of the county's true hidden gems – the 7th century Church of St John the Evangelist, built using stone from the nearby Binchester Roman fort. It is one of only three complete Saxon churches in Britain.

PIERCEBRIDGE

10 miles E of Barnard Castle on the A67

The picturesque village green stands on the site of a once

important Roman fort, one of a chain of forts on Dere Street. The remains of the fort, which are visible today, can be dated from coin evidence to around AD 270.

To the northwest lies **Gainford**, County Durham's most beautiful village. It sits just north of the River Tees and its core is a jostling collection of 18th and 19th century cottages and houses grouped around a green.

MIDDLETON-IN-TEESDALE

8 miles NW of Barnard Castle on the B6277

Middleton is the centre for some magnificent walks in Upper Teesdale; the most famous of these is the **Pennine Way** on its 250-mile route from Derbyshire to Kirk Yetholm in Scotland. It passes through Middleton-in-Teesdale from the south, then turns west along Teesdale, passing traditional, whitewashed

169 THE SHIP INN

Middlestone Village, nr Bishops Auckland

One of the most popular pubs in the area, bringing in the crowds with superbly kept cask ales and excellent home cooking.

 see page 479

170 FIR TREE COUNTRY HOTEL

Fir Tree, nr Crook

On the A68 close to Hamsterley Forest, the **Fir Tree** is a perfect stopping-off place for refreshment or a break in the motel-style accommodation.

 see page 478

171 THE CALBURY ARMS

Piercebridge, nr Darlington

A popular, sociable pub-lover's pub with real ales and home-cooked food.

 see page 480

Auckland Castle, Bishop Auckland

Middleton-in-Teesdale

Honest food, honestly cooked makes **Café 1618** one of the most likeable eating places in the region. Also rooms for B&B and a self-catering cottage.

 see page 480

173 THE ROSE & CROWN

Durham

Good-value, practical accommodation in a hotel a short drive from the city centre and from J62 of the A1 (M).

 see page 481

Weardale Museum, Ireshopeburn

farmsteads and spectacular, riverside scenery, including the thrilling waterfalls at **Low Force** and **High Force**.

IRESHOPEBURN

18 miles NW of Barnard Castle on the A689

This small village is home to the **Weardale Museum** that includes a carefully re-created room in a typical Weardale lead miner's cottage, with furnishings and costumes in period. There is also a room dedicated to John Wesley, who visited the area on more than one occasion.

To the northwest lies **Killhope Mine**, the focal point of what is now the remarkable **North of England Lead Mining Museum**, which is dominated by the massive 34-feet high water wheel.

Essex

Bordering the north bank of the River Thames, southern Essex has long been a gateway to London, and while it contains much heavy industry, it also encompasses some very important marshland wildlife habitats. History, too, abounds in this part of the county - Henry VIII built the riverside Block Houses at East and West Tilbury, which later became Coalhouse and Tilbury Forts. Southend-on-Sea is one of the country's best-loved venues for a family holiday or a day trip from London, and there are numerous nature reserves, the ancient royal hunting ground of Epping Forest and the yachting centre at Burnham-on-Crouch. Maldon remains famous for its traditionally produced sea salt.

Although Chelmsford is the county town, Colchester, which was first established in the 7th century BC, has the greater character. The country's oldest recorded town was the capital of Roman Britain until Queen Boudicca (Boadicea) burned the town to the ground. Other ancient towns abound in the county including Tiptree, home to the famous

jam factory, Coggeshall, which is well known for its lace, and Saffron Walden which takes its name from the Saffron crocus that was used to make dyestuffs. Along the east coast, dubbed the 'Sunshine Holiday Coast', are the resorts of Clacton-on-Sea, Frinton-on-Sea and Walton-on-the-Naze that were all developed in the 19th century. Seafaring, fishing and shipbuilding were all once the mainstays of many of the settlements along this stretch of coast and Brightlingsea has the distinction of being the only limb of the Cinque Ports outside Kent and Sussex.

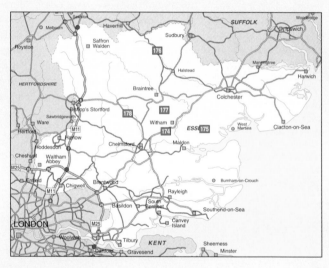

174 THE WILLIAM
BOOSEY

Hatfield Peverel, nr Chelmsford

A long-established public house open long hours and well patronised by the local community and motorists escaping the busy A12. Cask ales and home-cooked pub dishes.

 see page 482

•

At Highwood, three miles southwest of Chelmsford, lies Hylands House that was built in 1728 and has been painstakingly restored. The beautiful grounds that surround the neo-classical villa host a varied programme of outdoor events throughout the year.

•

CHELMSFORD

Situated at the confluence of the Rivers Chelmer and Can, the town was first settled by Romans, who built a fort and brought Christianity to Essex. It was not until 1914 that the diocese of Chelmsford was created, though **Chelmsford Cathedral** (formerly the Parish Church of St Mary) dates from the 15th century and was built on the site of a much earlier church. The Marconi Company set up the world's first radio company in Chelmsford in 1899. To the east of Chelmsford, and close to the village of **Danbury** (thought to take its name from the Danes who invaded this area in the Dark Ages), is **Danbury Country Park**, a pleasant stretch of open countryside with woodland and old pollarded trees, an 18th century ice house, a lake and ornamental gardens.

AROUND CHELMSFORD

MALDON

9 miles E of Chelmsford on the A414

Situated on the busy Blackwater estuary, Maldon's most distinctive feature is undoubtedly the 15th century **Moot Hall**, where an ambitious tapestry commemorates the 1,000th anniversary of the **Battle of Maldon**. Just outside the town, on **Northey Island**, lies the site of one of the most decisive battles of England's early history when, in AD 991, the English leader, Byrthnoth, was killed by the

invading Danes after a fierce three-day conflict. Following the defeat, the English king, Ethelred the Unready, was obliged to pay an annual tribute to his conquerors but the Danes soon tired of this arrangement and, overthrowing Ethelred, they put Canute on the throne. The island, in the Blackwater Estuary, has a large area of undisturbed salt marsh. Maldon's **Millennium Gardens** were named in commemoration of the battle.

Sea salt has been produced here for generations, and the history of this industry is one of the topics explored in the **Maldon District Museum**. To the north, at **Langford**, is the **Museum of Power**, an ex-waterworks pumping station that houses engines, pumps and other interesting artefacts.

SOUTH WOODHAM FERRERS

9½ miles SE of Chelmsford on the B1012

Surrounded by the empty marshland of the Crouch estuary, South Woodham Ferrers is a successful 20th century new town that, surprisingly, boasts a traditional market square overlooked by buildings constructed in the old Essex style – with brick, tile and weatherboard. To the northwest of the town, at **Hyde Hall**, is the **Royal Horticultural Society Garden**, which includes a woodland garden, large rose garden, ornamental ponds, herbaceous borders and the national collections of *malus* and *viburnum*.

BASILDON

12 miles S of Chelmsford on the A13

In **Wat Tyler Country Park**, 120 acres of meadows, woodland, marshland and ponds, is the **Motorboat Museum**, the only museum in the world devoted to the history of motor boats, concentrating on sports and leisure.

BURNHAM-ON-CROUCH

16½ miles SE of Chelmsford on the B1012

An attractive old village that is the county's main yachting centre. On the town's bustling quay is the **Burnham-on-Crouch and District Museum** featuring agricultural and maritime exhibits relating to this ancient area of Essex.

    Mangapps Farm Railway Museum on the edge of town houses an extensive collection of railway relics, historic buildings and one of the largest collections of signalling equipment. Train rides are available when the museum is open.

    To the northeast of Burnham, on the northern shore of the Dengie Peninsula, lies **Bradwell-on-Sea**, a village whose name is derived from the Saxon words 'brad pall' meaning 'broad wall'. Here is the site of **Bradwell Bay Secret Airfield**, which was used during World War II by aircraft that were unable to return to their original base. The village also has what could be the country's oldest church. **St Peter's-on-the-Wall**, built by St Cedd in the 7th century, was abandoned in the 14th century and forgotten for 600 years; it has been restored and reconsecrated.

St Peter's-on-the-Wall, Bradwell-on-Sea

SOUTHEND-ON-SEA

17 miles SE of Chelmsford on the A127

One of the country's best loved family resorts, Southend-on-Sea has seven miles of beaches, endless amusements and the longest pleasure pier in the world (1.33 miles), served by its own electric railway and with a little museum telling its story. The **Central Museum, Planetarium and Discovery Centre** features local history exhibits as well as astronomical displays. Several museums and galleries provide ample culture, and other attractions include the **Sealife Centre** and the renowned **Kursall** entertainment complex.

    Canvey Island has two unusual museums, the **Dutch Cottage Museum** with many traditional Flemish features, built by one of Vermuyden's marshland drainage workmen, and the **Castle Point Transport Museum**, housed in a 1930s bus garage, with a fascinating collection of Eastern

•

One of the most important archaeological finds of recent years is the burial chamber of a Saxon king, unearthed near the railway line at Prittlewell on the western edge of Southend. The chamber, dating from the early 7th century, is remarkably intact, and among the treasures recovered are glass vessels, gilded wooden drinking cups, gold foil crosses and solid gold buckles and brooches.

•

National buses and coaches and other commercial vehicles made between 1944 and 1981. At the Waterside Farm Centre, an attraction for the whole family is the Canvey Miniature Railway.

STANFORD-LE-HOPE

15 miles S of Chelmsford on the A1014

Lying between the town and the Thames estuary are **Stanford Marshes**, an ideal location for birdwatching and also the home to various species of wildlife. Close by is **Langdon Hills Country Park**, some 400 acres of ancient woodland and meadows that is home to many rare trees and from where there are spectacular views out over the Essex countryside.

TILBURY

19 miles SW of Chelmsford on the A1089

Chosen as the site for the Camp Royal in 1588 when the threat of invasion by Spain was imminent, **West Tilbury** (northeast of Tilbury) remains a quiet and hidden away backwater overlooking the Thames estuary whereas its larger neighbour is a busy, industrial centre. However, **Tilbury Fort**, the unusual 17th century building with a double moat, acts as a reminder of the past and it stands on the site of a military Block House built during the reign of Henry VIII. Close by, at the town's power station, is the **Tilbury Energy and Environment Centre** that includes a nature reserve. Another fortification, **Coalhouse Fort**, was constructed as a primary defence against invasion of the Thames area.

Despite the industry that lines the Thames estuary, the area around Tilbury is also rural, and the **Mardyke Valley**, which runs from Aveley to Orsett Fen, provides pleasant views and open spaces.

BRENTWOOD

10½ miles SW of Chelmsford on the A1016

Attractions in this town on the old pilgrim and coaching routes to and from London include a classically-styled modern cathedral, a picturesque cottage museum in a disused cemetery and a top entertainment venue. Just southeast of the town centre is **Thorndon Country Park** and **Hartswood**, formerly a Royal deer park. To the northwest, at **South Weald**, is **Weald Country Park**, a former estate which was partially landscaped in the 18th century and features a lake, woodland and an ancient deer park. To the northeast of Brentwood and situated beside a Roman road is **Mountnessing Post Mill**, a traditional

Tilbury Fort

weatherboarded mill dating from 1807 that was restored to working order in the 1980s.

WALTHAM ABBEY

Originally a Roman settlement and home to a hunting lodge belonging to the early Saxon kings, the town grew up around this and an **Augustinian Abbey** that was built in 1177 by Henry II. The Abbey's **Crypt Centre** explains the history of both the town and the Abbey, which was once one of the largest in the country and was the last to fall victim to the Dissolution in 1540.

Royal Gunpowder Mills, Waltham Abbey

Gunpowder production started here in the 17th century and by the 19th century the **Royal Gunpowder Mills** employed 500 workers. The once secret buildings and the surrounding parkland are now open to the public as part of the **Lea Valley Regional Park**, an important area of high biodiversity that sustains a large range of plant life and bird life. The park stretches 26 miles along the River Lea from East India Dock Basin, on the north bank of the Thames in East London, to Hertfordshire..

AROUND WALTHAM ABBEY

HARLOW

10 miles NE of Waltham Abbey on the A414

Though much of it is modern, Harlow has several sites of historic interest. **Harlow Museum** occupies a Georgian manor house set in picturesque gardens, while **Harlow Study and Visitors Centre** is set in a medieval tithe barn and adjacent 13th century church. At Chingford stands the **Queen Elizabeth Hunting Lodge**, a timber-framed building first used by Henry VIII. This unique Tudor survivor is situated in **Epping Forest**, the magnificent and expansive tract of ancient hornbeam coppice that offers miles of leafy walks and bridle paths along with some rough grazing and the occasional distant view. The Elizabethan Hunting Lodge was once the destination for thousands of Londoners who came by bus to enjoy a day in the open air, and at the end of the day queued patiently and orderly for the journey home.

CHIPPING ONGAR

8 miles SE of Harlow on the A414

In 1155, Richard de Lucy built a castle here, of which only the

The Greenwich Meridian runs through Waltham Abbey's main thoroughfare, Sun Street, and is marked out on the pavement and also through the Abbey Gardens.

117

To the south of Chipping Ongar, at Kelvedon Hatch, a rural bungalow is the deceptively ordinary exterior of the Kelvedon Secret Nuclear Bunker, which was built in 1952 as a regional base from which the Government and military commanders could run operations in the event of a nuclear war; it is now open to the public.

mound and moat remain today. However, a contemporary building, the **Church of St Martin of Tours**, still stands. It was here that the explorer David Livingstone spent time as a pupil pastor before beginning his missionary work in Africa.

The town is surrounded by rural Essex and several ancient villages, including **Fyfield**, home to **Fyfield Hall**, the oldest inhabited timber-framed building in England; **Blackmore**, a village that was almost totally destroyed by the plague; and **Greensted**, which became the home of several of the Tolpuddle martyrs after their sentences had been commuted. Greensted's **Church of St Andrew** is the single surviving log church in England, the oldest wooden church in the world and the oldest wooden building in Europe.

To the west of the town lies **North Weald Airfield Museum**, which details the history of flying in this area from 1916 to 1964.

COLCHESTER

First established in the 7th century BC and England's oldest recorded town, Colchester was an obvious target for the Romans, and the Emperor Claudius took the surrender of 11 British kings here. However, in AD 60 Queen Boudicca took revenge on the invaders and burned the town to the ground before going on to destroy London and St Albans. The walls, the oldest in the country, still surround the ancient part of the town and **Balkerne Gate** is the largest surviving Roman gateway in the country.

A thousand years later the Normans built Colchester Castle on the foundations of the Roman temple of Claudius and it boasts the largest Norman keep ever built in Europe. The **Castle Museum**, housed in the keep, is now one of the most exciting hands-on historical attractions in the country. Located in a fine Georgian building, the **Hollytrees Museum** displays a fine collection of toys, costumes, curios and antiquities from the last two centuries; the **Natural History Museum** concerns itself with the flora and fauna of Essex; and **Tymperleys Clock Museum** in Queen Street is home to a magnificent collection of 18th and 19th century Colchester-made clocks. Due to open in late 2008 is **firstsite:newsite**, a new social space with a programme of exhibitions, workshops, lectures and films.

Colchester is famous for its **Zoo**, where the attractions include

Colchester Castle

Playa Patagonia - the Underwater Sea Lion Experience and the Dragons of Komodo, and a new orang-utan enclosure. The town is even more famous for its oysters which are still cultivated on beds in the lower reaches of the River Colne – a visit to the **Oyster Fisheries** is a fascinating experience. Jane Taylor, daughter of a Colchester vicar, wrote the words of *Twinkle, Twinkle Little Star*.

To the east of Colchester, at **Elmstead Market**, are the **Beth Chatto Gardens** that were designed and are still presided over by the famous gardener. Close by is the **Rolts Nursery Butterfly Farm**.

Beth Chatto Gardens, nr Colchester

AROUND COLCHESTER

MANNINGTREE

7 miles NE of Colchester on the B1352

Situated on the River Stour, this ancient market town was a centre of the cloth trade in Tudor times before becoming a port serving the barges taking their wares to London. Manningtree is a centre for sailing, and from **The Walls** there are unrivalled views of the Stour estuary – a favourite subject of artists down the years.

DEDHAM

6 miles N of Colchester off the A14

This is Constable country, and the church at Dedham featured in many of the artist's paintings. Here, too, are a fascinating **Arts and Crafts Centre**; a **Toy Museum**; and **Dedham Vale**

Family Farm with a comprehensive collection of British farm animals. Another artist associated with this area is Sir Alfred Munnings and, just outside the village, his former home, Castle House, now contains the **Sir Alfred Munnings Art Museum**.

HARWICH

16 miles NE of Colchester on the A120

This town has an important maritime history, the legacy of which continues through to the present day. The Elizabethan seafarers Hawkins, Frobisher and Drake sailed from here, Christopher Jones, master of *The Mayflower*, lived here and Samuel Pepys, the diarist, was an MP for the town in the 1660s.

When the town's two lighthouses, built in 1818, were aligned they indicated a safe shipping channel into Harwich harbour. **Harwich Maritime**

119

Redoubt Fort, Harwich

To the southwest of Walton-on-the-Naze, lies the former fishing village of Frinton-on-Sea that was developed as a quiet resort and which expanded in the 1880s into the genteel family town of today.

Museum can be found in the **Low Lighthouse**, and another museum well worth a visit is the **Lifeboat Museum**, whose exhibits include Calcton's last off-shore 34 feet lifeboat. Harwich's importance as a port in the 19th century is confirmed by the **Redoubt**, a huge grey fort similar in style to the Martello Towers, which has been opened as a museum. Another interesting building is the **Electric Palace Cinema** that dates from 1911 and is the oldest purpose-built cinema in Britain.

WALTON-ON-THE-NAZE

16½ miles E of Colchester off the B1034

A traditional resort that is focused on its **Pier**, which was first built in wood in 1830, and the **Marine Parade**, which dates from the same period.

The wind-blown expanse of **The Naze**, to the north of Walton, is constantly changing shape as it is eroded by the wind and the tide but it remains a pleasant place for

walking and for picnics. The **Naze Tower** was originally built as a beacon in 1720 to warn seamen off the West Rocks just offshore.

CLACTON-ON-SEA

13 miles SE of Colchester on the A133

First settled by hunters in the Stone Age, Clacton is another traditional family resort with a **Victorian Pier**, long sandy south-facing beach and lovely gardens, including the **Clifftop Public Gardens**. Close by are the ancient ruins of **St Osyth Priory** that was founded by Augustinian Canons and named after St Osytha, the martyred daughter of Frithenwald, the first Christian King of the East Angles, who was himself beheaded by the Danes in AD 653. In a **Martello Tower** at **Point Clear** is the **East Essex Aviation Museum** that contains interesting displays of wartime aviation, military and naval photographs, uniforms and other memorabilia with local and USAAF connections. To the north of Clacton is the **Holland Haven Country Park** that is an ideal place for watching the marine birds and other wildlife of this region.

BRIGHTLINGSEA

7½ miles SE of Colchester on the B1029

As well as a long tradition of shipbuilding and seafaring, Brightlingsea has the distinction of being the only limb of the Cinque Ports outside Kent and Sussex. It is also home to one of the oldest occupied buildings in Essex – the

13th century **Jacobes Hall** – that was used as a meeting hall during the reign of Henry III. There are numerous walks along Brightlingsea Creek and the River Colne which provide the opportunity to watch the birdlife on the saltings. Across the water from Brightlingsea, reached by a causeway, is **Mersea Island**, much of which is now a National Nature Reserve. The story of the Island, with special reference to its maritime heritage, is told in the **Mersea Island Museum** at West Mersea. A notable vicar of East Mersea (and father of 13 children) was Sabine Baring-Gould, who wrote the stirring hymn *Onward Christian Soldiers*.

TOLLESHUNT D'ARCY
9½ miles SW of Colchester on the B1026

The birthplace of Dodie Smith, the author of *101 Dalmatians*, this modest village lies close to the **Maldon District Agricultural and Domestic Museum** at Goldhanger, featuring a large collection of vintage farm tools and machinery as well as printing machinery and domestic artefacts.

TIPTREE
8½ miles SW of Colchester on the B1022

Tiptree is famous as the home of the **Wilkin and Sons Jam Factory**, a Victorian establishment that now boasts a fascinating visitors' centre in the grounds of the original factory. Just to the east of Tiptree lies **Layer Marney** where a mansion to rival Hampton Court was planned but never completed.

However, the massive eight-storey Tudor gatehouse was finished in 1525, and provides spectacular views out over the estate's formal gardens and across the surrounding countryside.

COGGESHALL
9½ miles W of Colchester on the A120

An ancient town whose prosperity was based on cloth and lace in the Middle Ages. Its attractions include the delightful half-timbered

175 THE QUEENS HEAD

Tolleshunt D'Arcy

Everything an English country pub should be, with a capable, friendly landlord, a choice of cask ales and a wide variety of home-cooked snacks and meals

🍴 *see page 483*

Layer Marney Tower, nr Tiptree

121

In the village church at Gestingthorp is a handsome memorial to Captain Lawrence Oates, who died in an attempt to save the lives of his companions on Scott's ill-fated Antarctic expedition in 1912.

Paycockes House that dates from around 1500 and features unusually rich panelling, wood carvings and a display of Coggeshall lace. The National Trust also owns the restored **Coggeshall Grange Barn**, which dates from around 1140 and is the oldest surviving timber-framed barn in Europe.

To the south is the **Feering and Kelvedon Museum**, which is dedicated to manorial history and houses artefacts from the Roman settlement of Canonium; to the west are the **Cressing Temple Barns** which were commissioned in the 12th century by the Knights Templar and contain the timber of over 1,000 oak trees.

HALSTEAD

12 miles NW of Colchester on the A1124

Like Coggeshall and Braintree, Halstead was once an important weaving centre. The picturesque **Townsford Mill** is a reminder of the town's industrial heritage and this three-storey mill beside the River Colne, once a landmark site for the Courtauld empire. is now an antiques centre. Halstead's most famous product was once life-sized, mechanical elephants built by W Hunwicks; they could carry a load of eight adults and four children at speeds of up to 12 miles per hour!

To the east, at **Chappel**, is the **East Anglian Railway Museum**, where a comprehensive collection of period railway architecture, engineering and memorabilia can be seen. Railway enthusiasts should also visit the **Colne Valley Railway and Museum** at **Castle Hedingham**, where a mile of the Colne Valley and Halstead line has been restored to run steam trains. The village itself is dominated by its **Norman Castle** that was, in the 11th century, one of the country's strongest fortresses.

To the west of Halstead is the **Gosfield Lake Leisure Resort**, the county's largest freshwater lake, which lies in the grounds of **Gosfield Hall**, a Tudor mansion remodelled in the 19th century by its then owner, Samuel Courtauld.

Castle Hedingham, Halstead

SAFFRON WALDEN

This typical market town is named after the saffron crocus that was ground in the area to make dyestuffs and fulfil a variety of other uses in the Middle Ages. **Saffron Walden Museum** contains a wide range of exhibitions and displays, and among the many fascinating items are the gloves worn by Mary, Queen of Scots on the day that she died; here, too, are the ruins of historic Walden Castle. On the Common, once Castle Green, is the largest surviving **Turf Maze** in England, believed to be some 800 years old. Once the home of the 1st Earl of Suffolk and of Charles II, 17th century **Audley End House**, with its two large courtyards, was a rival in magnificence to Hampton Court. Though much of the house was demolished as it fell into disrepair, it remains one of the country's most impressive Jacobean mansions and its distinguished stone façade is set off perfectly by Capability Brown's lake. A new attraction for 2008 is 'Experience the Service Wing at Work'.

To the north of Saffron Walden is the village of **Hadstock** whose parish **Church of St Botolph** claims to have the oldest church door in England – it is Saxon. The village of **Hempstead**, near Saffron Walden, was the birthplace in 1578 of William Harvey, the chief physician to Charles I and the discoverer of the circulation of the blood, and in 1705 of the highwayman Dick Turpin, whose parents kept the Bell Inn.

AROUND SAFFRON WALDEN

THAXTED

6 miles SE of Saffron Walden on the B184

Originally a Saxon settlement, this small and thriving country town has numerous attractively pargeted and timber-framed houses along with a magnificent **Guildhall** that dates from around 1390. Built as a meeting place for cutlers, it later became an administrative centre, then part of a school. It contains a small display of work by Thaxted artists. Built in 1804 by John Webb, the town's famous **Tower Windmill** remained in use until 1907 and now contains a rural life museum.

FINCHINGFIELD

10 miles SE of Saffron Walden on the B1053

A charming village of thatched cottages around a sloping village green, this is one of the most photographed villages in Essex. To the southwest lies the old market town of **Great Bardfield** whose most notable feature is its restored windmill that goes by the name of 'Gibraltar'.

BRAINTREE

16½ miles SE of Saffron Walden on the A131

Situated at the crossing of two Roman roads, Braintree and its close neighbour Bocking were

176 THE THREE BOTTLES

Great Yeldham

A snug bar in winter, a seclude garden in summer, and all year round a good variety of drinks and a popular Sunday lunch.

see page 484

177 THE CROSS KEYS

White Notley, nr Witham

A quaint little inn with a strong local following for a good selection of drinks and good, honest bar food.

see page 484

123

178 THE BUTCHERS ARMS

North End, Great Dunmow

A popular country pub with friendly family hosts, a good choice of real ales and menus to suit appetites large and small

🍽 see page 485

brought together by the cloth industry when Flemish and then Huguenot weavers settled here. One Huguenot, Samuel Courtauld, established a silk mill here in 1816 and the **Braintree District Museum** has a number of associated displays. The town's magnificent former Town Hall is another legacy of the Courtauld family.

To the southwest of Braintree can be found the **Great Leighs Great Maze**, one of the most challenging in the world, while to the northwest, at **Great Saling**, is the charming **Saling Hall Garden**.

GREAT DUNMOW

12 miles SE of Saffron Walden on the A120

This town is famous for the 'Flitch of Bacon', an ancient ceremony that dates back to the early 12th century when a flitch, or side, of bacon is awarded to the local man who "does not repent of his marriage nor quarrel, differ or dispute with his wife within a year and a day after marriage." In the parish church at **Broxted** a window

Stansted Windmill, Stansted Mountfichet

commemorating the captivity and release of John McCarthy and the other Beirut hostages was dedicated in 1993.

STANSTED MOUNTFICHET

9 miles SW of Saffron Walden on the B1383

Though close to Stansted Airport, this village is worth a visit as it is home to a Norman Village, complete with domestic animals and the reconstructed **Mountfichet Castle**. The **Mountfichet Castle Experience** incorporates a Norman Village, the **House on the Hill Toy Museum**, reputedly the largest in the world, with over 80,000 items on display, and Dinosaur Encounters. New for 2008 is the **Greats of British TV Comedy**, featuring *Only Fools & Horses*, *Dad's Army* and *Open All Hours*. Nearby is **Stansted Windmill**, which dates from 1787 and is one of the best-preserved tower mills in the country. To the north, at **Widdington**, lies **Mole Hall Wildlife Park** where visitors can see a range of wild and domestic animals along with butterflies, snakes and insects; the village is also home to Prior's Hall Barn, a fine medieval 'aisled' barn.

Between Stansted Mountfichet and Hatfield Broad Oak lies **Hatfield Forest**, a former Royal hunting forest where many features of a medieval forest can still be seen.

Gloucestershire

For many, Gloucestershire is the Cotswolds, the delightful limestone hills that sweep across the county from Tetbury in the south to Chipping Campden in the north. As well as providing some of the most glorious scenery and the prettiest villages in the country, the county is also home to the historic towns of Cirencester and Cheltenham. However, Gloucestershire is not only about the Cotswolds. To the west, on the River Severn, is the ancient city of Gloucester, while further downriver is the Vale of Berkeley, and historic Berkeley Castle. On the opposite bank of the river lies the old royal hunting ground of the Forest of Dean, once an important mining and industrial area. Bounded by the Rivers Severn and Wye, the area has been effectively isolated from the rest of England and Wales and so has developed a character that is all its own.

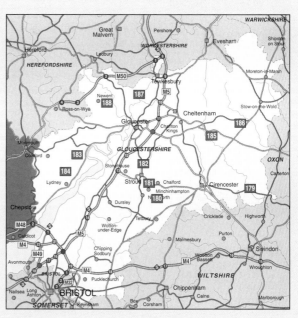

Fairford

This welcoming, family-friendly inn has plenty to please both real ale fans and lovers of good home cooking.

 see page 486

Avening

A pleasant village setting for a family-friendly pub serving cask ales and a choice of excellent traditional and less familiar dishes.

 see page 485

CIRENCESTER

As **Corinium Dobonnorum**, this was the second largest Roman town in Britain and, although few signs remain of their occupation today, the award winning **Corinium Museum** features one of the finest collection of antiquities from Roman Britain as well as several room reconstructions.

Now dubbed the 'Capital of the Cotswolds', the Cirencester of today is a lively market town which has built upon the medieval wealth that was generated by its wool trade. One of the many legacies of this era is the magnificent **Church of St John**, perhaps the greatest of all the Cotswold 'wool churches', whose 120 feet tower dominates the town.

AROUND CIRENCESTER

FAIRFORD

9 miles E of Cirencester on the A417

Wealthy wool merchants financed the building of the splendid

Church of St Mary, whose greatest glory is a set of 28 medieval stained-glass windows depicting the Christian faith in picture-book style.

BIBURY

7 miles NE of Cirencester on the B4425

Described by William Morris, founder of the Arts and Crafts Movement, as "the most beautiful village in England", Bibury remains a delightful place. The most photographed building here is **Arlington Row**, a superb terrace of medieval stone cottages built as a wool store in the 14th century and converted, 300 years later, into weavers' cottages and workshops. The fabric produced here was sent to nearby **Arlington Mill** for fulling and, today, the mill houses a Museum that includes pieces made in the William Morris workshops.

TETBURY

9½ miles SW of Cirencester on the A433

In the heart of this charming old wool town is the superb 17th century **Market House** which is connected to the old trading centre by the ancient Chipping Stones. Among other places of interest is **Tetbury Police Museum** in the cells of the old police station.

Just to the northwest of the town stands **Chavenage House**, a beautiful Elizabethan mansion constructed in the characteristic E-shape of the period. Still occupied by descendants of the original owners, the house contains many relics from the Cromwellian period

Chavenage House, Tetbury

and Cromwell himself is known to have stayed here.

To the southwest of Tetbury lies **Westonbirt Arboretum**, one of the finest collections of trees and shrubs in Europe that was founded by Robert Stayner Holford and added to by his son. Now managed by the Forestry Commission, it offers numerous delightful walks along some 17 miles of footpaths.

CHIPPING SODBURY

23 miles SW of Cirencester on the A432

A pleasant market town that still retains its ancient street pattern, Chipping Sodbury once enjoyed prosperity as a weaving centre, and it was during this period that the large parish church was built. A mile or so to the east lies **Old Sodbury**, whose church contains the tomb of David Harley, the Georgian diplomat who negotiated the treaty that ended the American War of Independence. Just beyond Old Sodbury is the **Badminton Park** estate, founded by Edward Somerset, the son of the Marquis of Worcester. The house is known for its important collection of Italian, English and Dutch paintings and the estate is the venue for **Badminton Horse Trials**, which were started by the 10th Duke of Beaufort in 1949.

To the south of Chipping Sodbury and standing on the slope of the Cotswold ridge is **Dyrham Park**, a striking baroque mansion with a fine collection of Delft porcelain and several Dutch paintings among its treasures.

NAILSWORTH

11 miles W of Cirencester on the A46

Another town that thrived on the local wool trade, Nailsworth still has several of its old mills and associated buildings.

Just to the east of the town, in Hampton Fields, is the extraordinary **Avening Long Stone**, a prehistoric standing stone pierced with holes that is said to move on Midsummer's Eve. Another ancient monument, **Nan Tow's Tump**, a huge round barrow tomb that is said to contain the remains of a local witch, can be found to the south near Ozleworth.

BERKELEY

21½ miles W of Cirencester on the B4066

This small town lends its name to the fertile strip of land known as the Vale of Berkeley. Its largely Georgian centre is dominated by the Norman **Berkeley Castle**, said to be the oldest inhabited castle in Britain. Built between 1117 and 1153 on the site of a Saxon fort, the castle has a rich and colourful history and as well as seeing the many treasures that the Berkeley family have collected over the centuries, visitors can explore the dungeons, the grounds and the medieval bowling alley.

Berkeley was also the home of Edward Jenner, the pioneering doctor and immunologist whose beautiful Georgian house, **The Chantry**, is now the **Jenner Museum**. At **Slimbridge** is the **Wildlife and Wetlands Centre** founded in 1946 by the great

The game of badminton is said to have started here during a weekend party in the 1860s, when the 8th Duke of Beaufort and his guests wanted to play tennis in the entrance hall but, worried about damaging the paintings, they used a cork studded with feathers instead of a ball.

Slimbridge has the world's largest collection of ducks, geese and swans, as well as flamingos and many other exotic wildfowl. Sir Peter Scott died in 1989 and his ashes were scattered at Slimbridge, where he had lived for many years.

181 THE SHIP INN

Brimscombe, nr Stroud

A popular public house and restaurant with plenty to please real ale drinkers and lovers of wholesome home cooking.

🍽 see page 487

182 THE EDGEMOOR INN

Edge, nr Stroud

Interesting locally brewed real ales and a wide variety of home-cooked dishes in a delightful, family-friendly village pub on the Cotswold Way.

🍽 see page 488

Painswick Rococo Gardens, nr Stroud

naturalist, artist, sailor and broadcaster Peter (later Sir Peter) Scott.

STROUD

11 miles W of Cirencester on the A419

With the surrounding hill farms providing a constant supply of wool and the several Cotswold streams which join the River Frome here supplying water power, it is not surprising that Stroud became the capital of the Cotswold woollen industry. By the 1820s there were over 150 textile mills in and around the town though only six survive today – one of these specialises in green baize for snooker tables.

To the east of Stroud lies the delightful village of **Bisley**, which stands some 780 feet above sea level and is known as 'Bisley-God-Help-Us' because of the bitter winter winds that sweep across the hillside. Below the village's impressive church are the **Seven Wells of Bisley** that are blessed and decorated with flowers each

year on Ascension Day.

Just to the north of Stroud is the beautiful little wool town of **Painswick** which is known as the 'Queen of the Cotswolds'. Hidden away, to the north, amidst the magnificent Cotswold countryside is **Painswick Rococo Garden**, a unique 18th century garden that features plants from around the world along with a maze, planted in 1999, which commemorates the gardens 250th anniversary.

Further north again is **Prinknash Abbey Park** (pronounced Prinnage) to where the Benedictine monks of Caldey Island moved in 1928. Part of the abbey gardens are given over to the **Prinknash Bird and Deer Park**.

FRAMPTON-ON-SEVERN

17½ miles W of Cirencester off the B4071

Frampton's large village green, which incorporates a cricket ground and three ponds, was formed when the marshy land outside the gates of **Frampton Court** was drained in the 18th century. The Court is an outstanding example of a Georgian country house and has been the seat of the Clifford family ever since it was completed in the 1730s. On the opposite side of the green is **Frampton Manor**, also owned by the Cliffords, a much-restored medieval manor whose lovely walled garden contains many rare plants.

To the west of Frampton, on a great bend in the river, is the **Arlingham Peninsula**, part of the **Severn Way Shepperdine-Tewkesbury Long Distance Footpath**.

The land on which the village of Arlingham stands once belonged to the monks of St Augustine's Abbey, Bristol, and is believed to be the point where St Augustine crossed the Severn on his way to convert the heathen Welsh tribes.

COLEFORD

A former mining town, Coleford developed into an important iron-processing centre due to the availability of local ore deposits and of the ready supply of timber for the smelting process. Still regarded as the capital of the **Royal Forest of Dean**, Coleford is also home to the **Great Western Railway Museum**, which is housed in an 1883 goods station and numbers several steam locomotives among its exhibits. Another treat for railway enthusiasts is the **Perrygrove Railway**, with its narrow-gauge steam train and treasure hunt through the woods.

To the southeast lies **Parkend**, which, like many communities in the area, was once based around the extraction of minerals. At the northern terminus of the Dean Forest Railway, just west of the village, is the RSPB's **Nagshead Nature Reserve**.

Just to the south of Coleford are **Clearwell Caves**, the only remaining working iron mine in the Forest of Dean, where ochres for use as paint pigments are produced. Visitors can tour the nine impressive caverns, and several marked walks explore surface mining remains.

Clearwell Caves, nr Coleford

AROUND COLEFORD

WESTBURY-ON-SEVERN

9 miles NE of Coleford on the A48

This village is best known as the home of **Westbury Court Garden**, a formal Dutch water garden laid out between 1696 and 1705 that is home to many historic varieties of apple, pear and plum. To the west lies **Littledean Hall**, reputedly the oldest inhabited house in England, which has both Saxon and Celtic remains in its cellars and is thought to date from the 6th century. Westbury is an excellent place to view the famous **Severn Bore**, a tidal wave that several times a month makes its often dramatic way along the river.

LYDNEY

5½ miles SE of Coleford on the B4234

Lydney is the largest settlement between Chepstow and Gloucester, with a harbour and canal that

183 THE WHITE HORSE INN

Soudley, Forest of Dean

Well-kept ales and tasty, wholesome cooking in a convivial Forest of Dean inn.

‖ ⊨ see page 487

184 THE BAILEY INN

Yorkley, Forest of Dean

A handsome Victorian with an across-the-board menu of dishes using organic and free-range produce.

‖ see page 489

Gustav Holst was born in a terraced Regency house in Clarence Road in 1874 and this is now the Holst Birthplace Museum and Period House. The composer's original piano is the centrepiece of the collection that tells the story of the man and his works. Other notable sons of Cheltenham are Sir Frederick Handley Page (born 1885), Sir Arthur 'Bomber' Harris (1892) and Sir Ralph Richardson (1902).

served the iron and coal industries. The town is the southern terminus of the **Dean Forest Railway,** which operates a regular service of steam and diesel trains between here and Parkend. At Norchard Railway Centre, the line's headquarters, there is a railway museum, souvenir shop and details of restoration projects.

One of the key attractions in the area is **Lydney Park Gardens and Museum** on the western outskirts of the town. The gardens are not only a riot of colour, particularly in May and June, but they contain the site of an Iron Age hill fort and the remains of a Roman temple.

ST BRIAVELS

4 miles SW of Coleford on the B4228

Named after a 5th century Welsh bishop, St Briavels became an important administrative centre in the Middle Ages and was a leading manufacturer of armaments that supplied both weapons and ammunition to the Crown – in 1223 it is believed that Henry III ordered 6,000 crossbow bolts (called 'quarrels') from the village.

CHELTENHAM

This was a small, insignificant village until a mineral spring was accidentally discovered here in 1715 by a local man, William Mason, who built a pump room and began Cheltenham's transformation into one of Europe's leading Regency spa towns. In 1788, the spa received the royal seal of approval when George III spent five weeks here taking the waters with his family. As an entirely new town was planned and built on the best features of neo-classical Regency architecture there are very few buildings of any real antiquity left, but one is the **Church of St Mary** that dates back in parts to the 12th century. Cheltenham Boys' College was the location for Lindsay Anderson's 1968 film *If...*

The tree-lined **Promenade** is one of the most beautiful boulevards in the country, and its crowning glory is the wonderful Neptune's Fountain modelled on the Fontana di Trevi in Rome. Housed in Pittville Park, in the magnificent Pump Room overlooking gardens and lakes, is the **Pittville Pump Room Museum**, which uses original period costumes to bring alive the

Cheltenham Art Gallery and Museum

story of Cheltenham from its Regency heyday to the 1960s.

Cheltenham Racecourse, two miles north of town at Prestbury Park, is the home of National Hunt Racing and stages numerous top-quality race meetings throughout the season, culminating in the prestigious March Festival when the Gold Cup and the Champion Hurdle find the year's best steeplechaser and hurdler. The chaser Denman and the hurdler Katchit took the honours in 2008.

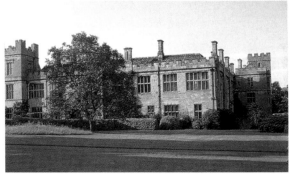

Sudeley Castle, Winchcombe

AROUND CHELTENHAM

WINCHCOMBE

5½ miles NE of Cheltenham on the B4632

The **Winchcombe Folk and Police Museum** tells the history of the town from prehistoric times, and the **Winchcombe Railway Museum and Garden** has one of the largest collections of railway equipment in the country: visitors can work signals and clip tickets and generally go misty-eyed about the age of steam. The Cotswold garden surrounding the building is full of old and rare plants. Set against the beautiful backdrop of the Cotswold Hills stands **Sudeley Castle**, a treasure house of Old Masters (Turner, Rubens, Van Dyck), tapestries, furniture, costumes and toys; the lovely grounds include a lake, formal gardens and a 15 feet double yew hedge.

Catherine Parr, the sixth and last wife of Henry VIII, was brought to Sudeley Castle after the King died. She married Sir Thomas Seymour,

Baron Seymour of Sudeley and died at the Castle in 1548.

STANTON

10½ miles NE of Cheltenham off the B4632

One of the prettiest spots in the Cotswolds, the whole village was restored by the architect Sir Philip Scott in the years before World War I; his home from 1906 to 1937 was **Stanton Court**, an elegant Jacobean residence built by Queen Elizabeth I's Chamberlain. Beyond Stanton, on the road to Broadway, is **Snowshill Manor**, an elegant mansion dating from Tudor times, which was once the home of Catherine Parr. It now contains a fascinating collection of crafts and artefacts assembled by the last private owner, Charles Paget Wade.

CHIPPING CAMPDEN

16 miles NE of Cheltenham on the B4081

The 'Jewel of the Cotswolds' and full of beautifully restored buildings, Chipping Campden was a regional capital of the wool trade from the 13th to the 16th century and much of the town dates from that era. The **Market Hall** was

Just to the north of Winchcombe stands the ruins of Hailes Abbey, which was founded in 1246 by Richard, Earl of Cornwall and became a place of pilgrimage after a wealthy patron donated to the Cistercian monks a phial said to contain the blood of Christ.

185 GLOUCESTERSHIRE & WARWICKSHIRE RAILWAY

Toddington
The railway offers a 20-mile round trip between Toddington and Cheltenham Race Course through some of the most spectacular scenery in the Cotswolds

🏛 see page 489

131

186 THE PLOUGH

Cold Aston, nr Cheltenham

A picture-postcard pub in a quiet village, popular far and wide for its friendly ambience, local ales and an interesting menu of excellent dishes.

❙❙ *see page 490*

built in 1627 by the wool merchant, Sir Baptist Hicks; he also endowed a group of almshouses and **Old Campden House**, which was burnt down by Royalists to prevent it falling into the hands of the enemy.

STOW-ON-THE-WOLD

15½ miles E of Cheltenham on the A429

At 800 feet above sea level, this is the highest town in the Cotswolds and at one time held a twice-yearly sheep fair on the market square where the town stocks still stand today. In Park Street is the **Toy and Collectors Museum**, housing a charming display of toys, trains, teddy bears and dolls, along with textiles and lace, porcelain and pottery.

BOURTON-ON-THE-WATER

13 miles E of Cheltenham on the A429

Probably the most popular of all the Cotswold villages, Bourton has the willow-lined River Windrush flowing through its centre, crossed by several delightful pedestrian bridges. Here, among the golden stone cottages, is **Miniature World – the Museum of Miniatures** that houses a unique collection of miniature scenes and models. Miniatures seem to be something of a feature here as Bourton is also home to a famous Model Village and a Model Railway. Those with a keen nose will want to visit the unique **Perfumery Exhibition**, where the extraction and manufacture of perfume is explained and where there is also a perfume garden.

To the north, at **Lower Slaughter**, is the **Old Mill**, a restored 19th century flour mill with a giant water wheel, while, to the southwest, near the traditional market town of **Northleach**, is the **Cotswold Heritage Centre**, housed in an old country prison. In the centre of the town, in a 17th century merchant's house, **Keith Harding's World of Mechanical Music** is a fascinating museum of antique self-playing musical instruments.

To the west of Northleach is **Chedworth Roman Villa**, a large, well-preserved villa that was discovered by chance in 1864. Excavations have revealed more than 30 rooms and buildings and some wonderful mosaics.

GLOUCESTER

In the 1st century AD, the Romans established a fort here to guard

Chedworth Roman Villa

what was then the lowest crossing point of the River Severn; it was soon replaced by a much larger fortress and the settlement of Glevum quickly became one of the most important military bases in Roman Britain. It was at Gloucester that William the Conqueror held a Christmas parliament and also ordered the rebuilding of the abbey, an undertaking that included a magnificent church that was the forerunner of the superb Norman **Gloucester Cathedral**. The exquisite fan tracery in the cloisters of the Cathedral is the earliest and among the finest in existence and the great east window is the largest surviving medieval stained glass window in the country, measuring 72 feet by 38 feet. It was built to celebrate the English victory at the Battle of Crécy in 1346 and depicts the coronation of the Virgin surrounded by assorted kings, popes and saints. The young Henry III was crowned at the Cathedral, with a bracelet on his little head rather than a crown.

Gloucester Docks were once the gateway for waterborne traffic heading into the Midlands and the handsome Victorian warehouses are home to several award-winning museums. The **National Waterways Museum**, which is entered by a lock chamber with running water, tells the fascinating story of Britain's canals, and the **Robert Opie Collection** at the **Museum of Advertising and Packaging** takes a nostalgic look at the 1940s through to the 1970s with the aid of toys and food,

fashions, packaging and a continuous screening of vintage TV commercials.

In the southwestern suburbs of Gloucester are the ruins of **Llanthony Abbey**, which was moved in the 12th century from its original site in the Black Mountains of Wales - bringing with it its Welsh name - because the monks were terrified of the Welsh.

AROUND GLOUCESTER

NEWENT

5 miles NW of Gloucester on the B4215

This is the capital of an area of northwest Gloucestershire that is known as the Ryelands, home of the renowned Ryelands sheep – an ancient breed famed for the quality of its wool. Naturally, therefore, this was one of the county's principal wool trading centres and there are a number of grand merchant's houses in the town. The most distinctive building, however, is the splendid timber-framed **Market House** which was built as a butter market in the 16th century with its upper floors supported on 16 oak pillars. The **Shambles Museum of Victorian Life** is virtually a little Victorian town, a jumble of cobbled streets and alleyways with shops and even a mission chapel.

There are not a great many windmills in Gloucestershire but at **Castle Hill Farm** is a working wooden mill which provides great views from its balcony. A short distance south is the **National**

187 THE HAWBRIDGE INN

Hawbridge, nr Tirley

A superb setting alongside the River Severn for a friendly inn serving real ales and classic pub dishes.

‖ ⊨ see page 491

188 THE TRAVELLERS REST

Malswick, nr Newent

Easy-to-like dishes based on the best raw ingredients make this a popular place for lunch or dinner.

‖ see page 492

A couple of miles east of Newent lies Pauntley Court where, in 1350, Richard Whittington, the penniless orphan of the pantomime, was born. Neither poor nor an orphan, Whittington became a mercer in London, then a financier, and he was indeed Mayor three times (though not Lord Mayor, as that title had not yet been created).

'The Warwickshire Avon falls into the Severn here, and on the sides of both, for many miles back, there are the finest meadows that were ever seen'. So wrote Cobbett in 1820 of Tewkesbury's soil.

Bird of Prey Centre that houses one of the largest collections of birds of prey in the world.

DYMOCK

10 miles NW of Gloucester on the B4215

In the years before World War I, this village became the base for a group of writers who became known as the **Dymock Poets**. The Dymock Poets included Rupert Brooke, Wilfred Gibson, Edward Thomas, John Drinkwater and Lascelles Abercrombie and was later joined by Robert Frost; they sent out its New Numbers poetry magazine from Dymock's tiny post office and it was also from here that Brooke published his War Sonnets, including *The Soldier*. Brooke and Thomas died in the Great War, which led to the dissolution of the group.

TEWKESBURY

A town of historic and strategic importance, the rivers restricted the town's lateral expansion, which accounts for the unusual number of tall buildings. Its early prosperity was based on the wool and mustard trades and the movement of corn by river also contributed to its wealth. Tewkesbury's main thoroughfares, High Street, Church Street and Barton Street, form a Y shape, and the area between is a marvellous maze of narrow alleyways and small courtyards hiding many grand old pubs and medieval cottages. At the centre of it all is **Tewkesbury Abbey**, one of the largest parish churches in the country, which was founded in the 8th century and completely rebuilt in the 11th. After the Dissolution, it was saved from destruction by the townspeople, who raised £453 to buy it from the Crown.

The **Battle of Tewkesbury**, which took place in 1471 in a field south of town, was one of the fiercest in the War of the Roses and the battle site has been known as Bloody Meadow ever since. Following the Lancastrian defeat, those who had not been slaughtered in the battle fled to the Abbey, where the killing began again. The 17-year-old son of Henry VI, Edward Prince of Wales, was killed in the conflict and a plaque marking his final resting place can be seen in the abbey.

Hampshire

Hampshire's coastal crescent, which stretches from Havant to New Milford in the west, is home to two of the country's most famous ports, Southampton and Portsmouth, and the maritime and naval traditions here remain strong. This contrasts greatly with the grand scenery in the northern part of the county and the ancient landscape of the North Downs, home to the historic towns of Winchester and Andover. On the western bank of Southampton Water lies the New Forest, the largest wild area of lowland in Britain, which William the Conqueror set aside as his own private hunting ground over 900 years ago.

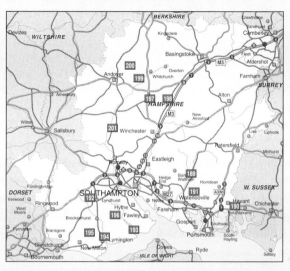

189 THE WHITE HORSE

Droxford
Former coaching inn
specialising in authentic
Indian cuisine; beer garden
and patio.

¶ see page 493

SOUTHAMPTON

It was from this historic port that
Henry V sailed for Agincourt in
1415 and the *Titanic* steamed out
into the Solent on her tragic first
and last voyage. The town was an
obvious target for enemy bombing
during World War II, but despite
the numerous attacks several
ancient buildings have survived
including a section of the town's
medieval walls and their most
impressive feature – Bargate.
Southampton's links with the sea
are never far away and the story of
the luxury liners that sailed from
here, along with the port, is told at
the **Maritime Museum** housed in
the 14th century Wool House.
Along with its maritime heritage,
the town was at the centre of the
developing aircraft industry and this
connection is explored at the Solent
Sky, where the centrepiece is the
spectacular Sandringham flying
boat.

On the northern outskirts of
Southampton lie **Itchen Valley**
Country Park and **West End**, the
village to which the Captain of the
liner *Carpathia*, which rescued
passengers from the *Titanic*, retired.
His grave lies in an old burial
ground near the village's **Local
History Museum**.

AROUND
SOUTHAMPTON

BISHOPS WALTHAM
8 miles NE of Southampton on the B3035

This charming small town was, for
nearly 1,000 years, home of the
country residence of the Bishops
of Winchester and at their
sumptuous **Bishop's Palace** they
played host to numerous monarchs.
Built in 1136 by Henri de Blois, the
palace was largely destroyed during
the Civil War although the ruins
remain an impressive sight.

PETERSFIELD
21 miles NE of Southampton on the B2070

The oldest building in this pleasant
market town is the 12th century
Church of St Peter. Also of
interest are the town museum, the
Teddy Bear Museum, the first of
its kind in Britain, and the **Flora
Twirt Gallery**.

HORNDEAN
17 miles E of Southampton off the A3

This village has a long association
with brewing and the company of
George Gale, founded in 1847,
offers guided tours that include the
techniques of brewing. To the
northwest lies **Queen Elizabeth
Country Park**, an Area of

Bishop's Palace, Bishops Waltham

Outstanding Natural Beauty which contains many Roman and Iron Age sites as well as the three hills of Butser, War Down and Holt Down. Nearby, **Butser Ancient Farm** is a living, working reconstruction of an Iron Age farm.

Further northwest lies **Hambledon**, the village where the rules of cricket were laid down in 1774 and where a monument stands on **Broadhalfpenny Down**, where the early games were played.

HAVANT

18 miles SE of Southampton on the A27

Originally a Roman crossroads, the town developed into a leading manufacturing centre; the whole history of the town is explored and explained at the **Havant Museum**. To the north lies one of the south of England's most elegant stately homes, **Stansted Park**, which houses numerous treasures and stands in particularly attractive grounds. To the southeast is the picturesque village of **Emsworth**, for many years the home of the novelist PG Wodehouse.

To the south of Havant is **Hayling Island**, a traditional family seaside holiday resort with a five-mile sandy beach.

PORTSMOUTH

15 miles SE of Southampton on the A3

Portsmouth is the country's leading naval base, and **Portsmouth Historic Dockyard** is home to three of the greatest ships ever built. The most famous of all is HMS *Victory*, from which Nelson

masterminded the decisive encounter with the French navy off Cape Trafalgar in 1805. Here, too, lies the *Mary Rose*, the second largest ship in Henry VIII's fleet, which foundered on her maiden voyage and was raised in 1983. HMS *Warrior*, the Navy's first ironclad warship, can also be seen. Also within the Dockyard are the **Dockyard Apprentice and Action Stations**, an exciting exhibition that brings the modern Navy to life. Dominating the Portsmouth skyline is the **Spinnaker Tower**, representing a billowing sail and extending some

190 THE BLUE BELL INN

Emsworth

Only yards from the Quay, a traditional family-owned pub serving great home-cooked food with fish a speciality.

see page 493

Spinnaker Tower, Portsmouth

Bursledon Windmill

191 THE TRAVELLERS REST

Newtown

Traditional 18th century country inn offering superb value-for-money menu; large beer garden and aviary.

see page 494

550 feet into the sky. Southsea, the southern part of the city, also has much to offer: the D. Day Museum that commemorates the Allied invasion of France in 1944; the **Royal Marines Museum** housed in Eastney Barracks; and **Portsmouth Sea Life Centre** which reflects the city's rich maritime history.

A plaque in Britain Street in Portsmouth marks the place where Isambard Kingdom Brunel was born in 1806, and the house in Old Commercial Road where Charles Dickens was born in 1812 is now a museum.

Southsea Castle, built in 1545 by Henry VIII, was altered in the early 19th century to accommodate more guns and men. Just offshore lies **Spitbank Fort**, a huge Victorian defence that is reached by ferry from Southsea pier.

At the head of Portsmouth Harbour stands **Portchester Castle**, one of the grandest medieval castles in the country, built on the site of a Roman fort.

FAREHAM

10 miles SE of Southampton on the A27

Many aspects of this charming old

town are exhibited in **Westbury Manor Museum**, housed in a 17th century farmhouse on the town's outskirts. Nearby are the **Royal Armouries** at **Fort Nelson** where the display of artillery, dating from the Middle Ages, is one of the finest in the world.

To the southeast lies Gosport, home to another of Lord Palmerston's forts, the circular **Fort Brockhurst**, and of the **Royal Naval Submarine Museum** located at HMS *Dolphin*, where visitors can look over several submarines. **Explosion! The Museum of Naval Firepower** is dedicated to the brave people who prepared Navy armaments from Trafalgar to the present day.

HAMBLE

5 miles SE of Southampton on the B3397

A major medieval trading port and once a centre of the shipbuilding industry on the River Hamble, this village is now famous throughout the world as a yachting centre, and some 3,000 boats have berths in the Estuary. To the south lies **Hamble Common**, an area of coastal heath with a wide range of habitats.

Just to the north of Hamble lies **Bursledon**, another village with a strong maritime heritage: it was here that King Alfred's men sank 20 Viking longships, and Nelson's flagship at the Battle of Copenhagen, *The Elephant*, was built here. Close by, on a hilltop setting, is **Bursledon Windmill**, fully restored to working order. The village of Bursledon also has a relic of the county's industrial heritage – **Burlesdon Brickworks**, built in 1897 and after closing in 1974, restored and opened to the public.

ROMSEY

6½ miles NW of Southampton on the A3057

Romsey Abbey was founded in AD 907 by Edward the Elder, son of Alfred the Great, though most of what remains dates from the 12th and 13th centuries. Close to the Abbey stands the oldest secular building in the town, **King John's House**. Other places of interest here include **Romsey Signal Box**, home to numerous railway artefacts, and **Broadlands**, a gracious Palladian mansion set in grounds landscaped by Capability Brown which was the family home of Lord Palmerston, three times Prime Minister in the 1850s and 1860s. The house passed to the Mountbatten family, and it was Lord Louis who first opened it to the public, shortly before his death in 1979. The **Mountbatten Exhibition** commemorates his life.

To the northeast lies the **Sir Harold Hillier Garden and Arboretum**, which is based on the collection of this renowned gardener and now houses 11 National Plant Collections. Southeast of Romsey lies **East Wellow**, where Florence Nightingale was buried beneath the family monument on her death in 1910.

To the northwest is **Mottisfont Abbey**, which was originally an Augustinian priory but was adapted into a country mansion in the 16th century.

Broadlands, Romsey

LYNDHURST

The only town of any size in the New Forest, Lyndhurst still remains its administrative centre. Next to the compact **Church of St Michael and All Angels** in whose churchyard is the grave of Alice Liddell, the inspiration for Alice in Lewis Carroll's novels, stands **Queen's House**. Originally a medieval hunting lodge, the house is now the Headquarters of the Forestry Commission and also home to the **Verderers' Court**, an institution dating back to Norman times that still deals with matters concerning the Forest's ancient common rights. In the High Street, the **New Forest Museum and Visitor Centre** has numerous displays covering all aspects of the forest.

To the northeast, at Ashurst, is the **Otter, Owl and Wildlife Conservation Park**.

To the northwest, near the

192 THE WATERLOO ARMS

Lyndhurst
In the heart of the New Forest, a great place to relax and enjoy a drink and a meal.

see page 494

Sir Arthur Conan Doyle bought a house at Bignell Wood, near Minstead, and is buried in the village churchyard with his wife. He had initially been buried in a garden grave at his house called Windlesham in Crowborough, East Sussex, where he lived for many years until his death in 1930. When the house was sold in 1955 his body and that of his wife were moved to the churchyard at All Saints' Church.

193 BUCKLER'S HARD

Bucklers Hard, Beaulieu

With a beautiful setting, Riverside Walk and River Cruises to enjoy, Buckler's Hard is one of the most attractive and unusual villages in England.

🏛 *see page 495*

picturesque village of **Minstead**, lie **Furzey Gardens**, which were laid out in the 1920s and provide excellent views over the New Forest to the Isle of Wight.

Near Minstead stands the **Rufus Stone** that is said to mark the spot where William Rufus, King William II, son of William the Conqueror, was accidentally killed by an arrow from Sir Walter Tirel's bow while out hunting. Sir Walter made good his escape, and William's brother, who was also hunting in the Forest, lost no time in riding to Westminster to be crowned king Henry I. William's body was found by the charcoal burner Perkis, who carried it on his cart to Winchester, where he was buried without ceremony under the central tower of the Cathedral.

AROUND LYNDHURST

BEAULIEU

7 miles SE of Lyndhurst on the B3056

Cistercian monks built an abbey by the River Beaulieu in the 13th century, and some of the abbey's buildings survive today, incorporated into a country estate now owned by Lord Montagu. The estate is most famous for its **National Motor Museum**, where over 300 historic vehicles are on display. Many Montagu family treasures can be seen in **Palace House**, the former Great Gatehouse of Beaulieu Abbey.

At the mouth of the River Beaulieu lies **Buckler's Hard**, a popular place for yachts and cruisers. Facing Buckler's Hard across the River Beaulieu stands **Exbury** where, in the 1920s, Lionel de Rothschild created **Exbury Gardens** with their world-renowned displays of rhododendrons, camellias and azaleas.

FAWLEY

10 miles SE of Lyndhurst on the A326

Despite the vast oil terminals and refineries of one of Europe's largest oil plants dominating the village, Fawley has retained some links with the past: the gardens of **Cadland House**, which were designed by Capability Brown, house the National Collection of *leptospermums*.

To the southeast lies **Calshot**, home to RAF bases during both World Wars; at the very end of a shingle spit stands **Calshot Castle**, built by Henry VIII, now restored as a pre-World War I garrison.

LYMINGTON

8 miles S of Lyndhurst on the A337

An ancient seaport and market town, Lymington was once a major manufacturer of salt and the **St Barbe Museum** tells the story of this area, between the Solent and the New Forest, with special reference to the salt industry.

Just up the River Lymington is the pretty village of **Boldre** whose charming 13th century church has become a shrine to HMS *Hood* which was sunk by the Bismarck in 1941 with the loss of 1,400 lives.

NEW MILTON

9½ miles SW of Lyndhurst on the A332

The best-known landmark in this lively little town is its splendid **Water Tower** of 1900. A particularly striking octagonal building with a castellated parapet, it has the look of a castle rather than part of the town's water system. Just to the west of the town, the **Sammy Miller Museum and Farm Trust** holds the finest collection of fully restored machines in Europe.

To the southeast lies the unspoilt resort of **Milford-on-Sea**, from where a shingle spit extends out to sea; from its end it is less than a mile to the Isle of Wight. Here stands **Hurst Castle**, another in the chain of fortresses built by Henry VIII, while just inland are **Braxton Gardens**, with their beautiful roses and knot garden.

RINGWOOD

10 miles W of Lyndhurst on the A31

Despite extensive modernisation, this town on the western edge of the New Forest still boasts a number of elegant old buildings; notable among these are **Ringwood Meeting House**, now a museum, and **Monmouth House**, which both date from the early 18th century. At **Crow**, to the southeast, is the **New Forest Owl Sanctuary**, home to a vast collection of owls and several pairs of breeding red squirrels.

FORDINGBRIDGE

10 miles NW of Lyndhurst on the A338

The main feature here is the medieval Great Bridge which has seven elegant arches and is upstream from the original ford. The town was loved by painter Augustus John and he spend much

Hurst Castle

194 LOUNGES OF LYMINGTON

Lymington

The friendliest of welcomes and a daytime selection of sweet and savoury delights.

see page 495

195 THE FOREST HEATH HOTEL

Sway, New Forest

Two pleasant bars, classic pub dishes and en suite accommodation in a smart village near Lymington.

see page 496

196 THE BEAULIEU ROAD INN

Brockenhurst

A lovely New Forest setting, well-kept cask ales and fine cooking using prime local produce.

see page 496

197 COACH & HORSES

Sutton Scotney

Charming 18th century traditional village inn offering superb food and en suite rooms.

  see page 497

of the last 30 years of his life at Fryern Court, an austere Georgian house.

To the north lies the unspoilt village of **Breamore** and 16th century **Breamore House** which overlooks the Avon Valley. The house has a fine collection of 17th and 18th century paintings of the Dutch School, and the grounds are home to the **Countryside Museum** and its reconstruction of a Tudor village. Close by, on Breamore Down, is a mizmaze, a circular maze cut into the turf – why, nobody knows.

To the northwest is **Rockbourne Roman Villa** where excavations have revealed the remains of a large villa, with some 40 rooms, superb mosaics and part of its underfloor heating system.

WINCHESTER

Winchester was the capital of King Alfred's Kingdom of Wessex in the 9th century, and two centuries later work began on the Cathedral. **Winchester Cathedral** is filled with priceless treasures, including copies of the Winchester Bible and Bede's Ecclesiastical History. The tombs of William II (William Rufus – see under Lyndhurst above), Jane Austen and Izaak Walton are among the many here, along with that of St Swithin, a 9th century bishop to whom the Cathedral is dedicated.

The area round the Cathedral holds a wealth of interest: the **Deanery**, occupied continuously since the 13th century; the **Pilgrims' Hall** with its marvellous hammerbeam roof; Cheyney Court, once the Bishops' courthouse; **Jane Austen's House** where she spent the last six weeks of her life; and the renowned **College**, with its beautiful chapel, founded in 1382. Here too is **Wolvesey Castle**, the chief residence of the medieval bishops, where, in 1554, Queen Mary first met Philip of Spain; the wedding banquet was held the very next day.

The only surviving part of **Winchester Castle** is its Great Hall, behind which is **Queen Eleanor's Garden**, a faithful representation of a medieval garden; the grounds are also the site of the **Peninsula Barracks**, which includes several military museums.

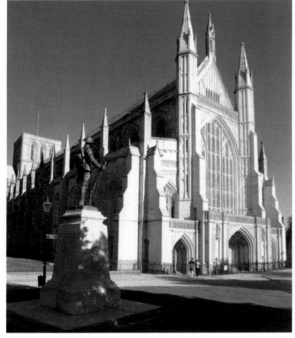

Winchester Cathedral

The story of the Red Cross in Hampshire is told at the **Balfour Museum**, and at the **Historic Resources Centre** there is a vast collection of historic records for this area. This centre is near the site of **Hyde Abbey**, which recent excavations have revealed as being the probable site of King Arthur's final burial place.

AROUND WINCHESTER

WHITCHURCH

11½ miles N of Winchester on the B3400

Once an important coaching stop between London and Exeter, Whitchurch has a unique attraction, **Whitchurch Silk Mill**, the last working silk mill in the south of England.

BURGHCLERE

19 miles N of Winchester off the A34

This village is home to the **Sandham Memorial Chapel** where, in the 1920s, Stanley Spencer was commissioned to paint murals on the walls depicting scenes from World War I. The moving paintings are best seen on a bright day as the chapel has no lighting.

Southwest lies **Highclere Castle**, the largest mansion in the county, on the site of a former palace of the Bishops of Winchester.

BASINGSTOKE

17 miles NE of Winchester on the A30

Despite the extensive building work of the 1960s, there are still reminders of old Basingstoke to be seen including the evocative ruins of the 13th century **Chapel of the Holy Ghost** and the 19th century old Town Hall that is now home to the **Willis Museum**.

To the north lies **The Vyne**, a fine 16th century country house that is noted for its linenfold panelling, Gothic painted vaulting and a Tudor chapel with Renaissance stained glass.

To the east of Basingstoke is **Old Basing**, a place of narrow streets and old cottages and the ruins of **Basing House**. Built on a massive scale within the walls of a medieval castle, the house was once the largest private residence in the country.

SILCHESTER

22 miles NE of Winchester off the A340

This village is home to the famous Roman site of **Calleva Atrebatum** where on-going excavations have revealed one of the most complete plans of any Roman town in Britain. East of Silchester is the estate of **Stratfield Saye House**, which was presented to the Duke of Wellington as a reward for his defeat of Napoleon at Waterloo. It is full of Wellington artefacts, including books, flags and his ornate funeral carriage, and one whole room of the house is devoted to his beloved charger, Copenhagen.

FARNBOROUGH

29 miles NE of Winchester on the A325

Famous for the Farnborough Air Show, the town is also home to **St**

198 THE HALFMOON & SPREAD EAGLE

Micheldever, nr Winchester

A very friendly, sociable village inn serving a good range of drinks and excellent home-cooked food.

see *page 497*

199 THE HURSTBOURNE INN

Hurstbourne Inn, nr Whitchurch

A charming inn in the lovely Hampshire countryside, with super food and comfortable B&B rooms.

see *page 498*

200 THE GEORGE INN

St Mary Bourne, nr Andover

A lovely village pub where bar and restaurant menus offer plenty of choice for all tastes and appetites.

see *page 498*

143

Michael's Abbey. St Michael's Abbey was built in a flamboyant French style by the Empress Eugénie in honour of her husband Napoleon III. Deposed at the end of the Franco-Prussian War, Napoleon III, nephew of the first Napoleon, was exiled to England in 1870 and died at Chislehurst in 1873. The grieving Eugénie founded the Abbey as a mausoleum for her husband, and later for their son Leopold, who died in the Zulu Wars in 1879. Eugénie herself was buried here when she died n 1920.

To the south lies **Aldershot**, a little-known village until the Army established the town as the most famous military centre in the country. The **Aldershot Military Museum**, housed in the only two surviving Victorian barrack blocks, tells the history of the military town and the adjoining civilian town.

ALTON

16 miles NE of Winchester on the A339

The town's impressive double-naved **St Lawrence's Church** was the scene of a dramatic episode during the Civil War when a large force of Roundheads drove 80 Royalists into the church, killing 60 of them. Elsewhere in the town, the **Allen Gallery** contains a fine collection of porcelain and pottery including the famous Elizabethan Tichborne spoons.

Just to the south is **Chawton House**, the home of Jane Austen from 1809 until shortly before her death in 1817, and now home to the **Jane Austen Museum**. A little further from Alton lies the attractive village of Selborne which was, in 1720, the birthplace of the naturalist Gilbert White. His house, **The Wakes**, is now the **Gilbert White Museum**. The Wakes also contains the **Oates Museum**, which is dedicated to Francis Oates, the Victorian explorer, and his nephew, Captain Lawrence Oates, who was a member of Captain Scott's ill-fated South Pole expedition.

NEW ALRESFORD

7 miles E of Winchester on the A31

Founded in about 1200, New Arlesford has long been a world centre of the watercress industry – so much so, that the railway line that carried the commodity to London was dubbed the **Watercress Line**. Now kept going by enthusiasts as a steam railway, it runs between here and Alton.

Close by is one of the finest stately homes in England, **Avington Park**, which stands on a site that was once used by the Romans. The **River Itchen**,

Watercress Line, New Alresford

renowned for its trout and watercress beds, rises close to the village of **Hinton Ampner** and here can be found **Hinton Ampner House and Gardens**.

STOCKBRIDGE

8 miles NW of Winchester on the A30

Situated on the trout-rich River Test, which flows through, under and alongside its broad main street, Stockbridge attracts visitors with its antique shops, art galleries and charming tearooms. To the south of the town lies **Houghton Lodge Gardens and Hydroponicum**, a charming 18th century cottage with glorious views over the Test Valley that also has a hydroponic greenhouse.

To the northwest is **Danbury Iron Age Hillfort** and nearby is the village of **Middle Wallop** which became famous during the Battle of Britain, when the nearby airfield was a base for squadrons of Spitfires and Hurricanes. The **Museum of Army Flying** houses an important collection that traces the development of Army flying from its beginnings during World War I.

ANDOVER

11 miles NW of Winchester on the A3057

A picturesque market town with a history going back to Saxon times,

Hinton Ampner Gardens

the market place is dominated by a handsome Guildhall; many of its coaching inns survive from the days when Andover was an important stopping place on the routes between London, Oxford and Southampton.

Just to the west of Andover, at **Weyhill**, is the **Hawk Conservancy and Country Park**, home to over 150 birds of prey from around the world. It was at the Weyhill October Fair that the future mayor in Thomas Hardy's novel *The Mayor of Casterbridge*, sold his wife and child.

201 THE CROWN

Kings Somborne

Thatched 17th century former coaching inn serving traditional pub fare and cask ales.

🍴 see page 499

145

Herefordshire

With its rolling landscape, pretty villages and charming market towns, Herefordshire is a delightful place to visit and, as it has few natural resources, there are few industrial scars to mar the countryside. Apples and hops are the traditional crops of the county and cider producing remains a thriving industry. Sheep and cattle are also a familiar sight. Hereford cattle still abound and their stock are now to be found in many parts of the world.

Skirmishes with the Welsh were a common occurrence for many centuries and one of the county's best known landmarks, Offa's Dyke, was built in the 8th century as a defence against these marauders. The River Wye, which enters England at Hay-on-Wye, winds its way through some of the most glorious countryside in all the land before finally joining with the River Severn at its estuary. The whole length, which takes in many ancient villages and small towns, provides excellent walking, and the Wye Valley Walk follows the river for 112 miles, the majority in

Herefordshire. The valley is a designated Area of Outstanding Natural Beauty, while the river itself was the first to be recognised as a Site of Special Scientific Interest.

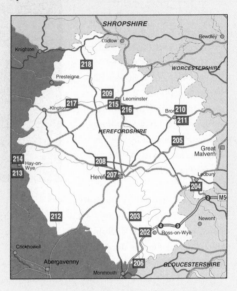

ROSS-ON-WYE

This lovely old market town is signalled from some way out by the towering spire of **St Mary's Church**, which stands on a sandstone cliff surrounded by a cluster of attractive houses. Opposite the church is a row of rosy-red Tudor almshouses. In 1637, the town was visited by the Black Death and over 300 victims to the plague are buried in the churchyard, where their graves are marked by a simple cross. They were buried in the dead of night in an effort to avoid panicking the townspeople.

In the town's market square is the splendid 17th century **Market House**, with its open ground floor and pillars that support the upper floor, which is now the local Heritage Centre.

Opposite the Market House in Ross-on-Wye is a half-timbered house (now shops) that was the home of the town's greatest benefactor, John Kyrle. A wealthy barrister who had studied law at the Middle Temple, Kyrle settled in Ross in around 1660 and dedicated the rest of his life to philanthropic works: he donated the town's main public garden, The Prospect; he repaired St Mary's spire; he provided a constant supply of fresh water; and he paid for food and education for the poor.

Another interesting building to look out for is **Thrushes Nest** that was once the home of Sir Frederick Burrows, a gentleman who began his working life as a railway porter and rose above his station to

become the last Governor of Bengal. The town has two very different museums: the **Lost Street Museum**, which is a time capsule of shops and a pub dating from 1885 to 1935, and the **Button Museum**, which is unique as it is the only museum devoted entirely to buttons.

Ross-on-Wye is well known for its International Festival of music, opera, theatre, comedy and film that takes place annually in August. Among the examples of modern public art littered around the town is a mural celebrating the life of the locally born playwright Dennis Potter.

To the south of Ross-on-Wye is **Hope Mansell Valley**, one of the loveliest and most fertile valleys in the region.

AROUND ROSS-ON-WYE

BROCKHAMPTON

4½ miles N of Ross-on-Wye off the B4224

This charming village is home to one of only two thatched churches in the country. The **Church of All Saints** was designed by William Lethaby and built in 1902 by Alice Foster, a wealthy American lady, as a memorial to her parents. The Norfolk thatch is one of many lovely features of this beautifully situated church, which also has stained glass from Christopher Whall's studio and tapestries designed by Burne-Jones.

This is great walking country, and the once busy mining community of **Mordiford** is an

202 THE WHITE LION

Ross-on-Wye
Home cooking and B&B rooms in a pub with a long history – it was once the town police station.

see page 499

203 THE NEW HARP INN

Hoarwithy
Great food and a vast range of draught and bottle beers in a pleasant country setting.

see page 500

147

204 THE PRINCE OF WALES

Ledbury

A delightful, traditional tavern serving lunchtime food and an impressive selection of draught and bottled beers.

 see page 501

205 THE CHASE INN

Bishops Frome

A nice mix of traditional and modern in a charming country pub with accommodation.

 see page 502

excellent place from which to explore the Forestry Commission's **Haugh Wood**.

LEDBURY

11 miles NE of Ross-on-Wye on the A449

Mentioned in the Domesday Book as Ledeberge and granted its market status in the 12th century, this classic rural town is filled with timber-framed black and white buildings. Its most famous son was the Poet Laureate John Masefield, born in 1878 in a house called the Knapp, who wrote of his birthplace as 'A little town of ancient grace'. A much earlier poet born here was William langland, born in 1332, the aouthor of *Piers Plowman*. In the centre is the **Barrett Browning Institute** that was erected in 1892 in memory of Elizabeth Barrett Browning whose family lived at nearby Colwall. The town's symbol is the 17th century **Market House**, which stands on wooden pillars and

is attributed to the royal carpenter John Abel. Another notable landmark is the Norman parish church of **St Michael and All Angels**, with a soaring spire set on a separate tower, some magnificent medieval brasses, fine monuments - and bullet holes in the door, the scars of the Battle of Ledbury.

Overlooking the Malvern Hills, just to the east of Ledbury, lies **Eastnor Castle**, a fairytale castle that has the look of a medieval fortress but was actually built between 1881 and 1924. Wanting a magnificent baronial castle, the 1st Earl Somers engaged the young architect Robert Smirke, and the result is a fine example of the great Norman and Gothic architectural revival that was taking place at that time.

SYMONDS YAT

5½ miles SW of Ross-on-Wye on the B4432

This inland resort and well-known

Eastnor Castle, nr Ledbury

beauty spot offers glorious views, walks, river cruises, wildlife, history and adventure including canoeing down the River Wye and rock climbing. The village is divided into east and west by the river and, with no vehicular bridge at this point, pedestrians cross by means of a punt ferry that is pulled across the river by a chain. Walking in the area is a delight, and among the many landmarks nearby are **Seven Sisters Rocks**, a collection of oolitic limestone crags; **Merlin's Cave**; **King Arthur's Cave**, where the bones of mammoths and other prehistoric creatures have been found; **Coldwell Rocks**, where peregrine falcons nest; **The Biblins** with a swaying suspension bridge that provides a vertiginous crossing of the river; and **Yat Rock** itself, which rises to 500 feet above sea level at a point where the river performs a long, majestic loop.

The **Jubilee Maze** is an amazing hedge puzzle created to celebrate Queen Elizabeth II's Silver Jubilee and, on the same site, there is a **Museum of Mazes** and a puzzle shop.

Upriver from Symonds Yat, at the little settlement of **Kerne Bridge**, where coracles are still made, walkers can hike up to the majestic ruins of **Goodrich Castle** in a commanding position overlooking the River Wye. Built of red sandstone in the 11th century by Godric Mapplestone, Goodrich Castle was the last bastion to fall in the Civil War when it finally gave way after a four and a half month siege.

WORMELOW

10 miles NW of Ross-on-Wye on the A466

The **Violette Szabo GC Museum** celebrates the bravery of the young woman who parachuted into Nazi-occupied France to work with the Resistance.

HEREFORD

Founded as a settlement near the unstable Welsh Marches after the Saxons had crossed the River Severn in the 7th century, Hereford grew to become an important centre of the wool trade. Fragments of the Saxon and medieval walls can still be seen today but Hereford's crowning glory is its **Cathedral**, often called the Cathedral of the Marches. Largely Norman, the Cathedral has, in its impressive New Library building, two of the country's most important historic treasures. The **Mappa Mundi** is a renowned medieval world map, drawn on vellum, which has Jerusalem as its

206 THE ROYAL LODGE HOTEL

Symonds Yat East

A splendid hotel in a glorious setting, offering top-class food and accommodation.

 see page 503

Goodrich Castle, nr Symonds Yat

149

207 WATERWORKS MUSEUM

Broomy Hill, Hereford
Water is the most precious
substance on earth. Learn at
the Museum why every drop
is important and have fun at
the same time.

 see page 504

208 THE PRIORY HOTEL

Stretton
A comfortable and charming
country house hotel set in 3
acres of grounds with 9
spacious ensuite bedrooms.

  see page 505

Cider Museum, Hereford

centre and East at the top,
indicating that East was the source
of all things good and was
religiously significant. Richard of
Haldingham, the creator of the
Mappa Mundi, was the Treasurer
of Lincoln Cathedral; that explains
why Lincoln appears rather more
prominently on the map than
Hereford. The other great treasure
is the **Chained Library**, which
houses 1,500 rare books that are all
chained to their original 17th
century book presses. At nearby All
Saints Church is another impressive
Chained Library of some 300
bokks donated by William Brewster
in the 1730s.

The city's restored pumping
station is now home to the
Waterworks Museum where a
wide range of Victorian technology
is still very much alive in the shape
of the collection of pumps along
with Britain's largest triple
expansion engine on display.
Hereford and cider are old friends

and the Cider Museum tells the
interesting story of cider
production down the ages. Also on
the outskirts of the city are the
Cider Mills of HP Bulmer, the
world's leading cider producer,
where visitors can take guided tours
with tastings.

AROUND HEREFORD

HOPE UNDER DINMORE

7½ miles N of Hereford on the A49

South of the village stretch the
green spaces of **Queen's Wood
Country Park**, a popular place for
walking that also provides
panoramic views over the
surrounding countryside; its
arboretum has a wonderful variety
of specimen trees.
Adjoining Queen's Wood Country
Park is **Dinmore Manor**, where
the Knights Hospitallers had their
local headquarters, but today it is
the manor's magnificent sheltered
gardens that draw most people.

Just outside the village is **Hampton Court, Herefordshire**, not to be mistaken with the London version. Founded in 1430 as a reward for a knight's bravery at Agincourt, the castle and gardens have been remodelled several times during their long history, each generation adding new features according to the fashions of the day. The estate declined after World War Two until its sale in 1994 to the Van Kampen family, when a massive programme of building restoration was begun. Attention turned to the gardens in 1996 and designers Simon Dorrell and David Wheeler were chosen to provide an appropriately elaborate setting for the newly restored castle. Today, water canals, island pavilions, avenues and borders complement the established planting of earlier eras.

BROMYARD

13 miles NE of Hereford on the A44

This charming little market town on the banks of the River Frome is home to the **Teddy Bear Museum** housed in an old bakery. The **Bromyard Heritage Centre** tells the story of the local hop growing industry and illustrates life in the town down the centuries.

ABBEY DORE

10 miles SW of Hereford on the B4347

In the 12th century a **Cistercian Abbey** was founded here and the building, which was substantially restored in the 17th century, is still used as the parish church. The

Hampton Court and Gardens, Hope under Dinmore

209 THE PLOUGH

Stoke Lacy, nr Bromyard

A much-loved village local and a popular venue for functions and special occasions.

see page 506

210 THE ROYAL OAK

Bromyard Downs

Family run, family friendly pub serving local ales and home cooking in the Herefordshire countryside.

see page 506

211 LINTON BROOK FARM

Bringsty, nr Bromyard

Glorious views enhance peace and comfort in a civilised Bed & Breakfast farmhouse.

see page 507

212 THE CROWN

Longtown

Real ales, home cooking and a choice of family rooms and a bunkhouse for 6 in an old cider house in beautiful border country.

 see page 507

213 THE HOLLYBUSH INN

Hay-on-Wye

Down-to-earth pub with an exceptional welcome, real ales, wholesome home cooking and a wide range of indoor and outdoor activities.

 see page 508

214 THE OLDE BLACK LION HOTEL

Hay-on-Wye

The Olde Black Lion is not just a great place for a meal, it's also a delightful place to stay with quality en suite bedrooms

 see page 509

Dore Abbey, Abbey Dore

gardens of **Abbey Dore Court**, through which the River Dore flows, are home to many unusual shrubs and perennials including a specialist collection of euphorbias, hellebores and peonies.

Another delightful garden, **Pentwyn Cottage Garden**, can be found just to the north at nearby **Bacton**.

HAY-ON-WYE

17 miles W of Hereford on the B4348

Situated on the border with Wales, Hay-on-Wye is a must for bookworms as there are nearly 40 secondhand bookshops in this small town. Richard Booth, known as the King of Wye, opened the first bookshop here more than 40 years ago and he was also instrumental in setting up the annual **Hay Book Festival** that now draws people from all over the world. However, Hay is not just bookshops - there are plenty of antique shops here, too.

A few miles southeast of the town lie the ruins of **Craswall Priory**, which was founded in the 13th century by the rare Grandmontine order and abandoned just 200 years later.

EARDISLEY

13 miles NW of Hereford on the A4111

Inside the village's **Church of St Mary Magdalene** is an early 12th century font that is decorated with figures that depict not only familiar religious themes but also two men engaged in an armed struggle. It is believed that these are a 12th century lord of the manor, Ralph de Baskerville, and his father-in-law, whom he killed in a dispute over land. As a penance, Ralph was ordered by the authorities to commission the extraordinary font. Outside the village, standing majestically by an old chapel, is a Great Oak that is thought to be some 800 years old.

Almeley Castle, just to the north east of Eardisley, was once the home of Sir John Oldcastle, who is believed to be the model for Shakespeare's Falstaff.

WEOBLEY

9½ miles NW of Hereford on the B4230

The steeple of this pretty town's parish **Church of St Peter and St Paul** is the second highest in Herefordshire and is a reminder that this was once a thriving market town.

As well as supporting the local farming communities, one of Weobley's more unusual sources of wealth was a successful glove making industry that flourished in the early 19th century when the traditional French source of gloves was cut off due to the Napoleonic Wars.

One of the town's many interesting buildings is the Throne Inn, where Charles I took refuge after the Battle of Naseby in 1645.

LEOMINSTER

The largest town in this part of Herefordshire, Leominster's unusual name is thought to be linked to the 7th century King of Mercia, Merewald, who was renowned for his bravery and so earned himself the nickname of 'the Lion'. The priory **Church of St Peter and St Paul**, which was originally King Merewald's convent, became a monastery in the 11th century and its three naves attest to its past importance. Close by, in Priory Park, is **Grange Court**, a fine timbered building that for many years stood in the Market Place. Built in 1633, the court is the work of the royal architect John Abel and displays his characteristic flamboyance in its elaborate carvings.

AROUND LEOMINSTER

ASHTON

3½ miles N of Leominster on the A49

This village is home to **Berrington Hall**, an elegant 18th century mansion designed by Henry Holland, who later became architect to the Prince Regent. The house is noted for its fine furniture and paintings, a nursery, a Victorian laundry, a tiled Georgian dairy and above all its beautifully decorated ceilings: in the drawing room is the highlight, the central medallion of Jupiter, Cupid and Venus. The surrounding parkland was laid out by Holland's father-in-law, Lancelot 'Capability' Brown.

PEMBRIDGE

6½ miles W of Leominster on the A44

The influential Mortimer family were responsible for the medieval prosperity of historic Pembridge and the many handsome buildings bear witness to their patronage.

215 SAVERYS LICENSED CAFÉ

Leominster

A popular town-centre licensed café open for a daytime variety of snacks and meals.

see page 508

216 THE LAMB

Stoke Prior, nr Leominster

Family run and family friendly in a traditional village pub.

see page 510

217 LOWE FARM

Pembridge, nr Leominster

A 14th century farmhouse offering exceptional standards of accommodation and local food

 see page 511

218 YE OLDE OAK INN

Wigmore

Traditional English dishes, including excellent fish and meat pies, in a friendly village inn.

 see page 510

The delightful 16th century **Market Hall** stands on eight oak pillars, the **Old Chapel Gallery** is housed in a converted Victorian chapel, and the 14th century church has a marvellous timber belfry.

SHOBDON

8 miles W of Leominster on the B4362

The **Church of St John the Evangelist** is one of the most flamboyant in the whole country, its 'wedding cake rococo' interior a jaw-dropping sight for first-time visitors.

Just north of the village of Shobdon is a collection of Norman sculptures known as the **Shobdon Arches** that, though greatly damaged by centuries of exposure to the elements, still demonstrate the superb skills of the 12th century sculptors.

KINGTON

12 miles W of Leominster on the A44

Close to the Welsh border, Kington, like other towns in Marches, was for centuries under threat of attack from the west. Its castle was destroyed many years ago, but outside the town, on Wapley Hill, are the earthworks of an ancient hill fort that is thought to be the site of King Caractacus' last stand. The most notable of all the defences in this border country is **Offa's Dyke**, the imposing ditch that extends for almost 180 miles from the Severn Estuary at Sedbury Cliffs to Prestatyn on the North Wales coast. Remnants of the wooden stakes unearthed down the years suggest that the dyke had a definite defensive role, rather than merely acting as a psychological barrier. This truly massive construction was in places almost 60 feet wide, and the stretch north of Kington is especially well preserved today and provides excellent and invigorating walking.

To the west of the town lies the impressive **Hergest Ridge**, which rises to around 1,400 feet, and on its southern edge is **Hergest Court**, once owned by the Vaughan family. Several of these feisty Vaughans are buried in the Vaughan Chapel in Kington's parish church. **Hergest Croft Gardens** provide a dazzling display of colour from spring to autumn.

YARPOLE

3½ miles NW of Leominster off the B4361

Close to this delightful village with its jumble of cottages is **Croft Castle**, whose parkland contains many ancient oak trees and an avenue of 350-year-old Spanish chestnut trees.

Behind the defensive exterior of Croft Castle, the elegant staterooms contain rare furniture, fine plasterwork and portraits of the Croft family, who have almost continuously occupied the castle since it was built in the 14th century.

Just a short walk from the castle is **Croft Ambrey**, an Iron Age fort from which there are stunning views.

Hertfordshire

Although Hertfordshire borders London, it remained essentially a rural county until the construction of the Grand Union Canal. There are still peaceful walks to be enjoyed along the canal's towpath, which flows through a gap in the Chiltern Hills on its journey to the Midlands. It was in the Edwardian era that the first Garden Cities were conceived and built here following the plans of Ebenezer Howard. Later, after World War II, several old market towns were developed as New Towns to provide pleasant housing primarily for those made homeless during London's Blitz. Further north, the countryside remains chiefly rural and there are numerous villages of timber-framed cottages and quiet market towns to explore. Hertfordshire has its fair share of

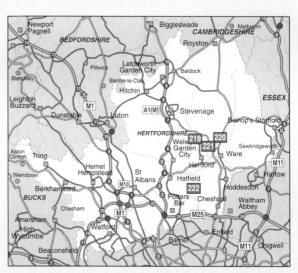

Roman remains, particularly at St Albans and Welwyn, and there are also several grand stately homes tucked away in the rolling countryside.

ST ALBANS

To the north of St Albans lies Redbournbury Mill, an 18th century watermill that once belonged to St Albans Abbey; it has been restored to full working order. To the southwest is one of Hertfordshire's biggest attractions, the Gardens of the Rose, with one of the most important rose collections in the world.

As **Verulamium**, this was one of the most important major Roman cities in Britain. It was attacked and sacked by Boudicca in the 1st century and today, the remains of the rebuilt city, including the walls and the only Roman theatre in Britain, can be seen in **Verulamium Park**. Close to the park, on the banks of the River Ver, is the restored 16th century Kingsbury Watermill with its collection of agricultural implements.

The city's cathedral, **St Albans Abbey**, was built on the site where Alban, the first British martyr, was beheaded in the 4th century. The Abbey dates from the 11th century but was designated a **Cathedral** as recently as 1887. Among the many features inside are medieval paintings that are thought to be unique in England.

Another historic building lies in the market place – the **Clock Tower**, built between 1403 and 1412, is the only medieval town belfry in England and its original bell, Gabriel, is still in place. Also worthy of a visit are the city's two museums. The **Museum of St Albans** tells the history of the city from Roman times to the present day, and **St Albans Organ Museum** houses an amazing collection of working mechanical musical instruments.

AROUND ST ALBANS

HARPENDEN

4½ miles N of St Albans on the A1081

Harpenden's High Street is lined with many listed 17th and 18th century buildings, and the whole of the town centre is a conservation area. The **Harpenden Local History Centre** is the ideal place to find out more about this charming agricultural community, and another place well worth a visit is the **Experimental Station for Agricultural Research** housed in Rothamsted Manor. The **Harpenden Railway Museum** has a small private collection of railway memorabilia.

HATFIELD

5 miles E of St Albans on the A1057

This historic town grew up around the gateway of the palace of the Bishops of Ely but all that remains of the **Royal Palace of Hatfield**, where Elizabeth I spent her early life, is a single wing. This can be seen in the delightful gardens of the impressive Jacobean mansion, Hatfield House, which now stands on the site.

Verulamium Park, St Albans

KING'S LANGLEY

5 miles SW of St Albans on the A4251

This historic village has a long and illustrious royal past: in the 13th century a palace was built from which Edward I governed England for a short period, while close by was a Dominican friary. Both sites are now occupied by the Rudolf Steiner School.

BERKHAMSTED

10 miles W of St Albans on the A4251

First settled by the Saxons, it was here, two months after the Battle of Hastings, that the Saxons finally submitted to William of Normandy; shortly afterwards, building work began on a castle. **Berkhamsted Castle** had a double moat, a very necessary precaution in this low-lying situation; an important fortification up until the 15th century, the castle is now in ruins. Of the few buildings that have survived from the past is **Dean John Incent's House**, an impressive black and white timbered jettied building – Dean Incent was the founder of the original Grammar School of 1554 that is now incorporated into Berkhamsted School.

TRING

13 miles NW of St Albans on the A4251

This bustling market town on the edge of the Chiltern Hills has been greatly influenced by the Rothschild family. However, they are not the only people associated with Tring and in **St Mary's Church** lies the grave of the grandfather of the first US president, George Washington, while the 17th century Mansion House was reputedly used by Nell Gwynne. Another building of note is the Market House, which was built by public subscription in 1900 to commemorate Queen Victoria's Diamond Jubilee. The old Silk Mill, first opened in 1824, once employed over 600 people, but towards the end of the 19th century the silk trade fell into decline and Lord Rothschild ran the mill at a loss to protect his employees rather than see them destitute. From 1872 to the 1940s, the Rothschild family lived at Tring Park and their greatest lasting legacy is, perhaps, the **Walter Rothschild Zoological Museum**, first opened in 1892, which, on Walter's death in 1937, became part of the British Museum (Natural History).

Just north of Tring lies the Tring Reservoirs National Nature

• *Hatfield House is famous for its collection of beautiful tapestries and paintings as well as its exquisite interior and the beautiful gardens that were laid out in 1611, before the house was completed.*

•

•

Just to the north of Berkhamsted is Northchurch, which lies on the Grand Union Canal. All of its length in Hertfordshire can be walked, but the towpath between Northchurch and Tring has been developed particularly for recreational use.

•

Quagga at the Walter Rothschild Zoological Museum, Tring

In Walkern, a mile east of Stevenage, lived Jane Wenham, the last person in England to be sentenced to death for being a witch, in 1711. Though found guilty and condemned to death, she was pardoned by Queen Anne and lived on in seclusion in Hertingfordbury. The case led to the law against witchcraft being repealed in 1736.

Reserve, four reservoirs built between 1802 and 1839 and declared a reserve in 1955.

MARKYATE

8 miles NW of St Albans off the A5

This quiet village of charming 18th and 19th century cottages and houses is home to a large mansion that stands on the site of Markyate Cell, a medieval nunnery.

STEVENAGE

Following World War II, Stevenage became the first of Britain's New Towns and it expanded as a pleasant residential town after the first houses were occupied in 1951.

It was at Stevenage that the novelist EM Forster lived with his widowed mother from the age of 4 to 14 and **Howards End**, which featured in the book of the same name, is the house in which they lived; in the book, the village of Hilton is an adaptation of Stevenage. **Stevenage Museum** uses all the latest technology to tell the history of the town and surrounding area.

To the northeast lies one of Hertfordshire's last surviving post mills, **Cromer Windmill**, which dates from 1800 and ceased working in the 1920s. To the south stands **Knebworth House**, the home of the Lytton family since 1490. The present magnificent mansion was built during the 19th century and has played host to many famous visitors, including Charles Dickens, Benjamin Disraeli and Sir Winston Churchill.

AROUND STEVENAGE

LETCHWORTH

5 miles N of Stevenage on the A505

Letchworth is the first garden city where the ideals of Ebenezer Howard (to create a comfortable living environment with residential, industrial and commercial areas all within easy reach) were put into practice in the early 20th century. The offices of the town's architects are now home to the **First Garden City Heritage Museum**, a unique place that traces the history and development of Letchworth.

To the southeast lies **Hitchin**, an old market town which

Classic Car Show, Knebworth House

prospered from straw that was traded here for the local cottage industry of straw plaiting. Though the market declined, many of the town's older buildings have survived, including The Biggin, which was built in the early 17th century on the site of a Gilbertine Priory and became an almshouse for the poor. **Hitchin Museum** is home to the largest collection of period costume in the county and it also includes the **Museum of Hertfordshire Imperial Yeomanry**, a Victorian chemist's shop and a physic garden.

ROYSTON

12 miles NE of Stevenage on the A10

Situated at the intersection of the Ickneild Way and Ermine Street, this was a favourite hunting base for royalty, and James I's Hunting Lodge still stands. Just below the intersection of the two ancient thoroughfares the man-made **Royston Cave** was discovered in 1742 but its purpose remains a mystery.

BISHOP'S STORTFORD

16 miles E of Stevenage on the A120

The completion of the **Stort Navigation** in 1769 aided the development of the town's two industries, malting and brewing, and during the age of the stagecoach this was a major stopping point on the route between London and Norwich. The excellent **Local History Museum** brings the town's long history to life.

To the west is the unspoilt village of **Much Hadham** and the **Forge Museum** and **Victorian Cottage Garden**. Further west again is **Standon**, where, in a field, lies the Balloon Stone, a giant boulder that marks the spot where in 1784 Vincenzo Lunardi completed the first balloon flight in England.

WARE

10 miles SE of Stevenage on the A1170

Situated at the point where Ermine Street crosses the River Lea, Ware was the scene of a famous encounter between King Alfred and the Danes in AD 895. By the Middle Ages this was a market town to rival Hertford and several ancient buildings remain, including **Place House**, which is possibly one of Ware's two Domesday manor houses. The town's most interesting feature is **Scott's Grotto**, a series of passageways and artificial caves built by the poet John Scott in the late 18th century.

To the south, at **Great Amwell**, are the impressive buildings of **Haileybury College**, which was established in 1809 as a training school for the East India Company. The buildings are not open to the public, but the **Museum of Street Lighting**, with its collection of over 150 street lamps, is open by appointment.

Further south lies **Hoddesdon**, a town that dates back to Saxon times and which was a thriving market place by the 13th century. Housed in a Georgian building, the **Lowewood Museum** concentrates its collections on the region's illustrious history.

219 PAPILLON RESTAURANT AT THE WOODHALL ARMS

Stapleford

A charming Spanish landlord, top-notch food and comfortable, practical B&B rooms.

see page 512

220 THE WHITE HORSE

High Cross, nr Ware

A long history of hospitality at a splendid village inn serving a fine selection of food that includes dishes cooked on the healthy, fat-free Black Rock Grill.

see page 513

221 ROBIN HOOD & LITTLE JOHN

Tonwell, nr Hertford

A cosy village inn with a good choice of real ales, a menu of favourite English dishes and comfortable, practical B&B rooms.

see page 512

222 THE BEEHIVE

Epping Green, nr Hertford

A popular, cosy country pub with a fine choice of home-cooked snacks and meals. Accommodation planned.

see page 514

In Lea Valley Park stands **Rye House Gatehouse**, where, in 1683, a plot to assassinate Charles II was formulated. The plot failed and the conspirators, including the tenant of Rye House, were executed.

HERTFORD

8½ miles SE of Stevenage on the A119

Another Saxon town on the once important waterway of the River Lea that linked the town with London. The **Hertford Nature Walk** leads through the meadows between the Rivers Lea and Beane and takes in the canal basin that is known as The Folly. Hertford is very much a mix of old and new and among its interesting buildings is the Quaker Meeting House, said to be the oldest purpose-built meeting house in the world – it dates from 1669.

WELWYN GARDEN CITY

8 miles S of Stevenage on the A1000

One of the two garden cities in Hertfordshire that followed the ideas and plans of Ebenezer Howard (the other is Letchworth), the land for Welwyn Garden City was acquired in 1919 and building began a year later. Just to the south of the town lies **Mill Green Museum**, housed in the workers' cottages for the adjoining mill, which displays local artefacts from Roman times to the present day. Mill Green Mill is a delightful watermill that has been restored to working order and stands on the site of one of the four such mills that were listed in the *Domesday Book*. A famous son of Welwyn Garden City is the golfer Nick Faldo, born here in 1957.

Just to the north is the historic town of **Welwyn** that grew up along the route of the Great North Road. During excavations for the new A1(M) motorway, the famous **Welwyn Roman Baths** were discovered, part of a 3rd century villa or farm that was occupied for over 150 years.

AYOT ST LAWRENCE

5½ miles SW of Stevenage off the B651

A picturesque rural village whose most famous resident was Sir George Bernard Shaw, who lived here from 1906 until his death in 1950. His house, **Shaw's Corner**, is preserved as it was in his lifetime and contains many literary and personal mementoes.

Shaw's Corner House, Ayot St Lawrence

Isle of Man

The Isle of Man has an unusual status as a Crown Protectorate, with the Queen as Lord of Mann represented in the Island by the Lieutenant-Governor. Best known for its motorcycle races, its tailless cats and its kippers, it has plenty to interest the visitor with a wide range of wildlife, diverse geographical features, plenty of entertainment and a rich history. The TT (Tourist Trophy) races take place in May/ June, and the Manx GP in August/September.

223 THE WYNDHAM HOTEL

Douglas

Comfortable, practical B&B accommodation a few yards from the promenade.

 see page 515

224 THE WELLBECK HOTEL

Douglas

A fine family-owned and run hotel with high standards of comfort, service and food.

 see page 515

225 JAKS

Loch Promenade, Douglas

On Loch Promenade, with views out to sea, **Jaks** is one of the liveliest and most popular eating and drinking places on the Island.

see page 516

DOUGLAS

The island's capital, Douglas, is a lively resort where visitors can take a leisurely ride along the promenade aboard the **Douglas Bay Horse Tramway**, a remarkable and beautiful reminder of a bygone era. Another delightful means of travel is the **Victorian Steam Railway** that runs between Douglas and Port Erin. Following the line of the cliff tops, the memorable journey also takes in bluebell woods and steep-sided rocky cuttings. The **Manx Electric Railway**, completed in 1899, operates the oldest working tramcars in the world and runs between Douglas and Ramsey.

No trip to the island is complete without a visit to the **Manx Museum**, where the Story of Man film gives a dramatic and vivid portrayal of the island's unique history.

On a headland overlooking Douglas Bay is a camera obscura known as the Great Union Camera.

Manx Electric Railway, Douglas

Here, natural daylight is focused on to a white panel through a system of lenses to provide a living image of the scene outside.

AROUND DOUGLAS

RAMSEY

12 miles N of Douglas on the A18

This northernmost resort on the island is an attractive coastal town with a cosy harbour that is popular with visiting yachtsmen. Just to the north of the town stands the **Grove Rural Life Museum**, housed in a pleasantly proportioned Victorian house.

LAXEY

5 miles N of Douglas on the A2

Set in a deep, wooded valley, this village is home to one of the island's most famous sights, the **Great Laxey Wheel** that marks the site of a once thriving mining community. Known as the Lady Isabella Wheel, with a circumference of 228 feet, a diameter of 72 feet, and a top platform some 72 feet off the ground, it is the largest waterwheel in the world. The wheel lies in Laxey Glen, one of the island's 17 National Glens. The Great Laxey Mine Railway, opened in 2004, carries passengers in tiny carriages along a stretch of the line where loaded wagons once rolled.

Situated above Laxey, in a beautiful glen, are the magnificent **Ballalheanagh Gardens**, while from Laxey station the **Snaefell Mountain Railway** carries visitors to the top of the island's only mountain. Built in 1895, the six original tram cars still climb the steep gradients to Snaefell's 2,036 feet summit from which there are outstanding views of the whole island and out over the sea to Ireland, Scotland and England.

PEEL

9 miles W of Douglas on the A1

On the western side on the island, Peel, which is renowned for its sunsets, typifies the unique character and atmosphere of the Isle of Man. It is traditionally the centre of the Manx fishing industry, including the delicious oak-smoked kippers and shellfish. Its narrow winding streets exude history and draw the visitor unfailingly down to the harbour, sandy beach, and magnificent castle of local red sandstone. The museum in Peel is well worth a visit.

Peel Castle, one of Isle of Man's principal historic monuments, occupies the important site of St Patrick's Isle. In the 11th century the castle became the ruling seat of the Norse Kingdom of Man and the Isles.

CASTLETOWN

9 miles SW of Douglas on the A7

The original capital of the island, the town's harbour lies beneath the imposing battlements of the well-preserved 12th century **Castle Rushen**. Castletown is also home to the island's **Nautical Museum**, where the displays centre on the late 18th century armed yacht *Peggy* that sits in her contemporary boathouse.

Perched right on the southwestern tip of the island, **Cregneash Village Folk Museum** offers a unique experience of Manx traditional life within a 19th century crofting community. The centrepiece of Cregneash is Harry Kelly's Cottage. Kelly was a renowned Cregneash crofter and a fluent speaker of the Manx language who died in 1934.

PORT ERIN

16 miles S of Peel on the A5

Situated between magnificent headlands, Port Erin has its own Arts Centre, which since 1975 has hosted the annual Mananan International Festival of Music and the Arts, now recognised as one of the island's most prestigious cultural events. Port Erin also has a small steam railway museum.

CALF OF MAN

15 miles W of Douglas

This small island, situated just off the southwestern tip of the island, is a National Trust bird sanctuary. In **Calf Sound**, the stretch of water between the island and the Isle of Man, the largest armada of Viking longships ever assembled in the British Isles congregated before setting off to invade Ireland.

Peel gave its name to the only production car ever made on the Island. The three-wheel Peel was one of the tiniest cars ever made - the claim that it could carry a driver and a shopping bag was disputed by some, who thought that it was a question of one or the other!

226 DUNCANS DINER & COFFEE SHOP

Michael Street, Peel

On one of Peel's busy main streets, **Duncans Diner & Coffee Shop** is open all day Monday to Saturday for a good choice of home cooking.

see page 517

On the road between Castletown and Douglas, visitors should look out for the Fairy Bridge. For centuries, people on the Isle of Man have taken no chances when it comes to the little people and it is still customary to wish the fairies, who live under the bridge, a 'Good Morning' when crossing.

Isle of Wight

Separated from the mainland by the Solent, is the Isle of Wight, where Queen Victoria sought solitude at Osborne House after the premature death of her husband. John Keats wrote his Endymion (first line: A thing of beauty is a joy for ever) while staying on the Island. Other notable visitors have described it as the Garden Isle and England's Madeira; about half of its 147 square miles have been designated Areas of Outstanding Natural Beauty.

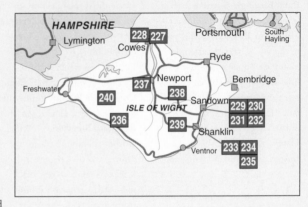

COWES

East and West Cowes are linked across the River Medina by a chain ferry. West Cowes is the home of the **Royal Yacht Squadron**, which organises Cowes Week, the famous regatta that is a firm fixture in the sailing and social calendar. The links with ships and shipbuilding go back centuries and Royal Navy craft, lifeboats, flying boats and seaplanes have all been built at Cowes. The Isle of Wight's maritime history is charted at the **Cowes Maritime Museum**, which also houses a collection of racing yachts, while the **Sir Max Aitken Museum** has a collection of nautical paintings, instruments and artefacts. The Isle of Wight Model Railways Exhibition includes models spanning the whole history of railways.

On the eastern bank of the Medina lies 18th century Norris Castle, where the 12-year-old Princess Victoria stayed; she was so charmed by the island that she returned with her husband, Prince Albert, and built **Osborne**

House, a mile to the south, in the style of an Italian villa. The **Isle of Wight Steam Railway** runs renovated steam trains along a preserved 5-mile track between Wootton and Smallbrook Junction. Wootton is also home to **Butterfly World & Fountain World**, which includes an indoor sub-tropical garden with hundreds of exotic free-flying butterflies.

AROUND COWES

RYDE

6½ miles SE of Cowes on the A3054

For many visitors to the island, Ryde is their arrival point. The largest town on the Island has five miles of sandy beach and with all the usual seaside attractions and a

Osborne House, Cowes

227 THE WATERSIDE

Cowes

A sociable pub on the waterfront at Cowes, with a nautical look and feel and a good selection of food and drink.

🍴 *see page 517*

228 THE OCTOPUS' GARDEN CAFÉ

Cowes

An amazing place, which is unbeatable for its combination of vibrant setting, great music, great food and great company.

🍴 *see page 518*

229 THE BELMORE
GUEST HOUSE

Sandown

A spotless, friendly, family-run guest house where guests can expect the best in comfort, service and hospitality.

 see page 518

230 THE SANDHILL

Sandown

Excellent accommodation in a comfortable, quiet hotel in a pleasant residential area of Sandown.

 see page 519

231 THE FOUNTAIN

Sandown

A busy, popular pub open from 11 every day for a wide range of drinks and good honest pub grub.

 see page 519

marina, it remains a popular holiday spot. One of Ryde's Victorian churches, St Thomas, is now a Heritage Centre that features the transportation of convicts to Australia - many of the unfortunates left England in ships moored off Ryde. In the middle of Appley Park stands Appley Tower, which houses a collection of fossils, crystals and rune readings.

To the east lies **Seaview Wildlife Encounter Flamingo Park**, whose colonies of flamingos, penguins, macaws and waterfowl are among the largest in the country, while inland from Ryde is **Brickfields Horse Country**, a centre with more than 100 animals including magnificent Shire horses and miniature ponies.

BEMBRIDGE

10½ miles SE of Cowes on the B3330

Once a thriving fishing village, Bembridge is now a popular holiday and sailing centre that maintains its maritime links through the **Maritime Museum and Shipwreck Centre**. The village is also home to the **Ruskin Gallery**, displaying an impressive collection of the 19th century artist's work.

Maritime Museum and Shipwreck Centre, Bembridge

Here, too, is one of the island's best-known landmarks, the 18th century Bembridge Windmill.

Further along the coast lies **Sandown**, the island's leading holiday resort, which has drawn such distinguished visitors as Lewis Carroll, Charles Darwin and George Eliot. The beaches and the museums are among the attractions, and to the north, near **Brading**, is a Roman Villa discovered in 1880. One of the island's oldest towns, Brading is also home to the **Isle of Wight Wax Works** and the **Lilliput Museum of Antique Dolls and Toys** while, close by, are two notable historic houses. **Nunwell House**, where Charles I

Nunwell House, Brading

Shanklin Chine

spent his last night of freedom, is set within a glorious garden, and 13th century **Morton Manor** features an Elizabethan sunken garden surrounded by a 400-year-old box hedge.

SHANKLIN

12 miles SE of Cowes on the A3055

To the south of Bembridge lies Sandown's more sedate neighbour Shanklin, which stands at the head of one of the island's most renowned landmarks, **Shanklin Chine**, a 300 feet deep wooded ravine. First opened in 1817 and a former refuge of smugglers, this ravine,

232 DRIFTWOOD BEACH BAR

Sandown

No visit to the Island is complete without a visit to this super beach bar, which offers an amazing range of food and drink in a friendly, laid-back atmosphere.

see *page 520*

233 MELBOURNE ARDENLEA HOTEL

Shanklin

A well-appointed hotel with outstanding leisure and family facilities.

see *page 521*

234 THE ORCHARDCROFT HOTEL

Shanklin

Family-friendly accommodation in a comfortable hotel with indoor pool, sauna and games room.

see *page 521*

235 CLAREMONT GUEST HOUSE

Shanklin

Quiet, comfortable, civilised accommodation in a guest house convenient for all Shanklin's attractions.

 see page 522

236 THE THREE BISHOPS AT BRIGHSTONE

Brighstone

A delightful family-friendly village pub serving an excellent selection of real ales and home-cooked food.

see page 523

237 THE WORLD'S END

Newport

A drinker's pub, offering a selection of simple pub grub that fits the bill perfectly.

 see page 522

mysterious and romantic, has long fascinated visitors with its waterfalls and rare flora. In the Heritage Centre at the top of the chine is an interesting exhibtion on the PLUTO (Pipe Line Under the Ocean) project for pumping fuel across the Channel to supply the troops involved in D-Day. The Chine also has a memorial to the Royal Marines of 40 Commando who used the Chine as an assault course before the disastrous assault on Dieppe in 1942.

NEWPORT

4 miles S of Cowes on the A3020

The island's capital and once a busy shipping centre on the River Medina, Newport still has many of its old riverside warehouses; one of them houses the **Classic Boat** **Museum**, and next door is the Isle of Wight Bus Museum with its impressive collection of passenger transport vehicles. In St Thomas' Church lies the tomb of Princess Elizabeth, Charles I's daughter, who died of a fever while the family were held prisoner at **Carisbrooke Castle**. She was buried by the altar in the church at Newport. Queen Victoria restored the grave and dedicated a monument. Here, too, a 3rd century Roman Villa has been excavated, offering an insight into the sophistication of the late Romano-British designers and builders.

It was to the Isle of Wight that Charles I fled to get help to reach France. He was imprisoned in Carisbrooke Castle, from where, after a night at Nunwell House, he

Carisbrooke Castle, Newport

was taken for execution on Whitehall in January 1649.

VENTNOR

8 miles S of Cowes on the A3055

With much of its Victorian charm still intact, the town has much to offer today's visitors including the Ventnor Botanic Garden on the site of the former Royal National Chest Hospital, the Smuggling Museum, and the Coastal Visitor Centre dedicated to the island's marine environment. Away from the town, St Boniface Down provides excellent walking country as well as spectacular views across the island. At nearby **Bonchurch**, the poet Algernon Swinburne is buried in the graveyard of the Church of St Boniface. Inland lies **Appuldurcombe House**, once the grandest mansion on the island, which is now home to the **Owl and Falconry Centre** where daily flying displays and courses in the age old art of falconry are held.

The **Isle of Wight Donkey Sanctuary** lies close by, as does the village of **Godshill** with its magical **Model Village** and the **Nostalgia Toy Museum**.

Nestling in the heart of the Undercliff, to the southwest of Ventnor, is the ancient village of **St Lawrence** which is home to the **Rare Breeds Waterfowl Park**. From here the coast road continues round to **St Catherine's Point**, the wildest part of the island, where steps lead down to **St Catherine's Lighthouse**. On the most southerly tip of the island is **Blackgang Chine**, a Victorian scenic park that has been developed into a modern fantasy park.

CALBOURNE

9 miles SW of Cowes off the B3401

The most enchanting part of this picturesque village is Winkle Street, which has a row of charming old cottages opposite the village stream

238 THE WHITE LION

Arreton

An atmospheric one-time staging post, now a cheerful village pub serving well-kept beer and a good choice of home-cooked food.

🍴 *see page 524*

239 LITTLE SPAN FARM

Rew Lane, nr Wroxall

High-quality B&B and self-catering accommodation in a beautiful farmhouse setting.

🛏 *see page 524*

Appuldurcombe House, nr Ventnor

240 THE SUN INN

Calbourne

A delightful village pub run by two sisters, who serve well-kept ales and excellent home-cooked food.

¶ see page 525

Calbourne Water Mill

and an ancient sheepwash. Close by, in a lovely landscaped valley, is a superb 17th century **Water Mill** that incorporates a fascinating Rural Museum.

FRESHWATER

11 miles SW of Cowes on the A3054

This bustling town was the home of Alfred, Lord Tennyson, who was persuaded to move here by the pioneer photographer, Julia Cameron. Her home, **Dimbola Lodge**, houses a permanent exhibition of her work.

To the west lies the popular holiday spot of Totland and the famous multi-coloured sands of **Alum Bay**, and on the very western tip of the island are **The Needles**, three jagged slabs of rock with a lighthouse at the end of the most westerly.

North of Freshwater lies Yarmouth, a picturesque place with narrow streets, old stone quays and a castle built by Henry VIII after the town had been sacked by the French.

The Needles Park, Alum Bay

Kent

'*Kent, Sir – everybody knows Kent – apples, cherries, hops and women*'. That's how Charles Dickens described Kent in *The Pickwick Papers*.

Kent is the first county that most cross-channel visitors encounter when visiting England (though for many the tunnel has removed the thrill of the sight of the White Cliffs of Dover), and few counties combine glorious open landscapes with such a rich history. It was here that Julius Caesar landed in 55 BC; the Vikings followed 1,000 years later and the land was widely settled by the Normans following the defeat of King Harold in 1066. Throughout the centuries there has been a threat of invasion and, with the north Kent coast situated on the Thames estuary, it is not surprising that this area became the scene of great naval activity. On the south coast, the Cinque Ports were set up in the 11th century as a commercial alliance of significant ports – but the silting up of channels over the centuries has left some of them high and dry miles from the sea.

Visitors have flocked to the seaside resorts of Ramsgate, Herne Bay and Margate since Victorian times, but centuries ago Kent was a favourite place of pilgrimage as Christians made their way to Canterbury Cathedral.

The county's reputation as the 'Garden of England' is well earned, and green fields and orchards still abound. Rolling wooded countryside is dotted with windmills, and oast houses are still a common sight. In contrast are the remote, flat lands of Romney Marsh, sometime haunt of smugglers, and, of course, the White Cliffs of Dover, one of the most evocative sights in the land, a symbol of the country's strength that was immortalised in song by Vera (now Dame Vera) Lynn.

Rochester Castle

AROUND ROCHESTER

GRAVESEND

7 miles NW of Rochester on the A226

Gravesend marks the point at which ships entering the broad River Thames take on board a river pilot. On the A207, in Bexleyheath, is one of the National Trust's most recent acquisitions. This is **The Red House**, which was designed in 1859 by Philip Webb for the newly married William and Janey Morris. The interior was decorated by Webb, Morris, Burne-Jones, Madox Brown and Rossetti; William Morris described the house as 'a joyful nook of heaven in an unheavenly world'. For Dante Gabriel Rossetti it was '.....more a poem than a house - but an admirable place to live in too'.

Nearby **Dartford** is best known nowadays for the Tunnel that runs under the Thames to emerge on the Essex side near West Thurrock. Robert Trevithick, the first man to carry passengers on a steam vehicle, spent the last years of his life working on inventions in a factory in Dartford and died in poverty in 1833 in the Bull public house (now the Royal Victoria and Bull). The factory workers paid for his funeral, and he is buried in Holy Trinity churchyard. Dartford is one of several places which claims to be the birthplace of Wat Tyler, leader of the Peasants Revolt (others include Deptford, Colchester and Maidstone). What is not in doubt is the place where he met his end – it

•

The graveyard of St George's in Gravesend is thought to be the final resting place of the famous Red Indian princess, Pocahontas, who died on board ship in 1617 while she was on her way back to America, where she had reputedly saved the life of the British settler John Smith in Virginia. The precise site of her grave is not known, but there is a statue of her and two memorial windows in the church.

•

ROCHESTER

The site was first settled by the Romans, but it was following the Norman invasion that William the Conqueror ordered his architect, Bishop Gundulph, to design a fortification to protect this strategic crossing point of the River Medway. Today, **Rochester Castle** remains one of the finest surviving examples of Norman architecture in the country. Bishop Gundulph was also ordered to build Rochester Cathedral on the site of a Saxon church that was founded in AD 604.

The city has close connections with the novelist Charles Dickens. An Elizabethan building houses the Charles Dickens Centre, The Royal Victoria and Bull Hotel featured in both *The Pickwick Papers* and *Great Expectations*, and Restoration House became Satis House in *Great Expectations*.

was Smithfield in London, where in 1381 he was killed by the Mayor of London and one of the King's esquires in the presence of the 15-year-old King Richard II.

CHATHAM
1 mile SE of Rochester on the A229

Visitors to the historic **Chatham Dockyard** – now the **World Naval Base** – can appreciate the scale of modern fighting ships in the dry dock as well as the architecture of the most complete Georgian dockyard in the world. Rope is still made in the traditional way in the long Ropery building, and the history of lifeboats is told at the **National Collection of the RNLI**. The **Museum of the Dockyard** tells the 400-year-old story of the site. Close to the dockyard lies **Fort Amherst Heritage Park and Caverns**, the country's premier Napoleonic fortress that was home to a secret underground telephone exchange that co-ordinated air raid warnings during World War II.

To the east of Chatham lies **Gillingham**, the home of the fascinating **Royal Engineers Museum** where the diverse skills of this distinguished Corps are on display.

SITTINGBOURNE
10½ miles E of Rochester on the A2

Once a stopping point for pilgrims on their way to Canterbury, Sittingbourne has developed into a thriving market town. Visitors today can also take a nostalgic ride on a steam train along the

Fort Amherst Heritage Park.

Sittingbourne and Kemsley Light Railway. In 1533, in nearby Teynham, Richard Harris, Henry VIII's fruiterer, planted England's first cherry tree along with apple trees and thus established the village as the birthplace of English orchards.

At **Milton Creek**, just north of the town centre, lies **Dolphin Yard Sailing Barge Museum**, which aims to preserve the traditional Thames barges that were built in their hundreds in boatyards around Sittingbourne.

Sheerness Heritage Centre

ferry port, and the **Sheerness Heritage Centre** tells the history of the dockyard and its influence on the town's development. Sheppey is closely linked with the early years of British aviation: the Short brothers set up a factory here, and other notable pioneers who visited here include the future Lord Brabazon, the Hon Charles Rolls and the Wright Brothers.

To the southeast lies the seaside town of Minster where the 15th century abbey gatehouse is home to the Minster Abbey Gatehouse Museum.

On the southern tip of the island is the Swale National Nature Reserve, home to numerous wildfowl, while to the west lies Elmley Marshes Nature Reserve, an area of salt marsh.

241 THE GEORGE & NEW TERRITORIES RESTAURANT

Teynham, nr Sittingbourne

A most unusual combination – a traditional English country pub and a top-notch Chinese restaurant.

see page 526

242 THE PEPPERBOX INN

Fairbourne Heath, nr Ulcombe

Secluded down leafy lanes, a fine old country pub with friendly family owners, well-kept ales and interesting home cooking.

see page 525

SHEERNESS

12 miles NE of Rochester on the A249

On the **Isle of Sheppey**, this town was once the site of a naval dockyard, the first to be surveyed by Samuel Pepys as Secretary to the Admiralty in the reign of Charles II, and it was here in 1805 that HMS *Victory* docked when it brought Nelson's body back to England following the Battle of Trafalgar. It is now a busy container and car

LEEDS

11 miles SE of Rochester on the B2163

This village is synonymous with the beautiful **Leeds Castle**, which

Leeds Castle

Cobtree Manor Park, Maidstone

243 THE BEACON

Rusthall

Glorious views, superb, imaginative cooking and comfortable accommodation in a beautifully appointed late-Victorian house.

¶ ⊨ see page 527

stands in glorious landscaped gardens on two islands in the middle of the River Len. Built on a site once owned by Saxon kings, the castle was immaculately modernised by the last owner, Olive Paget, later Lady Baillie. The castle contains many superb antiques and tapestries, and in one of the medieval outbuildings is an idiosyncratic **Dog Collar Museum**. One of the gardens is named in honour of Lady Baillie, who put so much back into the Castle until her death in 1974.

MAIDSTONE

8½ miles S of Rochester on the A229

Despite extensive development in modern times, Maidstone has retained many handsome historic buildings including **Chillington Manor**, a particularly fine Elizabethan residence that is now home to the **Maidstone Museum and Art Gallery**. Part of the museum's collection, The **Tyrwhitt-Drake Museum of Carriage** can be found in the stables that once belonged to the

Archbishops of Canterbury. Opposite the stables is the 14th century **Archbishop's Palace**, where the clergy rested while travelling between London and Canterbury, and elsewhere in the town are the College of Priests, founded in 1395, and the 13th century Corpus Christi Fraternity Hall.

Just north of Maidstone town centre stands Allington Castle, the home of Sir Thomas Wyatt, the 16th century poet who takes some credit for introducing the sonnet into English poetry.

On the opposite bank of the River Medway is Tyland Barn, a beautifully restored 17th century building that houses the **Museum of Kent Life**.

ROYAL TUNBRIDGE WELLS

Surrounded by the unspoilt beauty of the Weald, Royal Tunbridge Wells is an attractive town that

244 BARNFIELD OAST

Lamberhurst

A beautifully converted oast house and adjacent buildings provide luxurious self-catering accommodation in the lovely Kentish countryside.

⊨ see page 527

245 THE SWAN AT THE VINEYARD

Lamberhurst

One of the top eating pubs in the land, in a picturesque setting overlooking vineyards.

¶ see page 528

175

developed into a
fashionable health
resort in the 18th
and 19th centuries
after the discovery
of chalybeate
springs in 1606.
One of the most
famous features of
the town is **The
Pantiles**, a lovely
shaded walk lined
with elegant shops
that were, in the
days of the spa, the
central focus of the
hectic social life
arranged by the
Master of
Ceremonies, Beau
Nash.

To the east of
Royal Tunbridge Wells, close to
Goudhurst, is a charming
Georgian manor house,
Finchcocks, which contains a
magnificent collection of historic
keyboard instruments. Also in this
area is **Scotney Castle**, with its
romantic gardens, and **The Owl
House**, a pretty little cottage that
has associations with night
smugglers or 'owlers'. There are
more superb gardens at nearby
Groombridge Place, and to the
northwest of the town there are
three wonderful places that are well
worth exploring. **Penshurst Place**
dates back to 1341 and is
surrounded by glorious gardens
that are a rare survivor of the
Elizabethan age. A little further on
is **Chiddingstone Castle**, a
traditional squire's house with the

Hever Castle, nr Tunbridge Wells

appearance of a grand castle, while,
close by, is one of the county's star
attractions, **Hever Castle**, the
childhood home of Anne Boleyn.

The Hever Castle Estate was
bought in the early 20th century by
the millionaire William Waldorf
Astor; his extensive restoration
work has created award winning
gardens along with a castle filled
with fine collections of paintings,
furniture, tapestries and objets
d'art.

SEVENOAKS

The pride of this ancient market
town is **Knole House**, one of the
largest private homes in the
country, with 365 rooms. In 1603,
Elizabeth I granted the house to
the Sackville family, and it was here,

249 YE MAYDES
RESTAURANT

Biddenden

An intimate, romantic and
very comfortable setting for
enjoying superb food based
on Kentish produce.

see page 530

Knole House, Sevenoaks

250 THE KING
WILLIAM IV

in 1892, that Vita Sackville-West
was born.

To the east, close to the small
village of **Ivy Hatch**, lies **Ightham
Mote**, one of England's finest
medieval houses. In the opposite
direction, near the hamlet of

French Street, stands **Chartwell**,
Sir Winston Churchill's home from
the 1920s until his death in 1965.

To the northwest of Sevenoaks
is Biggin Hill RAF Station, whose
entrance is flanked by a Spitfire and
a Hurricane that act as silent

Benenden

A 16th century inn with a
father-and-son team at the
helm. Excellent cooking
using locally sourced
ingredients.

see page 532

251 THE CHEQUERS
INN

High Halden

A lively, popular village inn
with bar and restaurant
menus of home-cooked
dishes.

see page 531

Ightham Mote, Sevenoaks

Wittersham

Cooked-to-order food, a wide variety of real ales and three annual beer festivals in a homely 17th century pub.

🍴 see page 533

•

To the south of Fordwich, close to Canterbury, lies Howletts Wild Animal Park which was created by John Aspinall and is dedicated to the preservation of rare and endangered animals, including gorillas and both Indian and Siberian tigers.

•

reminders of the stalwart service these two aircraft, and their crews, gave during the dark days of World War II. Close to the station is **Down House**, where Charles Darwin lived for over 40 years until his death in 1882. The house is now a Museum dedicated to his life and work.

At nearby **Westerham**, a pleasant town near the Surrey border, are two statues of British heroes who had connections with the town. One is a tribute to Sir Winston Churchill, who made his home at nearby Chartwell, the other remembers General Wolfe, who defeated the French at Quebec in 1759. Wolfe was born in Westerham and his childhood home, renamed Quebec House, stands east of the town centre. Wolfe also has connections with nearby Squerryes Court, where one of the rooms has been set aside to display mementoes relating to the General.

CANTERBURY

It was here, in AD 597, that St Augustine founded an abbey which was to become the roots of Christianity in England. Lying just outside the city walls, **St Augustine's Abbey** is now in ruins, but a museum displays artefacts excavated from the site while, close by, is **St Martin's Church**, England's oldest parish church. However, both these buildings are overshadowed by the Mother Church of the Anglican Communion, **Canterbury Cathedral**, which was founded in AD 597 although the oldest part of the present building is the early 12th century crypt. Canterbury Cathedral is best known as the scene of the murder of Archbishop Thomas à Becket rather than for its ecclesiastical architecture. At the **Canterbury Tales Visitor Attraction** visitors are taken back to the 14th century and can meet the Knight, the Miller and other characters that tell their stories to keep the 'pilgrims' amused.

Canterbury predates its cathedral by many centuries and was the capital of the Iron Age kingdom, Cantii, as well as being settled by the Romans. The **Roman Museum** centres on the remains of a Roman town house, while the **Canterbury Heritage Museum** presents a full history of the city over the last 2,000 years. In the **Kent Masonic Library and Museum** the history of freemasonry is explored.

Canterbury Cathedral

Canterbury Tales Visitor Attraction

AROUND CANTERBURY

HERNE BAY

7 miles NE of Canterbury on the A299

Originally a fishing village and a notorious haunt for smugglers, this chiefly 19th century town has developed into one of the main resorts on the north Kent coast. Its story is told at the **Herne Bay Museum Centre**.

East of Herne Bay is Reculver. The Normans built two huge towers within the remains of the Roman fort, providing sailors with a landmark to guide them into the Thames estuary. Today, Reculver Towers and Roman Fort is in the care of English Heritage. During World War II, the Barnes Wallace

'bouncing bomb' was tested off the coast here. Several bombs were found here on the shore in 1997 – none of them containing explosives.

GOODNESTONE

6½ miles SE of Canterbury off the B2046

Close to the village lies Goodnestone (pronounced Gunston) Park, an estate that was frequently visited by Jane Austen and, today, **Goodnestone Park Gardens** are considered some of the finest in the southeast of England.

STELLING MINNIS

6½ miles S of Canterbury off the B2068

Close to this village on the edge of what remains of the once great

•

In the heart of the Elham Valley, the Rural Heritage Centre at Parsonage Farm explores over 600 years of farming, while the Elham Valley Railway Trail provides the opportunity to observe both wildlife and plant life that have made their home along this disused track.

•

Built on a Roman foundation, Chilham Castle was originally a Norman keep but a Jacobean mansion house was added and the grounds first laid out by Charles I's gardener John Tradescant and reworked in the 18th century by Capability Brown.

Lyminge Forest is **Davison's Mill**, a mid-19th century smock mill that is now home to a Museum of milling implements and tools.

CHALLOCK

10 miles SW of Canterbury on the A252

Set in the dense woodlands known as Challock Forest, this pretty village is home to **Beech Court Gardens**, which are a riot of colour from spring through to autumn. To the north, close to the village of **Sheldwich**, lies the **National Fruit Collection** – home to what is probably the largest collection of fruit trees and plants in the world. Tucked away in the orchards and close to the village of **Throwley** is **Belmont**, a beautiful Georgian mansion house that is renowned for its impressive clock collection assembled by the 5th Lord Harris.

To the northeast, towards Canterbury, is one of the county's best-preserved villages, **Chilham**, which is often used as a film location.

FAVERSHAM

9 miles NW of Canterbury on the A2

First settled by the Romans, the town grew steadily as a market town. For 400 years it was the centre of the country's explosives industry and **Chart Gunpowder Mills** is a lasting monument to the industry based here between 1560 and 1934. Faversham boasts over 400 listed buildings, among them the 16th century Guildhall and a 15th century former inn that is now the **Fleur de Lis Heritage Centre**.

WHITSTABLE

5½ miles NW of Canterbury on the A2990

Sometimes referred to as the 'Pearl of Kent', this town, centred on its busy commercial harbour, is as famous for its oysters today as it was in Roman times. On the harbour's East Quay, the **Oyster and Fishery Exhibition** tells the story of Whitstable's connections with fishing, and **Whitstable Museum and Gallery** explores the traditions and life of this ancient seafaring community. In Whitstable's Museum will be found references to some of the 'firsts' to which the town lays claim: the first scheduled passenger train ran between Whitstable and Canterbury; the first steamship to sail to Australia from Britain left here in 1837; the diving helmet was invented in the town; and the country's first council houses were built here.

Just inland from Whitstable is Druidstone Wildlife Park, home to a wide variety of animals and birds including otters, owls, rheas, wallabies and parrots.

Lancashire

For some, Lancashire is the brash seaside resort of Blackpool, for others a county dominated by cotton mills. However, there is much more to Lancashire than candyfloss and cotton. It is an ancient county, with many of its towns and villages dating back to Saxon times and beyond, and during the Civil War it remained fiercely loyal to the King and saw some of the bloodiest incidents of the whole bitter conflict. Away from the brash resorts, which developed to provide attractions and amenities for the mill workers who made use of the new railway network to escape for a day or even a week's holiday, there are the more genteel towns of Lytham St Anne's and Southport with its elegant mile-long main boulevard. Inland lies beautiful countryside that includes the ancient hunting ground of the Forest of Bowland and, to the south, Pendle Hill, the scene of the notorious 17th century witch hunts. Morecambe Bay, beautiful but occasionally treacherous, offers glorious views and sunsets and is an important habitat for a variety of birdlife and other wildlife.

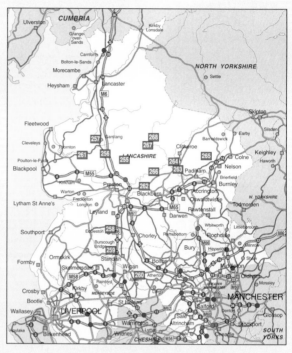

255 YE HORNS INN

Goosnargh

Outstanding food, drink, service and accommodation in one of Lancashire's very finest inns.

 see page 535

256 OLDE DUNCOMBE HOUSE

Bilsborrow, nr Preston

Excellent B&B rooms in a handsome family-run canalside hotel. The other part of the business is a 65' luxury party barge.

see page 536

257 THE CHURCH INN

Garstang

Quality is to the fore in the hospitality, drink and food that caters for all tastes and appetites.

 see page 537

PRESTON

Preston is strategically positioned on the highest navigable point of the River Ribble, and although the port activity has declined, the docklands, now called Riversway, have become an area of regeneration with a marina. The complex is in the **Millennium Ribble Link**, itself part of a three-mile water park. The **Ribble Steam Railway** boasts the largest single collection of standard-gauge industrial locomotives in the country.

Dominating the Market Square is a magnificent neoclassical building, reminiscent of the British Museum, which houses the **Harris Museum and Art Gallery**. Fulwood Barracks is home to the Queen's Lancashire Regiment Museum.

On the northern outskirts of Preston is one of its most popular visitor attractions, the **National Football Museum**. In 1888, Preston North End was one of the 12 founder members of the

Football League and its first champion. In 1887 the team recorded the biggest win in the FA Cup's history – 26-0 against Hyde United. Sporting stars hailing from Preston include Bill Beaumont and Andrew 'Freddie' Flintoff.

Preston saw the first stretch of motorway; the Preston-By-Pass was opened in 1958.

AROUND PRESTON

GARSTANG

10½ miles N of Preston on the A6

This ancient market town dates back to the 6th century when a Saxon named Garri made his base here. At the excellent **Discovery Centre** displays deal with various aspects of the region, including the history of the nearby Forest of Bowland.

Just to the east of the town, on the top of a grassy knoll, are the remains of **Greenhalgh Castle**, built in 1490 by Thomas Stanley, the 1st Earl of Derby. Severely damaged in a siege against Cromwell in 1645-6, the Castle was

Greenhalgh Castle, Garstang

one of the last strongholds in Lancashire to hold out against Parliament. To the north, on the A6, are the remains of a 17th century tollhouse built when parts of the turnpike from Garstang to Lancaster were realigned.

CHORLEY

8 miles SE of Preston on the A6

A bustling and friendly market town, Chorley was the birthplace, in 1819, of Henry Tate, who founded the world famous sugar business of Tate and Lyle. A great benefactor, Henry gave vast sums of money to worthy causes, and endowed the art gallery that now bears his name.

The jewel in Chorley's crown is undoubtedly **Astley Hall**, built in the late 16th century and set within some beautiful parkland.

To the southeast is the charming village of Rivington, surrounded by moorland that forms the western border of the Forest of Rossendale.

Overlooking the village of Rivington, and with splendid views over west Lancashire, **Rivington Pike**, at 1,191 feet, is one of the area's high peaks. Just to the south of the village lies **Lever Park**, situated on the lower slopes of Rivington Moor, which was the home of William Hesketh Lever, who later became Lord Leverhulme.

LEYLAND

5 miles S of Preston on the B5253

The name is the clue: the town is best known for its associations

with the manufacture of cars and lorries and the **British Commercial Vehicle Museum** is housed on the site of the former Leyland South Works, where commercial vehicles were produced for many years.

WIGAN

15 miles S of Preston on the A49

Wigan's development as an industrial town centred on coal mining, which began as early as 1450. By the 19th century, there were over 1,000 pit shafts in operation in the surrounding area, supplying the fuel for Lancashire's expanding textile industry. The Leeds and Liverpool Canal, which runs through the town, was a key means of transporting the coal to the cotton mills of Lancashire and Wigan Pier, the major loading bay, remains one of the most interesting features of the waterway.

There is some fine countryside around Wigan, including the Douglas Valley Trail; Pennington Flash, a large lake formed by mining subsidence that is now a wildlife reserve and a country park; and Haigh Country Park, one of the first to be designated in England.

RUFFORD

10 miles SW of Preston on the A59

In this attractive village of pretty houses stands the ancestral home of the Hesketh family, the splendid 15th century Rufford Old Hall. In the outbuildings is the **Philip Ashcroft Museum of Rural Life**, with its unique collection of items

258 THE ORIGINAL FARMERS ARMS

Eccleston, Chorley

Original décor and brilliant original cooking in a much-loved family-run village pub.

 see page 538

259 THE WHITE LION

Wrightington

A charming old inn open all day for food and drink: real ales, quality cooking on a very varied menu.

see page 538

260 THE CUMBERLAND ARMS

Hindley

A popular destination for locals and visitors, with a fine range of drinks and hearty home cooking

see page 539

that illustrate village life in pre-industrial Lancashire.

SOUTHPORT

15 miles SW of Preston on the A565

The rise of this popular seaside resort lies in the tradition of sea bathing that began at nearby Churchtown centuries ago. As the number of people celebrating Bathing Sunday grew, so did the need for a more accessible beach and a stretch of sand two miles south of Churchtown was deemed suitable. From the first simple hotel Southport has grown into an elegant and sophisticated resort that is centred on its main boulevard, Lord Street, a mile-long wide road built between the lands of the two neighbouring lords of the manor. Southport's Promenade is bordered by grand hotels on the land side and a series of formal gardens on the other. From the centre of the promenade extends Southport's Pier that, at 1,460 yards, was for a time the longest in the country.

A unique Southport attraction is the **British Lawnmower Museum**, a tribute to the garden machine industry.

Along the coast to the southeast is the **Freshfield Nature Reserve**, with a pine forest that has one of the few colonies of red squirrels in England.

BLACKPOOL

15 miles NW of Preston on the A583

This classic British resort, with piers, funfairs, gardens, amusement arcades and a promenade, was until the middle of the 19th century little more than a fishing village among the sand dunes of the Fylde coast. However, the fashion for taking day trips and holidays, assisted by the very expanding railway network, saw Blackpool develop rapidly. In 1889, the original Opera House was built in the Winter Gardens complex and two years later a start was made on the world famous Tower. Completed in 1894, **Blackpool Tower**, modelled on the

Meols Hall, Southport

Eiffel Tower in Paris, stands 518 feet high. The **North Pier**, designed by the peerless Eugenius Birch, was opened at the beginning of the 1863 season; it soon became the place to promenade and is now a listed building. The **Pleasure Beach**, which boasts its own railway station, is an attraction that continues to be extended and improved. The famous Blackpool Trams provide enjoyable trips along the front and out to these less busy sides of the town.

A couple of miles inland, **Marton Mere** is a Wildlife Trust bird reserve where more than 160 species have been recorded.

South of Blackpool lies **Lytham St Anne's**, a quiet place that was a small port before the expansion of Blackpool. As its neighbour grew, Lyham developed into a genteel, elegant resort famous for its Victorian and Edwardian architecture. Royal Lytham and St Anne's golf course is one of the finest links courses in the country and a regular host of the Open.

POULTON-LE-FYLDE

13 miles NW of Preston on the A586

The Romans were in the area and it was probably their handiwork that constructed the Danes Pad, an ancient trackway. The town developed as a commercial centre for the surrounding agricultural communities and its Market Place remains its focal point.

Strolling around Poulton-le-Fylde now, it is hard to imagine that the town was once a seaport. But

until relatively recently ships sailed up the River Wyre to **Skippool Creek**, now home to the Blackpool and Fleetwood Yacht Club.

Along the banks of the River Wyre is the Wyre Estuary Country Park, an excellent place for walking and discovering the area.

FLEETWOOD

17 miles NW of Preston on the A587

The town's **Museum**, overlooking the River Wyre, illustrates Fleetwood's links with the fishing industry that suffered greatly from the Icelandic cod wars. However, Fleetwood's real claim to fame is the Fisherman's Friend – a staggeringly successful lozenge made from liquorice, capsicum, eucalyptus and methanol that was used by fishermen to relieve sore throats and bronchial trouble caused by the freezing conditions found in the northern Atlantic waters.

BLACKBURN

The largest town in east Lancashire, Blackburn is notable for its shopping malls, celebrated three-day market, modern cathedral, and Thwaites Brewery, one of the biggest independent brewers of real ale in the north of England. Hard though it may be to imagine today, at the height of the textile industry, Blackburn was the biggest weaving town in the world. In 1931, it received arguably its most influential visitor when Mahatma Gandhi toured the area on a study trip of Lancashire's textile

261 THE FARMERS ARMS

Great Eccleston

A much-loved village inn serving a fine selection of home-cooked dishes.

🍴 *see page 540*

262 THE MYERSCOUGH

Balderstone, nr Blackburn

A handsome inn on the A59, with wide-ranging menus, Robinsons ales, a good wine list and comfortable rooms for B&B.

🍴 🛏 *see page 541*

263 THE DOG INN

Whalley

A popular village inn serving 6 real ales and a good choice of lunchtime food.

see page 542

264 THE ASPINALL ARMS

Mitton, nr Clitheroe

A very pleasant, civilised refreshment stop or a base for anyone with business in the area or tourists discovering the local places of interest.

see page 543

Whalley Abbey, nr Blackburn

manufacture. Examples of the early machines, including James Hargreaves' Spinning Jenny and his carding machine, invented in 1760, can be seen at the **Lewis Textile Museum**.

In 1926 the Diocese of Blackburn was created and St Mary's Church, built in 1826, became the Cathedral of the Bishop of Blackburn.

Just to the northeast of Blackburn lies the charming village of Whalley, home of the well-preserved 13th century **Whalley Abbey**.

AROUND BLACKBURN

CLITHEROE

10 miles NE of Blackburn on the A671

This old stone town, just south of the Forest of Bowland, has always been considered the forest's capital

and it is also Lancashire's second oldest borough, receiving its first market charter in 1147. Clitheroe is dominated by its 800-year-old **Castle**, standing on a limestone crag high above the town but now little more than a ruin. The **Castle Museum** includes reconstructions of a clogger's workshop, a printer's shop, and a lead mine. Nearby **Pendle Hill** is a place rich in history and legend, famous for the tragic story of the Pendle Witches. In the early 17th century, several women of the area were imprisoned in Lancaster Castle as a result of their seemingly evil practices and, having been found guilty, were publicly hanged.

To the west of Pendle Hill's summit is Apronfull Hill, a Bronze Age burial site. Also to the northeast lies Sawley Abbey, founded in the 13th century by the Cistercian monks of Fountains Abbey.

COLNE

14½ miles NE of Blackburn on the A6068

Before the Industrial Revolution turned this area into a valley devoted to the production of cotton cloth, Colne was a small market town that specialised in wool. In the centre of the town, next to the War Memorial, is the statue of Lawrence Hartley, the bandmaster on the ill-fated *Titanic* who heroically stayed at his post with his musicians and played *Nearer my God to Thee* as the liner sank beneath the waves of the icy Atlantic in 1912. Colne is also the unlikely home of the **British in India Museum**, where exhibits covering many aspects of the British rule over the subcontinent are housed.

To the northeast lies the **Earby Mines Museum** with a collection of lead mining tools and equipment used in the Yorkshire Dales.

ACCRINGTON

4½ miles E of Blackburn on the A680

This attractive Victorian market town is the home of the **Haworth Art Gallery**, which houses the largest collection of Tiffany glass in Europe. The collection was presented to the town by Joseph Briggs, an Accrington man, who worked with Louis Tiffany in New York for nearly 40 years.

Close by is another typical Lancashire textile town, **Oswaldtwistle**, which could be considered to be the birthplace of the industry since it was while staying here that James Hargreaves invented his famous Spinning Jenny in 1764.

BURNLEY

10 miles E of Blackburn on the A646

A cotton town rich in history and the largest in this area of east Lancashire. With the Industrial Revolution and the building of the Leeds and Liverpool Canal, Burnley grew to become the world's leading producer of cotton cloth. A walk along the towpath of the canal leads through an area known as the Weavers' Triangle – an area of spinning mills and weaving sheds; foundries where steam engines and looms were made; canal-side warehouses and domestic buildings. On the outskirts of town is the **Towneley Hall Art Gallery and Museum**.

To the west of Burnley is Gawthorpe Hall, a splendid 17th century house that was restored with a flourish of Victorian elegance during the 1850s. Beautiful period furnishings are enhanced by the ornately decorated ceilings and the original wood-panelled walls, making the perfect setting for the nationally important Kay-Shuttleworth needlework and lace collection.

DARWEN

4 miles S of Blackburn on the A666

The town is dominated by **Darwen Tower**, built to commemorate the Diamond Jubilee of Queen Victoria in 1897 and situated high on the moor. Another striking landmark is the chimney of the **India Mill**, constructed out of hand-made bricks and built to resemble the

265 THE PENDLE INN

Barley, nr Burnley

An outstanding family-run country inn, with local ales, excellent food and superb accommodation.

see page 542

187

266 THE WHITE BULL

Ribchester

Food is the star at an outstanding hostelry that attracts patrons from all over the region.

 see page 544

campanile (belltower) in St Mark's Square, Venice.

BOLTON

12 miles S of Blackburn on the A666

During the Civil War, the town saw one of the bloodiest episodes of the conflict when James Stanley, Earl of Derby, was brought back here by Cromwell's troops after the Royalists had been defeated. In a savage act of revenge for the massacre his army had brought on the town early in the troubles, Stanley was executed and his severed head and body, in separate caskets, were taken back to the family burial place at Ormskirk.

Impressive buildings here include 14th century **Smithills Hall** and the late 15th century **Hall-i'-th'-Wood**, a fine example of a wealthy merchant's house. One of Bolton's most recent attractions is the state-of-the-art **Reebok Stadium**, home of Bolton Wanderers FC.

Six miles east of Bolton lies **Bury**, another typical Lancashire mill town that is more famous for

its inhabitants that its buildings. Over the centuries the town has given the world the Pilkington family of glassworks fame, John Kay, the inventor of the flying shuttle, and Robert Peel, the politician who repealed the Corn Laws and founded the modern police force. On the outskirts of the town lies **Burrs Country Park** which, as well as offering a wide range of activities, also has an interesting industrial trail around the historic mill site.

Further east again is **Rochdale**, another cotton town, most famous as being the birthplace of the Co-operative Movement; in carefully restored Toad Lane, to the north of the town centre, is the world's first Co-op shop, the Rochdale Pioneers.

RIBCHESTER

5 miles NW of Blackburn on the B6245

Situated on the banks of the River Ribble, the village is famous for its **Roman Fort** on the northern riverbank, first established by Gnaeus Julius Agricola in AD 79. Although little of the fort's walls remain, the granary and its hypocaust have been excavated, revealing interesting finds that can be seen in the fort's **Roman Museum**.

LANCASTER

The capital town of Lancashire boasts a long and interesting history. It was in the 10th century that Athelstan, the grandson of Alfred the Great, had lands in the area, and during the reign of

Ribchester Roman Fort

188

William the Conqueror large parts of what is now Lancashire were given by the grateful king to his cousin Roger of Pitou, who made his base at Lancaster. Queen Elizabeth II retains the title of Duke of Lancaster. Within yards of the railway station lies **Lancaster Castle**, a great medieval fortress founded by the Normans to keep out Scottish invaders and strengthened by John of Gaunt, Duke of Lancaster. In Church Street stands the 17th century Judge's Lodging, which now houses two separate museums, the **Museum of Childhood** and the **Gillow and Town House Museum**.

The town's rich maritime history is celebrated at St George's Quay, which, with its great stone warehouses and superb Custom House, is now an award-winning **Maritime Museum**.

One of the first sights visitors see of Lancaster is the great green copper dome of the impressive **Ashton Memorial**, built by the linoleum manufacturer Lord Ashton in memory of his wife and a landmark for miles around that stands on a hilltop in the centre of the splendid Edwardian Williamson Park. Pevsner described it as 'the grandest monument in England'.

Lancaster Castle

AROUND LANCASTER

CARNFORTH

5 miles N of Lancaster on the A6

Not many towns are best known for their stations, but Carnforth is one of them: it was used as the setting for the 1940s film classic *Brief Encounter*. The old engine sheds and sidings are now occupied by Steamtown, one of the largest steam railway centres in the north of England.

Just to the north lies **Leighton Hall**, a fine early 19th century house that is now owned by a branch of the Gillow family; the fine furniture seen in the hall

189

267 THE COBBLED CORNER

Chipping

Home-made savoury and sweet treats in a delightful village café

 see page 544

268 THE SUN INN

Chipping, Forest of Bowland

A handsome old village inn serving four real ales and excellent traditional pub food.

see page 545

•

The Hark to Bounty inn in Slaidburn was originally called The Dog, but one day in 1875 the local Hunt gathered here. A visiting squire, listening to the hounds outside, clearly made out the cry of his favourite hound rising above the others and exclaimed "Hark to Bounty!". The landlord was so impressed by this unrestrained show of delight that he changed the name of his pub there and then.

•

reflects the trade that made the family fortune.

FOREST OF BOWLAND

3 miles E of Lancaster

Designated an Area of Outstanding Natural Beauty in February 1964, this large and scenic area is a paradise for walkers and country lovers that is dotted with picturesque villages. Following the Norman Conquest, Bowland became part of the Honour of Clitheroe and the vast estates that belonged to the de Lacy family. In 1399, when the then Duke of Lancaster came to the throne as Henry IV, Bowland finally became one of nearly 100 royal hunting forests.

The remains of a Roman road can be clearly seen traversing the land and many of the villages in the area have names dating back to the Saxon period. Perhaps the most celebrated of the many routes across Bowland is the minor road from Lancaster to Clitheroe that crosses the Abbeydale Moor and the Trough of Bowland before descending into the lovely Hodder Valley around Dunsop Bridge.

At the heart of the Forest is **Slaidburn**, a pretty village of stone cottages and cobbled pavements whose 13th century public house Hark to Bounty contains an old court room where, from around 1250, the Chief Court of Bowland, or Halmote, was held.

MORECAMBE

3 miles W of Lancaster on the A589

Featuring prominently on the Lancashire coastline, Morecambe has long been one of the most popular seaside resorts in the North, and it can truly be said to enjoy one of the finest views from its promenade of any resort in England – a magnificent sweep of coastline and bay, looking across to the Lakeland mountains. Many buildings date from Morecambe's heyday as a holiday destination, including the Midland Hotel, built in the early 1930s to designs by Oliver Hill.

Near the Stone jetty is the **Eric Morecambe Statue** with words from the song *Bring Me Sunshine* carved into the granite steps. The comedian was born John Eric Bartholomew in 1926.

Morecambe Bay, a vast wide, flat tidal plain situated between Lancashire and Cumbria, is the home of many forms of marine life as well as being a very popular and important habitat for birds. It's also famous for a great delicacy – Morecambe Bay potted shrimps. The Bay is also very treacherous, and over the years many have fallen victim to the tides and the quicksands. In medieval times this perilous track formed part of the main west coast route from England to Scotland, and the monks of Furness would act as guides for travellers who wished to avoid the long overland route. Today, **Cross Bay Walks** are led by the Queen's Guide to the Sands.

Leicestershire

Rolling fields, wooded gorges and meandering waterways make Leicestershire a perfect place for exploring – on foot, by bicycle or by boat. The county is divided into two almost equal parts by the River Soar, which flows northwards into the River Trent. The Grand Union Canal threads its way through South Leicestershire, while the Ashby Canal passes close to Bosworth Battlefield, in the west of the county. Leicester, the capital, is one of the oldest towns in the country and retains outstanding monuments of almost every age of English history. Agriculture and industry go hand in hand here: the long-haired local sheep produced fine woollens, and by the end of the 17th century the now worldwide hosiery trade had been established. Loughborough has been famous for making bells for more than 100 years, while at Melton Mowbray pork pies have been made on a commercial scale since 1830. King Richard III spent his last days in the county before his death at the Battle of Bosworth in 1485, a battle that changed the course of British history.

ACCOMMODATION

FOOD & DRINK

LEICESTER

Designated Britain's first 'environment city' in recognition of its commitment to green issues, Leicester has numerous parks and open spaces but also a rich architectural heritage, with no fewer than 350 listed buildings. At the heart of Leicester's heritage is **Castle Park**, the old town, an area of gardens, churches, museums and other fine buildings. Here are concentrated many of the city's main attractions: **Castle Gardens** opened as a park in 1926; Castle Motte, a man-made mound built around 1070 by Leicester's first Norman lord; the **Church of St Mary de Castro**, founded in 1107 and still in use; the Great Hall of **Leicester Castle** built in the 12th century; and **Newarke Houses Museum**, a museum of social and domestic history contained in two 16th century houses.

Leicester's diverse cultural and religious heritage is represented by the **Jain Centre**, the **Guru Nanak Sikh Museum**; the **Jewry Wall and Museum**; and the **Church of St Martin**, which was in existence before 1086, was extended in the 14th and 15th centuries, restored in the 19th century and hallowed as the Cathedral of Leicester in 1927. One of the very finest buildings in the city is the **Guildhall**, built around 1390 for the Guild of Corpus Christi and used as the Town Hall from the late 15th century until 1876. Across the road from the Cathedral is **Wygston's House**, a part timber-framed building, one of the oldest in the city, which now houses displays of fashion, textiles and crafts.

AROUND LEICESTER

HINCKLEY

11½ miles SW of Leicester on the A47

An old town whose Fair is mentioned in Shakespeare's Henry IV. In Lower Bond Street, a row of restored 17th century thatched framework knitters' cottages is home to Hinckley and District Museum. It was in Hinckley that Joseph Hansom invented and demonstrated his Patent Safety Cab in 1835. To the east lies Burbage Common and Woods Country Park, which contains one of the largest areas of grassland in the area.

MARKET BOSWORTH

11 miles W of Leicester off the A447

This market town is most famous as the battle site for the turning point in the Wars of the Roses, when in 1485 the forces of King Richard III were routed by those of Henry Tudor, who took the throne as Henry VII. The battle was immortalised in Shakespeare's play *Richard III*, where the King is heard to cry, "*My kingdom for a horse.*" **Bosworth Battlefield** lies to the southwest of the town and the Visitor Centre has details of the Battle and numerous artefacts and displays on the Tudor period.

Market Bosworth Country Park is one of many beautiful open spaces in the area whilst another is Bosworth Water Trust's Leisure and

Water Park to the west of town. This is a 50-acre leisure park with 20 acres of lakes for sailing, boardsailing and fishing.

To the northwest of Market Bosworth lies **Twycross Zoo**, home to a wide variety of animals that include a famous primate collection, from tiny pygmy marmosets to huge Western lowland gorillas. To the north of Market Bosworth is a village with the wonderful name of Barton-in-the-Beans. The county was apparently once known as 'bean-belly' Leicestershire, on account of the heavy reliance on bean crops that formed part of the staple diet in needy times.

The composer George Frederick Handel regularly stayed at the nearby Gopsall Estate, where he composed the music for his glorious *Messiah*. The grandson of the estate's owner completed the job by writing the words.

MOUNTSORREL

6 miles N of Leicester off the A6

Situated on the banks of the River Soar, the village is home to **Stonehurst Family Farm and Motor Museum**, where the highlights range from baby rabbits and guinea pigs in cuddle corner to an impressive collection of vintage vehicles, including Leicestershire's first motor bus.

LOUGHBOROUGH

10 miles N of Leicester on the A6

There are two attractions at Loughborough that visitors certainly should not miss. In 1858,

the bell foundry of John Taylor moved here from Oxford and the **John Taylor Bell Foundry Museum** covers all aspects of bell-founding from early times. The town is also the headquarters of the **Great Central Railway**, which runs steam trains every weekend and Bank Holiday, and daily in June, July, August and local school holidays.

COALVILLE

11 miles NW of Leicester on the A511

Originally called Long Lane, the town sprang up on a bleak common when Whitwick Colliery was opened in 1824. **Snibston Discovery Park**, built on the site of the former Snibston Colliery, provides the opportunity to explore a unique mixture of nature, history, art, science and technology with the help of the latest interactive technology.

To the northeast of Coalville, in a beautiful elevated position in Charnwood Forest, is **Mount St Bernard Abbey**, the first Catholic

270 THE GRANGE COURTYARD GUEST ACCOMMODATION

Shepshed

Twenty cottage rooms provide comfortable B&B or self-catering accommodation in a quiet courtyard.

 see page 545

271 THE CROFT GUEST HOUSE

Shepshed

A friendly, well-kept guest house in the centre of Shepshed, with nine comfortable bedrooms and good secure parking.

 see page 547

Snibston Discovery Park, Coalville

193

Ashby-de-la-Zouch Castle

multipurpose forest providing a full range of environmental, recreational and social benefits for current and future generations.

KEGWORTH

15½ miles NW of Leicester on the A6

A large village with many architectural reminders of its days as a framework-knitting centre. Topics covered at the **Kegworth Museum** include the knitting industry, saddlery, air transport and photography, and postcards of the 1920s. To the west lies **Donington Park**, home of the **Donington Grand Prix Collection** with over 130 exhibits in five halls covering 100 years of motor racing history.

MELTON MOWBRAY

272 THE OLD THATCHED INN

Stanton-under Bardon

A smartly refurbished village inn with a varied menu of home-cooked dishes.

🍴 see page 548

abbey to be founded in England after the Reformation.

ASHBY-DE-LA-ZOUCH

16 miles NW of Leicester on the A511

During the Civil War, **Ashby Castle** was besieged for over a year by the Parliamentarian Army until the Royalists surrendered in 1646. After the war the castle was partly destroyed to prevent its further use as a centre of resistance and almost wholly forgotten until Sir Walter Scott used the castle as the setting in Ivanhoe for the archery competition that Robin Hood won by splitting the shaft of his opponent's arrow in the bull's eye.

To the east lies the **National Forest**, a truly accessible,

This bustling market town is, of course, home to the pork pie, one of the most traditional of English delicacies. The Melton Hunt Cake is another local speciality and Stilton, the 'king of English cheeses', is also made here. The cheese has the longest history, dating back possibly as far as the 14th century, and the town became the market centre for Stilton.

In the town's oldest surviving bakery, **Ye Olde Pork Pie Shoppe**, visitors can watch the traditional hand-raising techniques and taste the pies and the Hunt cake. The **Melton Carnegie Museum** has displays devoted to Stilton cheese, pork pies and the history of fox hunting in the area; visitors can also learn about 'Painting the Town Red', an occasion in 1837 when the Marquis of Waterford and his pals decided to decorate the town with red paint after a night's drinking.

AROUND MELTON MOWBRAY

BELVOIR CASTLE

12 miles N of Melton off the A607

The present **Belvoir Castle**, the Leicestershire home of the Duke of Rutland, was completed in the early 19th century after previous buildings had been destroyed during the Wars of the Roses, the Civil War and in the major fire of 1816. Over-looking the lovely Vale of Belvoir, the castle's stunning interior contains notable collections of furniture and porcelain, silks and tapestries, sculptures and paintings, along with the **Queen's Royal Lancers Museum**. The grounds are as splendid as the castle and are used for medieval jousting tournaments on certain days in the summer.

WYMONDHAM

8 miles E of Melton off the B676

The six-sailed **Windmill**, dating from 1814, and partially restored, is one of only four of its kind in the country.

BURROUGH-ON-THE-HILL

5 miles S of Melton off the B6074

Burrough House, set in five acres of beautiful gardens, was a favourite meeting place of the Prince of Wales and Mrs Wallis Simpson in the 1930s. To the northeast of the village is **Burrough Hill**, an Iron Age hill fort.

MARKET HARBOROUGH

In 1645 Charles I made Market Harborough his headquarters and held a council of war here before the **Battle of Naseby**. The development of turnpike roads led to prosperity and the establishment of coaching inns in the town, many of them still in business. The canals and the railways transformed communications and manufacturing industry became established, the most notable company being R W & H Symington, creators of the Liberty Bodice. The **Harborough Museum** incorporates the **Symington Collection of Corsetry**.

AROUND MARKET HARBOROUGH

FOXTON

2 miles NW of Market Harborough off the A6

The most famous site on the county's canals is the **Flight of Ten Locks** on the Grand Union Canal, one of the great engineer Thomas Telford's most impressive constructions. In the **Canal Museum**, halfway down the flight, the steam-powered boat lift of 1900 is undergoing restoration, and there are several other buildings and bridges of interest (including a swing-bridge) in this pretty village.

273 THE CROWN

Asfordby

A warm welcome and good honest home cooking in an old coaching inn a short drive from Melton Mowbray.

see page 549

274 THE ROSE AT HOSE

Hose

A family-friendly village inn combining traditional values with contemporary styling.

see page 550

275 THE ROYAL HORSESHOES

Waltham-on-the-Wolds, nr Melton Mowbray

A convivial food-oriented pub with a warm welcome for families and comfortable rooms for B&B.

see page 551

276 THE TAVERN INN

Walcote

A great local favourite with a terrific host and a fine variety of food and drink

 see page 552

Rockingham Castle, nr Market Harborough

LUTTERWORTH

12 miles W of Market Harborough on the A4304

John Wycliffe was rector here under the tutelage of John of Gaunt. His instigation of an English translation of the Bible into English caused huge dissent. He died in 1384 and was buried in the church here, but when he was excommunicated in 1428 his body was exhumed and burned and his ashes scattered in the River Swift. Close to the church, **Lutterworth Museum** contains a wealth of local history from Roman times to World War II. Lutterworth is where Frank Whittle perfected the design of his jet engine.

About 3 miles southeast of Lutterworth and set in meadows beside the River Avon, **Stanford Hall** has been the home of the Cave family since 1430. The present house – pleasantly proportioned, dignified and serene, was built by the celebrated architect William Smith of Warwick in the 1690s. A superb staircase was added in around 1730, one of very few structural alterations to the house in its 300-year history: another was the Ballroom, which contains paintings that once belonged to Bonnie Prince Charlie's younger brother, Henry Stuart.

Lincolnshire

Although it is the second largest county in England, Lincolnshire remains relatively unknown. It is largely rural and has some of the richest farmland in the country producing, particularly, potatoes, sugar beet and flowers. The county has strong historical connections with Holland and Scandinavia and is blessed with many picturesque villages and towns including the majestic county capital Lincoln with its marvellous cathedral, historic Stamford, acclaimed as the finest stone town in England, and Grantham, the birthplace of Margaret Thatcher. Along with its extensive coastline, which boasts a number of traditional seaside resorts, Lincolnshire has also played a part in history. It is home to the world's first military air academy, RAF Cranwell; the Dambusters – 617 Squadron – were stationed near Woodhall Spa; and RAF Coningsby is home to the Battle of Britain Memorial Flight. The port of Grimsby is England's main fishing port.

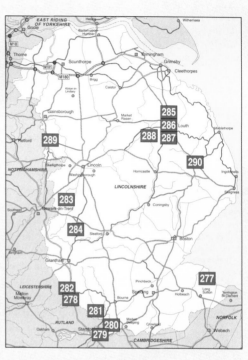

ACCOMMODATION

FOOD & DRINK

SPALDING

This small market town is known for its annual **Flower Parade**, which is held in early May, when marching bands lead a succession of colourful floats through the town. Spalding is an interesting place to stroll around, and the jewel in its crown is undoubtedly **Ayscoughfee Hall Museum and Gardens**, a well-preserved medieval mansion standing in attractive riverside gardens that houses, among other displays, a permanent exhibit honouring the explorer and oceanographer Captain Matthew Flinders.

A couple of miles south of Spalding, the **Gordon Boswell Romany Museum** has a colourful collection of Romany Vardos (caravans), carts and harnesses. To the north is the **Pinchbeck Engine and Land Drainage Museum**, which illustrates how the South Holland Fen was drained. Also here, at Pinchbeck, are the **Spalding Bulb Museum** and the **Spalding Tropical Forest**.

AROUND SPALDING

HOLBEACH

10 miles E of Spalding on the A151/B1168

An agreeable market town in one of the county's largest parishes. The antiquarian William Stukeley and the shot-putter Geoff Capes are sons of Holbeach.

BOSTON

15 miles NE of Spalding on the A16

Boston's most famous landmark is the tower of the massive 14th century **St Botolph's Church**; it's popularly known as the **Boston Stump** – a real misnomer since it soars to 272 feet and is visible for 30 miles or more.

Another striking building is the 15th century **Guildhall** that for 300 years served as the Town Hall and now houses the town Museum. It was here, in the Guildhall cells, that the Pilgrim Fathers were held in 1607 while they tried to escape to the religiously tolerant Netherlands. The town is home to the tallest working windmill in Britain, the **Maud Foster Windmill**, which is unusual in having five sails.

CROWLAND

8½ miles S of Spalding on the B1166

Founded by King Ethelbald of Mercia in the 8th century, the now ruined **Crowland Abbey** seen today dates from the 12th century and is the third to have been built on the site. The town is noted for its extraordinary 'Bridge without a River': when it was built in the 1300s, **Trinity Bridge** provided a dry crossing over the confluence of three small streams which have since dried up.

GRIMSTHORPE

12 miles W of Spalding on the A151

The village is home to **Grimsthorpe Castle**, which when viewed from the north is a stately 18th century palace; from the south, it is a homely Tudor dwelling. The Tudor part of the house was built at incredible speed in order to provide

---

On the outskirts of the town can be seen more of Spalding's heritage: the Pode Hole Pumping Station preserves one of the steam engines installed in 1825 to drain the local fens.

•

277 THE RISING SUN

Gedney Drove End

Secluded country inn well worth seeking out for its cosy ambience and good honest home cooking.

 see page 553

278 THE BLUE COW INN

South Witham

A delightful village inn serving decent food and beer from its own brewery. Also rooms for B&B.

 see page 553

a convenient lodging place in Lincolnshire for Henry VIII on his way north to meet James V of Scotland in York. The royal visit took place in 1541 but the honour of the royal presence was tarnished by the adultery that allegedly took place here between Henry's fourth wife, Catherine Howard, and an attractive young courtier, Thomas Culpepper. A subsequently passed law declared it treason for an unchaste woman to marry the king, and both Catherine and her ardent courtier paid the ultimate price for their night of passion.

STAMFORD

An attractive market town with unspoilt Georgian streets and squares, Stamford is also noted for its rich cluster of outstanding churches. The most ancient ecclesiastical building is **St Leonard's Priory**, founded by the Benedictines in the 11th century,

and a fine example of Norman architecture.

Secular buildings of note include the **Museum of Almshouse Life** and the **Stamford Museum**, which includes a display celebrating one of the town's most notable residents, Daniel Lambert, the keeper of Leicester Jail, who earned a solid living by exhibiting himself as the world's heaviest man; on his death in 1809 he weighed nearly 53 stone. Other famous residents include the flamboyant conductor and Promenaders' favourite Sir Malcolm Sargent ('Flash Harry'), who lies buried in the town cemetery, and William Cecil, 1st Lord Burghley, who was Elizabeth I's Chief Secretary of State. **Burghley House** is a wonderfully opulent Elizabethan mansion that houses a magnificent collection of treasures. The **Burghley Horse Trials** are held in the glorious grounds each year at the end of August.

279 THE JOLLY BREWER

Stamford

A convivial pub serving cask ales and old favourites on the chalkboard menu.

see page 554

280 THE HARE 'N' HOUNDS

Greatford, nr Stamford

A hospitable village pub serving a good choice of beers, wines and food. Four pitches for caravans.

see page 554

281 THE WILLOUGHBY ARMS

Little Bytham, nr Stamford

A handsome hostelry serving a good range of real ales (quarterly beer festival) and a varied choice of home-cooked dishes. Three superior rooms for B&B.

see page 555

Burghley House, nr Stamford

Skillington

A lovely old village inn with traditional home cooking and three new and luxurious guest bedrooms.

 see page 555

Norton Disney

A traditional village inn with a fine reputation for its locally sourced home-cooked food.

 see page 556

Caythorpe, nr Grantham

Well-loved classic English country pub serving a good range of home cooking.

 see page 556

AROUND STAMFORD

WOOLSTHORPE-BY-COLSTERWORTH

14 miles N of Stamford off the B6403

It was at Woolsthorpe Manor that Isaac Newton was born in 1642 and where the Father of Modern Science made some of his greatest discoveries. Descendants of the tree from which that famous apple dropped can still be seen in the garden. In a bedroom in the house is displayed Pope's famous epitaph on Newton's birth: *'Nature and Nature's laws lay hid in night: God said, Let Newton be! And there was light'*. A 17th century barn holds a **Science Discovery Centre** that helps to explain some of his achievements.

Newton's achievements were legion, including research into colour and light. He also took a major role in reforming the corrupt system of the nation's coinage and from 1699 until his death in 1727 he held the post of Master of the Mint. Widely praised, he was more modest about his own achievements: *'If I have seen further than others, it is because I was standing on the shoulders of giants.'*

GRANTHAM

This ancient market town on the banks of the River Witham has some pleasing old buildings including Grantham House, which dates back to around 1380, and the Angel and Royal Hotel, where King John held court and where Richard III signed the death warrant of the 2nd Duke of Buckingham in 1483.

Grantham is perhaps best known as being the childhood home of Margaret Roberts, later Thatcher. **Grantham Museum** has special exhibits devoted to both Lady Thatcher and Sir Isaac Newton.

AROUND GRANTHAM

SLEAFORD

10 miles E of Grantham on the B1517

Inhabited since the Iron Age and home to a massive Roman mint, Sleaford is a busy market town with one of the oldest stone church towers in the country. Other features of interest include the Money's Mill, a 70 feet high tower that was erected in 1796 to allow large quantities of corn to be brought here by barge and offloaded right outside the door.

To the northwest of Sleaford is the RAF College, **Cranwell**, which opened in 1920 as the first Military Air Academy in the world. The **Cranwell Aviation Heritage Centre** tells the Cranwell story and that of the many other RAF bases in the region.

LINCOLN

Lincoln Cathedral occupies a magnificent hilltop location, its towers soaring high above the Lincolnshire lowlands being visible for miles around. Among its many superb features are the magnificent open nave, stained-glass windows incorporating the 14th century Bishop's Eye and Dean's Eye, and the glorious Angel Choir, whose carvings include the Lincoln Imp, the unofficial symbol of the city. The imposing ruins of the **Bishops Old Palace**, in the shadow of the Cathedral, reveal the sumptuous lifestyle of the wealthy medieval bishops whose authority stretched from the Humber to the Thames.

Other notable buildings include **Lincoln Castle**, which dates from 1068 and houses one of the four original versions of the Magna Carta; the **Jews House**, which dates from about 1170 and is thought to be the oldest domestic building in England to survive intact; and the most impressive surviving part of the old town walls, the Stonebow, which spans the High Street pedestrianised shopping mall. Lincolnshire's largest social history museum is the **Museum of Lincolnshire Life** that occupies an extensive barracks built for the Royal North Lincoln Militia in 1857. The newest museum in the county, opened in 2005, is **The Collection**, a major centre of art and archaeology running alongside the Usher Gallery.

Bishops Old Palace, Lincoln

AROUND LINCOLN

MARKET RASEN

14 miles NE of Lincoln on the A631

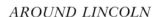

Taking its name from the River Rase, Market Rasen was described by Charles Dickens as being "the sleepiest town in England." Much of the central part is a conservation area and includes two ecclesiastical buildings of some note: the **Centenary Wesleyan Chapel** of 1863 boasts an impressive frontage, while **St Thomas's Church** has a typical 15th century tower of local ironstone. Market Rasen Racecourse stages popular National Hunt meetings throughout the year.

LOUTH

24 miles NE of Lincoln off the A16

One of the county's most appealing towns, Louth lies on the Greenwich Meridian beside the River Lud on

•

To the west of Lincoln is Doddington Hall, a grand Elizabethan mansion completed in 1600 by the architect Robert Smythson, and standing now exactly as then, with wonderful formal gardens, a gatehouse and a family church.

•

285 MELANIE'S

Louth

Top-notch cooking with fine wines and impeccable service in a superb new restaurant.

see page 557

286 THE NEWMARKET INN & HURDLES BISTRO

Louth

A friendly, traditional inn where a great choice of cuisine is a magnet for food-lovers.

see page 558

287 YE OLD WHYTE SWANNE

Louth

The oldest pub in Louth, with old-world charm, great-value food and six rooms for B&B guests.

 see page 558

the eastern edge of the Wolds. The town is best known for being the home of Alfred Lord Tennyson, who lodged here with his grandmother while attending the King Edward VI School. **Broadbank**, which now houses the **Louth Museum**, is an attractive little building with some interesting artefacts, including some amazing locally-woven carpets that were displayed at the Paris Exhibition in 1867. Louth's magnificent **Church of St James** has a wonderful Perpendicular Gothic steeple, the tallest steeple in Britain at almost

300 feet. To the southwest of Louth lies Donignton-on-Bain, a peaceful Wolds village on the Viking Way that runs 147 miles from the Humber Bridge to Oakham in Rutland. The way is marked by Viking helmet symbols.

GAINSBOROUGH

15 miles NW of Lincoln on A156

Britain's most inland port is located at the highest navigable point on the River Trent for seagoing vessels. During the 17th and 18th centuries in particular, the town prospered greatly, and although

Gainsborough Old Hall

many of the lofty warehouses lining the river bank have been demolished, enough remain to give some idea of its flourishing past.

The town's most famous building is the enchanting Gainsborough Old Hall, a complete medieval and Tudor hall house, and one of the most striking architectural gems in the county. The hall was built in the 1470s by Sir Thomas Burgh, who entertained Richard III in the Great Hall. The hall is generally considered one of the best preserved medieval manor houses in the country.

Another notable building in Gainsborough is Marshall's Britannia Works, a proud Victorian reminder of Gainsborough's once thriving engineering industry.

OLD BOLINGBROKE

22 miles E of Lincoln off the A155

Originally built in the reign of William I, **Bolingbroke Castle** later became the property of John of Gaunt whose son, later Henry IV, was born at the castle in 1367. During the Civil War, Bolingbroke Castle was besieged by Parliamentary forces in 1643 and fell into disuse soon after.

Just to the south, at East Kirkby, is the **Lincolnshire Aviation Heritage Centre**, based in the old control tower. Exhibits include a Lancaster bomber, a Shackleton, military vehicles and a wartime blast shelter.

WOODHALL SPA

14 miles SE of Lincoln on the B1191

Woodhall became a spa town by

accident when a shaft sunk in search of coal found mineral-rich water. In 1838 a pump room and baths were built, to be joined later by hydro hotels, and the arrival of the railway in 1855 accelerated Woodhall's popularity. By the early 1900s, the spa had fallen out of favour and the associated buildings disappeared one by one, but this beautifully maintained village has retained its decorous spa atmosphere.

Woodhall Spa had close connections with 617 Squadron, the **Dambusters**, during World War II. The Petwood House Hotel was used as the officers' mess and memorabilia of those days is displayed in the hotel's Squadron Bar. By the front door of the hotel lies one of Barnes Wallis' famous 'Bouncing Bombs' that were used in the attack on the Ruhr dams.

SKEGNESS

In the early 1800s Skegness was still a tiny fishing village but it was already becoming famous for its firm sandy beaches and bracing sea air. As late as 1871, the resident population of Skegness was only 239 but two years later the railway arrived and three years after that the local landowner, the Earl of Scarborough, built a new town to the north of the railway station. A huge pier, 1,843 feet long, was built in 1880, chosen from 44 designs submitted.

The famous slogan 'Skegness is SO Bracing', was first used on posters by the Great Northern

288 THE BLACK HORSE

Donnington-on-Bain

A fine old country inn with abundant period charm, a great choice of food and eight smart bedrooms.

 see page 559

289 THE BLACK SWAN GUEST HOUSE

Marton, nr Gainsborough

A very comfortable and characterful guest house in a Grade II listed former coaching inn. Super breakfasts.

see page 561

290 THE HAY WAIN MOTEL & RESTAURANT

Alford

Comfortable, practical accommodation and the warmth of a favourite local in a prime location on the A16.

see page 560

Railway in 1908 and appeared in many designs subsequently. In the best known of all the famous posters a jolly pipe-smoking fisherman is shown bouncing along the beach.

Natureland Seal Sanctuary on North Parade provides interest for all the family with its seals and baby seal rescue centre and numerous other animal attractions.

Just outside Skegness **Gibraltar Point National Nature Reserve** is a field station among the salt marshes and dunes with hides, waymarked routes and guided tours.

Yellowhammers and whitethroats nest here, and skylarks are more numerous than anywhere else in Britain.

AROUND SKEGNESS

MABLETHORPE

15 miles N of Skegness on the A52

The northernmost of the three popular Lincolnshire holiday resorts (Skegness and Sutton-on-Sea are the others) that almost form a chain along this stretch of fragile coast. Much of the original village of Mablethorpe has disappeared into the sea, including the medieval **Church of St Peter**. The Seal Sanctuary at North End is open every day from Easter to the end of September.

ALFORD

10 miles NW of Skegness on the A1104

Alford Manor House, built around 1660, claims the distinction of being the largest thatched manor house in England. Alford's **Five Sailed Windmill**, built of brick in 1813, stands a majestic six floors high and has five sails and four sets of grinding stones.

SCUNTHORPE

Much of Scunthorpe's industrial and social heritage is on display at the **North Lincolnshire Museum & Art Gallery** with exhibits that include an ironmonger's cottage.

Scunthorpe has also created a Heritage Trail which takes visitors through three of the parks created

Five Sailed Windmill, Alford

by Victorian benefactors - Scunthorpe is proud of its parks and gardens and has claimed the title of 'The Industrial Garden Town of rural North Lincolnshire'.

AROUND SCUNTHORPE

NORMANBY

4 miles N of Scunthorpe off the B1430

Normanby Hall was built in 1825 for the Sheffield family and extended in 1906. The 300-acre Park has plenty to see and enjoy, including a deer park, duck ponds, an ice house in the middle of the miniature railway circuit, a Victorian laundry and a walled garden. The **Normanby Hall Farming Museum** majors on rural life in the age of the heavy horse. Near the park gates, some picturesque estate cottages bear witness to the Sheffield family's reputation as good landlords.

BRIGG

7 miles E of Scunthorpe on the A10

King John was not universally admired but one of his more popular deeds was the granting of a charter (in 1205) which permitted this modest little town to hold an annual festivity on the 5th day of August. **Brigg Fair**, along with Widdecombe and Scarborough, has joined the trio of 'Best Known Fairs in England', celebrated in a traditional song and in a haunting tone poem based on Lincolnshire folk songs, composed by Frederick Delius in 1907. 800 years later, the fair still attracts horse traders from around the country, along with all the usual fun of the fair.

GRIMSBY

According to tradition it was a Dane called Grim who founded Grimsby. He had been ordered to drown the young Prince Havelock after the boy's father had been killed in battle. Grim could not bring himself to murder the child so he fled Denmark for England. After a tempestuous crossing of the North Sea, Grim and the boy arrived at the Humber estuary where he used the timbers of their boat to build a house on the shore. They lived by selling fish and salt, thus establishing the foundations of an industry for which Grimsby would become known the world over. A statue of Grim and the infant prince can be seen at the ~~Humberside~~ Polytechnic.

GRIMSBY COLLAGE

•

A question for football anoraks. Why does Grimsby Town Football Club play all its games away? Answer: Because the Mariners' ground is actually in Cleethorpes, a resort which has spread northwards more or less to merge into Grimsby.

•

Norfolk

Norfolk is home to Britain's finest wetland areas, the Broads, which cover some 220 square miles to the northwest of Great Yarmouth. Three main rivers, the Ant, the Thurne and the Bure, thread their way through the marshes, providing some 120 miles of navigable waterways. This area is also a refuge for many species of endangered birds and plants, and during the summer and autumn the Broads are a favourite stopping off point for migrating birds. The eastern coast, from Great Yarmouth to Sheringham, is almost one continuous strip of excellent sandy beaches, dotted with charming holiday resorts such as Caister-on-Sea, Mundesley and Cromer. Inland lies the county town, Norwich, which is famous for its Norman cathedral, its castle and a wealth of other historic buildings. Norwich is also the home of mustard and its best-known producer J & J Colman.

It is surprising to find one of England's most important medieval ports, King's Lynn, at the southern end of the underwater maze of sandbanks of the Wash but then, of course, keels were shallower. King's Lynn is still a busy port today; several ancient ports along the North Norfolk coast are now holiday resorts. A little way inland is the Royal family's country estate of Sandringham.

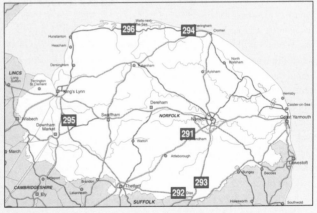

ACCOMMODATION

291 Elm Lodge, Wymondham   pg 207, 561
296 The Globe Inn, Wells-next-the-Sea   pg 214, 563

FOOD & DRINK

292 Amandines Café Restaurant, Diss   pg 208, 562
293 The Crown Inn, Pulham Market   pg 208, 561
294 The Lantern Restaurant, Sheringham   pg 210, 562
295 The Kings Arms, Shouldham,
        nr King's Lynn   pg 213, 562
296 The Globe Inn, Wells-next-the-Sea   pg 214, 563
297 The Maltsters Country Inn, Badby   pg 219, 563

THETFORD

The town's strategic position, at the confluence of the Rivers Thet and Little Ouse, have made this an important settlement for centuries and excavations have revealed an Iron Age enclosure that is thought to have been the site of Boudicca's Palace.

In the charming heart of the town is the striking **Ancient House**, a 15th century timber-framed house that is home to the **Museum of Thetford Life** containing replicas of the Thetford Treasure. The **King's House** is named after James I who was a frequent visitor here from 1608-18. The town's 12th century **Cluniac Priory** is mostly in ruins, though the impressive 14th century gatehouse still stands. Thetford's industrial heritage is vividly displayed in the **Burrell Steam Museum**, which has full-size working steam engines, re-created workshops and vintage agricultural machinery.

To the west of the town lies **Thetford Forest**, the most extensive lowland forest in Britain, planted by the Forestry Commission in 1922. In the heart of the forest are **Grimes Graves**, the earliest major industrial site discovered in Europe. At these Neolithic flint mines, Stone Age labourers extracted materials for their axes and knives from the chamber 30 feet below ground.

On the edge of Thetford Forest are the ruins of **Thetford Warren Lodge**, built in the early 15th century when the surrounding area was preserved for farming rabbits – a major element of the medieval diet.

AROUND THETFORD

WYMONDHAM

19 miles NE of Thetford on the B1172

The town is home to one of the oddest ecclesiastical buildings in the country, **Wymondham Abbey**, which was founded in 1107 by William d'Albini, butler to King Henry I. Its two towers dominate the town's skyline.

Although many of the town's oldest houses were destroyed by fire in 1615, some older buildings escaped, including 12th century **Becket's Chapel**. Also of interest is **The Bridewell** which was built in 1785 as a model prison and reputedly served as a model for the penitentiaries established in the United States. It is now the **Wymondham Heritage Museum**. Displays include brushmaking and Kett's Rebellion.

Burrell Steam Museum, Thetford

292 AMANDINES CAFÉ RESTAURANT

Diss

A charming courtyard setting for this top-notch Vegetarian café restaurant open Tuesday to Saturday from 10am until 4pm plus Special Saturday nights

 see page 562

293 THE CROWN INN

Pulham Market

A charming old thatched village inn with a welcome for all who pass through the door. Bar and fine dining menus.

 see page 561

Wymondham's historic Railway Station was built in 1845 on the Great Eastern's Norwich to Ely line and, still in use, the buildings house a railway museum.

BANHAM

12 miles E of Thetford off the B1077

To the southwest of the village lies **Banham Zoo**, home to some of the world's most endangered animals including monkeys and apes – a particular concern here. A new giraffe enclosure opened at Easter 2008.

DISS

16 miles E of Thetford on the A1066

Situated on the northern bank of the River Waveney, which forms the boundary between Suffolk and Norfolk, Diss is an old market town that developed on the hill overlooking The Mere. **Diss Museum** in the market place is packed with information about the town's past, its trade, famous people and 'orrible murders.

Just northeast of Diss, is the **100th Bomb Group Memorial Museum**, a tribute to the US 8th Air Force that was stationed here at Dickleburgh Airfield during World War II. The museum has a fine collection of USAAF uniforms, decorations, combat records, equipment and wartime photographs. Two other interesting museums can be found at nearby Bressingham. The **Bressingham Steam Museum** boasts a fine collection of locomotives and traction engines, a Victorian steam roundabout and three narrow-gauge

railway rides. On the same site are two delightful gardens – the Dell and Foggy Bottom – and the **National Dad's Army Collection**.

NORWICH

By the time of the *Domesday Book*, Norwich was the third most populous city in England and the Normans built a Castle here that was replaced in the late 12th century by a mighty stone fortress. **Norwich Castle** never saw military action and, as early as the 13th century, it was already being used as the county gaol – a role it filled until 1889. The Castle is now a lively Museum with exhibitions ranging from Norfolk painters and Norwich silver to natural history, Lowestoft porcelain and a vast collection of ceramic teapots. Visitors can also tour the dungeons and battlements.

While the Castle's function has changed over the years, the **Cathedral**, consecrated in 1101, remains the focus of ecclesiastical life in Norfolk. The most completely Norman cathedral in England after Durham, this superb building has the largest Norman cloisters in the country and is noted for its 400 gilded bosses that depict scenes from medieval life. Among the cathedral's numerous treasures are the Saxon Bishop's Throne in the Presbytery, the 14th century altar painting in St Luke's Chapel and the richly carved canopies in the Choir. By the open market place is the Gothic masterpiece **St Peter Mancroft Church** with its massive embellished tower, 15th century windows depicting the New Testament, and a celebrated peal of bells. **City Hall**, which was modelled on Stockholm City Hall, was opened in 1938 by George VI. No mention of Norwich is complete without telling the story of Jeremiah Colman who, in the early 1800s, perfected his blend of mustard flours and spice to produce a condiment that was smooth in texture and tart in flavour. Together with his nephew James, he founded J & J Colman in 1823 and The Mustard Shop commemorates the company's history.

To the south of the city are the remains of Venta Icenorum, the Roman town that was established here after Boudicca's rebellion in AD 61. Three miles to the north, next to Norwich International Airport, is the City of Norwich Aviation Museum, whose exhibits include a Vulcan bomber.

Famous sons of Norwich include the recorder of Parliamentary proceedings Luke Hansard (1752), Rupert Everett (1959) and Matthew Parker (1509) sometime Archbishop of Canterbury, dubbed 'Nosey Parker' by Queen Elizabeth I.

Norwich Cathedral

AROUND NORWICH

AYLSHAM

12 miles N of Norwich off the A140

In the churchyard of **St Michael's Church** is the tomb of one of the greatest English 18th century landscape gardeners, Humphry Repton, who created some 200 parks and gardens around the country.

One of Repton's commissions was to landscape the grounds of **Blickling Hall**, which lies just to the north of the town. Built for Sir Henry Hobart in the 1620s, the Hall is perfectly symmetrical and its most spectacular feature is the Long Gallery that extends for 175 feet and has a glorious plaster ceiling.

Within a few miles of the Hall are two other stately homes, **Mannington Hall** and **Wolterton Park**. Repton also landscaped the grounds for the latter, an 18th

• *In the 16th century weavers from Holland introduced the canary to Norwich, which perhaps explains why Norwich City Football Club is called The Canaries and their strip is yellow.* •

Muckleburgh Collection, Sheringham

**294 THE LANTERN
RESTAURANT**

Sheringham

A charming little restaurant
on Sheringham's High Street,
serving a good choice of
snacks, hot and cold main
dishes and home baking.

❦ see page 562

century mansion that was built for
the brother of Sir Robert Walpole,
England's first Prime Minister.

SHERINGHAM

22 miles N of Norwich on the A149

A former fishing village which still
has a fleet of fishing boats that are
launched from the shore,
Sheringham was transformed into a
seaside resort with the arrival of
the railway.

Although Sheringham's railway
line was closed in the 1960s, it was
reopened in 1975 as the **North
Norfolk Railway**; it is also known
as the **Poppy Line** because these
brilliant flowers can still be seen in

the fields along the scenic five-mile
route.

Just to the west of the town,
footpaths lead to the lovely Repton-
landscaped grounds of
Sheringham Park from where
there are grand views along the
coast. Yet more glorious scenery
can be found at the aptly named
Pretty Corner, a particularly
beautiful area of woodland.

A little further along the coast
is the shingle beach known as
Weybourne Hope (or Hoop) that
slopes so steeply that an invading
force could brings its ships right up
to the shore. The garrison camp
that defended this vulnerable
stretch of beach during both World
Wars now houses the
Muckleburgh Collection, a
fascinating museum of military
equipment. East of Sheringham, at
West Runton, is the highest point in
Norfolk – **Beacon Hill**. Although
only 330 feet high, it commands
glorious views from the summit.
Close by is the Roman Camp,
which excavations have shown to
have been an iron-working
settlement in Saxon and Medieval
times. The village, too, is home to
the **Norfolk Shire Horse Centre**
where the heavy horses give
demonstrations of the valuable
work they once performed on
farms.

CROMER

21 miles N of Norwich on the A149

A popular seaside resort since the
late 18th century, Cromer is famous
for its crabs, reckoned to be among
the most succulent in England.

Cromer Pier is the genuine article, complete with a Lifeboat Station and theatre, and on the promenade is a museum dedicated to the coxswain Henry Blogg and 200 years of Cromer lifeboats. **Cromer Museum** is housed in a row of restored fishermens' cottages.

Just inland from Cromer is one of Norfolk's grandest houses, **Felbrigg Hall**, a wonderful Jacobean mansion dating from the 1620s.

NORTH WALSHAM

13½ miles NE of Norwich on the A149

A busy country town with an attractive market cross dating from 1600, North Walsham was the home of Horatio Nelson, who came to the town's Paston School at the age of 10. A dual place of interest is the **Cat Pottery and Railway Junk Yard**, dealing in lifelike handmade pottery cats and transport memorabilia. To the west of North Walsham, near the village of Erpingham, is **Alby Crafts and Gardens** which promotes the excellence of mainly East Anglian and British craftsmanship and where there is also a **Bottle Museum**.

To the northeast is the quiet seaside village of **Mundesley**, whose **Maritime Museum** in a former coastguard lookout is believed to be the smallest museum in the country.

HAPPISBURGH

17 miles NE of Norwich on the B1159

The coastal waters of Happisburgh (pronounced Hazeborough) have seen many shipwrecks over the centuries and the victims lie buried in the graveyard of **St Mary's Church**. The large grassy mound on the north side of the church contains the bodies of the crew of the ill-fated HMS *Invincible* which was sunk on sandbanks here in 1801. On its way to join up with Nelson's fleet at Copenhagen, the ship sank with the loss of 110 sailors.

WROXHAM

7 miles NE of Norwich on the A1151

This riverside village, linked to Hoveton by a bridge over the River Bure, is the capital of the Norfolk Broads, and during the high season its boatyards are full of craft of all shapes and sizes. The village is also the southern terminus of the **Bure Valley Railway**, a nine-mile long steam railway that follows the course of the River Bure through glorious countryside to the market town of **Aylsham**.

Just to the north lies the **Wroxham Barns**, a delightful collection of beautifully restored 18th century barns that house a community of craftspeople, and to the east is **Hoveton Hall Gardens**, which offer visitors a splendid combination of lovely plants and both woodland and lakeside walks.

Further up the River Bure is the charming village of **Coltishall**, home to the **Ancient Lime Kiln**, a reminder of Norfolk's industrial heritage.

RANWORTH

9 miles E of Norwich off the B1140

A beautiful Broadland village, from

To the south of Happisburgh, at Stalham, stands the tallest windmill in England, the 80 feet high Sutton Windmill that dates from 1789 and that finally ceased grinding in 1940. Here, too, is the Museum of the Broads, with boats, displays, exhibits and videos telling the story of the broads. Stalham Fire Museum, next to the church, houses the town's original fire engine.

Caister Castle

where five Norfolk Broads, the sea at Great Yarmouth and the spire of Norwich Cathedral can be seen from the tower of **St Helen's Church**. Also to be seen is the National Trust's **Horsey Mill**. Along with the views, the church houses one of the county's greatest ecclesiastical treasures - an early 15th century Gothic choir screen.

•
Yarmouth's literary connections include Anna Sewell, the author of
Black Beauty, *born here in 1820, and Charles Dickens, who stayed at the Royal Hotel in 1847 to 1848 while writing* David Copperfield.
•

GREAT YARMOUTH

In Saxon times, Great Yarmouth was an island, but changes in the flow of the River Bure means that it is now a promontory. The seaward side has a five-mile stretch of sandy beach and numerous family amusements, as well as the **Maritime Museum of East Anglia** and the **Elizabethan House**, a merchant's house of 1596 which is now a museum of domestic life. Behind South Beach is the 144 feet Nelson's Monument crowned by a statue of Britannia.

Most of Yarmouth's older buildings are concentrated in the riverside part of the town, including the historic South Quay

with an array of museums, including one celebrating the life and times of Horatio Nelson.

For centuries, incredible quantities of herring were landed at Yarmouth and the trade involved so many fishermen that there were more boats registered here than in London. It was a Yarmouth man, John Woodger, who developed the process to produce that great essential of a proper English breakfast – the kipper.

When the Romans established their fortress, Garionnonum, now known as **Burgh Castle** a few miles west of Great Yarmouth, the surrounding marshes were still under water and the fort stood on one bank of a vast estuary commanding a strategic position. Today's ruins are impressive, its walls of alternating layers of flint and brick rising to some 15 feet in places.

To the north of Yarmouth lies **Caister-on-Sea**, a holiday resort that was an important fishing village for the Iceni tribe. The Romans built a castle here of which little remains; the **Caister Castle** seen today dates from 1432 and was built by Sir John Fastolf who distinguished himself leading the English bowmen at the Battle of Agincourt. The castle is home to a **Motor Museum** which houses an impressive collection of vintage and veteran cars, the oldest being a Panhard Levassor from 1893.

KING'S LYNN

An ancient town that is a

harmonious mix of medieval, Tudor, Jacobean and Flemish architecture and with some of the finest old streets anywhere in England. It is not surprising that King's Lynn was chosen by the BBC to represent early 19th century London in their production of *Martin Chuzzlewit*. One of the most striking sights in the town is the 15th century **Guildhall of the Holy Trinity** with its distinctive chequerboard design of black flint and white stone. Next to it, in the late-Victorian Town Hall, is the **Museum of Lynn Life**, whose greatest treasure is King John's Cup, a dazzling piece of medieval workmanship. Close by, standing proudly on the banks of the River Purfleet, is the handsome **Custom House** of 1683 that was designed by the local architect Henry Bell. Other buildings of note, and there are many, include the **Hanseatic Warehouse**, the South Gate, the Greenland Fishery Building and the Guildhall of St George, the oldest civic hall in England and now home to the **King's Lynn Arts Centre**.

The pretty village of **Castle Rising**, just northeast of King's Lynn, is overshadowed by its massive Castle Keep, whose well-preserved walls rise to some 50 feet. Built in 1150 to guard what was then the sea approach to the River Ouse, Castle Rising was much more a residential building than a defensive one and it was to here, in 1331, that Edward III banished his ferocious mother Isabella who had been instrumental in his father's murder.

Castle Rising

AROUND KING'S LYNN

DERSINGHAM

8 miles NE of King's Lynn on the B1440

A large village close to some pleasant walks through Dersingham Wood and the adjoining Sandringham Country Park. The Royal family's country retreat, **Sandringham House** is a relatively recent addition to the family and was purchased by the Prince of Wales, later Edward VII, as a country refuge to match the retreats his parents enjoyed at Balmoral and Osborne.

To the north of Dersingham lies **Snettisham**, which is best known for its spacious, sandy beaches and the **RSPB Bird Sanctuary**.

295 THE KINGS ARMS

Shouldham, nr King's Lynn
A delightful family friendly free house with a rural setting and a good choice of food and drink.

see page 562

213

A few miles south of Hunstanton stands the five-storey Great Bircham Windmill, one of few in Norfolk to have found a hill to perch on, and it's still working.

296 THE GLOBE INN

Wells-next-the-Sea

A lovely place to relax and unwind, for a drink, a snack, a meal or an overnight or longer stay.

see page 563

HUNSTANTON

14½ miles N of King's Lynn on the A149

A busy seaside resort, Hunstanton boasts two unique features: its cliffs of colourful layers of red, white and brown strata and its west-facing position - unique for an east-coast resort! Developed in the 1860s with the arrival of the railways, the town was assured of its social standing after the Prince of Wales, later Edward VII, came here to recover from typhoid fever and it retains a distinct 19th century charm.

To the north lies **Old Hunstanton**, a charming village at the beginning of the Norfolk Coastal Footpath which leads eastwards, around the coast, to Cromer. Just a little further up the coast is **Holme next the Sea**, which lies at the northern end of another long distance footpath, the 50-mile long Peddars Way which starts at Thetford. This village is the site of **Sea Henge**, a 4,500-year-old Bronze Age tree circle discovered on the beach.

To the south lies Heacham, the home of **Norfolk Lavender**, the largest lavender growing and distilling operation in the country. Visitors can take a guided tour around the working farm, which also contains the National Collection of Lavenders.

BURNHAM MARKET

19 miles NE of King's Lynn on the B1155

The largest of the seven Burnhams strung along the valley of the River Burn, Burnham Market has an outstanding collection of Georgian buildings surrounding its green. To the southeast lies **Burnham Thorpe**, the birthplace of Horatio Nelson, whose father was the rector here for 46 years. He was born in 1758 at the now demolished Parsonage House, and both the local inn and the church contain memorabilia from his life.

WELLS-NEXT-THE-SEA

23½ miles NE of King's Lynn on the A149

Wells was a working port from the 13th century, and in 1859, to prevent the harbour silting up completely, an embankment, cutting off an area of marshland, was built; today, the harbour lies more than a mile from the sea. Running alongside the embankment, which provides a pleasant walk, is the **Harbour Railway** that runs from the quay to the lifeboat station by the beach. This narrow-gauge railway is operated by the same company as the Wells and

Holkham Hall, Wells-next-the-Sea

Walsingham Railway which carries passengers on the delightful ride on the old Great Eastern route to Little Walsingham.

Just west of the town lies **Holkham Hall**, a glorious classical mansion built by Thomas Coke that was completed in 1762. The magnificent rooms are only overshadowed by the superb collections they contain, including classical sculptures, paintings by Rubens and Van Dyck, and tapestries. A museum at the Hall has exhibits of social, domestic and agricultural memorabilia.

Further along the coast, to the east, lies the pretty village of **Stiffkey** (pronounced Stewkey) and the **Stiffkey Salt Marshes**, a National Trust nature reserve that turns a delicate shade of purple in July when the sea lavender is in bloom. Away from the coast can be seen the picturesque ruins of **Binham Priory**, founded in 1091 and once one of the most important religious houses in Norfolk.

CLEY-NEXT-THE-SEA

30 miles NE of King's Lynn on the A149

In early medieval times, Cley was a more important port than King's Lynn, a fact that is hard to believe today as the town lies a mile from the sea. The subject of thousands of paintings, **Cley Mill** was built in 1713, remained in use until 1921 and is now open to visitors during the season.

Another fine old mill can be found at the village of Glandford, which is also home to the **Glandford Shell Museum**, featuring seashells gathered from around the world, and the Natural Surroundings Wild Flower Centre that is dedicated to gardening with a strong ecological emphasis.

To the west of Cley is one of the most enchanting of Norfolk's coastal villages, Blakeney, where the silting up of the estuary has created a fascinating landscape of serpentine creeks and channels twisting their way through mudbanks and sand hills. Down the B1156 from Blakeney is Langham Glass, where visitors can see regular demonstrations of glass-making and walk through the 2005 Lord Nelson Maize maze.

THURSFORD GREEN

24 miles NE of King's Lynn off the A148

This village is home to one of the most unusual museums in Norfolk, the **Thursford Collection** – a fascinating collection of steam-powered traction engines, fairground organs and carousels. At the regular live music shows, the most astonishing exhibit, a 1931 Wurlitzer

At Stiffkey are also found the famous Stewkey Blues – cockles that are highly regarded as a delicacy.

From Cley there is a walk along the shoreline to Blakeney Point, a spit of land that stretches three miles out to sea and which is the most northern extremity of East Anglia.

Windmill, Cley-next-the-Sea

Shirehall Museum and Abbey, Little Walsingham

organ, displays its virtuosity.

To the northwest lies the village of **Little Walsingham** that still attracts pilgrims who come to worship at the **Shrine of Our Lady of Walsingham**. In 1061, the Lady of the Manor had a vision in which she was instructed to build a replica of the Holy House of Nazareth and her Holy House soon became a place of pilgrimage. In the mid 12th century, an Augustinian Priory was established to protect the shrine and, today, the largest surviving part, a stately gatehouse, can be seen on the east side of the High Street. Henry VIII went on to Slipper Chapel, a beautiful 14th century building at nearby Houghton St Giles.

Other buildings of interest in the attractive village of Little Walsingham are the 16th century octagonal Clink in Common Place; the scant ruins of a 14th century Franciscan Friary; and the former Shire Hall that is now a museum.

FAKENHAM

20 miles NE of King's Lynn off the A148

A prosperous market town and home to a National Hunt Racecourse, Fakenham is a major agricultural centre for the region. An attractive town, it must be one of the few places in the country where the former gasworks have become an attraction and here they house the **Museum of Gas and Local History**. A mile from Fakenham on the A1067 Norwich road lie **Pensthorpe Nature Reserve & Gardens**, the Natural Centre of Norfolk, and a multi-award winning attraction for lovers of nature, wildlife, bird life and the great outdoors.

CASTLE ACRE

12 miles SE of King's Lynn on the A1065

William de Warenne, William the Conqueror's son-in-law, came here very soon after the Conquest and built a **Castle** that was one of the first, and largest, in the country to be built by the Normans. Of that vast fortress, little remains apart from the gargantuan earthworks and a squat 13th century gateway.

Much more has survived of **Castle Acre Priory**, founded in 1090 and set in fields beside the River Nar. Its glorious West Front gives a powerful indication of how majestic a triumph of late Norman architecture the complete Priory must have been.

SWAFFHAM

14 miles SE of King's Lynn on the A47

A town with many handsome and interesting buildings, including the **Assembly Rooms** of 1817 and the elegant **Butter Cross**, a classical lead-covered dome standing on eight columns. Swaffham was the birthplace in 1874 of Howard Carter, who found and opened Tutankhamen's tomb.

Swaffham Museum is located in the Town Hall, and just to the southwest of the town, archaeologists have reconstructed a village from the time of Boudicca - Cockley Cley Iceni Village and Museums. A more recent addition to Swaffham's attractions is the **EcoTech Centre**, opened in 1998, which explores current innovations as well as technologies of the future. There's a climbable wind turbine in the grounds.

Southwest of Swaffham lies Oxburgh Hall, a lovely moated house dating from the 15th century which was visited by Henry VII and his Queen in 1497.

DEREHAM

23 miles SE of King's Lynn off the A47

One of the most ancient towns in Norfolk, where in AD 654 St Withburga founded a nunnery. Her name lives on in **St Withburga's Well**, which marks the place where she was laid to rest. The poet William Cowper lived here for the last four years of his life, and in the nearby hamlet of **Dumpling Green**, one of the country's most celebrated travel writers, George

Borrow, was born. A much less attractive character connected with the town is Bishop Bonner, the enthusiastic arsonist of Protestant heretics during the reign of Mary Tudor. Rector here before being appointed Bishop of London, he lived in the exquisite thatched terrace that is known as Bishop Bonner's Cottages, now the home of a small Museum.

To the north of the town, at Gressenhall, is the **Roots of Norfolk Museum** housed in an imposing late-18th century former workhouse. The many exhibits here concentrate on the working and domestic life of Norfolk people over the last 150 years.

DOWNHAM MARKET

10 miles S of King's Lynn off the A10

A compact little market town on the very edge of the Fens, with the River Great Ouse and the New Bedford Drain running side by side at its western edge. Of particular note here in the market place is the elegant and highly decorated cast-iron **Clock Tower** that was erected in 1878.

Just to the south, at the village of Denver, is the **Denver Sluice** which was built in 1651 by the Dutch engineer, Cornelius Vermuyden, as part of a scheme to drain 20,000 acres of land owned by the Duke of Bedford.

Running parallel to this is the modern **Great Denver Sluice** that was opened in 1964. Also here is **Denver Windmill**, built in 1835 and reopened in 2000 after being carefully restored.

•

Castle Acre village is extremely picturesque, the first place in Norfolk to be designated a Conservation Area, in 1971. Most of the village, including the 15th century parish church, is built in traditional flint, with a few later houses of brick blending in remarkably happily.

•

•

The Mid Norfolk Railway, headquartered at Dereham Station, is the longest heritage railway in East Anglia, linking Dereham and Wymondham. Heritage diesel railcars work the line most weekends with occasional steam services at peak times. The station has recently been restored to a 1950s/1960s appearance.

•

217

Northamptonshire

Although a relatively small county, Northamptonshire has a lot to offer. The county town, Northampton, along with other local towns, is famed for its shoe industry, but outside the towns Northamptonshire remains essentially a farming county littered with ancient market towns and rural villages. Its history is as interesting as most – the decisive battle of Naseby was fought on its soil, and it was at Fotheringay Castle that Mary, Queen of Scots was executed. There are many magnificent stately homes here but the most famous now is Althorp, the country estate of the Spencer family and the last resting place of Diana, Princess of Wales. There are also some more eccentric buildings to discover, including the creations of Sir Thomas Tresham – notably the unique Triangular Lodge at Ruston.

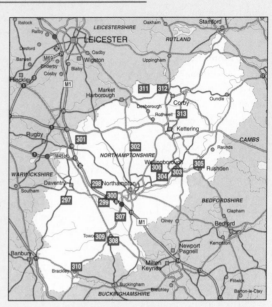

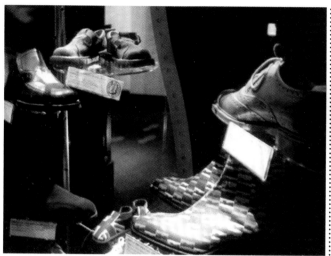

297 THE MALTSTERS COUNTRY INN

Badby, nr Daventry

A friendly pub at the heart of village life: real ales, good honest home cooking, en suite accommodation and a thriving social side.

see page 563

298 THE SARACEN'S HEAD

Little Brington, nr Northampton

A quintessential English inn of great character, with real ales, home cooking and four comfortable en suite bedrooms.

see page 564

Central Museum and Art Gallery, Northampton

NORTHAMPTON

By the 13th century Northampton was a major market town and its market square is reputed to have been the second largest in the country. The town is best known for its shoemaking and the first large order came in 1642 when 4,000 pairs of shoes and 600 pairs of boots were made for the army. The industry grew rapidly throughout the county and by the end of the 19th century 40% of the population was involved in the shoe trade. The **Central Museum and Art Gallery** has the world's largest collection of footwear, while the **Abington Museum**, set in a 15th century manor house, tells the county's military history.

There are many fine buildings here and, in particular, notably the wonderful 12th century **Church of the Holy Sepulchre**, one of only a handful of round churches in

Britain. The Welsh House, one of the few buildings to survive a disastrous fire in 1675, recalls the time when Welsh drovers would bring their cattle to the market. The town's most prestigious building is the **Guildhall**, a gem of Victorian architecture built in 1864 by Edward Godwin.

In the south part of Northampton town stands one of the three surviving Eleanor Crosses of the original 12 that marked the journey of King Edward with his wife's body from Nottinghamshire to London.

AROUND NORTHAMPTON

DAVENTRY

11½ miles W of Northampton on the A45

A historic town, which holds a colourful market along the High Street every Tuesday and Friday. In the Market Place stands the Moot

299 THE OLDE SUN INN

Nether Heyford

A wonderful village pub filled with interesting bygones, serving cask ales and good simple food.

see page 565

300 THE RED LION & TRUCK STOP

Weedon Road (A45), Heyford

Two enterprises in one: a busy truckers stop and a quaint, traditional local.

 see page 564

301 THE KNIGHTLEY ARMS

Yelvertoft

A popular village pub with a friendly, inviting feel, a good choice of real ales and good honest food.

 see page 566

302 THE OLD HOUSE

Scaldwell, nr Northampton

Comfortable Bed & Breakfast and Self-Catering accommodation in adjacent properties in lovely countryside.

 see page 566

220

Hall, built in 1769 as a private residence; it now houses Daventry Museum.

Just north of the town lies Daventry Country Park; close by is **Borough Hill**, the third largest Iron Age hill fort in Britain, and also the site of a Roman villa.

In 1925 the recently established BBC built a broadcasting station on Borough Hill, and from 1932 it transmitted the BBC Empire Service (later the BBC World Service) from here. In 1935 the station was used by Robert Watson-Watt for the first demonstration of radar.

To the southeast of Daventry lies **Flore**, an ancient village whose wide green slopes down to the banks of the River Nene. Adams Cottage was the home of the ancestors of John Adams, President of the United States.

ALTHORP
5 miles NW of Northampton off the A428

The home of the Spencer family since 1508, **Althorp** remains exactly that - a classic family-owned English stately home. The present house was begun in 1573, and behind the stark tiling of the exterior is a wealth of fine paintings, sculpture, porcelain and furniture. Known widely by connoisseurs for generations, Althorp is now known across the whole world since the death of Diana, Princess of Wales, in 1997; she lies at peace in the beautiful, tranquil setting of the Round Oval, an ornamental lake.

To the north is **Holdenby Hall**, which was built by Elizabeth I's Lord Chancellor, Sir Christopher Hatton, for the purpose of entertaining the Queen. At the time, it was the largest Elizabethan house in England but Elizabeth I only visited the house once. Later it became the palace and eventually the prison of Charles I, who was held here for five months after the Civil War.

Also north of Althorp is Cottesbrooke Hall, a magnificent Queen Anne house that is reputed to be the model for Jane Austen's *Mansfield Park*; close by is Coton Manor Garden, a traditional garden originally laid out in 1925 that embraces several delightful smaller gardens.

ASHBY ST LEDGERS
12½ miles NW of Northampton on the A361

From 1375 to 1605 the manor house at Ashby was the home of the Catesby family and it was in a room above the gatehouse that Guy Fawkes is said to have met Robert Catesby and hatched the Gunpowder Plot.

KELMARSH
12 miles N of Northampton on the A508

This village is home to **Kelmarsh Hall**, an early 18th century house that was designed by James Gibb, best known as the architect of St Martin in the Fields, London, and surrounded by beautiful gardens, woodland and farmland. To the southeast is another fine country house, 16th century **Lamport**

Kelmarsh Hall

303 THE RISING SUN

Wellingborough

Friendly, cosy bars provide a homely setting for enjoying a drink and a meal in the centre of busy Wellingborough.

see page 567

Hall. Its grounds include the first Alpine garden and the first garden gnomes in England, along with the Hannington Vintage Tractor Club.

West of Kelmarsh is the site of the **Battle of Naseby**, where in 1645 Oliver Cromwell's Parliamentarian forces defeated Charles I and determined the outcome of the Civil War. The king finally surrendered in Newark some months later. **Naseby Battle and Farm Museum**, in Naseby village, contains a model layout of the battle, relics from the fight and a collection of bygone agricultural machinery.

WELLINGBOROUGH

10 miles NE of Northampton on the A509

An important market and industrial town, known for its iron mills, flourmills and tanneries, Wellingborough sits near the point where the River Ise joins the River Nene. One of many fine buildings is **Croyland Abbey**, now a Heritage Centre, and nearby is a

splendid stone-walled, thatch-roofed 15th century Tithe Barn.

An attraction in the centre of town is the **Millennium Rose Garden** at Swanspool Gardens while to the south is **Summer Leys Nature Reserve**, a year round haven for large numbers of birds.

Two miles south of Wellingborough lies Irchester Country Park, 200 acres of woodland walks and nature trails in a former ironstone quarry.

304 THE STAGS HEAD

Earls Barton

The social hub of the village, with a ready welcome for one and all, four cask ales and simple lunchtime food.

see page 567

Lamport Hall, nr Kelmarsh

305 EAT 'N' ENJOY COFFEE SHOP

Rushden

A delightful, cosy little coffee shop open for daytime snacks both savoury and sweet.

¶ see page 568

306 THE GRIFFINS HEAD

Mears Ashby

Everything a village inn should offer: a warm greeting, a convivial atmosphere, well-kept ales and a good choice of food.

¶ see page 568

307 THE ROYAL OAK

Blisworth

A 17th century pub that's a convivial spot for meeting or making friends over a drink or a meal.

¶ see page 569

CASTLE ASHBY

6 miles E of Northampton off the A428

Dating from 1574, Castle Ashby is a fine Elizabethan mansion on the site of a demolished 13th century castle. The surrounding parkland was landscaped by Capability Brown.

STOKE BRUERNE

6½ miles S of Northampton off the A508

This picturesque village lies on the Grand Union Canal, at the southern end of the famous **Blisworth Tunnel**. In addition to towpath walks and boat trips to the tunnel, the fascinating **Canal Museum**, housed in a converted corn mill, is a popular attraction.

Just south of the village is **Stoke Park**, a great house that was built by Inigo Jones in the 1630s. The main house burnt down in 1886 and only the pavilions and a colonnade remain, but they are an impressive sight.

SULGRAVE

16 miles SW of Northampton off the B4525

Along with its old village stocks, the remains of a castle mound and its church, Sulgrave is home to **Sulgrave Manor**, a Tudor manor house built by the ancestors of George Washington, first President of the United States of America.

Lawrence Washington, sometime Mayor of Northampton, bought Sulgrave Manor from Henry VIII in 1539 and the family coat of arms, which is said to have inspired the stars and stripes design of the American flag, is prominent above the front door. The house is a treasure trove of George Washington memorabilia, including documents, a velvet coat and even a lock of his hair.

CANONS ASHBY

12 miles SW of Northampton off the A361

A monastery belonging to the Black Canons once stood here, but after the Dissolution some of the ecclesiastical buildings were used to create **Canons Ashby House**, one of the finest stately homes in Northamptonshire. Home of the Dryden family since the 1550s, it contains some marvellous

Canons Ashby House

Elizabethan wall paintings and sumptuous Jacobean plasterwork.

TOWCESTER

9 miles SW of Northampton off the A43

Called Lactodorum by the Romans and situated on their major route, Watling Street, this town became an important staging post on the route between London and Holyhead. By the end of the 18th century there were 20 coaching inns in the town, servicing up to 40 coaches every day. Charles Dickens stayed here at the Saracen's Head, then called the Pomfret Hotel, and immortalised it in *The Pickwick Papers*. The parish **Church of St Lawrence**, on the site of a substantial Roman building, is one of the loveliest in the county, and close by is the Chantry House, formerly a school, founded by Archdeacon Sponne in 1447.

Towcester Racecourse is set in the beautiful parkland estate of Easton Neston, the family home of Lord Hesketh. There is racing of a different kind at nearby **Silverstone**, the home of British motor racing and the British Grand Prix.

BRACKLEY

18 miles SW of Northampton on the A43

Dating back to Saxon times, the Castle built here in the early 12th century is said to have been the meeting place for the rebel barons who drew up the first version of Magna Carta in 1215.

To the southwest, lies the former manor house, **Aynho Park**, a very grand 17th century country house that was originally the property of the Cartwright family, who, it is said, claimed the rents from their tenants in the form of apricots.

CORBY

True industry arrived at Corby only in the latter years of the 19th century with the building of the Kettering-Manton Railway. Many of the bricks used in the building of the viaduct at Harringworth were made at Corby brickworks, which closed at the beginning of the 20th century.

Corby was still essentially a small village until the 1930s, when Stewarts and Lloyds built a huge steel-making plant based on the area's known reserves of iron ore. That industry virtually stopped in 1980 but Corby remains a forward-looking modern town, with many cultural and leisure opportunities.

Just to the north lies **Rockingham Castle**, built by William the Conqueror on the slopes of Rockingham Hill overlooking the Welland valley. The grand rooms are superbly furnished, and the armour in the Tudor Great Hall recalls the Civil War, when the castle was captured by the Roundheads. Owned and lived in since 1530 by the Watson family, it was here that Charles Dickens wrote much of *Bleak House*. East of Corby lies East Carlton Countryside Park, with its nature trails and steel-making heritage centre.

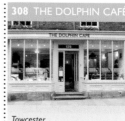

308 THE DOLPHIN CAFÉ

Towcester

A friendly licensed café open all day for snacks, light meals, cakes, pastries and drinks.

see page 569

309 THE BUTCHERS ARMS

Greens Norton, Towcester

A traditional village inn offering a good choice of cask ales and good honest home cooking.

see page 570

310 THE RED LION

Brackley

The best public house in Brackley, with real ales, home cooking and practical B&B accommodation.

see page 571

223

311 THE GEORGE

Ashley

A traditional village hostelry in the Welland Valley, with great hosts, well-kept beers, country cooking and superb guest accommodation

see page 572

312 THE SPREAD EAGLE

Cottingham

Food is the star of the show at a convivial village pub with exciting menus catering for all tastes and appetites.

see page 573

AROUND CORBY

DEENE

4 miles NE of Corby off the A43

Originally a medieval manor, **Deene Park** was acquired in 1514 by Sir Robert Brudenell and has been occupied by the family ever since. It is surrounded by beautiful gardens filled with old-fashioned roses, and parkland containing rare trees. Close by is Kirby Hall, one of the loveliest Elizabethan ruins in England.

FOTHERINGHAY

11½ miles NE of Corby off the A605

The first **Fotheringhay Castle** was built in around 1100 by the son-in-law of William the Conqueror, and the second, in the 14th century, by Edmund of Langley, a son of Edward III. The future Richard III was born here, but Fotheringhay is best known as being the prison and the place of execution of Mary, Queen of Scots, who was brought here in bands of steel and beheaded in the Banqueting Hall in 1587. The castle was pulled down in 1627.

At Nassington, just to the north, stands **Prebendal Manor House**, dating from the early part of the 13th century and the oldest

Deene Park, nr Corby

house in Northamptonshire.

Oundle, which lies 10 miles east of Corby, on the A427, is a town rich in architectural interest, with many fine 17th and 18th century buildings. Oundle is best known for the Public School that was founded by Sir William Laxton in 1556; an inscription to his memory is written above the doorway in Greek, Latin and Hebrew.

BRIGSTOCK

5 miles SE of Corby on the A6116

On the banks of a tributary of the River Nene called Harpers Brook, this Saxon village has many delightful old cottages, a 16th century manor house, and a church with an unusual circular extension to its tower.

To the east lies **Lyveden New Bield**, a cross-shaped Elizabethan garden lodge erected to symbolise the Passion.

KETTERING

An important town standing above the River Ise, Kettering gained fame as a producer of both clothing and shoes and it was here that the missionary William Carey and the preacher Andrew Fuller founded the Baptist Missionary Society in 1792. Much of the old town has been swallowed up in modern development but there are still a few old houses in the narrow lanes. The **Heritage Quarter** around the church gives a fascinating, hands-on insight into the town's past, as does the **Manor House Museum**.

Just to the north lies **Geddington**, an attractive village that is home to the best preserved of the three surviving **Eleanor Crosses** that marked the funeral procession of Queen Eleanor, who had died at Harby in Nottinghamshire in 1290.

Just south of the village is one of the finest houses in the country, **Boughton House**, the Northamptonshire home of the Duke of Buccleuch. Originally a small monastic building, it has been transformed over the years into a magnificent mansion that holds numerous treasures, notably French and English furniture, paintings (El Greco, Murillo, 40 van Dycks) and collections of armoury and weaponry.

AROUND KETTERING

RUSHTON

4 miles NW of Kettering off the A6

Rushton Triangular Lodge is a unique folly built in 1597 and symbolising the Holy Trinity: three walls each with three windows, three gables and three storeys, topped by a three-sided chimney.

313 THE STAR INN

Geddington

A convivial inn of immense appeal, a happy hunting ground for lovers of real ale and real food.

see page 574

Northumberland

In the far north, beyond the city of Newcastle-upon-Tyne, Northumberland has one of the least populated and least well known of the country's 11 National Parks. An area of remote, wild and haunting landscapes, the most famous features of the Northumberland National Park are the Cheviot Hills and Kielder Forest. Elsewhere in the county there are stretches of Hadrian's Wall and also border towns that were constantly under the threat of Scottish raids. However, two of the county's most dramatic castles lie on the coast – Dunstanburgh and Bamburgh. Along this coastline is also Lindisfarne, or Holy Island, home to one of the most famous and evocative ecclesiastical ruins.

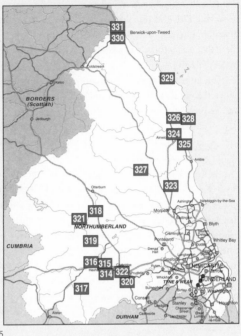

HEXHAM

Founded in AD 674 by St Wilfrid, **Hexham Abbey** was once described as 'the largest and most magnificent church this side of the Alps'. Only the crypt of the original building survives, but the 13th century church that now occupies the site has many outstanding features, including marvellous carved stonework and a superb 16th century rood screen. The nearby early 14th century Moot Hall, built of Roman stone and once used as the courtroom of the Archbishop of York, now houses the Border History Library. The **Border History Museum**, housed in the 14th century gaol, tells the story of the border struggles between Scotland and England. Hexham is on the **Hadrian's Wall Path**, which runs the entire length of the Wall.

Hexham National Hunt racecourse is one of the most attractive in the country.

AROUND HEXHAM

BARDON MILL
10 miles W of Hexham on the A69

This former mining village is a convenient starting point for walks along Hadrian's Wall, particularly to the two Roman forts of Vindolanda and Housesteads nearby. Both have extensive Roman remains and accompanying exhibitions.

HALTWHISTLE
15 miles W of Hexham on the A69

The origins of the name Haltwhistle are unknown but two suggestions are the watch 'wessel' on the high 'alt' mound, or the high 'haut' fork of two streams 'twysell'. It is difficult to imagine that this pleasant little town with its grey terraces was once a mining area, but evidence of the local industries remain. An old pele tower is incorporated into the Centre of Britain Hotel in the town centre.

Three miles northwest of Haltwhistle, off the B6318, is

314 MRS MIGGINS COFFEE HOUSE

Hexham
A delightful little café serving snacks and meals Monday to Saturday daytimes.

¶ see page 575

315 THE QUEENS ARMS HOTEL

Acomb
Warm hospitality, hearty home cooking and well-priced B&B rooms close to Hadrian's Wall.

¶ ⊨ see page 575

316 THE RAILWAY INN

Fourstones, Hexham
An immaculate village inn serving an impressive selection of imaginative, superbly cooked dishes.

¶ see page 576

Hadrian's Wall

227

317 THE KINGS HEAD

Kielder Forest Park

Allendale

A handsome old village inn serving cask ales, dozens of malts and hearty, wholesome food. Five rooms for B&B guests.

see page 576

318 THE BAY HORSE INN

West Woodburn, Kielder

A mellow sandstone hostelry where drinkers, diners and overnight guests are all made equally welcome.

see page 577

Walltown Quarry, a recreation area on the site of an old quarry. Today, part of the Northumberland National Park, it contains laid out trails and it is possible to spot oystercatchers, curlews, sandpipers and lapwings.

KIELDER

20 miles NW of Hexham off the B6357

Kielder village was built in the 1950s to house workers in the man-made **Kielder Forest**, which covers 200 square miles of spectacularly beautiful scenery to the west of the Northumberland National Park. The forest is one of the few areas in Britain that contains more red squirrels than greys and is also home to deer and rare birds and plants. Within the forest is **Kielder Water**, the largest man-made lake in northern Europe. A pleasure cruise stops at several points of interest on the Lake, and an art and sculpture trail is laid out around its shores and in the trees. To the northwest is **Kielder Castle**, once a hunting lodge for the Duke of Northumberland and now a fascinating visitor centre.

CHOLLERFORD

4 miles N of Hexham on the B6318

The remains of the Roman fort of **Chesters**, on Hadrian's Wall, include a well-preserved bathhouse and barracks and the museum houses a remarkable collection of Roman antiquities.

Chester Roman Fort, Chollerford

228

Cheviot Hills at Catcleugh Reservoir

OTTERBURN

19 miles N of Hexham on the A696

Almost in the centre of what is now the **Northumberland National Park**, on a site marked by 18th century Percy Cross, the **Battle of Otterburn** took place in 1388 between the English and the Scots. This was a ferocious encounter, described by a contemporary as 'one of the sorest and best fought, without cowards or faint hearts'. **Otterburn Mill** dates from the 18th century, and on display are Europe's only original working 'tenterhooks', where newly woven cloth was stretched and dried.

North of the village are the remains of the Roman fort built by Julius Agricola in the 1st century.

PRUDHOE

10 miles E of Hexham on the A695

When **Prudhoe Castle** was built in the 12th century it was one of the

finest in Northumberland, and a Georgian manor house in the courtyard tells its interesting story. To the west, at Mickley Square, is **Cherryburn**, the birthplace in 1753 of Thomas Bewick, the renowned illustrator and engraver.

Wylam, not far from Prudhoe, has a strong connection with the early history of the railway. George Stpehenson was born there in 1781 and Timothy Hackworth in 1786. They often worked together, and Stephenson put Hackworth in charge of his locomotive works in Newcastle. They were in competition at the famous Rainhill Trials of 1829, when Stephenson's *Rocket* proved superior to Hackworth's *Sans Pareil*.

WALLSEND

3 miles E of Newcastle on the A193

Wallsend, on the eastern edge of Newcastle and actually in Tyne & Wear, is the site of mighty

319 BATTLESTEADS

Wark

A family owned and run country inn and restaurant serving local cask ales and home-cooked local produce. 17 rooms for B&B guests.

 see *page 578*

320 THE HADRIAN HOTEL

Wark, nr Hexham

Tourists, walkers and lovers of the countryside will find excellent hospitality and comfortable accommodation close to Hadrian's Wall.

see *page 577*

321 RIVERDALE HALL COUNTRY HOUSE HOTEL

Bellingham, nr Hexham

Northumberland's premier country house hotel, with outstanding accommodation, superb food and extensive sporting and leisure facilities.

see *page 579*

229

322 THE ANGEL INN AND THE ANGEL RADCLIFFE

Corbridge

Two facing properties, both recently splendidly refurbished, one for B&B, the other with accommodation and a restaurant.

 see page 580

323 THE OAK INN

Morpeth

The only pub on the A1 for many miles around attracts a steady stream of visitors with its well-kept ales and hearty home cooking.

 see page 579

324 THE ODDFELLOWS ARMS

Alnwick

A friendly, down-to-earth dining pub opposite Alnwick Castle.

 see page 581

shipyards and of the reconstructed **Segedunum Roman Fort**, the last outpost on Hadrian's Wall. **Whitley Bay** is a resort at the mouth of the River Tyne, with safe beaches and spectacular views from the top of **St Mary's Lighthouse**.

SEATON SLUICE

8 miles NE of Newcastle on the A193

Inland from Seaton Sluice is **Seaton Delaval Hall**, a superb Vanbrugh mansion. The ancestral home of the Delavals was built in the early 18th century for Admiral George Delaval.

BLYTH

12 miles NE of Newcastle on the A193

This small industrial town at the mouth of the River Blyth claims its own piece of railway history with one of the country's earliest wagonways, the 17th century Plessey Wagonway, built to carry coal from the pits to the riverside. The building, now the headquarters of the Royal Northumberland Yacht Club, was a submarine base during the Second World War.

MORPETH

28 miles NE of Hexham on the A192

Northumberland's county town has some distinguished buildings: its **Town Hall** was built to designs by Vanbrugh and the handsome bridge over the River Wansbeck was designed by Telford. The 13th century **Morpeth Chantry** has been over the centuries a cholera hospital, a mineral water factory and a school where the famous Tudor botanist William Turner was educated. The 14th century Church of St Mary in Morpeth has some of the finest stained glass in Northumberland, and in its cemetery is the grave of suffragette Emily Davison, who died under the hooves of the King's horse *Anmer* at the 1913 Epsom Derby meeting. Her funeral attracted thousands of mourners to Morpeth.

To the east is Ashington and the **Wansbeck Riverside Park**, which has been developed along the embankment and offers sailing and angling facilities, plus a four-mile walk along the mouth of the River Wansbeck. The famous footballing brothers Bobby and Jackie Charlton and the cricketer Steve Harmison are sons of Ashington.

ALNWICK

This impressive Northumberland town is dominated by the massive **Alnwick Castle**, which began as a Norman motte and bailey and was replaced in the 12th century by a stone castle. In the mid 19th century, the 4th Duke of Northumberland transformed the castle into a great country house which, still the home of the Dukes of Northumberland, contains many treasures, including paintings by Canaletto, Titian and Van Dyck. The **Museum of the Northumberland Fusiliers** is housed in the Abbot's Tower. The Castle is a favourite location for films, most famously doubling as Hogwart's School in the Harry Potter films.

The only surviving part of the town's fortifications is 15th century **Hotspur Tower**, while all that is left of **Alnwick Abbey** is its 15th century gatehouse. **Hulne Park**, landscaped by Northumbria-born Capability Brown, encompasses the ruins of Hulne Priory, the earliest Carmelite foundation in England (1242).

AROUND ALNWICK

WARKWORTH
6 miles S of Alnwick on the A1068

Alnwick Castle

At the southern end of Alnmouth Bay, on the River Coquet, lies **Warkworth Castle**. The site has been fortified since the Iron Age, though what can be seen now is mainly late 12th and 13th century, including the great Carrickfergus Tower and the West Postern Towers. An unusual and interesting walk is signposted to The Hermitage, along the riverside footpath below the castle, where a ferry takes you across the river to visit the tiny chapel hewn out of solid rock. It dates from medieval times and was in use until late in the 16th century.

St Lawrence's Church is almost entirely Norman, though its spire - an unusual feature on medieval churches in Northumberland - dates from the 14th century.

AMBLE
7 miles SE of Alnwick on the A1068

Amble is a small port situated at the mouth of the River Coquet, once important for the export of coal, but now enjoying new prosperity as a marina and sea-fishing centre.

Alnwick Gardens Tree House

325 THE HOPE & ANCHOR

Alnwick

A very cheerful and convivial inn with local ales, imaginative cooking and stylish accommodation.

🍴 🛏 see page 581

326 THE MASONS ARMS

Rennington, nr Alnwick

A handsome country inn with a fine restaurant and top-quality guest accommodation.

🍴 🛏 see page 582

231

Rothbury

Super English cooking in a traditional hostelry with rooms for B&B.

 see page 583

Craster, nr Alnwick

Farmhouse B&B in a glorious location on the Coast & Castle Cycle Route.

 see page 583

A mile offshore lies **Coquet Island**, where St Cuthbert landed in AD 684. The Island had a reputation in former times for causing shipwrecks, but is now a celebrated bird sanctuary, noted for colonies of terns, puffins and eider ducks. Managed by the Royal Society for the Protection of Birds, Coquet Island can be visited by boat trips departing from Amble quayside throughout the summer.

ROTHBURY

10½ miles SW of Alnwick on the B6341

This attractive town is a natural focal point from which to explore the valley of the River Coquet. The best-known of many delightful walks leads to the Rothbury Terraces, a series of parallel tracks along the hillside above the town. Just outside Rothbury is the house and estate of **Cragside**, whose owner, the industrialist, engineer and arms manufacturer Sir William Armstrong, devised a system with man-made lakes, streams and underground piping that made his home the first to be lit by hydroelectricity. The National Trust has sympathetically restored Cragside to show how upper middle class Victorians were beginning to combine comfort and opulence with the latest technological advances.

CRASTER

7 miles NE of Alnwick off the B1339

To the northeast of Alnwick is Craster, a small, unpretentious fishing village that is nationally known for its oak-smoked kippers. At one time, herring were caught in vast quantities around this coast, but a combination of over-fishing and pollution resulted in a dramatic decline in numbers, so the fish now mainly have to be imported. During the curing season visitors can sniff around the sheds where the herring are hung over smoking piles of oak chips. Craister Quarry was closed in

Cragside, Rothbury

1939 and is now a small nature reserve called the Arnold memorial Site. It was this quarry that supplied London and other large cities with its kerbstones. This is the start point of a pleasant walk along the coastal footpath to Dunstanburgh Castle.

EMBLETON

7 miles NE of Alnwick on the B1339

The dramatic ruins of **Dunstanburgh Castle** stand on a cliff top east of the village, on a site that was originally an Iron Age fort. The castle, by far the largest in Northumberland, was built in 1313 by Thomas, Earl of Lancaster, and in the Wars of the Roses it withstood a siege from troops led by Margaret of Anjou, Henry VI's Queen.

BAMBURGH

13½ miles N of Alnwick on the B1340

Built on an epic scale and dominating the village, **Bamburgh Castle** dates back to the 6th century although the mighty fortress seen today was originally built in the 12th century. The tour of the Castle takes in the magnificent King's Hall, the Cross Hall, the Bakehouse, the Scullery, the Armoury and the Dungeons. The village was the birthplace of Grace Darling, the Victorian heroine, who, in 1838, rowed out with her father from the Longstone Lighthouse in a ferocious storm to rescue five survivors from the wreck of the steam ship *Forfarshire* which had foundered on the Farne

Craster Harbour

Islands rocks. Though earning instant wide acclaim and celebrity, she remained at the lighthouse, where she died of tuberculosis only four years later, still in her twenties; she was buried in a ceremony that attracted thousands of mourners and a message of sympathy from Queen Victoria in a canopied tomb in St Aidan's churchyard. The **Grace Darling Museum**, in Radcliffe Road, contains memorabilia of the famous rescue.

The Farne Islands are a group of 28 little islands that provide a sanctuary for many species of sea birds, including kittiwake, fulmar, puffin, and tern. They are also home to a large colony of Atlantic Grey seals which can often be seen from the beach of the mainland. Boat trips to the islands leave from the harbour at Seahouses, down the coast from Bamburgh. It was on Inner Farne that St Cuthbert landed in AD 687, and a little chapel was built in his memory.

329 BAMBURGH CASTLE

Bamburgh
Standing on a rocky outcrop overlooking miles of beautiful sandy beach, **Bamburgh Castle** dominates the Northumbrian landscape.

🏛 *see page 584*

233

Farne Islands

hermit before seeking further solitude on the Farne Islands.

Benedictine monks renamed Lindisfarne "Holy Island" when they came here in the 11th century and established **Lindisfarne Priory**. **Lindisfarne Castle** was established in Tudor times as yet another fortification to protect the exposed flank of Northumbria from invasion by the Scots. In 1902 it was bought by Edward Hudson, the owner of *Country Life*, who employed the great Edwardian architect Sir Edward Lutyens to rebuild and restore it as a private house. It is now in the care of the National Trust and is open to the public in the summer.

Lindisfarne is the finishing point of the 62-mile St Cuthbert's Way, a long-distance footpath opened in 1996; the trail begins at Melrose, across the Scottish border, and along the way passes through the Northumberland National Park and the Cheviot Hills.

330 CARA HOUSE

Berwick-upon-Tweed

A very cosy, friendly guest house close to the centre of Berwick.

🛏 see page 584

331 MEADOW HOUSE INN

Berwick-upon-Tweed

A busy, sociable pub with a vast selection of drinks and menus to cater for all appetites.

🍴 see page 585

CHILLINGHAM

11½ miles NW of Alnwick off the B6348

Chillingham is a pleasant estate village best known for the herd of wild, horned white cattle that roam the parkland of **Chillingham Castle**. They are perhaps the purest surviving specimens of the wild cattle that once roamed the hills and forests of Britain.

LINDISFARNE

18 miles NW of Alnwick off the A1

Northumberland's northern coastline is dominated by one outstanding feature – **Lindisfarne**, also known as **Holy Island**. Reached by a three-mile causeway, the island was settled in the 7th century by St Aidan and his small community of Irish monks from Iona. It was these monks who produced some of the finest surviving examples of Celtic art, the richly decorated Lindisfarne Gospels. St Cuthbert also came here, living on a tiny islet as a

BERWICK-UPON-TWEED

For centuries, this former Royal burgh of Scotland was fought over by the Scots and the English, and changed hands no fewer than 14 times until it finally became part of England in 1482. But even now, Scotland exerts a great influence. The local football team, Berwick Rangers, plays in the Scottish League, and in 1958 the Lord Lyon, who decides on all matters armorial in Scotland, granted the town a coat-of-arms - the only instance of armorial bearings being granted in Scotland for use in England.

Berwick's original medieval walls, built in the 13th century by Edward I, are regarded as being the finest preserved fortifications of their age in Europe. The walk around the walls (about 1.5 miles) provides fine views of the town and the Northumberland coastline.

Housed in the clock tower of the Hawksmoor-designed barracks is the **Berwick-upon-Tweed Borough Museum and Art Gallery**, which explores the history of the town, and the **King's Own Scottish Borderers Museum**.

The Berwick skyline is dominated by the imposing **Town Hall** with its clock tower and steeple that rise to 150 feet, and which is often mistaken for a church. Guided tours in the summer enable visitors to explore the upper storeys, where there are civic rooms and the former town gaol as well as a small Cell Block Museum.

Barracks Square, Berwick-upon-Tweed

AROUND BERWICK-UPON-TWEED

HORNCLIFFE

4 miles W of Berwick off the A698

The village of Horncliffe, five miles upstream of Berwick, can only be reached by one road that leads into and out of the village, making it feel rather remote. Many visitors are unaware of the existence of the river, but there is nothing more pleasant than wandering down one of the paths leading to the banks to watch the salmon fishermen on a summer's evening.

Not far from the village the Tweed is spanned by the **Union Suspension** Bridge linking England and Scotland. It was built in 1820 by Sir Samuel Browne, who also invented the wrought-iron chain links used in its construction. This graceful structure, 480 feet long, was Britain's first major suspension bridge to carry vehicular traffic. Though not carrying a major road, it is still possible to drive over the bridge.

Lady Waterford Hall, Ford

14th century castle, destroyed in 1497 by King James IV of Scotland on his way to Flodden.

Ford is a 'model' village with many beautiful stone buildings and well-tended gardens. Dating originally from the 14th century, but heavily restored in the 19th century, **Ford Castle** was the home of Louisa Ann, Marchioness of Waterford. In 1860 she built the village school and from 1862 until 1883 spent her time decorating it with murals depicting biblical scenes. As models she used local families and their children thus creating a pictorial gallery of life and work in the area at that time. Now known as **Lady Waterford Hall**, it is open to the public.

DUDDO

7 miles SW of Berwick on the B6354

Close to the village are the **Duddo Stones**, one of Northumberland's most important ancient monuments. This ancient stone circle, which now consists of five upright stones over seven feet high, dates back to around 2000 BC, and can only be reached from the village by foot.

FORD & ETAL

13 miles SW of Berwick off the B6354

The twin estate villages of **Ford** and **Etal** were built in the late 19th century. Etal is an attractive village, within which are the ruins of the

TILLMOUTH

9 miles SW of Berwick on the A698

The village of Tillmouth lies along the banks of the River Till, a tributary of the Tweed which is crossed by the imposing 15th-century **Twizel Bridge**, although a more modern structure now carries the A698 over the river. There are some lovely walks here and a well-signed footpath leads to the ruins of Twizel Castle and the remains of St Cuthbert's Chapel on the opposite bank.

Nottinghamshire

Nottinghamshire is the home of the legendary Robin Hood and various exhibitions in Nottingham tell his story. Sherwood Forest, part of a great mass of forest land that once covered much of Central England, is officially designated 'Robin Hood Country'. The Industrial Revolution saw the mechanisation of the lace and hosiery industry of which Nottingham was a centre and on which many of the surrounding towns and villages were dependant. Mills sprang up in the towns, taking the industry away from the homes, and the Nottinghamshire coalfields, which had been mined for centuries, saw their scale of operation expanded dramatically. It was into this environment that DH Lawrence was born in the late 19th century and the family's terrace house is now a museum dedicated to the novelist. One of the gems of the county is Southwell Minster, a wonderfully graceful building that is probably the least well known of England's Cathedrals. The medieval town of Newark has many reminders of the Civil War, while the ancient village of Scrooby, in the far north of the county, is closely associated with the Pilgrim Fathers, who sailed to America on the Mayflower in 1620.

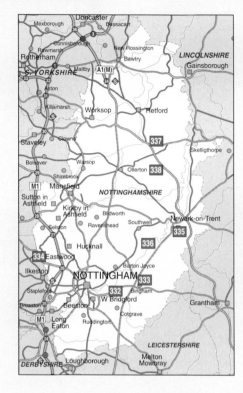

ACCOMMODATION

FOOD & DRINK

NOTTINGHAM

To the north of the city of Nottingham lies Bestwood Country Park, which encompasses part of the old royal hunting ground; to the west is Wollaton Hall, one of the most elaborate Elizabethan country mansions in the Midlands.

At the heart of the city is its **Old Market Square**, believed to be the largest market square in the country. This was the setting for the famous Nottingham Goose Fair that began in medieval times and continues today; it is now held at Forest Fields on the edge of Nottingham. Not far from the square, **The Tales of Robin Hood** tells the story of the celebrated outlaw who is forever linked with the city.

On a rocky outcrop high above the city centre stands **Nottingham Castle**, home now to a museum and art gallery and to the **Sherwood Foresters Regimental Museum**.

At the base of Castle Rock lies the famous **Trip to Jerusalem Inn**, where the crusaders are said to have stopped for a pint before setting off on their long journey to the Holy Land. Dating back to around 1189, it has claims to being the oldest pub in England; it was

once the brewhouse for the castle. Close by, and set in the heart of Nottingham's historic **Lace Market**, is the **Museum of Nottingham Lace**, where the story of Nottingham's famous industry is told.

Nottingham is built on sandstone, and one of the many caves tunnelled down the years to provide shelter or hiding places has been left as a memorial to the black days of the Second World War.

AROUND NOTTINGHAM

RAVENSHEAD

9 miles N of Nottingham on the A60

This village is home to **Longdale Lane Rural Craft Centre**, established in the 1970s and the oldest such centre in the country. Just to the southwest lies **Newstead Abbey**, a magnificent 13th century ruin attached to a Victorian reworking of a Tudor mansion that is one of the county's most historic houses. The abbey was founded by Henry II in the 12th century as part of his atonement for the murder of Thomas à Becket.

BINGHAM

8 miles E of Nottingham on the A52

Celebrities connected with Bingham, the unofficial capital of the Vale of Belvoir, include Edward VII's mistress, Lily Langtry, who is commemorated on the chancel screen in the church. Bingham was also the third Nottinghamshire town to provide

Newstead Abbey, Ravenshead

an Archbishop of Canterbury – George Abbot.

To the east of Bingham lies **Aslockton**, the birthplace in 1489 of Thomas Cranmer; the church is appropriately dedicated to St Thomas, and the village school also bears his name.

RUDDINGTON

4 miles S of Nottingham on the B680

This historic village was once the home of many hosiery workers and several of their cottages still remain. There are two museums here: the **Ruddington Framework Knitters' Museum** and the **Ruddington Village Museum**, housed in the old village school building of 1852.

BEESTON

4 miles SW of Nottingham on the A6005

Lying on the outskirts of Nottingham, Beeston is the home of Boots the Chemist, which was started by Jesse Boot in the late 19th century. Jesse Boot was born in Beeston in 1850 and left school at the age of 13 to work in his mother's herbalist shop in the centre of Nottingham. In 1888 Jesse set up the Boots Pure Drug Company, which became the Boots the Chemist empire. Boot, a great benefactor, was knighted in 1903, created a baronet in 1917 and raised to the peerage as Lord Trent in 1929, two years before his death. From 1880 it was also home to the Humber bicycle factory, which expanded to include motor cars before moving to Coventry in 1908.

Just to the north, in **Stapleford** churchyard, can be found the best preserved Saxon carving in the county in the form of a 10 feet cross shaft that dates from the late 11th century.

EASTWOOD

8 miles NW of Nottingham on the A610

This mining town was the birthplace of DH Lawrence and the Lawrence family home, a two up, two down, terrace house at 8a Victoria Street is now the **DH Lawrence Birthplace Museum**. A place of pilgrimage for devotees of Lawrence, Eastwood also attracts those with an interest in railway history. It was at the Sun Inn in the Market Place that a group of 'Iron Masters and Coal Owners' gathered in 1832 to discuss the construction of a railway that would eventually become the mighty Midland Railway. A plaque on the wall of the inn commemorates the meeting.

The railway was formed to compete with the Erewash Canal, completed in 1779 and effectively put out of business by the 1870s. Almost a century later, following years of neglect, the canal was cleared and made suitable for use by pleasure craft.

HUCKNALL

7½ miles NW of Nottingham on the A611

Hucknall attracts a constant stream of visitors who come to **St Mary Magdalene Church** to gaze not so much at the 14th century font or the Kempe stained glass but at a simple marble slab set in the floor

332 THE BLACK LION

Radcliffe-on-Trent

A big, bold landmark pub with an exceptional range of real ales and home-cooked pub classics.

see page 586

333 THE WHITE LION

Bingham

A very sociable pub close to the town centre, serving a full range of drinks

see page 586

334 THE GREAT NORTHERN

Langley Mill

A family friendly pub with friendly family owners. Real ales, good honest pub food, lots of quizzes and music.

see page 587

of the chancel that marks the last resting place of Lord Byron. He died in Greece in 1824 and his body was returned to England to be buried in the family vault. Also buried here is his daughter Ada, Countess of Lovelace, a noted mathematician and friend and colleague of Charles Babbage, inventor of the Analytical Engine, a predecessor of the computer.

Hucknall boasts another famous son, Eric Coates, who is best remembered as a composer of light music: his *Sleepy Lagoon* is immediately recognisable as the signature music of BBC Radio's long-running programme *Desert Island Discs*.

NEWARK-ON-TRENT

The market square of this elegant medieval town is lined with handsome houses and inns. The most remarkable of these is the 14th century former **White Hart**

Inn, whose magnificent frontage is adorned with 24 plaster figures of angels and saints. Dominating one side of the square is the noble Georgian **Town Hall**, which now houses the town's civic plate and regalia and an art gallery displaying works by Stanley Spencer, William Nicholson and notable local artists.

The most glorious days of the 12th century castle were during the Civil War, when the townsfolk, who were fiercely loyal to Charles I, endured three separate sieges before finally surrendering to Cromwell's troops.

Newark possesses several other reminders of the Civil War and of the two small forts that were built to guard this strategic crossing over the River Trent only the **Queen's Sconce** has survived. Nearby is the **Governor's House**, where the governors of Newark lived during the Civil War and also where Charles I quarrelled with Prince Rupert after the prince had lost Bristol to Parliament.

With such a wealth of history inside its boundaries, Newark naturally has its fair share of museums and, along with those in the town, to the east is the **Newark Air Museum**, one of the largest privately managed collections in the country.

AROUND NEWARK-ON-TRENT

SIBTHORPE

6 miles S of Newark off the A46

All that remains above ground of a priests' college, founded here in the

Newark Air Museum

240

14th century, is the parish church and a Dovecote that stands in the middle of a field. Of the three Archbishops of Canterbury born in Nottinghamshire, Thomas Cranmer is by far the best known, but Sibthorpe was the childhood home of Thomas Secker, Archbishop from 1758 to 1768.

SOUTHWELL

6 miles W of Newark on the A612

Undoubtedly one of England's most beguiling towns, Southwell is dominated by its **Minster**, whose twin towers, with their pyramidal Rhenish Caps, are unique in this country. Perhaps the least well-known of England's cathedrals, Southwell's history goes back to AD 956 when Oskytel, Archbishop of York, established a church here. The present building was erected in three phases between 1150 and 1290. Octagonal in design, the Chapter House has been hailed as the pinnacle of the Decorated period of architecture. The Cathedral stands in a delightful precinct surrounded by attractive buildings, while to the south stand the ruins of the palace of the archbishops of York built in the 14th and 15th centuries. **The Workhouse**, in the care of the National Trust, tells what life was like for 19th century paupers.

Southwell can claim to be the birthplace of the Bramley apple. The story goes that in the early 19th century, two ladies planted some apple pips in their cottage garden in the nearby village of Easthorpe. Nature took its course

Southwell Minster

and one of the seedlings grew into a tree. By this time, Matthew Bramley owned the cottage and the quality of the tree's fruit began to excite public interest. Henry Merryweather, a local nurseryman, persuaded Bramley to let him take a cutting, which he subsequently propagated with enormous success.

MANSFIELD

16 miles W of Newark on the A617

The second largest town in the county, Mansfield stands at the heart of what were once the great North Nottinghamshire coalfields. That industry has now vanished but Mansfield still has the atmosphere of an industrial town although its economy is now based on a broader spread of varying businesses. The most distinctive structure in Mansfield is undoubtedly the great railway viaduct, built in 1875, which sweeps through and above the town, carried by 15 huge arches of rough-hewn stone.

336 THE FULL MOON

Morton, nr Newark

A secluded setting, family-friendly hosts, lots of real ales and excellent home cooking make this popular with a wide range of patrons.

🍴 see page 588

337 THE QUEEN'S HOTEL

East Markham

Long-serving hosts provide excellent hospitality and a good range of food sand drink served all day.

¶ see page 588

338 BRECKS COTTAGE

Moorhouse, nr Newark

A delightful redbrick house offering five bedrooms for Bed & Breakfast guests.

⊨ see page 589

LAXTON

9 miles NW of Newark off the A616

Laxton is one of the few places in the country that has managed to retain its open field farming system. Devised in the Middle Ages, this system was generally abandoned in the 18th and 19th centuries when the enclosure of agricultural land took place. The site has a **Visitor Centre and Museum**. Another unique feature of this interesting village is the magnificent **Dovecote Inn** that is owned by the Queen.

Just north of the village, along a lane close to the church, is the Norman motte, known as **Castle Mound**, which lies almost hidden beneath the trees. At the beginning of the 12th century, the stewardship of Sherwood Forest moved to Laxton and the village became the administrative centre for the forest. As a consequence, the motte and bailey castle was one of the biggest in this part of the country.

OLLERTON

12½ miles NW of Newark on the A6075

Ollerton is a delightfully preserved cluster of old houses, a charming Georgian coaching inn, a church set beside the River Maun and the ancient **Ollerton Water Mill**.

To the south lies the pretty conservation village of **Wellow**, whose village green has the tallest permanent Maypole in England, 60 feet high and colourfully striped like a barber's pole, with a cockerel perched on the top.

Close by lies **Rufford Country Park**, in the grounds of Rufford Abbey, which contain nine formal gardens near the house along with a display on Nottinghamshire's history.

EDWINSTOWE

13½ miles NW of Newark on the A6075

Lying at the heart of **Sherwood Forest**, the life of this village is still dominated by the forest, as it has been since the 7th century when Edwin, King of Northumbria died in the Battle of Hatfield in AD 632; the village developed around the church built on the spot where he was slain. The **Church of St Mary** was the first stone building in Edwinstowe and, according to legend it was here that the marriage took place between Robin Hood and Maid Marian.

CRESSWELL

21 miles NW of Newark on the A616

Cresswell village is actually in Derbyshire but its most famous feature lies just inside the

Rufford Abbey and Country Park

Nottinghamshire border. **Cresswell Crags** form a dramatic limestone gorge pitted with deep, dark and mysterious caves and here the bones of prehistoric bison, bears, wolves, woolly rhinos and lions twice the size of their modern descendants have been found. The Visitors' Centre contains some fascinating archaeological finds and there are some pleasant walks past the lakes to the crags.

RETFORD

Retford is actually two communities, East and West Retford, set either side of the River Idle. **Cannon Square** takes its name from a Russian cannon dating from 1855 and weighing over two tons. It was captured by British soldiers at Sebastopol and brought to Retford at the end of the Crimean War. One of Retford's most infamous visitors was the highwayman Dick Turpin, and several historic inns still stand as a reminder of the days of stage coach travel. Another man who stood and delivered here, though in a more respectable fashion, was John Wesley, who conducted many open air meetings in East Retford. The **Bassetlaw Museum** is housed in Amcott House, an imposing late 18th century town house.

AROUND RETFORD

MATTERSEY

5 miles N of Retford off the B6045

To the east of the village lie the ruins of **Mattersey Priory**,

founded in 1185 for the Gilbertine Order, the only monastic order to be established by an Englishman, Roger de Mattersey. The original priory buildings at Mattersey were destroyed by fire in 1279 so the remains seen today are of the 14th century dormitory, refectory, and the walls of the Chapel of St Helen.

NORTH WHEATLEY

4 miles NE of Retford off the A620

Famous for its strawberries that are sought after for their delicious taste and excellent quality, North Wheatley is also home to a peculiar 17th century brick house, known as the **Old Hall**, where all the external features, including the vase-like decorations, are made from bricks. Just to the south is the splendid **North Leverton Windmill**, which was built in 1813 and still grinds corn today.

WORKSOP

7 miles W of Retford on the A60

One of the major attractions of Worksop is the 14th century **Priory Gatehouse** that was originally the portal to a large Augustinian monastery; the gatehouse and the **Church of St Mary and St Cuthbert** are all that remain today. There is also a wayside shrine, which makes it a unique ecclesiastical attraction.

Mr Straw's House, along with an endowment of one million pounds, was bequeathed to the National Trust by William Straw in 1990. It was found that nothing in this seemingly ordinary Edwardian

•

Tracing the stories of Robin Hood is a difficult task, as the tales, which have been told for over 600 years, were spoken rather than written. Visitors still flock to see the great hollow tree that Robin Hood and his band of outlaws purportedly used as a meeting place and as a cache for their supplies. The mighty Major Oak is located about 10 minutes walk along the main track in the heart of the forest. A little way up the road leading northwards out of Edwinstowe is the Sherwood Forest Visitor Centre, which houses a display of characters from the Robin Hood stories with appropriate scenes of merrymaking.

•

To the southeast of Worksop lies the 3,800-acre Clumber Park, created in 1707 when the 3rd Duke of Newcastle was granted permission to enclose part of the Forest of Sherwood as a hunting ground for Queen Anne. Only the foundations of Clumber House remain, but other buildings still stand in this lovely setting. The estate houses feature high-pitched gables and massive chimneys, and the redbrick stables are surmounted by a clocktower crowned by a domed cupola. The Clumber, one of the largest of the spaniels, was first bred here in the 19th century.

semi-detached house had been altered or added to since 1932, though it had been occupied by Straws until the death of the last Straw in 1990. **Worksop Museum** has a Pilgrim Fathers exhibition and is the start of the **Mayflower Trail** that guides visitor around the local sites connected with the Fathers.

SCROOBY

7 miles NW of Retford on the A638

This ancient village is best known for its links with the Pilgrim Fathers and, particularly, with William Brewster. Having formed his radical ideas on religion at

Cambridge and in the Netherlands, Brewster returned to England, settling in Scrooby. In 1598 he was summoned before the ecclesiastical court for poor church attendance, but he continued to maintain his battle for religious belief to be free of State control and was imprisoned for a short time before going back to Amsterdam. After some years he returned to England and became an Elder of the Separatist Church; it was a group of some 40 members of this church who, in 1620, boarded the Mayflower for the famous voyage which eventually landed at what is now Plymouth, New England.

Oxfordshire

A county of ancient towns and villages, whose capital, Oxford, 'that sweet city of dreaming spires', has dominated the surrounding area for centuries. The first scholars arrived at this walled Saxon town in the 12th century and, since then, this great seat of learning has influenced thinking and scientific research around the world. The southeastern part of the county is dominated by the River Thames and among the charming riverside towns and villages is Henley-on-Thames, the country's home of rowing and known worldwide for its annual Regatta. To the west lie the Vale of the White Horse and an area of downland which is littered with ancient monuments. Here, too, is Wantage, the birthplace of Alfred the Great. However, Oxfordshire's most famous feature is undoubtedly Blenheim Palace, the magnificent 18th century mansion that was the gift of a grateful queen to her loyal subject the Duke of Marlborough. A World Heritage Site, the palace is grand and opulent - it was also the birthplace of Sir Winston Churchill, whose modest room can be seen.

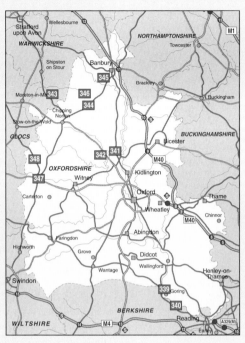

ABINGDON

One of England's oldest towns, Abingdon grew up around a 7th century Benedictine **Abbey**. Twice sacked by the Danes, it was all but derelict by the 10th century, but under the guidance of Abbot Ethwold it again prospered and in its heyday was larger than Westminster Abbey. Little remains today except the late 15th century Gatehouse.

AROUND ABINGDON

THAME

14½ miles NE of Abingdon on the A418

Founded in AD 635 as an administrative centre for the Bishop of Dorchester, Thame became a market town in the 13th century and its main street is lined with old inns and houses. The imposing **Church of St Mary** and the **Prebendal House** both date from the 13th century, while the town's famous school was founded in 1558.

DORCHESTER

5½ miles SE of Abingdon off the A4074

All that remains of the Augustinian Abbey, which was built on the site of the original Saxon church, is the Abbey **Church of St Peter and St Paul**, whose chief glory is the huge Jesse window showing the family tree of Jesus.

WALLINGFORD

8 miles SE of Abingdon on the A4130

It was here that William the Conqueror crossed the river on his

Wallingford was besieged in 1646 by the Parliamentary forces under Sir Thomas Fairfax and its walls were breached after a 12-week siege; it was the last place to surrender to Parliament. The Castle, built by William the Conqueror, was destroyed by Cromwell in 1652 but substantial earthworks can still be seen and the museum tells the story of the town from earliest days.

six-day march to London, and during the Civil War the town was a Royalist stronghold defending the southern approaches to Oxford, the site of the Royalist headquarters.

STONOR

16 miles SE of Abingdon on the B480

The village is the home of Lord and Lady Camoys and their house, **Stonor**, which has been in the family for over 800 years. Set in a wooded valley and surrounded by a deer park, the house contains many rare items and a medieval Catholic Chapel.

HENLEY-ON-THAMES

19 miles SE of Abingdon on the A4155

In 1829, the first University boat race between Oxford and Cambridge took place here and, within a decade, the event was enjoying royal patronage. Today, **Henley Regatta** is a stylish as well as a sporting occasion that remains a popular annual event.

Beside the town's famous 18th century bridge is the **Leander Club**, the headquarters of the world famous rowing club and here, too, is the River and Rowing Museum, which traces the rowing heritage of Henley.

MAPLEDURHAM

17 miles SE of Abingdon off the A4074

Hidden down a little lane that leads to the River Thames, this tiny village is home to the Elizabethan **Mapledurham House**, which has several notable literary connections. Alexander Pope was a frequent visitor in the 18th century; the final chapters of John Galsworthy's *The Forsythe Saga* were set here; and it became the fictional Toad Hall in *The Wind in the Willows*.

GORING-ON-THAMES

12 ½ miles SE of Abingdon on the B4526

Situated on a particularly peaceful stretch of the River Thames, this ancient town began to develop in the 19th century after Brunel had laid the tracks for the Great Western Railway through Goring Gap.

DIDCOT

5 miles S of Abingdon on the A4130

Although this town is overshadowed by the giant cooling towers of Didcot power station, it has a saving grace in the form of the **Didcot Railway Centre**, which is a shrine to the days of the steam locomotive and the Great Western Railway.

To the north lies the pretty village of **Sutton Courtenay** where, in the churchyard of the Norman church, are the graves of Herbert Asquith, the last Liberal Prime Minister, and Eric Blair, who is better known as novelist George Orwell.

WANTAGE

The birthplace of Alfred the Great in AD 849, Wantage remained a royal manor until the end of the 12th century and in the central market place is a huge statue of the King of all the West Saxons. Only the **Church of St Peter and St Paul** has survived from medieval times. Opposite the church is the **Vale and Downland Museum Centre** which is housed in a 16th century building and a reconstructed barn.

AROUND WANTAGE

UFFINGTON

6 miles W of Wantage off the B4507

This large village was the birthplace, in 1822, of Thomas Hughes, the author of *Tom Brown's Schooldays*, and he incorporated many local landmarks in his well-known work. The **Tom Brown's School Museum** tells the story of Hughes's life and works. The village is best known for the **Uffington White Horse**, a mysteriously abstract figure of a horse, some 400 feet long, which was created by removing the turf on the hillside to expose the gleaming white chalk beneath. Close by lies the **Blowing Stone** (or Sarsen Stone), a piece of glacial debris that is perforated with holes and, when blown, emits a sound like a foghorn.

339 THE JOHN BARLEYCORN

Goring-on-Thames

A picture-postcard country inn with home-cooked food, real ales and excellent modern bedrooms.

🍴 🛏 see page 589

340 THE FERRY BOAT INN

Whitchurch-on-Thames

A convivial pub with a warm, welcoming atmosphere, real ales, good home cooking and three cosy B&B rooms.

🍴 🛏 see page 591

Vale and Downland Museum Centre, Wantage

William Morris is buried in the graveyard of St George's Church in a grave whose ridge-shaped stone, inspired by Viking tomb houses, was designed by his friend and partner, the architect Philip Webb. His wife Jane , who died in 1914, was buried with him. One of William Morris' best known paintings is of his future wife dressed as Queen Guinevere.

BUSCOT

12 miles NW of Wantage on the A417

This small village is home to two National Trust properties: **Buscot Old Parsonage**, a William and Mary house with a small garden beside the River Thames, and **Buscot Park**, a grand late Georgian house that houses the Faringdon Art Collection, which includes paintings by Rembrandt, Rubens, Reynolds and Burne-Jones.

Just downriver from the village lies 16th century **Kelmscott Manor House**, which was the home of William Morris between 1871 and his death in 1896.

Further along the river again is the tiny hamlet of **Radcot**, which boasts the oldest bridge across the Thames – Radcot Bridge dates from 1154.

OXFORD

A walled town in Saxon times, Oxford grew around the angle of two rivers, the Thames (called the Isis locally) and the Cherwell. The first students arrived here in the 12th century when they were forced out of Europe's leading academic centre, Paris. The first colleges as we know them were **Merton**, **Balliol** and **University**. The colleges all have their own distinctive features, and one of the most beautiful is **Christ Church** (known as 'The House'), which was founded in 1525 as Cardinal College by Thomas Wolsey. The main gateway leads through the bottom of **Tom Tower** (designed by Christopher Wren) and into Tom Quad, the largest of the city's quadrangles, and the college's chapel is the official seat of the Bishop of Oxford; **Christ Church Cathedral** is also England's smallest.

As well as the college buildings, Oxford has many interesting places for the visitor to explore. The 18th century **Radcliffe Camera** is England's earliest example of a round reading room and this splendid building still serves this purpose for the **Bodleian Library**, which was refounded by Sir Thomas Bodley, a fellow of Merton College, in 1602. One of Oxford's most famous buildings is the magnificent **Sheldonian Theatre**, which was designed and built in the Roman style by Christopher Wren between 1664 and 1668 while he was Professor of Astronomy at the University. The ceiling has 32 canvas panels, depicting Truth descending on the Arts, and the theatre is used for such events as matriculation and degree ceremonies.

Pitt Rivers Boat Museum, Oxford

The **Ashmolean Museum**, which first opened in 1683, was originally established to house the collection of John Tredescant and his son; this internationally renowned museum is home to many treasures, including archaeological collections from Europe, Egypt and the Middle East. The Ashmolean's original building is now home to the **Museum of the History of Science** where among a remarkable collection are Einstein's blackboard and a large silver microscope made for George III. The **Botanic Gardens** are a peaceful place, founded in 1621, a teaching garden where the plants grown were studied for their medicinal and scientific uses. The rose garden commemorates the work of Oxford's scientists in the discovery and use of penicillin. The University is also responsible for the lovely **Harcourt Arboretum** at **Nuneham Courtenay**, 4 miles south of Oxford.

To the southeast of the city lies the 16th century **Garsington Manor**, the home of the socialite Lady Ottoline Morrell between 1915 and 1927. With her husband Philip she played host to a whole generation of writers, artists and intellectuals including Katherine Mansfield, Siegfried Sassoon, TS Eliot, Rupert Brooke and Bertrand Russell.

AROUND OXFORD

BICESTER

11½ miles NE of Oxford on the A41

Established in Saxon times, Bicester (pronounced Bister) later acquired both an Augustinian priory and a Benedictine nunnery, but much of the old part of the town was lost during a disastrous fire in the early 18th century. The founding here of the Army's ordnance depot in 1941 brought much new development, which continued up until the 1960s in what had hitherto been a chiefly agricultural community.

EYNSHAM

6½ miles W of Oxford on the A40

To the south of this ancient market town lies **Stanton Harcourt Manor**, which dates back to the 14th century and is noted for its well-preserved medieval kitchen. It was while staying here that Alexander Pope translated Homer's *Iliad*, working in a 15th century tower that is now called Pope's Tower.

WOODSTOCK

8 miles NW of Oxford off the A44

Woodstock is known the world over and attracts visitors by the million to the magnificent **Blenheim Palace**, one of the very few sites in the country on the World Heritage List. The estate was a gift from Queen Anne to John Churchill, 1st Duke of Marlborough, for his victory at the Battle of Blenheim during the Spanish War of Succession, but the Queen's gratitude ran out before the building work was finished and the Duke had to meet the remainder of the costs himself. Designed by Sir John Vanbrugh and built between 1705 and 1722,

---

•

Aldous Huxley based an account of a country house party at Garsington Manor in his satirical novel Crome Yellow *on his experiences there and, in so doing, caused a rift between himself and his hostess. DH Lawrence also fell out with Lady Morrell when he drew a less than flattering portrait of life at her house in* Women in Love.

•

341 STURDY'S CASTLE

Tackley

A traditional inn, a destination restaurant and a comfortable hotel close to Woodstock and Blenheim Palace.

see page 590

342 THE DUKE OF MARLBOROUGH

Woodleys, Woodstock

Long-established tenants have made the **Duke of Marlborough** one of the finest destination restaurants in the region and a very comfortable base for exploring the area.

see page 592

The Cross at Banbury is immortalised in the nursery rhyme 'Ride a cockhorse to Banbury Cross, to see a fine lady upon a white horse; rings on her fingers and bells on her toes, and she shall have music wherever she goes' It is not known who the fine lady was. Banbury's other legendary claim to fame is its spicy, fruity cakes, though at one time it was also famous for its cheeses, which were only about an inch thick.

---

343 THE KING'S HEAD

Fritwell

A popular steak house in a super country inn.

see page 591

---

the house is also famously associated with Sir Winston Churchill, who was born here in 1874, and among the grand collections, there are intimate mementoes from the great statesman's life. The surrounding parkland was landscaped by Capability Brown. The graves of Sir Winston and his parents lie in the churchyard of St Martin, which was formerly the parish church of Woodstock.

LOWER HEYFORD

12 miles NW of Oxford on the B4030

To the south of the village, which stands on the banks of the River Cherwell, is **Rousham**, a fine 17th century house built for the Dormer family, with magnificent gardens laid out by William Kent in 1738; they represent the first phase of English landscape gardening and remain the only complete William Kent garden to have survived.

Bloxham Museum, Banbury

CHIPPING NORTON

At 650 feet above sea level, this is Oxfordshire's highest town and was once an important centre of the wool trade. This medieval prosperity can be seen in the grandeur of the spacious **Church of St Mary**, which, like many other buildings in the town, endured substantial remodelling in the 19th century. To the west of the town centre is the extraordinary 19th century **Bliss Tweed Mill**, which was designed by George Woodhouse, a Lancashire architect, in the style of Versailles.

To the north, beyond **Over Norton**, are the **Rollright Stones** – one of the most fascinating Bronze Age monuments in the country. These great slabs of stone stand on a ridge which affords fine panoramic views.

AROUND CHIPPING NORTON

BANBURY

12½ miles NE of Chipping Norton on the A361

This historic market town has managed to preserve many of its old buildings and to retain its status as a leading livestock market. The famous **Banbury Cross** in Horsefair dates only from 1859 as the previous cross was destroyed by the Puritans during the Civil War. It was erected to commemorate the marriage of Queen Victoria's oldest daughter to the Crown Prince of Prussia, and the figures around the base, of Queen Victoria, Edward VII and George V, were added in 1914.

To the southwest of Banbury, in an old courthouse, is the **Bloxham Village Museum**, where the displays concentrate on the lives of Oxfordshire's rural inhabitants. Close by is the 14th century moated mansion, **Broughton Castle**, which was remodelled into a fine Tudor home in the 16th century. The castle figured prominently in the Civil War, when its secret room was used by leaders of the Parliamentary forces to lay their plans.

CHARLBURY

5½ miles SE of Chipping Norton on the B4022

Charlbury was once famous for its glove-making as well as being a centre of the Quaker Movement – the simple **Friends Meeting House** here dates from 1779 and there is also a Friends cemetery. Close to the Meeting House is **Charlbury Museum**, where the town's charters can be seen. Close by are two interesting great houses. On the opposite bank of the River Evenlode from the main town lies **Cornbury Park**, a large estate that Elizabeth I gave to Robert Dudley. Although most of the house now dates from the 17th century, this was originally a hunting lodge in Wychwood Forest and it had been used since the days of Henry I. Just to the west is **Ditchley Park**, a restrained, classical, early 18th century house with superb interiors; it was used as a weekend

headquarters by Sir Winston Churchill during World War II when Chequers was thought to be unsafe.

WITNEY

10½ miles S of Chipping Norton on the A4095

Situated at the bottom of the valley of the River Windrush, Witney developed as a planned town in the early Middle Ages. Wool was the economic base of life here and Witney developed weaving and, in particular, the making of blankets. The **Blanket Hall**, which sports the arms of the Witney Company of Weavers, was built for the weighing and measuring of blankets in an age before rigid standardisation.

Just outside the town is the **Cogges Manor Farm Museum**, which tells the stories of the lives of those who have worked the surrounding land for centuries.

Just to the west of Witney lies **Minster Lovell**, one of the prettiest villages along the River Windrush and home to the once impressive 15th century manor house, **Minster Lovell Hall**. Built between 1431 and 1442, this was one of the aristocratic houses of Oxfordshire and home of the influential Lovell family. Although the hall was dismantled in the 18th century and the ruins turned into lowly farm buildings, the remains in this serene setting are extremely picturesque.

SHIPTON-UNDER-WYCHWOOD

6 miles SW of Chipping Norton off the A361

The suffix 'under-Wychwood' is derived from the ancient royal

344 THE MASONS ARMS

Swerford, nr Chipping Norton

A fine country pub widely acclaimed for its outstanding food.

see page 593

345 THE SAYE & SELE ARMS

Broughton, nr Banbury

Cask Marque approved ales and well-chosen wines accompany top-notch cooking at this welcoming village inn.

see page 594

346 THE WHITE SWAN

Wiggington

Thirsts are quenched and fresh-air appetites satisfied at a fine old pub in excellent walking country.

see page 594

347 THE CARPENTERS ARMS

Fulbrook, nr Burford

Patrons come form many miles around to enjoy the superb food and the outstanding hospitality at a marvellous country inn.

 see page 595

348 THE MERRYMOUTH INN

Fifield, nr Stow-on-the-Wold

An outstanding country inn with a history going back to the 13th century. Widely acclaimed for its superb food and accommodation.

 see page 596

hunting forest, **Wychwood Forest**, the remains of which lie to the east of this village. Though cleared during the Middle Ages, it was still used as a royal hunting ground until well into the 17th century; 150 years later there was little good wood left and the forest was rapidly cleared to provide arable land. The forest was one of the alleged haunts of Matthew Arnold's *Scholar Gypsy*.

BURFORD

11 miles SW of Chipping Norton on the A361

The site of a battle between the armies of Wessex and Mercia in AD 752, the town and surrounding area were given after the Norman Conquest to Bishop Odo of Bayeux, William the Conqueror's brother.

An important centre of the wool trade for centuries, Burford saw something of a revival with the stage coaching era and many of the old inns still survive.

With the atmosphere of a small cathedral, the wonderful **Church of St John** was built on the wealth of the wool trade and has several interesting features, including the Guild of Merchants Chapel, glass by Charles Kempe and a memorial to Edmund Harman, Henry VIII's barber and courtier, that contains what could be the first representation of a native American Indian in this country.

The town's 16th century courthouse, with its open ground floor, is now home to the **Tolsey Museum**.

Rutland

The motto of England's smallest county is, appropriately, 'multum in parvo' ('much in little'). It has two delightful market towns, Oakham and Uppingham, and 52 small, unspoilt villages of thatch and ironstone cottages clustered round their churches. The county's central feature is **Rutland Water**, which extends over 3,300 acres and is the largest man-made reservoir in Europe. Started in 1971 to supply water to East Midlands towns, it was created by damming the valley near Empingham. There's good walking around its 26-mile shoreline, some great bird-watching (including wild ospreys), excellent trout and pike fishing, and a wide variety of water sports.

Curiously for such a pastoral, peaceful county, it was Rutland men who were prime movers in two of the most dangerous conspiracies in England's history. In a room over the porch of **Stoke Dry Church**, the Gunpowder Plot was hatched with the local lord of the manor, Sir Everard Digby, as one of the ringleaders. Some 75 years later, Titus Oates and his fellow conspirators hatched the anti-Catholic 'Popish Plot' at his home in Oakham.

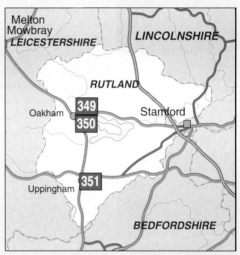

349 THE GRAINSTORE
BREWERY

Oakham

A working brewery in a converted Victorian grainstore, with superb home-brewed beer and an excellent lunchtime menu.

 see page 597

350 NICK'S
RESTAURANT
WITH ROOMS

Oakham

Part of Lord Nelson House Hotel offering an unbeatable combination of great food, comfort and impeccable service.

 see page 598

OAKHAM

Just off the Market Place of Rutland's county town is **Oakham Castle**, a romantic, evocative fortified manor house built between 1180 and 1190, with the earliest surviving example of an aisled stone hall in the country. Only the Great hall survives. One of the most unusual attractions is a collection of horseshoes presented by royalty and nobility to the Lord of the Manor. Notable natives of Oakham include the infamous conspirator Titus Oates, born here the son of a Baptist minister in 1649. The famed midget Jeffrey Hudson was born in 1619 in a cottage that still stands today. His father worked for the Duke and Duchess of Buckingham at nearby Burley-on-the-Hill. The Duchess was much taken with Jeffrey and dressed him in fine clothes, keeping him as a sort of mascot. During a visit to Burley by Charles I and his wife Henrietta Maria, the story goes that little Jeffrey delighted the

assembled company by springing out of a pie. He became a great favourite at court in London, where he was knighted and had his portrait painted by Van Dyck.

One of Rutland's best-known landmarks, **Normanton Church**, stands on the very edge of Rutland Water, which was formerly part of the Normanton Estate and now houses a display dedicated to the construction of the reservoir by Anglian Water and a history of the area. On the north shore of Rutland Water, the **Butterfly Farm & Aquatic Centre** contains a walk-through jungle with tropical butterflies and birds; ponds with koi carp and terrapins; an insect cave with tarantulas, scorpions and other mini-beasts; a monitor lizard enclosure; and a display of local coarse and game freshwater fish. Tel: 01780 460515.

Ospreys can be seen between May and September and the famous British Bird Watching Fair takes place in August.

To the northeast of Oakham is **Cottesmore**, the home of the **Rutland Railway Museum**, a working steam and diesel museum open some weekends.

In the tiny village of **Tickencote**, off the A1 west of Stamford, stands the **Church of St Peter**, famed for its glorious sexpartite vaulting over the chancel. Equally breathtaking is the chancel arch, and other treasures include a fine 13th century font and a life-size wooden effigy of a 14th century knight.

Rutland Railway Museum, Cottesmore

UPPINGHAM

This picturesque stone-built town is the major community in the south part of the county. The town is known for its bookshops and art galleries, but whereas other places are dominated by castles or cathedrals, in Uppingham it's the impressive **Uppingham School** that gives the town its special character. The school was founded in 1584 by Robert Johnson, Archdeacon of Leicester, who also founded Rutland's other celebrated public school at Oakham. For more than 250 years, Uppingham was just one of many such small grammar schools, giving rigorous instruction in classical languages to a couple of dozen sons of the local gentry. Then, in 1853, the Reverend Edward Thring was appointed headmaster. During his 43-year tenure the sleepy little school was transformed.

The Old School Building still stands in the churchyard, with trilingual inscriptions around the walls in Latin, Greek and Hebrew. In its place rose a magnificent complex of neo-gothic buildings: not just the traditional classrooms and a (splendid) chapel, but also a laboratory, workshops, museum, gymnasium and the most extensive school playing fields in the country.

The old school, the 18th century studies, the Victorian chapel and schoolrooms, and the 20th century great hall, all Grade I or Grade II listed, can be visited on a guided tour on Saturday afternoons in summer.

LYDDINGTON

3 miles SE of Uppingham off the A6003

A quiet village where English Heritage oversees the **Bede House**, one of the finest examples of Tudor domestic architecture in the country. This house of prayer was once part of a retreat for the Bishops of Lincoln and was later converted to almshouses, a role it fulfilled until 1930.

351 THE VAULTS

Uppingham

A much-loved old hostelry on the market square, with a friendly bar, an excellent restaurant and comfortable guest accommodation.

see page 598

Shropshire

The glorious border county of Shropshire hides a turbulent past, when the Marcher Lords divided their time between fighting the Welsh and each other. The remains of their fortresses can be seen in various places, and one of the finest Roman sites in the country is at Wroxeter - Viroconium was the first Roman site to be developed in this part of the country. There are ancient market towns that serve the rich farmland and some magnificent stately homes; and Shropshire saw the birthplace of the Industrial Revolution that began at Ironbridge Gorge. This stretch of the Severn Valley is now a World Heritage Centre, which ranks it alongside the Pyramids, the Grand Canyon and the Taj Mahal, and several interesting museums can be found here. Along with man-made places of interest, visitors will find spectacular scenery around Wenlock Edge, Long Mynd and Clun Forest and the extraordinary Tar Tunnel.

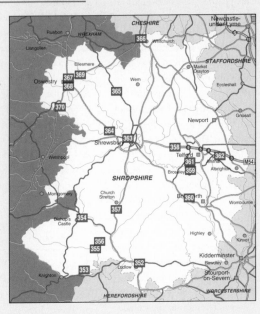

LUDLOW

Often referred to as 'the perfect historic town', Ludlow has more than 500 listed buildings along with a medieval street pattern that remains virtually intact. **Ludlow Castle** was built on a rocky promontory above a curve of the River Teme by the Normans in the 11th century as one of a string of castles along the Marches. It has been home to many distinguished families and to royalty, including Edward V and Prince Arthur; it was also the headquarters of the Council of the Marches, which governed Wales and the border counties until 1689.

The parish **Church of St Laurence** is one of the largest in the county; the ashes of AE Housman, author of *A Shropshire Lad*, lie beneath the north door, and he is commemorated by a tablet on the outer wall. Other places to see are **Castle Lodge**, which was once a prison and later the home of the officials of the Council of the Marches, the Georgian **Dinham House**, the Feathers Hotel and the **Museum**.

Ever since 1960, the town has played host to the annual Ludlow Festival, one of the country's major arts festivals that lasts for a fortnight in June and July and the centrepiece of the event is an open-air performance of a Shakespeare play in the castle's inner bailey.

Just northwest of the town lies Ludlow Racecourse, a charming, rural National Hunt course, while a few miles to the southeast lies the village of **Burford**. On the banks of the River Teme stands **Burford House**, whose four acre garden is filled with well over 2,000 varieties of plants. The garden is also the home of the National Collection of Clematis.

AROUND LUDLOW

BISHOP'S CASTLE

14 miles NW of Ludlow on the B4385

Surrounded by the great natural beauty of the border country, little remains of the castle that was built here in the 12th century for the bishops of Hereford. The **House on Crutches Museum** is situated in one of the oldest and most picturesque of the town's buildings – its gable end is supported on wooden posts that explain the unusual name. North of Bishop's Castle lie the **Stiperstones**, a rock-strewn quartzite outcrop rising to a height of 1,700 feet at the Devil's Chair. A bleak, lonely place, the ridge is part of a 1,000-acre National Nature Reserve.

CHURCH STRETTON

12 miles N of Ludlow on the A49

Just behind the High Street is the **Church of St Laurence** that has Saxon foundations and, over the aisle, is a memorial to three boys who were tragically killed in a fire in 1968. The memorial takes the form of a gridiron – the symbol of St Laurence, who was burned to death on one in AD 258. A mile from the town centre are Carding Mill Valley and the **Long Mynd**.

352 THE UNICORN

Ludlow

A friendly pub near the centre of Ludlow, particularly popular for its home cooking.

see page 599

353 THE BARON OF BEEF

Bucknell, nr Knighton

Relaxed eating, real ales, fine wines, good value and great service in a family-run country inn. Adjacent caravan site.

see page 600

354 THE SIX BELLS

Bishops Castle

A favourite place for lovers of hearty home cooking and connoisseurs of real ale, with its own micro-brewery.

see page 601

355 ROCKE COTTAGE TEAROOMS

Clungunford, nr Craven Arms

Light lunches, homemade cakes, scones and puddings in a delightful, very English setting.

 see page 602

356 THE ENGINE & TENDER

Broome, nr Craven Arms

A sociable, family-friendly pub with plenty of eating choice and a caravan/camping park.

 see page 602

357 THE GREEN DRAGON INN

Little Stretton

Real ales from national and local breweries and wholesome home cooking in a friendly pub close to the famous Long Mynd.

 see page 603

Stokesay Castle, Craven Arms

The valley and the moorland into which it runs are very popular for walking and picnicking.

Just to the southwest lies the pretty village of **Little Stretton** that nestles in the Stretton Gap. The most interesting building here is the black and white timber-framed **All Saints Church**, with its thatched roof and general cottage-like appearance.

BRIDGNORTH

16½ miles NE of Ludlow on the A458

Straddling the River Severn, this ancient market town comprises Low Town and, some 100 feet up on sandstone cliffs, High Town. In 1101, Robert de Belesme built a Castle here but all that remains now is part of the keep tower. Bridgnorth's oldest complete building is 16th century **Bishop Percy's House**, a handsome townhouse that

was one of the few timber-framed buildings to survive a devastating fire in 1646. The **Northgate Museum** is a good place to start a tour of this interesting town, and the **Costume and Childhood Museum** is guaranteed to appeal to all ages. On the outskirts of the town, in the grounds of **Stanmore Hall**, is the **Midland Motor Museum** that holds an outstanding collection of more than 100 vehicles.

Bridgnorth is the northern terminus of the wonderful **Severn Valley Railway** but the town has another irresistible attraction in the **Castle Hill Cliff Railway**, a funicular railway built in 1892 that

Dudmaston Hall, nr Bridgnorth

links the two parts of the town. Sir John Betjeman likened a ride on this lovely little railway to a journey up to heaven. The alternative to the railway is seven sets of steps or the meandering, historic Cartway.

MUCH WENLOCK

16½ miles NE of Ludlow on the A4169

Among the mellow buildings of this delightful small town are some places of real beauty, including the timber-framed **Raynald's Mansion** and the magnificent 16th century **Guildhall**.

The most interesting building is the **Priory of St Milburga** that was originally founded as a nunnery in the 7th century by King Merewald, who installed his daughter Milburga as head of the house. Among the remains, the

Jackfield Tile Museum, Ironbridge

Prior's Lodge, dating from around 1500, is particularly impressive, while away from the main site is St Milburga's Well, whose waters are reputed to cure eye diseases.

TELFORD

Telford is a sprawling modern town that absorbed several existing towns in the Shropshire coalfield. The name chosen in the 1960s commemorates Thomas Telford, whose influence can be seen all over the county.

AROUND TELFORD

IRONBRIDGE

3 miles S of Telford off the B4373

This town, at the centre of **Ironbridge Gorge**, is part of an area of the Severn Gorge where the world's first cast-iron bridge was constructed and where, over 250 years ago, the Industrial Revolution first began in earnest. In this locality, now designated a World Heritage Centre, the first iron wheels, the first iron rails and the first steam railway locomotive were made.

The **Ironbridge Visitor Centre** offers the ideal introduction to the series of museums here, including the **Museum of Iron** at **Coalbrookdale**, and

358 THE RED LION

Wellington, nr Telford

Local ales and classic pub dishes in a pleasant inn opposite The Wrekin.

 see page 603

359 THE SWAN

Ironbridge

A splendid pub at the heart of England's industrial heritage, with a menu full of quality and variety. 13 rooms for B&B.

see page 604

360 THE ACTON ARMS

Morville, nr Bridgnorth

A popular village pub with all the traditional virtues – warm welcome, friendly hosts and staff, good food and drink.

see page 604

Coalbrookdale, nr Ironbridge

Outstanding hospitality, a great range of real ales and generous servings of home-cooked food in a historic setting.

 see page 605

Shifnal

Excellent, imaginative modern cooking in a popular restaurant open Tuesday to Saturday evenings.

 see page 606

Shrewsbury

Housed in Shrewsbury Castle the **Shropshire Regimental Museum** tells the proud story of the four Shropshire Regiments.

 see page 606

the neighbbouring furnace that was used by Abraham Darby when he first smelted iron with coke; the **Jackfield Tile Museum**, which houses a fine collection of wall and floor files from Victorian times through to the 1950s; and the **Coalport China Museum** with its marvellous displays of porcelain that span over two centuries.

Nearby is the extraordinary **Tar Tunnel**, which was a popular tourist attraction in the 18th century as well as being one of the most interesting geological phenomena in Britain. Further upstream from Ironbridge is one of the finest ruined abbeys in England, **Buildwas Abbey**, virtually complete, though roofless, after 850 years.

SHIFNAL

4 miles E of Telford on the A464

On the A41 at **Cosford**, near Shifnal, the **RAF Museum** houses an important collection of aircraft, aero engines and weapons of war from all over the world.

TONG

6 miles E of Telford on the A41

Charles Dickens set the closing chapters of The Old Curiosity Shop in Tong and Little Nell's home was right by the church.

To the east of the village lie the ruins of White Ladies Priory, a 12th century nunnery dedicated to St Leonard. Nearby is **Boscobel House**, a timber-framed building where Charles II hid after his defeat at the Battle of Worcester in 1651. The secret room where he hid can be seen, as can the Royal Oak, which was grown from an acorn taken from the original tree in which the King escaped a house search by Cromwell's men.

SHREWSBURY

Situated in a horseshoe bend in the River Severn, this lovely county town occupies, almost, an island site and it was on the two well-protected hills here that the Saxon town developed. Later, the Normans built a **Castle**, which last saw action in the Civil War, and a great Benedictine Abbey on the site of a Saxon wooden church. The **Abbey Church** remains a place of worship to this day, and the Castle is now home to the **Shropshire Regimental Museum**. Close to the abbey is the **Shrewsbury Quest**, which presents the sights and sounds of medieval Shrewsbury as it grew and prospered on the wealth generated by the woollen trade.

It was at Shrewsbury that Charles Darwin was born and educated and, earlier, Robert Clive, Clive of India, lived in the town and was Mayor in 1762. His home, **Clive House**, contains mementoes from his life along with a display dedicated to Charles Darwin, whose statue can be seen opposite the castle. Just outside Shrewsbury, at **Longden Coleham**, is a museum with a difference – the **Coleham Pumping Station** – which houses the splendid Renshaw pumping engines that powered Shrewsbury's sewerage system until

1970. There are more than 30 churches in Shrewsbury and one of the finest is St Mary's, the town's only complete medieval church.

One of the many guided tours and suggested walks in this marvellous town leads north to a place known as the **Battlefield**. It was here, in 1403, that the armies of Henry IV and the insurgent Harry Hotspur met; in the brief but bloody battle there were many casualties, including Hotspur.

To the southeast of the town lies the village of **Atcham**, and close by is one of the finest houses in Shropshire, the splendid neo-classical **Attingham Park** with grand Regency interiors and delightful grounds that were landscaped by Humphry Repton.

A little further from Shrewsbury lies **Wroxeter**, home to one of the most important Roman sites to have been excavated. Known as **Viroconium**, it was the first town to be established by the Romans in this part of the country. Six miles north of Shrewsbury on the A49 stands the village of **Grinshill**. This is a neat, quaint little place and the area is a walker's paradise; the hill rises to 630 feet above sea level, and its greatest asset is the substance from which it is made – sandstone. The Romans quarried it for the construction of Wroxeter, and in more recent times it was used for the door surrounds of No 10 Downing Street. The quarry has revealed many rare fossils and has accordingly been designated a Site of Special Scientific Interest.

AROUND SHREWSBURY

WEM

10½ miles N of Shrewsbury on the B5476

Although this is a peaceful place today Wem was virtually destroyed during the War of the Roses and, later, it was again attacked during the Civil War.

Fortunately some notable buildings survived the great fire that devastated much of the town in the 17th century and these

364 THE WINGFIELD ARMS

Montford Bridge, nr Shrewsbury

A super pub for all the family, with three real ales and excellent home cooking. Caravan site; fishing rights on the Severn.

 see *page 607*

Wroxeter Roman City, nr Shrewsbury

Burlton, nr Shrewsbury

Good food, good wine, good service and superior B&B accommodation in an immaculate country inn.

 see page 609

Grindley Brook

A popular roadhouse with menus strong on flavours and value for money. Camping/caravan site at the back.

 see page 608

Oswestry

Roomy, relaxing and very professionally run, **The Walls** is the top place in Oswestry for food and entertainment.

 see page 610

include **Astley House**, the home of the painter John Astley. Another famous person associated with the town is Judge Jeffreys, of the Bloody Assizes, whose official residence was at Lowe Hall.

Wem is the home of the modern sweet pea, which was developed by the 19th century nurseryman, Henry Eckford, and the Sweet Pea Show and carnival take place here annually.

WHITCHURCH

19 miles N of Shrewsbury on the A49

First developed by the Romans and known as Mediolanum, Whitchurch has been the most important town in the northern part of the county for centuries. The main street is dominated by the tall sandstone tower of **St Alkmund's Church**, while hidden away in the heart of the town are the Old Town Hall Vaults, where the composer Edward German was born in 1862. Whitchurch is also the home of **Joyce Clocks**, the oldest tower clockmakers in the world.

The long-distance footpath, the Shropshire Way, passes near Whitchurch, as does the Llangollen Canal, and nature lovers can explore the local wetland habitats at Brown Moss, which lies just to the south of the town.

MARKET DRAYTON

17 miles NE of Shrewsbury on the A529

Mentioned in the *Domesday Book* as Magna Draitune, Market Drayton changed its name when Abbot Simon Combermere obtained a

Royal Market charter in 1245; a market continues to be held here every Wednesday.

To the east of town is the village of **Moreton Say**, where locally born Robert Clive, Clive of India, is buried in St Margaret's Church.

A few miles southwest of Market Drayton lies a beautiful Georgian mansion, **Hawkestone Hall**, which was the ancestral home of the Hill family from 1556 until 1906. Hawkestone Park is a woodland fantasy of caves, follies, grottoes and secret tunnel and pathways.

NESSCLIFFE

9 miles NW of Shrewsbury on the A5

Close to the village is **Nesscliffe Hill Country Park** where paths lead up through woodland to the hill, a sandstone escarpment, from which there are glorious views out across Shropshire and to Wales.

A short distance north of Nesscliffe is the village of **Ruyton-XI-Towns**, which acquired its curious name in medieval times when 11 communities were united into the one borough of Ruyton.

OSWESTRY

17 miles NW of Shrewsbury off the A5

This important market town takes its name from Oswald, a Saxon king who was killed in a battle in AD 642 and whose dismembered body was hung on the branches of a tree. Local legend then tells an eagle swooped down and carried off one of his arms and, where the limb fell to the ground, a spring bubbled up to mark the spot and it was around St Oswald's Well that the town developed while the well became a place of pilgrimage.

Due to several fires that ravaged the town's old timber-framed buildings, Oswestry's architecture is chiefly Georgian and Victorian but various fine old buildings do still remain including **St Oswald's Church**. Standing in the grounds of the church is the 15th century **Holbache House** that was once a grammar school and now houses a Heritage Centre.

In 1559, a plague killed almost a third of the town's inhabitants and the Croeswylan Stone commemorates this disaster as well as marking the spot to which the market was moved during the days of the infection.

Oswestry was the headquarters of the Cambrian Railway Company until it amalgamated with the Great Western Railway in 1922 and as recently as the 1960s there were over 1,000 railwaymen in the area. One of the old engine sheds now houses the **Cambrian Museum of Transport**, where a collection of railway memorabilia, along with some old bicycles and motorbikes, is on display.

About five miles south of Oswestry lies the village of **Llanymynech** that was once a town of some standing, with a major canal and a thriving industry based on limestone. The quarried limestone was taken, after processing, to the nearby canalside wharf on the Montgomery Canal that was built at the end of the 18th century chiefly for this purpose.

ELLESMERE

15½ miles NW of Shrewsbury on the A495

The most impressive building here is undoubtedly the parish **Church of St Mary the Virgin**; built by the Knights of St John, it has an exceptional 15th century carved roof in the chapel. This church overlooks **The Mere**, the largest of several local lakes, which is home to herons, Canada geese and swans, and an ideal place for boating enthusiasts and anglers.

368 THE RED LION

Oswestry

Great food, great hospitality and comfortable B&B rooms in the heart of Oswestry.

see page 609

369 THE PENRHOS ARMS

Whittington

A convivial, family-friendly country hostelry with excellent home cooking and little caravan/camping site.

see page 611

370 THE BLACK HORSE INN

Maesbrook, Oswestry

Super home cooking and the warmest of welcomes in a friendly pub close to the Welsh border.

see page 611

Somerset

Somerset has more than its fair share of natural beauty. The wilds of Exmoor and the ranges of spectacular hills such as the Quantocks and the Mendips add to this county's allure. In the far northwest is Exmoor, once wild hunting country: its abundance of prehistoric sites, ancient packhorse bridges and wild deer and ponies easily make it one of the more romantic and mysterious spots. As the

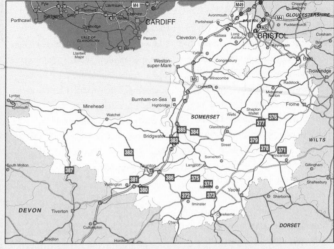

Mendips are limestone, the hills are full of holes, and, in particular, this area is known for its caves at Wookey Hole and the spectacular Cheddar Gorge, which carves a path right through the hills as well as lending its name to the cheese.

Below the hills is the charming and ancient city of Wells, from where the county's plain stretches out to Glastonbury, a place shrouded in mystery and steeped in early Christian and Arthurian legends.

YEOVIL

In the 1890s, James Petter, a local pioneer of the internal combustion engine, founded a business here that was to become one of the largest manufacturers of diesel engines in Britain. It later moved to the Midlands, but a subsidiary was established during World War I to produce aircraft and Yeovil became well known as the home of Westland Helicopters. Situated in Wyndham House, the **Museum of South Somerset** documents the social and industrial history of the town and surrounding area.

To the south lies **Barwick Park**, an estate that is littered with bizarre follies, while to the west is the magnificent Elizabethan mansion, **Montacute House**, which has one of the grandest long galleries in the country. **Montacute** village is also the home of the **TV and Radio Memorabilia Museum**. In the lanes to the southeast of Montacute and close to the village of **West Coker** is the magnificent **Brympton d'Evercy Manor House** dating from Norman times but with significant 16th and 17th century additions.

AROUND YEOVIL

SPARKFORD
7 miles NE of Yeovil off the A303

Home to the **Haynes Motor Museum**, which holds one of the largest collections of veteran, vintage and classic cars and motorbikes in the country. Just to the east of Sparkford is **Cadbury**

Castle, a massive Iron Age hill fort that is also believed by some to be the location of King Arthur's legendary Camelot.

CASTLE CARY
11½ miles NE of Yeovil on the B3152

Once the site of an impressive Norman castle, this little rural town has some interesting old buildings, including a handsome 18th century post office, a tiny 18th century lock-up called the Round House, and a splendid Market House that is now home to the **Castle Cary District Museum**.

WINCANTON
13 miles NE of Yeovil off the A303

This attractive old cloth-making town was also a bustling coaching town, lying almost exactly half way between London and Plymouth. Modern day Wincanton is a peaceful light industrial town whose best-known attraction is the **National Hunt Racecourse**. Also worth visiting are the beautiful Hadspen House Gardens that are situated to the northwest.

CREWKERNE
8 miles SW of Yeovil on the A356

A thriving agricultural centre during Saxon times, Crewkerne even had its own mint in the decades that led up to the Norman invasion. The town lies close to the source of the River Parrett, from where the 50-mile long River **Parrett Trail** follows the river through some of the country's most ecologically sensitive and fragile areas. Just a couple of miles southwest of

In the church at East Coker were buried the ashes of the poet and playwright TS Thomas (Stearnes) Eliot. This village, where his ancestors lived, is mentioned in **Four Quartets**, *a poem written by Eliot, and two lines from that poem are quoted on his memorial tablet.*

371 THE BULL INN

Brewham, nr Bruton

Fresh local produce is to the fore in the splendid dishes served in this friendly village inn

see page 612

372 THE WYNDHAM ARMS

Kingsbury Episcopi

A traditional country pub that sets the highest standards in hospitality, food and drink

🍴 see page 613

373 THE WHEATSHEAF

South Petherton

One of the most sociable and likeable pubs in the region, a great place to pause for a drink or a meal

🍴 see page 614

Forde Abbey, nr Chard

Crewkerne, close to the village of **Clapton**, are the interesting **Clapton Court Gardens**.

CHARD

15 miles SW of Yeovil on the A30

Although Chard has expanded rapidly since World War II, it still retains a pleasant village-like atmosphere; its museum is located in the attractive thatched **Godworth House**.

To the northwest of the town is a 200-year old corn mill, **Hornsbury Mill**, whose impressive water wheel is still in working order; to the northeast lies **Chard Reservoir Nature Reserve**, a conservation area that is an important habitat for wildlife.

Close to the county border lies **Forde Abbey**, which was founded in the 12th century by Cistercian monks. The remains of the Abbey were incorporated into the grand private house of the Prideaux family, and among the many treasures are the renowned Mortlake Tapestries brought from Brussels by Charles I. The gardens are equally superb.

ILMINSTER

13 miles W of Yeovil on the A358

On the outskirts of the ancient agricultural and ecclesiastical centre of Ilminster is the handsome part-Tudor mansion, **Dillington House**, the former home of the influential Speke family.

John Speke of Dillington House was an officer in the Duke of Monmouth's ill-fated rebel army and, following the rebellion's disastrous defeat at the Battle of Sedgemoor, Speke was forced to flee abroad, leaving his brother George, who had done no more than shake the Duke's hand, to face the wrath of Judge Jeffreys and the inevitable death sentence. Jeffreys justified his decision with the words 'His family owes a life and he shall die for his brother.'

MARTOCK

6 miles NW of Yeovil on the B3165

The old part of Martock is blessed with an unusually large number of fine buildings, including the **Treasurer's House**, a small two-storey house dating from the late 13th century, and a 17th century Manor House, the home of Edward Parker, the man who exposed the Gunpowder Plot.

To the east of Martock are the enchanting **Tintinhull House Gardens**.

YEOVILTON

5 miles NW of Yeovil off the A37

Here is one of the world's leading aviation museums, the **Fleet Air Arm Museum**, which contains a unique collection of aircraft, many on permanent display.

MUCHELNEY

9½ miles NW of Yeovil off the A372

Muchelney is the location of an impressive part-ruined Benedictine monastery, **Muchelney Abbey**, thought to have been founded by King Ine in the 8th century. Opposite the parish church stands the Priest's House, a late medieval hall house that was built by the abbey.

WELLS

The first church here is believed to have been founded by King Ine in around AD 700 but the present **Cathedral of St Andrew** was begun in the 12th century. Taking over three centuries to complete, the treasures of this wonderful place include the 14th century **Astronomical Clock**, one of the oldest working timepieces in the world. Set in the pavement outside the Cathedral walls is a length of brass that extends over the prodigious distance leapt by local girl Mary (Bignall) Rand when she set a world record for the long jump. To the south of the cathedral's cloisters is the **Bishop's**

374 THE WYNDHAM ARMS

Ilton, nr Ilminster

A friendly free house with ales from local breweries and a fine variety of excellent home-cooked dishes.

see page 615

375 THE LAMB & LION

Hambridge

A superb country inn serving a good selection of drinks and home-style cooking.

see page 616

Fleet Air Arm Museum, Yeovilton

267

376 THE STRODE ARMS

**West Cranmore,
nr Shepton Mallet**

A charming, picturesque inn
with well-kept ales and a
choice of bar and restaurant
menus.

 see page 616

377 THE PRESTLEIGH INN

Prestleigh, nr Shepton Mallet

A super country inn with
food and drink served all
day long and comfortable,
practical B&B rooms.

 see page 617

378 THE PILGRIMS AT LOVINGTON

Lovington

The pub that thinks it's a
restaurant – with rooms.
Outstanding in every aspect,
and a place to put on top of
any visitor's list

 see page 618

Palace, a remarkable
fortified medieval building
that is surrounded by a moat
fed by the springs that give
the city its name. On the
northern side of the
cathedral green is 14th
century Vicar's Close, one of
the oldest planned streets in
Europe.

To the north of the city
lies **Wookey Hole**, where
the carboniferous limestone
has been eroded away over
the centuries to create over
25 caverns. During
prehistoric times, lions, bears
and woolly mammoths lived
in the area.

The **Great Cave** at
Wookey contains a rock
formation known as the Witch of
Wookey that casts a ghostly shadow
and is associated with the gruesome
legends of child-eating. Nearby lies
the dramatic **Ebbor Gorge**, now a
National Nature Reserve managed
by English Nature.

AROUND WELLS

CHEW MAGNA

11½ miles N of Wells on the B3130

The nucleus of this former wool
village is its three-sided green at the
top of which is the striking early
16th century **Church House**
while, behind a high wall adjacent
to the churchyard, lies **Chew
Court**, a former summer palace of
the Bishops of Bath and Wells.

To the south of Chew Magna
are the two reservoirs constructed
to supply Bristol with fresh water

East Somerset Railway, Shepton Mallet

but that also provide a first class
recreational amenity.

NORTON ST PHILIP

15½ miles NE of Wells on the A366

The monks who founded the now-
ruined Priory were also responsible
for building the village's most
famous landmark – the splendid
George Inn – that was originally
established as a house of hospitality
for those visiting the priory.

To the west is one of the finest
Neolithic monuments in the west
of England, **Stoney Littleton
Long Barrow** that was built over
4,000 years ago.

SHEPTON MALLET

5 miles E of Wells on the A371

From before the Norman Conquest
and through the Middle Ages
Shepton Mallet was at first a centre

of woollen production and then a weaving town. Several fine buildings date back to those prosperous days including the 50 feet **Market Cross**, which dates from around 1500, and The Shambles, a 15th century wooden shed where meat was traded. Each year, Shepton Mallet plays host to two agricultural shows: the **Mid-Somerset Show** in August and, in May, the **Royal Bath and Wells Show**.

FROME
14½ miles E of Wells on the A362

Frome's old quarter is an attractive conservation area where can be found the **Blue House** that was built in 1726 as an almshouse and a boy's school and is one of the town's numerous listed buildings.

GLASTONBURY
5½ miles SW of Wells on the A39

This ancient town of myths, legends and tales of King Arthur and the early Christians is an attractive market town dominated by the dramatic ruins of its abbey. If the legend of Joseph of Arimathea is to be believed, **Glastonbury Abbey** is the site of the earliest Christian foundation in the British Isles. However, it is the Abbey's connection with King Arthur and his wife Queen Guinevere that draws most visitors to Glastonbury, as this is thought by some to be their last resting place. Even the **Somerset Rural Life Museum** cannot escape from the influence of the Abbey as the impressive 14th century barn here

once belonged to the Abbey.

To the east of the town lies **Glastonbury Tor**, a dramatic hill that rises above the surrounding Somerset Levels. The 520 feet Tor has been inhabited since prehistoric times and excavations have revealed evidence of Celtic, Roman and pre-Saxon occupation. It has long been associated with myth and legend (Joseph of Arimathea is said to have built a church here) and has been identified as the Land of the Dead, the Celtic Otherworld, a Druid temple, an Arthurian hill fort and a rendezvous point for passing UFOs.

In the nearby village of **Street**, the Clark family began to produce sheepskin slippers in the 1820s; the oldest part of the Clark's factory is now a fascinating **Shoe Museum**.

BURNHAM-ON-SEA
15 miles W of Wells on the B3140

A large and popular seaside resort whose most distinctive landmark is the **Low Lighthouse**, a curious square structure that is raised above the beach on tall stilts. To the

379 THE TRAVELLERS REST

Stone, East Pennard, nr Shepton Mallet

An aptly named country inn offering classic pub food, good beers and wines and 2 comfortable B&B rooms.

🍴 🛏 *page 619*

Glastonbury Abbey

As the name 'Cheddar Cheese' refers to a recipe and not a place, Cheddar can be made anywhere in the world. However, North Somerset is dotted with cheese manufaucturers, some of which offer guided tours, craft demonstrations and catering facilities for those who come to gorge on the renowned speciality.

380 THE WHITE HART INN

Corfe, nr Taunton

A cosy, likeable village inn that served real ales and excellent home cooking.

see page 619

northeast lies Brent Knoll, whose 445 feet summit is crowned with the remains of an Iron Age hill fort.

CHEDDAR

7½ miles NW of Wells on the A371

This sprawling village is best known for its dramatic limestone gorge, **Cheddar Gorge**, which is characterised by its high vertical cliffs, from which there are outstanding views.

This village is also renowned for its caves and, of course, its cheese. The term 'Cheddar cheese' refers to a recipe that was developed in the mid 19th century by Joseph Harding, a farmer and pioneer food scientist from near Bath who made the first scientific investigation into cheese making.

From the nearby remote village of **Charterhouse** a footpath leads up onto **Black Down**, which at 1,067 feet is the highest point in the Mendips; from here, to the northwest, the land descends down into Burrington Combe, a deep cleft that is said to have inspired the Reverend Augustus Toplady to write *Rock of Ages*.

The Mendip Hills were once a royal hunting ground and, to the northwest of Cheddar, lies **King John's Hunting Lodge**, home to an excellent **Local History Museum.**

Cheddar Gorge

TAUNTON

Founded by the Saxon King Ine in the 8th century, Taunton, the county town of Somerset, had by Norman times grown to have its own Augustinian monastery, a Minster and a Castle – an extensive structure whose purpose had always been more as an administrative centre than as a military post. The **Castle** is now the home of the **Somerset County Museum** and the **Somerset Military Museum**. Somerset's famous County Cricket Ground occupies part of the priory grounds and a section of the old monastic gatehouse now houses the fascinating **Somerset**

County Cricket Museum.

Taunton's attractive **National Hunt Racecourse** is one of the best country courses in Britain.

In the lanes to the north of Taunton lie the beautiful Hestercombe Gardens on the south-facing foothills of the Quantocks just north of the village of Cheddon Fitzpaine.

AROUND TAUNTON

WELLINGTON

6 miles SW of Taunton on the A38

It was from this pleasant old market town that the Duke took his title and, to the south, stands the **Wellington Monument**, a 175 feet obelisk erected to commemorate his great victory at Waterloo.

BISHOP'S LYDEARD

4½ miles NW of Taunton off the A358

This large village is the southern terminus of the **West Somerset Railway**, the privately operated steam railway that runs to Minehead on the Bristol Channel coast.

NETHER STOWEY

9½ miles N of Taunton on the A39

It was while staying in a friend's cottage here that Samuel Taylor Coleridge wrote most of his famous works, including *The Rime of the Ancient Mariner*. When not writing, he would go on long walks with his friend and near neighbour William Wordsworth. The Coleridges stayed here for three years and Coleridge Cottage now displays mementos of the poet.

HINKLEY POINT

13½ miles N of Taunton off the A39

Hinkley Point is perhaps best known for its great power stations and, at the **Hinkley Point Visitor Centre**, visitors can find out just how the adjacent power station creates electricity while, the **Hinkley Point Nature Trail** leads walkers through a wide diversity of habitats.

BRIDGWATER

9 miles NE of Taunton on the A38

Situated at the lowest bridging point of the River Parrett, Bridgwater is an ancient inland port and industrial town. As the river began to silt up, Bridgwater underwent something of an industrial renaissance, as the river mud that closed the port also proved to be an excellent scourer when baked.

To the southwest, near Enmore, is the small redbrick country mansion of **Barford Park**, a delightfully proportioned Queen Anne house that is set in extensive grounds which incorporate a large area of woodland. Further southwest again is **Fyne Court**, which is the headquarters of the **Somerset Wildlife Trust** and whose grounds have been designated a nature reserve.

BURROW BRIDGE

9 miles NE of Taunton on the A361

This village on the River Parrett is home to one of several pumping stations that were built in Victorian times to drain the Somerset Levels - the **Pumping Station** is open to

381 THE WHITE HORSE INN

Bradford-on-Tone, nr Taunton

A handsome old village inn with CAMRA-accredited ales and a fine reputation for home-cooked food

 see page 620

382 THE FARMERS ARMS

Combe Florey, nr Taunton

A friendly, sociable family-run village pub with a good choice of ales and an award-winning chef.

 see page 620

383 THE BOAT & ANCHOR

The Boat & Anchor, Huntworth, nr Bridgwater

One of two well-run inns in the same ownership, both offering excellent hospitality, good food and comfortable guest accommodation.

 see page 621

271

Chilton Polden, nr Bridgwater

The Olive Mill is a striking modern pub offering real ales, a large Mediterranean-inspired menu and well-appointed bedrooms. Excellent wheelchair access.

 see page 621

Bawdrip, nr Bridgwater

Traditional surroundings in which to enjoy Cask Marque accredited ales and superb home cooing with an emphasis on zingy fresh seafood.

 see page 622

Wrantage, nr Taunton

Good food, good beer and a good friendly atmosphere are a winning combination at a popular village inn

 see page 623

the public occasionally throughout the year; here, too, is the **Somerset Levels Basket and Craft Centre**.

Just west of Burrow Bridge, the **Bridgwater and Taunton Canal** winds its way through some of the most attractive countryside in the Somerset Levels and the restored locks, swing bridges and engine houses add further interest to this picturesque walk.

Just northwest of the village of **Westonzoyland** is the site of the last battle to be fought on English soil when, in July 1685, the forces of James II heavily defeated the followers of the Duke of Monmouth in the bloody Battle of Sedgemoor.

EXMOOR & THE QUANTOCK HILLS

The characteristic heartland of the **Exmoor National Park** is a high, treeless plateau of Devonian shale carved into a series of steep-sided valleys by the prolonged action of the moor's many fast-flowing streams.

Exmoor is crisscrossed by a network of paths and bridleways, which provide superb opportunities for walking and pony-trekking. Many follow the routes of the ancient ridgeways across the high moor and pass close to the numerous hut circles, standing stones, barrows and other Bronze and Iron Age remains which litter the landscape. The remarkable medieval packhorse bridge known

as **Tarr Steps** lies to the north of the village of **Hawkridge**, near Dulverton.

MONKSILVER

13 miles NW of Taunton on the B3188

To the southwest of this pretty village of charming old houses and thatched cottages are the **Brendon Hills**, the upland area within the Exmoor National Park from where, in the mid 19th century, iron ore was mined in significant quantities and then carried down a steep mineral railway to the coast for shipment to the furnaces of South Wales.

WATCHET

15 miles NW of Taunton on the B3191

It was at Watchet that, in the 6th century, St Decuman is said to have landed from Wales with the cow that he brought along to provide sustenance. It was also from Watchet that Coleridge's imaginary crew set sail in *The Rime of the Ancient Mariner*.

To the south of Watchet, in the village of **Williton**, are the diesel locomotive workshops of the **West Somerset Railway** and the **Bakelite Museum**, a fascinating place providing a nostalgic look at the 'pioneer of plastics'. Just to the west lies **Cleeve Abbey**, the only monastery in Somerset that belonged to the austere Cistercian order.

MINEHEAD

21½ miles NW of Taunton off the A39

A popular seaside town at the foot of the wooded promontory of

North Hill, now a nature reserve, Minehead is one of the county's oldest settlements. As the port declined, the town began to expand as a seaside resort and in 1962 a popular holiday camp was opened.

To the west of Minehead lies the village of **Selworthy**. This picturesque and much photographed village is situated on the side of a wooded hill. Just to the northwest lies **Selworthy Beacon**, one of the highest points on the vast Holnicote Estate. Covering some 12,500 acres of Exmoor National Park, it includes a four-mile stretch of coastline between Minehead and Porlock Weir. **Dunkery Beacon**, the highest point on Exmoor, rises to 1,700 feet.

To the southeast lies **Dunster**, dominated by **Dunster Castle**, a medieval fortification that was remodelled in 1617 and was one of the last Royalist strongholds in the West Country to fall during the Civil War. In the castle's parkland is 18th century **Dunster Working Watermill**; little remains of Dunster Priory apart from its priory church and an unusual 12th century dovecote.

PORLOCK WEIR

26½ miles NW of Taunton off the A39

Once an important seaport, Porlock Weir is a picturesque place where a Submerged Forest, a relic of the Ice Age, can be seen at low tide. From Porlock Weir a pretty mile-long walk leads up through walnut and oak woodland to **Culbone Church**, the smallest church in

Dunster Watermill

regular use in England, and certainly one of the most picturesque. A true hidden treasure, measuring only 33 feet by 14 feet, this superb part-Norman building is set in a wooded combe that once supported a small charcoal-burning community and was at other times home to French prisoners and lepers. The **South West Coast Path** passes this lovely secluded church.

To the west lies **Doone Valley**, a long enclosed sweep of green pasture and mature woodland that was immortalised by RD Blackmore in his classic romantic novel *Lorna Doone*.

DULVERTON

19 miles W of Taunton on the B3222

Situated in the wooded Barle Valley on the edge of Exmoor, Dulverton is a pretty little town where the

387 THE ANCHOR INN

Exebridge, Dulverton

A picturesque village inn that's equally popular as a much-loved local, a destination restaurant and a comfortable holiday base

see page 624

One of Bristol's most famous features is the graceful Clifton Suspension Bridge that spans the River Avon. Opened in 1864, five years after the death of its designer Brunel, it provided magnificent views over the city and the surrounding countryside. The land just to the west of the Bridge is now the Avon Gorge Nature Reserve.

headquarters of the Exmoor national park can be found in an old converted workhouse.

BRISTOL

Situated at a strategically important bridging point at the head of the Avon gorge, the West Country's largest city and sometime administrative centre of the county of Avon, Bristol was founded in Saxon times and soon became a major port and market centre. During the Middle Ages, it expanded as a trading centre and at one time was second only to London as a seaport. In the early 19th century, the harbour was expanded when a semi-artificial waterway, the Floating Harbour, was created by diverting the course of the River Avon to the south.

Today, the main docks have moved down stream to Avonmouth and the **Floating Harbour** has become home to a wide assortment of pleasure and small working craft. Much of Bristol's waterfront has now been redeveloped for recreation, and several museums tell of the city's connections with the sea. The **Maritime Heritage Centre** is dedicated to the history of shipbuilding in Bristol and has a number of historic ships moored at the quayside, including Brunel's mighty SS *Great Britain*, the world's first iron-hulled passenger liner, launched in 1843.

AROUND BRISTOL

WESTON-SUPER-MARE

17 miles NW of Wells on the A370

A popular seaside resort with all the trappings, including the Edwardian **Grand Pier** (one of the last traditional iron-piled piers), the Winter Gardens and an Aquarium, as well as the fascinating **North Somerset Museum**. Close by is the start of the Mendip Way, a 50-mile long footpath that takes in the whole length of the Mendip Hills and ends at Frome.

CLEVEDON

18½ miles NW of Wells on the B3133

Clevedon Pier is a remarkably slim and graceful structure that was built in the 1860s from iron rails intended for Brunel's ill-considered South Wales Railway. When part of the pier collapsed in the 1970s, its long-term future looked bleak but, following an extensive restoration programme, the pier is now the landing stage in the summer for large pleasure steamers.

BATH

The ancient Celts were the first to become aware of the healing powers of the mysterious steaming spring here but it was the Romans who were the first to enclose the spring. The restored Roman remains centre on the Great Bath, a rectangular lead-lined pool that stands at the centre of the complex system of buildings. In the 8th century the Saxons founded a nunnery here but the present-day **Bath Abbey** dates from the 15th century and is considered to be the ultimate example of English Perpendicular church architecture.

Bath developed into a magnificent Georgian spa resort under the influence of three gentlemen: Beau Nash, who became the Master of Ceremonies; the architect father and son, both called John Wood; and the entrepreneur Ralph Allen, who made his first fortune developing an efficient postal system for the provinces and his second as the owner of the local quarries that supplied most of the honey-coloured stone for the city's wonderful Georgian buildings.

Among the many fine buildings here are **Queens Square**; the **Royal Crescent**, the first terrace in Britain to be built to an elliptical design; the **Pump Room** completed in 1796; and the **Assembly Rooms**. Spanning the River Avon is the magnificent

Bath Postal Museum

Pulteney Bridge that was inspired by Florence's Ponte Vecchio. Among the most interesting of Bath's several museums are the **Bath Postal Museum**, with its reconstruction of a Victorian sorting office, and the **Jane Austen Centre** – the novelist spent a good deal of time here.

Just to the east of the city lies the 16th century country mansion, Claverton Manor, now the **American Museum and Gardens**.

Staffordshire

Southern Staffordshire encompasses many changing landscapes, from the busy industrial towns of Stafford and Burton upon Trent to the peace and quiet of Cannock Chase. Along with the Hednesford Hills, the Chase provides a wonderful open area of woodland and moorland that is one of the county's great recreational areas. One legacy of the Industrial Revolution and a feature throughout the whole of Staffordshire is the canal network. The motorways of their day, the network linked not only the industrial centres of the county with each other but also with the rest of the country. The northeast of the county, some of which lies in the Peak District National Park, is an area of undulating moorland that makes ideal walking and cycling country. However, the Industrial Revolution has left its mark here in the form of two great reservoirs – Rudyard and Tittesworth. Staffordshire is, of course, home to the Potteries, the area around Stoke-on-Trent that is world famous for its pottery industry. The natural resources of coal and clay found here and the foresight of such men as Wedgwood and Minton saw what began as a

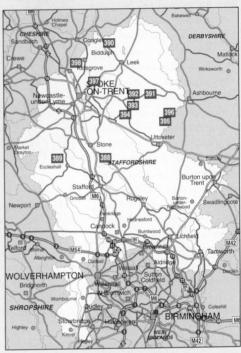

cottage industry explode into one of the great factory systems of the 18th century.

LICHFIELD

Lichfield Cathedral is particularly renowned for the three magnificent spires that dominate the city's skyline. Inside there are many treasures, including the beautiful 8th century illuminated manuscript The Lichfield Gospels and Sir Francis Chantrey's famous sculpture *The Sleeping Children*. The surrounding Cathedral Close is regarded by many as the most original and unspoilt in the country, and, being separated from the rest of the city by Stowe and Minster Pools, it is also a peaceful haven of calm.

Lichfield's most famous son is Dr Samuel Johnson, the poet, novelist and author of the first comprehensive English dictionary. The son of a bookseller, Johnson was born in 1709 in Breadmarket Street, and the house is now the **Samuel Johnson Birthplace Museum**. Another famous son is Erasmus Darwin, the doctor, philosopher, inventor, botanist and poet, and the grandfather of Charles Darwin. **Erasmus Darwin's House** has touch-screen computers to access Darwin's writings and inventions, and a garden with herbs and shrubs that would have been familiar to the good doctor.

The Wall Roman Site, **Letocetum**, has the remains of a bath house and mansion, the most substantial in the country.

AROUND LICHFIELD

ALREWAS

5 miles NE of Lichfield off the A38

The **National Memorial Arboretum**, to the east of this pretty village, is the first large arboretum and wildlife reserve to be created in Britain for 200 years. A substantial grant from the Millennium Commission has transformed this 150-acre former gravel quarry into a sylvan temple whose themes are remembrance and reconciliation. The central

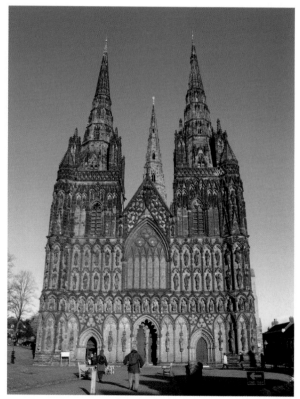

Lichfield Cathedral

Tamworth Castle

William Bass began brewing at Burton in 1777 and by 1863 the brewery produced half a million barrels of beer each year. Now the biggest brewery site in the UK, it brews 5.5 million barrels a year. The brewery is open for tours, and the entry fee includes a tour of the Coors Visitor Centre in Horninglow Street.

feature is the Millennium Avenue, created from cuttings from a 2,000-year-old lime tree.

BURTON UPON TRENT
11 miles NE of Lichfield on the A38

Burton has long been famous for its brewing industry that began many centuries ago - even the monks of the Benedictine Abbey, founded here in 1100, were not the first to realise that Burton well water was specially suited to brewing.

TUTBURY
13 miles NE of Lichfield on the A511

This historic small town is dominated by the imposing remains of **Tutbury Castle**, where Mary, Queen of Scots, was imprisoned for a while. During the Civil War, Tutbury Castle remained loyal to the Crown while the town was under the control of Parliament. After a three-week siege, the castle surrendered and in the following

year, 1647, Parliament ordered its destruction.

TAMWORTH
7 miles SE of Lichfield on the A51

Dominating Tamworth is the fine Norman motte and bailey **Castle** that originally dates from the 1180s. The Town Hall, built in 1701, was paid for by Thomas Guy, the local Member of Parliament, who was the founder of the London hospital that bears his name.

To the south of Tamworth lies **Drayton Manor Family Theme Park**, and further on stands **Middleton Hall**, the former home of Francis Willoughby, a 17th century naturalist and a founder member of the Royal Society.

To the northwest of Tamworth is the village of Whittington that is home to the **Museum of the Staffordshire Regiment** (The Prince of Wales's) at the Victorian Whittington Barracks.

BURNTWOOD
4 miles W of Lichfield on the A5190

The 700 acres of land and water known as **Chasewater Heaths** are an unexpected find in this otherwise urban setting. Criss-crossed by paths and bridleways, it supports many and varied plants and animals, some so rare that a large area has been designated a Site of Special Scientific Interest. The volunteer-run Chasewater Railway, a former colliery railway, operates passenger services behind tank engines between Brownhills West and Norton Lakeside stations.

STAFFORD

The county town of Staffordshire is Saxon in origin, though little of its early history is visible except for the extensive earthworks close to the castle and the foundations of a tiny Saxon chapel in the grounds of **St Mary's Church**. The grounds of the impressive Norman fortress, **Stafford Castle**, are used for historical re-enactments and also include a medieval herb garden.

One of the most interesting of the many old buildings in Stafford is the **Ancient High House**, a beautiful Elizabethan house built in 1595 that is the largest timber-framed town house in England. It now houses the **Museum of the Staffordshire Yeomanry**.

Close to the High House is the **Collegiate Church of St Mary**, an unusual building that dates in part from the late 12th century and was added to in the early English, Gothic and Victorian styles. Sir Izaak Walton was baptised here on 21st September 1593 and his bust can be seen on the north wall of the nave. Each year, at a civic service, a wreath is placed around the bust to commemorate his probable birthday (9th August).

To the north of Stafford lies the ancestral home of the Earl of Harrowby, **Sandon Hall**, which was rebuilt in 1850 after the earlier house had been damaged by fire.

Stafford Castle

AROUND STAFFORD

STONE

7 miles N of Stafford on the A51

The Trent and Mersey Canal played a large part in Stone's early economic development and, today, it still brings work to the town through the building of holiday canal cruisers and a growing tourist trade.

UTTOXETER

12 miles NE of Stafford on the A518

Today, the town is perhaps best known for its Racecourse, a popular National Hunt track with around 20 days of racing including the stamina-sapping Midlands Grand National held in the spring. Uttoxeter is a traditional, rural market town, with a busy livestock and street market on Wednesdays.

GREAT HAYWOOD

5 miles E of Stafford on the A51

This ancient village has the longest

388 THE GREYHOUND INN

Burston, nr Sandon, Stafford

A popular family-run village pub serving an impressive range of excellent home-cooked dishes.

 see page 625

279

Shugborough Hall, nr Great Haywood

packhorse bridge in England. Built in the 16th century, the **Essex Bridge** still has 14 of its original 40 arches spanning the River Trent.

To the southwest lies one of the most impressive attractions in the county, **Shugborough Hall**, the 17th century seat of the Earls of Lichfield. The wonderful staterooms and former servants' quarters have been beautifully restored, and the magnificent 900-acre estate includes **Shugborough Park Farm**, home to rare breed animals and host to demonstrations of traditional farming.

ABBOTS BROMLEY

10 miles E of Stafford on the B5234

This delightful 13th century village in the Vale of Trent is best known for its annual **Horn Dance**, the origins of which are lost in the mists of time. It is thought that the Horn Dance was first performed at the three-day Bartelmy Fair, granted to the Abbots of Burton by Henry III in 1226 to celebrate St Bartholomew's Day. In early September each year six male dancers carry the ancient reindeer horns around the village with six others and a fool, a hobby horse, a bowman and Maid Marian, the last being a man in drag. The reindeer horns used in the ceremony are kept in the Hurst Chapel of the Church of St Nicholas.

RUGELEY

7½ miles SE of Stafford on the A51

To the west of Rugeley lies **Cannock Chase**, a surprisingly wild place of heath and woodland that has been designated an Area of Outstanding Natural Beauty. Covering some 20,000 acres, the Chase was once the hunting ground of Norman kings and, later, the Bishops of Lichfield. In the unique military cemeteries near **Broadhurst Green**, some 5,000 German soldiers from World War I lie buried. Cannock Chase was used as a training ground during that war and was the last billet for many thousands of soldiers before they left for France. The **Museum of Cannock Chase** at the Valley Heritage Centre illustrates the social and industrial heritage of the area, and there are special exhibits in the Toys Gallery and the Coal Face Gallery.

CANNOCK

9 miles S of Stafford on the A34

To the southwest of Cannock is the Elizabethan **Moseley Old Hall**, which retains much of the original panelling and timber framing. The Hall sheltered King Charles II for a short time following his defeat at the Battle of Worcester in 1651.

WESTON-UNDER-LIZARD

10 miles SW of Stafford on the A5

Situated on the site of a medieval manor house, **Weston Park** has been the home of the Earls of Bradford for 300 years. Disraeli was a frequent visitor here and on one visit presented the house with a grotesque stuffed parrot, which still enjoys the hospitality of Weston Park. Fallow deer and rare breeds of sheep roam the vast grounds that also include nature trails, a miniature railway and a **Museum of Country Bygones**.

In the very south of the county, west of Wolverhampton, lies the village of **Perton**, scene of the Tough Guy Challenge. Started in 1987 and held twice a year, it is an eight-mile cross-country run followed by a series of obstacles such as flame pits, barbed wire and underwater tunnels. In what must be one of the toughest endurance tests in the world casualties are not unusual: in 1997 seven competitors broke legs, and 700 developed hypothermia in 2001.

ECCLESHALL

6½ miles NW of Stafford on the A5013

For over 1,000 years **Eccleshall Castle** was the palace of the bishops of Lichfield before becoming a family home when the Carter family moved from Yorkshire. The present simple sandstone house is typical of the best architecture of the William and Mary period and incorporates part of the 14th century castle.

A little way north of Eccleshall is **Mill Meece Pumping Station**, where two magnificent steam engines are kept in pristine condition. An exhibition tells the story of water and the history of the station.

Set in beautiful grounds in the tiny hamlet of **Shallowford**, to the northeast of Eccleshall, is **Izaak Walton's Cottage**, a pretty 17th century half-timbered cottage that was once owned by the famous

389 THE STAR INN

Copmere End, Eccleshall

A popular place to drink and dine, with the bonus of a beautiful garden.

See page 625

390 THE ROYAL OAK INN

Rushton Spencer

A good choice of real ales and a fine selection of home cooking in a characterful old coaching inn.

see page 626

391 THE CROSS INN

Caulden Lowe, nr Waterhouses, Leek

Well-kept ales, super food, quality accommodation and a caravan site in a delightful rural location.

see page 627

Izaak Walton's Cottage, Shallowford

392 THE RAILWAY INN

Froghall

Good food, a great family atmosphere and excellent accommodation in a fine old inn near Alton Towers.

 see page 628

393 THE ROYAL OAK HOTEL

Cheadle

A town-centre inn that's equally popular with locals, trusts and the passing trade, and a good stopover for nearby Alton Towers.

 see page 629

394 THE HUNTSMAN

Cheadle

A convivial former coaching inn serving popular pub dishes from 12 to 6 (12 to 4 Sunday).

see page 629

biographer and author of *The Compleat Angler* and is now a museum.

LEEK

William Morris, founder of the Arts and Crafts movement, lived and worked in Leek for many months between 1875 and 1878 and much of his time here was spent investigating new techniques of dyeing while also reviving the use of traditional dyes. **Leek Art Gallery** has displays on the intricate work of the famous Leek School of Embroidery that was founded by Lady Wardle in the 1870s.

Leek was the home of James Brindley, the 18th century engineer who built much of the early canal network. A water-powered corn mill built by him in 1752 in Mill Street has been restored and now houses the **Brindley Water Museum**, which is devoted to his life and work.

To the northwest of Leek is the village of **Rudyard**, the name chosen for their son by Mr and Mrs Kipling in fond memory of the place where they first met in 1863. The nearby two-mile long Rudyard Lake was built in 1831 by John Rennie to feed the Caldon Canal. The west shore of the reservoir is also a section of the Staffordshire Way, the long distance footpath that runs from

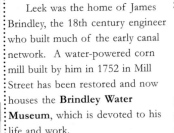

Blackbrook Zoological Park, Leek

Mow Cop to Kinver Edge, near Stourbridge.

AROUND LEEK

LONGNOR

8½ miles NE of Leek on the B5053

Found on a gentle slope between the River Manifold and the River Dove, Longnor was the meeting point of several packhorse routes. The **Market Square** is one of the oldest in England, dating back to medieval times. The village also has some fascinating narrow flagged passages that seem to go nowhere but suddenly emerge into the most beautiful scenery.

FROGHALL

6½ miles SE of Leek on the A52

Froghall Wharf was built along

the banks of the **Caldon Canal** to act as a trans-shipment area for limestone as it came down a railway incline from the quarries to the south of Waterhouses. Here, the limestone was tipped into narrow boats and later into railway wagons to be carried to Stoke-on-Trent. The once-busy Wharf declined after 1920 following the construction of the Manifold Valley Light Railway, which directly linked the quarries with Leek and the national railway network.

To the southeast lies **Hawksmoor Nature Reserve** and bird sanctuary that covers some 300 acres of the Churnet Valley and includes glorious landscapes, abundant natural history and industrial architecture.

CROXDEN

12 miles SE of Leek off the B5032

Tucked away in this secluded hamlet are the romantic ruins of **Croxden Abbey**, founded by the Cistercians in 1176. Although only the west front, south transept wall and a few of the eastern cloisters remain, the Abbey is well worth a visit.

CHEDDLETON

3 miles S of Leek on the A520

As well as being home to the **Churnet Valley Railway and Museum**, this village is also home to the restored Cheddleton Flint Mill, which lies in the rural surroundings of the Churnet valley. The water-powered machinery was used to crush flint that had been brought in by canal and then

transported, again by water, to Stoke, where it was used in the hardening of pottery. The small museum includes a rare 18th century 'haystack' boiler and a Robey steam engine, and there are also exhibits that relate to the preparation of raw materials for the pottery industry

To the south, **Consall Nature Park** is an RSPB reserve, a quiet and peaceful haven with much to delight the avid birdwatcher.

STOKE-ON-TRENT

It was the presence of the essential raw materials for the manufacture and decoration of ceramics, in particular marl clay, coal and water, that led to the concentration of pottery manufacturers in this area. Though production started in the 17th century, it was the entrepreneurial skills of Josiah Wedgwood and Thomas Minton, who brought the individual potters together in factory-style workplaces, that caused the massive leap forward in production in the 18th century. The Wedgwood and Minton factories were large, but there were also hundreds of small establishments producing a whole range of more utilitarian chinaware; production in The Potteries reached its height towards the end of the 19th century.

Among the many centres and museums telling the story of Stoke and pottery are the **Spode Museum and Visitor Centre**; the **Royal Doulton Visitor Centre**,

395 THE TAVERN

Denstone

Food is king at a popular village inn close to Alton Towers.

🍴 see page 630

396 MANOR HOUSE FARM

Prestwood, nr Denstone

The farmhouse and adjacent cottages provide outstanding accommodation in serene, scenic surroundings.

🛏 see page 631

397 CASTRO'S RESTAURANT & LOUNGE

Cheddleton, nr Leek

The coolest eating place for miles around, specialising in the palate-tingling tastes of Latin America.

🍴 see page 632

283

Apart from one of the most gifted football players who ever kicked a ball Stoke city has two other famous sons – Arnold Bennett, who immortalised the five pottery towns of Tunstall, Burslem, Hanley, Longton and Stoke in his novels, and John Smith, captain of the ill-fated Titanic.

and the **Wedgwood Visitor Centre and Museum**. The **Potteries Museum and Art Gallery** houses the world's finest collection of Staffordshire ceramics.

Etruria, to the west of the city centre, was created by Josiah Wedgwood in 1769 as a village for the workers at the pottery factory. Though the factory has gone (it moved to Barlaston in the 1940s), **Etruria Hall**, Wedgwood's home, is still standing in what is now the National Garden Festival site.

Stoke has a famous football team, Stoke City, and a local footballing hero, Sir Stanley Matthews.

To the south of Stoke-on-Trent are **Trentham Gardens** that were landscaped by Capability Brown and given a more formal style by Sir Charles Barry, whose work can be seen in the lovely Italian gardens. Although the Hall was demolished in 1911, this style can still be recognised in such buildings as the orangery and sculpture gallery.

AROUND STOKE-ON-TRENT

NEWCASTLE-UNDER-LYME

2 miles W of Stoke-on-Trent on the A53

One of Newcastle-under-Lyme's oldest buildings is the **Guildhall**, built in 1713 to replace an earlier timber building, which stands beside the base of a medieval cross. The **Borough Museum and Art Gallery**, set in eight acres of parkland, houses a wonderful collection of assorted items from clocks to teapots and paintings to clay pipes. A mile from the town centre, the **New Victoria Theatre** was Europe's first purpose-built 'theatre-in-the-round'.

To the southwest, on an ancient packhorse route from Newcastle-under-Lyme, is the village of **Madeley**, much of which has been designated a conservation area. Its charming focal point is The Pool, formed by damming the River Lea to provide waterpower for the corn mill, and now a haven for birds. Further southwest again is the **Dorothy Clive Garden** that was designed in the 1930s by

Dorothy Clive Gardens, nr Newcastle-under-Lyme

Biddulph Grange Gardens

398 THE CHESHIRE VIEW

Mow Cop, nr Stoke-on-Trent

The glorious views add to excellent home cooking at an outstanding village inn on the Staffordshire-Cheshire border.

see page 633

who first dreamt of building a canal to link the area with the major Trent and Mersey navigation and thus create a waterway link right across the country from Liverpool to Hull. He fought long and hard to get the necessary Bill passed through Parliament, undaunted by the fact that a 3,000-yard long tunnel would be needed to go through Harecastle Hill. The Bill was passed and, though many scoffed at his plans, Wedgwood's canal and tunnel were built by James Brindley over an 11-year period.

Colonel Harry Clive in memory of his wife. The original garden was a woodland garden created from a gravel pit that had become overgrown with all kinds of trees.

KIDSGROVE
5 miles N of Stoke-on-Trent on the A50

Now chiefly a residential town, Kidsgrove is home to the two **Harecastle Tunnels**, major engineering feats of their time, which carry the **Trent and Mersey Canal** from Cheshire into The Potteries. It was Josiah Wedgwood

BIDDULPH
5 miles N of Stoke-on-Trent on the A527

The gardens at **Biddulph Grange** are among the most unusual and remarkable in the whole country. The numerous high points include the Egyptian garden with a pyramid and clipped yew obelisks, and the Chinese garden features a joss house, a dragon parterre, a temple and a watch tower. The parterres and the Shelter House and Dahlia Walk have been restored to the way they were in the middle of the 19th century.

Suffolk

For much of its length the River Stour forms the county boundary between Suffolk and Essex, and here lies some of the county's most attractive and peaceful countryside. The beauty is largely unspoilt and those travelling through the area will come upon a succession of picturesque, ancient wool towns and villages, historic churches, stately homes and nature reserves. There is the wonderful preserved medieval town of Lavenham, the atmospheric old wool town of Long Melford and, of course, East Bergholt. This was the birthplace, in 1776, of John Constable, and two of his most famous subjects – Flatford Mill and Willy Lot's Cottage – can still be seen today looking much as they would have done in the great artist's day.

Much of inland Suffolk remains rich farmland, with ancient towns and villages along with some of the finest windmills and watermills in the country. While Suffolk has few equals in terms of picturesque countryside and settlements, it is also very much a maritime county, with more than 50 miles of coastline. The whole stretch is a conservation area, with miles of waymarked walks and cycle trails and an abundance of bird and wildlife. This coast has also been a constant source of inspiration for distinguished writers, artists and musicians. Between the major port of Ipswich in the south and the fishing port of Lowestoft in the north are some charming and popular seaside resorts, such as Southwold and Aldeburgh, which have tried their hardest to escape any brash commercialism and retain the charming and genteel atmosphere of a bygone age.

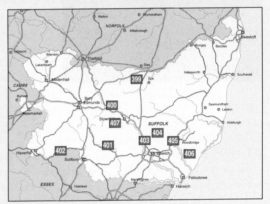

ACCOMMODATION

FOOD & DRINK

BURY ST EDMUNDS

This glorious Suffolk town takes its name from St Edmund, who was born in Nuremberg in AD 841 and came here as a young man to become the last king of East Anglia and the patron saint of England before St George. A staunch Christian, he was tortured and killed by the Danes in AD 870 and, after he was canonised in AD 910, his remains were moved to the abbey at Beodricsworth (later St Edmundsbury) where his shrine became incorporated into the Norman Abbey Church. The town grew up around the Abbey and soon became an important place of pilgrimage.

The **Abbey** was dismantled after the Dissolution but the imposing remains can be seen in the colourful **Abbey Gardens**. Originally the Church of St James, **St Edmundsbury Cathedral** was accorded cathedral status in 1914 and the 15th century building has been added to over the years. The latest work was a Millennium project to crown the Cathedral with a 140 feet Gothic-style lantern tower. Also in the complex is **St Mary's Church**, whose detached tower stands just as it did when erected in the 12th century. The **Abbey Visitor Centre**, situated in Samson's Tower, has displays concerning the abbey's history.

Along with its fine ecclesiastical buildings, there are many other places of interest in Bury, including museums, galleries and the **Theatre Royal**. Built in 1819 by William Wilkins, who was responsible for the National Gallery, and recently magnificently restored, it is still very much a working theatre; it once staged the premiere of Charley's Aunt. To the southwest, near **Horringer**, stands the extraordinary **Ickworth House**. Built in 1795 by the eccentric 4th Earl of Bristol, the massive structure comprises a central rotunda and curved corridors; it was designed to house his various collections that include paintings by Titian, Gainsborough, Hogarth and Reynolds and a magnificent collection of Georgian silver. The house is surrounded by an Italian garden and a park landscaped by Capability Brown.

•

To the northwest of Bury is Hengrave Hall, a rambling Tudor mansion that was built between 1525 and 1538 by Sir Thomas Kytson, a wool merchant. Later owners of the house were the Gage family, one member of which imported various kinds of plum tree from France. Most of the bundles arrived labelled but one had lost its name tag and, when it produced its first crop of luscious green fruit it became known as the green Gage and the name has stuck to this day.

•

Theatre Royal, Bury St Edmunds

Mellis, nr Eye

A handsome village pub providing a traditional setting for a drink or a meal. Also B&B rooms for overnight guests.

 see page 634

Elmswell

A popular pub by the station, with a convivial public bar and a menu of freshly prepared dishes

 see page 634

Chelsworth, nr Lavenham

A fine 14th century inn with a traditional bar, a lovely garden, well-kept real ales and a super choice of excellent home cooking.

 see page 635

AROUND BURY ST EDMUNDS

IXWORTH

6 miles NE of Bury St Edmunds on the A143

This is superb walking country and **Knettishall Heath Country Park**, close to the border village of **Barningham**, is the official starting point of the **Peddars Way National Trail**. Nearby is the pretty village of **Walsham-le-Willow** with its weatherboarded and timber-framed cottages and its ancient parish church.

WOOLPIT

7½ miles E of Bury St Edmunds off the A14

Famous for its bricks, the majority of the old buildings here are faced with 'Woolpit Whites', the yellowish-white brick that looked very much like more expensive stone. Some of the brick was used in the building of the senate wing of the Capitol in Washington DC. Red bricks were also produced and the village's **Bygones Museum** includes a brick-making display.

A charming Woolpit legend concerns the Green Children, a brother and sister with green complexions who appeared one day in a field, apparently attracted by the church bells. Though obviously hungry, they would eat nothing until some green beans were produced. The boy survived for only a short time, but the girl thrived, lost her green colour and was baptised and married a man from King's Lynn – no doubt leaving many a Suffolk man green with envy!

To the southeast is the group of villages collectively known as the **Bradfields** – St George, St Clare and Combust – that lie in a particularly delightful part of the countryside. Here, too, are **Bradfield Woods**, which have been managed by coppicing for hundreds of years.

LAVENHAM

10½ miles SE of Bury St Edmunds on the A1141

Lavenham is the most complete of all the original medieval wool towns. The medieval street pattern still exists, along with the market place and cross, and the finest of its many listed buildings is the superb 16th century timbered **Guildhall** which was originally the meeting place of the Guild of Corpus Christi, an organisation that regulated the production of wool.

Originally a 13th century home for Benedictine monks, **The Priory** is now a beautiful half-timbered house dating from around 1600 and, in the original hall, is an important collection of paintings and stained glass whilst the extensive grounds include a kitchen garden, herb garden and a pond.

John Constable went to school in Lavenham and one of his school friends was Jane Taylor, who wrote the words to *Twinkle, Twinkle Little Star.*

SUDBURY

The largest of the wool towns and once a busy port on the River Stour. Along with its three medieval churches, Sudbury is famous as being the birthplace, in 1727, of the painter Thomas Gainsborough; **Gainsborough's House** has more of the artist's work on display than any other gallery.

Northwest of Sudbury lies the attractive village of **Cavendish** where, housed in a 16th century rectory, the **Sue Ryder Foundation Museum** was opened by the Queen in 1979. Further upriver lies the medieval wool town of **Clare**, 'a little town with a lot of history' that is renowned for its **Ancient House**, a timber-framed building dating from 1473 noted for its remarkable pargeting. Another place of historical significance is **Nethergate House**, once the workplace of dyers, weaver and spinners. **Clare Castle Country Park** contains the remains of the castle and moat and has a visitors' centre in the goods shed of a disused railway line.

Gainsborough House, Sudbury

AROUND SUDBURY

LONG MELFORD

2 miles N of Sudbury off the A134

The heart of this atmospheric old wool town is its long and, in places, fairly broad main street filled with antique shops, bookshops and art galleries. Some of the town's houses are washed in the characteristic Suffolk pink that was originally created by mixing ox blood or sloe juice into the plaster. At the northern end of the street lies a 14-acre green and also **Holy Trinity Church**, an exuberant manifestation of the prosperity of the town in ages past. Edmund Blunden lived in Long Melford from 1965 to 1974 and is buried in the churchyard. To the east of the town lies 16th century **Melford Hall**, whose attractions include the panelled banqueting hall where Elizabeth I was entertained and a Beatrix Potter room where some of her watercolours and first editions of her books are on display. She was a frequent visitor to the house as her cousins, the Hyde Parkers, were the then owners. Further north is **Kentwell Hall**, a beautiful moated Tudor mansion.

HAVERHILL

15 miles W of Sudbury on the A1307

Although fire destroyed much of the town in 1665, **Anne of Cleves House**, (where the fourth wife of Henry VIII spent the remainder of

402 THE GLOBE

Clare, nr Sudbury

A handsome 16th century inn equally popular with locals and visitors to Clare. Greene King ales, traditional pub food.

🍴 see page 635

National Horseracing Museum, Newmarket

•

As far back as medieval times, the area around Newmarket was popular with riders, and in 1605 James I paused here on a journey north to enjoy a spot of hare coursing and so taken was he with the town, that he moved the royal court here. The tradition continued with Charles I but it was Charles II who really established the royal sport here when he initiated the Town Plate, a race that he won twice as a rider and that, in a modified form, still exists today.

•

her days), has been restored. To the northeast lies **Kedington**, home to the 'Cathedral of West Suffolk', the **Church of St Peter and St Paul**.

NEWMARKET

The historic centre of British horse racing, Newmarket is home to some 60 training establishments, 50 stud farms, the world famous thoroughbred sales and two racecourses. The majority of the population is involved in racing in one way or another and, among the racing art and artefact shops and galleries, there are the saddlers – one even has a preserved horse on display - Robert the Devil, the runner-up in the 1880 Derby.

The **National Horseracing Museum** chronicles the history of the sport from its royal beginnings through to the top trainers and

jockeys of today. Close by is **Palace House**, which contains the remains of Charles II's palace, while in the same street is **Nell Gwynn's House** that some say was connected to the palace by an underground tunnel. Other places in the town associated with horses are **Tattersalls**, where the leading thoroughbred sales take place between April and December; the **British Racing School**; and the **National Stud** that has, at one time, been home to three Derby winners – Blakeney, Mill Reef and Grundy.

To the southeast of Newmarket is the pretty village of **Dalham**, where the vast majority of the buildings are still thatched. The village is also the home of **Dalham Hall** which was built in the early 18th century on the orders of the Bishop of Ely. The home of the Duke of Wellington for several years it was, much later, bought by Cecil Rhodes who, unfortunately, died before taking up residence.

The ancient village of **Exning**, to the northwest of Newmarket, has been the home of Roman, Iceni, Saxon and Norman settlers. Struck by the plague during the Iceni occupation, its market was moved to the next village and thus the town of Newmarket acquired its name.

AROUND NEWMARKET

MILDENHALL

9 miles NE of Newmarket on the A11

For an insight into the town's heritage, the excellent **Mildenhall** and **District Museum** contains a wealth of local history exhibits, including the artefacts from the nearby RAF and USAAF base and the story of the **Mildenhall Treasure**, a cache of 4th century Roman silverware found by a ploughman in 1946 and now in the British Museum. This parish is the largest in Suffolk and it is fitting that it also boasts the magnificent **Church of St Mary**, which dominates the heart of the town.

In the village of **Barton Mills**, Sir Alexander Fleming had a country house and perhaps worked on the discovery of penicillin in his garden shed.

WEST STOW

9 miles NE of Newmarket off the A1101

In 1849, a Saxon cemetery was discovered here and further excavations have revealed traces of a Roman settlement and the Saxon layout of this village. Several buildings have been constructed using 5th century tools and methods and this fascinating village is now part of the **West Stow Country Park**.

IPSWICH

A Roman port and the largest in Anglo Saxon Britain, Ipswich prospered on the exportation of wool, textiles and agricultural products. Of the great Victorian buildings here the most memorable are the **Old Custom House**, the **Town Hall** and the splendid **Tolly Cobbold Brewery**, rebuilt at the end of the 19th century.

Christchurch Mansion survives from an older age, a beautiful Tudor home in glorious parkland, with a major collection of works by, most notably, Constable and Gainsborough. The town's **Museum** displays a wealth of exhibits from natural history through to a reconstructed Roman villa, while the **Ipswich Transport Museum** concerns itself with vehicles both mechanical and self-propelled.

The town's most famous son is undoubtedly Thomas Wolsey, who was born here in 1475 and who went on to become Lord Chancellor under Henry VIII.

On the outskirts of the town lies **Orwell Country Park**, an area of wood, heath and reed beds by the Orwell estuary. (George Orwell, born Eric Blair, took his name from the river; he often stayed with his parents in Southwold.) The **Ipswich & Gipping Valley Local Nature Reserves Management Project** comprises ten nature reserves

403 THE GREYHOUND

Claydon

A much-loved local with a much-loved landlady. Lunchtime snacks Monday to Friday and a thriving sporty side – football, darts and pool teams.

see page 636

West Stow Anglo Saxon Village

404 THE MOON & MUSHROOM

Swilland, nr Ipswich

A fine country inn with bags of character, less familiar locally brewed ales and top-notch cooking.

 see page 636

405 THE CHERRY TREE

Ridgmont

A flagship pub in Woodbridge, with a good choice of real ales, popular pub dishes and quiet, comfortable accommodation.

 see page 637

406 THE SORREL HORSE

Shottisham, nr Woodbridge

A splendid thatched 16th century inn set in tourist country southeast of Woodbridge. Great atmosphere, well-kept ales and a fine selection of home cooking.

see page 638

292

stretching up from Ipswich to Stowmarket.

Three miles south of Ipswich stands a tall, slender redbrick tower. Perhaps it is just a folly, perhaps a look-out tower, but the favourite story is that Freston's Tower was built by Lord de Freston as a place of study for his daughter Ellen, with a different one-room storey for each subject that filled her day: charity, tapestry, music, literature and astronomy.

AROUND IPSWICH

HELMINGHAM

8 miles N of Ipswich on the B1077

This village is home to **Helmingham Hall**, a moated Tudor house, and there's another moated hall in the nearby village of **Otley**, the home of Bartholomew Gosnold, who sailed to the New World, discovered Cape Cod and founded the settlement of Jamestown, Virginia.

WOODBRIDGE

7 miles NE of Ipswich on the A12

A market town for over 1,000 years, Woodbridge stands at the head of the Deben estuary and is a place of considerable charm, character and history. Shipbuilding flourished here and it was in a Woodbridge ship that Sir Francis Drake sailed in the 16th century.

The town's splendid Shire Hall now houses the **Suffolk Horse Museum** which is devoted to the Suffolk Punch breed of heavy working horse – the oldest such breed in the world. Other buildings

of note are the town's two marvellous mills, both still in working order – **Tide Mill** dates from the late 18th century and uses the power of the sea to turn its wheels and **Buttrum's Mill**, named after the last miller, is a tower mill standing just west of the town centre.

On the opposite bank of the River Deben, lies **Sutton Hoo**, a group of a dozen grassy barrows that hit the headlines in 1939 when excavations unearthed the outline of an 80 feet long Saxon ship filled with a great hoard of treasure. It is believed that the ship was the burial place of Raedwald, a King of East Anglia who died in about AD 625. This is one of the most important archaeological sites in the country, and the National Trust provides impressive facilities for visitors.

In the churchyard of St Michael in the little village of **Boulge**, a short distance northwest of Woodbridge, is the grave of Edward Fitzgerald, translator of the *Rubaiyat of Omar Khayyam*. The church stands in the grounds of his parents' house.

ORFORD

16½ miles NE of Ipswich on the B1084

Although the keep is all that remains of Henry II's **Castle**, it remains an impressive sight and the climb up the spiral staircase provides some splendid views. The Castle and the grand 14th century **St Bartholomew's Church** are a reminder that Orford was once an important town and a thriving port until the steadily growing shingle bank of Orford Ness gradually cut it off from the sea.

Though the sea has gone the river remains and, in the summer, the quayside is alive with yachts and pleasure craft. Across the other side of the river lies **Orford Ness**, the largest vegetated shingle spit in England and home to a variety of rare flora and fauna as well as a lighthouse. Now owned by the National Trust, the Ness can be reached by ferry, and there are also boat trips to the RSPB reserve of **Havergate Island**, the haunt of avocet and tern.

FELIXSTOWE

10 miles SE of Ipswich on the A14

The original fishing hamlet from which the Victorian town was developed is now called **Felixstowe Ferry** – a cluster of holiday homes, fishing sheds and a Martello Tower. The southernmost tip of this peninsula is **Landguard Point** where a nature reserve supports rare plants and migrating birds. Close by is **Landguard Fort**, which was built in 1718 to protect Harwich Harbour, and is now home to the **Felixstowe Museum** with its displays of local history, model aircraft and model paddle steamers.

EAST BERGHOLT

9 miles SW of Ipswich on the B1070

It was in this picturesque village that John Constable was born and, although his actual house is no longer standing, the site is marked by a plaque. Close by is Moss Cottage, which he once used as his studio, and the parish **Church of St Mary**, which contains memorials to Constable, his family and his friends.

A leafy lane leads south from the village to the River Stour and two of Constable's favourite subjects, **Flatford Mill** and **Willy Lot's Cottage**. At nearby **Flatford**, **Bridge Cottage** houses a Constable display.

The villages of Capel St Mary, Brantham and Stratford St Mary all have links with Constable, and it was in Stratford that Henry Williamson, author of *Tarka the Otter*, saw his first otter.

NAYLAND

14 miles SW of Ipswich on the B1087

A charming village found on a particularly beautiful stretch of the River Stour, Nayland has two fine 15th century buildings – **Alston Court** and the **Guildhall** – while its original 15th century wooden Abels Bridge was replaced a century later by a humped-back bridge that allowed barges to pass underneath.

HADLEIGH

8½ miles W of Ipswich on the B1070

This once prosperous wool town has a harmonious variety of architectural styles – from timber-framed buildings to elegant Regency and Victorian houses – but the gem here is the 15th century **Guildhall** with its two overhanging storeys.

There are two good walks from Hadleigh: over the medieval

In the early 19th century Colonel Tomline of Orwell Park created a port at Felixstowe to rival Harwich and went on to develop Felixstowe as a resort. By the time of his death in 1887, most of his dreams had been realised, but he did not live to see the completion of the Pier. Along with all the other usual attractions for holidaymakers, there is also the Felixstowe Water Clock, a curious piece that is assembled from industrial bits and pieces.

293

Suffolk Owl Sanctuary, Stowmarket

407 THE BUXHALL CROWN

Buxhall

A fine timber-framed country inn widely acclaimed for its cosy ambience, its well-kept ales and its superb cooking.

see page 639

Toppesfield Bridge and along the River Brett; and along the disused railway track between the town and Raydon to the south.

To the northwest is the photogenic postcard village of **Kersey**, whose main street has a Water Splash; this and the 700-year-old Bell Inn have featured in many films.

STOWMARKET

11 miles NW of Ipswich on the A14

In the heart of Suffolk, Stowmarket enjoyed a period of rapid growth when the River Gipping was still navigable to Ipswich, and again when the railway arrived. Much of the town's history is brought to life at the **Museum of East Anglian Life** which is surrounded by meadowland on the old Abbot's Hall estate, where the aisled barn dates from the 13th century. At **Stonham Barns**, to the east of Stowmarket, are the **Redwings Horse Rescue Centre**, with grazing for over 30 rescued horses, ponies and donkeys, and the **Suffolk Owl Sanctuary**.

ALDEBURGH

24 miles NE of Ipswich on the A1094

This is yet another town that had flourishing fishing and shipbuilding industries – Drake's *Greyhound* and *Pelican* were built at Slaughden, which was long ago taken by the sea. This village was also the birthplace, in 1754, of the poet George Crabbe, who created the character Peter Grimes, a solitary fisherman, who later became the subject of an opera by another Aldeburgh resident, Benjamin Britten. It was Britten who, in 1948, started the **Aldeburgh Festival**, a world-renowned arts festival based mainly at **The Maltings** at nearby **Snape**.

One of the town's major benefactors was Newson Garrett, a wealthy businessman who was the town's first mayor. As well as developing the Maltings, he produced a remarkable daughter, Elizabeth, who was the first woman doctor in England (she qualified in Paris) and the first woman mayor (of Aldeburgh in 1908).

The most interesting of Aldeburgh's older buildings is the **Moot Hall**, a 16th century timber-framed hall which has a little museum of the town's history. Aldeburgh also has a Martello Tower, built in 1814; it never saw action, though its guns were manned until the middle of the 19th century.

Benjamin Britten's grave, along with those of his friend Peter Pears and Imogen Holst, is in the churchyard of **St Peter and St**

Paul, and in the church itself is a wonderful stained glass window by John Piper depicting three Britten oratorios. The latest tribute to Britten is a huge metal clam shell designed by Maggie Hambling. The words on its rim – 'I hear those voices that will not be drowned' – are taken from Britten's opera *Peter Grimes*. It stands on the beach between Aldeburgh and the unique holiday village of **Thorpeness** with its mock-Tudor houses and the general look of an eccentric film set. Further up the coast is the Sizewell nuclear power station, while inland the busy town of **Leiston** is home to the fascinating **Long Shop Museum**, once the works of the renowned Garrett engineering works. Back along the coast is what remains of the one-time capital of East Anglia, **Dunwich**, which over the centuries was claimed by the sea. **Dunwich Heath** is one of Suffolk's most important conservation areas, while nearby **Minsmere**, best reached through the village of Westleton, is a marvellous RSPB sanctuary.

Aldeburgh Moot Hall

LOWESTOFT

The most easterly town in Britain, Lowestoft's heyday as a major fishing port came during the late 19th and early 20th centuries and, although the industry has declined since World War I, it remains a fishing port, and is also a popular holiday resort. Its main attractions are its lovely golden sands, safe swimming and two piers - one of these, **Claremont Pier**, built in 1902, was a landing place for daytrippers arriving on the famous Belle steamers.

The history of the town and its links with the sea are detailed in the **Lowestoft and East Suffolk Maritime Museum** and, nearby, the **Royal Naval Patrol Museum** remembers the minesweeping service.

Just north of the town is the largest theme park in East Anglia, **Pleasurewood Hills**. A little further afield lies **Somerleyton Hall**, one of the country's grandest and most distinctive stately homes, built in the Italian style by Samuel Morton Peto. Along with magnificent wood carvings and notable paintings, the grounds include a renowned yew-hedge

Lowestoft Maritime Museum

its classic Georgian exterior, actually dates from the mid 16th century and was built for a wealthy Tudor merchant. Many features from that age survive, including the brickwork and heavy timbered ceilings.

The town's maritime heritage is recorded in the **Museum**, which is housed in a Dutch-style cottage, and in the **Sailors Reading Room**.

On the other side of the River Blyth is **Walberswick** which was also once a flourishing fishing port. Today, it is best known for its bird sanctuary, Walberswick and Westleton Heaths. Inland lies one of the wonders of Suffolk, the **Church of the Holy Trinity** at **Blythburgh** that rises from the reed beds and is visible for miles around. Dubbed the 'Cathedral of the Marshes', its grandeur reflects the days when Blythburgh was a prosperous port until the river silted up.

HALESWORTH

14 miles SW of Lowestoft on the A144

An ancient market town, Halesworth reached its peak as a trading place when the River Blyth was made navigable as far as here in 1756. Along with some fine architecture the chief attraction here is the **Halesworth and District Museum**, housed in the town's station buildings.

FRAMLINGHAM

25 miles SW of Lowestoft on the B1119

This old market town is dominated by the **Castle** that was built by Roger Bigod, 2nd Earl of Norfolk, in the 12th century. It remained the

maze created in 1846, a little miniature railway and, still part of the estate, **Fritton Lake Countryworld**. Close by is **Herringfleet Windmill**, a beautiful black-tarred smock mill which is the last survivor of the Broadland wind pumps whose job it was to assist in draining the marshes. A little way south of Lowestoft, at **Carlton Colville**, is the **East Anglia Transport Museum** where visitors can enjoy rides on buses, trams and trolleybuses. Further south again is the small resort of **Kessingland**, the home of the **Suffolk Wildlife Park**, which includes a re-creation of the Plains of Africa.

AROUND LOWESTOFT

SOUTHWOLD

10 miles S of Lowestoft on the A1095

The most interesting building at this civilised seaside resort is **Buckenham House** which, despite home of the Earls and Dukes of Norfolk for generations before they moved to Arundel in 1635. Still in remarkably good condition, nine of the castle's 13 towers are accessible and, on one side, the view is of a noted bird sanctuary. In the splendid **Church of St Michael** is the beautifully adorned tomb of Henry Fitzroy, the illegitimate son of Henry VIII.

On the village green at **Saxtead Green** is a particularly attractive white 18th century **Post Mill** which dates back to 1796 and is, arguably, the best example of such a mill in the world.

BECCLES

8 miles W of Lowestoft on the A145

One of the few buildings to survive the fires that ravaged Beccles in the 16th and 17th centuries is **Roos Hall**, a gabled Dutch-style building dating from 1583. Another Dutch-style building houses the **Beccles and District Museum**, while the town's printing industry is remembered at its own **Printing Museum** at the Newgate works of printer William Clowes.

Norfolk and Suffolk Aviation Museum, Flixton

BUNGAY

13½ miles W of Lowestoft on the A144

An ancient town on the River Waveney, Bungay is best known for its **Castle**, which was built by Hugh Bigod, 1st Earl of Norfolk, as a rival to Henry II's castle at Orford. It was another Bigod, Roger, who came to Bungay in 1294 and built the round tower and mighty outer walls that still stand today. At **Flixton** is the **Norfolk and Suffolk Aviation Museum** which stands on the site of the USAAF Liberator base of World War II.

• *Situated at the southernmost point of the Broads, Beccles is an ancient town that was once a major supplier of herring to St Edmundsbury Abbey.* •

Surrey

Although the northern part of Surrey, which once ran all the way up to the south bank of the River Thames through the capital, has seemingly been engulfed by Greater London, this is an area rich in stately homes, notably the most magnificent royal palace of all – Hampton Court. In among this prosperous commuter land there are also several excellent racecourses, including Epsom, home of The Derby and The Oaks. The influence of London is soon lost as the countryside to the south and west gives way to leafy lanes, green fields and two famous natural features – the Hog's Back and the Devil's Punch Bowl.

Guildford, the county town of Surrey, is home to one of only two Anglican cathedrals built in England since the Reformation – the other is in Liverpool. While many travel through the county on their way to the south coast, it is

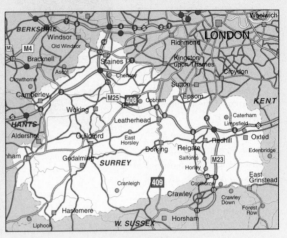

well worth pausing here and taking in the quintessentially English villages, such as Chiddingfold, the old Georgian market towns of Godalming and Farnham, and the genteel Victorian towns such as Haslemere that developed with the arrival of the railway.

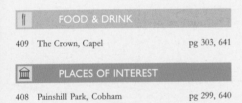

FOOD & DRINK

PLACES OF INTEREST

WEYBRIDGE

A surprisingly old settlement on the River Wey, this town once possessed a palace, Oatlands Park, where, in 1540, Henry VIII married his fifth wife, Catherine Howard. In 1907, the world's first purpose-built motor racing track was constructed on the nearby **Brooklands** estate and, although racing on this world-famous banked circuit came to an end with the outbreak of World War I, the old Edwardian clubhouse still stands, home to the **Brooklands Museum**.

Just to the southwest lies the remarkable **Whiteley Village**, a 200-acre model village founded on the instructions of the owner of a famous Bayswater department store who in 1907 left money in his will to house his retired staff.

AROUND WEYBRIDGE

RICHMOND

9 miles NE of Weybridge on the A316

Situated on a sweeping bend on the River Thames, the older part of this charming town is centred on **Richmond Green**, a genuine village green. Handsome 17th and 18th century houses flank the southern edges of the green, while the southwestern side was the site of 12th century Richmond Palace, where Elizabeth I died in 1603.

Richmond Hill leads upwards from the town centre and commands breathtaking views that both Turner and Reynolds have

captured. A little further up the hill is an entrance to **Richmond Park**, some 2,400 acres of open land on which deer roam.

KINGSTON UPON THAMES

7 miles NE of Weybridge on the A308

Kingston was a thriving medieval market town and ancient and modern buildings can be found side by side; close to the functional 1930s Guildhall is the **Coronation Stone**, which is said to have been used in the crowning of at least six Saxon kings.

A couple of miles southwest of Kingston lies one of the most magnificent royal residences, **Hampton Court**, which was built in 1516 by Cardinal Wolsey, Henry VIII's Lord Chancellor. After Wolsey's fall from power, the palace came into royal possession and the buildings and magnificent gardens seen today are the work of Henry VIII, Charles II and William III. The most famous feature in the 60 acres of grounds is undoubtedly the Maze, first planted in 1713.

ESHER

4½ miles E of Weybridge off the A3

The town has an excellent racecourse, **Sandown Park**, and is also home to the beautiful **Claremont Landscape Garden**, begun in 1715 and believed to be one of the earliest surviving examples of an English landscape garden. Over the years, some of the greatest names in garden history were involved in its creation, including Capability

On the banks of the Thames, south of Richmond, is Ham House, *one of the best examples of a Stuart stately home in the country.*

408 PAINSHILL PARK

Cobham
A beautiful 18th century landscape garden with many interesting walks to view all the attractions.

🏛 *see page 640*

To the west of Woking is Brookwood cemetery, the largest in the country (it once even had its own railway station) and the final resting place of the painter John Singer Sargent, the novelist Dame Rebecca West, King Edward the Martyr, the dance-band leader Carroll Gibbons, the murderess Edith Thompson and the society beauty Margaret, Duchess of Argyll, the subject of Cole Porter's popular song Youre' the Top.

Brown, John Vanbrugh and Charles Bridgeman.

COBHAM
4 miles SE of Weybridge on the A245

A busy residential town, Cobham has a **Bus Museum** with the largest collection anywhere of London buses. To the north lies 19th century **Foxwarren Park**, a bizarre house with eerie gables and multi-coloured bricks, while to the west is **Painshill Park**, a white 18th century house with particularly fine grounds. Just beyond Painshill, on Chatley Heath, is a unique Semaphore Tower that was once part of the Royal Navy's signalling system for relaying messages between Portsmouth and the Admiralty in London.

WOKING
6 miles SW of Weybridge on the A320

Amidst the largely Victorian buildings in this commuter town is the **Shah Jehan Mosque**, the first purpose built mosque in Britain.

To the east of Woking is the Royal Horticultural Society's

internationally renowned **Wisley Garden**.

LIGHTWATER
9½ miles SW of Weybridge on the A322

For many Londoners, Lightwater represents the first taste of countryside from the metropolis. The visitor centre at **Lightwater Country Park** has a fascinating collection of exhibits about the history and natural history of this area of heath and woodland.

VIRGINIA WATER
6 miles NW of Weybridge on the B389

The water referred to here is a large artificial lake that is set within the mature woodland at the southern end of Windsor Great Park. The picturesque ruins on the lakeside are the genuine remains of a Roman temple that once stood at Leptis Magna in Libya and the Valley Gardens contain an unusual 100 feet totem pole that was erected here in 1958 to mark the centenary of British Columbia. Just to the west of this selected residential community is the famous **Royal Wentworth Golf Course**, while to the north are the historic fields of Runnymede where King John sealed the Magna Carta in 1215.

GUILDFORD

The ancient county town of Surrey, where Henry II built a Castle on high ground, is the home of one of only two new Anglican cathedrals to have been built since the Reformation (the other is Liverpool); the impressive

RHS Garden, Wisley

Guildford Cathedral was consecrated in 1961. A few years later, in 1968, the **University of Surrey** was relocated from London to Guildford and on its pleasant, leafy hillside site, the campus contains a number of striking buildings.

Back in the city centre, **Guildford Museum** has an exhibition devoted to Lewis Carroll, who died here in 1898, and at the foot of the castle is the famous **Yvonne Arnaud Theatre**.

Just east of Guildford lies **Clandon Park**, a magnificent 18th century country mansion renowned for its superb marble hall, sumptuous decorations and fine plasterwork. Further on lies the distinctive brick house of **Hatchlands Park**, which was designed in the mid-18th century for Admiral Boscawen after his famous victory at the Battle of Louisburg.

To the west of Guildford lies a ridge, known as the **Hog's Back**, which dominates the surrounding landscape; the main road following the ridge offers fantastic views.

Guildford Castle

building is arguably the **Pepperpot**, the former early-19th century town hall that used to house an interesting **Museum of Local History**, which has since found new premises in **Wealden House** opposite. However, the town is best known for **Charterhouse**, the famous public school that moved from London to a hillside site north of the town in 1872. Among its most striking features are the 150 feet Founder's Tower and the chapel designed by Giles Gilbert Scott as a memorial to the First World War dead.

HASLEMERE

12 miles SW of Guildford on the A286

This genteel town owes much of its development to the arrival of the railway in 1859 that saw it become a comfortable residential place for well-to-do commuters. However, some notable pre-Victorian buildings still exist, among them the Town Hall of 1814 and the Tolle House Almshouses.

AROUND GUILDFORD

GODALMING

4 miles SW of Guildford on the A3100

A market town since the early 14th century, Godalming later became a centre for the local textile industry before becoming an important staging post between London and Portsmouth in the 18th century. The town's most interesting

•

To the southeast of Godalming lies the renowned Winkworth Arboretum, a wooded hillside that contains a magnificent collection of rare trees and shrubs.

•

The **Haslemere Educational Museum** was founded in 1888 by local surgeon and Quaker, Sir James Hutchinson.

ELSTEAD

6½ miles SW of Guildford on the B3001

An attractive village on the River Wey, Elstead is home to an 18th century watermill – **Elstead Mill**, standing four storeys high and topped with a Palladian cupola. To the northeast of Elstead one of the best collections of Surrey farm buildings can be seen at **Peper Harrow Farm** where a large early 17th century granary standing on 25 wooden pillars is a striking sight.

FARNHAM

10 miles W of Guildford on the A31

After the Norman Conquest, the Bishop of Winchester built himself a castle on a rise above the town centre. An impressive building, **Farnham Castle** remained in the hands of the Bishops of Winchester until 1927.

Farnham Castle

Other historic buildings here include a row of 17th century gabled almshouses and Willmer House, a handsome Georgian building that is now home to the **Farnham Museum**.

Just to the southeast are the atmospheric ruins of 12th century **Waverley Abbey**, the first Cistercian abbey to be built in England. Close by, near the attractive village of **Tilford**, is the **Rural Life Centre and Old Kiln Museum**, a museum of rural life covering the years from 1750 to 1960.

REIGATE

Once an important outpost for the de Warenne family, the assertive Norman rulers whose sphere of influence stretched from the south coast to the North Downs, Reigate retains an attractive mix of Victorian, Georgian and older buildings, despite its rapid postwar expansion.

Just to the northwest lies Reigate Heath, a narrow area of open heathland that is home to the unique **Windmill Church**, the only church in the world to be situated in a windmill.

AROUND REIGATE

LIMPSFIELD

9 miles E of Reigate off the A25

In the churchyard here lies the grave of the composer Frederick Delius, who died in France in 1934 but had wished to be buried in an English country graveyard. Sir

Thomas Beecham, a great admirer of Delius, read the funeral oration and conducted an orchestra playing works by Delius. Sir Thomas died in 1961 and was originally buried at Brookwood Cemetery near Woking. In 1991 his body was transferred to Limpsfield, where he was buried close to Delius. Also lying here are the conductor Norman del Mar and the pianist Eileen Joyce. **Detillens**, a rare 15th century hall house, contains collections of period furniture, china and militaria.

LINGFIELD

9½ miles SE of Reigate on the B2028

'Leafy' Lingfield's **Church of St Peter and St Paul** has been enlarged down the years to create what has become known as the 'Westminster Abbey of Surrey'. Features include a rare double nave and an exceptional collection of monumental brasses. Near the village of **Outwood**, the **Post Mill**, built in 1665, is recognised as the country's oldest working windmill.

Lingfield racecourse stages a year-round programme of all-weather racing and still retains its turf circuit.

DORKING

5½ miles W of Reigate on the A25

An ancient settlement that stands at the intersection of Stane Street and the Pilgrims' Way, Dorking owes much of its character to the Victorians.

Just to the north of the town lies **Box Hill**, whose 563 feet summit rises sharply from the valley floor.

To the northwest of Dorking is **Polesden Lacey**, a Regency villa that was extensively modified by the Edwardian hostess Mrs Ronald Greville. Four miles southwest of Dorking, **Leith Hill** is the highest point in the southeast of England, at 965 feet above sea level. On the southern slopes of the hill is a lovely rhododendron wood planted by Josiah Wedgwood, grandson of the illustrious potter.

EPSOM

7 miles NW of Reigate on the A24

The old market town of Epsom is known throughout the world as the home of the world's premier classic race, **The Derby**. Racing was formalised in 1779 when a party of aristocratic sportsmen, led by Lord Derby, established a race for three-year-old fillies that was named after the family home at Banstead – The Oaks. This was followed a year later by a race for all three-year-olds, The Derby, which was named after the founder himself.

409 THE CROWN

Capel

Everyone can expect a warm genuine welcome at a fine old country pub serving four real ales and a good choice of food on lunch and evening menus.

see page 641

British Wildlife Centre, Lingfield

Sussex

Sussex saw one of the most momentous events in England's history when, in 1066, William, Duke of Normandy landed with his army at Pevensey and went on to defeat the Saxon King Harold at Battle on the 14th of October. Battle Abbey was built on the spot where Harold fell, and both here and in nearby Hastings there are museums and exhibitions detailing this historic victory. The south coast has been no stranger to invasion and, in the days before the establishment of the Royal Navy, the confederation of Cinque Ports provided fleets of ships to defend the coast. Today, the Sussex coast is best known for the elegant and genteel resorts of Eastbourne, Bexhill, Rottingdean, Worthing and, of course, Brighton.

Inland the rolling landscape of the South Downs provides glorious walking country and the South Downs Way long distance footpath follows the crest of the hills from Winchester to Beachy Head near Eastbourne. Here there are numerous ancient market towns and a wealth of fine stately homes but Sussex is also renowned for its glorious gardens such as Wakehurst Place, Herstmonceux and Leonardslee.

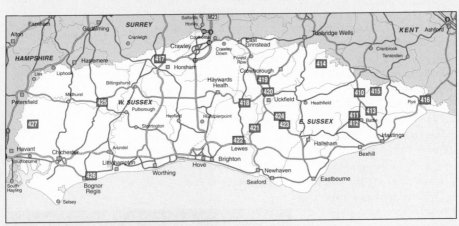

♑ ACCOMMODATION

415	The White Dog Inn, Ewhurst Green	pg 307, 645
416	The Cinque Ports Inn, Rye	pg 307, 645
418	The Bull Inn, Newick	pg 309, 646
420	The Pig & Butcher, Five Ash Down	pg 309, 648
424	The Black Lion Inn, Halland	pg 312, 651
426	The Thatched House, Felpham	pg 315, 652

⫙ FOOD & DRINK

410	The Salehurst Halt, Salehurst	pg 305, 641
411	The Kings Head, Battle	pg 305, 642
412	The Chequers Inn, Battle	pg 306, 643
413	The Queens Head, Sedlescombe	pg 306, 644

414	The White Hart, Wadhurst	pg 306, 643
415	The White Dog Inn, Ewhurst Green	pg 307, 645
416	The Cinque Ports Inn, Rye	pg 307, 645
417	The Sussex Oak , Warnham	pg 308, 647
418	The Bull Inn, Newick	pg 309, 646
419	Duddleswell Tea Rooms, Fairwarp	pg 309, 647
420	The Pig & Butcher, Five Ash Down	pg 309, 648
421	The Cock Inn, Ringmer	pg 311, 649
422	The Garden Room Café Gallery, Lewes	pg 311, 650
423	The Foresters Arms, East Hoathly	pg 311, 650
424	The Black Lion Inn, Halland	pg 312, 651
425	The Black Horse, Byworth, nr Petworth	pg 314, 651
426	The Thatched House, Felpham	pg 315, 652
427	The Coach & Horses, Compton	pg 315, 652

HASTINGS

This was the principal town of a small Saxon province long before William the Conqueror landed nearby but it was to Hastings that the victorious William returned after the battle that took place six miles away. The **Castle** he built is now in ruins, but a medieval siege tent contains a permanent display – the **1066 Story at Hastings Castle**. After the Conquest, Hastings became a leading Cinque Port, a role it played until the harbour began to silt up in Elizabethan times. However, the fishing industry has managed to survive and the tall wooden huts used for drying nets remain a familiar feature. The Church of St Nicholas is home to the **Fishermen's Museum**, where the centerpiece is the old sailing lugger *The Enterprise*. The town also has its own version of the Bayeux Tapestry, the Hastings Embroidery.

Hastings Castle

AROUND HASTINGS

BEXHILL

5 miles W of Hastings on the A259

This small seaside resort was founded in the 1880s by the influential De La Warr family and among the many late-Victorian buildings is the striking **De La Warr Pavilion**, built in the 1930s and now a beautifully maintained,

Maritime Stade, Hastings

410 THE SALEHURST HALT

Salehurst, nr Robertsbridge

Rescued from threatened closure in 2006, now once again a thriving village inn with a growing clientele who come to enjoy good food, good drink and good company.

see page 641

411 THE KINGS HEAD

Battle

Affable leaseholders are rightly proud of their convivial pub, cask-conditioned ales and good honest pub food.

see page 642

305

412 THE CHEQUERS INN

Battle

A cosy, family-friendly pub offering warm hospitality, award-winning ales and a good choice of food.

🍴 see page 643

413 THE QUEEN'S HEAD

Sedlescombe, nr Battle

A handsome redbrick village pub equally popular with locals, motorists and visitors to the area. Tip-top beers and excellent food.

🍴 see page 644

414 THE WHITE HART

Wadhurst

A distinctive High Street pub with an all-day bar and good lunchtime food.

🍴 see page 643

Battle Abbey

renowned centre for arts and culture. A seemingly conservative resort, Bexhill played host to the birth of British motor racing in 1902, an event that is remembered annually with the **Bexhill Festival of Motoring** held in May. Bexhill was also the first seaside town to allow mixed bathing on its beaches - a very daring move back in 1900!

HERSTMONCEUX

11½ miles NW of Hastings on the A271

This village is famous as being the home of 15th century **Herstmonceux Castle** - to where, in 1948, the Royal Observatory at Greenwich moved. Although the Observatory has since moved on again, the castle is now home to the **Herstmonceux Science Centre**.

BATTLE

6 miles NW of Hastings on the A2100

This historic settlement is renowned as being the site of the momentous battle, on 14 October 1066, between the armies of Harold, King of England, and William, Duke of Normandy. Battle Abbey was built on the spot where Harold fell.

BURWASH

13 miles NW of Hastings on the A265

An exceptionally pretty village and one time centre of the Wealden iron industry, Burwash is home to **Rampyndene**, a handsome 17th century timber-framed house. Just outside the village stands **Bateman's**, a Jacobean house that was the home of Rudyard Kipling from 1902 until his death in 1936.

To the south of Burwash is **Brightling**, the home of the Georgian eccentric, 'Mad' Jack Fuller. One of the first people to recognise the talents of the great painter Turner, Fuller also built several imaginative follies including Brightling Needle, a 40 feet stone obelisk.

NORTHIAM

9 miles N of Hastings on the A28

The picturesque village of Northiam is the southern terminal for the **Kent and East Sussex Railway** that runs steam trains to Tenterden during the summer. Just to the northwest lies **Great Dixter House**, one of the finest late medieval hall houses in the country, with superb gardens designed by Lutyens.

To the west lies **Bodiam Castle**, begun in 1385 and one of the last great medieval fortresses to be built in England. Bodiam was once the centre of a thriving hop-growing region, served by 'The Hoppers' Line' of the Kent & East Sussex Railway.

RYE

9 miles NE of Hastings on the A259

A picturesque town and Cinque Port; its harbour gradually silted up and it now lies further down the Rother estuary. **Rye Harbour Nature Reserve**, at the river mouth, is a large area of sea, saltmarsh, sand and shingle that supports a wide range of plant, animal and bird life. A strategically important place due to its hilltop position, Rye had a substantial perimeter wall to defend its northern approaches and the Landgate, one of its four gateways,

still survives. One of Rye's many interesting buildings is the handsome Georgian residence, **Lamb House** (National Trust), which was the home of the novelist Henry James from 1898 to his death in 1916. A later occupant was the prolific writer EF Benson, best remembered for his Mapp and Lucia novels and various volumes of reminiscences.

To the south lies **Camber Castle** (English Heritage), a fine example of the coastal defences built by Henry VIII.

HAYWARDS HEATH

The oldest part of this town is centred on the conservation area around Muster Green, an open space where the 16th century Sergison Arms can be found. Modern Haywards Heath grew up around its station on the Brighton

Rye Harbour Nature Reserve

415 THE WHITE DOG INN

Ewhurst Green

A cheerfully unpretentious pub/restaurant with well-kept ales, very interesting menus and three super rooms for B&B.

🍴 🛏 see page 645

416 THE CINQUE PORTS INN

Rye

A welcoming hostelry where both the hosts cook, from snacks to full meals. Three pleasant en suite rooms for B&B guests.

🍴 🛏 see page 645

Horsham Museum

417 THE SUSSEX OAK

Warnham

A gem of a country inn with wide appeal. Four or more real ales and a fine selection of home-cooked British and European dishes.

see page 647

line – other local villages refused to allow the railway to run through them.

AROUND HAYWARDS HEATH

SHIPLEY

12 miles W of Haywards Heath off the A272

A pleasant village which is home to Sussex's only remaining working smock mill, Shipley Mill. Shipley was the home of the celebrated Sussex writer, Hilaire Belloc.

HORSHAM

10½ miles NW of Haywards Heath on the A281

An ancient town that dates back to Saxon times, Horsham's architectural gem is **The Causeway**, a tree-lined street that runs from the town hall to the Church of St Mary and the gabled 16th century Causeway House that is now home to the **Horsham Museum**. Just outside the town is the famous **Christ's Hospital**

School, a Bluecoat school founded in London in 1552 by Edward VI that moved here in 1902.

To the southeast is the village of **Lower Beeding**, home to the beautiful **Leonardslee Gardens** that were laid out in this natural valley in the late 19th century.

CRAWLEY

8½ miles NW of Haywards Heath on the A23

One of the original new towns created after the New Towns Act of 1946, Crawley has swallowed up several ancient villages. Just to the north lies **Gatwick Airport**, which first opened to commercial air traffic in 1936 and where Gatwick Airport Skyview provides an interesting insight behind the scenes of this busy airport. To the south of Crawley, near Handcross, are the superb gardens of **Nymans** created by William Robinson and Gertrude Jekyll. Close by are the smaller but equally delightful High Beeches Gardens.

WEST HOATHLY

5 miles N of Haywards Heath off the B2028

A historic settlement whose most impressive building is the **Priest House**, a 15th century house that was the estate office for the monks of Lewes Priory and is now a museum.

To the southwest lies **Ardingly**, home of Ardingly College public school, the showground for the South of England Agricultural Society and, at the top of Ardingly Reservoir, **Wakehurst Place**, the Tudor home of the Culpeper family. Today, the magnificent gardens are administered by the Royal Botanic Gardens at Kew; Wakehurst is also home to the **Millennium Seed Bank**, a project that aims to ensure the survival of over 24,000 plant species worldwide.

EAST GRINSTEAD

9 miles N of Haywards Heath on the A22

East Grinstead was an important centre for the Wealden iron industry and a busy market town, and several buildings remaining from those prosperous days. The **Town Museum** in East Court is a fine building that was originally constructed in 1769 as a private residence; the Greenwich Meridian passes through the town at this point.

To the south lies **Standen**, a remarkable late Victorian country mansion that is a showpiece of the Arts and Crafts Movement. From near Standen, the famous **Bluebell Railway** offers a pleasant steam-powered journey through the Sussex Weald.

To the east of East Grinstead is the old hunting settlement of Hartfield, which was the home of AA Milne, the creator of *Winnie the Pooh*. The village's 300-year-old sweet shop, **Pooh Corner**, is now full of Winnie the Pooh memorabilia; Poohsticks Bridge spans a small tributary of the River Medway.

BUXTED

10½ miles E of Haywards Heath on the A272

The village has long been dominated by the great house of **Buxted Park**, built along classical lines in 1725, restored after a fire by Basil Ionides and now a hotel. To the southwest, on the other side of Uckfield in the village of **Piltdown**, an ancient skull was discovered in 1912 by an amateur archaeologist that was, for a time, believed to have been the 'missing link' until exposed as a hoax in 1953. Advanced testing methods showed that the skull was a combination of a human skull and

418 THE BULL INN

Newick

Historic country pub, destination restaurant and luxury hotel in a 15th century former coaching inn.

 see page 646

419 DUDDLESWELL TEA ROOMS

Fairwarp, Ashdown Forest

A traditional team rooms serving homemade cakes and cream teas.

 see page 647

420 THE PIG & BUTCHER

Five Ash Down, nr Uckfield

A distinctive gabled redbrick building offering a good selection of drinks and excellent dishes that take their inspiration for the UK, Europe and beyond.

 see page 648

Standen House, East Grinstead

Brighton Royal Pavilion

the lower jaw of an orang-utan, both treated to suggest fossilisation. To the west lies Sheffield Green, home to the splendid 18th century mansion **Sheffield Park** whose superb Capability Brown gardens are open to the public.

BRIGHTON

It was Dr Richard Russell's enthusiasm for sea bathing, taking the sea air and even drinking seawater that saw Brighton grow from an insignificant little fishing village called Brighthelmston into a popular seaside resort. But it was the patronage of the Prince Regent, who first came here in 1783, which saw the village completely transformed. Wishing to have a permanent base here, the Prince built his famous **Royal Pavilion**, and the magnificent, exotic building seen today was the creation of the architect John Nash. The gardens surrounding this early 19th century pleasure palace based on a

maharajah's palace are also Nash's work.

The Metropole Hotel marked the end of the Emancipation Run of 1896, celebrating the abolition of the law that demanded that motorised vehicles had to be preceded by a man with a red flag. The London-Brighton run is an annual institution, with some of the cars dating back almost as far as the original run.

As the Prince took up almost permanent residence in the resort a period of rapid expansion took place of which the Royal Crescent is probably the greatest feature. However, **The Lanes**, the tiny alleyways of the old village, are equally interesting with their antique shops, restaurants and smart boutiques.

The best-known features on the seafront are the **Palace Pier** which has for more than a century been one of Brighton's greatest attractions, the **Volk's Electric Railway**, the first public electric railway in Britain, and the **Sea Life Centre**, home to the longest underwater tunnel in Europe.

Just to the west lies **Hove**, a genteel place that developed alongside its neighbour. At the **Hove Museum and Art Gallery** stands a wooden pavilion, the **Jaipur Gateway**, which was transported here from Rajashtan in 1886. History of a different kind is on view at the **British Engineerium** which contains all manner of engines from steam powered to electric housed in a restored 19th century pumping station.

AROUND BRIGHTON

HURSTPIERPOINT

7 miles N of Brighton on the B2116

This ancient village is dominated by **Hurstpierpoint College** and its chapel while, to the south of the village lies **Danny**, the ancestral home of the Norman Pierpoint family. It was in this impressive E-shaped Elizabethan mansion that Lloyd George drew up the terms of the armistice that ended World War I. Closer to Brighton, at Poynings, is one of the greatest natural features of the South Downs. The **Devil's Dyke** is a huge steep-sided ravine that attracts tourists, walkers and hang-gliders.

LEWES

7 miles NE of Brighton on the A27

It was in this historic settlement, the county town of East Sussex, that William the Conqueror's powerful friend, William de Warenne, constructed a **Castle** and founded the great Priory of St Pancras. A substantial part of the castle remains today.

HAILSHAM

18 miles NE of Brighton on the A295

A pleasant market town that was once the centre of a thriving rope and string industry. To the southwest lies **Michelham Priory**, which was founded in 1229. Many of the priory's buildings are now incorporated into a grand Tudor farmhouse, whose rooms contain many treasures, and the gardens cover an attractive range of planting styles.

NEWHAVEN

10 miles E of Brighton on the A26

Two early visitors on the packet boat from Dieppe were the fleeing King and Queen of France, Louis Philippe and Marie Amelie. They spent a night in 1848 at the Bridge Inn (registering as Mr & Mrs Smith!) before taking a train to

421 THE COCK INN

Uckfield Road (A26), nr Ringmer

A fine old family-run country inn serving exceptional food and a full range of drinks.

see page 649

422 THE GARDEN ROOM CAFÉ GALLERY

Lewes

A gem of a café with a wonderful lady owner and a an excellent choice of home baking and home cooking.

see page 650

423 THE FORESTERS ARMS

East Hoathley

Splendid hosts, a full range of drinks and varied menus in a village inn by the church.

see page 650

Newhaven Harbour

424 THE BLACK LION

Halland

An attractive tile-hung inn offering a long-hours bar, a good choice of home-cooked dishes and comfortable rooms for B&B guests.

 see page 651

London, where they were met by Queen Victoria's coach and taken to Buckingham Palace.

Along the coast to the east lies **Seaford**, a once thriving port that is home to **Martello Tower No 74**, the most westerly of these defensive structures, which now houses the **Seaford Museum of Local History**. Seaford Head, a nature reserve, is an excellent place from which to view the **Seven Sisters** - a spectacular series of clifftop undulations.

To the west of Newhaven, in a gap in the cliffs, lies **Rottingdean** and **North End House**, the home of the artist Sir Edward Burne-Jones. Inland is the village of **Rodmell**, where **Monk's House** was the home of Virginia and Leonard Woolf from 1919 until her death in 1941. The house, now in the care of the National Trust, is filled with books and paintings and is surrounded by a lush garden.

SELMESTON

13 miles E of Brighton off the A27

Selmeston is best known as the

home of the artist Vanessa Bell, who shared **Charleston Farmhouse** with her husband Clive and her lover, Duncan Grant.

To the south, beyond Alciston with its medieval dovecote, is the beautiful village of **Alfriston**, whose splendid 14th century church is often referred to as the **Cathedral of the Downs**. Beside the church is the **Clergy House**, the first building acquired by the National Trust (for £10 in 1896) and a marvellous example of a 14th century Wealden hall house. To the north lies **Drusillas Park**, a child friendly zoo set in attractive gardens.

To the west of Selmeston lies **Firle Beacon** which, at 718 feet, dominates the surrounding countryside and **Firle Place**, a wonderful Tudor manor that houses superb collections of European and English Old Masters, French and English furniture and Sèvres porcelain.

EASTBOURNE

20 miles E of Brighton on the A259

A stylish and genteel seaside resort, Eastbourne's rapid growth from two small villages was instigated by the 7th Duke of Devonshire from the 1850s. Several buildings predate this expansion, including the Georgian residence that houses the **Towner Art Gallery and Museum; Martello Tower No 73** which is home to a **Puppet Museum;** and the Redoubt Fortress that is now the **Military Museum of Sussex**. The sea has always played an important part in

Charleston Farmhouse, Selmeston

312

the life of Eastbourne and there is an **RNLI Lifeboat Museum** close to the lifeboat station.

To the southwest of Eastbourne lies **Beachy Head**, one of the most spectacular chalk precipices in England, almost 600 feet high. This is also the end of the South Downs Way, a long distance bridleway established in 1972.

To the northeast lies **Pevensey**, landing place for invading Roman legions and in 1066 for William the Conqueror and his troops; it was William's half-brother, Robert de Mortain, who built **Pevensey Castle**.

SHOREHAM-BY-SEA

6 miles W of Brighton on the A259

An ancient port that has suffered from the silting up of its river; its earlier importance is reflected in the construction of Shoreham Fort, which was part of Palmerston's coastal defence system. The history of Shoreham, particularly its maritime past, is explored at **Marlipins Museum**, while at Shoreham Airport, which first opened in 1934, is the **Museum of D-Day Aviation**.

WORTHING

10 miles W of Brighton on the A259

An ancient fishing community, Worthing developed into a fashionable seaside resort in the late 18th century and boasts one of the oldest piers in the country. The **Worthing Museum and Art Gallery** has a nationally important costume and toy collection along with displays on smuggling and the town riots of the 19th century. A plaque on the esplanade marks the site of the house where Oscar Wilde wrote *The Importance of Being Earnest.*

CHICHESTER

Founded by the Romans in the 1st century, Chichester has also been an ecclesiastical centre for over 900 years and its **Cathedral** is unique on two counts: it is the only medieval English cathedral which can be seen from the sea, and it has a detached belfry.

One of its most distinctive modern buildings is the **Chichester Festival Theatre**, opened in 1962 and the focal point of the annual Chichester Festival.

Just east of the city are the splendid remains of **Fishbourne Roman Palace** that was built in around AD 75 for the Celtic King Cogidubnus.

Further west again is the pleasant village of Bosham, where legend has it that King Canute ordered back the waves.

Inland from Eastbourne is the Polegate Windmill and Museum, a superb tower mill built in 1817. Near Wilmington is its famous Long Man, cut into the chalk of Windover Hill. At 235 feet, this is the largest such representation in Europe, and its chalk outline is so unmistakable that it was covered up during World War II lest it should act as a navigation aid to German bombers.

Beachy Head, nr Eastbourne

313

Goodwood House

425 THE BLACK HORSE

Byworth, nr Petworth

Patrons come from all over the county to enjoy the excellent hospitality, the well-kept ales and the extensive menu of home-cooked dishes.

see page 651

AROUND CHICHESTER

GOODWOOD

2 miles N of Chichester off the A286

The spectacular country home of the Dukes of Richmond, **Goodwood House** was built in the late 18th century by the architect James Wyatt and, along with a fine collection of paintings, gruesome relics from the Napoleonic Wars are on display. The house is the focal point of the vast Goodwood Estate that incorporates the world famous **Goodwood Racecourse**, the venue of the fashionable 'Glorious Goodwood' meeting first held in 1814.

Nearby Singleton is the location of the famous **Weald and Downland Open Air Museum**, an exemplary museum with over 40 reconstructed historic rural buildings. At West Dean lies **Charleston Manor**, an ancient house that was originally built in 1080 for William the Conqueror's cupbearer and is now the centrepiece of a remarkable garden

created by members of the Bloomsbury Group.

Just to the southwest, and overlooked by Bow Hill, is **Kingley Vale National Nature Reserve**, home to the finest yew groves in Europe – several trees here are more than 500 years old.

PETWORTH

13 miles NE of Chichester on the A285

What brings most people here is the grand estate of 17th century **Petworth House**, which has the look of a French château and is home to the National Trust's finest collection of art from the 15th to 19th centuries, and some superb ancient and neo-classical sculpture.

To the south of the Petworth Estate is the Coultershaw Water Wheel and Beam Pump, one of the earliest pumped water systems; it was installed in 1790 to pump water two miles to the house.

PULBOROUGH

14½ miles NE of Chichester on the A29

Situated on Roman Stane Street, Pulborough was an important staging post along the old coaching route between London and Chichester. To the southeast lies the **RSPB's Pulborough Brooks Nature Reserve**, where a nature trail leads to views overlooking the wet meadows of the Arun Valley.

To the southwest of Pulborough, near **Bignor**, is one of the largest Roman sites in Britain – some 70 buildings surround a central courtyard and many of the fine mosaics uncovered can be seen in the Museum.

TANGMERE

2½ miles E of Chichester off the A27

This village is associated with the nearby former Battle of Britain base, RAF Tangmere, which is now home to the **Tangmere Military Aviation Museum**.

The heroic deeds of the pilots are also remembered in the local pub, the Bader Arms.

ARUNDEL

9½ miles E of Chichester on the A27

A settlement since before the Roman invasion, this peaceful town lies beneath the battlements of the impressive 11th century **Arundel Castle**. The town is also the seat of the Catholic bishopric of Brighton and Arundel; the Cathedral of Our Lady and St Philip Howard was originally designed by JA Hansom and Son, the inventors of the Hansom cab. Another historic site is the **Maison Dieu**, a medieval hospital that was founded in 1345.

To the north lies the attractive village of **Amberley** and **Amberley Castle**, originally a fortified summer palace for the bishops of Chichester.

BOGNOR REGIS

5½ miles SE of Chichester on the A259

A quiet fishing village with some elegant Georgian features. King George V came here in 1929 to convalesce and granted the town the title Regis. The town is best known nowadays for its annual international **Birdman Rally**, when competitors hurl themselves off the pier in an attempt to make the longest unpowered flight.

SELSEY

7½ miles S of Chichester on the B2145

A modest yet popular resort, whose town's most impressive building is **Selsey Windmill**, built in 1820. A Lifeboat Station was established here in 1860 and there is now an interesting **Lifeboat Museum** along with a more recent station.

The town's East Beach was the scene for smuggling in the 18th century and during World War II sections of the famous Mulberry Harbour were gathered here before D-Day.

WEST WITTERING

6½ miles SW of Chichester on the B2179

Situated close to the beautiful inlet that is Chichester's natural harbour, this charming seaside village is home to **Cakeham Manor House**, once a summer palace of the bishops of Chichester.

To the north lies Birdham, the setting for Turner's famous painting of Chichester Harbour, and site of the **Sussex Falconry Centre**.

SOUTH HARTING

10 miles NW of Chichester on the B2146

One of the most attractive villages on the South Downs, South Harting stands at the foot of Harting Down where the South Downs Way footpath skirts around Beacon Hill, one of the highest points on the Downs. The magnificent house **Uppark** lies on the crest of a hill to the south. The grounds and gardens were laid out by Humphry Repton.

426 THE THATCHED HOUSE

Felpham, Bognor Regis

A pleasant old inn just moments from the sea, with a cheerful host, a good range of drinks, classic pub dishes and two cosy rooms for B&B guests.

🍴 🛏 *see page 652*

427 THE COACH & HORSES

Compton, nr Chichester

A 17th century village pub with a warm welcome for all-comers, a fine range of real ales and plenty of good home cooking.

🍴 *see page 652*

The story of King George's last words 'Bugger Bognor' in response to his doctor telling him that he would soon be well enough to visit his favourite resort is open to doubt. His doctor's account has the King saying 'God Damn You' on being given a large injection of morphine, while The Times quotes his last words as 'How is the Empire?'

Warwickshire

A rich vein of medieval and Tudor history runs through Warwickshire, and the romantic ruins of Kenilworth Castle, the grandeur of Warwick Castle and the elegance of Royal Leamington Spa set the tone for this most delightful of counties. But Stratford-upon-Avon is most visitors' focal point, a town dominated by William Shakespeare and all things Shakespearian. Another town that has found fame through one of its citizens is Rugby, as it was the young scholar William Webb Ellis who, in the early 19th century, broke the rules of football and picked up the ball and in so doing founded the game that bears the name of the town. Close by is the ancient village of Dunchurch that is often dubbed the 'Gunpowder Plot Village' as it was here that the conspirators waited to hear if their mission had been accomplished.

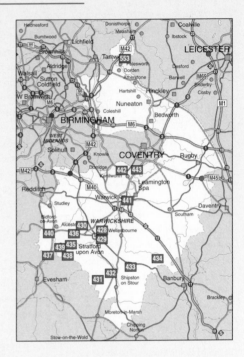

STRATFORD-UPON-AVON

It was here, in 1564, that William Shakespeare was born and having found fame in London, retired to his birthplace and lived here until his death in 1616. Few towns are so completely dominated by one man. The half-timbered house that is **Shakespeare's Birthplace** has been returned to the way it must have looked in his day and a room thought to have been his father's workshop has been re-created with the help of the Worshipful Company of Glovers. Further along, on Chapel Street, stands **Nash's House**, another half-timbered building that belonged to Shakespeare's granddaughter, Elizabeth Hall; it now contains an exceptional collection of Elizabethan furniture and tapestries, as well as displays on the history of Stratford. Its spectacular Elizabethan-style knot garden is an added attraction.

In Old Town is one of the best examples of a half-timbered gabled house in Stratford, **Hall's Croft**, which was named after Dr John Hall, who married Shakespeare's daughter Susanna in 1607. This impressive house, along with outstanding 16th and 17th century furniture and paintings, has a reconstruction of Dr Hall's consulting room,

accompanied by an exhibition detailing medicinal practices during Shakespeare's time. Outside, the beautiful walled garden features a large herb bed. In a beautiful setting by the River Avon, is 13th century **Holy Trinity Church** where Shakespeare is buried by the north wall of the chancel. The grave of his wife Anne Hathaway is close by.

The town is also home to three theatres, as well as the internationally renowned Royal Shakespeare Company, and the most famous is, of course, the **Royal Shakespeare Theatre** that opened in 1879 with a performance of *Much Ado About Nothing* starring Ellen Terry and Beerbohm Tree. The Royal Shakespeare Theatre Summer House in Avonbank Gardens is home to the **Stratford Brass Rubbing Centre**, which

428 RUSSONS RESTAURANT

Stratford-upon-Avon

A bright, cheerful restaurant with excellent seasonal menus including super seafood specials.

see page 653

429 THE OLD THATCH TAVERN

Stratford-upon-Avon

Period appeal aplenty, along with real ales and classic English food, in Stratford's oldest and only thatched pub.

see page 653

Hall's Croft Museum, Stratford-upon-Avon

430 LARKRISE COTTAGE

Upper Billesley

Excellent B&B accommodation in a lovely old gamekeeper's cottage with a pretty garden and superb views.

see page 653

431 FOLLY FARM COTTAGE

Ilmington

A cottage offering luxurious B&B and self-catering accommodation in a beautiful and serene part of the Cotswolds.

see page 654

432 THE FOX & GOOSE COUNTRY INN

Armscote

A fine country inn of wide appeal – as a much-loved local, as a destination restaurant and as a comfortable hotel.

see page 654

433 THE PEACOCK

Oxhill, nr Stratford-upon-Avon

A friendly village inn serving a good range of home-cooked dishes.

see page 655

contains a large collection of exact replicas of brasses of knights and ladies, scholars, merchants and priests.

To the west of the town is an Elizabethan farmhouse that is now known as **Anne Hathaway's Cottage**, as it was here that Shakespeare's wife was born. Another notable house connected with the Bard is that of his mother, situated in the village of Wilmcote: **Mary Arden's House** is a striking Tudor farmhouse that contains the Shakespeare Countryside Museum of farming and rural life.

AROUND STRATFORD-UPON-AVON

WELLESBOURNE

5 miles E of Stratford off the A429

The village is home to **Wellesbourne Watermill**, a brick-built working flourmill on the River Dene. Demonstrations of the art and skill of milling stoneground flour are enacted and explained by the miller and there

Stratford Brass Rubbing Centre

are guided walks alongside the river.

To the southeast lies **Compton Verney Manor House**, a magnificent manor that is home to a fine art collection that includes British portraiture, European Old Masters and modern works, along with a unique collection of British

Wellesbourne Watermill

Folk Art. On the other side of Wellesbourne lies 16th century **Charlecote Park**, a magnificent stately home occupying landscaped grounds overlooking the River Avon that were laid out by Capability Brown.

Used as the location for the filming of the BBC adaptation of George Eliot's *The Mill on the Floss*, 18th century Charlecote Mill is situated on the site of an earlier mill mentioned in the *Domesday Book*.

ILMINGTON

7 miles S of Stratford off the B4632

This pretty village at the foot of Ilmington Downs had its moment of history on Christmas Day 1934, when the first radio broadcast by George V was introduced by Walton Handy, the village shepherd, and relayed to the world from Ilmington Manor, the fine Elizabethan house once owned by the de Montfort family.

ALCESTER

7½ miles NW of Stratford off the A435

An ancient Roman market town built on the Icknield Street Encampment, Alcester boasts several very pretty cottages on Maltmill Lane and a handsome Norman church. Just to the south lies the village of **Arrow** and the 17th century home of the Marquess of Hertford, **Ragley Hall**. One of England's great Palladian country houses, it was inherited by the 8th Marquess in 1940 when he was only nine, and during World War II it was used as a hospital. Completely renovated in a style befitting its age, the Hall boasts a wonderful collection of treasures, and out in the landscaped park there are formal gardens, an impressive collection of carriages and a country trail. **Roman Alcester Heritage Centre** explores everyday life in and around Roman Alcester. At nearby Kinwarton stands the National

Roman Alcester Heritage Centre

434 THE ROSE & CROWN

Ratley, nr Stratford-upon-Avon

A delightful old country inn with a good range of real ales and menus catering for all appetites.

¶ see page 655

435 THE GOLDEN CROSS COUNTRY INN & DINING HOUSE

Ardens Grafton

One of the most attractive inns in the area, and one of the very best for food and drink.

¶ see page 656

436 THE STAG AT RED HILL

Red Hill, nr Stratford-upon-Avon

A lovely location adds to the pleasure of enjoying outstanding hospitality and great food.

¶ see page 656

437 THE VINEYARD COUNTRY PUB & RESTAURANT

Abbot's Salford

A superb country pub and restaurant with a warm, friendly ambience and a wide variety of drinks and excellent food.

🍴 🛏 see page 657

438 THE COTTAGE OF CONTENT

Barton, nr Bidford-on-Avon

The **Cottage of Content** – the perfect name for a great place to wine, dine and make merry.

🍴 🛏 see page 657

439 THE PLOUGH INN

Bidford-on-Avon

Smart and comfortable, with a good choice of food and traditional pub games

🍴 see page 657

440 THE ARROW MILL

Arrow, nr Alcester

An outstanding hotel and restaurant in an attractive riverside setting opposite Ragley Hall.

🛏 🍴 see page 658

Warwick Castle

Trust's **Kinwarton Dovecote**, a 14th century circular dovecote that still houses doves and retains its 'potence', a pivoted ladder giving human access to the nesting boxes.

WARWICK

Standing by the River Avon, Warwick is in a good defensive position and became part of Crown lands just after the Norman Conquest. Dominating the town, much of **Warwick Castle** was destroyed during the Barons' revolt in 1264, led by Simon de Montfort, and the majority of the present castle dates from the 14th century. The towers at each end are very impressive - one is known as Caesar's Tower and is shaped rather like a cloverleaf.

The castle's exterior is best viewed from Castle Bridge, where the 14th century walls can be seen reflected in the waters of the River Avon. There is much to explore

along the ramparts and in the 60 acres of grounds, which include a re-created Victorian formal rose garden, the Peacock Gardens and an expanse of open parkland designed by Capability Brown. Events throughout the year include Medieval Tournaments, open-air fireworks concerts and special entertainment days.

The centre of Warwick is dominated by elegant Queen Anne architecture and there is also a wealth of museums including several honouring the county's regiments. One of the most important buildings in Warwick is St John's House, dating from 1666, which contains the **Museum of the Royal Warwickshire Regiment**. Two of Warwick's medieval town gateways have survived, complete with chapels and one of these, Westgate Chapel, forms part of **Lord Leycester's Hospital**, a spectacularly tottering and beautiful collection of 15th century half-timbered buildings enclosing a pretty galleried courtyard.

To the west of Warwick lies **Hatton Country World**, a uniquely charming blend of family fun and country shopping that is situated on a farm built by the descendants of Sir Richard Arkwright, the inventor of the Spinning Jenny. Along with the extensive craft village, the farm is home to the largest collection of rare breed farm animals in Britain.

Hatton Country World, nr Warwick

AROUND WARWICK

KENILWORTH

4 miles N of Warwick on the A452

Although the town was here before the *Domesday Book* was compiled, Kenilworth's name is invariably linked with its castle and, today, the remains of **Kenilworth Castle** stand as England's finest and most extensive castle ruins. The tales of this great fortress, immortalised in Sir Walter Scott's novel Kenilworth, are many and varied. The marvellous Norman keep, the oldest part of the ruins, was built between 1150 and 1175 and John of Gaunt's Great Hall once rivalled London's Westminster Hall in palatial grandeur. The remains of Kenilworth's Abbey can be seen in the churchyard of the Norman parish Church of St Nicholas in the High Street.

ROYAL LEAMINGTON SPA

2 miles E of Warwick on the A452

This attractive town boasts a handsome mixture of smart shops and Regency buildings and **The**

Parade is undoubtedly one of the finest streets in Warwickshire. Rapidly taking advantage of the fashion for taking the waters, Leamington Spa developed in the first few decades of the 19th century and was given the title 'Royal' by the grace of the new Queen, Victoria. The **Pump Rooms** were opened in 1814 by Henry Jephson, a local doctor who was largely responsible for promoting the spa's medicinal properties and therefore the popularisation of this elegant spa resort by the rich. Immediately opposite the spa itself are Jephson's Gardens containing a Corinthian temple that houses his statue.

SOUTHAM

8½ miles SE of Warwick on the A423

It was in this attractive town by the River Itchen that Charles I spent the night before the battle of Edge Hill. The Roundheads also came into the town, and Cromwell himself arrived with 7,000 troops in 1645. In the main street is the

441 ROBBIES OF WARWICK

Warwick

Top-quality cooking on an imaginative modern British menu; lunch every day, with evening meals by arrangement.

see page 658

442 KENILWORTH CASTLE

Kenilworth

Explore the Medieval Living Village within the castle walls as it would have been in the Middle Ages

see page 658

Coughton Court

examples of almost every kind of English architecture from the 15th century onwards, including many old timber-framed houses built from Arden oak. Little remains today of the **Forest of Arden**, the setting adopted by William Shakespeare for *As You Like It*, as its stocks were diminished in the 18th century by the navy's demand for timber. The town emerged initially under the protection of Thurston de Montfort, Lord of the Manor in 1140, and Beaudesert Castle, home to the de Montfort family, lies behind the **Churches of St John and St Nicholas**, where remains of the castle mound can still be seen.

The gatehouse and the half-timbered courtyard of Coughton Court are particularly noteworthy, while inside there are important collections of paintings, furniture, porcelain and other family items from Tudor times to the present day. Treasured possessions include the chemise that Mary, Queen of Scots wore at her execution and the Throckmorton Coat, the subject of a 1,000 guinea wager in 1811.

surprisingly named Old Mint Inn, a 14th century stone building that takes its name from an occurrence following the battle of Edge Hill. Charles I commanded his local noblemen to bring him their silver treasure, which was then melted down and minted into coins with which he paid his army.

SHERBOURNE
2½ miles S of Warwick on the A429

Set in lovely countryside with views across fields to the River Avon, **Sherbourne Park** is one of the very finest gardens in the county. Highlights of the gardens, which were designed by Lady Smith-Ryland in the 1950s, include a paved terrace covered by clematis, wisteria and a magnolia; an 'orchard' of sorbus trees; a box-edged, rose-filled parterre and the White Garden surrounded by yew hedges.

HENLEY-IN-ARDEN
9 miles W of Warwick on the A3400

Henley's mile-long High Street has

COUGHTON
13 miles W of Warwick off the A435

The crowning glory of this village, **Coughton Court**, has been the home for almost 600 years of the Throckmorton family who were very prominent in Tudor times and were instigators of Catholic emancipation, playing a part in the Gunpowder Plot - the wives of some of the Gunpowder Plotters awaited the outcome of the Plot in the imposing central gatehouse.

SHREWLEY
5 miles NW of Warwick off the B4439

Shrewley boasts a marina on the Grand Union Canal but its well-known landmark is the **Hatton Flight** of 21 locks that stretches for a couple of miles up Hatton Hill. Just to the northwest, at

Lapworth, the Grand Union and Stratford Canals meet and, close by, is Baddesley Clinton, a romantic, medieval moated manor house that has changed little since 1633.

RUGBY

Rugby's Market Place is surrounded by handsome buildings that act as reminders of the town's origins during the reign of Henry III. **Rugby Town Trail**, a two-hour walk that brings to life the town's history from its Saxon beginnings to the present day, begins at the Clock Tower in Market Place. The tower was intended to commemorate the Golden Jubilee of Queen Victoria in 1887, yet it was not completed until 1889 because over-indulgent citizens had dipped too deep into the Tower funds to feast and drink at the Jubilee. Also along the trail is the house where Rupert Brooke was born (his statue stands in Regent Place), and **Caldecott Park** with its beautiful floral displays, trees and a herb garden.

Rugby is bounded by two of the greatest Roman roads, Fosse Way and Watling Street, which meet just northwest of Rugby, at High Cross, one of the landmarks of the area.

The town is best known for **Rugby School**, founded in 1567 and moved to its present site in 1750. It was here that the game of Rugby originated when, in 1823, the story goes that William Webb Ellis broke the rules during a football match by picking up the ball and running with it.

The **James Gilbert Rugby Museum** is housed in the original building where, since 1842, the Gilberts have been making their world-famous rugby footballs. The most famous headmaster of Rugby school was Dr Thomas Arnold, Head from 1828 to 1842. He is buried in the school chapel. One of his pupils was Thomas Hughes, who wrote *Tom Brown's Schooldays* based on his experiences at the school. Another old boy was Rupert Brooke, whose father was a housemaster.

AROUND RUGBY

DUNCHURCH

2 miles SW of Rugby on the A426

On the 5th of November 1605, the Gunpowder Plot conspirators met at the **Red Lion Inn**, Dunchurch, to await the news of Guy Fawkes' attempt to blow up the Houses of Parliament. The Red Lion still exists today but as a private residence known as Guy Fawkes House.

RYTON-ON-DUNSMORE

6 miles W of Rugby off the A45

This village is home to the **Henry Doubleday Research Association** at Ryton Gardens, an organic farming and gardening organisation that leads the way in research and advances in horticulture. The grounds are landscaped with thousands of plants and trees, all organically grown. Ryton Pools Country Park, which opened in 1996, has a 10-acre lake that is home

The evidence for the origins of the game of rugby may not be watertight but the story was, literally set in stone when a granite plaque was erected in 1923 on the Doctor's Wall, commemorating 'William Webb Ellis, who, with a fine disregard for the rules of football as played in his time, first took the ball in his arms and ran with it, thus originating the distinctive features of the Rugby game. AD 1823.'

Arbury Hall, nr Nuneaton

443 THE THREE HORSESHOES INN

Bubbenhall, nr Coventry

A smartly modernised village pub serving traditional ales and English, Anglo-Indian and Indian food. Seven spacious rooms for B&B.y

 see page 659

to great crested grebes, swans, moorhens and Canada geese. Pagets Pool, near the northeastern end of the park, is one of the most important sites in Warwickshire for dragonflies.

To the north is **Brandon Marsh Nature Centre**, 200 acres of lakes, marshes, woodland and grassland that provide a home and haven for many species of wildlife.

NUNEATON

13½ miles NW of Rugby on the A444

Originally a Saxon town known as Etone, the 'Nun' was added when a wealthy Benedictine priory was founded here in 1290. The Priory ruins are adjacent to the **Church of St Nicholas**, a Victorian building occupying a Norman site that has a beautiful carved ceiling dating back to 1485. **Nuneaton Museum and Art Gallery** features displays of archaeological interest ranging from prehistoric to medieval times.

Nuneaton Museum also has a permanent exhibition of the town's most illustrious daughter, the novelist George Eliot. Born at Arbury Hall in 1819, Eliot, whose real name was Mary Ann Evans, was an intellectual giant and free thinker. Her father was a land agent on the estate; she portrays this, her first home, as Cheverel Manor in her novel *Mr Gifgil's Love Story*.

NEWTON REGIS

6 miles NW of Atherstone off the B5493

One of the most unspoilt villages in Warwickshire, Newton Regis has been voted Best Kept Small Village on numerous occasions. Near the Staffordshire border and between the M42 and B5453, this lovely village is built around an attractive duck pond which was once a quarry pit. The village's name is thought to derive from its former royal ownership, having once been the property of King Henry II.

Wiltshire

A county rich in prehistoric remains, Wiltshire also has one of the highest concentrations of historic houses and gardens in the country as well as some fine downland and woodland that provide excellent walking or cycling. The industrial heritage of the county takes many forms – Brunel's Great Western Railway centred on Swindon, brewing at Devizes, carpet making at Wilton and the Kennet and Avon Canal. The jewel in Wiltshire's crown is the fine city of Salisbury with its magnificent cathedral. But it is for its ancient monuments, white horses and the intriguing crop circles that the county is best known. Along with the Stone Circles at Avebury, Silbury Hill, West Kennet Long Barrow and the White Horse at Westbury, Wiltshire is, of course, home to Stonehenge. A World Heritage Site, these massive stone blocks are one of the greatest mysteries of the prehistoric world. Close by is an even more ancient monument that is often overlooked – Woodhenge.

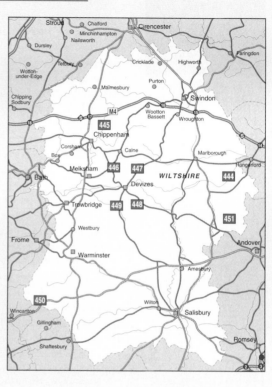

444 THE CROSS KEYS

Great Bedwyn, nr Marlborough

A very cheerful, friendly pub with a fine reputation for its food. Also B&B rooms

see page 659

SWINDON

The largest town in Wiltshire, lying in the northeast corner between the Cotswolds and the Marlborough Downs, Swindon was an insignificant agricultural community before the railway line between London and Bristol was completed in 1835. In 1843, Isambard Kingdom Brunel, the Great Western Railway's principal engineer, decided that Swindon was the place to build his locomotive works.

Within a few years it had grown to be one of the largest in the world, with as many as 12,000 workers on a 320-acre site that incorporated the Railway Village: this was a model development of 300 workmens' houses built of limestone extracted from the construction of Box Tunnel. This unique example of early Victorian town planning is open to the public at the **Railway Village Museum**.

The Great Western Railway Museum, now called **Steam**, houses a collection of locomotives, nameplates and signalling equipment along with exhibitions on the life of Brunel and of the men and women who built and repaired the rolling stock for God's Wonderful Railway. The site also contains the **National Monuments Record Centre** - the public archive of the Royal Commission on the Historical Monuments of England, with 7 million photographs, documents and texts.

On the western outskirts of Swindon is **Lydiard Park**, one of Wiltshire's smaller stately homes, which is the ancestral home of the Viscounts Bolingbroke.

Just south of the town lies Wroughton Airfield, a historic World War II airbase which is home to the National Museum of Science and Industry's collection of large aircraft.

AROUND SWINDON

MARLBOROUGH

10 miles S of Swindon on the A346

Marlborough College was founded in 1843 primarily for sons of the clergy. Built on the site of a Norman castle, the first mansion here was replaced in the early 18th century by a building that became the Castle Inn and is now C House, the oldest part of the college.

To the southeast of the town lies the ancient woodland of **Savernake Forest** where Henry VIII hunted wild deer.

STEAM, Swindon

Situated in a beautiful valley that bears its name, **Pewsey** is a charming village that was once the property of Alfred the Great. The **Heritage Centre**, housed in an 1870 foundry building, is well worth a visit, but the most interesting feature here lies just south of the village on Pewsey Down. The original **Pewsey White Horse** was cut in 1785 and apparently included a rider, but it was redesigned by George Marples and cut by the local fire brigade to celebrate the coronation of George VI.

Silbury Hill, nr Avebury

AVEBURY

10 miles SW of Swindon on the A4361

This village is home to the **Avebury Stone Circles**, the most remarkable ritual megalithic monuments in Europe and now a World Heritage Site. Many of the archaeological finds from the site are displayed in the Alexander Keiller Museum, which also describes the reconstruction of the site by Keiller in the 1930s.

Avebury also has a gem from more recent times: **Avebury Manor** dates from the Elizabethan era and is surrounded by a walled garden that features a wishing well, topiary and an Italian walk.

This area abounds with ancient monuments. To the south lies **West Kennet Long Barrow**, one of the country's largest Neolithic burial tombs; on nearby Overton Hill is The Sanctuary, an early Bronze Age monument of giant standing stones.

To the west of West Kennet, by the A4, lies the largest man-made prehistoric mound in Europe, **Silbury Hill**, which dates from around 2800 BC and rises some 300 feet. No bones or any other clues as to the purpose of the mound has been found, but it might have some connection with the nearby Avebury Stone Circles.

CRICKLADE

6½ miles NW of Swindon on the B4040

The only Wiltshire town on the River Thames, Cricklade was an important post on the Roman Ermin Street and, in Saxon times, had its own mint. There are many buildings of interest here, including the famous school founded by the London goldsmith Robert Jenner in 1651, and the elaborate Victorian clock tower. Nearby, North Meadow is a National Nature Reserve where the rare snakeshead fritillary grows.

CHIPPENHAM

An important administrative centre in King Alfred's time, Chippenham

327

Foxham, nr Chippenham

The inn highlights local produce in serving anything from a light snack to a full meal in friendly, relaxed surroundings.

🍴 *see page 660*

later gained prominence from the wool trade and was a major stop on the London to Bristol coaching route. In the flood plain to the east of Chippenham lies the footpath known as **Maud Heath's Causeway**, a remarkable and ingenious walkway consisting of 64 brick and stone arches that was built in the 15th century at the bequest of Maud Heath. She had spent most of her life as a poor pedlar trudging her way between the village of Bremhill and Chippenham but she died a relatively wealthy woman and her will provided sufficient funds for the construction and upkeep of the causeway.

To the south lies **Lacock Abbey**, which was founded in 1232 by Ela, Countess of Salisbury, in memory of her husband William Longsword, stepbrother to Richard the Lionheart. The estate later passed into the hands of the Talbot family, whose most distinguished member was the pioneering

photographer, William Henry Fox Talbot, who carried out his experiments here in the 1830s. Today, the National Trust's estate village of **Lacock** is one of the county's real treasures, with its delightful assortment of mellow stone buildings seemingly remaining unaltered over the centuries. The **Fox Talbot Museum** commemorates the life and achievements of a man who was not just a photographer but a mathematician, physicist, classicist and transcriber of Syrian and Chaldean cuneiform. The cloisters of Fox Talbot's house were used as a classroom at Hogwart's School in the Harry Potter films.

AROUND CHIPPENHAM

MALMESBURY
9 miles N of Chippenham on the B4040

England's oldest borough is dominated by the impressive remains of the Benedictine **Malmesbury Abbey**, founded in the 7th century by St Aldhelm. In the 10th century, King Athelstan, Alfred's grandson and the first Saxon king to unite England, granted 500 acres of land to the townsfolk in gratitude for their help in resisting a Norse invasion. This land is still known as King's Heath and is now owned by 200 residents who are descended from those far-off heroes.

In the **Athelstan Museum** are numerous displays, including one of lace making and another of early bicycles, while a more recent piece

Malmesbury Abbey

of local history concerns the Tamworth Two – the pigs who made the headlines with their dash for freedom.

To the east lies **Easton Grey**, whose elegant 18th century manor house was used as a summer retreat by Herbert Asquith, Prime Minister between 1908 and 1916.

CALNE

5 miles E of Chippenham on the A4

Calne is a former weaving centre in the valley of the River Marden and the prominent **Wool Church** reflects the town's early prosperity; inside, is a memorial to Dr Ingenhousz, who is widely credited with creating a smallpox vaccination before Edward Jenner.

A short distance from Calne, to the west, stands **Bowood House**, which was built in 1625 and is now a treasury of Shelborne family

heirlooms, paintings, books and furniture. It was in the Bowood Laboratory at Bowood House that Dr Joseph Priestley, tutor to the 1st Marquis of Lansdowne's son, conducted experiments that resulted in the identification of oxygen.

The **Atwell Motor Museum**, to the east of Calne, has a collection of over 70 vintage and classic cars and motorcycles from the years 1924 to 1983.

DEVIZES

9 miles SE of Chippenham on the A342

Devizes was founded in 1080 by Bishop Osmund, nephew of William the Conqueror, who built a timber castle here between the lands of two powerful manors; this act brought about the town's name, which is derived from the Latin 'ad divisas', or 'at the boundaries'.

After the wooden structure burnt down, the Bishop of Sarum built a stone castle in 1138 that survived until the end of the Civil War, when it was demolished.

Devizes **Visitor Centre** is based on a 12th century castle and takes visitors back to medieval times, when Devizes was home not just to its fine castle but also to anarchy and unrest during the struggle between Empress Matilda and King Stephen.

Many of the town's finest buildings are situated in and around the old market place, including the

Caen Hill Flight of Locks, Devizes

446 THE OLIVER CROMWELL

Bromham

Home-cooked pub grub in a traditional country inn with a large garden.

see page 660

447 THE CROWN INN

Bishop's Canning, nr Devizes

The warmest of welcomes for one and all, great food and well-kept ales in a picturesque village setting.

see page 661

448 THE LAMB INN

Urchfont, nr Devizes

A traditional country inn in a picturesque village setting providing a relaxing ambience for enjoying a drink and a meal.

see page 661

329

449 THE ROSE & CROWN

Worton, Devizes

A pleasant place to meet for good drink, good conversation and a fine across-the-board menu of excellent home cooking.

🍴 see page 662

Town Hall and the Corn Exchange. Devizes stands at a key point on the Kennet and Avon Canal and the **Kennet and Avon Canal Museum** tells the complete story of the waterway in fascinating detail. Many visitors combine a trip to the museum with a walk along the towpath; the town really buzzes in July when the Canalfest is held at the Wharf.

TROWBRIDGE

11 miles S of Chippenham on the A361

The county town of Wiltshire and another major weaving centre in its day, Trowbridge still has a number of old industrial buildings, and an interesting waymarked walk takes in many of them. The parish **Church of St James** contains the tomb of the poet and former rector George Crabbe, who wrote the work on which Benjamin Britten based his opera *Peter Grimes*. Trowbridge's most famous son was Isaac Pitman, the shorthand man, who was born in Nash Yard in 1813.

BRADFORD-ON-AVON

10 miles SW of Chippenham on the A363

A historic market town at a bridging point on the River Avon, which is spanned by a superb nine-arched bridge with a lock-up at one end. The town's oldest building is the **Church of St Lawrence** that is believed to have been founded by St Aldhelm in around AD 700. It 'disappeared' for over 1,000 years, during which time it was used variously as a school, a charnel house for storing the bones of the dead and a residential dwelling; it was re-discovered by a keen-eyed clergyman who looked down from a hill and noticed its cruciform shape.

Another of the town's outstanding buildings is the mighty **Tithe Barn**, which was once used to store the grain from local farms for Shaftesbury Abbey.

On the edge of the town, **Barton Farm Country Park** offers delightful walks in lovely countryside beside the River Avon and the Kennet and Avon Canal. **Barton Bridge** is the original packhorse bridge that was built to assist the transportation of grain from the farm to the tithe barn.

Half a mile south of the town, by the River Frome, is the Italian-style **Peto Garden** laid out between 1899 and 1933 by the architect and landscape gardener Harold Ainsworth Peto.

To the west, in the middle of the village of Holt, stands **The Courts**, an English country garden of mystery with unusual topiary, water gardens and an arboretum.

Bradford-on-Avon

CASTLE COMBE

5½ miles NW of Chippenham on the B4039

The loveliest village in the region, and for some the loveliest in the country, Castle Combe was once a centre of the prosperous wool trade, famed for its red and white cloth. Many of the present buildings date from the 15th and 16th centuries, including the covered **Market Cross** and the **Manor House**, which was built with stones from the Norman castle that gave the village its name.

SALISBURY

The glorious medieval city of Salisbury stands at the confluence of four rivers, the Avon, the Wylye, the Bourne and the Nadder. Originally called New Sarum, it grew around the present Cathedral, which was built between 1220 and 1258 in a sheltered position two miles south of the site of its windswept Norman predecessor, Old Sarum.

Surely one of the most beautiful buildings in the world, **Salisbury Cathedral** is the only medieval cathedral in England to be built all in the same Early English style – apart from its spire, the tallest in England, which was added some years later and rises to an awesome 404 feet. The Chapter House opens out of the cloisters and contains, among other treasures, one of the four surviving originals of the Magna Carta. The oldest working clock in Britain, and possibly in the world, is situated in

the fan-vaulted north transept; it was built in 1386 to strike the hour and has no clock face. **The Close**, the precinct of the ecclesiastical community serving the Cathedral, is the largest in England and contains a number of museums and houses open to the public, including, in the 17th century King's House, **Salisbury Museum**, home of the Stonehenge Gallery and The **Royal Gloucestershire, Berkshire and Wiltshire Museum**, housed in a 13th century building called **The Wardrobe**, which was originally used to store the bishop's clothes and documents. **Mompesson House** is a perfect example of Queen Anne architecture that is noted for its plasterwork, an elegant carved oak staircase, fine period furniture and the important Turnbull collection of 18th century drinking glasses.

There are many other areas of Salisbury to explore, and on a huge mound to the north are the ruins of **Old Sarum**, abandoned when the bishopric moved into the city. Old Sarum became the most

The view of the Cathedral across the water meadows of the Avon is one of the loveliest in England; Constable painted it from the garden of the Bishops Palace.

Old Sarum, nr Salisbury

A mile to the north of Amesbury lies Woodhenge, a ceremonial monument that is even older than its more famous neighbour, Stonehenge, and was the first major prehistoric site to be discovered by aerial photography.

---

450 STOURHEAD HOUSE AND GARDENS

Stourton

Often referred to as 'Paradise', lying in secluded privacy in its own valley, **Stourhead** is one of the finest landscape gardens in the world.

 see page 662

---

451 THE CROSS KEYS INN

Upper Chute, nr Andover

A traditional village inn with Fullers ales, a good choice of home-cooked food and four en suite bedrooms

see page 663

---

notorious of the 'rotten boroughs', returning two Members of Parliament, despite having no voters, until the 1832 Reform Act stopped the cheating. A plaque on the site commemorates Old Sarum's most illustrious Member of Parliament, William Pitt the Elder.

AROUND SALISBURY

AMESBURY

7 miles N of Salisbury on the A345

It was here that Queen Elfrida founded an abbey in AD 979, in atonement for her part in the murder of her son-in-law, Edward the Martyr, at Corfe Castle. Henry II rebuilt the abbey's great **Church of St Mary and St Melor**, whose tall central tower is the only structure to survive from the pre-Norman monastery.

Two miles west of Amesbury stands **Stonehenge**, perhaps the greatest mystery of the prehistoric world, one of the wonders of the world and a monument of unique importance. Stonehenge's orientation on the rising and setting sun has always been one of its most remarkable features, leading to theories that the builders were from a sun-worshipping culture or that the whole structure is part of a huge astronomical calendar.

WILTON

3 miles W of Salisbury on the A30

The third oldest borough in England, and once the capital of Saxon Wessex, Wilton is best known for its carpets and the

Wilton Carpet Factory, on the River Wylye, continues to produce top-quality Wilton and Axminster carpets.

To the south of the town stands **Wilton House**, the home of the Earls of Pembroke that was designed by Inigo Jones in the 17th century after the original house had been destroyed by fire in 1647. Later remodelled by James Wyatt, Wilton House features the amazing Double Cube Room and a fine art collection.

To the west lies **Dinton**, a lovely hillside village that is home to **Little Clarendon House**, a near perfect Tudor manor house, and **Philipps House**, a handsome early 19th century mansion that stands in the beautiful grounds of Dinton Park. Further west again are the ruins of **Old Wardour Castle**, a unique six-sided castle that dates from the 14th century.

STOURTON

23 miles W of Salisbury off the B3092

The main attraction of this beautiful village is **Stourhead**, one of the most famous examples of an early 18th century English landscape garden, and a place renowned for its striking vistas and woodland walks. **Stourton House** is a classical masterpiece dating from the 1720s and on the edge of the estate is the imposing King Alfred's Tower, a redbrick folly erected in 1772 that commemorates the king who reputedly raised his standard here against the Danes in AD 878.

WARMINSTER

19 miles NW of Salisbury off the A36

This historic town on the western edge of Salisbury Plain has a number of distinguished old buildings and some interesting monuments of varying age. **The Obelisk**, with its feeding troughs and pineapple top, was erected in 1783 to mark the enclosure of the parish; the Morgan Memorial Fountain stands in the Lake Pleasure Grounds; and Beyond Harvest is a statue in bronze by Colin Lambert of a girl sitting on sacks of corn.

To the west of town, **Cley Hill** is an Iron Age hill fort with two Bronze Age barrows; it is renowned as a place for sighting UFOs. The region is also noted for the appearance of crop circles, and some have linked the two phenomena.

Just to the west of Warminster is **Longleat House**, the magnificent home of the Marquis of Bath that dates from the 1570s and is filled with a superb collection of old masters, beautiful furniture, rare books and murals by Lord Bath. The glorious grounds, landscaped by Capability Brown, are famous as the home of the Safari Park established in the 1960s.

Longleat House, Warminster

North of Warminster is **Westbury**, a major centre of the wool and cloth trades in the Middle Ages and with many fine buildings still standing as a legacy of those prosperous days.

To the east of Westbury is the town's best known feature, the famous Westbury **White Horse** that dates from 1778 and replaces an earlier horse carved to celebrate King Alfred's victory over the Danes in AD 878. Above the horse's head are the ruins of Bratton Castle, an Iron Age hill fort covering 25 acres.

Worcestershire

The southern part of Worcestershire is dominated by the spectacular ridge of the Malvern Hills in the west, which provides excellent walking country along with breathtaking views, and the Vale of Evesham in the east, an attractive area with charming towns and villages built of the warm Cotswold stone. Most of the county's industry is centred in the northern part, where there are numerous examples of industrial archaeology to interest the historian. Canals here were once as important as roads and the area around Kidderminster and Redditch is dominated by three such waterways: the Worcester & Birmingham Canal, the Staffordshire & Worcester Canal and the Droitwich Canal. The arrival of the railways saw a rapid decline in water transport and, although this network is now much smaller than it was, the Severn Valley Railway, from Kidderminster to Bridgnorth, has survived and flourishes today as people flock here to relive the days of steam travel.

Between these two very different sections of Worcestershire lies the county town of Worcester, an ancient place that is well known for its glorious cathedral and as being the home of Royal Worcester porcelain. It was near here that one of Britain's greatest composers, Sir Edward Elgar, was born.

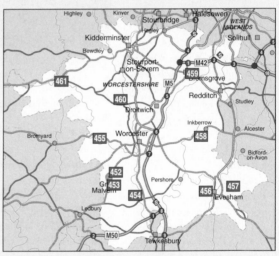

WORCESTER

Situated on the River Severn, Worcester is a bustling county capital that is dominated by its **Cathedral**. Built by St Wulstan, the only English bishop not replaced by a Norman following the Conquest, the Cathedral, with its 200 feet tower and 11th century crypt, is a magnificent example of classic medieval architecture. One of the many tombs here is that of King John, adorned with a fine sculpture showing the King flanked by Bishops Oswald and Wulstan; outside is a statue of Sir Edward Elgar, who was born at nearby Lower Broadheath.

Right in the centre of the city stands a wonderful survivor from the past - **Greyfriars**, a medieval house with a pretty walled garden. By contrast, the imposing Guildhall is a marvellous example of Queen Anne architecture that was designed by a local man, Thomas White. At the **City Museum and Art Gallery** there are displays of contemporary art and archaeology, a 19th century chemist's shop and the military collections of the Worcestershire Regiment and the Worcestershire Yeomanry Cavalry. The history of the city and its people is explored at the **Museum of Local Life**.

During the Civil War the **Battle of Worcester** was fought in 1651 and the **Commandery**, a stunning complex of buildings behind a small timber-framed entrance, was used as the Royalist headquarters. Now the **Commandery Civil War**

Centre is home to a series of period rooms that offer a fascinating glimpse of the architecture and style of Tudor and Stuart times while also acting as the country's only museum devoted to the story of the Civil War.

With charming old buildings, a splendid cathedral, interesting museums and a compact **National Hunt Racecourse**, Worcester certainly has much to offer visitors, but no trip to the city would be complete without a visit to the **Royal Worcester Porcelain Visitor Centre**. Royal Worcester is Britain's oldest continuous producer of porcelain and the factory was founded in 1751 by Dr John Wall,

Lea & Perrins Worcestershire sauce was made from a recipe brought back from India in 1835 by Lord Sandys. He commissioned two chemists, John Lea and William Perrins, to make up the recipe, but the result was unpalatable. Thy put the bottle away and when it came to light years later, hey presto! – the maturing process had transformed it into the delicious concoction that had so delighted Lord Sandys in India.

Greyfriars, Worcester

452 THE EXPRESS INN

Malvern

A landmark local open for drinks from noon to midnight every day of the week.

see page 663

453 THE COTFORD HOTEL & L'AMUSE BOUCHE RESTAURANT

Malvern

Outstanding food and accommodation in a superb hotel set in extensive gardens at the foot of the Malvern Hills.

see page 664

454 THE THREE KINGS

Hanley Castle

A traditional country inn with a lively little bar serving a fine selection of real ales.

see page 665

who intended to create "a ware of a form so precise as to be easily distinguished from other English porcelain." Just to the southeast is Worcester Woods Country Park, a glorious place with ancient oak woodland, wildflower meadows and waymarked trails.

To the south of Worcester lies **Powick Bridge**, the scene of the first and last battles in the Civil War – the last, in 1651, ending with Charles II hiding in the Boscobel Oak before journeying south to nine year's exile in France.

It was at **Lower Broadheath**, just to the west of Worcester, that Edward Elgar was born in 1857, and, although he spent long periods away from the village, it remained his spiritual home. There are various **Elgar Trails** to follow, and the **Elgar Birthplace Museum** is housed in a redbrick cottage.

AROUND WORCESTER

MALVERN

7½ miles S of Worcester on the A449

Best known for its porcelain, annual music and drama festivals, Malvern water and Morgan cars, Malvern, beneath the northeastern slopes of the Malvern Hills, was a quiet and little known place with a priory at its centre before the discovery of its spring waters started its growth. The hotels, baths and pump room were built in the early 19th century and the arrival of the railway provided easier access. The station is one of the many charming Victorian buildings,

and a Regency cottage houses one source of the spring waters, St Anne's Well, where visitors can still sample the waters. The first Morgan car was developed in 1909 in the school workshops of Malvern College; the famous Morgan three-wheeler stayed in production, with few changes, until 1950.

The centre of the town is dominated by a much older building, the priory **Church of St Mary and St Michael**, whose east and west windows (gifts from Henry VII and Richard III respectively) contain a wonderful collection of stained glass. Outside, in the churchyard, are some interesting graves including that of Jenny Lind, the 'Swedish Nightingale', who was born in Stockholm in 1820 but who died in Malvern while on a summer retreat in 1887. The 14th century Abbey Gateway still remains, now the home of the **Malvern Museum**. The town's heritage as an agricultural and market centre has not been lost, as close by is the permanent site of the **Three Counties Show**, one of the country's premier agricultural shows.

Great Malvern is the largest of the six settlements that make up the Malverns. To the south lies **Little Malvern**, where a simple headstone in the churchyard marks the grave of Sir Edward Elgar and his wife Caroline. In the churchyard at West Malvern is the grave of Peter Mark Roget of Thesaurus fame.

UPTON-ON-SEVERN

9 miles S of Worcester on the A4104

As one of the few bridging points on the River Severn, this unspoilt town was a Roman station and an important medieval port. It also played a role in the Civil War when in 1651 Charles sent a force to Upton to destroy the bridge; but after a long and bloody struggle the King's troops were defeated and Cromwell's men regained the town.

The **Tudor House** contains a museum of Upton past and present, and the 16th century White Lion Hotel was the setting for some of the scenes in Henry Fielding's novel *Tom Jones*.

Northeast of Upton, close to Earls Croome, lies **Croome Landscape Park**, which was Capability Brown's first complete landscape commission.

Little Malvern Court and Gardens

ALFRICK

6½ miles W of Worcester off the A44

The village church's claim to fame is that Charles Dodgson (better known as Lewis Carroll) once preached here but, today, it is nature lovers who are drawn to this charming village. To the northwest lies **Ravenshill Woodland Nature Reserve** where waymarked trails lead through woodland that is home to many breeding birds while, to the south, is Knapp and Papermill Nature Reserve, whose woodland and meadow are rich in flora and fauna.

To the east is the spectacular valley of Leigh Brook, a tributary of the River Teme, which winds its way through glorious countryside, and in the village of **Leigh**, in the grounds of **Leigh Court**, stands a massive 14th century Tithe Barn with great cruck beams and wagon doors.

EVESHAM

'*Who travels Worcester county takes any road that comes, when April tosses bounty to the cherries and the plums*'. Thus did the poet John Drinkwater describe his favourite county.

This bustling market town lies at the centre of the Vale of Evesham, an area that has long been known as the Garden of England as it produces a prolific

455 THE ROYAL OAK

Broadwas-on-Teme

Food is the star of the show at this popular village pub, classic pub grub at lunchtime and a huge choice from display cabinets in the evening.

see page 665

337

456 YE OLDE RED HORSE

Evesham

Locals and visitors from afar are equally welcome at this attractive pub in the centre of Evesham.

 see page 666

457 THE FLEECE INN

Bretforton, nr Evesham

A quintessential English village inn, and a must for anyone who appreciates proper ale and decent food.

 see page 667

458 THE WHEELBARROW CASTLE

Radford

The social hub of the village, with plenty to please anyone who enjoys good food, drink and entertainment in convivial surroundings.

 see page 668

harvest of soft fruits, apples, plums and salad vegetables. The **Blossom Trail**, which starts in the town, is a popular outing, particularly when the fruit trees are in blossom, and the waymarked trail follows a route from the town's High Street to Greenhill, where the **Battle of Evesham** took place.

At this point, the River Avon meanders in a loop around the town and Abbey Park is an excellent place for a riverside stroll although all that remains of the **Abbey**, which was built in around AD 700 by Egwin, Bishop of Worcester, is the magnificent bell tower and the home of the Abbey Almoner that dates from around 1400. At the **Almonry Heritage Centre**, visitors can view a unique collection of artefacts that include displays showing the history of the Abbey and the defeat of Simon de Montford at the Battle of Evesham in 1265. He was buried by the high altar, and a stone marking the site was unveiled by the Speaker of the House of Commons in 1965, the 700th anniversary of his death.

AROUND EVESHAM

INKBERROW

9 miles N of Evesham on the A422

William Shakespeare stayed at the village inn, **The Old Bull**, in 1582, and it later won fame as the original of The Bull at Ambridge, the home of The Archers. Another handsome building in the village, the 18th century Old Vicarage, played host, in an earlier guise, to Charles I, while he was on his way

to Naseby. Some maps that he left behind are now kept in the church.

MIDDLE LITTLETON

4 miles NE of Evesham off the B4085

Situated close to the River Avon along with the other Littletons – North and South – this village is home to a huge **Tithe Barn** that dates from the 13th century and that was once the property of the Abbots of Evesham; it is still in use as a farm building. Just to the north, in an area of fertile limestone, is **Windmill Hill Nature Reserve** while, to the southeast, near **Honeybourne**, is the **Domestic Fowl Trust and Honeybourne Rare Breeds Centre** where pure breeds of poultry, along with rare farm animal breeds, are conserved.

BROADWAY

5 miles SE of Evesham on the B4632

One of the most beautiful villages in England, this quintessential Cotswold village has a broad main street that is lined with houses and cottages built of golden Cotswold stone. It was settled as far back as 1900 BC, the Romans occupied the hill above Broadway, and the village was probably re-established after the Battle of Dyrham in AD 557 by conquering Saxons as they advanced on Worcester.

Housed in a picturesque 18th century shop on the High Street is the **Teddy Bear Museum**, where visitors of all ages will be enchanted with the numerous displays. The hall of fame tells of celebrity bears, including Paddington, Pooh and the three in the story of Goldilocks, while bears of all ages and sizes are for sale. Old bears and much-loved dolls are also lovingly restored here at – where else! – the St Beartholomew's Hospital.

On top of Broadway Beacon stands **Broadway Tower**, a folly that was built by the 6th Earl of Coventry at the end of the 18th century. Designed by James Wyatt, the tower now contains various displays and exhibitions, while the surrounding area is a delightful country park.

BREDON

8 miles SW of Evesham on the B4079

The most outstanding building here is undoubtedly **Bredon Barn**. This huge 14th century Cotswold stone barn has a dramatic aisled interior, marvellous beams and two porches at the wagon entrances.

PERSHORE

6 miles NW of Evesham on the A44

This glorious market town, with its fine Georgian architecture, occupies an attractive location on the banks of the River Avon. Its crowning glory is undoubtedly its 7th century **Abbey**, which combines outstanding examples of both Norman and Early English architecture. Although only the choir remains of the original church, it is still a considerable architectural treasure, and the vaulting in the chancel roof is magnificent.

Pershore Bridge, which is now a favourite picnic spot, still bears the scars of damage it sustained during the Civil War.

KIDDERMINSTER

Standing on the banks of the River Stour, Kidderminster is known chiefly as a centre of the carpet-making industry that began here as a cottage industry in the early 18th century. The introduction of the power loom instigated the move to a more industrialised method and carpet mills were built – the enormous chimneys still dominate the skyline. The industry also brought wealth to the town and surrounding area and this is reflected in the size of **St Mary's Church**, the largest parish church in the county, which stands on a hill overlooking the town. Outside the Town Hall is a statue to Kidderminster's best known son, Rowland Hill, a teacher, educationalist and inventor who founded the modern postal system and introduced the penny post.

The **Severn Valley Railway** runs from Kidderminster to Bridgnorth, in Shropshire, and at the town's station is the **Kidderminster Railway Museum**, where a splendid collection of railway memorabilia can be seen in an old Great Western Railway grain store.

AROUND KIDDERMINSTER

HAGLEY

6 miles NE of Kidderminster on the A456

In 1756, George, 1st Lord Lyttleton, commissioned the creation of what was to be the last great Palladian mansion in Britain,

Just to the northwest of Broadway, near the village of Childswickham, is the Barnfield Cider Mill Museum, where visitors can see a display of cider-making down the years before sampling cider, perry or one of the wines produced from local plums and berries.

To the northeast of Bredon lies Bredon Hill that dominates this area of Worcestershire and around which there are some delightful villages. Almost circular, this limestone outcrop rises to over 900 feet, and on the crest of the northern slope are the remains (part of the earthworks) of the pre-Roman settlement that is known as Kemerton Camp. At the top is a curious black tower called Parson's Folly that was built by a Mr Parson in the 18th century.

Hagley Hall

Just to the southeast of Hagley lie the Clent Hills, an immensely popular area for walking and enjoying the panoramic views. On the top of the hills are four upright stones that look as if they could be a work of modern art - in fact, they were erected over 200 years ago by Lord Lyttleton.

459 BROMSGROVE MUSEUM

Bromsgrove
Much of the earlier history of Bromsgrove can be seen at **Bromsgrove Museum**, which contains exhibits of the glass, salt and rail industries, and of the Bromsgrove Guild

 see page 669

340

Hagley Hall, an imposing building with a restored rococo interior. In the surrounding parkland, there are temples, cascading pools and a ruined castle along with a large herd of deer.

BROMSGROVE

8½ miles SE of Kidderminster on the A448

Along with some very handsome timber-framed buildings in the High Street, there stands a statue of AE Housman, Bromsgrove's most famous son.

Close to the town centre is the **Bromsgrove Museum** where there are displays of local crafts and industry, including the Bromsgrove Guild, an organisation of craftsmen that was founded in 1894. The skilled craftsmen of this guild designed and made the gates and railings of Buckingham Palace.

Two popular annual events are held here: the Music Festival, which hosts a wide range of musical entertainment from orchestral concerts to jazz, and the

Court Leet, the ancient form of local administration whose annual colourful procession has been revived.

Just northeast of Bromsgrove near the village of **Burcot** is the notorious **Lickey Incline**. This stretch of railway is, at 1 in 37.7, the steepest gradient in the whole of Britain's rail network. One especially powerful locomotive, No. 58100, '*Big Bertha*', the Lickey Banker, spent its days up until the late 1950s helping trains up the bank, a task that was later performed by massive double-boilered locomotives that were the most powerful in the whole BR fleet. The steepness of the climb is due to the same geographical feature that necessitated the construction of the unique flight of locks at Tardebigge (to the southeast of Bromsgrove), where in the space of 2½ miles the canal is lifted by no fewer than 30 locks.

In the churchyard of St John the Baptist in Bromsgrove are the graves of Thomas Scaife and Joseph Rutherford, who were killed in 1840 when the boiler of their locomotive blew up as they were climbing Lickey Incline.

To the south of Bromsgrove is the **Avoncraft Museum of Historic Buildings** that takes visitors on a walk through seven centuries of English history and where each building provides a snapshot of life in its particular period. Behind the museum's shop is another unique attraction, the **BT National Telephone Kiosk Collection**.

REDDITCH

*14½ miles SE of Kidderminster
on the A448*

It was along the banks of the River Arrow that the town's famous needle-making industry was founded. Housed in one of the historic buildings in the beautiful valley is the **Forge Mill Needle Museum** and Bordesley Abbey Visitor Centre that offers a unique glimpse into a past way of life.

DROITWICH

8½ miles SE of Kidderminster on the A38

Salt deposits, a legacy from the time when this area was on the seabed, were mined here for 2,000 years, and the Romans named it Salinae, the place of salt. The natural Droitwich brine, which is pumped up from an underground lake 200 feet below the town, contains about 2½ pounds of salt per gallon – ten times that of sea water – and it is often likened to the waters of the Dead Sea. The first brine baths were built here in the 1830s and by 1876, under the influence of the 'Salt King' John Corbett, Droitwich had developed into a fashionable spa.

Many of the buildings in present day Droitwich were owned by Corbett, including the Raven Hotel, but his most remarkable and lasting monument is undoubtedly **Chateau Impney** on the eastern side of the town at Dodderhill. Designed in the style of an ornate French château by a Frenchman, Auguste Tronquois, the house has soaring turrets, a mansard roof and classical French gardens.

To the east of Droitwich lies **Hanbury Hall**, a fine redbrick mansion in William & Mary style. Along with a splendid collection of porcelain, the interior of the house is famous for its murals by Sir James Thornhill, who is perhaps best known for his frescoes in the dome of St Paul's Cathedral. The surrounding grounds include a formal garden, an orangery and an 18th century icehouse.

STOURPORT-ON-SEVERN

3½ miles S of Kidderminster on the A451

Situated at the centre of the Worcestershire waterways, Stourport-on-Severn is a canal town of glorious Georgian buildings with an intricate network of canal basins. Prosperity and growth came quickly once the Staffordshire and Worcestershire Canal had been dug, and although the commercial trade has now gone the town still prospers, as the barges laden with coal, timber, iron and grain have given way to pleasure craft.

Just to the east of the town lies **Hartlebury Castle**, a historic sandstone castle that was once owned by the Bishops of Worcester and was used as a prison for captured Royalist troops during the Civil War. It now houses the **Worcester County Museum**.

GREAT WITLEY

8½ miles SW of Kidderminster on the A443

This village is home to two remarkable buildings. Once one of the largest houses in Europe, **Witley Court** was a palatial

• *Leading southwestwards from Droitwich, the Droitwich Canal, which opened in 1771, was built by James Brindley to link the town with the River Severn at Hawford, where a half-timbered 16th century dovecote is sited. For some of its short length the canal passes close to the Salwarpe Valley Nature Reserve, one of the very few inland sites with salt water, which makes it ideal for a variety of saltmarsh plants.* •

460 THE LENCHFORD INN

Shrawley

A lovely riverside setting for a handsome inn serving a fine selection of drinks and food. Nine rooms for B&B guests.

🍴 🛏 *see page 669*

461 THE TALBOT HOTEL

Tenbury Wells

Family-run hotel with the warmest of welcomes and handsome bedrooms and day rooms.

🛏 🍴 *see page 670*

The Forestry Commission's Wyre Forest covers a vast area to the west and northwest of Bewdley and extending into Shropshire. The Wyre Forest Visitor Centre, just west of Bewdley, contains information on the forest, and the nearby Discovery Centre offers a wide range of holiday activities and educational programmes.

mansion that was funded by the riches of the Dudley family but, following a devastating fire in 1937, the shell stood neglected for many years. The ruins have been made safe and accessible and along with the massive Poseidon and Flora fountains inspired by Bernini's fountains in Rome, they are a sight not to be missed. Adjacent to these haunting ruins is St **Michael's Church**, whose rather nondescript exterior does nothing to prepare visitors for the spectacularly flamboyant Baroque interior: stained glass by Joshua Price, plasterwork by Bagutti, canvas ceiling paintings by Bellucci.

BEWDLEY

3 miles W of Kidderminster on the B4190

Situated on the western bank of the River Severn and linked to its suburb, Wribbenhall, by a fine Thomas Telford bridge, Bewdley was once a flourishing port but it lost some of its importance when the Staffordshire and Worcestershire Canal was opened. It has now won fame with another form of transport, the **Severn Valley Railway**, which operates a full service of trains hauled by a variety of steam locomotives. Running from Kidderminster to Bridgnorth, the home of the railway since 1965, the route takes in several scenic attractions including the Wyre Forest and the Severn Valley Country Park and Nature Reserve. There are six stations along the track, each of them an architectural delight.

The **Bewdley Museum** contains exhibitions that are themed around the River Severn and the Wyre Forest and depicts local crafts such as charcoal burning, coopering and brass making. The town was the birthplace of Stanley Baldwin, Earl Baldwin of Bewdley, who was Prime Minister in 1923-1924, 1924-1929 and 1935-1937. He died at his home, **Astley Hall** (5 miles south of Kidderminster), opposite which is a memorial stone inscribed 'Thrice Prime Minister'. His ashes lie with those of his wife in the nave of Worcester Cathedral.

Yorkshire

	ACCOMMODATION	
465	Wuthering Heights, Stanbury	pg 346, 672
466	The Greyhound, Riccall	pg 348, 673
468	The Kings Head, Pollington	pg 348, 674
469	The New Globe Inn, Malton	pg 349, 674
471	The Cross Keys, Thixendale	pg 350, 675
473	The Star Country Inn, Weaverthorpe	pg 350, 677
475	The New Crown Hotel, Bridlington	pg 351, 678
479	The Black Bull Inn, Pickering	pg 354, 681
480	The Riviera, Whitby	pg 354, 680
482	The Captain Cook Inn, Staithes	pg 355, 683
483	Estbek House, Sandsend, nr Whitby	pg 355, 684
488	Woody's At The Black Swan, Thornton-Le-Moor	pg 357, 689
491	Lastingham Grange Country House Hotel, Lastingham, nr Kirkbymoorside	pg 358, 691
492	The Blacksmiths Arms, Lastingham	pg 358, 691
494	The Greyhound Inn, Hackforth	pg 359, 692
496	Dalegarth & The Ghyll Holiday Cottages, Buckden, nr Skipton	pg 360, 694

Yorkshire

The largest county in England, Yorkshire has a rich industrial and ecclesiastical heritage along with a wide diversity of countryside that helps to make it one of the most intriguing regions of England. The Yorkshire Dales National Park is an area of rich farmland, high moorland and deep valleys. The predominant limestone has given rise to a host of interesting natural features, none more so than Malham Cove, Malham Tarn and Aysgarth Falls. South of the Dales is Brontë country, an area forever associated with the tragic family, but one that also has strong links with the textile industry. The northeast of the county is dominated by the North York Moors National Park that incorporates not only the Cleveland Hills but also some spectacular coastline, including the old port of Whitby. Here, too, are elegant market towns such as Richmond and Ripon, and the famous spa town of Harrogate. Above all, there is York, a fabulous city centred on its magnificent cathedral that has a long and colourful history going back over 2,000 years.

343

HALIFAX

*Halifax is the home of
Mackintosh's Toffee. In
1936 a new toffee and
chocolate mixture took its
name from a play by
James Barrie – the
sentimental comedy
Quality Street.*

Halifax boasts one of Yorkshire's
most impressive examples of
municipal architecture, the glorious
18th century **Piece Hall**, a large
quadrangle surrounded by
colonnades and balconies behind
which are some 40 specialist shops.
Adjacent to the hall is the
Calderdale Industrial Museum,
which provides an insight into
Halifax's textile heritage as well as
celebrating the town's greatest
contribution to modern motoring,
the cats-eye. Halifax also has one of
the largest parish churches in
England.

On the outskirts of the town is
the **Bankfield Museum**, the home
between 1837 and 1886 of Edward
Akroyd, the largest wool
manufacturer in Britain, which now
houses an internationally important
collection of textiles and costumes
from around the world.

To the east of Halifax lies
Shibden Hall and Park, a
distinctive timber-framed house

Shibden Hall, nr Halifax

dating from 1420, situated in 90
acres of parkland.

AROUND HALIFAX

KEIGHLEY

10 miles N of Halifax on the A650

Lying at the junction of the Rivers
Worth and Aire, Keighley still retains
a strangely nostalgic air of the
Victorian Industrial Revolution.
Several of the old mill buildings
survive, and at the **Keighley
Museum** is the hand loom,
complete with unfinished cloth, that
was used by Timmy Feather, the last
hand-loom weaver in England.

Just northeast of the town lies
17th century **East Riddlesden
Hall**, which has one of the largest
and most impressive timber-framed
barns in the North of England that
now houses a collection of farm
wagons and agricultural equipment.

ILKLEY

14 miles NE of Halifax on the A65

One of the most famous West
Yorkshire attractions has to be
Ilkley Moor, immortalised in the
well-known song; like any of the
Yorkshire moors, Ilkley Moor can
look inviting and attractive on a
sunny day but ominous and
forbidding when the weather is bad
– best to wear a hat.

BRADFORD

10 miles NE of Halifax on the A650

The **Bradford Industrial Museum**
and Horses at Work, housed in an
original worsted spinning mill
complex built in 1875, re-creates life
in Bradford in late Victorian times as

well as offering horse-bus and tram rides. Of related interest is Britain's only **Museum of Colour**, where the fascinating story of dyeing and textile printing from Ancient Egypt to the present day is explained. The **National Museum of Photography, Film and Television** houses an IMAX, one of the largest cinema screens in the world.

HUDDERSFIELD
6½ miles SE of Halifax on the A629

Huddersfield flourished in Victorian times and its most impressive buildings date from that era: the stately railway station, the Italianate **Town Hall** and the lofty **Jubilee Tower**, built in 1897 to celebrate Queen Victoria's Diamond Jubilee.

HOLMFIRTH
11 miles SE of Halifax on the A635

As the location for the television comedy, *The Last of the Summer Wine*, Holmfirth is familiar to millions who have never visited this little Pennine town. The town is home to the **Holmfirth Postcard Museum**, which has a comprehensive collection of the traditional saucy seaside postcard produced by Bamfords of Holmfirth in the first half of the 20th century.

HAWORTH
8 miles NW of Halifax off the A6033

Haworth is the home of the Brontë family and in its time was also a thriving industrial town. **The Parsonage**, built in 1777, is the focus of most Brontë pilgrimages and is now given over to the **Brontë Parsonage Museum**.

The **Brontë Way**, a 40-mile footpath with a series of four guided walks, links the places that provided inspiration to the sisters. All the siblings were buried in the family vault except Anne, who was

462 THE GREAT WESTERN INN

Marsden, Huddersfield
The warmest of welcomes, cask ales and good wholesome food generously served in an outstanding country pub.

 see page 670

463 THE CASK & SPINDLE

Shepley, Huddersfield
Home cooking is a magnet for lovers of good food, with children's and senior citizens' menus supplementing the main menu and Sunday roasts.

 see page 672

464 THE OLD FARMHOUSE

Netherton, Huddersfield
Outstanding food sourced on the farm or locally is the basis of daytime tea room and evening restaurant menus.

 see page 671

Last of the Summer Wine Exhibition, Holmfirth

345

465 WUTHERING HEIGHTS

Stanbury, nr Haworth

An outstanding village inn open all day for drinks and at lunchtime for food.

 see page 672

buried at Sacrborough. The town is the headquarters of the **Keighley and Worth Valley Railway,** a thriving volunteer-run railway that serves six stations (most of them gas-lit) in the course of its length.

SHEFFIELD

In recent years Sheffield has re-invented itself. England's fourth largest city, it is still busy with its steel, cutlery, engineering and toolmaking industries but is also a vibrant, international, multi-cultural city whose image was given a fillip by the worldwide success of *The Full Monty* which was filmed in and around Sheffield.

The city's premier museum is the **Kelham Island Museum**

which tells the story of Sheffield in a living museum. Sheffield's industrial heritage is celebrated in a number of museums, the most picturesque of which is undoubtedly the **Bishop's House Museum** which dates from around 1500 and is the earliest timber-framed house still standing in the city. A museum of a very different nature is the **Sheffield Bus Museum**, housed in the Tinsley Tram sheds on Sheffield Road. Sheffield also has three outstanding galleries devoted to the visual arts: the **Millennium Galleries** that not only showcase Sheffield's impressive metalware collection but also provides space to show the city's wonderful collection of paintings, drawings and natural history exhibits; the **Graves Art Gallery** with a wide-ranging collection of British art from the 16th century to the present along with European paintings and a fine collection of watercolours, drawings and prints; and the **Site Gallery**, devoted to photographic and new media exhibitions and events.

AROUND SHEFFIELD

RENISHAW

9 miles SE of Sheffield on the A616

This sizeable village gives its name to **Renishaw Hall**, home of Sir Reresby and Lady Sitwell and located about a mile or so to the northwest. The beautiful formal Italian gardens and 300 acres of wooded park are open to visitors, along with a nature trail and a Sitwell family museum, an art gallery, a display of Fiori de

Bishop's House Museum, Sheffield

Henriques sculptures in the Georgian stables, and a café.

ROTHERHAM

7 miles NE of Sheffield on the A630/A631

The town's most striking building is undoubtedly the **Church of All Saints**. With its soaring tower, pinnacled buttresses and battlements, and imposing porch, it is one of the finest examples of perpendicular architecture in Yorkshire. It dates mainly from the 15th century although there is evidence of an earlier Saxon church on the site.

Dramatically set within the former Templeborough steelworks, Magna was the UK's first science adventure park.

BARNSLEY

10 miles N of Sheffield on the A61

The county town of South Yorkshire, Barnsley stands on the River Dearne and derived its Victorian prosperity from the rich seams of coal hereabouts. It has an appropriately imposing Town Hall although the building is comparatively recent, completed in 1933. The town's most impressive museum is actually located a few miles to the west, in the village of **Cawthorne**. **Cannon Hall** is a magnificent 18th century country house set in formal gardens and historic parkland. It offers unique collections of pottery, furniture, glassware and paintings, along with the 'Charge Gallery' which documents the story of the 13th/ 18th Royal Hussars.

About a mile to the south of

Barnsley is the **Worsbrough Mill and Country Park**. The Grade II listed mill dates from around 1625. A steam mill was added in the 19th century and both have been restored to full working order to form the centrepiece of an industrial museum. Another three miles to the southeast, situated in attractive South Yorkshire countryside just off the M1 (J36), the **Elsecar Heritage Centre** is an imaginative science and history centre which is fun and educational for all the family.

DONCASTER

Originally a Roman settlement, Doncaster later had one of the country's most important railway works, where steam locomotives were turned out in their thousands, including the A4 Pacifics, among which was the record-breaking *Mallard*. Doncaster is also a renowned centre of horse-racing,

•

From the mid 18th century, the Walker Company of Rotherham was famous for cannons, their products serving to lethal effect in the American War of Independence and at the Battle of Trafalgar. They also built bridges, amongst them Southwark Bridge in London and the bridge at Sunderland. Another famous bridge builder was born here in 1901. Sir Donald Coleman Bailey invented the Bailey Bridge which proved to be of great military value, especially during World War II.

•

Elsecar Heritage Centre, Barnsley

466 THE GREYHOUND

Riccall

A warm and friendly village pub serving four cask ales and a fine choice of food cooked by the leaseholder.

 see page 673

467 THE PERCY ARMS

Airmyn, nr Goole

A cheerful, sociable, family-friendly village pub with a good menu based on fresh seasonal produce.

 see page 673

468 THE KINGS HEAD

Pollington

A familiar village landmark with a welcome for one and all, food to satisfy a wide range of tastes and appetites and five wheelchair-friendly chalet-style bedrooms.

 see page 674

and the venue for the final classic of the racing year, the St Leger.

On the northwestern outskirts of Doncaster lies **Cusworth Hall**, home to the Museum of South Yorkshire Life while, a little further on, is **Brodsworth Hall**, a remarkable example of a Victorian mansion that has survived with most of its original furnishings and decorations intact.

AROUND DONCASTER

SELBY

18 miles N of Doncaster on the A63

Selby Abbey was completed in the 13th century and has suffered more than most down the centuries. It was severely damaged by

Cromwell's troops during the Civil War and in 1690 the central tower collapsed. Major restoration work was carried out during the 19th century, but in 1906 a disastrous fire swept through the Abbey. Despite all this, the building is still a beautiful edifice, and the famous Washington Window that depicts the coat of arms of John de Washington, a 15th century Prior of the Abbey and a direct ancestor of George Washington, remains intact.

CONISBROUGH

5 miles SW of Doncaster on the A630

The town is best known for its 11th century **Conisbrough Castle**, which features prominently in one of the most dramatic scenes in Sir

Conisbrough Castle

Walter Scott's novel *Ivanhoe*. The most impressive medieval building in South Yorkshire, Conisbrough Castle boasts the oldest circular keep in England.

PONTEFRACT

15 miles NW of Doncaster on the A639

When it was built in the 11th century, **Pontefract Castle** was one of the most formidable fortresses in Norman England. In medieval times it passed to the House of Lancaster and became a Royal Castle – Richard II was imprisoned here and murdered in its dungeons on the orders of Henry Bolingbroke, who then assumed the crown as Henry IV. The castle was a major Royalist stronghold during the Civil War, after which it was destroyed by Cromwell's troops. Today it is a gaunt ruin with only sections of the inner bailey and the lower part of the keep surviving intact.

The town is most famous for its Pontefract Cakes. Liquorice root has been grown here since monastic times and there is even a small planting of liquorice in the local park.

YORK

At the centre of this glorious city is **York Minster**, which stands on the site of an even older building, the headquarters of the Roman legions. Its stained glass windows – there are more than a hundred of them – cast a celestial light over the many treasures within. A guided tour of the Great Tower gives spectacular views across the city, while a visit to the crypt reveals some of the relics from the Roman fortress that stood here nearly 2,000 years ago.

The network of medieval streets around the Minster is one of the city's major delights. Probably most famous of these ancient streets is **The Shambles** – its name comes from 'Fleshammels', the street of butchers and slaughterhouses.

Continuing to prosper into the 19th century, York became the hub of the railway system in the north at the instigation of the entrepreneur George Hudson, founder of what became the Great Northern Railway. Close to the magnificent railway station is the **National Railway Museum**, the largest of its kind in the world.

One of York's most unusual attractions is the **Jorvik Centre**, an innovative exhibition of Viking York complete with authentic sounds and even smells.

AROUND YORK

MALTON

17 miles NE of York on the B1248

Malton has been the historic centre of Ryedale ever since the Romans came and built a large fort beside the River Derwent. Many relics from the site can be seen in the **Malton Museum**, along with items from the Iron Age settlement that preceded the Roman garrison.

The River Derwent has always been vitally important to Malton as it provides an essential element for what was once a major industry in

---

469 THE NEW GLOBE INN

Malton

A friendly family-run pub serving real ales and freshly prepared pub food. Three rooms for B&B guests.

see page 674

470 THE HIDDEN MONKEY TEA ROOMS

Malton

The appetising smell of home cooking tempts customers inside to enjoy a fine range of home-cooked savoury and sweet goodies.

see page 675

349

471 THE CROSS KEYS

Thixendale, nr Malton

A delightful one-roomed pub in a quiet scenic location. Home cooking, real ales and three rooms for B&B guests.

 see page 675

472 THE SCHOOL HOUSE INN

Low Marishes, nr Malton

A hidden gem in a peaceful, picturesque setting, serving excellent home-cooked dishes in a very friendly ambience.

 see page 676

473 THE STAR COUNTRY INN

Weaverthorpe, nr Malton

A scenic country location for a pleasant village inn with an all-day bar, home cooking and 5 rooms for B&B guests.

 see page 677

Malton - brewing. In the 19th century there were nine breweries here, but now only the Malton Brewery Company survives.

Old Malton is located just to the north of the Roman Fort, an interesting and historic area on the edge of open countryside. To the north is **Eden Camp**, a themed museum dedicated to re-creating the dramatic experiences of ordinary people living through World War II, and next door is **Eden Farm Insight**, a working farm with a fascinating collection that includes old farm machinery and lots of animals.

To the southwest, lying in the folds of the Howardian Hills, stands one of the most glorious stately homes in Britain, **Castle Howard**. Well known to television viewers as the Brideshead of *Brideshead Revisited*, Castle Howard has impressed visitors ever since it was completed in the early 1700s.

SLEDMERE

22 miles NE of York on the B1253

The village is home to **Sledmere House**, a noble Georgian mansion built by the Sykes family in the 1750s. Inside, there is fine furniture by Chippendale and Sheraton; outside, gardens and parkland landscaped by Capability Brown.

Across the road from Sledmere House are two remarkable, elaborately detailed, monuments: an Eleanor Cross, modelled on those set up by Edward I in memory of his queen, and the **Waggoners Memorial**, which commemorates the 1,000-strong company of men the Sykes family raised from the Wolds during World War I.

BRIDLINGTON

38 miles NE of York on the A165

The old town lies a mile inland from the bustling seaside resort,

Castle Howard, nr Malton

Sewerby Hall and Gardens, nr Bridlington

474 THE WHITE HORSE INN

Bempton, nr Bridlington
Smiles, hospitality and a good choice of food and drink in a friendly pub in a coastal village.

see page 677

with its amusements and ten-mile stretch of sandy beach. Bridlington Priory was once one of the wealthiest in England but it was ruthlessly pillaged during the Reformation.

On the northern outskirts of Bridlington is **Sewerby Hall**, a monumental mansion built between 1714 and 1720. Set in 50 acres of garden and parkland, the house was first opened to the public in 1936 by Amy Johnson, the dashing, Yorkshire-born pilot who captured the public imagination with her daring solo flights to South Africa and Australia. The Museum here houses some fascinating memorabilia of Amy's pioneering feats. Close by is **Bondville Miniature Village**, one of the finest model villages in the country.

A few miles north of Bridlington is the picturesque and dramatic scenery of **Flamborough Head**. The Head's first, and England's oldest surviving Lighthouse, was built in 1674 and its original beacon was a basket of burning coal.

STAMFORD BRIDGE
6 miles E of York on the A166

Just a few days before the Battle of Hastings, King Harold II, the last Anglo-Saxon king of England, had clashed at **Stamford Bridge** with his half-brother Tostig and Hardrada, King of Norway, who between them had mustered some 60,000 men. Harold's troops were triumphant but immediately after this victory they marched hurriedly southwards to the south coast, where William the Conqueror had landed, and to defeat at the Battle of Hastings.

DRIFFIELD
26 miles E of York on the A166

Located on the edge of the Wolds, Driffield was once the capital of

475 THE NEW CROWN HOTEL

Bridlington
A handsome three-storey pub popular with locals and visitors to the town; tasty home cooking, well-priced B&B rooms.

see page 678

476 THE OLD STAR INN
& RESTAURANT

Kilham, nr Driffield

A 'Wold famous' pub
offering the very highest
standards of food, drink and
service.

 see page 679

477 THE TROUT INN

Wansford, nr Driffield

Keg beers and good
wholesome home cooking in
a comfortable, welcoming
village pub.

 see page 678

478 ARABIAN HORSE

Aberford, Leeds

Quality is the keynote at a
handsome village pub
serving excellent home
cooked snacks and meals.

 see page 680

352

the Saxon Kingdom of Dear, a vast
domain extending over the whole
of Northumbria and Yorkshire. It
was a king of Dear who divided the
southern part of his realm into
three parts, 'thriddings', a word
which gradually evolved into the
famous Ridings of Yorkshire.

To the northeast lies **Burton
Agnes Hall**, an outstanding
Elizabethan house with fabulous
gardens.

HORNSEA

37 miles E of York on the B1242

This small coastal town can boast
not only the most popular visitor
attraction in Humberside, **Hornsea
Pottery**, but also Yorkshire's
largest freshwater lake, **Hornsea
Mere**, a refuge for over 170 species
of birds. Also here, housed in a
converted 18th century farmhouse,
is the North Holderness **Museum
of Village Life**.

BEVERLEY

27 miles SE of York on the A1035

In medieval times, Beverley was
one of England's most prosperous
towns and it remains one of the
most gracious, with its great
Minster, built between 1220 and
1450, dominating the landscape. An
unusual feature of the **Guildhall** is
a figure of Justice with her scales
but without her blindfold. When an
18th century Town Clerk was asked
the reason for this, he replied, "In
Beverley, Justice is not blind."

Exhibits at Beverley's **Museum
of Army Transport** include a
wagon in which Lord Roberts
travelled during the Boer War and

the Rolls-Royce used by Field
Marshal Montgomery as a staff car
in France.

TADCASTER

9 miles SW of York off the A64

Situated on the River Wharfe, since
the 14th century Tadcaster's major
industry has been brewing and
three major breweries are still based
here: John Smiths, Samuel Smiths
and the Tower Brewery, owned by
Bass Charrington. The distinctive
brewery buildings dominate the
town's skyline and provide the basis
of its prosperity.

The oldest building in
Tadcaster is **The Ark**, dating back
to the 1490s. During its long
history, The Ark has served as
many things and it now houses the
Town Council offices.

WETHERBY

10 miles W of York on the A1

Situated on the Great North Road,
at a point midway between
Edinburgh and London, Wetherby
was renowned for its coaching inns,
of which the two most famous
were The Angel and The Swan &
Talbot. It is rumoured that serving
positions at these inns were
considered so lucrative that
employees had to pay for the
privilege of employment in them!

To the northeast, in 1644, one
of the most important encounters
of the Civil War took place on
Marston Moor. The forces of
Thomas Fairfax and Oliver
Cromwell inflicted a heavy defeat on
Prince Rupert's army. Wetherby has
a popular National Hunt racecourse.

BOROUGHBRIDGE

16 miles NW of York on the B6265

This attractive and historic town dates from the reign of William the Conqueror and the bridge over the River Ure, from which the village takes its name, was built in 1562, forming part of an important road link between Edinburgh and London. To the west are the great **Devil's Arrows**, three massive Bronze Age monoliths, which are the most famous ancient monument in Yorkshire. Further on is one of the area's finest stately homes, 18th century **Newby Hall**, standing in magnificent gardens.

To the east of Boroughbridge is **Aldborough Roman Museum** housing relics from this once thriving Roman city.

Aldborough Roman Museum, nr Boroughbridge

EASINGWOLD

12 miles NW of York off the A19

Easingwold's prosperity dates back to the 18th century when it flourished as a major stage coach post. Later, it enjoyed the distinction of having its own private railway.

A little to the southeast of Easingwold is **Sutton Park**, a noble early 18th century mansion that contains some fine examples of Sheraton and Chippendale furniture.

HULL

Extensively battered by the Luftwaffe during World War II, this ancient port has risen from those ashes to be once again one of the country's busiest ports. Its most famous son is William Wilberforce, born here in 1759. After becoming the town's Member of Parliament, Wilberforce began a campaign to outlaw the slave trade, which was successful after a 30-year struggle; the **Wilberforce House Museum** presents a history of the trade and Wilberforce's efforts to eradicate it forever. Many other museums and trails tell the story of Hull's connection with the sea and fishing.

The other great point of interest here is the **Humber Bridge**, one of the world's longest single-span bridges with an overall length of 2,428 yards that was opened in 1981.

PICKERING

The largest of the four market towns in Ryedale and possibly the oldest, claiming to date from 270

To the southeast of Hull is Spurn Point that leads to Spurn Head, the narrow hook of ever-shifting sands that curls around the mouth of the Humber estuary. This bleak but curiously invigorating part of Yorkshire is home to hundreds of species of rare and solitary wild fowl, playful seals, and also to the small contingent of lifeboatmen who operate the only permanently manned lifeboat station in Britain.

353

479 THE BLACK BULL INN

Pickering

Fine hospitality, a splendid variety of home-cooked dishes and practical chalet-style accommodation.

  see page 681

480 THE RIVIERA

Whitby

High standards of décor and comfort in a pleasant small hotel in the heart of historic Whitby.

 see page 680

481 THE STATION INN

Whitby

The **Station Inn** provides a wonderful place to enjoy cask ales, morning coffee, home-cooked lunches, afternoon tea and regular live entertainment.

 see page 682

BC, Pickering lies at the heart of the fertile Vale of Pickering. Housed in a gracious Regency mansion, the **Beck Isle Museum** has intriguing re-creations of typical Victorian domestic rooms, shops, workshops and even a pub. The town is the southern terminus of the **North York Moors Railway**, whose steam trains run to Grosmont.

To the south lies Flamingo Land, a zoo and fun park in the wooded parkland of Kirby Misperton Hall.

AROUND PICKERING

WHITBY

17½ miles NE of Pickering on the A171

Whitby was one of the earliest and most important centres of Christianity in England, and high on the cliff that towers above the old town stand the imposing and romantic ruins of **Whitby Abbey**. It was here in the 7th century the Synod of Whitby met and settled, once and for all, the precise date on which Easter should be celebrated. As an apprentice, James Cook, later the renowned Captain Cook, lived in Whitby, and the handsome house in Grape Lane where he lodged is now the **Captain Cook Memorial Museum**. According to Bram Stoker, Whitby was the place where Count Dracula, in the form of a wolf or large dog, came ashore from a crewless ship that had drifted into harbour.

A popular souvenir of Whitby is jet, a lustrous black stone that enjoyed enormous popularity in Victorian times when, after the death of Prince Albert, jewellery in jet was the only ornament the Queen would allow herself to wear.

The **Esk Valley Line** from Whitby to Middlesbrough runs across the North York Moors on a 90-minute journey that rivals the Settle-Carlisle line in scenic splendour.

Whitby Abbey

Newburgh Priory, nr Coxwold

482 THE CAPTAIN COOK INN

Staithes
A great place for a drink, a meal, an overnight stay or a longer break in a popular fishing village.

see page 683

483 ESTBEK HOUSE

Sandsend, nr Whitby
One of the county's very finest restaurants with rooms, in an outstanding location close to the sea and on the edge of the North York Moors National Park.

see page 684

To the south of the town lies **Robin Hood's Bay**, where once smuggling was as important as fishing.

SCARBOROUGH

15½ miles E of Pickering on the A170

With its two splendid bays and dramatic cliff-top castle, Scarborough was targeted by the early railway tycoons as the natural candidate for Yorkshire's first seaside resort. Even before the advent of the railway, Scarborough had been well-known to a select few who travelled to what was then a remote little town to sample the spring water.

Anne Brontë came to Scarborough in the hope that the spa town's invigorating air would improve her health, a hope that was not fulfilled. She died at the age of 29 and her grave lies in **St Mary's** churchyard at the foot of the castle.

Built between 1158 and 1168, **Scarborough Castle** occupies the site of a Roman fort and signal station and its gaunt remains stand high on Castle Rock Headland, dominating the resort's two sweeping bays.

Down the coast from Scarborough lies **Filey**, one of the first Yorkshire resorts to benefit from the early 19th century craze for sea bathing.

COXWOLD

16½ miles SW of Pickering off the A170

At the western end of the village stands the 500-year-old **Shandy Hall**, home of Laurence Sterne, vicar of Coxwold in the 1760s. Sterne was the author of *Tristram Shandy*, a wonderfully bizarre novel which opened a vein of English surreal comedy inherited by the likes of the Goons and Monty Python.

Just to the south of Coxwold is **Newburgh Priory**, founded in 1145 as an Augustinian monastery and now a mostly Georgian country house with fine interiors and a beautiful water garden.

Thirsk

The original and cosy home of James Herriot providing a fascinating insight into his life.

 see page 685

Bagby, nr Thirsk

A fine country inn with a talented team producing outstanding food to satisfy all tastes and appetites.

 *see page 686*

Carlton Miniott, nr Thirsk

A genuinely warm welcome, well-kept beer and hearty home-cooked food all contribute to the popularity of this convivial village inn.

 see page 687

To the north are the lovely, cream-coloured ruins of **Byland Abbey** that was built by the Cistercians in 1177.

HELMSLEY

11 miles W of Pickering on the A170

One of North Yorkshire's most popular and attractive towns, Helmsley lies on the banks of the River Rye at the edge of the North York Moors National Park. Founded in the early 1100s, **Helmsley Castle** was badly damaged during the Civil War and is today a romantic and picturesque ruin. Just to the west of Helmsley are the hauntingly beautiful remains of **Rievaulx Abbey**, standing among wooded hills beside the River Rye. Founded in 1131, this was the first Cistercian abbey in Yorkshire and, with some 700 people eventually living within its walls, became one of the largest.

To the southeast lies **Nunnington Hall**, a late 17th century manor house set beside the River Rye with a picturesque packhorse bridge within its grounds.

THIRSK

23 miles W of Pickering on the A61

Thirsk has become famous as the home of veterinary surgeon Alf Wight, better known as James Herriot, author of *All Creatures Great and Small*, who died in 1995. **The World of James Herriot** is housed in his original surgery in Kirkgate and offers visitors a trip back in time to the 1940s, exploring the life and times of the world's most famous country vet.

On the edge of town, the **Trees to Treske Visitor Centre** is an imaginative exhibition exploring how trees grow, the character of different woods and examples of the cabinetmaker's craft. Nearby is **Thirsk Racecourse**, known to devotees of the turf as the 'Country Racecourse'.

Nunnington Hall, nr Helmsley

Rydale Folk Museum, Hotton-le-Hole

To the northwest of Thirsk is **Sion Hill Hall**, one of the last great country houses. Completed in 1913, the rooms have not altered since they were built and they are home to one of the best collections of Georgian, Victorian and Edwardian artefacts in the north of England.

HUTTON-LE-HOLE
6½ miles NW of Pickering off the A170

Long regarded as one of

Yorkshire's prettiest villages, Hutton-le-Hole has a character all its own. Facing the green is the **Ryedale Folk Museum**, an imaginative celebration of 4,000 years of life in North Yorkshire; among the historic buildings is a complete Elizabethan Manor House rescued from nearby Harome.

NORTHALLERTON
27½ miles NW of Pickering on the A168

The county town of North Yorkshire, and once an important stop on the coaching route from Newcastle to London.

To the northeast is **Mount Grace Priory**, a 14th century building where a well-appointed two-storey monks' cell has been restored to give a vivid impression of what life was like in

Mount Grace Priory, Northallerton

487 CARPENTERS ARMS

Felixkirk, nr Thirsk

A scenic setting, the friendliest of hosts and outstanding cooking on bistro and restaurant menus.

see page 688

488 WOODY'S AT THE BLACK SWAN

Thornton-le-Moor

A popular public house incorporating a superb destination restaurant and four superb guest bedrooms.

see page 689

489 THE WHEATSHEAF INN

Borrowby, nr Thirsk

An impressive village pub with well-kept ales and superb food that combines skill with imagination at a high level.

see page 690

490 THE OLD ROYAL GEORGE

Morton-upon-Swale

Five miles from the A1 (M), an ideal refreshment stop for motorists and tourists.

see page 690

357

491 LASTINGHAM GRANGE COUNTRY HOUSE HOTEL

Lastingham, nr York

A fine country hotel that's an ideal base for a walking, touring holiday – or for simply relaxing in the picturesque surroundings.

 see page 691

492 THE BLACKSMITHS ARMS

Lastingham

A neat stone inn offering high standards of hospitality, food, drink and accommodation.

 see page 691

493 THE COACH HOUSE INN

Rosedale Abbey, nr Pickering

A warm and sociable inn with home cooking, real ales and well-chosen wines.

see page 692

what was clearly one of the more comfortable 14th century monastic houses.

GREAT AYTON

22 miles NW of Pickering on the A173

This appealing village set around the River Leven is an essential stopping point for anyone following the **Captain Cook Country Tour**, a 70-mile circular trip taking in all the major locations associated with the great sailor. Cook's family moved to Great Ayton when he was 8 years old and he attended the little school that is now the **Captain Cook Schoolroom Museum**.

GOATHLAND

11 miles N of Pickering off the A169

A major attraction in this pleasant moorland village is **Mallyan Spout**, a 70 feet waterfall locked into a crescent of rocks and trees. Just to the north is Beck Hole, a little village that plays host to the World Quoits Championship. The game, which appears to have originated in Eskdale, involves throwing a small iron hoop over an iron pin set about 25 feet away.

Rosedale Abbey Cross

PATELEY BRIDGE

Considered to be one of the prettiest towns in the Dales, Pateley Bridge is perfectly situated as a base from which to explore Upper Nidderdale. Much of the town seen today was built in the prosperous years when it was a flourishing textile town with a local mining industry.

The **Nidderdale Museum** is housed in one of the town's original Victorian workhouses and presents a fascinating record of local folk history. To the east are

Brimham Rocks, an extraordinary natural sculpture park where the millstone grit boulders have been formed into fantastic shapes by years of erosion.

AROUND PATELEY BRIDGE

LEYBURN

16 miles N of Pateley Bridge on the A684

The main market town and trading centre of mid Wensleydale, Leyburn is an attractive town with a broad market place lined by handsome late Georgian and Victorian stone buildings.

To the east, and surrounded by walled and wooded parkland, is **Constable Burton Hall**, famous for its gardens. To the south, on the banks of the River Ure, is **Jervaulx Abbey**, one of the great Cistercian sister houses to Fountains Abbey, set in beautiful gardens.

RICHMOND

22 miles N of Pateley Bridge on the A6108

Alan Rufus, 1st Earl of Richmond, built the original **Richmond Castle** in 1071 and the site, 100 feet up on a rocky promontory overlooking the River Swale, is both imposing and well chosen. The first completely Norman stone castle in the country, it is now a ruin, though much of the original stonework remains intact. One of the grandest buildings in the town is the **Culloden Tower**, which was erected in 1747 by the Yorke family, one of whose members had fought at the Battle of Culloden the

previous year. Richmond is also home to England's oldest theatre, the Georgian **Theatre Royal**, which opened in the 1780s and originally formed part of a circuit that included Northallerton, Ripon, and Harrogate. The **Georgian Theatre Royal Museum** contains a unique collection of original playbills as well as the oldest and largest complete set of painted scenery in Britain.

Just outside the town lies **Easby Abbey**, founded in 1155 and now a delightful monastic ruin which looks down to the River Swale.

MASHAM

10½ miles NE of Pateley Bridge on the A6108

Set beside the River Ure, picturesque Masham is best known for its beer. **Theakston's Brewery** was founded in 1827 by two brothers, Thomas and Robert Theakston, and its modern visitor centre illustrates the process of brewing and the art of cooperage. The **Black Sheep Brewery** is also well worth a visit. It too offers a guided tour and visitors get the chance to sample the traditionally made ale.

RIPON

10 miles NE of Pateley Bridge on the A61

This attractive city, on the banks of the Rivers Ure, Skell, and Laver, dates from the 7th century, when Alfrich, King of Northumbria, granted an area of land to the church. Later that century, St Wilfrid built a church on the high

•

South of Leyburn lies Middleham, an enchanting little town with strong racing connections. Among the illustrious trainers based here were Sam Hall, a master trainer on the Flat, and Neville Crump, who trained the winner of the Grand National on three occasions. Rising high above the town are the magnificent ruins of Middleham Castle, a once-mighty fortress whose finest days were in the 15th century, when most of northern England was ruled from here by the Neville family.

•

494 THE GREYHOUND INN

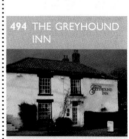

Hackforth, nr Bedale

A friendly refreshment stop for motorists (the A1 is nearby), with home cooking, Yorkshire ales and 3 rooms for B&B guests.

🍴 🛏 see page 692

359

495 THE LAMB INN

Rainton, nr Thirsk

A village pub full of charm and character and a popular choice for a meal.

❚❚ see page 693

496 DALEGARTH AND
THE GHYLL
HOLIDAY
COTTAGES

Buckden, nr Skipton

Luxuriously appointed cottages provide an ideal base for a self-catering holiday in the most serene and picturesque Dales setting.

⬌ see page 694

ground between the three rivers but the crypt is all that remains of his church; the magnificent 12th century **Cathedral of St Peter and St Wilfrid** now stands on the site.

The **Spa Baths**, opened in 1905 by the Princess of Battenberg, are a reminder of Ripon's attempt to become a fashionable spa resort. Not far from the Cathedral is the 17th century House of Correction, which now houses the **Ripon Prison and Police Museum**.

To the southwest of the city are the magnificent **Studley Royal Gardens**, created in the early 18th century. Adjoining the gardens is the glorious **Fountains Abbey**, the pride of all the ecclesiastical ruins in Yorkshire and a World Heritage Site. The abbey, which was founded in 1132, was one of the wealthiest of the Cistercian houses and its remains are the most complete of any Cistercian abbey in Britain.

A few miles east of Ripon, by the River Swale, is the village of

Cundall, one of the few villages in the country named **Thankful Village** by Arthur Mee. The term refers to villages whose serving soldiers all came home safely from the Great War.

RIPLEY

7½ miles SE of Pateley Bridge off the A61

Ripley Castle has been home to the Ingilby family for over 600 years, granted to them when Thomas Ingilby killed a wild boar that was charging at King Edward III. The castle stands in an outstanding Capability Brown landscape, and the walled garden contains the National Hyacinth Collection.

HARROGATE

12 miles SE of Pateley Bridge on the A61

One of England's most attractive towns, Harrogate retains many of its original spa buildings including the **Royal Pump Room** and the **Royal Baths Assembly Rooms**, which in their heyday were full of rich visitors sampling the waters.

To the east lies the town of **Knaresborough** and **Mother Shipton's Cave**, the home of a Petrifying Well where the lime-rich water has seemingly turned to stone an array of objects from old boots to bunches of grapes.

SKIPTON

14 miles SW of Pateley Bridge on the A59

Skipton's origins can be traced to the 7th century, when the farmers christened it Sheeptown. The Normans decided to build a castle to guard the entrance to Airedale

Royal Pump Room Museum, Harrogate

and Skipton became a garrison town. **Skipton Castle**, home of the Cliffords, is one of the most complete and well-preserved medieval castles in England, and its most striking feature is the impressive 14th century gateway.

For many years Skipton remained just a market town, until, with the development of the factory system in the 19th century, textile mills were built and cottages and terraced houses constructed for the influx of mill workers. The **Leeds and Liverpool Canal**, which flows through the town, provided a cheap form of transport as well as linking Skipton with the major industrial centres of Yorkshire and Lancashire.

To the east, in a village that is part of the Duke of Devonshire's estate, are the substantial ruins of **Bolton Priory**, an Augustinian house that was founded in 1155 by monks. Upstream from the ruins is one of the most visited natural features in Wharfedale, a point where the wide river suddenly narrows into a confined channel of black rock through which the water thunders. This spectacular gorge is known as **The Strid** because, over the centuries, many heroic (or foolhardy) types have attempted to leap across it as a test of bravery.

GRASSINGTON
11 miles W of Pateley Bridge on the B6265

One of the best loved villages within the Yorkshire Dales National Park, Grassington in many ways typifies the Dales' settlement with its characteristic market square.

Skipton Castle

Known as the capital of Upper Wharfedale, the historically important valley roads meet here and the ancient monastic route from Malham to Fountains Abbey passes through the village. The **Upper Wharfedale Folk Museum** is housed in two converted 18th century lead-miners' cottages.

To the east is the wonderful 500,000-year-old-cave at **Stump Cross Caverns**, a large show cave with a fantastic array of stalactites and stalagmites.

MALHAM
17 miles W of Pateley Bridge off the A65

Malham village was originally two settlements, Malham East and Malham West, which came under the influence of a different religious house: Bolton Priory and Fountains Abbey respectively.

To the north is **Malham Cove**, a limestone amphitheatre that is the most spectacular section of the

A walk around Skipton town reveals many interesting buildings, including the Town Hall, now also the home of the Craven Museum. It seems appropriate that a town that was so dedicated to trade and commerce should be the birthplace, in 1851, of Thomas Spencer, co-founder of Marks and Spencer.

To the west of Settle, near Giggleswick, is the famous Ebbing and Flowing Well, one of many in the area that owe their unusual names to the porous limestone that causes water to be sometimes there and sometimes not.

A bleak and exposed site, the Ribblehead Viaduct is often battered by strong winds that can, on occasion, stop a train literally in its tracks. The regular service is worked by two-car diesel Sprinters, but there are also special excursions and charter trains.

mid-Craven fault; as recently as the 1700s, a massive waterfall that was higher than Niagara Falls cascaded over its edge! These days the water disappears through potholes at the top, called water-sinks, and re-appears through the cavern mouth at **Aire Head** near the village. Not far away is the equally inspiring **Gordale Scar**, a huge gorge carved by glacial melt water with an impressive waterfall leaping, in two stages, from a fissure in its face. Further north of the scar is **Malham Tarn**, a glacial lake that, by way of an underground stream, is the source of the River Aire.

SETTLE
22½ miles W of Pateley Bridge on the B6480

This small market town is best known today as the home of the scenically unrivalled **Settle-Carlisle Railway**, a proudly preserved memento of the glorious age of steam. The line took six years to build, being completed in 1876, and incorporated 21 major viaducts and 14 tunnels. The workmen on the

line endured the harshest of conditions, and many lost their lives; over 100 lie buried in the graveyard at Chapel-le-Dale. Settle is dominated by one of the huge viaducts and by the towering limestone cliffs of Castleberg Crag.

INGLETON
30 miles W of Pateley Bridge off the A65

Ingleton Waterfalls have been delighting visitors since 1885, and along the four miles of scenic walks, the stretch of waterfalls includes interesting names such as Pecca Twin Falls, Holly Bush Spout, Thornton Force, and Baxengill Gorge. The second principal network of caves in the area is **White Scar Caves**. Discovered in 1923, this network has been under exploration ever since. At Ingleborough, the peak has been used as a beacon and a fortress for 2,000 years.

RIBBLEHEAD
28½ miles NW of Pateley Bridge on the B6255

Lying close to the source of the River Ribble is an impressive structure, the 24-arched **Ribblehead Viaduct**, which was built to carry the Settle-Carlisle Railway. It took five years to build (the work was completed in 1876) and claimed the lives of more than 200 workers.

HAWES
25½ miles NW of Pateley Bridge on the A684

One of the local industries was rope-making and at the **Hawes Ropeworkers**, next to the **Dales Countryside Museum**, visitors

Dales Countryside Museum, Hawes

can see experienced ropers twisting cotton and man-made fibres to make halters, hawsers, picture cords, dog leads and clothes lines. Wensleydale's most famous product (after its sheep) is its soft, mild cheese, and at the **Wensleydale Cheese Experience** its history is told through a series of interesting displays.

Just to the north and located in a natural amphitheatre of limestone crags, is **Hardraw Force**, the highest unbroken waterfall in England above ground. Because of an undercut in the cliff, walkers can view the water from behind, just as Turner and Wordsworth famously did.

Swaledale Folk Museum, Reeth

AYSGARTH

18 miles NW of Pateley Bridge on the A684

The village is famous for the spectacular **Aysgarth Falls** where the River Ure thunders through a rocky gorge and drops some 200 feet over three huge slabs of limestone which divide this wonderful natural feature into the Upper, Middle and Lower Falls. The **Dales National Park** has a Visitor Information Centre here and, just a short walk away, is the **Yorkshire Museum of Horse-Drawn Carriages**, where a collection of nearly 60 Victorian coaches is housed in a 200-year-old mill overlooking the Falls.

To the northwest lies the once important market town of **Askrigg**, which became **Darrowby** in the popular television series *All Creatures Great and Small*. The village has been popular with tourists since the days of Turner and Wordsworth, many of them coming to see the impressive waterfalls at **Whitfield Fill Force** and **Mill Gill Force**.

REETH

23 miles NW of Pateley Bridge on the B6270

At the junction of the River Swale and its main tributary Arkle Beck, Reeth is home to the **Swaledale Folk Museum**, housed in what was once the old Methodist Sunday School. The Museum tells how local mining, farming and craft industries have shaped the lives of those living in this beautiful dale. Other aspects of Swaledale life, including the impact of Wesleyan Methodism are also revealed.

To the northeast of Aysgarth is Bolton Castle, which has dominated mid Wensleydale for more than 600 years ever since the lord of the manor, Richard le Scrope, was granted permission to fortify his manor house in 1379. Today, this luxurious fortified manor house is still occupied by a direct descendant of the 1st Lord Scrope and it remains an impressive sight with its four square towers acting as a local landmark.

Accommodation, Food &Drink and Places to Visit

The establishments featured in this section includes hotels, inns, guest houses, bed & breakfasts, restaurants, cafés, tea and coffee shops, tourist attractions and places to visit. Each establishment has an entry number which can be used to identify its location at the beginning of the relevant county chapter. This section is ordered by county and the page number in the column to the right indicates the first establishment in each county.

In addition full details of all these establishments and many others can be found on the Travel Publishing website - www.travelpublishing.co.uk. This website has a comprehensive database ocovering the whole of Britain and Ireland.

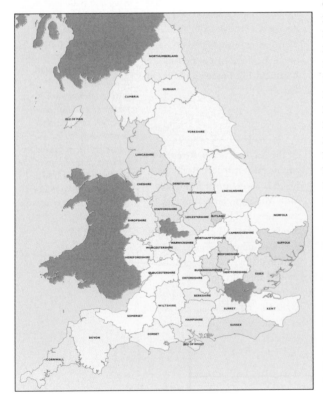

THE SUN INN

Grange Road, Felmersham,
Bedfordshire MK43 7EU
☎ 01234 781355

Felmersham is an attractive village lying off the A6 between Bedford and Rushden, signposted and easily reached from Milton Ernest. One of the best-known landmarks in the village is the **Sun Inn**, built of local stone in the 18th century and once known as the Felmersham Arms. It's very much the stuff of picture postcards and chocolate boxes, with a thatched roof, white-painted window surrounds and red-tiled eaves over the ground-floor windows. Colourful flower displays add to the lovely scene in the spring and summer, and inside is equally delightful at any time of the year, with exposed stone, low beams and an open fire to keep the winter chill at bay.

The whole place is looking immaculate after a major refurbishment programme carried out by the new hosts, Susan and Bill, who took over the Sun in the spring of 2008. Bill is an engineer by trade and Susan ran a successful wine bar in London, and this is their first venture into the licensed business. The bar is open all day, seven days a week, for serving drinks, which usually include Eagle IPA and another Charles Wells brew. The refurbishment was just the first of many plans that Bill and Susan are putting into effect. In their first few months the food side of the enterprise was limited to bar snacks and a hot dish of the day, but by the end of 2008 they hope to have created a brand new 40-cover restaurant with its own lounge bar. The professional chef will make use of fresh local ingredients to create a wide choice of dishes both traditional and more contemporary.

A popular local meeting place for many generations, the Sun is certain to appeal to an even wider catchment area with the new developments. The proximity of the A6 makes it a pleasant and convenient spot to take a break on a journey, and it will enhance its popularity as a popular place to escape from the bustle of Bedford and enjoy the fresh air, the excellent hospitality and the new amenities of this grand pub. The River Great Ouse runs nearby, so the Sun also attracts walkers, cyclists and fishermen. Other local attractions include the Harrold-Odell Country Park and the Santa Pod Raceway.

20 High Street, Blunham,
Bedfordshire MK44 3NL
☎ 01767 640620
e-mail: salutation110@btconnect.com

The **Salutation** is a handsome brown and white building, with records dating back to 1649, located in the village of Blunham, east of Bedford, north of Sandy and easily reached off the A1, the A421 or the A603. The quiet rural village of Blunham was the home of poet John Doone while he was the rector here from 1622 until his death in 1632. It was here that he wrote Devotions, which contains the well known lines "No man is an island, entire of itself" and "Never send to know for whom the bell tolls; it tolls for thee".

The bell might well have been tolling for the Salutation until Victoria and Michael came here at the end of March 2008. They immediately set about giving the place the care and attention it needed. They have lost no time in putting the inn back on the map, and the locals are impressed at the transformation they have made in this, their first venture in running their own business. They are also beginning to attract visitors from a wider catchment area as the news of the inn's revival spreads. The old- world bar, with open fires, period pictures of old Blunham, and assorted bygones is open lunchtime and evening throughout the week and all day Friday, Saturday and Sunday for drinks, which include at least four real ales, usually Greene King IPA, Moorlands Bitter, Greene King XX (Mild) and a guest ale. In the bar, the 30 cover restaurant or out in the garden a good variety of familiar dishes are served 7 days a week from midday to 2pm and from 6.30pm to 9pm. All food is prepared using locally sourced produce. Thursday night is steak night and Sundays sees traditional roasts.

Barbeques are popular occasions in the summer in the garden and the inn hosts regular charity events and beer festivals. The Salutation also fields two skittles teams in the local league, a petanque team, pool team and darts team. There are plenty of opportunities to work up a thirst and appetite in the vicinity of the Salutation.

The River Ivel flows nearby and numerous walks and cycle ways include the Kingfisher Way, which follows the course of the Ivel from its source in Baldock to its confluence with the River Ouse at Roxton Lock. It's a great place not just for walkers and ramblers but also for nature lovers, the wildlife around the banks include kingfishers and terns, water voles, water shrews and otters.

3 THE ROSE & CROWN

89 High Street, Ridgmont,
Bedfordshire MK43 0TY
☎ 01525 280245

The Rose & Crown is a charming 300 year old inn on the main street of Ridgmont, just 2 miles from junction 13 of the M1 [take the A421 to Bedford then immediate right signposted Ridgmont {A507} and only 5 minutes from Woburn Safari Park.

Once the property of the Duke of Bedford, it's a real stunner inside and out, with a low ceilinged public bar, a comfortable lounge and lots of interesting bric a brac. Outside is a secure, tree sheltered garden with a children's play area. Hosts Peggy and Dave have it back on the map as a place to seek out for top-notch hospitality, well-kept beer and a fine choice of home cooking. The locals love it, and visitors are coming from further afield as its reputation spreads.

Pub classics span door step sandwiches, jacket potatoes, basket meals, beer battered fish and chips, burgers, meatballs, home-made pies and some more 'restauranty' dishes like chicken in orange and tarragon sauce and a choice of rump or sirloin steaks with all the trimmings.

The bar is open lunchtime and evenings Monday to Friday and all day Saturday and Sunday and food is served every session with the exception of Sunday evening. The pub's annexe is a popular venue for functions and private parties and the pub benefits from the added amenity of a camping site for caravans and tents open all year and equipped with electric hook ups. Other facilities include outside toilet and washbasin and recently added showers.

4 THE CARPENTERS ARMS & SUNFLOWER RESTAURANT

93 High Street, Cranfield,
Bedfordshire MK42 0DP
☎ 01234 750232
e-mail: Karen@thecarps.org.uk

Easy on the eye both inside and out, the redbrick **Carpenters Arms & Sunflower Restaurant** stands on the main street of Cranfield, reached off the A421 or A509 and not far from the M1 (J13 or 14). Dennis Pole and his daughter Karen greet their

customers with smiles and a fine choice of food and drink. In the bar, the 28-cover restaurant or out in the lovely garden, classic pub fare, from sandwiches to pizza, honey-roast ham, burgers, steaks and beer-battered haddock can be enjoyed lunchtime Tuesday to Saturday and from 12 to 4 on Sunday. The inn is closed Mondays except on Bank Holidays.

HIDDEN PLACES GUIDES

Explore Britain and Ireland with *Hidden Places* guides - a fascinating series of national and local travel guides.

Packed with easy to read information on hundreds of places of interest as well as places to stay, eat and drink.

Available from both high street and internet booksellers

For more information on the full range of *Hidden Places* guides and other titles published by Travel Publishing visit our website on

www.travelpublishing.co.uk
or ask for our leaflet by phoning
01752 276660 or emailing
info@travelpublishing.co.uk

5 THE WINTERBOURNE ARMS

Winterbourne, nr Newbury,
Berkshire RG20 8BB
☎ 01635 248200
e-mail: winterbournearms@tiscali.co.uk
⊕ www.winterbournearms.tablesir.com

Overlooking the green in the village from which it takes its name, the **Winterbourne Arms** has a reputation for friendly hospitality that brings patrons from many miles around. The premises date back some 300 years and part was once a bakery – the old ovens can still

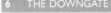

be seen in the pub's restaurant.
The intimate restaurant and bar extends into fine gardens for summer dining, and in winter the roaring log fire and candlelight create a warm atmosphere. The food is big and gutsy traditional British and European fare with an occasional oriental twist using the best local produce. The friendly staff here know their stuff and add humour to their daily work, and all this just 5 minutes from Junction 13 on the M4.

6 THE DOWNGATE

New Park Street, Hungerford,
Berkshire RG17 0ED
☎ 01488 682708
e-mail: davidyates@tiscali.co.uk
⊕ www.the-downgate.co.uk

David and Janet Yates are pleased to welcome visitors to their classic country pub, which enjoys a delightful setting on the edge of the ancient Hungerford Common, overlooking open fields and the Kennet valley. **The Downgate** is a splendid place for a drink, a lunchtime snack or a leisurely meal, and great company is guaranteed throughout the long opening hours. Arkell's real ales are always on tap (CAMRA recommended) and excellent home-cooked food is served every lunchtime and evening. Tried and tested pub classics include home-made faggots, macaroni cheese, steaks and steak & ale or steak & kidney pie, with apple pie and custard to round things

off in style. Children can choose from their own menu, and all the old favourites are on the over-60s menu served Monday to Thursday lunchtimes. Our special offers include Fish and Chips on Tuesday evening for £5.50 and 8oz Sirloin Steak and chips on Wednesday evening for £6.95. On the social side, league darts are played on Thursday, with an open darts challenge at 8 o'clock on Sunday evening.

7 THE PHEASANT INN

Ermin Street, Shefford Woodlands,
nr Hungerford, Berkshire RG17 7AA
☎ 01488 648284 Fax: 01488 648971
⊕ www.thepheasant-inn.co.uk

Behind the white clapboard frontage **The Pheasant** is an inn of great charm and character and a popular spot to meet for a drink and a chat or a meal. It's also an ideal place to spend a night or two in one of the eleven new contemporary hotel rooms when exploring the surrounding countryside or enjoying the top-class racing at nearby Newbury. The interior is very traditional, with beams, flagstone floors and country furniture – some tables for four are separated booth-style by wooden partitions. This is horse-racing territory, and much of the décor (as well as the conversation) has a racing theme, with photos, cartoons and sketches of jockeys, trainers and owners, including the exploits of Charlie Brooks, jockey, trainer and onetime part owner of the pub. Much of the pub's success is due to the energy and personality of Johnny Ferrand, who also owns a fish company in Cornwall. In the bar, which is open from 11am to midnight (Sunday 12 to 10.30), an excellent selection of drinks includes cask ales from local breweries such as Butts, an extensive wine list with six house wines, spirits, liqueurs and non-alcoholic choices. A very talented team in the kitchen is kept busy preparing traditional British dishes, many with a modern twist. Perennial favourites such as steaks, burgers and fish & chips are joined by restaurant classics like Dover sole, interesting ways with local ingredients (pheasant, duck and wild boar terrine) and

exotic options such as coconut-spiced tempura of red mullet fillets. Lunchtime brings bar snacks, baguettes and light meals from the main evening menu. For guests staying awhile the Pheasant has 11 top-of-the-range bedrooms in a modern extension. With Newbury racecourse and the training centre of Lambourn nearby, the pub is naturally the first choice for many racing folk, but it also offers a convenient refreshment stop for motorists on the busy M4 – leave at J14, take the A338 Wantage road and immediately turn left on to the B4000 Lambourn road.

8 THE CASTLE INN

Cold Ash Hill, Cold Ash, nr Thatcham,
Berkshire RG18 9PS
☎ 01635 863232

Nick and Maggie Hex have held the lease at the **Castle Inn** since 1994, and they continue to win new friends at their delightful mid-Victorian

hostelry. The West Berkshire Brewery's Mr Chubb's Lunchtime Bitter is one of four real ales always on tap, and the pub has been Cask Marque accredited for many years. An open fire banishes winter chills in the bar, and in summer the sunny south-facing terrace is a popular spot, enhanced by colourful window boxes and hanging baskets. Maggie's cooking ensures that everyone who eats here leaves well filled and happy. Her home-made pies, curries and Sunday roasts are great favourites, but everything is good and fresh, and there's plenty of choice on the printed menus and blackboard specials. Booking is recommended at the weekend. Food is served every session except Monday night, when players stay mean and hungry for the fortnightly quiz.

9 THE POT KILN

Frilsham, nr Yattendon, Berkshire RG18 0XX
☎ 01635 201366
e-mail: info@potkiln.org
⊕ www.potkiln.org

Dating back some 400 years and named after the kilns that once stood at the back, the **Pot Kiln** enjoys an idyllic rural setting with views over fields and woodland. Owner Mike Robinson, a well-known TV chef and presenter, heads a busy team

of chefs preparing a superb, daily changing choice of dishes of British and European inspiration with a strong emphasis on seasonal game. Mike himself shoots nearly all the venison on the menu, and all other game and meat is sourced locally. Most of the vegetables and salads come from their own kitchen garden and bread is baked daily in the wood-fired oven. Signature dishes on an always interesting menu include warm salad of pigeon, bacon and black pudding and pave of venison, alongside delights such as terrine of pork & venison, slow-cooked wild rabbit with white wine & rosemary, and

braised shin of beef with Madeira and wild mushrooms. Mike has made the Pot Kiln one of the most popular dining pubs in the whole county, and booking is strongly recommended, particularly at the weekend. Real ales include Brick Kiln brewed specially for the pub, Mr Chubb's and Magg's Mild. The pub, which stands a mile south of Yattendon, is open lunchtime and evening and all day Saturday and Sunday.

10 THE SIX BELLS

The Green, Beenham, nr Reading,
Berkshire RG7 5NX
☎ 0118 971 3368
e-mail: info@thesixbells.net
🌐 www.thesixbells.net

Walkers, cyclists and tourists from near and far join a loyal band of regulars at the **Six Bells**, which enjoys a picturesque village setting surrounded by fields and woodland. Some parts of the redbrick pub date back 200 years, and in the public areas African and Oriental art and carvings combine with more traditional décor, comfortable leather

sofas and real fires to create a homely, welcoming atmosphere. Proprietors Chris Harman from New Zealand and Glynis Snow, who was born in Beenham, run the pub in a friendly, relaxed style, and Chris, a talented chef, prepares an excellent choice of dishes from bar and restaurant menus. Anything from a lunchtime light bite to a full meal can be enjoyed in the bar or in the bright conservatory, and booking is recommended at peak times, particularly for Sunday's roast lunch. The pub is a popular venue for functions and parties, and for guests touring the area it offers Bed & Breakfast accommodation in four en suite rooms. The Six Bells is open lunchtime Wednesday to Sunday and evenings seven days a week.

11 FROGMORE HOUSE

Home Park, Windsor Castle, Windsor,
Berkshire SL4 1NJ
☎ 020 7766 7305
e-mail: information@royalcollection.org.uk
🌐 www.royalcollection.org.uk

Frogmore House has been a royal retreat since the 18th century and is today used by the Royal Family for private entertaining. It is especially linked with Queen Charlotte, the wife of George III, and her daughters, whose love of botany and art is reflected throughout the house. Many works

by other royal artists are on display at Frogmore. Queen Victoria loved Frogmore so much that she broke with royal tradition and chose to build a mausoleum for herself and Prince Albert there.

12 THE GEORGE & DRAGON

74 High Street, Princes Risborough,
Buckinghamshire HP27 0AX
☎ 01844 343087 Fax: 01844 347339
e-mail:
Christopher@georgeanddragonrisborough.co.uk
🌐 www.georgeanddragonrisborough.co.uk

The **George & Dragon** has long been a popular place to meet for a drink or a meal. It's on top form under tenants Margaret and Frenchman Christophe Rondelot, who have enhanced its role as one of the social hubs of the town. Christophe, a chef with 25 years' experience, prepares a selection of popular English and Continental dishes. The two-course lunch served Monday to Saturday is particularly popular. The bar is open all day, every day, and food is served lunchtime and evening Tuesday to Saturday and Sunday lunchtime.

14 THE PLOUGH INN

**The Common, Hyde Heath, nr Amersham,
Buckinghamshire HP6 5RN
☎ 01494 783163 Fax: 01494 774408
e-mail: ploughin@gobadsl.co.uk
🌐 www.hydeheath.com/plough**

A newly-opened 40-cover restaurant is testimony to the popularity of the **Plough Inn**, which has been run by Chris Herring and his family since 2004.

Chris, a chef with more than 30 years' experience, has made his 19th century free house overlooking the village green a great favourite not just with the good folk of Hyde Heath but with lovers of good food and good company from way beyond the locality, as well as a favourite venue for parties and wedding celebrations. The pub is open lunchtime and evening and all day at the weekend for drinks, which include Fullers London Pride and two guest real ales.

Chris seeks out the very best local produce for his international menus, which can be enjoyed every day from 12 to 3 and 6.30 to 9.30. Typical dishes on his always tempting menu include tempura king prawns,

chicken liver, orange & cranberry pâté, Dover sole, halibut, spiced lamb with spinach & garlic, and beef medallions with a peppered stilton sauce. The themed food evening on the last Wednesday of the month is a popular event for which booking is necessary. Hyde Heath lies between the A143 west of Amersham and the B485 west of Chesham.

14 THE BELL

**Chartridge Lane, Chartridge, nr Chesham,
Buckinghamshire HP5 2TF
☎ 01494 782878**

A quiet country road leads northwest from Chesham to the tiny village of Chartridge, where **The Bell** lies at the very heart of the community. It's the domain of Philip and Elvire Bailey, who have rung all the right bells with the locals ever since they came here in 2003.

Their warm, genuine hospitality and Philip's fine cooking have magnets not just for the good folk of Chartridge but for visitors from well outside the area. Philip's

printed menu and specials board offer a tempting choice of cooked-to-order dishes both familiar and less usual, from whitebait, scampi, fish & chips, liver & bacon and steaks to prawn and avocado salad, pasta with bacon & chorizo, beef bourguignon and gilthead bream with a tomato and basil sauce. Sunday brings traditional roasts, and delicious homemade sweets add the finishing touch to a very fine meal. Drinks include selected wines and three rotating real ales. Food is served from 12 to 2 Tuesday to Sunday and from 7 to 9 Tuesday to Saturday. It's best to book at the weekend.

15 THE KINGS ARMS 🍴

King Street, Old Town, Chesham,
Buckinghamshire HP5 1LZ
☎ 01494 774466
🌐 www.kingsarmschesham.co.uk

Ronan, Samantha and their staff have the warmest of welcomes for visitors to the **Kings Arms**, which enjoys a pleasant villagey setting close to the centre of Chesham. It was first licensed as a public house in the early 19th century, having been an ale house before that, and it retains a good deal of old-world charm while adding up-to-date comfort and amenities. Ronan has been in the catering and licensed trade for more than 30 years, and he has made the Kings Arms a popular destination restaurant.

The bar menu, served from 12 to 2 Monday to Saturday, offers a selection of classic pub snacks and meals, and a well-priced 2- or 3-course Over-60s Lunch is available from Tuesday to Saturday. Sunday lunch (12-4; must book) brings a good choice of roasts with fish, vegetarian and other meaty options. The evening restaurant menu showcases the chef's talents with such dishes as oyster mushroom & champagne risotto, king prawn fricassee and a nut roast with roasted vegetables, cranberries and goat's cheese. There's also an excellent children's menu. A short, well-chosen wine list accompanies the food, and the bar stocks three real ales and a selection of Continental lagers.

The pub is closed Monday except Bank Holidays, otherwise open lunchtime and evening and from 12 to 6 on Sunday. The bijou sun-trap patio is a pleasant place for summer sipping.

16 THE BOOT & SLIPPER 🍴

2 Rickmansworth Road, Amersham,
Buckinghamshire HP6 5JN
☎ 01494 727082 Fax: 01494 433184

The **Boot & Slipper** is a large, imposing property with a traditional look and a very roomy, comfortable drinking and eating area. It stands on the A404 Rickmansworth Road near the junction with the A416 and a short drive from Junction 18 of the M25. Landlord Adam Szczypior and his staff use the best seasonal produce for the menu, which includes top-notch British meat dishes, fish & chips, salmon, sea bass and vegetarian options. The main menu is served all day from noon, and a lighter menu is available until 6. Drinks include up to six cask ales and an extensive choice of wines, with most available by glass and bottle.

97 High Street, Old Amersham,
Buckinghamshire HP7 0DT
☎ 01494 726410
e-mail:
theelephantamersham@hotmail.co.uk

The Romans were farming around Amersham
in the 3rd and 4th centuries, so it has plenty
of history – much of it told in the town's
museum. It became an important stopping
point in coaching days, and it was in the early
part of the 16th century that the **Elephant
& Castle** first saw the light of day. It was a
well-known stop on the London to Stratford-
upon-Avon run, with stables for a change of
horses and its own smithy and saddle and harness maker. That's
all long gone, but what remains is the ambience, the character,
the hospitality and a new emphasis on the food side of the
business.

Michelle was the manager here before taking over the lease
with her partner Nick towards the end of 2006. Under this
hardworking pair the place is really thriving, with a following
that grows day by day. Michelle is a popular presence front of
house, and Nick's background as a builder assists greatly in
ensuring that everything is kept in excellent working order. The
bar is open all day, every day of the week, for drinks, and
Fullers London Pride and Spitfire are among the favourite real
ales. These are backed up by a full range of other draught and
bottled beers, lagers, cider, wines, spirits, liqueurs and non-
alcoholic drinks.

Until recently the food side was franchised to a family and
the menu offered both Thai and English dishes but Michelle and
Nick have taken back the catering, seeking out the best local produce for a range of traditional
English dishes, from light snacks (sandwiches, jacket potatoes) to home-cooked full meals. Food times
are 12 to 9.30 (12 to 7 Friday, Saturday and Sunday). Children are welcome until 7 o'clock, and the
pub accepts the major credit cards. The Elephant & Castle has a lovely conservatory to the rear and a
garden, with a patio and smoking area, that reaches down to the River Misbourne.

Amersham has many fine old buildings, including the 17th century Market hall and the Church
of St Mary with some notable stained glass. A stroll around town will build up a thirst and appetite,
so will a walk or cycle on the South Bucks Way or one of the many other footpaths in the area.

Clifden Road, Worminghall,
Buckinghamshire HP18 9JR
☎ 01844 339273

On the South Bucks/Oxford border tucked away in the attractive village of Worminghall, the **Clifden Arms** is a quintessential English country inn, with a smartly re-thatched roof, beams and timbers, log fires and country memorabilia, along with some sympathetic modern elements. Starting life in the 16th century, it has been a public house for 150 years and the long tradition of hospitality is now in the safe hands of Lin and Mike. They brought valuable experience in the trade when they took over in August 2006, re-opening the following month after overseeing a programme of refurbishment. That experience, combined with their talents, hard work and enthusiasm, guarantees that they have a real success on their hands, and the appeal, both among the local community andd with visitors from outside the are, is growing week by week as the good news spreads.

Fullers London Pride, Adnams and a guest ale are on tap in the bar and a blackboard in the dining area lists the day's dishes. Local produce takes pride o place and all the starters and main courses are prepared and freshly cooked to order in the busy kitchen. Among the starters are home-made soups, deep-fried whitebait, brie wedges. The favourite main courses range from home-made beef or vegetable lasagnes, Wornal steak pies, home-made fishcakes, fresh haddock fillet plus a choice of steaks to mixed grills plus roasts on Sundays also not forgetting seasonal fayre.

The Clifden Arms is a family friendly pub with a safe childrens play area and a superb separate beer garden. Worminghall is reached by minor roads A40 east of Oxford Wheately exit, north off the A418 Thame to Wheately and is only a short drive from junction 8 of the M40 (follow signs for Waterperry Gardens which is approx one-mile away). The pub is closed on Mondays during the winter otherwise open Monday evening thro to Friday serving food lunchtime noon to 2.30 pm, 6-9 pm in the evening Open all day Saturday noon to 3.00 pm and 6-9.30 pm evening. Sunday open all day for food from 12 till 7pm. Booking is advisable and essential on Sundays. The pub accepts most credit cards. Lin and Mike hope to offer bed and breakfast accommodation later this year which will make the inn an excellent base for touring the region. Also we welcome caravans and motor homes by appointment. We also cater for wedding venues by arrangement.

19 THE WHITE SWAN

Main Street, Stow cum Quy,
Cambridgeshire CB25 9AB
☎ 01223 811821
e-mail: sandraallsebrook@yahoo.co.uk

The **White Swan** public house and restaurant stands on the main street of the quiet little village of Stow cum Quy. This lovely Grade II listed pub is in the capable hands of Colin and Sandra Allsebrook, who brought many years' experience in running pubs when they took over here in the autumn of 2007. The public rooms are cosy, warm and inviting, and there are seats outside on the patio. The locals love the place, and the atmosphere is chatty and convivial in the little bar, where Sharps Doom Bar, Greene King IPA, Adnams Bitter and Woodforde's Wherry provide an excellent choice for real ale enthusiasts. In the bar or restaurant pub classics like fish & chips, steaks and steak & ale pie take care of fresh-air appetites. This is fine walking country, and rural attractions include Wilbraham

Fen and Quy Fen, a Site of Special Scientific Interest. An important annual event is the Fenland Country Fair held at Stow cum Quy Park – the 2008 renewal is 24 and 25 August. Also nearby is Anglesey Abbey, with a magnificent collection of paintings and lovely gardens. The White Swan lies five miles east of Cambridge on the B1102, off the A1303 Newmarket Road and a short drive from Junction 35 of the A14.

Green End, Fen Ditton,
Cambridgeshire CB5 8SX
☎ 01223 793264
🌐 www.theploughfenditton.co.uk

The **Plough** is a stylish modern riverside inn situated at Green End, close to Fen Ditton, on the eastern outskirts of Cambridge between Bottisham and Girton. For long one of the area's best-kept secrets, it's been discovered by a wide cross-section of visitors, from riverbank ramblers and boating folk on the Cam to tourists, motorists and anyone looking to take a break from the bustle of Cambridge.

The pub's sign depicts a Spitfire plane flying above a horse-drawn plough. It was at nearby Fen Ditton aerodrome that the first public demonstration of the Spitfire took place in October 1938. Fen Ditton was also the site of one of the UK's first public flying schools, in 1930, and the Plough was known as a pilots' pub. The aerodrome's duties have now been transferred to Cambridge Airport, but the Plough is still a favourite place to touch base when food, drink and hospitality are what's needed. Leaseholder Sharon Turner and her team provide the warmest of welcomes, and the bar – smart and stylishly modern – has plenty of comfortable seats to relax in and a real fire to keep the chill at bay.

The bar stocks a good range of drinks, which include Timothy Taylor Landlord, Adnams Bitter and Greene King Abbot Ale, along with a selection Continental lagers and a great wine list. The Plough is also a terrific place to enjoy a leisurely meal at any time of the day, every day of the week. The lunch menu (served Monday to Friday until 6) and the evening and weekend menu (served all day Saturday and Sunday and from 6 Monday to Friday) provide a fine variety of pub favourites and modern dishes such as royal bream with sugar snaps, crispy duck and orange salad with a sweet chilli dressing, spiced crab & crayfish cocktail and roast chicken supreme stuffed with sun-blush tomatoes with a black olive and basil compote.

The well-chosen, helpfully annotated wine list, with most available by the glass, includes a section of draught wines served by the glass and 500ml, 750ml and 1 litre carafes.

The Plough has a large beer garden with a decked dining area, and a capacious car park. The garden is the perfect place to enjoy a snack or meal from the Garden Menu, which lists a range of light dishes. The accompanying drinks list offers juices, smoothies, fizzy soft drinks, sparkling wine and Pimms.

High Street, Babraham,
Cambridgeshire CB22 3AG
☎ 01223 833800
e-mail: george@inter-mead.com
🌐 www.georgeinnbabraham.co.uk

The **George** is a popular beamed and timbered dining pub in a peaceful setting in the village of Babraham. The short detour off the A11, M11 and A1307 southeast of Cambridge is well worth while to enjoy the hospitality, the well-kept ales and the fine food provided by host George A Wortley, a perfectionist whose philosophy is that only the best will do for his patrons. His grand old inn, which started life as a coaching inn in the middle of the 18th century, has been stylishly and sympathetically updated to combine the handsome beams and other original features with a rich

contemporary feel. It's a comfortable, convivial place to meet or make friends and enjoy a drink from a wide choice that includes Greene King IPA, Abbot Ale and Old Speckled Hen. When the sun shines, the large dining terrace overlooked by a huge old oak tree is a popular place to be. But above all this is a place to take time to relax over a meal, and the reputation earned by the talented team at the stoves brings in discerning patrons from an ever-widening catchment area. Freshly baked ciabattas make a tasty quick lunch, and the menu offers a wide choice of dishes that combine technique and imagination at a very high level. Typical dishes run from hot-smoked salmon with penne pasta to pan-fried lamb kidneys, yellow Thai curry, roasted Cumberland sausage with clapshot mash and garlicky rosemary jus, and haddock, leek and gruyere cheese tartlet on a wild rocket and pea shoot salad dressed with a chive cream vinaigrette. The evening menu is even more exciting, with dishes that take their inspiration from around the world: sesame tempura of salmon nori roll with Oriental dips; spiced chicken and vegetable balti; grilled plaice fillet with crayfish and capers; and scallops with black pudding and a celeriac and grain mustard purée. Room should definitely be left for one of the delectable desserts, perhaps pear & cinnamon tarte tatin or peanut butter & honeycomb panna cotta. George A Wortley is adding another string to his bow with the bringing on stream of eight en suite letting rooms (one disabled friendly) in converted outbuildings. These are due to open in the autumn of 2008, making the George not just a top-class pub and restaurant but a comfortable, convenient base for both leisure and business guests. The A11 and M11 provide easy access to all areas, and attractions in the area include the wonderful city of Cambridge, the zoo at Linton and the Duxford Aviation Museum with its outstanding collection of historic aircraft.

High Street, Hildersham,
Cambridgeshire CB21 6BU
☎ 01223 891680
e-mail: peartree@btconnect.com

There are many reasons for visiting this very pleasant part of Cambridgeshire, and one of the best is the **Pear Tree**. This friendly old pub, adorned in spring and summer with colourful flower tubs and hanging baskets, stands in the picturesque village of Hildersham, which is not far from the busy A11 and just 500 yards from the A1307 (leave at Little Abington or Linton).

John and Gillian Harris came here at the beginning of 2008 after running a guest house in Thirsk, North Yorkshire, and they are quickly making their mark and making new friends in their new venture. The pub, much altered down the years, has a neat, bright bar with a stone floor, oak-beamed ceiling and lots of interesting bric-a-brac and memorabilia. There are papers and games to pass the time in the unlikely event of conversation flagging, and tables and chairs are set out in the garden in the summer. Greene King IPA and Abbot Ale and a guest cask ale head the list of drinks, and good honest home cooking is served in the bar and dining areas. The home-made pies, including beef, Guinness and stilton, have immediately been declared a hit by the regulars. Other choices might include scampi, home-cooked ham, steaks and a hearty beef bourguignon, and many a meal ends on a memorable note with an old-fashioned steamed pudding.

This popular pub facing the village green is open Monday evening and lunchtime and evening on other days, and food is served every day except Monday lunchtime and all day Tuesday. A recent addition to the Pear Tree's amenities is a cottage converted to provide two cosy, comfortable en suite bedrooms. They offer a very quiet, peaceful and civilised base for walkers, cyclists, motorists and tourists.

The River Granta flows through the village, which, thanks to a Millennium grant, is a riot of daffodils in the spring. It's a pleasant area for walking and rambling, and attractions within an easy drive include Linton Zoo, with its collections of birds, wild cats, snakes and insects; the fine Church of St Mary the Virgin, also in Linton; and Chilford Hall Vineyard on the B1052 between Linton and Balsham.

23 THE OLD RED LION

Horseheath, nr Haverhill,
Cambridgeshire CB21 4QF
☎ 01223 892909
e-mail: info@theoldredlion.co.uk

The **Old Red Lion** occupies a prominent site in the village of Horseheath, on the A1307 between Haverhill and Linton. Dating from the late-1940s, with extensions and alterations over the last 20 years, it provides a roomy, comfortable refreshment stop and a comfortable, practical base for motorists, tourists, bikers and people passing through on business or working in the area. The interior is very handsome, with slab floors and heavy wooden furnishings, and outside there's a beer garden and a huge off-road car park. Greene King IPA and Old Speckled Hen are accompanied by two rotating guest ales and a full range of other drinks. Leaseholder Ian Holt, Nuneaton born and bred, has really turned the place round since taking over the reins, making it a popular choice to relax and unwind with a drink or a leisurely meal.

Most of the dishes are prepared and cooked on the premises, and the food offers excellent value for money on bar and restaurant menus and a menu that combines the two. Starters on the main menu include home-made chicken liver pâté served with onion marmalade, crispy duck spring rolls with hoisin sauce and locally grown asparagus with cured ham and aïoli. Main courses include classic moules marinière, confit of Gressingham duck, wild mushroom risotto, chargrilled rib-eye steak and chargrilled swordfish loin marinated with lime and ginger. In addition to the beers and wines the menu lists a selection of teas and coffees, including liqueur coffees. The pub is open all day Monday to Saturday and from midday to 5pm on Sunday. Food is available lunchtime and evening and all day on Saturday; Sunday carvery from midday to 4.

The accommodation at the Old Red Lion is in roadhouse style and the 12 guest bedrooms all have en suite facilities; two of the rooms are wheelchair accessible. Horseheath is well placed for visiting Linton, with its renowned zoo, and other attractions in the vicinity include Chilford Hall Vineyard and Bartlow Hills, the site of the largest Roman burial site to be unearthed in Europe. And just along the road in the other direction is the fine little town of Haverhill, noted for its handsome Victorian architecture and the house occupied by Henry VIII's fourth wife Anne of Cleves.

24 THE DOG & DUCK

High Street, Linton,
Cambridgeshire CB21 4HS
☎ 01223 891257
e-mail: cnvarian@yahoo.co.uk

For many visitors to Linton, the Zoo is a major attraction, with creatures ranging from red-kneed tarantulas to Sumatran tigers. But in the High Street two rather more familiar creatures have long been attracting visitors. The **Dog & Duck** is a quintessential English pub, with an immaculate thatched roof, hanging baskets and a cosy old-world bar (originally two 16th century cottages) with low beams, an open fire, brasses and period pictures.

Chris Varian, who took over at the end of 2007, is a friendly, enthusiastic host, adding his personal charm to the warm, inviting ambience. Three Greene King cask ales – IPA, Abbot Ale and Old Speckled Hen – are on tap in the bar, which is open all day, every day, starting with morning coffee. Food is an important and growing part of the business, served every session except Sunday evening. The

menus combine classic pub dishes like battered cod fillet, rump steaks and the day's roast with less familiar choices such as mussel, squid & stilton chowder, Russian-style chicken & veal meatballs and Italian vegetable layer bake. Sunday lunchtime brings four roasts, with fish and vegetarian options and smaller portions for young gourmets. Another major asset at this lovely old inn is a pretty garden alongside the River Granta.

25 THE HARE & HOUNDS

6 High Street, Harlton,
Cambridgeshire CB23 1ES
Tel: 01223 262672
🌐 www.thehareandhoundspub.net

The **Hare & Hounds** is a cosy, compact pub in the tranquil village of Harlton, which lies a few miles southwest of Cambridge on a minor road that runs off the A603 across to the A10. Gordon Sweeting and Susan Davies are the welcoming hosts at this attractive thatched free house, a listed building dating from the middle of the 17th century. Recent refurbishment has enhanced the appeal of the beamed, carpeted bar, where a coal-burning fire keeps things snug in the cooler months. It's a great favourite with the locals, who meet for a chat over a glass of beer – Charles Wells Bombardier and Eagle IPA are the resident cask ales together with a guest beer, which changes on a weekly basis. Susan prepares a good variety of traditional bar food, which spans hot and cold baguettes, home-made soups, ploughman's platters, mushrooms with garlic mayonnaise,

scampi and hearty main dishes like egg, sausage or ham with chips, beef or vegetarian lasagne,

chicken curry and rump steak. In addition there is a home-made specials board which includes casseroles and pies in the winter and salads and a pint of prawns in the summer. The Sunday 1-, 2- or 3-course lunch centres round a choice of roasts – booking is recommended for this very popular occasion. There is a large beer garden to the rear of the pub overlooking open countryside and including a petanque pitch. Pub hours are 5pm-11pm Monday, 12-3pm and 5pm-11pm Tuesday to Thursday, all day Friday and Saturday and 12-5pm and 7pm-10.30pm on Sunday.

26 QUEENSBERRY

196 Carter Street, Fordham,
Cambridgeshire CB7 5JU
☎ 01638 720916
e-mail: queensberry196@btconnect.com

Resident owners Jan and Malcolm Roper provide quiet, comfortable Bed & Breakfast accommodation at **Queensberry**, their fine period house on the edge of the village. Fordham lies on the B1102, just off the A142 Newmarket to Ely

road and a short drive from Junction 37 of the A14. The accommodation provided at Queensberry is in the house and adjacent cottage comprising of seven double/twin rooms with four with ensuite facilities. All rooms enjoy garden views; some can be booked on a self-catering basis.

The house is an ideal base for visiting CAmbridge, Duxford Imperial War Museum, Newmarket and Ely. Among the other places of interest nearby are the National Trust's Wicken Fen, a delight for both ramblers and naturalists, Wicken's

St Lawrence's Church, where Oliver Cromwell is buried, and the imposing Wicken Smock windmill. Newmarket is known throughout the world as the headquarters of British horseracing, and Malcolm is a tour guide for the National Stud.

Breakfast at Queensberry is guaranteed to set up guests for a day's racing or discovering the local sights, with an excellent choice served in the pretty, leafy conservatory. Cash only. WiFi available.

27 CHESTER ZOO

Cedar House, Caughall Road,
Upton by Chester, Chester CH2 1LH
☎ 01244 380280
e-mail: j.benn@chesterzoo.org
🌐 www.chesterzoo.org

Chester Zoo is the UK's number one charity zoo, with over 7000 animals and 400 different species, including some of the most endangered species on the planet. With more than one million visitors

every year, the zoo – a conservation charity - is an all-year round favourite attraction for kids of all ages!

Café Tsavo is the eco-friendly cafeteria where visitors can eat under the watchful eyes of some of the animals including rhinos, mongoose and warthogs, and The Secret World of the Okapi enclosure which is home to the elusive Okapi. Come and see the Zoo's Bornean and Sumatran orang-utans in their new tropical environment, along with a wide variety of Indonesian Forest species including gibbons, reptiles and birds as well as indigenous plants, trees and shrubs. Experience the largest free-flight bat zone in Europe, now home to the Livingstone's Fruit Bat - one of the world's largest bats. Watch in awe as 300 Seba's Bats and Rodrigues Fruit Bats, whizz past, plus over 120 new baby bats – 'pups' - gaining their

flying wings! At your feet, Red-tailed Catfish swim with Freshwater Stingrays. Watch out too for the Turkish Spiny Mice and the Madagascan Hissing Cockroaches!

The 110-acre Zoo is open all year, except Christmas Day and Boxing Day, from 10am. Last entry and closing times vary with the seasons. Car parking is free. Restaurants, shops, monorail and summer time boat bus. Facilities for disabled visitors, including self-drive electric scooters and wheelchairs.

28 BEESTON CASTLE 🏛

Beeston, Tarporley, Cheshire CW6 9TX
☎ 01829 260464
🌐 www.english-heritage.org.uk

Standing majestically on a sheer rocky crag, Beeston has perhaps the most stunning views of any castle in England. Excavations indicate that a Bronze Age settlement and Iron Age hillfort occupied the site long before the castle was begun in 1225. For centuries

an impregnable royal fortress, it finally fell to Parliamentarian forces in the Civil War. The 'Castle of the Rock' exhibition outlines the 4,000 year history of this strategic site. There are family-friendly books and activities.

30 THE HORSE SHOE INN ⁋

Newcastle Road, Willaston, nr Nantwich, Cheshire CW5 7EP
☎ 01270 569404

Two miles east of Nantwich, between the A534 and A500, Willaston put itself on the map as the home of the World Worm Charming championships. It's also where the **Horse Shoe Inn** can be found, a homely, inviting old inn where tenant Mike Follett welcomes old friends

and new with well-kept ales (Unicorn and Old Stockport are the regulars) and a good choice of familiar pub snacks and meals. This attractive redbrick inn has a large garden and plenty of off-road parking. Close Monday lunchtime except on Bank Holiday weekends.

29 THE GLOBE INN ⁋

100 Audlem Road, Nantwich, Cheshire CW5 7EA
☎ 01270 623374
e-mail: info@woodlandsbrewery.co.uk
🌐 www.woodlandsbrewery.co.uk

John and Glenda Skeaping, their son Peter and grandson Joseph run the Globe Inn, which stands on the A529 Audlem road close to Nantwich railway station. The family came here in August 2007 and undertook a major refurbishment and redecoration programme that has made the old place once again spick and span. The Globe is a real magnet for connoisseurs of real ales, with eight brews always available from the range of ten produced by the family's own award-winning Woodlands Brewery at nearby Wrenbury (the Brewery also supplies many pubs in the region and beyond). The

printed menu and the specials board provide an admirable choice that runs from sandwiches and snacks to three-course meals. Among the main-course favourites are fish and seafood specials, lasagne, steaks and a super steak & ale pie made with Woodlands Midnight Stout. The Globe is closed Monday lunchtimes in winter, otherwise it's open lunchtime and evening and all day in the summer.

31 THE SWAN AT WYBUNBURY

2 Main Road, Wybunbury, nr Crewe,
Cheshire CW5 7MA
☎ 01270 841280 Fax: 01270 842916
e-mail: jacqueline.harris7@btinternet.com
🌐 www.theswanwybunbury.co.uk

South Cheshire's answer to the Leaning Tower of Pisa is the 100ft tower of St Chad's Church, built in 1470 above an unsuspected ancient salt bed. In the shadow of the tower stands the **Swan at Wybunbury**, one of the prettiest buildings in a village of pretty buildings. It dates back to the 16th century, and the old beams in the bar are staunch reminders of its origins. Jacky and Martin Harris took over in July 2007 and have lost no time in giving the old place a new lease of life with their

brand of hospitality. They have five real ales on tap – Unicorn, Hartley's Cumbrian Way and three rotating guests, all kept in tip-top condition – and a fine selection of other draught and bottle beers and lagers, cider, wines, spirits and non-alcoholic drinks. The food, served lunchtime and evening Monday to Saturday and from midday to 8pm on Sunday, is also excellent. The menus combine classics like beer-battered cod and pie of the day with dishes that are just that little bit different: typifying a winter menu are beef broth with pearl barley; smoked bacon, chicken and wild mushroom terrine with cranberry relish; salmon wrapped in Parma ham served with roasted fennel with a prawn and dill butter sauce; stilton and walnut quiche; and roast vegetable casserole topped with herb scones and cheesy mashed potato. This is a very popular eating place so booking is recommended at the weekend to be sure of a table. Old outbuildings in the grounds have been converted into seven en suite letting rooms with lots of space, large bathrooms and lovely views. It's a very comfortable, civilised base for a break, with plenty to see and do in the vicinity. A pleasant walk from that church tower, now stabilised on a reinforced concrete bed, leads to Wybunbury Moss National Nature Reserve, home to a number of rare moss-loving plants.

32 THE ROYAL OAK

Main Road, Worleston, nr Nantwich,
Cheshire CW5 6DN
☎ 01270 624138 Fax: 01270 611663

The **Royal Oak** stands at the heart of the
village of Worleston, on the B5074 a short
drive north of Northwich and the A51.
Robert and
Rachel
Hollinshead's
spacious,
stylish,
family-
friendly inn
is open
lunchtime
and evening,
seven days a

week, for a good range of drinks (three real
ales always on tap) and an excellent selection
of home-cooked food. Steaks and fish dishes
are particularly popular, but everything is
good, from sandwiches, salads and jacket
potatoes to duck à l'orange, rack of ribs and
tuna pasta bake. Robert and Rachel also run a
successful outside bar and catering business.

HIDDEN PLACES GUIDES

Explore Britain and Ireland with
Hidden Places guides - a fascinating
series of national and local travel
guides.

Packed with easy to read information
on hundreds of places of interest as
well as places to stay, eat and drink.

Available from both high street and
internet booksellers

For more information on the full range
of *Hidden Places* guides and other
titles published by Travel Publishing
visit our website on

www.travelpublishing.co.uk
or ask for our leaflet by phoning
01752 276660   or emailing
info@travelpublishing.co.uk

VISIT THE TRAVEL PUBLISHING WEBSITE

Looking for:

• *Places to Visit?*
• *Places to Stay?*
• *Places to Eat & Drink?*
• *Places to Shop?*

*Then why not visit the Travel
Publishing website...*

• Informative pages on places to visit,
stay, eat, drink and shop throughout
the British Isles.

• Detailed information on Travel
Publishing's wide range of national
and regional travel guides.

www.travelpublishing.co.uk

385

22 High Street, Congleton,
Cheshire CW12 1BD
☎ 01260 272702

Amanda Thompson, a lovely, lively, friendly lady, has made **Ye Olde White Lion** a roaring success since the day she took over the tenancy in 1997. The much-photographed black-and-white frontage has for centuries been an unmissable landmark on the main street of Congleton, and inside all is old-world charm, with cosy bars featuring beams, brasses and assorted pictures of the locality.

At the back of the pub is a delightful, secluded beer garden with a little aviary on one side. A minimum of three real ales are always available – Greene King Abbot Ale is a regular, along with a changing local brew – and good simple home cooking has proved a winner with the local residents and the considerable passing trade. Familiar favourites are firmly to the fore on the long list of dishes served at lunchtime every day except Monday. Sandwiches, panini and hot baguettes cater for those with less time or smaller appetites, while for others more filling fish & chips, chilli con carne, steak pie, gammon & egg, lasagne or a giant Yorkshire pudding filled with hot roast beef or chilli and cheese should fit the bill nicely. The burgers are particularly popular, topped with just cheese; with bacon, cheese & BBQ sauce; with a creamy mushroom & stilton sauce; or a chicken version with mayonnaise and crisp lettuce. The meal could end in similarly traditional style with apple pie, rhubarb crumble, sticky toffee pudding or chocolate fudge cake.

The inn is almost a tourist attraction in its own right, with a long and fascinating history. The premises were once the offices of the solicitors firm of John Bradshaw, the man who was the first – even before Cromwell – to put his signature to the death warrant of King Charles I. Congleton, which lies in the foothills of the Pennines, was once known as the 'Venice of the North' on account of the number of lakes that were created in the vicinity. It has plenty for the visitor to see, including the town's first silk mill, the Church of St Peter and the imposing Gothic Town Hall, which has a museum telling the story of civic and commercial life in Congleton, with some fine civic regalia on display.

34 LOCK 57

The Canal Centre, Hassall Green, Sandbach,
Cheshire CW11 4YB
☎ 01270 762266 Fax: 01270 762270
e-mail: enquiries@lock57.co.uk
🌐 www.lock57.co.uk

Lock 57 is a superb café/brasserie in an outstanding location alongside the Trent & Mersey Canal by Lock 57 at Hassall Green, a picturesque village found a couple of miles south of Sandbach. It started life as a smithy and stables for the horses who once pulled the canal barges. Canal life is now almost exclusively leisure-oriented, and Edward Hark's marvellous eating place is a popular stop for boaters as well as motorists, cyclists, walkers and local residents. Lock 57 is stylishly decorated and furnished, with feature brick walls, beams and soft lighting. There are lovely views over the Cheshire Plains from the upstairs restaurant, which can seat 50 in great comfort.

The garden by the lock, which has seats for 60, is a popular alternative in the summer. Food is taken very seriously here, and Edward is an experienced and talented, award-winning chef. Local produce is cooked to order, and everything from the bread and biscuits to the ice cream is made on the premises. The main menu caters for both traditional and more adventurous palates. Typifying the former are steak, kidney & ale pie and bread & butter pudding, while less conventional are pressing of confit duck leg with beetroot purée and dressed salad leaves; carrot & orange crème brûlée with a baby carrot salad; roast fillet of cod with pan-fried potatoes, wild mushrooms, asparagus and pesto dressing; and soft-centred hot chocolate fondant with Bailey's ice cream. The café menu proposes breakfast (from 10 to 1), scones, tea cakes, shortbread and croissants for morning coffee and afternoon tea, sandwiches, salads jacket potatoes and lunchtime specials such as terrine of ham hock with apple chutney, poached haddock topped with a poached egg, or braised lamb shank. People come from many miles around to enjoy the food and the setting, and booking is advisable, particularly in the evening.

Lock 57 is open in summer from 10 to 4.30 every day and from 6.30 every evening except Monday; in winter from 10 to 3.30 (from 9.30 Saturday and Sunday) and from 6.30 Wednesday to Sunday.

The Square, Sandbach,
Cheshire CW11 1AT
☎ 01270 762099

The Market Tavern stands proudly as a prominent landmark on the Square in Sandbach, as it has done since starting life as a coaching inn more than 200 years ago. Kay and Mike took over the tenancy of this handsome three-storey black-and-white building in September 2006, and they have breathed new life into the old place, earning it a rapidly growing reputation for hospitality and fine food and ales. The bar is open all day, seven days a week, with plenty of space for enjoying something to drink – the choice includes Unicorn cask ales and a good selection of other keg and bottled beers.

Food is served from 12 to 3 Monday to Saturday and locals keep coming back for the sandwiches and toasties, the ploughman's lunch with pickles and a bap, the deep-fried golden scampi and plaice and haddock, the jumbo sausages, the steaks and steak pies, the gammon with egg and pineapple and the beef stews. The tenants hope to make food available in the evening and on Sundays – phone to check. Families with children are very welcome and the secluded rear garden, unseen from the front, has an area where children can romp in safety. A folk club plays good music on Tuesday evenings and the pub also hosts occasional other live music and karaoke evenings.

The pub is an excellent venue for wedding and christening parties and other celebrations and get-togethers. Sandbach was one an important stopover for coaches, as is shown by the number of half-timbered old inns and houses – it linked major towns and cities of the Midlands with those of the North.

On the same market square as the tavern are the best-known landmarks in Sandbach. Two remarkable stone crosses, one 16 feet high, the other 11 feet, date from the 9th century, and the scenes depicted are thought to represent the conversion of Mercia to Christianity during the reign of King Penda. A plaque at the base notes that the crosses were restored in 1816 after 'destruction by the iconoclasts' (that is to say, the Puritans). The restoration involved finding hundred of pieces and fragments that had been put to various uses (walls, steps, paving) in the village.

36 THE COURTYARD COFFEE HOUSE 🍴 🏛

Rear of 92 King Street, Knutsford,
Cheshire WA16 6ED
☎ 01565 653974

Hidden away at the back of Knutsford's main street, the **Courtyard Coffee House** has few equals in its field. Renowned throughout the county and far beyond, this outstanding eating place run by Matthew and Sharon Fay provides a unique ambience for enjoying high-quality food in the 50-cover main area or outside in the courtyard – a popular choice in the summer months. Morning coffee (served 9 to 12) comes with scones, toast, tea cakes, tea bread and croissants, and afternoon tea (2.30 to 4.30) with dainty sandwiches, home-made scones and lovely tempting cakes. Between the two,

Lunchtime favourites include Welsh rarebit, grilled smoked haddock, honey-baked ham or one of the many varied vegetarian options. In addition to the super hospitality and cooking, this top-notch coffee house has another, unexpected attraction. The walls and beams display a collection of Penny Farthings and other ancient bicycles, including an original Boneshaker. The Penny Farthing, which in its day was usually known as the Ordinary, was in vogue for only about 20 years from the early 1870s, but the Courtyard Coffee House has been going strong for longer than that.

37 CRANFORD CAFÉ & SANDWICH BAR 🍴

8-12 Canute Place, Knutsford,
Cheshire WA16 1BH
☎ 01565 633203 Fax: 01565 633203
e-mail: orders@cranfordcafe.co.uk
🌐 www.cranfordcafe.co.uk

The **Cranford Café and Sandwich Bar** in Canute Place takes its name from the novel by Mrs Gaskell, who spent most of her childhood in Knutsford, which was to be the basis for the book. Sally and Roger Freeman acquired the premises in 2001, and after gutting the place they redesigned, refurbished and redecorated it to a very high standard. They have created one of the most appealing daytime eating places in the region and one that attracts locals, returning regulars and first-timers who are determined to become regulars. In the pleasant spotless surroundings the café offers a huge range of

breakfasts as well as traditional and speciality sandwiches, hot toasted panini, jacket potatoes and salads as well as the chef's special board featuring a fresh daily soup and hot roast. The café is also licensed so you can enjoy a relaxing glass of wine or beer with your meal. There are also some very tempting sweet things - cherry and rhubarb sponge, yum yum pastries , tiffin, teacakes and flapjacks to name a few. The Sandwich Bar lists a huge variety of sandwiches , hot food and salad boxes as well as hot and cold drinks and freshly made cakes. Opening hours are 7.30am to 3.00pm Monday to Friday , 8.30am to 2.00pm Saturday. Though much changed since Mrs Gaskell's day, Knutsford still has something of a Victorian air, with narrow streets and cobbled alleyways that reward a leisurely stroll.

39 THE LEGH ARMS

Prestbury Village, Cheshire SK10 4DG
☎ 01625 829130 Fax: 01625 827833
e-mail: legharms@hotmail.co.uk
🌐 www.legharms.co.uk

Peter Myers runs one of the very finest inns in Cheshire, renowned far beyond the county, with a reputation second to none for food, accommodation, comfort and service.

Behind the handsome frontage in the village centre the beautifully appointed bar has several distinctive areas, each with its own decorative features, furnishings and mood – delightful spots to chat over a drink or to meet before dinner in the oak-beamed restaurant. In the summer months tables and chairs are set out in the garden. The talent in the kitchen ensures that a meal here is an occasion to remember, and the promise of the mouthwatering menu is more than fulfilled by results on the plate. A meal could start with pheasant roulade, seared scallops with a saffron and lemon risotto or king prawn and leek terrine, and move on to pan-fried calves' liver with caramelised onions, roasted figs and champ potatoes, lobster with garlic butter or Thermidor, or fillet steak with a stilton rarebit topping and a rich red wine sauce. Desserts like a superb apple pie ensure a fine end to the meal, and the outstanding food is complemented by an excellent wine list and cask-conditioned ales from Robinsons Brewery. The bar menu offers the same high standards, mixing old

favourites like fish & chips, burgers and steaks with spicy fishcakes with chilli & plum jam or slow-roasted belly of pork. Peter also owns the popular next-door restaurant Nice.

Prestbury, on the A538, is a charming, well-kept, prosperous place and both the village and the surrounding area are well worth taking time to explore. There's no better base for doing this than the **Legh Arms**, which has eight luxuriously and comprehensively en suite bedrooms. Two are in traditional, home-from-home style, the rest stylishly contemporary, and exceptional attention to detail is evident in the décor, furnishings, fixtures and fittings in every room.

38 THE DUKE OF YORK

Stockport Road, Romiley, nr Stockport,
Cheshire SK6 3AN
☎ 0161 430 2806 Fax: 0161 430 9445
e-mail: mail@dukeofyorkromily.co.uk
⊕ www.dukeofyorkromily.co.uk

Since arriving in 1992 Jim Grindrod has been extending a warm, genuine welcome to friends old and new at the **Duke of York**. Close to the Peak Forest Canal, it was built as a coaching inn, and the archway under which the coaches passed to the stables is still there. Inside, the pub has retained plenty of old-world character, providing a very inviting ambience for enjoying a drink and a chat. Up to six real ales are available, with John Smith's Cask, Fullers London Pride and Charles Wells Bombardier among the regulars. Old Rosie cider also has plenty of fans. The pub's unique feature.s is the variety of its cooking, with chefs taking their inspiration from English, French, Italian, Spanish, Greek, Turkish and other world cuisines.

Diners in the 30-cover Mediterranean Restaurant (booking is best) have a terrific choice: a short selection from the long menu includes spicy Turkish sausages, stuffed aubergines, calamari, a mezze platter for 2, lamb kebabs, moussaka and chilli king prawns. Halibut, sea bass and swordfish are cooked simply and served with a lemon sauce, and the chef's special chicken dish is cooked in a creamy walnut sauce. The Duke of York, which is open all day, every day, has a pleasant beer garden and an outdoor, undercover area where smokers can puff away.

40 THE SPINNERS ARMS

76 Palmerston Street, Bollington,
Cheshire SK10 5PW
☎ 01625 571515

The **Spinners Arms** stands a mile or so off the A523, north of Macclesfield on the edge of the Peak District National Park. Popular with the local community and with visitors, especially walkers, its main business is quenching thirsts, with four real ales heading the list (Boddingtons' Black Sheep and guests), but hot and cold snacks are available at lunchtime and early in the evening. Children are welcome up to 9 o'clock. Cash only.

Karen Farrow, leaseholder of the Spinners Arms, also runs the **Robin Hood Inn**, located just outside Macclesfield on the B5470 road to Whaley Bridge. Customers here can also enjoy

well-kept real ales (three always on tap) and good food is served lunchtime and evenings Monday to Saturday and from 12 to 6 on Sunday, when traditional roasts take centre stage. The inn also offers very comfortable accommodation for Bed & Breakfast guests in four top-of-the-range en suite bedrooms, two of them on the ground floor. Tel: 01625 574060.

391

Hawkins Lane, Rainow, nr Macclesfield,
Cheshire SK10 5TL
☎ 01625 424235
e-mail: morninablue@myway.com

The **Rising Sun** is a lovely old coaching inn on the edge of the Peak District National Park at Rainow, a short drive northeast of Macclesfield on the road to Whaley Bridge. That road, now the B5470, was once the haunt of highwaymen, but things are peaceful now and locals and visitors alike will arrive without standing and delivering to enjoy the warm, genuine welcome and friendly hospitality extended by Kathleen and Dickie and Kathleen's sister Linda, who took over the licence in May 2007.

A brew from Black Sheep is one of three real ales always available in the bar, alongside a

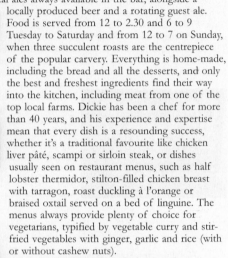

locally produced beer and a rotating guest ale. Food is served from 12 to 2.30 and 6 to 9 Tuesday to Saturday and from 12 to 7 on Sunday, when three succulent roasts are the centrepiece of the popular carvery. Everything is home-made, including the bread and all the desserts, and only the best and freshest ingredients find their way into the kitchen, including meat from one of the top local farms. Dickie has been a chef for more than 40 years, and his experience and expertise mean that every dish is a resounding success, whether it's a traditional favourite like chicken liver pâté, scampi or sirloin steak, or dishes usually seen on restaurant menus, such as half lobster thermidor, stilton-filled chicken breast with tarragon, roast duckling à l'orange or braised oxtail served on a bed of linguine. The menus always provide plenty of choice for vegetarians, typified by vegetable curry and stir-fried vegetables with ginger, garlic and rice (with or without cashew nuts).

Families with children are always welcome at the Rising Sun, which is closed on Monday except on Bank Holiday weekends, otherwise open lunchtime and evening and all day in the summer. Friday is quiz night. For spring 2008 a new conservatory has been built, with 40

additional seats and lovely views over the Cheshire countryside. The Peak District National Park, just moments away, offers glorious scenery and walking as gentle or rigorous as requires; and after the fresh air has generated a thirst and appetite, it's quick march to the Rising Sun, where the hosts are ready with exactly what's needed – a place to relax, unwind and enjoy a refreshing drink and a reviving meal!

42 THE CAT & FIDDLE

Buxton Road, Macclesfield Forest,
Cheshire SK11 0AR
☎ 01298 23364
e-mail: info@catandfiddle.co.uk
🌐 www.catandfiddle.co.uk

Within the Peak District National Park on the A537 between Buxton and Macclesfield, the **Cat & Fiddle** enjoys superb views in all directions. One of the best-known pubs in the region, it's popular with locals, walkers, cyclists, motorists, day-trippers and tourists from all over the UK and beyond – it's so well known that it's marked on many of the major road atlases. The isolated, scenic setting is just the first of many qualities to greet the visitor. Fine hospitality is dispensed by David and Natalie Barnes, both local people. David first worked here in the mid-1990s, later becoming head chef and now installed as co-tenant with his wife.

At 1,690 feet above sea level, the Cat & Fiddle is reputedly the second highest pub in England, and the lofty setting is matched by the sky-high reputation of its cooking. Local seasonal produce is the basis of the dishes, which are served from noon to 9 o'clock. The printed menu and specials board propose mainly tried and tested pub favourites such as scampi, beer-battered cod, steak & ale pie, burgers, honey-glazed ham, roast chicken, steaks and Cumberland sausage served in a giant Yorkshire pudding. Booking is advisable on Sunday, when a super carvery is added to the options.

This is wonderful walking country, and a hike up nearby Shining Tor or Axe Edge is guaranteed to create a thirst that David and Natalie are always happy to satisfy. For a more leisurely stroll, the River Goyt, a major source of the Mersey, runs close to the pub and can be walked along its whole length. Other nearby attractions include Poole's Cavern, a natural limestone cave, Grin Low Country Park and the prominent folly known as Solomon's Temple. The pub is closed on Monday evenings in winter – and on the occasional days when its exposed, elevated location is prey to weather conditions that close the road.

43 THE EGERTON ARMS

Knutsford Road, Chelford,
nr Macclesfield, Cheshire SK11 9BB
☎ 01625 861366 Fax: 01625 861132
🌐 www.chelfordegertonarms.co.uk

The **Egerton Arms**, built in the late-18th century, was named in deference to the great landowners in the area, the Egertons of Tatton Park, a few miles up the road. It was at first a simple ale house brewing its own beer using water from a well in the garden. On the edge of Chelford, on the A537 between Knutsford and Macclesfield, it has gone from strength to strength since Jeremy and Anne Hague arrived in October 2006 and patrons come from all over the region to enjoy the excellent hospitality, food and drink. The interior is delightfully traditional, with lots of beams and wood and pictures of local interest, and the extensive grounds have plenty of seating for the summer months. The inn is open all day for drinks (three real ales are always on tap), and food is served from midday to 9 o'clock. Professional chefs seek out the best seasonal produce,

some of it from the well-known Chelford Farmers Market, for dishes on the main menu and specials of the day. Pub classics run from soup to fish & chips, steaks, generously filled pies (chicken, leek & mushroom), curries and Sunday roasts. There are seats for 120 inside and another 80 outside, but such is the popularity of the inn that booking is recommended at peak times.

Photos used courtesy of Cyan Cat - www.cyancat.com

Holmes Chapel Road, Allostock,
nr Knutsford, Cheshire WA16 9JY
☎ 01565 722234 Fax: 01565 723216
e-mail: bookings@thethreegreyhounds.com
⊕ www.thethreegreyhounds.com

The Three Greyhounds is an impressive former coaching inn and smithy in the village of Allostock, situated at the junction of the B5081 and B5082 off the A50 seven miles south of Knutsford. It lies close to many of Cheshire's leading visitor attractions, including Jodrell Bank Observatory and Arboretum, the extraordinary Anderton Boat Lift and several National Trust properties.

When Simon and Elaine took over the Three Greyhounds in June 2007 they came out of the traps running to give the old place a new lease of life with their excellent hospitality and culinary skills. Theakstons Best is the regular among the real ales on tap, and super food is served from 12 to 8 Sunday to Wednesday and from 12 to 9 Thursday to Saturday. Ingredients are locally sourced as far as possible, and the wide-ranging menus offer plenty of choice for both traditional and more adventurous palates. Among the dishes that have made this such a popular place are beer-battered cod, beef & vegetable hotpot, moules marinière, steaks, lasagne (meat or vegetarian), rich game pie and the day's roast. A superb seafood platter includes smoked mackerel, prawns, flaked tuna and poached salmon with a honey mustard dill dressing, while sea bass with ginger and spring

onions, and duo of crab cakes with a coriander and lime dip bring a flavour of the Orient. An equally exciting dish is chicken breast flavoured with green pesto, wrapped in Black Forest ham and served on a roasted red pepper sauce. There's always a good choice for vegetarians, and desserts like apple & blackberry pie or Cointreau and marmalade bread & butter pudding provide a great finale to a memorable meal. A separate lighter bite menu offers sandwiches, tortilla wraps, hot baguettes and jacket potatoes as well as pub classics including burgers, fish & chips, Cumberland sausage ring and steak & kidney pudding. Booking is recommended, especially for Sunday lunch featuring a choice of roasts.

The inn has plenty of off-road parking and a major bonus in the shape of lovely gardens with lawns, picnic sets and a delightful gazebo. Tuesday is quiz night, local bands perform on Wednesdays and a function room for up to 100 is available for parties or other special occasions.

45 THE COTTAGE RESTAURANT & LODGE

London Road, Allostock, nr Knutsford,
Cheshire WA16 9LU
☎ 01565 722470
Fax: 01565 722749
e-mail: reception@thecottageknutsford.co.uk
🌐 www.thecottageknutsford.co.uk

Quality, comfort, service and food all excel at the **Cottage Restaurant & Lodge**, owned and personally run by the hardworking, hospitable Marr family. Their charming hotel stands in the beautiful Cheshire countryside, set back from the A50 between Knutsford and Holmes Chapel and just ten minutes' drive from the M6 (J10 or 19). It's an ideal spot for both leisure and business visitors, whether they've popped in for a quick drink and a snack, sat down to a leisurely meal or booked in for an overnight or longer stay.

The Cottage is well known throughout the area for serving a superb variety of modern British food from both à la carte and fixed-price menus. The owners take great pride and satisfaction in seeking out the very best seasonal produce, and results on the plate show that preparation, cooking and presentation all get full attention in the kitchen. Starters might include steamed mussels in a chilli & saffron broth, smoked duck terrine, tempura of vegetables with a sweet chilli dipping sauce and the super Rossini Piccolo – fillet of Cheshire beef with a pâté-topped crouton and a rich Madeira jus. Typical main courses are roasted local poussin stuffed with Cheshire cheese and sage served with a bacon-infused gravy; pan-fried fillet of sea bass with an orange & fennel salsa and a roquette & pine nut salad; and Moroccan lamb tagine – slowly braised Tabley lamb with raisins, almonds & honey herb couscous, dressed with mint yoghurt. The 60-cover waitress-served restaurant serves this delicious food from 12 to 2 and from 6 to 10.

The guest accommodation comprises 12 spacious bedrooms with bath and shower en suite, satellite TV, dial-out phone, radio-alarm clock, trouser press, ironing facilities and hot drinks tray. The four doubles and eight twins offer very versatile facilities, and the twins have zip & link beds which can convert them into doubles. The rooms can be booked on a room only or B&B basis, and the basic tariff remains static throughout the year. Discounts are given for longer stays. The Cottage is also a delightful venue for a function, meeting, conference, celebration or training course. Individually tailored, inclusive packages are available for 8hr and 24hr conferences.

46 THE DROVERS ARMS

I London Road, Allostock, nr Knutsford,
Cheshire WA16 9JD
☎ 01565 722214
e-mail: enquiries@droversarms.info

Standing on the main A50 in the village of Allostock, the **Drovers Arms** is a marvellous pub with a particularly warm and inviting atmosphere. Beyond the immaculate cream and burgundy frontage the bar is a comfortable, convivial spot for enjoying a drink and a chat.

The bar is open all day, every day of the week, for a wide selection of drinks headed by Black Sheep cask ale and two guests. The beer garden is a real bonus in the summer months and the inn also boasts one of the finest bowling greens in the county of Cheshire. When Pam Brazendale took over the tenancy in December 2006 she brought a wealth of experience in the licensed trade, and her welcome, the ambience and the excellent hospitality have made this a very popular destination for lovers of quality food and drink. Food is a major part of the business, with as many of the

ingredients as possible sourced locally and good honest flavours to the fore throughout. Some of the dishes are pub classics (lamb shank, fish pie, traditional beer-battered cod), while others are less familiar, like salmon with a pink peppercorn sauce or chicken fillet with roasted spices. Pan-fried king prawns cooked with roasted garlic and lemon butter served on a bed of crispy seaweed is a house special, as are the sizzling skillets – garlic chicken, ribbon of rump or king prawns wok-fried in hoi sin sauce with oriental-style vegetables. The main menu is served from 12 to 9 Monday to Saturday; on Sunday a popular carvery operates from midday to 4 o'clock, when the main menu takes over till 8 o'clock. A 'lite bite' menu served from 12 to 5.30 Monday to Saturday offers sandwiches, cold and hot baguettes, jacket potatoes and smaller portions of some of the all-time favourites from the main menu, including fish & chips, liver & bacon casserole, curries and steak & ale pie. A Pensioners Hot Buffet is served at lunchtime Tuesday to Thursday. Pam and her staff are happy to arrange special occasions at the inn, from meetings to christening parties, wedding receptions, office goodbyes – even funeral gatherings. The Drovers Arms has a 5-star graded caravan and camping site to the rear, reached through the car park.

Pam has recently taken over the tenancy of a second pub – the Potters Lodge (formerly the Waggon & Horses) at Audley, on the B500 near Newcastle-under-Lyme.

397

London Road, Northwich,
Cheshire CW9 8AA
☎ 01646 423333
Fax: 01646 46355

Tim Crank, his partner Marie, father Keith, mother Diane and sister Kim make it a real family affair at the **Bowling Green**. Five minutes' walk from the centre of Northwich, this lovely black-and-white inn was built in 1650 in a style that's very typical of many fine buildings to be found all over the county. Handsome at any time of the year, it is particularly enticing in spring and summer, when the frontage is adorned with colourful window boxes and hanging baskets.

The inn takes its name from the bowling green that, until the 1980s, stood alongside the building; the space that it occupied is now a very attractive children's play area. The inn also has a spacious and really lovely rear garden that overlooks the River Weaver and a railway viaduct, and there's ample off-road parking. The interior, much roomier than might appear from the outside, is an equally delightful place to be, with a number of striking features that include sturdy old beams, wood or quarry-tiled floors and a wealth of interesting bygones and memorabilia associated with the inn and the town.

Up to four real ales – typically Theakstons Best, Courage Directors and rotating guests – are available, along with a full range of other draught and bottled beers, lagers, stout, cider, wines, spirits, liqueurs and non-alcoholic drinks. Children are welcome, and the inn has a designated family area away from the main bar.

Kim is a super cook, and she and her talented team of helpers at the stoves attract lovers of good food from a wide area around the inn. Traditional and modern classics feature prominently on the menu, with jumbo battered cod, chilli, lasagne, gammon and rump steaks, minted lamb shank and chicken korma always in demand. A popular combo for two to share comprises a half-rack of ribs, chicken goujons, chunky potato wedges, onion rings, garlic bread, dips and barbecue sauce. A good choice of wines by bottle and two sizes of glass accompanies the food.

Tuesday is steak night, followed by a quiz, and the inn hosts regular seasonal themed nights. Sandwiches, baguettes, burgers, jacket potatoes and snacks on toasted batch bread cater for lighter appetites or those with less time to spare, and senior citizens can enjoy bargain lunches during the week.

The location, the welcome, the facilities and the resident expertise make the Bowling Green a popular choice for special occasions. The function room is an ideal venue for anniversaries, birthdays, christenings, wedding receptions, funerals and sportsmans dinners.

I Hartford Road, Davenham, nr Northwich,
Cheshire CW9 8JA
☎ 01606 42022
🌐 www.theoddfellowsofdavenham.co.uk

The **Oddfellows Arms**, which stands on the A533 two miles south of Northwich, started life as an ale house in the mid-19th century, becoming fully licensed premises in 1904. Since 2002 it has been run by carol

and Ross Boyle, who had previously opened and run a nearby golf club. They offer the hand of friendship not just to the odd fellow but to everyone who passes beyond the ornamental brick frontage and into the bar, where four real ales are always kept in prime condition. Carole and Ross's children Oliver, Sam, Lucia, Jon and William make this a real family affair, and Carol has the services of valued righthand girl Kerry to assist her in the kitchen. Traditional country cooking, using as much local produce as possible, covers an excellent variety of dishes, from mackerel pâté and prawn cocktail to cod & chips, sausages & mash, lamb

braised with root vegetables, curries, steaks, steak & ale suet pudding and chicken & mushroom suet pie. Sandwiches, baguettes and snacks are available for those in a hurry or with smaller appetites. The inn has won many awards for the seasonal floral displays that adorn the front; at the back is a secluded beer garden that's a perfect venue for wedding receptions and other celebrations. Also on the social side, the inn has a golf club that meets on Wednesday and Sunday.

85-87 Station Road, Winsford,
Cheshire CW7 3DE
☎ 01606 862008 Fax: 01606 591822
e-mail: winsfordlodge@btinternet.com
🌐 www.winsfordlodge.co.uk

A short walk from the centre of town and close to the railway station, the **Winsford Lodge Motel** and Guest House is owned and personally run by Steven and Rosemary Foster. The accommodation comprises 11 superbly furnished and decorated en suite bedrooms, seven of them on the ground

floor. They provide abundant comfort and practical modern facilities for an overnight stay or for longer periods while on business or touring the area. Guests enjoy the combination of the traditional hospitality and the up-to-date amenities; families with children are welcome, and pets can be accommodated by prior arrangement. The basic tariff is on a room only basis, but a full English breakfast is available with notice. Winsford lies on the River Weaver, on the A54 six miles south of Northwich. There's excellent walking hereabouts, and Oulton Park motor racing circuit is a short drive away.

50 THE PLOUGH INN

Beauty Bank, Whitegate, Northwich,
Cheshire CW8 2BP
☎ 01606 889455 Fax: 01606 301717
e-mail: info@ploughwhitegate.com
⊕ www.ploughwhitegate.com

David Hughes, the tenant of **The Plough Inn** since 1996, runs a real gem of a pub, a genuine "hidden place" tucked away down a No Through Road on top of Beauty Bank in the tiny hamlet of Foxwist Green near Whitegate. The setting, among fields, is serene and attractive, and the inn's two bars are full of charm and character. There are many reasons for seeking out this delightful place, the main one being the superb food cooked by 4 chefs (and occasionally by David himself) and served in generous helpings at very reasonable prices. The quality and choice are quite outstanding, whether it's a quick snack or a 3-course meal. The regular menu of sandwiches, salads, jacket potatoes and a dozen classic main courses is supplemented by the longest daily

specials list you'll ever see, with inspiration drawn from around the world. The inspiration may be worldwide, but the beef is all British and David is a great supporter of British farming. Real ales and a long list of well-chosen wines accompany this splendid fare. In summer, the garden has plenty of tables and chairs for alfresco quaffing.

51 THE FOREST VIEW

Gallowsclough Lane, Oakmere,
Cheshire CW8 2TG
☎ 01606 882860
e-mail: mail@forestviewinn.com
⊕ www.forestviewinn.com

Located in the picturesque hamlet of Oakmere, **The Forest View** is very appropriately named as the village stands on the edge of Delamere Forest. Mine hosts, Carol Gerrard and her parents Paula and Brian Aspinall first discovered this fine old traditional inn when, many years ago, Paula and Brian bought a caravan on the adjacent camping and caravan park. As a young girl Carol spent her holidays here and later started working at the pub and then ran it for the owners on and off for 10 years. Finally, in December 2007 she became the tenant. Since then she has built up the inn's reputation for superb food which is available every lunchtime and evening. On Sundays, a traditional roast lunch is added to the menu. Vegetarian options are available and there's also a children's menu. To accompany your meal, choose from the compact wine list with well-chosen selections from around the world. The inn also offers a choice of up to 4 real ales, including Theakston's Best, Theakston's Mild, Directors and Courage, and they are currently having a special beer brewed for them at a local brewery. The inn has an excellent beer garden and children's play area.

52 THE STANLEY ARMS HOTEL

Old Road, Anderton, Northwich,
Cheshire CW9 6AG
☎ 01606 75059

Standing right next to the famous Anderton Boat Lift, **The Stanley Arms Hotel** is known locally as "The Tip" because in the old days salt was tipped here down chutes into the canal barges. Dating back to 1753, this fine old hostelry occupies a superb position with a beer garden and terracing leading down to the canal and with views across to the Boat Lift. Mine hosts at this welcoming inn are Mick and Angela McCafferty, a local couple who took over in the spring of 2007 and have enhanced the inn's reputation for excellent home-made food. The extensive menu ranges from old favourites such as Steak & Ale Pie and Fish & Chips to dishes from around the world including curries, lasagne and Mexican Chilli & Tacos. Vegetarians

have a good choice of dishes, and for lighter appetites there are baguettes, sandwiches and jacket potatoes. Food is served all day, every day, from noon until 8.45pm (6.45 on Sundays) and to accompany your meal there's a choice of 3 well-kept real ales along with a comprehensive range of wines and spirits. And why not round off your visit with a boat trip along the canal on Canal Explorer which sails all year round.

53 THE ANTROBUS ARMS

Warrington Road, Antrobus,
Cheshire CW9 6JD
☎ 01606 891333
⊕ www.antrobusarms.co.uk

First licensed in 1760, the **Antrobus Arms** has been dispensing hospitality ever since. Leaseholders Trevor and Sandra Collins came back to Antrobus (Trevors birthplace) in 1990 after running two pubs in Burscough, Lancashire since the early eighties and the good people of Antrobus and the surrounding area are enjoying the relaxed, friendly ambience they have created at this traditional village local. Set in scenic countryside on the A559 between Warrington and Northwich, it's equally popular with passing trade and visitors to the area, who can drop in at any time for a spot of refreshment in convivial company. The inn is open all day seven days a week for drinks (offering a varied selection of cask ales) and professional chefs prepare excellent food served from 12 to 9 Monday to

Saturday and from 12 to 8 on Sunday. Prime local produce, including meat from Webbs Butcher in nearby Northwich, are the basis of dishes that run from sandwiches, salads and baked potatoes to steak & ale pie, liver & bacon, beer-battered cod and Caerphilly cheese & leek sausages in a Mediterranean tomato sauce. Sunday is quiz night, and the inn hosts a live entertainment evening on the first Friday of the month. A function room can be hired for private parties, and the inn has a pleasant patio, a 'secure' garden area and ample off-road parking.

550 Manchester Road, Hollins Green,
Rixton, Warrington, Cheshire WA3 6LA
☎ 0161 777 9673
Fax: 0161 776 9897

Once an important stop on the Liverpool-Manchester coaching route, the **Black Swan** has a history that dates back to 1667. It was originally called the Old Swan and acquired its present name when black swans, which were native to Australia, first appeared in the area on the nearby Mersey and Glaze rivers. The first recorded landlord was one Robert Clare, who was licensed to serve ale and food and to stable horses for 2/= (10p) a year. Since 1999 the tradition of hospitality (without the horses) has been carried on in fine style by Liz and Luke Morrison, who attract patrons from near and far with outstanding food, fine ales and wine and high-class service.

The bar at this venerable place is full of period charm and character, with beams, burnished brass and an interesting assortment of decorative memorabilia. Two or three real ales are always available, with Deuchars IPA the resident ale, and the bar also stocks a full range of other draught and bottled beers, lagers, cider, spirits, liqueurs and non-alcoholic drinks. The hosts aim to provide an excellent and enjoyable dining experience, and the talented in the kitchen certainly make it happen. And they make it happen for all tastes and appetites. The long menus run from sandwiches, burgers and starters like garlic mussels and mushrooms stuffed with stilton & bacon to chilli con carne, omelettes, battered cod, Cumberland sausage ring, the day's pie (ask the waitress) and toad-in-the-hole (when did you last see that on a menu?). Curries cooked to traditional, authentic recipes are always popular, and apple pie is just one of several tempting desserts. Sunday lunch is a favourite family occasion, with roasts the centrepiece; an interesting alternative way of serving this is as a 'Grandma Batty', with everything presented in a Yorkshire pudding. The pub is a popular venue for all occasions, including weddings, christenings, birthdays and business meetings, and an extensive buffet is available.

As well as being a fine destination restaurant, the Black swan is also very much at the social heart of the community: Monday and Wednesday are quiz nights, Tuesday it's fun bingo, Friday is once-a-month live entertainment and Saturday brings the bold and the brave to the mike for the karaoke session. Hollins Green lies on the A57 road from Warrington towards Salford and Manchester.

54 THE SLOW & EASY

Manchester Road, Lostock Gralam,
nr Northwich, Cheshire CW9 7PJ
☎ 01606 42148
e-mail: excelsounds@aol.com

Relaxation is the name of the game at the **Slow & Easy**, but the wonderful easy-going ambience has been achieved by the hard work of affable leaseholders Tony and Maria Beasant. Open every lunchtime and evening and all day on Saturday and Sunday, the

pub serves three real ales and hearty dishes cooked by Maria: burgers, jacket potatoes, cottage pie, lasagne, scampi, cod, plaice, steaks, curries, liver & onions, cidery pork hock. The pub is very much at the social heart of the community, with entertainment most days of the week: Bingo on Monday, poker on Tuesday, a jamming session on Wednesday, karaoke on Friday, a DJ and a quiz on Saturday. And there's never any shortage of convivial chat in the bar.

The pub's superb bowling green can be used by non-members of the bowling club when there's no match. The Slow & Easy, which takes its name from a racehorse owned in the 19th century by a prominent local landowner, stands in the village of Lostock Gralam, two miles east of Northwich where the A559 meets the A556. Well placed for both leisure and tourist visitors, the pub has eight excellent en suite rooms available all year for Bed & Breakfast guests, with evening meals also available.

56 THE STAR INN

64 Star Lane, Statham, nr Lymm,
Cheshire WA13 9LN
☎ 01925 753715

There's a human story behind the very survival of the **Star Inn**, the social hub of the tiny hamlet of Statham. The lucky locals, and visitors from outside the community, are grateful for the efforts of Ivan and Corinne Peers, who are bringing back the good times to this delightful place. Ivan had led a sadly unsuccessful campaign to save a pub in nearby Lymm, and when he heard that the Star was to be put in the hands of the developers he couldn't contemplate the disappearance of another traditional British pub, particularly one with strong family ties. He negotiated a 20-year lease from the Carlsberg Tetley Brewery and with Corinne and their daughter Chloe set about a complete revamp of the premises.

Once more it's a much-loved local, a proper drinkers' pub serving a selection of cask ales, and equally a place for all the family. The bar is warm and welcoming, with old beams, a feature fireplace and attractive prints of old Statham and Lymm. The premises were once a fustian cutters' work place (it was originally called the Cutters Arms) and their history is also on display.

Bar snacks are served all day, and Ivan's plans include hog roasts and barbecues in the garden, internet access, quizzes and karaoke/disco nights. The inn has three letting rooms for B&B guests, providing a friendly, convenient base for walkers and cyclists on the Trans Pennine Way.

Well Lane, St Cleer, nr Liskeard,
Cornwall PL14 5DG
☎ 01579 342091

The **Market Inn** stands in the moorland village of St Cleer, in former mining country two miles north of the main A38 at Liskeard. The promise of the frontage of this lovely old stone inn is more than fulfilled within, where beams and polished darkwood furniture assist the traditional look. With Penny and Paul as the hardworking and enthusiastic tenants, the inn has established a reputation for hospitality and fine food that extends far beyond the local community. Penny is the queen of the stoves, and her menus provide a good variety of dishes, based as far as possible on fresh local produce and all prepared and cooked to order. Fish-eaters, meat-eaters and vegetarians are all equally well catered for, and for anyone with a sweet tooth the list of daily desserts makes mouthwatering reading. The choice might include profiteroles, jam roly poly, spotted dick, chocolate fudge cake and lemon meringue ice cream cake. The main menu and the daily changing specials are served between 12 and 2pm (Sunday to 3pm) and from 6 to 8, booked tables only until 9. Monday hours 4pm to 11pm bar, no food is served on

Mondays except bank holidays and in summer the luscious cream teas, served between 12 and 4, are an extra treat. There are 40 covers in the dining area, but such is the popularity of Penny's cooking that booking is advisable on Friday, Saturday and Sunday to be sure of a table at the time you want.

Families with children are always very welcome, and the inn has a garden and patio area and a large off-road car park. Caravans and motor homes are welcome if the owners are members of the Caravan Club. The village of St Cleer is arranged round its 15th century parish church, close to which is a fine stone building that covers a holy well. Cornwall is renowned for its holy wells, and the well at St Cleer is thought to have curative powers, particularly from insanity. But, holy well or not, it would be madness to leave St Cleer without enjoying the hospitality and fine food at the Market Inn. The location, on the edge of Bodmin Moor, provides superb walking opportunities, and the many local attractions include the Neolithic chamber tomb Trevethy Quoit and the beauty spot and National Nature Reserve at Golitha Falls.

57 THE WHITE HORSE ¶ ⊨

14 Newport Square, Launceston,
Cornwall PL15 8EL
☎ 01566 772084
⊕ www.whitehorselaunceston.co.uk

The **White Horse** is located in the Newport area of Launceston, at the point where the main A388 turns a sharp corner and meets the B3254. Starting life in 1690 as a farmhouse, it became an inn in 1714, and the unbroken tradition of hospitality in the centuries since is in safe keeping in the hands of tenants William and Mary Drummond and managers Norman and Karen Pomery. They are enhancing the inn's reputation for good ale and food and hospitality, and their professional chefs are making it a magnet for lovers of good country cooking. Food is served lunchtime and evening, all day on Sunday (traditional roasts a speciality) and all day every day in the summer months. The bar is open all day for drinks, which include well-kept Tribute and HSD cask ales. The pub

has a covered patio area and a large off-road car park. Two upstairs bedrooms, one of them en suite, the other with private facilities, are available

for Bed & Breakfast guests. They provide a pleasant, well-priced base for exploring a town described by Sir John Betjeman as 'the most interesting inland town in Cornwall'. There is indeed plenty to interest the visitor, including the imposing ruins of the Castle, the magnificent Church of St Mary Magdalene and the National Trust's Lawrence House Museum.

59 THE SWAN COFFEE SHOP ¶

Broads Yard, Downderry, nr Looe,
Cornwall PL11 3LX
☎ 01503 250355
e-mail: robert.brough@btconnect.com

The **Swan Coffee Shop** is proof positive that good things come in small packages. Run since 2001 by Robert and Wendy, it stands in the picturesque seaside village of Downderry, on the B3247 east of Seaton. Quality and hospitality are both to be found in abundance at this super little place, which is open seven days a week from 9 to 3.30, with summer opening hours extended to 7 o'clock. The printed menu runs from all-day breakfast (standard, large, vegetarian and individual items on toast) to sandwiches and toasties, jacket potatoes, cod & chips, Cornish pasties, steak & kidney pie and Cornish cream teas. The specials board adds to the choice with the likes of macaroni cheese,

'mighty big lasagne',

fisherman's pie, vegetable tagine and some super curries – beef Madras, Thai green chicken, chicken tikka. The enjoyment level stays high to the end with delicious desserts such as rhubarb crumble, chocolate waffle meltdown and date & orange sponge with a spicy syrup sauce. Why not try one of our delicious coffees or speciality teas with your dessert? The Swan also sells a selection of books, maps, souvenirs and novelties. Closed November, December and January. Cash only.

405

Fore Street, Lerryn, nr Lostwithiel,
Cornwall PL22 0PT
☎ 01208 872374   mob: 07803 712653
e-mail: enquiries@ theshipinnlerryn.co.uk
⊕ www.theshipinnlerryn.co.uk

The **Ship Inn** enjoys an idyllic riverside setting in the quiet and peaceful village of Lerryn, which lies on a minor road two miles south of Lostwithiel. Cornwall is renowned for its creeks, and few are as delightful as the creek where the Ship Inn stands by the River Towey. A stroll along the wooded creekside is a perfect prelude to this beautifully appointed 16th century inn, where the hospitality extended by tenants Jonnie and Ronnie and the fine food prepared by chef Hasan attracts both the local community and visitors to this lovely part of the world. In the bar, in the conservatory, in the restaurant or out in the garden diners can enjoy an impressive choice of food freshly prepared and cooked by the talented Hasan and his assistants. The bar menu offers pub classics like burgers,

omelettes, beer-battered Cornish cod and ham, egg & chips. Typical dishes on the exciting main menu range from garlic prawns with a white wine and cream sauce and farmhouse pâté to pork chop with apple & swede mash, Moroccan lamb tagine, the pie of the week, mushroom carbonara tagliatelle and chicken Diablo – with a piquant chilli and tomato sauce. There's a special young diners menu, and Sunday brings a choice of four roasts with a vegetarian option. An extensive wine list, with many available by the glass, complements the excellent food, and the bar also keeps a good selection of real ales (four in winter, six in summer). Pub hours are 10 to 3 and 5 to 12 Monday to Thursday and all day Friday, Saturday and Sunday. Food is served every lunchtime and evening. The setting and the expertise of the management and staff make the Ship a great venue for wedding receptions, family get-togethers and other celebrations.

It's also a perfect choice for a relaxing break or as a base for tourists. Five bedrooms in the main building – four doubles and a family room – have en suite facilities, television and hot beverage tray, and guests start the day with a generous breakfast (also available fro non-residents). Close to the pub, and accessible through the garden, Tides Reach is a two-bedroom cottage with wonderful views up and down the creek. This can be let on a B&B or self-catering basis, and Jonnie and Ronnie have a nearby Georgian farmhouse for self-catering. It's a great place for a walking, riding, fishing or touring holiday, or a family holiday on the nearby beaches.

Bodmin General Station, Bodmin,
Cornwall PL31 1AQ
☎ 01208 73666 Fax: 01208 77963
🌐 www.bodminandwenfordrailway.co.uk

A trip on the **Bodmin & Wenford Railway**
is a must for the whole family and absolutely
irresistible for anyone who can remember the
days when steam was king. It runs mainly
steam-hauled trains on a six-mile track,
providing a wonderful experience for both
railway enthusiasts and lovers of the
countryside. Throughout the 1830s and
1840s Cornwall was at the forefront of the
great expansion of the railways. Over the next decades plans were laid to link Bodmin to the main
line from London Paddington to Truro and Penzance. In 1887 a line was opened from Bodmin
Road (now Parkway) to Bodmin (now Bodmin General). A further line, from Bodmin General to
Boscarne Junction was opened in 1888 to connect with the Bodmin to Wadebridge line. In 1983

British Rail announced the closure of these
lines, and soon afterwards the Bodmin Railway
Preservation Society was formed to save the
lines. To raise the money needed to save the
stretch from Bodmin Parkway to Boscarne
Junction via Bodmin General the Bodmin &
Wenford Railway plc was formed. The railway
held its first Open Day in 1986 and in 1990
regular steam-hauled passenger trains began
running for the first time since 1967, linking
the two Bodmin stations; in 1996 trains began
running on the Bodmin-Boscarne line. The
restored HQ station, Bodmin General, has a
buffet and souvenir shop, and on most days
visitors can see locomotives being restored in
the engine shed. At Parkway, the junction with
the main line, passengers can alight visit our café in the old signal box and take a scenic walk to
Lanhydrock House. At Colesloggett Halt there's an opportunity to enjoy a walk in lovely
Cardinham Wood, and Boscarne provides a direct line to the Camel walking and cycling trail –
bikes are carried free on the trains. Among the resident steam locomotives are 4612, an ex-GWR 0-
6-0 pannier tank; 5552, an ex-GWR 2-6-2 tank; 4247, an ex-GWR 2-8-0 tank; and 30587, a

venerable ex-LSWR 2-4-0 well tank dating from
1874. The line also uses a number of vintage
diesels and a wide variety of restored carriages
and wagons. Besides the regular timetable the
railway has a year-long programme of special
events. Highlights for 2008 include a Steam.n
Gala and Beer Festival (5-7 September), a Diesel
Gala (27-28 September) and a Branch Line
Weekend (11-12 October). This marvellous
railway is operated largely by volunteers, and all
support, active or 'armchair', is welcome.
Facilities for wheelchair users are available on
most trains, with level access to the platforms.
Limited free parking is available at Bodmin
General but not at the other stations.

Blisland, nr Bodmin, Cornwall PL30 4JF
☎ 01208 850739

The **Blisland Inn**, one of the most popular pubs in the whole county, stands in the heart of a village signposted off the main A30 and the B3266. The handsome stone building with white-shuttered windows stands opposite Blisland's large village green on the site of the previous Victorian inn and since arriving here in 1993 hosts Margaret and Gary Marshall have made it a magnet for those who appreciate the qualities of the traditional

English country inn. Every inch of the beams and ceilings are covered in beer mats and mugs, and beer-related posters and memorabilia fill the walls, along with a fascinating collection of clocks and barometers.

Up to seven real ales are on tap in the bar and lounge, including Blisland Bulldog and Blisland Special brewed for the pub by a local micro-brewery. That number increases considerably during the annual beer festival, and in their time here Margaret and Gary have offered up to 2,000 different real ales from breweries large and small all across the United Kingdom. They also stock local farm cider, apple juice and fruit wines, as well as a full range of other drinks both alcoholic and non-alcoholic. The outstanding choice for real ale connoisseurs is matched by an excellent variety of home cooking that caters for a range of palates and appetites. Sandwiches, salads and basket meals are among the lighter snacks and meals, and favourite main courses include the fresh fish specials, lasagne, rib-eye and fillet steaks with all the trimmings and hearty home-made pies cooked in a rich beer gravy. Other choices – the menu changes daily – could include a spicy cauliflower soup, a platter of smoked salmon & prawns, moussaka, beef & tomato Madras curry and, for vegetarians, a tasty leek & mushroom bake. Seasonal game is another speciality. The food is served at lunchtime between 12 and 2 and in the evening from 6.30 to 9. It's best to book to be sure of a table in the evening and for Sunday lunch, when traditional roasts are the centrepiece. Families with children are very welcome (and their dogs) and the pub has a separate family room. All the major cards are accepted.

Blisland, reached down a maze of pretty country lanes, is a pleasant village with some fine Georgian and Victorian houses. It also has a church which no less a figure than Sir John Betjeman described as 'dazzling and amazing'. This is excellent walking country, with the Camel Trail and Blisland Manor Common nearby, and Margaret and Gary are always pleased to deal with fresh-air thirsts and appetites.

63 TINTAGEL CASTLE

Tintagel, Cornwall PL34 0HE
☎ 01840 770328
🌐 www.english-heritage.org.uk

For over 800 years the tale has been told that **Tintagel Castle** was the birthplace of King Arthur, born to the beautiful Queen Igerna and protected from evil by the magician Merlin, who lived in a cave below the fortress. But the history of the site goes back even further. Fragments of a Celtic monastic house dating from the 6th century have been unearthed on the headland and their origins certainly coincide with the activities of the Welsh military leader on which the Arthurian legends are thought to be based. The castle was, in fact, built in the 12th century, some 600 years after the time of King Arthur, by Reginald, Earl of Cornwall, the illegitimate son of Henry I. Whatever the truth behind the stories, the magic of this site, with Atlantic breakers crashing against the cliffs, certainly matches that of the tales of chivalry and wizardry.

In 1998 the discovery of a 6th century slate bearing the Latin inscription 'Artognov' - which translates as the ancient British name for Arthur - renewed the belief that Tintagel was Arthur's home. The cave, found at the foot of The Island, is known as **Merlin's Cave** and is said still to be haunted by a ghost. Tintagel is also of great interest to nature-lovers: the cliffs are at the heart of a Site of Special Scientific Interest, providing breeding grounds for sea birds, lizards and butterflies. Tintagel Castle is one of over 400 historic sites in the care of English Heritage.

64 THE VICTORY INN

Victory Hill, St Mawes,
Cornwall TR2 5DQ
☎ 01326 270324 Fax: 01326 270238
e-mail: contact@victory-inn.co.uk
🌐 www.victory-inn.co.uk

A warm welcome is guaranteed at the **Victory Inn**, the only traditional public house in the charming little town of St Mawes. The hospitality and food offered by Phil and Deborah Heslip have made the family-friendly Victory a real winner, and the wonderful location looking down on the harbour is a real bonus. Patrons can park on the quay (a few steps away) or in the main car park (75 metres). A good selection of beers and wines is served in the open-plan bar or out on the terrace. Sharps Doom Bar is the regular real ale, with two or three regularly rotating guests. The chef and his team prepare an excellent variety of food served lunchtime and evening and all day in the summer months – in the bar, in the elegant upstairs restaurant or out on the terrace.

The menus offer something for everyone, including fresh local seafood, steaks, pasta and vegetarian options. The

specials board extends the choice with tempting dishes such as tomato & basil soup, Thai fishcakes, sole meunière, flambéed chicken liver bruschetta and braised lamb shank with wholegrain mustard mash. The Victory also offers a comfortable holiday base with two well-appointed bedrooms with double beds and en suite bathrooms.

65 THE FOUR WINDS INN

Dracaena Avenue, Falmouth,
Cornwall TR11 2EW
☎ 01326 311369 Fax: 01326 312930
e-mail: nicavery@tiscali.co.uk

Nick and Ruth Avery have put their experience to excellent use at the **Four Winds Inn**, which stands in its own grounds not far from the centre of Falmouth. Equally popular with locals and visitors, the inn is open for drinks lunchtime, evening and all day at the weekend, and lunchtime and evening for food – booking is recommended at weekends and always in the summer. Ruth uses local produce in her splendid dishes, which run from moules marinière and deep-fried crab cakes to liver & bacon, mushroom stroganoff, salmon with dill sauce and steak & Tribute ale pie. A carvery operates every night and all day Sunday.

66 THE HALFWAY HOUSE

Rame Cross, Penryn, Cornwall TR10 9ED
☎ 01209 860222
e-mail: arbataxuk@yahoo.co.uk

The **Halfway House** is a popular and sociable public house standing on the A394 halfway between Falmouth and Helston. Leaseholders Dennis and Jenny Ingate have a warm welcome for all their patrons and a good variety of food and drink. There are definitely no half measures in the kitchen, where the chefs prepare a selection of dishes using local produce as much as possible and catering for all appetites. For the truly ravenous the chefs issue the Halfway House Challenge: finish a mighty Grill Platter, a 10oz rump steak, full rack of ribs, chicken breast served with chips, mushrooms tomatoes, vegetables or salad and BBQ sauce. The reward is a certificate and a free dessert.

67 THE WHITE HART

The Square, St Keverne, Helston,
Cornwall TR12 6ND
☎ 01326 280325
e-mail: mark@saffill.fsworld.co.uk
⊕ www.whitehartcornwall.co.uk

"Eat. Drink. Relax."

That's the invitation extended by Mark and Lesley Saffill at the **White Hart**, which stands on the village square in the picturesque village of St Keverne on the Lizard Peninsula (from Helston take the A3083 then the B3293). The inn, parts of which date back to the early 17th century, has a comfortable bar and lounge, where cask-conditioned ales, premium lagers and wines are served lunchtime and evening and all day at the weekend. Outside is a pleasant beer garden with a children's play area. Lesley is a super cook, and her food is served from 12 to 2 and from 6 to 9. The choice runs from lunchtime light bites and snacks to a

main menu that typically includes fresh Newlyn fish cooked in Doom Bar beer batter, lasagne, steaks, burgers, mushroom stroganoff and pizzas (also available to take away). For guests exploring this lovely part of the world the White Hart has three newly refurbished letting rooms – a double, a twin and a family room – with en suite facilities, television and tea/coffee tray. One room is fully adapted (including a walk-in wet room) for disabled guests. Each room has its own reserved car parking space.

Porkellis, Cornwall TR13 0JR
☎ 01326 340237
e-mail: starporkellis@btconnect.com

The **Star** is a superb inn situated in the picturesque village of Porkellis, which can be reached off the A394 Helston-Penryn road or the B3297 Helston-Redruth road. The 300-year-old inn is very definitely picture postcard material both outside and in the cosy, old-world interior, where the scene is set by a log-burning stove in a massive stone hearth and a long bar counter with an attractive white-painted wooden front. Owners Gunton and Louise Robinson have a real success on their hands, and not just with the loyal and thriving local trade, as the quality of the food and drink and the outstanding welcome are drawing customers like a magnet from an increasingly wide area. First-time visitors soon become old friends, and no-one can fail to be impressed by the high standards achieved by Gunton and Louise in every department. Three real ales are on tap in the bar: Skinner's Betty Stoggs ('the Queen of Cornish Ales') is the regular, and the two rotating guests could be any national or local ale. Louise is a super cook, seeking out prime local produce and treating it with the respect it deserves in the wide selection of dishes that leave diners happy, satisfied and looking forward to their next visit. Typical starters include shell-on prawns, chicken liver & brandy pâté and

balsamic-dressed fresh figs with crumbled gorgonzola and a bed of rocket leaves. Main courses span moules à la crème, pan-fried cod with tartare sauce and sauté potatoes, venison sausages, lamb shank, steaks and, for vegetarians, an aubergine, mozzarella & tomato bake. A selection of Cornish cheeses is an alternative to luscious desserts like chocolate torte. A lighter lunch menu offers soup, sandwiches, salads and fish, meat and cheese platters. A compact but comprehensive wine list covers Old and New Worlds and most of the major grape varieties, all chosen to complement Louise's menus. The old coach house at the back of the main building is being converted into a self-catering cottage with two bedrooms with everything needed for a comfortable, carefree holiday. When it is complete (ring for progress) it will provide a splendid, civilised base for a relaxing break or for discovering all the attractions of the area.

69 THE STAR INN

Vogue, St Day, Redruth,
Cornwall TR16 5NP
☎ 01209 820242
e-mail: thestarinnvogue@aol.com
🌐 www.starinnvogue.biz

The **Star Inn** is the hub of the little
community of Vogue, a hamlet of St Day
that's easy to find on the road between St Day
and Redruth. It is only a few minutes' drive
from the A30, off the A393 or B3298. It's a
great place for food, drink, entertainment and good company, with excellent hosts in Mark and
Rachel Graham. Mark has been in the trade for 30 years and has run the Star with Rachel since
2004. Five real ales will keep beer-drinkers happy, and Mark, an experienced and talented chef,

produces a wide variety of snacks and meals on bar and
restaurant menus. The choice spans sandwiches, jacket
potatoes, burgers, ploughman's lunches, scampi, salmon,
curries and steaks, with specials such as pasta with peppers,
bangers & champits and super pies – steak & ale, pork &
apple, chicken & ham. Food is served from 12 to 2.30
every day and from 6.30 to 9 every day except Wednesday.
Sunday brings traditional roasts, and booking is advisable.
Pool and darts are played in the separate games room, and
outside is a boules pitch, as well as outside tables and chairs
and ample off-road parking. Cash and cheque only.

70 CLIFF HOUSE

The Square, Portreath,
Cornwall TR16 4LE
☎ 01209 843847
e-mail: simon.viv.haywood@gmail.com
🌐 www.cliffhouseportreath.com

Cliff House enjoys a splendid location on the
Square at Portreath, tucked under the cliff and
a short walk from the sandy beach. Dating
from the late-18th century, it's a first venture
into this type of business for Simon and Viv
Haywood. They took over the hotel in August
2007 and are rapidly building a fine reputation for the excellent hospitality and facilities they offer
their guests. The accommodation comprises five comfortable rooms, three with en suite, two with
private shower rooms (one ensuite room is downstairs for the less able) available all year round.
The tariff includes a generous breakfast (with lighter options) served at a time to suite the guest in
the pleasant flag-floored, white-walled sun room. Portreath is a thriving but pleasantly

uncommercialised holiday centre, once a busy port exporting
copper from the local, mines and importing coal. It's a popular
choice with families and surfers and a great base for walkers.
There are miles of walks in nearby Tehidy Country Park, and
some of the old tram-roads are now foot and cycle paths. The
village is the starting point of the Mineral Tramway Walks. One
of the most visited local attractions is the Cornish Goldsmiths
at Tolgus, with the largest collection of gold jewellery in the
West Country.

71 | THE TARBERT HOTEL

Clarence Street, Penzance,
Cornwall TR18 2NU
☎ 01736 363758 Fax: 01736 331336
e-mail: reception@anicelittlehotel.com
🌐 www.anicelittlehotel.com
🌐 www.tarberthotel.co.uk

The **Tarbert Hotel** has long been recognised as one of the very best in Penzance and the region for comfort, service and cuisine. Built in the 1830s for a sea captain, it is kept in shipshape condition thanks to the leadership of the owners and business partners Sam Ryan and Michael Dibben and the efforts of their hardworking, motivated staff.

No detail has been overlooked in the all-year accommodation, which consist of 12 bedrooms with ultra-modern en suite bathrooms with power showers, high-quality décor and furnishings, digital Freeview TV and wireless internet connection, hairdryer, shaver point and complimentary beverage tray. Guests have the services of an in-house laundry, and transport to and from coaches, railways, the ferries and the heliport can be arranged. Rooms can be hired on a Bed & Breakfast or Dinner, Bed & Breakfast basis, and in the bright, airy dining room a high-quality breakfast, with fruit, yoghurt and cereals before a generous cooked plateful, is served between 7.30 and 9.30.

Breakfast gives but a hint of the pleasure that awaits diners in this outstanding small hotel. Prime local produce, including fish and shellfish from the renowned Newlyn fish market, is the basis of the superb dishes that make up the lunchtime menu and the evening à la carte. The chefs display a combination of technique and innovation at the highest level, as shown by dishes that live up to their mouthwatering menu descriptions. Starters might include smoked Newlyn haddock on wilted spinach with melted ricotta, pan-seared scallops on sweet potato mash with a sweet chilli dressing, and brandied terrine of duck and pork, while main courses are typified by pan-fried cod fillet on a lemon scented mash with an oyster and coriander butter sauce, or best end of lamb with a heather honey and rosemary glaze on braised beetroot with a port sauce. The treat continues to the end with superb desserts like café au lait brûlée or malted bread pudding served with crème anglaise. The recently refurbished reception area makes an immediate favourable impression – an eyecatching fish tank is built into the counter – that continues throughout the public rooms. The fully stocked bar, with exposed stone walls and comfortable armchairs and settees, is open all day for teas and coffees as well as beers, lagers, wines and spirits.

413

The Digey, St Ives, Cornwall TR26 1HR
☎ 01736 797977

Remember as a child visiting your granny's house and going into her kitchen just as she was taking one of her special cakes or a loaf of home-baked bread out of the oven? The warm, wonderful smell left you with just one thought – to tuck into a piece or a slice. That's the sort of feeling you'll get at **Bumbles Tea Room**, with hospitality to match that irresistible aroma. A tea room for more than 20 years, the 200-year-old building stands on a corner site in the heart of busy St Ives, with views of the seashore.

The delightful owner and greeter Tammy Fraser has been here since 2003 and has made this a really popular tourist destination as well as a much-loved meeting and eating place among the local community. There are 24 seats in the bright, airy, well-decorated room, and a further eight outside at a couple of tables on the pavement. Tammy is lucky to have local cake-maker Yvonne Gail as a regular supplier of delicious cakes and pastries that has everyone licking their lips over the display cabinet: lemon meringue pie, apple pie, carrot cake, tray bakes, teacakes, scones, cheesecake.........and many more. Some wheat-free and gluten-free cakes are usually available. On the savoury side, sandwiches plain or toasted are made

to order on wholemeal, granary or white bread, jacket potatoes come with a dozen or more tasty fillings, and salads are based round ham, cheese, pâtés, crab in season or a hand-raised chicken & leek pie. Hot options include cheese on toast and scrambled eggs with smoked salmon. The finest Cornish butter and cream are used, and desserts include a selection of luscious Cornish ice cream. Children are welcome, even mothers with babies in buggies, and Bumbles keeps a supply of toys and games to keep the little ones happy.

The tea room is open from 10 to 6 between Easter and October, but if the weather is good and the tourists are hungry, it will open out of season – and St Ives attracts visitors throughout the year with its numerous scenic, historic and cultural delights. But nothing can beat the allure of Bumbles Tea Room, which once visited is never forgotten – just like those visits to grandma!

Longrock, nr Penzance,
Cornwall TR20 8JJ
☎ 01736 710416 Fax: 01736 710416

Mount View Hotel is a detached Victorian building standing 100 yards from the beach in the centre of Longrock, two miles east of Penzance. Longrock itself is in the middle of a three-mile stretch of beach that runs from Penzance to Marazion, and the views out into Mount's Bay are truly spectacular. The distinctive stone-built hotel has been run since 1990 by Doreen Capper, whose enthusiasm and personality ensure that the mood in the hotel is always friendly and relaxed. From 1986 to 1991 it was called the Rock Inn, but when Doreen took over she changed it back to its original name, which came from the fine views it commanded over St Michael's Mount and beyond.

The bar, which is open all day, seven days a week except between 4 and 7 on Sunday, is a popular local meeting place and also attracts many of the tourists who flock to this lovely part of the world to enjoy the scenery, the sights and the history. A fire in the feature stone hearth keeps the chill at bay in the smart dining area, where food is served from 12 to 3 and from 7 to 9. Doreen's cooking entices with a splendid selection of dishes on menus that cast their nets wide. Locally landed fish is very popular, and dishes that always go down a treat are her fisherman's pie and a trio of Cornish fish – perhaps lemon sole, haddock and monkfish. Crab and tomato soup is a subtle and delicious starter, and favourite main courses for meat-eaters include home-made pies – cottage, steak & kidney, chicken & mushroom – and steaks served with all the trimmings and a choice of pepper, creamy garlic & mushroom and wholegrain mustard sauces. Vegetarians are well catered for, too, with dishes like mushroom stroganoff or broccoli, potato & cream cheese bake, and diners should definitely leave room for delectable desserts such as home-made fruit pie or crumble or sticky toffee pudding. Sandwiches, salads and jacket potatoes are available for smaller appetites or those with less time to spare, but this really is a place to relax and enjoy the best of Cornish cooking to the full. Mount View is also a great place for a short break or longer holiday.

Five upstairs rooms, three of them with en suite facilities, are available all year for Bed & Breakfast guests, and to the rear of the main building is a newly refurbished self-catering cottage that is fully equipped for disabled guests. Two bedrooms and an easy-access wet room are on the ground floor, and a lift gives access to the lounge and kitchen above.

415

73 TATE ST IVES

Porthmeor Beach, St Ives,
Cornwall TR26 1TG
☎ 01736 796226
🌐 www.tate.org.uk

St Ives has attracted artists of renown for well over a century, and among early visitors were Turner, Whistler and Sickert. That tradition continues in **Tate St Ives**, housed in a superb modern three-storey building backing directly into the cliff face. The gallery offers a unique introduction to contemporary and modern art, and many works can be viewed in the surroundings that inspired them. Apart from the permanent and changing exhibitions, Tate St Ives stages regular special events and talks. It also manages the town's Barbara Hepworth Museum and Sculpture Garden.

75 THE KINGS ARMS

5 Market Square, St Just, Penzance,
Cornwall TR19 7HF
☎ 01736 788545

The **Kings Arms** stands by the 15th century church on the market square of mainland Britain's westernmost town. Rich in history and tradition, this fine old stone inn has a lovely old-world bar with beamed ceiling, exposed stone walls, panelling and country-style chairs set at polished darkwood tables. Reg Robinson and his daughter Krystie welcome visitors all day long with a good range of drinks, and the chef uses local produce for a selection of dishes that can also be enjoyed throughout the day (cold dishes only between 2 and 6). The red telephone box that stands outside is a nostalgic touch.

76 THE QUEENS ARMS

Botallack, St Just, Cornwall TR19 7QG
☎ 01736 788318
🌐 www.queensarms-botallack.com

The **Queens Arms** is a fine country inn located in the coastal village of Botallack, off the B3306 a mile north of St Just. In the Grade II listed building beams, exposed stonework, an open fire in a vast stone hearth, local photographs and hundreds of beer mats paint a traditional scene in the bar, where John and Helen Hulse, their son Matthew and his partner Terri ensure that the atmosphere is always warm and welcoming. The bar is open all day, every day, for drinks, which include three or four real ales. That number rises to up to 40 during the pub's September beer festival. The chefs do excellent work in the kitchen, putting the emphasis on fresh local produce. The fish specials – plaice, sea bream, gurnard, red mullet – are always popular, and other favourites include steaks, pasta, steak & mushroom pie, moules marinière and chilli con carne (as hot as you like). Room should be left for delicious desserts like treacle tart or Cornish saffron bread & butter pudding. Children are welcome, and the pub has a smartly refurbished family room. Outside is a pleasant garden with lawns, trees and shrubs, as well as ample off-road parking. In the grounds of the pub, the Queen's Lodge offers quiet, comfortable self-catering accommodation for two.

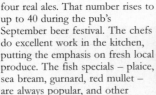

77 THE PUNCH BOWL

Barrows Green, Kendal,
Cumbria LA8 0AA
☎ 01539 560267
e-mail: caroline.dent@btconnect.com

Having been a member of staff for some years, Caroline Dent took over the tenancy of the **Punch Bowl** early in 2005. The handsome whitewashed roadside inn, which dates from the mid-19th century, stands a short distance from the A65 to the south of Kendal. Caroline has been the major

mover in creating the immaculate interior that greets visitors with beams, pillars, gleaming brass, comfortable banquettes and rustic furniture in the long bar. A beer garden at the back provides an equally pleasant alternative in the summer. The bar is open from 11.30 every day of the week, and traditional pub food, cooked to order from fresh local produce, is served from 12 to 2 and 6 to 9 Monday to Saturday and from 12 to 8.30 on Sunday. Sandwiches,

baguettes and baked potatoes make hearty quick snacks, while main courses include scampi, lasagne, chilli, rump and gammon steaks, roast chicken, steak pie and braised beef with dumplings. Specials like tuna pasts bake and lemon chicken tagliatelle provide even more choice, and vegetarians are well catered for with dishes such as mushroom stroganoff or three-cheese broccoli pasta bake. A choice of roasts is added to the menu on Sunday. Children are welcome, and the inn accepts the major credit cards.

79 WILF'S CAFÉ

Mill Yard, Back Lane, Staveley, nr Kendal,
Cumbria LA8 9LR
☎ 01539 822329 Fax: 01539 822969
e-mail: food@wilfs-cafe.co.uk
🌐 www.wilfs-cafe.co.uk

Overlooking the River Kent in the village of Staveley, a mile off the A591 Kendal-Windermere road, **Wilf's Café** has been serving fresh, wholesome snacks and meals to an appreciative public since 1997. Wilf, Charlotte, chef Martin and his team produce an excellent range that spans

breakfasts (classic English or vegetarian), sandwiches, salads, baked potatoes, rarebits, chilli and mouthwatering cakes, pastries, slices and shortbread. To drink, there's a choice of Fairtrade coffees and teas, hot chocolate, juices, soft drinks and milkshakes. The café is linked commercially to its neighbour the Hawkshead Brewery, and visitors can look round, sample a brew or two and bring back a glass to enjoy with a meal – or the other way round, taking the food to the brewery's bar area.

Wilf's Café (eat in or take away) is open from 10 to 5 all year

round, and the whole place can be hired for parties. The owners organise regular speciality evenings with guest speakers and offer a full outside buffet service. The café stands on the site of an old mill for the bobbin industry and is now home to a number of craft-related enterprises – the café's tables were made in the courtyard, as is the bread served in the café.

Yard 2, Stricklangdale, Kendal,
Cumbria LA9 4ND
☎ 01539 738480
⊕ www.dickiedoodles.com

Open every evening from 8 till late, **Dickie Doodles** is a magnet for lovers of good music and well-kept ales. Shaun Bainbridge dreamed of a live music venue open seven days a week and in 1999 he took over these premises, closed and empty at the time, and transformed them into what has become an unqualified success with a wide appeal. It is home to a multitude of musical talent covering many areas of the modern music spectrum and with performers ranging from talented amateurs to well-known professionals. It's music all the way, and the whitewashed walls are hung with musical instruments as well as modern artwork.

The week unfolds as follows:
· Monday: Acoustic jamming
· Tuesday: Electric jamming
  (there's a super in-house sound system)
· Wednesday: Traditional folk music
· Thursday: New and up-and-coming bands
· Friday and Saturday: Professional rock bands
· Sunday: Some or all of the above

Entrance (over-18s only) is free, and drinks (cash only) include a good choice of draught and bottled beers and lagers. Shaun and joint-owner Paul Crombie-Noble plan to make cask ale and food available in 2008.

Dickie Doodles also shows arts and crafts exhibitions showcasing the work of talented local artists and makers. Shaun is a blacksmith by trade and some of his forgework is also on display. Stricklandgate is one of the busy narrow streets at the heart of old Kendal, and the yards (alleyways) are a distinctive feature of the town. They were a defence against the constant threat posed by marauding Scots and could be sealed off by closing the single small entrance, keeping families and livestock safe inside. The Scottish have long since abated, and it's now tourists from around the world who come in peace to Kendal throughout the year. And for those who love their music, Dickie Doodles is definitely the place to head for.

Main Street, Dent, nr Sedbergh,
Cumbria LA10 5QL
☎ 01539 625256
e-mail: mail@thegeorgeanddragon.co.uk
⊕ www.thegeorgeanddragondent.co.uk

The **George & Dragon** stands on a prominent corner site on the cobbled main street of Dent, a charming village in one of Cumbria's finest Dales. With experienced licensees John and Anne Wilkins at the helm, it has everything a visitor could wish for, and has long been a favourite with both the local community and the many tourists who are attracted to this lovely part of the world.

The public rooms are relaxed and invitingly traditional in style, with roaring log fires to keep things cosy in even the coldest months. The bar is truly a place for the real ale connoisseur, with up to seven brews, most from their own brewery located some two miles away. Founded in 1990, the Dent Brewery is surely one of the most remote in the country, in a beautiful corner of the Yorkshire Dales National Park (though it is actually in Cumbria).

The choice of real ales served in the George & Dragon's bar jumps to around 40 during the 4-day Beer Festival held annually at the end of June. In the spacious dining areas outstanding food is produced by John and his talented team in the

kitchen, served from 12 to 2 and 6 to 8 in the winter and from 12 till about 9 in the summer. Traditional and contemporary dishes might include crispy black pudding with a tomato topping (a particularly tasty starter), grilled pork loin charcutière, cherry-glazed chicken with a port & walnut sauce, halibut joinville (cooked in white wine, with a mushroom, prawn and cheese sauce) and the chef's own game pie – rabbit, venison, partridge and pheasant cooked in red wine with apricots. The lunch and bar menu provides an equally excellent, less formal selection.

With its attractive setting and top-class service the George & Dragon is a popular venue for functions and special occasions. It also offers excellent guest accommodation in ten upstairs en suite bedrooms – doubles, twins and family rooms cater for most requirements. Right outside the inn is Dent's best-known landmark, the famous pinkish Shap granite memorial fountain to Adam Sedgwick, the 'Father of Geology', who was born here in 1785, the son of the local vicar.

Another landmark is the impressive St Andrew's Church with local marble paving and a three-decker Jacobean pulpit.

81 THE SNOOTY FOX HOTEL

Main Street, Kirkby Lonsdale,
Cumbria LA6 2AH
☎ 01524 271308
e-mail: snootyfoxhotel@talktalk.net
⊕ www.thesnootyfoxhotel.co.uk

For many regular visitors to Cumbria, the **Snooty Fox** is *the* place to stay. This charming, atmospheric Jacobean inn has long won acclaim for its food, beer, wine and accommodation, all of which

Glen and Lynn Massam have reinforced and enhanced since they took over in June 2007. They are already attracting new devotees by the day, whether they've dropped in for a drink and a snack, allowed time for an excellent meal or booked in for a relaxed short break or longer stay. The old-world ambience of the bar is perfect for enjoying a drink and a chat – the cask ales have earned Cask Marque recognition. The bar is open all day, every day, and for diners in the elegant restaurant a talented

team in the kitchen prepare an exciting, imaginative menu for lunch and dinner. Typical choices might be salmon & prawn cakes, risotto of artichokes, leeks & spinach with Cumbrian cheese and tarragon, and 28-day matured sirloin steak with a mustard crust, wild mushrooms and confit vegetables. For guests lingering awhile in this lovely part of the world the Snooty Fox has nine pretty bedrooms with en suite facilities, television and complimentary hot drinks tray.

82 THE CROSS KEYS HOTEL

1 Park Road, Milnthorpe,
Cumbria LA7 7AB
☎ 01539 562115 Fax: 01539 562446
e-mail: stay@thecrosskeyshotel.co.uk
⊕ www.thecrosskeyshotel.co.uk

'Come and unwind at the **Cross Keys**'
That's the invitation extended by Ian and Sandra Mills at their comfortably modernised three-storey inn standing on a corner site in the heart of Milnthorpe, where the

B5282 meets the A6. And indeed this *is* a great place to relax and unwind, as well as being a cosy, convenient base for touring a part of the country that abounds in places of scenic

and historic attraction. The cask ales, including Hartley's XB, are kept in perfect condition, earning the inn Cask Marque recognition.The menus offer a good choice for lunchers and diners, typified by crispy battered cod, Hartley's Cumbrian steak & ale pie, roast chicken and lamb rogan josh. Ian and Sandra are both keen and talented cooks, and in addition to the usual menus they organise regular cheese & wine evenings, steak nights and curry nights. The guest accommodation comprises eight super en suite rooms including two family rooms (a cot is available for wee ones). A two-bedroom self-catering cottage is also available. The inn has a large function room, ample off-road parking, a pleasant garden and a newly created covered and heated patio area complete with greenery and Sky TV.

420

83 THE ROYAL OAK INN

The Square, Cartmel, Cumbria LA11 6LB
☎ 01539 536259
⊕ www.royaloakcartmel.co.uk

The oldest pub in historic Cartmel is a magnet for locals and visitors from out of town who want the very best in well-kept ales and delicious food – with a warm welcome guaranteed and four rooms for Bed & Breakfast guests. The **Royal Oak Inn** is the first venture into the trade for Darren and Louise Allcock, who both come from nearby Windermere. The interior of the inn is beautifully decorated and furnished, and the cosy fires, the comfortable seats and the brass-adorned beams create a wonderfully relaxing ambience for meeting or making friends over a drink – Black Sheep, Castle Eden and Timothy Taylor Landlord are the regular real ales, and the inn keeps a good selection of Old and New World wines. Secluded at the back is a lovely riverside garden. Three chefs are kept busy preparing a superb variety of food featuring mainly local produce and served every day from 11.30 to 9. Typifying the tempting choice are traditional Cumberland sausage, Higginsons renowned black pudding, beer-battered haddock, salmon hollandaise, steak, mushroom & ale pie, Aberdeen Angus burgers, steaks and grilled smoked haddock topped with a poached egg. And what better way to finish than a helping of Cartmel's own sticky toffee pudding! Cartmel is a lovely place to spend a few days, and the Royal Oak provides a comfortable, civilised base with four en suite upstairs rooms for B&B guests; a full Cumbrian breakfast starts the day.

85 THE DEVONSHIRE ARMS

1 Bradley's Terrace, Ulverston,
Cumbria LA12 0DH
☎ 01229 582537

Hardworking hosts Julie and Cath run the most sociable of pubs, with a friendly greeting for all who enter the convivial bar. A changing real ale and draught keg ales are popular thirst-quenchers in the **Devonshire Arms**, and appetites large and small are satisfied by an excellent choice of home-cooked pub classics. It's also a sporty sort of  place, with darts, dominoes and quiz teams in action most days of the week. The pub, which has a secluded rear garden, is open from 7 on Monday and Tuesday and all day the rest of the week. Food is served from 12 to 2 and 5 to 8 Wednesday to Saturday and from 12 to 6 on Sunday. No credit cards.

Looking for:
- *Places to Visit?*
- *Places to Stay?*
- *Places to Eat & Drink?*
- *Places to Shop?*

COUNTRY LIVING MAGAZINE — RURAL GUIDES

HIDDEN INNS

HIDDEN PLACES

COUNTRY Pubs & Inns

off the motorway 3rd edition

www.travelpublishing.co.uk

84 UPLANDS COUNTRY HOUSE HOTEL

Haggs Lane, Cartmel, Cumbria LA11 6HD
☎ 01539 536248 Fax: 01539 536848
e-mail: enquiries@uplandshotel.co.uk
⊕ www.uplands.uk.com

Standing in its own grounds a short walk from the centre of Cartmel, **Uplands Country House Hotel** has for many years been among the leaders in its field. The setting is delightful, with truly magnificent views from the hotel and grounds over the rolling green countryside and the Leven estuary. To the outstanding location must be added a warm, welcoming atmosphere enhanced by the new proprietors, stylish

accommodation and excellent cuisine that brings patrons from many miles around.

Booking is essential for non-residents in the 60-cover restaurant, where top-quality food is served from 12 to 2 at lunchtime and from 7 o'clock in the evening. Technique and innovation combine at an admirably high level in lovely dishes like pheasant, duck & rabbit terrine; smoked salmon and gravlax on a bed of rocket leaves with a dill hollandaise; seared scallops set on a julienne of vegetables with a ginger & coriander dressing; and supreme of chicken with a wild mushroom sauce. Raspberry crème brûlée and home-made vanilla & praline ice cream provide delightful finales to a memorable meal. The five en suite bedrooms (5 Diamonds rating) are very comfortably furnished and prettily decorated, and the comfort and amenities, including books and magazines, contribute to a real home-from-home feel.

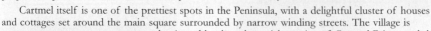

Guests can relax and unwind in the comfortable, stylish residents' lounge after a day spent exploring the beautiful Cumbrian countryside, meet the other guests and plan the next day's activities. Uplands is also a popular venue for wedding parties and other special occasions. It lies a few miles south of the Lake District proper and provides the ideal base for a peaceful, restful holiday.

Cartmel itself is one of the prettiest spots in the Peninsula, with a delightful cluster of houses and cottages set around the main square surrounded by narrow winding streets. The village is dominated by the substantial remains of Cartmel Priory, and the Church of St Mary & St Michael is among the most beautiful in the county. Cartmel also has one of the most delightful and intimate of all the country's racecourses, attracting happy crowds with several days of summer jumping. Other attractions in the vicinity include Cumbria's premier stately home, Holker Hall, set in formal gardens and grounds that include the Lakeland Motor Museum. The pleasant little bayside town of Grange-over-Sands, a favourite of Beatrix Potter, and the miniature village in Flookburgh are also close by.

86 THE DERBY ARMS

Horse Close Lane, Great Urswick,
nr Ulverston, Cumbria LA12 0SP
☎ 01229 586348
e-mail: thederbyarms@yahoo.co.uk
⊕ www.gocities.com/thederbyarms

Experienced licensees Judith and Stephen Davidson took over the reins at the **Derby Arms** at the end of 2007 after running inns in Yorkshire for many years. The whole place has a particularly warm, homely appeal, fully justifying its claim to be the 'local

friendly pub with traditional beer'. The traditional beer comes from the Robinson's Brewery range, and among other drinks favoured by the regulars are Carling Black Label and Cumbrian Lakeland Mild. Judith is expanding the food side of the business, expending the availability beyond the light snacks for Saturday lunch and the Sunday roasts served from 12 to 4 (phone for further food details).

Guest accommodation in an annexe comprises two double and two twin rooms, all with en suite facilities,

central heating, television, radio, hot drinks tray and hairdryer. The inn is ideal for a relaxing weekend break, a quiet retreat with good walking, birdwatching and fishing nearby (fishing permits can be obtained at the inn). It also provides easy access to many of the top tourist attractions in the Lakes and the Furness Peninsula. With pool and darts teams playing in the local leagues, the Derby Arms is very much the social hub of the picturesque village of Great Urswick, which lies off the A590 south of Ulverston. Cash and cheque only.

87 THE CROFTERS

Holbeck Park Avenue, Barrow-in-Furness,
Cumbria LA13 0RE
☎ 01229 825420
e-mail: alislaw@msn.com

With its excellent shopping, the largest indoor market in the area and an impressive heritage museum, Barrow-in-Furness has plenty to interest the visitor. And when the time comes for a break, the **Crofters** is one of the very best places to choose. This attractive, welcoming inn is run by Alison and David Lawson, who came here at the end of 2007 after running a pub in Lancaster, and before that a restaurant in Spain.

The very smart interior – red is a feature of the carpets and the stylish modern chairs – is a convivial place for enjoying a drink (Thwaites provides the real ales) and a meal. Most of the ingredients that go into the kitchen are locally sourced to produce a selection of dishes served

lunchtime and evening Monday to Friday and all day Saturday and Sunday. Tried and tested favourites such as cod in batter, sirloin steak and surf 'n' turf are typical choices on the specials board. Summer brings an additional attraction in the shape of barbecues and hog roasts. The inn has a large off-road car park and a lovely paved terrace with wooden picnic sets – a real boon in the summer months.

Princes Street, Broughton-in-Furness,
Cumbria LA20 6HQ
☎ 01229 716529
e-mail: dpike91556@aol.com
🌐 www.blackcockinncumbria.com

The **Black Cock Inn**, which stands at the heart of the attractive little town of Broughton-in-Furness, offers the very best in hospitality, food, drink and accommodation. In spring and summer, window boxes and hanging baskets add splashes of colour to the immaculate black-and-white frontage, and the promise of the exterior is amply fulfilled within. As befits a building that dates back as far as the 15th century, the interior is rich in old-world charm, and the lounge bar with its low-beamed ceiling and roaring winter log fires is the perfect spot for meeting friends and enjoying a drink.

The bar is open all day, every day, for drinks, which include a selection of five real ales – Theakston's Best and Marston's Pedigree are the regulars. That choice increases to about 15 during the inn's annual Beer Festival, which usually takes place in the first week in November. The inn also has a lovely leafy secluded beer garden, and tables and chairs are also set out at the front in the summer months. The inn is in the very capable hands of go-ahead landlord David Pike, whose enthusiasm and motivation have contributed greatly to the popularity of the old place. The improvements he has made, all carefully planned to blend with the inn's character and heritage, include a very smart and stylish extension.

Great credit also goes to the head chef and his talented team, who have made this a popular destination restaurant with excellent menus that provide a tempting mix of pub classics and more exotic and adventurous

choices. Black pudding & bacon salad, slow-roasted lamb shank, chicken breast filled with chorizo and cream cheese, salmon with a prawn, dill & lemon cream sauce – the choice is truly mouthwatering, and everything is prepared and cooked from the best seasonal ingredients. Food is served in the roomy dining area from 12 to 2 and 5 to 9 (12 to 9 on Sundays and in the summer months). Booking is recommended at the weekend. Children are very welcome, and they can even choose from their own special menu. The Black Cock is a great place to stay when touring the Furnesss and Cartmel Peninsulas, and the five en suite bedrooms include a family suite. Broughton is a very pleasant place for a stroll, with some fine Georgian houses including the house where Bramwell Brontë stayed while working as a tutor.

88 THE BLACK DOG INN

Broughton Road, Dalton-in-Furness,
Cumbria LA15 8JP
☎ 01229 462561
e-mail: jhoward@hotmail.com

James Howarth, keeper of the ales, and Andy Turner, master of the stoves, make a fine team at the **Black Dog Inn**, which lies a short walk from the centre of Dalton-in-Furness. It's a walk well worth taking, as the reward for a visit to this pristine 300-year-old inn is a superb choice of real ales and outstanding food. Six real ales from national and local breweries are kept in tip-top condition, and chalkboards give details of beers such as Hornbeam Top Hop (from Manchester) and Wyre Piddle in the Hole from the Worcestershire Wyre Piddle Brewery. The choice grows to more than 20 to sample during the inn's spring, autumn and winter Beer Festivals (phone for times). The pub was declared Furness CAMRA Pub of the

Season for autumn 2007. Other boards tempt the taste buds with a wide choice of dishes freshly cooked from prime local ingredients. Classics like beer-battered cod, lamb's liver and steaks share the menu with exciting options such as venison & chestnut pie, wild mushroom risotto cake stuffed with stilton and coffee-infused crème brûlée. This super food is served from 4 to 9 on Tuesday, from 12 to 9 Wednesday to Saturday and from 12 to 7 on Sunday, and it's wise to book at all times. The inn is closed on Monday except Bank Holidays, open from 4 on Tuesday and all day Wednesday to Sunday.

91 THE LUTWIDGE ARMS HOTEL

Holmrook, Cumbria CA19 1UH
☎ 019467 24230
Fax: 019467 24100
e-mail: mail@lutwidgearms.co.uk
⊕ www.lutwidgearms.co.uk

The **Lutwidge Arms Hotel** is the social hub of the village of Holmrook, which stands on the main A595 coastal road that runs all the way up from Barrow to Carlisle. Michael and Elena Law run this black-and-white Victorian

roadside inn, which takes its name from the Lutwidge family of nearby Holmrook Hall – its best-known member was Charles Lutwidge Dodson, better known as Lewis Carroll. The bar is open lunchtime and evening and all day in peak season for a wide range of drinks, and the chefs are kept busy producing excellent snacks and meals for bar and restaurant menus served from 12 to 2 and from 6 to 9. Local ingredients are used as much as possible in

dishes that span favourites like garlic mussels, crispy-battered haddock, curries, gammon and fillet steaks, meat and vegetable lasagne and the day's hearty stew. Desserts such as fruit crumble, sticky toffee pudding and ginger sponge keep up the enjoyment level to the end. The River Irt, famous for salmon and sea trout, flows past the front of the hotel, and there are many opportunities for walking and sightseeing close by. The Lutwidge Arms has 16 well-appointed bedrooms, en suite with bath or shower or both. Four rooms on the ground floor include one with wheelchair access.

Boot, Eskdale, Holmrook,
Cumbria CA19 1TH
☎ 019467 23230
e-mail: enquiries@woolpack.co.uk
🌐 www.woolpack.co.uk
🌐 www.bootbeer.co.uk

The **Woolpack Inn** lies in beautiful Eskdale, in a quiet, remote location far away from the tourist trails and the hubbub of city life. When Dave and Ann took over the inn in 2004 it needed a breath of life. And it certainly got one, with the result that it is one of the top destinations in the region, superb in every department and much loved by walkers and lovers of the great outdoors. The usual approach is on minor roads from the A595 at Holmrook or Ravenglass, but it can also be reached from the other direction. It stands on an old drovers road out of Boot towards Hardknott Pass and on to Wrynose Pass and into the Langdales. This is one of the most spectacular scenic routes in the Lake District, and one that is for intrepid travellers – it involves several arduous twists and turns and gradients as steep as 1 in 3. The reward for undertaking either journey is to arrive at an inn that excels in everything it does.

The Victorian frontage hides a much older interior, with parts dating back as far as 1578 and evidence in the thick stone and granite walls and the great trusses in the attic. One of the inn's most unusual assets is its own brewery in adjoining premises. In the **Hardknott Brewery** Dave oversees the production (and sampling!) of a range of cask-conditioned ales, usually from 6 to 10. They also champion several other Cumbrian micro-breweries and stock a selection of Continental draught and bottle beers, fruit beers and real ciders. In peak season they keep up to six real ales, which increases to around nine during the annual beer festival (the date for 2008 is June 5 to 8 and is normally the 2nd week in June).

The inn's daytime menu is mainly based on ploughman's platters and casseroles but the chefs really flex their wide-ranging talents on the exciting, innovative evening menu. The UK, Europe and the Far East provide the inspiration for dishes that make superb use of the best local produce. Guest accommodation (March to October, otherwise by arrangement) comprises eight characterful rooms, six with en suite facilities, all with satellite TV and beverage tray. One room is a romantic and luxurious four-poster room with a double spa bath. This marvellous place is open all day from March to October, Thursday to Sunday in November and February and more limited times (best to phone) in December and January. Guest accommodation is also available in November and February.

Nether Wasdale, nr Santon Bridge,
Cumbria CA20 1ET
☎ 01946 726237
Fax: 01946 726122
e-mail: info@strands hotel.com
🌐 www.strands hotel.com

One of the Lake District's premier hotels, the **Strands Hotel** enjoys a scenic location in the picturesque village of Nether Wasdale, close to Wast Water in the heart of Wasdale. Since the summer of 2006, the hotel has been owned and run by Mark and Lesley Corr, a friendly couple with a genuine welcome for all their customers.

The hotel has two bars with roaring log fires in winter where guests have the choice of a minimum of 4 real ales. In February 2007 Mark established his own micro-brewery which now produces a variety of ales including Errmmm Bitter, T'Errmmminator and Corrs Berg!

Food is taken seriously at the Strands. The printed menu and daily specials board present an appetising choice of meals which are served every lunchtime and evening; evenings only out of season. Amongst the starters there's always a tasty home-made soup and dishes such as Roasted Goats Cheese Stack - roasted goats cheese layered with roast peppers, served on a fresh leaf salad and with a pesto dressing. For the main course, how about Wild Local Venison Casserole, a fresh Whole Turbot or, for vegetarians, a Goats Cheese Tart? Such is the popularity of the Strands' restaurant that booking is strongly advised on weekend evenings, and for all evenings during the season. All major credit cards are accepted.

Strands also offers excellent accommodation in 14 attractively furnished and decorated guest bedrooms, 12 of which have en suite facilities. The other 2 rooms will also become en suite during the lifetime of this edition. All the rooms are upstairs. Guests have their own cosy residents' lounge; there's an attractive beer garden; and plenty of off-road parking. The Strands welcomes children and dogs. The B&B tariff includes a hearty traditional breakfast that sets guests up for a day of discovering the local attractions. These include lovely beaches just 6 miles away, golf, Muncaster Castle and the Owl Centre, the Roman fort at Hardknott and the La'al Ratty Steam Railway.

93 THE STANLEY ARMS HOTEL

Calderbridge, Seascale,
Cumbria CA20 1DN
☎ 01946 841235 Fax: 01946 841759
e-mail: info@stanleyarmshotel.com
🌐 www.stanleyarmshotel.com

The **Stanley Arms Hotel** is an 18th century former coaching inn that once had its own blacksmith's forge. It stands by the main A595 at Calder Bridge, in leafy lawned grounds that run down to the River Calder. It's a first venture into

this type of business for Wayne and Angela, who purchased the freehold in November 2007, and their effort and enthusiasm will ensure that they have a success on their hands. The bar is open every lunchtime and evening and all day at the weekend for a full range of drinks, which include three real ales from the Thwaites Brewery. An interesting selection of home-cooked dishes is served in the 30-cover restaurant, with typical dishes running from blue stilton & red onion tart to salmon with a lemon & dill sauce, Cumberland sausage, beef & ale pie and pork schnitzel with a fennel and green bean salad. Smaller portions are available for young diners. There's plenty to attract the visitor to the region, and for guests discovering the delights of coast and countryside the hotel has 12 en suite bedrooms that include some family rooms. They are available all year round, and the tariff includes a full cooked breakfast.

94 THE LAKES HOTEL

1 High Street, Windermere,
Cumbria LA23 1AF
☎ 01539 442751 Fax: 01539 446026
e-mail: admin@lakes-hotel.com
🌐 www.lakes-hotel.com

Andrew and Marie Dobson's hotel is a handsome mid-Victorian traditional stone building that was originally a bank. The **Lakes Hotel** stands in the heart of Windermere, about 150 yards from the railway and coach stations.

The ambience throughout is warm and inviting, and the bed rooms – doubles, twins and family rooms – offer space and comfort in abundance. They all have en suite facilities, central heating, television, beverage tray, fridge and hairdryer; three of the rooms are located on the ground floor. The tariff includes a full English breakfast. The owners and staff are always ready with advice for walkers, golfers and pursuers of other outdoor activities. Windermere and the surrounding area are rich in scenic, cultural and historic interest, and the best way to enjoy it all is through Andrew's other

excellent enterprise, **Lakes Supertours**. Luxury high-topped mini-coaches, with ample leg room and fine visibility, offer a number of half-and full-day tours around Lakeland. They are driven by friendly, well-informed driver-guides, and participants have ample opportunity to take a stroll and photograph the sites. The itineraries include the Complete Beatrix Potter's Lakeland and Wordsworth Tour, and by coach and boat on Borrowdale, Buttermere and Ullswater. And for extra convenience for guests at the Lakes Hotel, all the tours start from the hotel forecourt.

95 STORRS HALL HOTEL

Windermere, Cumbria LA23 3LG
☎ 015394 47111
Fax: (015394) 47555
Reservations: 08458 507506
e-mail: storrshall@elhmail.co.uk
🌐 www.elh.co.uk

Storrs Hall is an extraordinary hotel, providing an extraordinary experience. Its magical setting occupies seventeen acres of grounds and woodland on the shores of Lake Windermere. The hotel is a Grade II listed Georgian mansion, with an illustrious history. Its rich interiors are decorated in original Old English style and filled with genuine antiques and works of art, creating an air of relaxed ease and comfort.

From the Terrace Restaurant, a formal dining room at Storrs Hall, you can gaze in awe through enormous windows at the elegant terrace and picturesque gardens running right down to Lake Windermere.

This luxurious retreat offers attentive yet unobtrusive service accompanied by an artistically presented gastronomic extravaganza. The AA 2 rosette awards for food and the idyllic setting marry perfectly to offer something that is very special for any occasion.

The hotel has its own private boat jetty and landing for helicopters. You are also free to use its sister hotel's leisure facilities at the Low Wood Hotel, at any time during your stay.

97 OLD DUNGEON GHYLL HOTEL

Great Langdale, Ambleside,
Cumbria LA22 9JU
☎ 01539 437272
e-mail: neil.odg@lineone.net
⊕ www.odg.co.uk

For visitors approaching the **Old Dungeon Ghyll Hotel**, the magnificent, rugged setting at the head of the Great Langdale Valley is just the first of many outstanding features. For 300 years it has been attracting walkers, climbers, tourists and lovers of the great outdoors, and sine 1984 it has been in the more-than-capable hands of Neil Walmsley, himself a keen fell-walker, and his wife Jane. They have continued to improve and develop this popular family hotel while retaining as many of the old features as possible. Their reputation brings visitors from all over the world to the hotel, which takes its name from one of the most dramatic of the Lake District waterfalls, tumbling 60 feet down a nearby fell.

This marvellous place was originally an inn with a farmhouse (and was run as such until 1949) and the oldest part is the middle section; another part was added later and the stables at the north

end were converted into a dining room. The shippon at the other end became the Climbers Bar, where the old cow stalls still stand intact. In the Hikers Bar, real ales – usually at least four – are served in a delightfully charming and inviting ambience. Neil and Jane both cook, and the hearty home-made dishes on the bar and restaurant menus cater perfectly for appetites sharpened by the bracing surroundings; non-residents should book.

Guest accommodation at the Old Dungeon Ghyll comprises 14 warm, comfortable bedrooms, most with en suite facilities, some boasting four-poster beds. The residents' lounge is a great place to relax, meet the other guests, swap climbing stories and plan the day's activities, and the hotel has a drying room for wet clothes. In the days when coaches brought visitors from Little Langdale over Blea Tarn Pass, the driver would stop at the top and blow his horn – one toot for each passenger needing a meal. Down the years the hotel became very popular with climbing clubs and a favourite venue for club dinners, attracting many of the greatest names in the world of climbing. Clubs are still very welcome, and the hotel is the start point of several walks and climbs, including the famous and challenging peaks of Crinkle Crags, Bowfell and the Langdale Pikes. Great Langdale stands on the B5343 west of Ambleside – leave the A593 at Skelwith Bridge.

96 CONISTON GONDOLA 🏛

Gondola NT Bookings Office,
The Hollens, Grasmere,
Cumbria LA22 9QZ
☎ 015394 63831
⊕ www.nationaltrust.org.uk

The original steam yacht **Gondola** was first launched in 1859 and now, completely rebuilt by the National Trust, provides a passenger service in its opulently upholstered saloons. This is the perfect way to view Coniston's spectacular scenery. Gondola carries up to 86 passengers and can comfortably accommodate large groups. Enjoy a round trip of 45 mins. A buffet lunch or tea can be provided if Gondola is privately hired.

98 THE FISH HOTEL 🛏 🍴

Buttermere, nr Cockermouth,
Cumbria CA13 9XA
☎ 017687 70253
Fax: 017687 70287
⊕ www.fish-hotel.co.uk

For more than 40 years the Richardson family have been at the helm of the **Fish Hotel**, which combines period charm and character with up-to-date comforts and a truly

glorious setting. A short walk from beautiful Buttermere and Crummock Water at the foot of Honister Pass, it's a popular spot for tourists, walkers, climbers and lovers of the great outdoors, as well as a place where locals like to meet to swap news and put the world to rights over a glass or two of beer. For guests taking a break in this marvellous part of the world the Fish Hotel has ten

upstairs bedrooms, all en suite, with direct-dial phone, radio, hairdryer and beverage tray. The day starts with a generous cooked breakfast, and the hosts can arrange a packed lunch for guests setting out on a day's walking, fishing or sightseeing. Six real ales are usually on tap in the bar – typically two from Jennings Brewery, one from Hesket Newmarket, one from Keswick and two from other Cumbrian breweries. Keith, son of the owner, is in charge of the stoves, producing a selection of snacks and meals served lunchtime and evening in the bar.

99 THE GEORGIAN HOUSE HOTEL

8-11 Church Street, Whitehaven,
Cumbria CA28 7AY
☎ 01946 696611 Fax: 01946 696611
e-mail: Stephanie@thegeorgianhotel.net
🌐 www.thegeorgianhousehote.net

Stephanie and Lee have been in the hospitality business for more than 30 years, and after enjoying great success at the Distressed Sailor in nearby Hensingham they became the proprietors of the **Georgian House Hotel** in 2001. The 18th century premises were closed and empty when they came here, and they applied their considerable talents, experience and enthusiasm to create a top-quality enterprise that combines an elegant town house hotel with a widely acclaimed destination restaurant. Equally popular with the local community and with visitors from near and far, the Georgian House offers excellent accommodation and a fine variety of food and drink. Eight en suite upstairs bedrooms, all with double or king-size beds, are available all year round, providing a very comfortable and convenient base for both business and leisure visitors.

Hand in hand with the hotel side of the enterprise go all the traditional qualities of a favourite local and a destination restaurant. Lee is a wizard in the kitchen, and the food that he and his assistants produce is renowned throughout the county. The 70-cover restaurant, licensed for both non-residents and guests staying at the hotel, is open from 6 o'clock Tuesday to Saturday and from 12 to 2 on Sunday. Local produce takes pride of place on the menus, which provide patrons with an exceptional variety of dishes. A few examples show the range of the talented team in the kitchen: locally smoked kipper topped with a duck egg with a beetroot and horseradish chutney; sweet chilli crab cakes; lamb tattie hot pot; sea bass on wilted spinach with pine kernels; Cumbrian pork with apples, cinnamon and a Calvados sauce; sirloin, fillet and rib-eye steaks from locally reared beef cattle; and a Scottish-inspired trio of puds – black, haggis and fruit. The hosts plan to extend the already superb offerings of the hotel by opening an 80-seat wine bar at some time during 2008 – phone for details.

Whitehaven has plenty to attract the visitor: the conservation area of the harbour and its environs; the Met Office gallery, with news about the weather and the amazing story of the attack on the town by American ships; the Rum Story, which describes the town's connection with the Caribbean; and the Churches of St James, St Bergh and St Nicholas. And after a day's exploring the town and the surrounding area, it's good to know that the owners and staff at the Georgian House are ready to dispense their renowned hospitality.

100 THE SHEPHERDS ARMS HOTEL

Ennerdale Bridge, Cumbria CA23 3AR
☎ 01946 861249
e-mail: shepherdsarms@btconnect.com
⊕ www.shepherdsarmshotel.co.uk

The Shepherds Arms Hotel is a gem of a country house hotel offering en suite accommodation, home cooked cuisine and real ales. It is included in both the *Good Pub Guide* and the CAMRA *Good Beer Guide* and offers customers a choice of real ales with Jennings and Wainwright as the permanent brews, plus several guest ales. An extensive full bar menu is available every lunchtime and evening, with locally sourced homemade, vegetarian and daily special dishes being available. The comfortable accommodation here comprises three twin and three double rooms, all with en suite facilities, and one twin/one small double with private bath and shower. Family rooms are also available. All bedrooms are centrally heated and equipped with 9-channel digital TV, telephone, radio alarm, hospitality tray, and internet access. All

bathrooms have been refurbished in the past 12 months, along with two of the rooms. Breakfast is served in the Georgian panelled dining room where à la carte evening meals are also available. Ennerdale Bridge is situated on one of the most beautiful stretches of the world famous Coast to Coast walk and is close to Ennerdale water which is the only lake in the Lake District without a road alongside it.

101 THE CROWN HOTEL

Eamont Bridge, Penrith,
Cumbria CA10 2BX
☎ 01768 892892   Fax: 01768 892892
e-mail: crownhotel@msn.com

Located in the beautiful Eden Valley but only 1 mile from Penrith town centre, **The Crown Hotel** at Eamont Bridge is a welcoming former coaching inn that dates back to 1707. Owner Wendy Graham-Weston has presided over this fine old inn since 1993 and has established a glowing reputation for the quality of the appetising home-made food served here. The chalkboard menu offers a cosmopolitan selection of dishes, including Indian, Chinese and Italian, along with home-grown favourites such as Cod & Chips, Cumberland Sausage and Steak Pie. Vegetarian choices

might include a Broccoli & Pasta Bake or a vegetarian Balti. Only locally sourced meats and vegetables are used. Food is served every lunchtime and evening during the week, and all day on Saturday and Sunday. On Sundays, a Carvery with a choice of roasts is added to the menu . These are extremely popular so it is wise to book ahead. Pensioners are well looked after here with significant reductions in the prices of main meals. The Crown also has 15 beautifully appointed guest bedrooms, 6 of which have en suite facilities. All major credit cards apart from American Express and Diners are accepted.

433

102 THE KINGS ARMS HOTEL

Temple Sowerby, nr Penrith,
Cumbria CA10 1SB
☎ 017683 61211
e-mail: the-kings-arms@hotmail.co.uk
🌐 www.freewebs.com/thekingsarms

Approached along a delightful country lane, **The Kings Arms Hotel** is a 300-year-old former coaching inn that provides the opportunity for an idyllic and peaceful getaway. It has a beautiful beer garden that is flower-filled in

summer and has smoking facilities for colder nights. Inside, the hotel's bar stocks a wide range of spirits, beers, regularly rotated real ales and cocktails as well as non-alcoholic lagers, soft drinks, tea and coffee. The hotel's restaurant is in a more modern part of the building and has been recently redecorated to create a bright, warm dining area with an open log fire and gentle background music. The menu offers a wide choice of home-made dishes based on locally sourced ingredients. The

local Cumberland Sausage is particularly popular, as is the Steak & Ale Pie. Vegetarian options are available and there's also a children's menu. A popular amenity here is the newly decorated games room which has a full size pool table, golf games machine, dominoes tables, chess set, darts board with electronic score board, cards and a fruit machine. The accommodation at the Kings Arms comprises 10 classically styled, comfortably furnished rooms, 7 of which have en suite facilities. All rooms are equipped with colour TV and hospitality tray.

103 EDEN VALE INN

Bolton Village, Appleby,
Cumbria CA16 6AU
☎ 01768 361428
e-mail: theedenvale@google mail.com
🌐 www.edenvaleinnappleby.co.uk

An inviting old village hostelry with a spacious beer garden, the **Eden Vale Inn** dates back to the mid-1700s and has all the warmth and character you could hope to find. Nigel Duffin, who has some 20 years experience in the hospitality

business, took over here in the summer of 2006 and together with his chef, Richard Daffin, has made the inn a must-visit destination for discerning diners. Richard's imaginative menu offers amongst the starters a baked avocado stuffed with goat's cheese, wrapped in strips of Parma ham with a tangy lime and coriander dressing. Main course choices range from a mighty 16oz steak, through house specialities such as the Lamb

Shoulder or home-made Steak & Kidney Pudding, to vegetarian dishes such as Spinach and Ricotta Cannelloni. Children are welcome and there's also an Early Bird menu. The regular menu is supplemented by a good choice of daily specials, venison perhaps, or a swordfish steak. To complement your meal, there are 3 real ales to choose from, plus the contents of a fully stocked bar. And if you are planning to stay in this lovely part of the country, the inn has 4 recently refurbished guest bedrooms, all with en suite facilities.

4 High Wiend, Appleby-in-Westmorland,
Cumbria CA16 6RD
☎ 01768 351493
e-mail: jesveinsson@hotmail.com

The Golden Ball is a cosy, friendly pub which is open all day for drinks and great bar food. It also provides a relaxed and convenient base for touring the region. Licensees Andy and Jean took over the premises in October 2006 and quickly put their stamp on the place, making many improvements, creating a warm, welcoming ambience, and winning new friends all the time.

Located in the heart of this captivating little town, The Golden Ball features in the Good Beer Guide. Marstons Burton Bitter, Cumberland Ale and two guest real ales head the list of drinks to be enjoyed in the two bar areas or out in the secluded and sheltered garden which is illuminated and heated at night, and has a covered area for smokers.

Jean is the queen of the kitchen, producing a fine variety of country-style bar food which is available from noon until 8pm, (7pm in winter). The board lists the day's specials which include an

excellent home-made soup, cream cheese & mushroom, perhaps, or tomato & rocket. Classics such as cauliflower cheese, toad in the hole, cottage pie, scampi & chips, beef stew with dumplings and, a great favourite here, a chicken & leek pie, all feature on the menu. Children are very welcome and locals and visitors alike are invited to participate in the weekly Pub Quiz on Wednesday evenings.

The Golden Ball also has comfortable accommodation available all year round in 5 upstairs rooms for Bed & Breakfast guests. Please note that payment here is by cash only.

Appleby itself, the former county town of Westmorland, is one of England's most attractive towns. It's broad main street, Boroughgate, has been described as the finest High Street in the land. At one end of the street stands the 16th century Moot Hall, at the other stands the huge Norman Keep of Appleby Castle. Also worth visiting is St Lawrence's Church with its magnificent family tombs and historic organ of 1684 which is said to be the oldest still in use in Britain. And if you are visiting Appleby in early June, you will find the place transformed as the 300-year-old Gypsy Horse Fair takes place.

105 TUFTON ARMS HOTEL ⊨ ⫙

Market Square, Appleby-in-Westmorland,
Cumbria CA16 6XA
☎ 017683 51593   Fax: 017683 52761
e-mail: info@tuftonarmshotel.co.uk
🌐 www.tuftonarmshotel.co.uk

Located on the main square of the busy market town of Appleby, the **Tufton Arms Hotel** started life in the 17th century as a coaching inn. Owned and run for many years by the Milson family, it provides a charming, relaxing destination for an enjoyable break in the heart of the beautiful Eden Valley. Guests are welcomed with a smile at reception, which set the tone for the whole stay. The staff have a genuine desire that their guests will have a stay that's more than just pleasant, indeed a time to remember. It's quite likely that visitors will quickly meet one of the owners who speak not of guests but of 'friends who come to stay'.

Good food is a byword here and the award-winning team of chefs seek out the best and freshest local produce which they prepare with skill and flair to create delicious dishes with a modern twist. Dinner is served in the elegant Conservatory Restaurant overlooking the cobbled mews courtyard. Diners should allow time to peruse menus that are filled with good things. Fine food deserves fine wines and at the Tufton Arms an expertly chosen list that runs to some 200 wines provides the perfect marriage for any dish.

The standards of the hospitality and the cuisine are matched by the accommodation which caters admirably for a wide cross-section of guests, from holidaymakers and shooting/fishing parties to business and corporate individuals and groups. Each of the 22 bedrooms has its own charm and character, with furnishings that include the occasional antique piece from the Milson farmhouse. All the rooms have en suite facilities and all the amenities expected by today's guests.

The hotel is also completely geared up for banquets and conferences with 3 purpose-designed suites that combine the period elegance of the rest of hotel with up-to-date business requirements. Fly fishing and shooting can be arranged by the hotel which has access to some of the best stretches of the River Eden and has its own driven and rough pheasant shoot.

Appleby, the former county town of Westmorland, is a delightful place to explore. The surrounding area, too, is rich in historic and scenic glory, with a number of important country houses and castles, and the beauty of the tranquil Eden Valley.

Hoff, nr Appleby, Cumbria CA16 6TA
☎ 01768 351317
e-mail: mitchellderek@btconnect.com

Real ale expert Derek and talented cook Sue make a great team at **The New Inn** which stands amidst glorious scenery on the B6260 Tebay road running south from Appleby. A minimum of 5 well-kept real ales are always on tap in the bar where the centrepiece is a huge feature fireplace. The brews can be local or national, and many come from small micro-breweries.

Sue has built up a fine reputation for her honest, unpretentious cooking. Choose from either the printed menu or from the large blackboard which lists hearty dishes such as seafood crumble, 'fairly local' Cumberland sausage, 'very local' Westmorland sausage, chicken or vegetable Kiev, steaks, and the very popular Lamb Henry with a minty, winy sauce. There's also a children's menu. Food is served Wednesday to Sunday from noon until 3pm, and from 6pm to 9pm. The inn itself is open all day, Tuesday to Sunday, and from 6pm on Monday. Please note that payment at the New Inn is by cash or cheque only.

In addition to its good food and great ales, the inn is also renowned for its programme of live entertainment. Well-known musicians from around the world play and perform here in a variety of musical genres. As well as these performances, the inn also hosts live entertainment on Friday evenings from around 9pm.

Sue and Jean also hope that during the lifetime of this edition 4 double en suite letting rooms will become available on a bed & breakfast basis.

107 THE PENNINE HOTEL

Market Square, Kirkby Stephen,
Cumbria CA17 4QT
☎ 017683 71382
🌐 www.thepenninehotel.co.uk

Built in the mid-1800s, **The Pennine Hotel** stands at the heart of the bustling market town of Kirkby Stephen in the beautiful Eden Valley. It is run by the father and son team of Stephen and Craig Gardiner who arrived here in the autumn of 2007 and have given the hotel a new lease of life. With 9 years experience in the hospitality business, it's clear that they know how to look after their customers well.

In the bar, lovers of real ales will find a choice of two brews with Cumberland Ale as the regular plus a rotating guest ale. Popular draught keg drinks are Carling and Becks Vier. The hotel has established itself as a popular place to eat, with food served every day from noon until around 8.30pm. All the ingredients used here are sourced locally wherever possible. The Lite-Bites menu offers, amongst other choices, home-made soup, sandwiches of home-cooked beef or ham, or a chicken, bacon and melted cheese baguette. For heartier appetites, how about a 16oz T-bone Steak, or a giant Yorkshire pudding served with mashed potato and a home-made steak and ale filling. Also on offer are succulent Whitby scampi; chicken breast stuffed with a delicious creamy Wensleydale and cranberry cheese wrapped in bacon; and a vegetarian vegetable lasagne. Desserts include a delicious home-made crumble and custard, and the all time favourite here, a home-made sticky toffee pudding with custard. The regular menu is supplemented by daily specials - beef & Stilton baguette, perhaps - and on Sundays a roast is also available.

The Pennine is also noted for its entertainment. On Thursday and Friday evenings there's a Quiz starting at 8pm, and on Friday evenings a karaoke and music session from 8pm until late. Entertainments are listed on a chalk board at the side of the bar.

If you plan to stay in this lovely part of the county, The Pennine has 8 guest bedrooms available. At the time of going to press, 3 of them had en suite facilities but during the lifetime of this guide, all rooms will be upgraded.

The hotel accepts all major credit cards; has limited parking but there is a large public car park opposite; and has good disabled access to the ground floor.

438

108 THE SHAKESPEARE INN & RESTAURANT

117 London Road, Shardlow,
Derbyshire DE72 2GP
☎ 01332 792728

The **Shakespeare Inn** is a Grade II-listed building standing in the village of Shardlow, just off the A50 and only three miles from J24 of the M1. Kevin and Sue Johnson and their family are delightful hosts, and their recent refurbishment programme has made the public bar, lounge and restaurant all looking very smart. Marstons Pedigree is the resident cask ale, with two regularly changing guests, and the inn serves a great choice of straightforward home-cooked food. The Shakespeare, which has a pleasant beer garden and good off-road parking, is open from 11.30am to midnight every day. The first Friday of the month brings a popular jazz

session and the pub hosts other live music evenings on a regular basis. Shardlow stands on the River Trent and the Trent & Mersey canal and was once a busy canal port. Commerce has long since been overtaken by leisure and the port is now a n attractive modern marina.

109 THE RISING SUN

26 Rise End, Middleton, Matlock,
Derbyshire DE4 4LS
☎ 01629 822470
e-mail: info@therisingsuninn.biz
🌐 www.therisingsuninn.biz

The **Rising Sun** is a first pub for Dave and Lorraine Mountford, a cracking little country pub overlooking the village from its elevated position. Dave, who has a background in catering, was headhunted by Punch Taverns to run this fine old pub, which dates from the early 19th century. It's very much a place for ale lovers and food lovers, old-fashioned and unpretentious, with roaring open fires in winter and always a warm, welcoming ambience behind its white-painted, dark-shuttered façade. Bass, Old Speckled Hen and Marston's Pedigree are on tap to quench thirsts, and good simple, traditional food comes from the tiny kitchen, prepared as far as possible from fresh local produce. Popular choices run from sandwiches, wholemeal hoagies and jacket potatoes to omelettes, burgers, pasta, sausages & mash, smoked haddock fish cakes and giant battered fish. Open from noon seven days a week, the Rising Sun is a popular spot with walkers (it's on the High Peak Trail), cyclists and tourist as well as locals, and Carsington Water, with its glorious views, wildlife and sporting facilities is nearby. Two en suite bedrooms provide a very pleasant base for seeing this lovely part of the world. This is the Middleton near Wirksworth, not the one a few miles to the north near Youlgreave.

Market Place, Wirksworth,
Derbyshire DE4 4ET
☎ 01629 823340

By the old market place in Wirksworth, the **Hope & Anchor** is a sturdy three-storey building in local stone, easily the biggest pub in town and for centuries an unmissable landmark on the way into the centre. Originally three buildings, it has a long and interesting history, with the oldest parts dating back as far as 1590. The interior is delightfully traditional, with low beams, lots of dark wood, carpeted floors, gleaming brass and comfortable country-style furniture. By far the most eyecatching feature is the magnificent wooden fireplace surround, dating from 1610. At the back of the pub is a secluded patio with ivy-clad walls and tables and chairs for alfresco sipping.

The public bar, lounge and dining room are convivial spots to put the world to rights over a drink or to settle down to a snack or a meal. Owners Kevin and Lorraine Dowson took over in the summer of 2007 with the intention of carrying out a programme of refurbishment and creating a traditional ale house serving good food. They have made a great success of it, bringing back the locals and making new friends all the time. The resident real ale is Tribute from the St Austell Brewery, accompanied by two guests and a good selection of other draught and bottle beers, lagers, wines, spirits, liqueurs and soft drinks.

All the family cook, each bringing his or her own individual touches, and everything on the regular menu and the specials board is fresh, tasty and wholesome. Among the favourite dishes are cod & chips, 6oz cheeseburger, sirloin steak, home-made steak & ale pie and Kevin's super beef or roasted vegetable lasagne with tomato bread made specially to accompany the dish. The pub has a

pool table and big-screen TV to show the major sporting events.

Wirksworth has plenty to interest the visitor, including the Heritage Centre, housed in a former silk mill, the ancient Church of St Mary, The National Stone Centre and two delightful little light railways. The town of Matlock and the multi-activity Carsington Water are nearby, and there's excellent walking in the Peak District National Park. And when the sightseeing's done and thirst takes over, Kevin, Lorraine and their staff are ready to welcome one and all with their friendly, genuine hospitality.

The Hope & Anchor accepts cash or cheque only (credit cards are not accepted).

111 THE MINERS ARMS

Carsington, nr Matlock,
Derbyshire DE4 4DE
☎ 01629 540207

The **Miners Arms** is a lovely 200-year-old village inn located close to Carsington Water off the B5035 Ashbourne-Wirksworth road. The delightful hosts are Douglas and Lillibe Bunting, who took

over the tenancy in 2004 and continue to make new friends from near and far. The interior is rich in old-world charm, with heavy pine tables and chairs in the bar, low ceilings, gnarled beams, stone walls, antiques and objets d'art, gleaming brass and an open fire. In this atmospheric setting a good choice includes some local brews, and the chalkboard lists a tempting selection of dishes freshly prepared by Douglas. Typical choices include deep-fried haddock, salmon thermidor, tuna steak with a sweet chilli dip, lasagne, hearty pork and lamb casseroles and beef in ale. The steak dishes are always in demand, served plain or with a choice of black pepper, stilton, Diane or Rossini sauces.

Delectable desserts like apple & cranberry pie and treacle sponge finish a meal with a flourish. Wednesday is special steak night, Friday majors on fish & chips and Sunday brings a popular carvery. The pub is open lunchtime and evening and all day Saturday and Sunday.

112 THE BLACK SWAN

Church Street, Ashover,
Derbyshire SA45 0AB
☎ 01246 591648

The **Black Swan** lies just outside the boundary of the Peak District National Park at the heart of the largest parish in Derbyshire. Ashover, a village of limestone and gritstone dug from the local quarries,

lies off the B6036 six miles southwest of Chesterfield. It's a place well worth seeking out to enjoy the atmosphere and offerings of this picture-postcard pub, built of stone fro the nearby quarry in the early 18th century. Dawn and Malcolm Strange took over here at the end of 2006 and lost no time in putting their stamp on this fine village inn. This lovely place is a real magnet for connoisseurs of real ales, with six brews always available – a typical choice could include Peak Ales Swift Nick and, from the Thornbridge Brewery, Wild Swan and Kipling, the last a potent brew with a 5.3 ABV. The menu is based almost exclusively on fresh local produce, and the traditional

dishes are exemplified by super Sunday roasts, Cumberland sausage in a giant Yorkshire pudding and a hearty liver & bacon casserole. This splendid pub provides a great place to relax with friends, with a pool room, dart board and live entertainment every 1st and 3rd Saturday of the month. The Black Swan also has a function room perfect for parties and weddings. It is open for food from 12 midday everday except Monday. You can also pop in on a Sunday and enjoy a traditional sunday roast from 12 noon until 4pm.

113 THE HUNLOKE ARMS

Derby Road, Wingersworth,
nr Chesterfield, Derbyshire
☎ 01246 232458

The **Hunloke Arms** is a substantial, well-proportioned inn standing just off the A61 two miles south of Chesterfield. It dates back to the 18th century and was once a well-known coaching inn, named after a lord of the manor of the day. With is fine Georgian lines and porticoed entrance, it looks every inch the grand, welcoming inn, and the mellow interior, with old wood, coloured lead glass and comfortable furnishings, fully confirms that impression. It has an excellent host in Gavin Hibberd, an experienced chef who is restoring the inn's reputation as a place to seek out for food and drink, combined with outstanding service and good value for money. The inn is open all day every day for real ales and a wide selection of beers, lagers,

cider, wines, spirits and soft drinks. Food is definitely the star here, served lunchtime and evening Monday to Thursday, all day Friday and Saturday and from high noon to 5 on Sunday. The choice runs from sandwiches and light bites to burgers, grills and classic entrées like lamb's liver with onion gravy, mash & crisp pancetta, fillet of salmon with smoked salmon & chive butter sauce, and braised lamb shank with redcurrant gravy. Everyone is welcome to join in the Tuesday and Sunday quizzes.

114 SOMERSET HOUSE

1 Top Road, Calow, Chesterfield,
Derbyshire S44 5AF
☎ 01246 278225

Somerset House is a sturdy roadside inn standing large and proud next to the Royal Hospital in Calow, a village standing on the A632 a mile or so east of Chesterfield. A landmark almost as well known as its neighbour, the inn is a first venture into the licensed trade for Alan and Beverley Roberts, who arrived here as tenants in the autumn of 2007. The public bar and the large adjoining lounge bar are invitingly traditional in style, with lots of dark wood and burnished brass, comfortable spots for meeting the locals and enjoying a chat over a glass of Greene King Abbot Ale or Timothy Taylor Landlord. Somerset House is also gaining a spreading reputation as an excellent place for a meal, with a good variety of

familiar pub food served in generous portions at kind prices. Steaks, pies and curries are among the most

popular orders, and the printed menu is supplemented by a daily changing specials board. Pool and darts are played in the bar, and on Friday evenings inhibitions are cast aside at the karaoke session. The inn, which has a patio/beer garden and a large car park, is open from midday to 11 o'clock every day of the week.

Hollington, nr Ashbourne,
Derbyshire DE6 3AG
☎ 01335 360241
e-mail: info@redlionhollington.co.uk
🌐 www.redlionhollington.co.uk

Brothers Mark and Graham Gillespie are continuing a long tradition of hospitality at the **Red Lion Inn**, which attracts lovers of good food from near and far to the village of Hollington. It's also a much-loved local, with an excellent atmosphere, and behind the pretty yellow-painted shuttered frontage the interior is cosy and carpeted, with low dark-beamed ceilings, lots of snug little corners, half-panelled walls, brick fireplaces, smart polished tables and chairs, framed prints and ornaments and memorabilia on the walls and shelves.

The bar is a very pleasant, civilised place to relax and unwind, and when the sun shines the lawned area at the front comes into its own. Marston's Pedigree and Fuller's London Pride are the regular real ales.

In the elegant restaurant diners can sit back and enjoy at leisure the efforts of a very talented team in the kitchen. Food is definitely the star at the

Red Lion, and the menus really do offer something for everyone. Typical starters might be plum tomato & mozzarella tian with a basil dressing, creamy garlic mushrooms, chicken liver pâté served with onion marmalade and butterfly tiger prawns with a sweet chilli jam. Main courses include tried-and-tested favourites like lager-battered haddock, heart pies and succulent steaks. The fish and seafood specials are always in demand (baked sea bass stuffed with lime and herbs, wrapped in pancetta), and vegetarians are well catered for with dishes such as mushroom stroganoff or roasted vegetable lasagne.

To find this secluded gem of a place, take the A52 west from Derby or east from Ashbourne and turn south near Brailsford onto a minor road signposted for Hollington. The village and the pub are situated a mile along this road. There are plenty of things to see and places to discover in the area, including picturesque country lanes and little villages like Longford, home of the first cheese factory in England, the National Trust's Kedleston Hall, designed by Robert Adam with the look of a grand Roman temple, the town of Ashbourne with its Georgian architecture, the elegant parish church of St Oswald and plenty of interesting shops, and the important city of Derby. But no-one visiting the region should leave without sampling the excellent hospitality offered by the brothers and their staff at the Red Lion.

115 THE BLACK HORSE INN

Hulland Ward, Derbyshire DE6 3EE
☎ 01335 370206

The **Black Horse Inn**, personally owned and run since 1995 by Michael and Muriel Edwin, attracts ale-drinkers and food-lovers from a wide area. It's easy to find on the A517 halfway between Ashbourne and Belper on the Belper side of Hulland Ward. Four cask ales – Wadworth 6X and three guests – are on tap to satisfy fresh-air thirsts, and a good selection of home-cooked food is available daily. The menus combine traditional favourites with less familiar options such as roast duck with a rich wine and brandy sauce or chestnut, stilton & ale pie. The Sunday roasts are always

popular, and everything on the menu can be ordered to take away – even the roasts. Darts and dominoes are played in the public bar area, and the attractive lounge bar can be used for functions or small meetings. The Black Horse is an excellent base for discovering the many delights of the Derbyshire Dales, and the four centrally heated, double-glazed bedrooms have en suite bathrooms, TV, beverage tray and handsome four-poster beds.

118 THE BRAKENDALE RESTAURANT

Knockerdown Farm, Ashbourne,
Derbyshire DE6 1NQ
☎ 01629 540880 / 07891 839151
e-mail:
margaret@mchamberlain6.wanadoo.co.uk

The **Brackendale Restaurant** is part of a leisure complex set in the beautiful Derbyshire Peak District close to Carsington Water. Margaret proposes a menu that combines traditional home cooking with a generous splash of imagination. Typical dishes run from black pudding served

sizzling in a black pepper sauce to halibut with a Dijon mustard sauce, chicken tikka masala, leek & stilton crumble and the day's roast (served with the best Yorkshire pudding around). The restaurant is rightly very popular, so booking is advisable. Food is served from 12 to 2 and 6 to 9 Wednesday to Saturday and from 12 to 4 on Sunday.

119 STONE COTTAGE

Green Lane, Clifton, nr Ashbourne,
Derbyshire DE6 2BL
☎ 01335 343377
e-mail: info@stone-cottage.fsnet.co.uk
⊕ www.stone-cottage.fsnet.co.uk

Angela Whittle welcomes guests throughout the year at **Stone Cottage**, a charming little property standing in the quiet village of Clifton, a mile or so south of Ashbourne. The atmosphere is very friendly and informal, and the three en suite bedrooms are very smartly decorated and furnished. A hearty breakfast starts the day, and guests can relax and plan their days in the lounge or enjoy a stroll in the garden.

444

Osmaston, nr Ashbourne,
Derbyshire DE6 1LW
☎ 01335 342371

The **Shoulder of Mutton** is located in the quintessentially English village of Osmaston, which lies three miles from Ashbourne, just off the A52 Derby road. Personally run since 1993 by Paul and Tina, the pub occupies a unique position in the hearts and affections of locals from the village and surrounding area and first-timers. Anyone visiting the locality should definitely take time to enjoy the hospitality offered at this very special inn. Almost all the properties in the village are owned by the Walker Oakover estate (important local landowners).

A date stone from 1805 is the only extant proof of the inn's origins (other records were accidentally destroyed in a fire) but it certainly dates back much further than 200 years. The exterior is of red brick, which gives it a warm, inviting appearance, and it is an important feature of a village that boasts the fine old Church of St Martin and a village pond. The atmosphere at this cosy, traditional inn is invariably warm and welcoming, and the lounge is a lovely spot to meet or make friends over a drink. It leads straight out into attractive gardens, where tables and chairs are set outside in the warmer months.

The fully stocked bar offers a good selection of real ales as well as keg and bottled beers, lagers, ciders, wines, spirits, liqueurs and non-alcoholic drinks. The inn is open lunchtime and evening and all day in the summer, and patrons can enjoy something good to eat from 12 to 2 and 7 to 9 daily. The blackboard proposes a fine variety of delicious food cooked by Tina, including scampi, home-made steak & kidney pie, beef curry, lasagne and always a choice for vegetarians. The Sunday roasts are particularly popular, so you should turn up early to be sure of securing a table at the time you want. For lighter options, the snack menu offers sandwiches, rolls and baguettes, toasties on brown or white bread, jacket potatoes with a range of fillings that includes prawn Marie Rose and home-made steak & kidney, and beefburgers – just plain beef, cheese, Hawaiian with cheese & pineapple and the Shoulder of Mutton special loaded with melted cheese, mushrooms and crispy bacon.

Paul and Tina can provide outside bars and can cater for all kinds of functions and special occasions. Paul and Tina also run the village Post Office and general store next to the inn. This is open from 9 to midday Monday, Tuesday and Thursday and from 2 to 5 on Friday.

445

Kniveton, nr Ashbourne,
Derbyshire DE6 1JF
☎ 01335 342341 Fax: 01335 342341
e-mail: paul.wilson@unicombox.co.uk

The **Ketch at Kniveton** is a fine sight on summer days, with window boxes and tubs overflowing with colourful flowers and lush greenery. Behind the stone and whitewashed frontage the inside is really superb, thanks to a major refurbishment in 2007. Experienced chef and licensee Paul Wilson took over here in May of that year, and the inn was closed for three months during the revamp. It started life as a farmhouse, and since becoming a pub it has been called the Ketchum Inn and the Greyhound.

Now firmly established as the Ketch, it attracts well-deserved support from the local community as well as passing trade and the tourists who come here in their droves in season to discover the many attractions in the region. Everyone is welcome, including families with children, and the ambience is invariably notably warm and friendly.

Three real ales – Marston's Pedigree and two rotating guests – head the list of drinks, which include a good choice of other beers, lagers, wines, spirits and soft drinks. This is much more than a place to meet for a drink, it also serves really excellent food. Prime local raw materials go into the kitchen, where the chefs produce a wide variety of mainly classic pub food, from soup, prawn cocktail and deep-fried brie to lasagne, steaks, beer-battered haddock and stilton-stuffed chicken breast. There are also some more unusual choices such as South African-style peri peri chicken or fillet of pork with braised leeks in a paprika sauce. Sandwiches are added to the lunchtime menu (Monday to Saturday). Food is served from 12 to 3 and 6 to 9 Monday to Saturday and from 12 to 4 on Sunday, when there's a choice of four roast meats, with fish and vegetarian alternatives.

The pub is closed on Sunday nights in winter, but is otherwise open lunchtime and evening and all day Saturday and Sunday. It has a beer garden with plenty of seats and an area where children can play in safety, a good-size car park and a small caravan park with electric hook-ups for camper vans and towed vans. The Ketch celebrates all the usual red-letter days – Burns Night, St Valentine's Day, St Patrick's Day… and hosts regular themed jazz days.

The Ketch stands on the outskirts of Kniveton, three miles northeast of Ashbourne on the B5035. The start of the Peak District National Park is just a mile away, and other local attractions include Carsington Water (2 miles) and Alton Towers (9 miles).

121 PRIMROSE COTTAGE

Main Street, Hognaston, nr Ashbourne,
Derbyshire DE6 1PU
☎ 01335 370131

Primrose Cottage stands on the main street of Hognaston, a picturesque village on a hillside overlooked by Hognaston Winn, which rises to more than 1,000 feet. The stone-built cottage has recently been sympathetically converted as a self-catering let, with all the mod cons to guarantee a very enjoyable, comfortable break in quiet, civilised surroundings. The cottage is owned by Stephen and Lynda Allsopp, The cottage is a popular base for walkers, anglers and tourists exploring the region. The biggest magnet is Carsington Water, which is just a ten-minute walk away. This vast reservoir, owned by Severn Trent Water, was opened by the Queen in 1992, and brings thousands of visitors with its many attractions, including fishing, canoeing, sailing and walking in scenic surroundings. The reservoir is home to a wide variety of wildlife, and bird-watchers will look out

for the American ruddy duck, now well established in England after some escaped from a wildlife collection. In Hognaston itself, the parish church of St Bartholomew is well worth a visit. It boasts some extraordinary Norman carvings and a clock and bells that are a memorial to the renowned clock-maker John Smith, who was born in the village.

122 THE OLD SUN INN

33 High Street, Buxton,
Derbyshire SK17 6HA
☎ 01298 23452

The warmth and character of the traditional English pub is epitomised at the **Old Sun Inn**, which stands close to Buxton's market place. It dates back some 400 years, and the promise of the whitewashed outer walls and window boxes is amply fulfilled within. Open fires, cosy corners, bare boards or slate floors, stripped wood screens and period pictures make a perfect setting for a drink and meeting the regulars. The bar offers an impressive choice of cask ales, with three from Marston's Brewery – Bitter, Pedigree and Old Empire IPA – and three regularly changing guests. The inn, which since 2000 has been run by Rachel Cresswell, is not only a fine place for a drink, it also serves a fine range of great-value dishes prepared and cooked on the premises. The printed menu and specials board provide

abundant choice, from sandwiches and light bites to succulent steaks, steak & ale pie and seafood, pasta and vegetarian dishes. All are welcome to give their brains an airing at the Sunday night quiz. There's lots of local history in the pictures on the walls of the inn, and plenty more out and about in the town, the highest market town in Britain and the largest community in the Peak District National Park.

447

123 THE WOODROFFE ARMS

Main Street, Hope, Hope Valley,
Derbyshire S33 6SB
☎ 01433 620351
e-mail: wyjordan@hotmail.co.uk
⊕ www.thebullrib.co.uk

Investment by the owning brewery and the enthusiasm of the new hosts promises a rosy future for the **Woodroffe Arms**, which stands in the delightful village of Hope, nine miles northeast of Buxton. Wayne Jordan and Frazer Bradley are enhancing the inn's popularity with the local community and with visitors from further afield. Good honest English food is cooked on the premises using fresh local produce. The bar menu, served lunchtime and early evening (5 to 7) offers classics like fish & chips, sirloin steak and steak & kidney pudding, while typical dishes on the main evening menu (5 to 8) are lamb's kidneys, calves' liver, baby squid and slow-roasted duck leg. Five en suite bedrooms (more are planned) provide an ideal base for exploring the region. Hope is close to many of the Peak

District's top attractions, including superb scenery and the renowned mines and caves. Hope itself has an interesting church (next to the pub) and stages an Agricultural Show every August Bank Holiday. The Woodroffe Arms is open from midday Monday to Saturday and from 11am on Sunday. Monday is chilli night, Wednesday is quiz night and the last Friday of the month sees a disco session. The inn has a pleasant beer garden and good off-road parking.

124 CAUSEWAY HOUSE B&B

Back Street, Castleton, Hope Valley,
Derbyshire S33 8WE
☎ 01433 623291
e-mail: steynberg@btinternet.com

Causeway House offers outstanding Bed & Breakfast accommodation in an area of the Peak District National Park renowned for its beautiful scenery. The house is a classic Derbyshire 'cruck' house, built of local stone in the 14th century, and it retains some striking period features, including lots of solid timber. The little garden at the front is a cheerful, colourful spot in spring and summer. The accommodation comprises five comfortably appointed rooms, one with a four-poster, three with en suite facilities. A hearty English breakfast, with a lighter Continental and vegetarian alternatives, is included in the tariff and is sure to put a spring in the step for a day's exploring. The family-friendly house has been owned and run since May 2006 by Janet and Nick Steynberg, who are already attracting repeat visits with their amiable, welcoming style and excellent value for

money. They also have a wealth of information about places in the area to visit and explore.

Castleton, at the head of the Hope Valley, is overlooked by the ruins of Peveril Castle, built in 1080 by William Peveril, the King's bailiff for the Royal Manor of the Peak. Equally dominant is Mam Tor, where a walk to the summit (1700 feet) is rewarded with spectacular views.

Church Street, Ashford-in-the-Water,
nr Bakewell, Derbyshire DE45 1QB
☎ 01629 812931

Food lovers, ale lovers, pub lovers......the wide appeal of the **Bulls Head** brings patrons from near and far to this fine pub in Ashford-in-the-Water, where the proprietors are Carl and Debbie Shaw. Debbie is the third generation of her family to run this outstanding hostelry, which was built in the 17th century and retains a good deal of original character both inside and out. The setting and the lovely atmosphere make it a real pleasure to drop in here to relax, unwind and forget the cares of the world for a while.

Two real ales head the list of drinks served in the cosy bar, and there's an excellent selection of wines to enjoy on their own or to accompany a snack or meal. The menu changes frequently to reflect what's best and freshest in season and as many of the ingredients as possible are sourced locally. The steak & ale pie, cooked in award-winning Old Stockport Ale, is a sure-fire winner, and other choices – many of them you won't find on the average pub menu – could include chicken & pistachio terrine, omelette Arnold Bennett, rabbit & pear sausages and a ragout of monkfish and courgettes. A side order of dripping-roasted potatoes is more than many customers can resist, and sticky toffee pudding with black treacle sauce and fresh cream provides an equally naughty-but-nice finale. They try to accommodate anyone with any special dietary restrictions whenever possible and with a little notice. Tables are set outside in summer in the beer garden, and the pub also boasts a boules pitch.

Opening hours are Monday to Saturday 11am - 3pm & 6pm - 11pm, Sunday 12 noon - 3pm & 7pm - 10.30pm. Food is served 12 noon - 2pm & 6.30pm - 9pm. No food available Thursday evenings Nov - Mar.

Ashford-in-the-Water, one of the prettiest villages in the whole county, is located a mile northwest of Bakewell off the A6. It might not exactly be in the water, but it is certainly on the River Wye. Sheepwash Bridge is one of three bridges in the village, and a great favourite with artists and photographers, and the limestone Church of the Holy Trinity, is well worth a visit. Ashford is famous for its well-dressings, depicting biblical and other scenes. The date for 2008 is May 17 to 25.

126 THE OLD SMITHY TEA ROOMS & RESTAURANT

Church Street, Monyash, nr Bakewell,
Derbyshire DE45 IJH
☎ 01629 810190/814510
🖥 www.oldsmithymonyash.pizco.com
🖥 www.monyash.info.pizco.com

David Driscoll and his parents have forged the **Old Smithy** into one of the most popular eating places in the Peak District. Walkers and cyclists flock here for drinks, snacks and meals – all served in the friendly and informal surroundings. The setting itself is delightful – cosy little rooms with a woodburning stove and walls adorned with musical instruments. The food choice runs from hot snacks in baps or on toast to omelettes, Cornish pasties, the famous all-day breakfasts and home-made scones, cakes and pastries. Drinks include a choice of cask ales, draught and bottled beers and lagers and a full wine list. The tea rooms are open in winter from 10am to 4pm and in summer from 9am to 7pm; Saturday and Sunday open long hours all year round. The bistro-style restaurant

is open on Saturday evenings 7pm - 11pm. Monyash lies five miles west of Bakewell off the B5055. The area attracts many walkers throughout the season. Nearby Lathkill Dale is a noted road-free beauty spot and a designated National Nature Reserve. It's easy to work up a thirst and appetite in these lovely surroundings, and the Driscoll family are always ready to come to the rescue at the Old Smithy.

128 CHATSWORTH HOUSE

Chatsworth House
nr Edensor, Derbyshire DE45 IPP
☎ 01246 565300 Fax: 01246 583536
e-mail: visit@chatsworth.org
🖥 www.chatsworth.org

On the Outskirts of the village of Edensor lies the home of the Dukes of Devonshire, **Chatsworth House**, known as the "Palace of the Peak", is without doubt one of the finest of the great houses in Britain. The origins of the House as a great showpiece must be attributable to the redoubtable Bess of Hardwick, whose marriage into the Cavendish family helped to secure the future of the palace.

Bess's husband, Sir William Cavendish, bought the estate for £600 in 1549. It was Bess who completed the new House after his death. Over the years, the Cavendish fortune continued to pour into Chatsworth, making it an almost unparalleled showcase for art treasures. Every aspect of the fine arts is here, ranging from old masterpieces, furniture, tapestries, porcelain and some magnificent alabaster carvings.

The gardens of this stately home also have some marvellous features, including the Emperor Fountain, which dominates the Canal Pond and is said to reach a height of 290 feet. There is a maze and a Laburnum Tunnel and, behind the house, the famous Cascades. The overall appearance of the park as it is seen today is chiefly due to the talents of "Capability" Brown, who was first consulted in 1761. However, the name perhaps most strongly associated with Chatsworth is Joseph Paxton. His experiments in glasshouse design led him eventually to his masterpiece, the Crystal Palace, built to house the Great Exhibition of 1851.

Chapel Hill, Beeley, Derbyshire DE4 2NR
☎ 01629 734666

Situated in the lovely old village of Beeley, on the Chatsworth Estate, the **Old Smithy** combines the roles of village shop and licensed café – and both are outstanding in their field. Opened in 2004, it has been run since April 2007 by Sue and Neil Chatterton. As the name suggests, it was once the home and premises of the village blacksmith, and parts of it date back to the 17th century. The shop is housed in what was the forge, while the café occupies an extension to the rear.

Both the shop and the café specialise in prime local produce, with quality and flavour always to the fore.

The shop sells delicious delicatessen-style foods, including local meats and cheeses, jams and preserves, chutneys and pickles, as well as the delicious bread that Neil bakes (and which he also supplies to local markets and shops), cards, books, maps, guides....even the daily papers. The shop is open from 9 to 5 every day except Wednesday.

The licensed café has seats for 40 in comfort, with room for 50 more out on the patio and in the beautiful garden. The décor is an attractive mix of traditional and modern, with off stone walls and ceiling and a big brick hearth where a fire keeps things cosy even in the coldest snaps. Good wholesome produce is the order of the day; the breakfast menu, served from 10 to midday, offers a full English with free-range eggs, dry cure bacon, sausage, black pudding, mushrooms, tomatoes, toast and marmalade, tea or coffee – all for a very kind £8.95, and several lighter options. The lunch menu, available from midday to 3 o'clock, proposes soup, Neil's excellent pâté, and sandwiches with generous hot or cold fillings. Daily changing specials are marked up on a board, and the café serves a selection of home-made cakes, pastries and puddings. Sunday lunch is always a busy time, so it's best to book to be sure of getting a table at the time you want. The café is licensed, so visitors can enjoy a beer or a glass of wine, whether or not they're eating. The café is open from 10 to 4 every day except Wednesday.

The Old Smithy can be reached by turning off the main A6 Bakewell-Matlock road on to the B6012, which is signposted to Baslow and Beeley. After about three-quarters of a mile, take a left turn opposite the pub, and you'll find the shop and café on the right.

129 THE HALF MOON

Fore Street, Tiverton, Devon EX16 6LD
☎ 01884 253543 Fax: 01884 257554
e-mail: sdryhurst@sky.com

Top-notch home-cooked food keeps the customers happy at the **Half Moon**, where Shaun and Lynn Dryhurst have been at the helm for 20 years. Formerly located on the main street of Tiverton, it was rebuilt back from that road in the 1960s. It opens at 8.30 Monday to Saturday and at midday on Sunday, and food is served until 2 o'clock. The day starts with Lynn's excellent breakfasts – traditional, Special Half Moon, Special Full Moon, eggs or beans on toast, bubble & squeak with eggs & bacon, accompanied by tea, coffee or hot chocolate in cups or mugs. The main menu offers steaks, gammon, mixed grill, honey-roasted ham, pork chops, lamb chops and Lynn's homemade dishes – lasagne, chilli con carne, cottage pie, steak & kidney pie and

chicken, ham & mushroom pie. The pies can be ordered in large or small size. Daily specials could include scampi, roast pork and beef hot pot. Courage Best is the resident real ale, but the most popular draught ales are Fosters and John Smith Smooth. On the social side, the Half Moon hosts live music sessions every Sunday, a Friday/Saturday disco and a monthly quiz. Cash only.

130 THE MAD HATTERS RESTAURANT

5 Fore Street, Tiverton, Devon EX16 6LN
☎ 01884 252635
e-mail: david.hunter62@btinternet.com

The **Mad Hatters** on one of the main streets of Tiverton is a first venture into this type of business for David and Sue Hunter, who have made it one of the most popular eating places in town. A paved path flanked by tables, chairs,

trees and shrubs leads into this three-storey listed Georgian building, which is open from 9 to 3 Monday to Saturday, with longer hours in the summer. The good choice of home cooking spans the soup of the day, the fish of the day, filo king prawns, Cornish pasties, sweet & sour chicken and luscious Devon cream teas.

133 BROPHY'S

6 High Street, Sidmouth,
Devon EX10 8EL
☎ 01395 578998

Excellent home cooked food served in a relaxed atmosphere is what is on offer at **Brophy's** coffee shop and restaurant. Owned and run by Stephen and Shirley, it is open daily for breakfast, lunches and

afternoon teas. There is a day long selection of sweet and savoury delights. Most of the produce is sourced locally; the choice runs from light snacks to main meals such as Lamb and Apricot pie or Beer Battered Haddock. Sweeter treats include an array of super home baked cakes, scones and pastries. The fine food is accompanied by freshly ground coffee and teapigs speciality teas.

Rackenford, nr Tiverton,
Devon EX16 8DT
☎ 01884 881369
e-mail: sop_bb@hotmail.com
⊕ www.thestaginn.co.uk

History and charm abound at the **Stag Inn**, which is recorded as the oldest public house in Devon. Dating back to the end of the 12th century, this wonderful thatched pub stands in the village of Rackenford, about a mile off the main A361 Tiverton to South Molton road. A cobbled passage leads into an atmospheric bar with low beams, barrel tables and a huge fireplace flanked by old settles. Very much a local's local, it also appeals to a much wider clientele and is thriving under the management of Sophie, a local lady, and Matt, who hails from Australia and worked as a chef for

Gordon Ramsey in London at the Boxwood cafe in Knightsbridge. They arrived here towards the end of 2007 and through their hard work and enthusiasm, combined with the history of the place and the quality of the food and drink, they are well on the way to making this one of the most popular destination pubs in this part of the world.

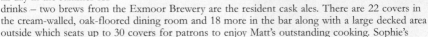

The bar is open lunchtime and evening and all day in the summer for drinks – two brews from the Exmoor Brewery are the resident cask ales. There are 22 covers in the cream-walled, oak-floored dining room and 18 more in the bar along with a large decked area outside which seats up to 30 covers for patrons to enjoy Matt's outstanding cooking. Sophie's family own and run a nearby organic farm, West Yeo, and a great deal of the produce that goes into Matt's kitchen comes from that source. West Yeo bacon is used in the Caesar salad; West Yeo chicken livers served with beetroot salad and a fried egg, and in the breast with a cider sauce; and West Yeo beef in the 10oz rib-eye served with proper chips and béarnaise sauce. On the fishy side, pollock is cooked in Stag Ale batter and hand-caught sea scallops from Brixham are served with pea shoots and brown sherry butter. Market fish is sourced daily by Noël from Channel Fisheries in Brixham. Sunday brings traditional roasts and a fish option. The bar menu, shorter and simpler but of equal excellence, offers dishes such as organic chicken sandwich and open toasted egg & cress sandwich as well as some dishes from the main restaurant menu. Diners would be missing another treat if they didn't round off their meal with one of the luscious desserts, perhaps white port trifle or champagne jelly raspberries with vanilla ice cream. Food is served from 12 to 2.30 and from 6.30 to 9.30 every day except Monday.

Families with children are welcome, and the pub accepts the major credit cards. There's ample off-road parking, and the patio commands wonderful views of the countryside.

Dalwood, nr Axminster, Devon EX13 7EG
☎ 01404 881342
e-mail: reservations@tuckersarms.co.uk
🌐 www.tuckersarms.co.uk

The **Tuckers Arms** is a classic English pub with a thatched roof, low beamed ceilings, flagstone floors and a handsome inglenook fireplace. Dating back some 800 years, it is the oldest building in Dalwood, a village signposted off the A35 Axminster to Honiton road. Hanging baskets, window boxes and flowering tubs make a lovely show in spring and summer, and the interior is equally delightful at any time of the year.

The two bars have an assortment of dining chairs, window seats and settles against the walls. The back bar has a huge collection of miniatures. The pub also has two skittle alleys that are used by teams in the local leagues nightly from Monday to Friday. Outside, there are plenty of chairs on the attractive paved terrace and picnic benches in the leafy lawned garden.

Otter Ale and Dorset Gold are the resident real ales, with another locally brewed guest ale in the summer months, and they also stock a good selection of wines by glass (two sizes) or bottle. Tracey, the licensee, her partner Craig, a chef with many years' experience, and Craig's mum Beverley make an excellent team at this outstanding old hostelry, and in the short time since they took over they have been attracting patrons from a wider area day by day. The hosts, together with the ambience and character of the pub, ensure that the atmosphere is always warm and relaxing.

They are also proud of the reputation they have gained for the quality of the food. Craig specialises in seasonal game, steaks and fresh fish and shellfish, including locally caught crab, lobster and lemon sole. The lunchtime menu offers pub classics like jacket potatoes, cod & chips, burgers, sausages and cold meat platters. From the specials board (lunch and dinner) could come salmon & dill fishcakes, spicy chicken open ravioli, herb-crusted rack of lamb and sirloin steak with a choice of sauces. There's a separate fishboard with the likes of moules et frites, baked mackerel with lemon butter and sea bass on potato gratin with a white wine and crevette sauce. Children are welcome in the restauarnt, where booking is advisable at the weekend. Pub hours are 12 to 3 and 6.30 to 11 (Sunday to 12 to 10.30) with extended hours in summer, and food is served every session except Sunday evening.

There are many attractions and places of interest near the inn, which is a very friendly and comfortable base for a short break or a longer holiday. The five upstairs rooms, including a family room, all have en suite facilities, television and tea/coffee tray, and a generous breakfast starts the day.

134 BICTON PARK BOTANICAL GARDENS

East Budleigh, near Budleigh Salterton,
Devon EX9 7BJ
☎ 01395 568465 Fax: 01395 568374
e-mail: info@bictongardens.co.uk
🌐 www.bictongardens.co.uk

Set in the picturesque Otter Valley, near the coastal town of Budleigh Salterton, **Bicton Park Botanical Gardens** span three centuries of horticultural history. The 63-acre park's oldest ornamental area is the Italian Garden that was created in the axial style of the Versailles landscaper, André le Notre in around 1735 by Henry Rolle, the park's owner. By that time, formal garden design was becoming unfashionable in England and this might explain why the garden was located out of view of the house.

However, today, the full grandeur of the Italian Garden can be seen from the spacious restaurant that is housed in the classically styled Orangery that was built at the beginning of the 19th century. Bicton's high-domed Palm House, one of the world's most beautiful garden buildings, was the first of many developments made here between 1820 and 1850 whilst others include the important collection of conifers in the Pinetum that is now the subject of a rare species conservation project. The gardens also contain St Mary's Church, where Queen Victoria once worshipped, and the exotic Hermitage that was built in 1839 by Lady Louise Rolle as a summerhouse. A large museum reflects changes in agricultural, and rural life generally, over the past 200 years. These Grade I listed gardens, which are open all year, also features a narrow-gauge railway that meanders through the gardens, a gift shop, a garden centre and children's indoor and outdoor play areas.

136 THE GREENHOUSE RESTAURANT

6 Lee Road, Lynton, Devon EX35 6HW
☎ 01598 753358
e-mail: paulking5@btconnect.com

What started in 1890 as a demure, typical late-Victorian tea room has developed into a thriving café and gastro-wine bar that's open from 9 in the morning to 9.30 in the evening every day in season and at the weekend off season. Owner Peter Bowes and manager Paul King have put their experience to fine use in the **Greenhouse Restaurant**, an outstanding enterprise that attracts good support both from the local community and from the large number of visitors who come to Lynton on holiday each year. The superb interior, which retains many original features, include a magnificent conservatory garden area. The extensive menus rely heavily on prime local produce including Exmoor meat and fish from local waters. Breakfast offers anything from toast to a traditional English full plate, and other choices – there really is something for

everyone – run from fishcakes and seafood linguine to seasonal salads, supreme of chicken, lamb casserole, steaks and Devon cream teas. Even the sandwiches are exceptional, with fillings like sun-blush tomato & brie, West Coast crab and pan-fried garlic chicken. The menu changes from café to restaurant at 6 o'clock. The Greenhouse has an extensive wine list (bottle or glass) and a range of beers, sherry, port, malts and liqueurs. Booking is recommended for evening tables.

135 MOTHER MELDRUM'S TEA GARDENS

The Valley of Rocks, Lee Road, Lynton,
Devon EX35 6JH
☎ 01598 753667 Fax: 01598 753667
e-mail: colinjoy@tiscali.co.uk

Mother Meldrum's is a magnet for lovers of home cooking, a popular refreshment stop for walkers and tourists in this dramatic part of the North Devon coast. Since 2000 it has been owned and personally run by Jacqui and Colin Joy. It has been a tea room and gardens for more than 50 years, but had been closed for seven years prior to the arrival of the Jays, who have given the old place a new and healthy lease of life. It stands in the amazing Valley of Rocks and can be reached by the unnumbered road west out of Lynton or on foot on the scenic North walk footpath.

There are seats for 40 inside in the tea room and for a further 40 outside at picnic benches on the lawn under trees in the beautiful garden – a real boon in the balmy summer months. The printed menu and the daily specials board provide plenty of choice to cater for appetites, large and small and palates savoury and sweet. Sandwiches and snacks on toast make a good start to the day (or at any time) and other choices include salads, scampi, pasties and a variety of all-day breakfast combinations. The Rock Climber Special is a burger topped with cheese in a bun, and Mother Meldrum's omelettes – ham, mushroom or tomato – are always popular. On the sweeter side are home-made cakes and pies, lattices and gateaux, Ragged Jack rock cakes and Devon cream teas. Families are always very welcome and children have their own special section of the menu. Ham, egg & chips, sausages, baked beans and spaghetti all go down a treat, and the reward for clearing the plate could be a helping of Witches Spell – wibble wobble jelly with ice cream.

The tea room takes its name from Mother Meldrum, a supposed witch who lived in caves in the area. The Valley of Rocks is one of the remarkable natural features in Devon. The poet Robert Southey was deeply impressed, and the author RD Blackmore transforms the site into the 'Devil's Cheesering' where Jan Ridd meets Mother Meldrum among the rocks. And it was after walking along the cliff path that Samuel Taylor Coleridge was inspired to write *The Rime of the Ancient Mariner*. The whole dramatic, atmospheric area is a paradise for ramblers and climbers. Hunger and thirst come quickly in the bracing air, and Jacqui, Colin and their staff know how to deal with both at Mother Meldrum's Tea Gardens, which are open every day from the end of March/Easter to the end of October. Cash only.

137 THE ROCK HOUSE HOTEL

Manor Green, Lynmouth,
Devon EX35 6EN
☎ 01598 753508 Fax: 01598 753796
e-mail: enquiries@rock-house.co.uk
🌐 www.rock-house.co.uk

The **Rock House Hotel** commands a breathtaking location in Lynmouth, looking seaward and across to the town and the famous cliff railway. The 17th century Grade II listed property stands alone at the harbour entrance between the sea and Manor Green, offering the ideal base for a relaxing holiday where the sounds of the river and the sea provide a soothing backdrop and woodland, coastal and riverside walks offer gentle exercise in the bracing Devon air.

The Rock House is a first venture for Mike and Glenys Haworth, who welcome guests all year round into the inviting surroundings of their lovely hotel. The accommodation comprises eight superbly appointed, centrally heated bedrooms – doubles, twins and a single – all with en suite facilities, television, alarm clock, complimentary hot drinks tray and hairdryer. Some of the rooms have romantic four-posters, and one is located on the ground floor, making it suitable for less mobile guests. All make the most of the wonderful location with views of the sea, the river, the harbour or the lovely Lyn Valley. Residents in

this magical setting wake up to a hearty English breakfast that provides the fuel for a day discovering all that the area has to offer – or just relaxing in the garden or enjoying a stroll round town. The tariff is on a Bread & Breakfast basis, but lunch and dinner are also available, served to non-residents and residents from 12 to 3 and from 6 to 9.

The bounty of the sea naturally features strongly on the menu, and a blackboard lists lunchtime specials such as deep-fried battered cod, breaded scampi or fishcakes. Evening meals are served in the bar or restaurant and booking is recommended to ensure a table in the elegant 20-cover harbourside restaurant. The evening menu tempts with such dishes as seafood jambalaya; sea bass with shallots, garlic, wine, herbs and a prawn and cream sauce; beef tournedos; and Gressingham duckling with rosemary, thyme and a raspberry liqueur sauce. Desserts like bread & butter pudding or a trio of chocolate truffle provide a delicious end to a memorable meal.

Lynmouth is a marvellous place for a holiday, with the constant pull of the sea (the tidal range is one of the highest in the world), the glorious scenery and the wonderful walks. One walk leads through woodland into Glen Lyn Gorge, where a stretch of the river is used to provide Lynmouth's hydro-electric needs. Another attraction is the water-powered Cliff Railway that connects Lynmouth to Lynton high on the cliff above.

457

138 CLEVERDON'S RESTAURANT

18 Mill Street, Bideford, Devon EX39 2JR
☎ 01237 472179 Fax: 01237 472179
e-mail: smsmith2007@aol.com

Sweet and savoury palates are equally well catered for at **Cleverdon's Restaurant**, where friends and partners Sue, Jock and Paul have built up a large and growing following both with the local community and with visitors to Bideford. The restaurant is easy to spot on a shopping street in the centre of town with its picture-windowed, blue-painted street-level floor and diamond-paned black-and-white upper storey. In the 64-seat dining room patrons can enjoy the chef's efforts between 9 and 4 Monday to Saturday, also Wednesday, Thursday and Friday evenings between May and October. The great majority of the ingredients are locally sourced on the wide-ranging menus. The main menu offers tried-and-tested favourites like toasties, omelettes, jacket potatoes, chilli, spaghetti bolognese (meat or vegetarian), salads, bangers & mash,

chicken curry and macaroni cheese. Home baking excels with the likes of Victoria sponge, coffee & walnut cake, carrot & orange cake, flapjacks, scones and almond slice, along scrumptious cream teas and gluten-free options of lemon cake and chocolate mousse cake. Families with children are always welcome and the little ones can choose from their own menu. No credit cards.

139 THE SWAN INN

49 Torrington Street, Bideford,
Devon EX39 4DD
☎ 01237 473460

Quality cooking and outstanding hospitality are a winning combination at the **Swan Inn**, which stands just over the bridge in the part of town called East-the-Water. Business partners and leaseholders Clint and Denise Duggan and Adam and Sharon Middleton have a real success on their hands, and the enjoyment of the fine food is complemented by the lovely setting overlooking the River Torridge. Clint is an experienced and talented chef, and in the bar and restaurant patrons can choose from a wide variety of snacks and meals. Local suppliers provide most of the produce, which is the basis of dishes that include something for everyone, served from 12 to 3 and 6 to 9 (till 10 at the weekend). Senior meals are served Tuesday and Thursday lunchtime and

Sunday sees a carvery with a choice of meats accompanied by five fresh vegetables. In addition, home-made cakes are served with tea or coffee throughout the day. The bar is open all day for drinks, which include three or four real ales, usually including Spitfire, Tribute and Old Speckled Hen. The Swan is closed between 3 and 5 in January and February, otherwise open all day every day.

140 THE BELL INN

Rectory Lane, Parkham, nr Bideford,
Devon EX39 5PL
☎ 01237 451201   Fax: 01237 452165
e-mail: enquiries@thebellinnparkham.co.uk
🌐 www.thebellinnparkham.co.uk

The **Bell Inn**, originally a smithy and two ancient cottages, has earned its reputation as one of the most popular destinations for food and drink in the whole of the county. Hosts Michael and Rachel Sanders and chef Pauline keep the customers happy with an excellent blend of outstanding hospitality and super

food based on the very best seasonal, West Country produce, including Exmoor trout, Devon saddle of lamb, Cornish brie and, for dessert, the local speciality Devon junket. Drinks include local cask ales and cider from Winkleigh.

141 HOLSWORTHY MUSEUM

Manor Offices, Holsworthy,
Devon EX22 6DJ
☎ 01409 259337
e-mail: holsworthy@devonmuseums.net
🌐 www.devonmuseums.net/holsworthy

Housed in an 18th century parsonage, this small museum gives you an insight into Holsworthy's heritage and traditions. Various themed displays cover the town, local railway, agriculture, trades, medical and the World Wars.

Researchers into family and local history may view, by prior arrangement, a selection of local parish registers on

microfiche, IGI fiche and Census data as well as information held in the Local History unit. The museum is run entirely by volunteers and is dependent on donations, a small entrance fee and support from local Councils.
Open February to December.

142 THE DART ROCK CAFÉ

6 Church Close, Dartmouth,
Devon TQ6 9DH
☎ 01803 834772
e-mail: info@dartrockcafe.com
🌐 www.dartrockcafe.com

The **Dart Rock Café** is a modern eating place located a stone's throw from Dartmouth's picturesque harbour. Susan Benjamin has quickly made it a popular place with the residents and tourists Susan works with local farmers, fishmongers and

other suppliers to ensure only the best produce goes into her kitchen, and out comes an excellent variety of dishes running from salads, burghers, home-made pizzas, cod & chips and griddled chicken to Sunday brunch. To drink, there's fair-trade tea and coffee, milkshakes, beer and wine by the glass. The café is open from 10 to 5 (to 4 in winter); closed Mondays in winter. Also open in the evening Thursday - Saturday.

143 THE STEAM PACKET INN

3 Fore Street, Kingswear,
Devon TQ6 0AD
☎ 01803 752208

The **Steam Packet** is a bright, welcoming inn looking out from Kingswear to Dartmouth harbour and the railway that runs to Paignton and beyond.

Run in fine style by experienced host Nessie Wilson, the inn is open all day for drinks, served in the warm, inviting

bar with real fires and lots of local pictures and photographs. The Steam Packet is a great place for a meal, whether it's a lunchtime baguette, burger, bangers & mash or battered cod or an evening curry, lasagne, salmon with parsley sauce, a succulent steak or a seasonal crab platter. Food is served from 12 to 3 and 6.30 to 9.30 (Sunday roasts 12 to 4; no food Sunday evening or Tuesday).

Church Street, Modbury, nr Ivybridge,
Devon PL21 0QR
☎ 01548 830239

The **Exeter Inn** is an outstanding public house located in the elegant little town of Modbury, on the A379 between Plymouth and Kingsbridge. Once a coaching inn, with origins going back to the 14th century, its bay-windowed frontage is adorned in spring and summer with a colourful show of flowers in tubs and hanging baskets. The rambling interior is equally delightful at any time of year, with flagstones, beams, an open fire in a hooded hearth and interesting period pictures and prints.

At the back of the inn is a secluded garden with tables and chairs surrounded by flowers and shrubs, and a partly covered patio area. Tenants Michelle and Paul, who took over the lease towards the end of 2007, have lost no time in building up a good local following by offering the very best in hospitality, beer, food and accommodation.

The bar is open throughout the day, seven days a week, for a full range of drinks, which include five well-kept real ales – Bass, Sharps Doom Bar, Tetley Dark, Greene King Abbot Ale and a rotating guest – and Addlestones and Thatchers ciders. Food is also served all day (midday to 9) and a blackboard lists the day's dishes, based whenever possible on local, seasonal ingredients. A typical selection might include sandwiches with assorted fillings; whitebait with tartare sauce; filo-wrapped tiger prawns with a sweet chilli sauce; turkey, ham & leek pie; gammon; lasagne and sausages & mash with onion gravy. There's always a vegetarian dish of the day, a children's menu, a specials menu and a dessert menu. It's best to book on Sunday, when the menu features traditional roasts. Families with children are welcome, and the inn accepts the major credit cards.

For guests staying overnight, the Exeter has six very well-appointed bedrooms, all en suite, in a variety of sizes. The tariff includes a generous breakfast or a packed lunch.

Modbury and the whole region are well worth taking time to explore. A short drive north brings visitors to the edge of Dartmoor, while to the south the coast at Bigbury-on-Sea is within equally easy reach. To the west the main road leads straight to Plymouth, to the east to Kingsbridge and Salcombe.

460

145 THE MARKET INN

2 Whitchurch Road, Tavistock,
Devon PL19 9BB
☎ 01822 613556
e-mail: sallysignature@aol.com

Five minutes' walk from the centre of Tavistock, the **Market Inn** has all the qualities of a traditional country inn – a cosy, friendly atmosphere, a fully stocked bar serving real ales, lagers, wines and spirits, home-cooked food served every day, a welcome for all the family, beer gardens, a pool table and ample off-road parking. The stand-alone stone building is easy to spot with its tall chimneys, white-painted pillars at the entrance and small-paned windows that give it a slightly ecclesiastical look. It was built as a mine-captain's residence in 1860 for Wheal Crelake, part of Devon United Mines producing copper, silver, pyrite and arsenic. It was previously known as the Cattle Market Inn, being located next to that once-thriving weekly market.

The interior is equally appealing, with a feature stone wall, pictures and plates and always a warm, inviting ambience. Sally and Godfrey Perkins, their son Neil, daughter Louise and Sally's sister Shirley make this a real family affair, and their efforts and enthusiasm have made it a very popular destination to enjoy a drink, a meal and genuine, spontaneous hospitality. The bar is open all day for drinks, which include two real ales – Courage Best and a regularly changing guest. Neil is the king of the kitchen, and his printed menu and the daily specials board provide an exceptional choice to satisfy a wide range of tastes and appetites. Traditionalists can tuck into much-loved classics like faggots with mushy peas, macaroni cheese, scampi, burgers, spaghetti Bolognese, the day's pie, the Sunday roasts, chilli con carne, steaks, lamb shanks and liver with bacon & onions. Neil puts an individual twist on other dishes such as pasta with crayfish, pork steak with a sweet apple & brandy sauce, cod & pancetta cakes, chargrilled chicken with coconut, chilli & lime, and duck leg in a plum sauce, served with stir-fried vegetables and rice. There's always a good choice for vegetarians, and a blackboard lists a selection of scrumptious desserts. Food is served from 11 to 9 Monday to Saturday and from 11 to 4 for the Sunday roasts (booking strongly recommended).

The summer Sunday barbecues are guaranteed to attract a good crowd, and other popular occasions are the quiz, held on the last Sunday of the month, and the live entertainment evening held every six weeks on a Saturday.

147 THE WHITE HART HOTEL

2 Plymouth Road, Buckfastleigh,
Devon TQ11 0DA
☎ 01364 642337
e-mail: her-ladyship49@hotmail.com

The **White Hart Hotel** stands in the former mill town of Buckfastleigh, which lies on the River Mardle on the B3380, close to the main A38 on the edge of Dartmoor. The historic premises, the oldest parts of which date back to the 16th century, were once a prominent coaching inn known for many years as the Golden Fleece. It also served for a time as a court house.

New licensees Dawn and Ian took over the reins at the beginning of 2008, bringing a new lease of life to the old place and implementing many changes to restore it to its former status as one of the top public houses in the area. The bar, with a feature stone hearth, exposed stone wall and an elaborate stone-fronted serving area, is an atmospheric spot for enjoying a chat and meeting the regulars. The bar is open all day, seven days a week, for a good selection of drinks, which include Highgate Mild and Jail Ale cask ales and a local cider. When the weather is warm, the secluded beer garden is a pleasant alternative. Dawn and Ian are lucky to have the services of Louise, a very talented chef whose cooking brings patrons from many miles around. A meal might start with a classic prawn cocktail or goat's cheese on a pesto crouton, and continue with a salmon dish or one of Louise's excellent pies – cottage, chicken & ham, steal & Jail Ale or fish (with haddock, prawns and salmon). To round off a splendid meal, home-made apple pie or whisky marmalade bread pudding fits the bill perfectly. Sandwiches, jacket potatoes, frittata and ham, egg & chips are additionally available on the lunchtime menu. Sunday lunch brings a choice of two roast joints and two vegetarian dishes – perhaps lasagne and a lentil loaf with a herb sauce.

Children are very welcome and they have a section of the menu just for them. Food is served from 12 to 3 at lunchtime and from 7 to 9 in the evening, and all day in high season. Cash or cheque only; no credit cards.

The hosts hope soon to have accommodation available, which will make the White Hart a pleasant place for a break and an ideal base for a walking holiday or discovering the many delights that Buckfastleigh and the surrounding area have to offer. With or without accommodation, the White Hart is a pub well worth seeking out for the excellent hospitality extended by Dawn and Ian and the fine food prepared by Louise.

146 THE FOX & HOUNDS

Bridestowe, nr Okehampton,
Devon EX20 4HF
☎ 01822 820206 Fax: 01822 820214
e-mail: info@foxandhoundshotel.com
🌐 www.foxandhoundshotel.com

Frank and Susy Ward have been the
proprietors of the **Fox & Hounds** since
1971, and with manager Dave they run one
of the most
popular pubs in
the region.
Standing by the
A386 between
Okehampton and
Tavistock, it's open
all day for drinks,
snacks and hot and

cold meals on a wide-ranging menu
supplemented by daily specials. Barbecues in
the beer garden are a popular summer
attraction. The inn also offers well-priced
accommodation in en suite rooms, a
bunkhouse and a caravan and camping park.
This most sociable of inns has a skittle alley
and a games room with pool and darts.

148 KNIGHTSTONE TEA ROOMS & RESTAURANT

Crapstone Road, Yelverton,
Devon PL20 6BT
☎ 01822 853679
e-mail: knightstonetea@yahoo.co.uk

Morning coffee, afternoon tea, cream teas,
home-made meals and Sunday roasts are
served in the popular licensed **Knightstone
Tea Rooms &
Restaurant**.
Dating from the
1890s, the
building later
became part of
the RAF Station

Harrowbeer. By 1960 it was sold and
converted into a restaurant then tea rooms.
Light snacks are served from 10 to midday
and after 2.30, with the main menu in
between. Everything is fresh and wholesome,
both the savoury items and the delicious
cakes and desserts. Open 10 to 6 in summer;
10 to 5 Wednesday to Sunday out of season.
Owners Francis and Lucy Hayes also have
two rooms for Bed & Breakfast guests.

149 THE LAUGHING POT TEA ROOMS

4 West Borough, Wimborne,
Dorset, BH21 1NF
☎ 01202 840676

The Fermor family – Lionel, Shirley, son Jason and
daughter-in-law Lisa – run the **Laughing Pot Tea
Rooms**, which are situated a short stroll from the
marvellous Wimborne Minster. What it lacks in size

(just 19 seats inside) it more than makes up for in
hospitality and the sheer quality of the food, and
cooks Shirley and Jason have firmly established it
as one of the finest tea rooms in the region.
Opening hours are 8ish to 4.30pm Monday to
Saturday. Breakfast, served from opening time to
3.30, offers a choice of full English, vegetarian
and lighter options, and light snacks, served from
9 to 4, include Welsh rarebit, macaroni cheese,
toasted sandwiches, hot filled baguettes and jacket

potatoes.
Sandwiches
can be
ordered to
take away.

The Laughing pot cream tea is another delight, and there's
always a mouthwatering display of home baking. Beverages
include teas (leaf, speciality, classic herbal) coffees, hot
chocolate, milkshakes and a variety of fruit blends. Families
with children are always made welcome, and the entrance is
wide enough to admit a wheelchair. Cash only.

Blandford Road, Sturminster Marshall,
nr Wimborne, Dorset BH21 4AQ
☎ 01258 857217

Sturminster Marshall is a village and parish on the River Stour, four miles west of Wimborne Minster, just off the A350 Poole to Blandford Forum road and just minutes from the A31. The whole area has a wealth of attractions both scenic and historic for visitors to discover, and one of the favourite places to pause for refreshment is the **Black Horse**. It's a former coaching inn dating from the middle of the 18th century, with beams, flagstones, real fires and a lovely old-world feel that makes the bar a really delightful place to meet for good conversation and something to quench a thirst. It has a large and loyal local following, and for visitors from outside the community it's the sort of place that once found is likely to become a must when returning to the area.

The Black Horse is the first pub venture for Jamie and Gemma, who took over the reins in September 2007. But they brought plenty of related experience, which, along with their excellent staff, has contributed to the success they are now enjoying here. In this warm, friendly ambience the bar is stocked with a full range of drinks, including award-winning ales – Badger Ale is one of the regular brews. Food is a major and still increasing side of the business, with separate lunchtime and evening menus – lunchtime from 12 to 3, evening from 6, weekends all day from 12 onwards. Lunch snacks include sandwiches and baguettes, jacket potatoes, omelettes and rumpsteak burgers ground and cooked to order – original, bacon & cheese or spicy, served in a ciabatta bun. The main lunch menu offers a long list of

tried-and-tested pub favourites, from battered cod, scampi and fish cakes to sausages, lasagne, the day's curry and ham, egg & chips. Most of the main courses are available in two sizes. An evening meal might start with chicken liver parfait served with an orange & beetroot marmalade, crab spring rolls or carpaccio of beef fillet or tuna. Next could come sea bass fillets on a bed of ribboned courgettes and carrots, 'posh' fish & chips (home-made chips, pea velouté), chicken in a cider and celery sauce, T-bone pork chop or sirloin steak served lain or with a Blue Vinney or pepper sauce. The menu lists a wine recommendation for each main course. There's always a good choice for vegetarians, and a blackboard lists the day's desserts.

151 THE CROWN

Winterborne Strickland,
Dorset DT11 0NJ
☎ 01258 880838
⊕ www.thecrownstrickland.co.uk

Easy to spot with its splendid thatched roof, the **Crown** is located in the village of Winterborne Strickland, off the A354 or A357 southwest of Blandford Forum.

James and Claire and James's mum Gill have made it once again the hub of village life, with well-kept ales, home-cooked food and a regular programme of events and entertainment. The menus offer a good selection of snacks and main meals, including pub classics such as fish & chips, steaks, steak & ale pie, hunter's chicken and lamb shanks. Families with children are very welcome and the Crown has a pleasant patio/beer garden area for alfresco sipping.

152 THE PLUME OF FEATHERS

Half Moon Street, Sherborne,
Dorset DT9 3LN
☎ 01935 816569

The **Plume of Feathers** is a 16th century inn built of mellow local stone and standing right across the road from the Abbey. This is the first inn together for Paul and Shirley Smith, but they bring a wealth of experience in the catering and hospitality trade. The bar is open every day of the week for drinks, which include four real ales (Greene King IPA, Wadworth's 6X, Horizon and a guest) and a real farm cider. Paul does most of the cooking, which gets going at 9 o'clock with traditional choices for breakfast. The main menu, freshly prepared from local produce, offers a choice of tried-and-tested favourites, from sandwiches and jacket potatoes to cottage pie, steak & kidney pie, scampi, steaks, cauliflower & broccoli cheese and Sunday roasts. Small portions are available of most main courses. There's lots to see in

Sherborne itself and the surrounding area, and the Plume of Feathers provides a very comfortable and convenient base for exploring the region. The two en suite rooms, which can be linked for use by a family, will during 2008 be augmented by two more rooms – a double and a family room – with views of the Abbey. The pub has a skittle alley and pleasant garden. Cash and cheque only

465

Middlemarsh, nr Sherborne,
Dorset DT9 5QN
☎ 01963 210966
e-mail: info@hunters-moon.org.uk
🌐 www.hunters-moon.org.uk

The **Hunters Moon** is a mid-18th century former coaching inn – once called the White horse – standing by the A352 at Middlemarsh, between Sherborne and Dorchester. Dean and Emma Mortimer, chef Andy and a hardworking team in support have made this an outstanding place to visit, whether it's for a refreshment stop, a snack, a leisurely meal or an overnight or longer stay. The interior of the inn is splendidly traditional, with a huge canopied hearth in a brick fireplace and handsome old beams, one of them home to a veritable army of miniature spirit and liqueur bottles.

The bar is an excellent place to meet at any time of the year, but when the sun shines or on balmy summer evenings a delightful alternative is provided by the superb lawned gardens with their picnic benches. The food here is outstanding, attracting regular visitors from far beyond the local area. Dean and Andy, both experienced and talented chefs, have devised a very tempting set of menus that provide a perfect balance between 'Great British Pub Favourites' and exciting, sometimes less familiar options. Representing the former are scampi, beer-battered cod, three-egg omelettes, a chunky club sandwich, burgers, lasagne and the

day's curry. Elsewhere on the menu are steaks; breast of chicken wrapped in bacon, topped with a smoked cheese cream; Portland scallops fried with garlic and thyme; pan-fried pork loin steak on a pool of apple and cider sauce; roasted salmon fillet with a vine tomato and basil ragout; and goat's cheese tart. Desserts include the local speciality Dorset apple cake. A carvery is added to the Friday evening menu and the Sunday roasts are guaranteed to bring in the crowds. Baguettes, bloomers and jacket potatoes are options for those with less time to spare. Children are welcome to enjoy starters or 'smaller appetites meals' from the menu, and the chefs are always ready to provide something else if they can – but be assured that it won't be turkey twizzlers!

The accommodation at the Hunters Moon comprises eight very comfortable en suite rooms, four of them family-size. They provide an ideal base for exploring the local attractions, which include the magnificent gardens at Minterne Magna and the club-wielding Cerne Abbas Giant carved into the hillside.

Trent, nr Sherborne, Dorset DT9 4SL
☎ 01935 850776
e-mail: hkirkie@hotmail.com
🌐 www.roseandcrowntrent.co.uk

At the heart of all things local

The picturesque village of Trent lies off the A30 or A359 a short drive from both Sherborne and Yeovil. In this attractive setting, with lovely views all round, the **Rose & Crown Trent** is a delightful place to relax, unwind and savour the excellent hospitality extended by Heather and Stuart. They brought considerable catering experience when they took over this, their first venture as publicans, in September 2007, and the reputation they have built up for fine cuisine and well-kept beer has quickly gained a dedicated following.

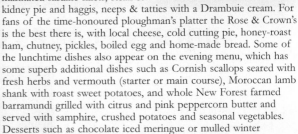

The promise of the part-thatched exterior is amply fulfilled inside, where the bar is a particularly pleasant spot for meeting or making friends over a glass of ale – Wadworth's 6X and Henry's IPA are the resident real ales, with two rotating guest ales in addition. The inn has a great asset in its delightful garden with lawns, a pond and a children's play area with swings and a slide.

The food at the Rose & Crown Trent is top class, and making a final choice from the always interesting menus can be a real problem! Prime produce from the South West takes pride of place in the kitchen, where the chefs produce a superb selection of dishes. The Trent Lunch Menu tempts with such delights as mushroom & Dorset Blue Vinny soup, basil-marinated sardine fillets, steak & kidney pie and haggis, neeps & tatties with a Drambuie cream. For fans of the time-honoured ploughman's platter the Rose & Crown's is the best there is, with local cheese, cold cutting pie, honey-roast ham, chutney, pickles, boiled egg and home-made bread. Some of the lunchtime dishes also appear on the evening menu, which has some superb additional dishes such as Cornish scallops seared with fresh herbs and vermouth (starter or main course), Moroccan lamb shank with roast sweet potatoes, and whole New Forest farmed barramundi grilled with citrus and pink peppercorn butter and served with samphire, crushed potatoes and seasonal vegetables. Desserts such as chocolate iced meringue or mulled winter pudding keep the enjoyment level high to the end. The menu notes that all diets are catered for and on request the chef will create a special dish from the seasonal stock.

The inn is closed on Mondays except Bank Holidays, and food is not served on Sunday evenings. Plans for the Rose & Crown Trent include the creation of rooms for B&B guests.

155 THE CROWN

High Street, Stalbridge, Dorset DT10 2LL
☎ 01963 362295
e-mail: ruth-panton@btconnect.com

The **Crown** has long been a landmark on the main street of Stalbridge, a lovely little village on the A357, south of the main A30 between Shaftesbury and Sherborne. Owners Ruth and Steve have made this a popular spot among the local community and a splendid place to pause on a journey. The ambience in the bar is always warm and welcoming, and the beer garden is a pleasant alternative in the summer months. Wadworth's 6X is the resident cask ale, with a changing guest, and good honest home cooking will satisfy a variety of tastes and appetites. The main menu is served at lunchtime every day except Monday and from 5 to 10.30 on Friday and Saturday. Home-made pies (steak & onion, beef & mushroom, chicken & mushroom, chicken & ham) are among the favourites,

which also include fish & chips, traditional breakfasts, ham & eggs and steaks. Sandwiches and snacks are served throughout the day, and the excellent homemade pizzas can be ordered to take away. Pub hours are from 6 on Monday, lunchtime and evening Tuesday to Thursday and all day at the weekend. The Crown has a thriving sporty/social side, with pool, skittles, darts and Sky TV.

HIDDEN PLACES GUIDES

Explore Britain and Ireland with *Hidden Places* guides - a fascinating series of national and local travel guides.

Packed with easy to read information on hundreds of places of interest as well as places to stay, eat and drink.

Available from both high street and internet booksellers

For more information on the full range of *Hidden Places* guides and other titles published by Travel Publishing visit our website on

www.travelpublishing.co.uk
or ask for our leaflet by phoning **01752 276660** or emailing **info@travelpublishing.co.uk**

468

Gold Hill, Child Okeford, nr Blandford
Forum, Dorset DT11 8HD
☎ 01258 860310
e-mail: peterturner@saxoninn.co.uk
🌐 www.saxoninn.co.uk

The premises that now comprise the **Saxon
Inn** were originally three farm cottages
believed to date back some 300 years. There
was a small shop in the middle cottage, selling
groceries, general supplies and drinks. The
Jug & Bottle did not become a hostelry until
the early 1950s, when it was known as the
New Inn. In 1965 it became the Saxon Inn,
one of the most delightful and picturesque
country inns you could ever encounter. It
nestles under Hambldeon Hill at Gold Hill,
by Child Okeford, signposted off the A350
or A357 northwest of Blandford Forum.

The white-painted exterior is adorned
with a colourful array of tubs and hanging
baskets, and at the back is a lovely garden
with trees, shrubs and plants and a Wendy
house that will keep the little ones busy and
happy. The interior is equally delightful, with
horse brasses on old beams, log fires and a
warm, welcoming ambience created by hosts
Peter and Helen Turner. The drinks served in
the bar include cask-conditioned ales from
local breweries and a small, select range of
wines from Old and New Worlds. The beers
are kept in A1 condition, earning CAMRA
approval and quenching the thirsts of
walkers, cyclists, motorists and tourists as well
as the local community.

The food is another excellent reason for seeking out this marvellous place. A wide choice of
traditional pub dishes makes up the à la carte menu, which is supplemented by a daily specials
board reflecting the best and freshest of what's in season at the time. Favourite dishes cooked by
Helen and the talented kitchen team include cottage pie, steak & ale pie, chicken provençale, cod in
batter, salmon with parsley butter and rump, fillet and gammon steaks. Sandwiches and jacket
potatoes provide lighter/quicker options. Food is
served lunchtime seven days a week and in the
evening Monday to Saturday. The Saxon Inn has
recently prepared for its continuing success by a
major programme to provide more bar and dining
space with no loss of the period character and
ambience.

The owners have also created four superbly
appointed upstairs guest rooms with state-of-the-art
en suite facilities: the inn is now not just a place to
find outstanding food and drink but a comfortable,
civilised base for touring a part of the world that's
rich in scenic and historic interest.

469

157 THE BREWERS ARMS

Winterborne St Martin/ Martinstown, nr
Dorchester, Dorset DT2 9LB
☎ 01305 889361
🌐 www.thebrewersarms.com

'It's also run by very nice people', which is what makes the **Brewers Arms** such a delightful place to visit. Hosts John and Jackie have a warm, genuine welcome for all who pass through the door into the bar, where the atmosphere is always chatty and relaxed. The décor includes an assortment of interesting ornaments and bric-a-brac, among them an old-style telephone bar counter – and it actually works!

The bar stocks an excellent range of real ales (Ringwood and Tribute Bitter are the regulars), draught and bottled beers, lagers, wines by the glass, spirits and soft drinks. For sunny days the large, secluded beer garden is a very pleasant spot for alfresco sipping. Hospitality is the name of the game, and John and Jackie have made their pub once again the hub of village life. That hospitality naturally extends to the food, which runs from bar snacks and sandwiches to hot and cold main meals and traditional Sunday lunches. Jackie's menu spans sandwiches with generous fillings, jacket potatoes and nachos; old favourites like cottage pie, sausages & mash; ham, egg & chips; burgers and steaks; traditional fish & chips; honey roast duckling; chilli con carne meatballs; salmon tagliatelle; chicken tikka masala; steak, mushroom & ale pudding and cheese & broccoli pasta bake. Favourites include sticky toffee pudding, spotted dick and pineapple upside-down cake. The Brewers Arms is a great place for families with children and dogs and it also has a thriving sporty/social side.

There are games machines, a pool table and a skittle alley, and regular events include a quiz every Wednesday, when visiting foursomes are invited to pit their wits against the local brains. The pub is closed at lunchtime on Mondays in winter and is otherwise open lunchtime and evening, all day on Friday, Saturday and Sunday and all day every day during the summer season. Food is served from 12 to 3 and from 6 to 9, and the pub is also open for morning coffee.

Winterborne St Martin, also known as Martinstown, lies on the B3159 near the junction with the A35, a short drive west of Dorchester. It's a pleasant spot, with a clear village stream running past the pub, and the area has plenty to interest the visitor: notable attractions include the ancient barrow of Nine Stones anf the impressive prehistoric site of Maiden Castle

158 THE DRAX ARMS

West Street, Bere Regis, nr Wareham,
Dorset BH20 7HH
☎ 01929 471386
e-mail: draxarms@btconnect.com
⊕ www.thedraxarms.co.uk

The **Drax Arms** is a traditional Dorset inn situated in the heart of Bere Regis. The village gained its royal suffix when it was a favourite stopping place for monarchs on their way to the West Country. It remains a popular place to pause for refreshment, and tenants Belinda and Martin Edge have breathed new life into the 400-year-old pub since taking over towards the end of 2007. The bar, with beams and a fine inglenook fireplace, is a convivial spot for enjoying a drink, and the beer garden, with lovely views of the surrounding countryside, is a pleasant alternative on sunny days or warm evenings. Belinda and Martin both cook, and their menu of classic pub dishes cater for appetites large and small. Service starts at 9 o'clock (10 on Sunday), when a wide breakfast choice is available

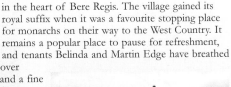

until midday. The main menu takes over until 2 and resumes in the evening at 7, with last orders at 9. The homemade steak & Tanglefoot Ale pie is a perennial favourite, and other popular choices include moules marinière, beer-battered cod, curries, lasagne (meat or vegetarian) and steaks. No credit cards. The pub hosts a live entertainment evening once a month (Friday or Saturday) and every Wednesday from 9 free guitar tuition is offered.

160 THE GREYHOUND INN

Sydling St Nicholas, nr Dorchester,
Dorset DT2 9PD
☎ 01300 341303
e-mail: info@thegreyhounddorset.co.uk
⊕ www.thegreyhounddorset.co.uk

The **Greyhound** is a picture-postcard inn that sits well in the attractive village of Sydling St Nicholas, which stands between the A37 and the A352 a short drive north of Dorchester. This splendid free house is owned and run by John and Karen, Ron and Cherry, who extend a warm and enthusiastic welcome for all who pass through the door. The bar is a convivial spot to meet friends and enjoy a drink, which could be a glass of Sydling Bitter that's brewed specially for the pub. Karen and the chefs prepare an excellent selection of dishes on the interesting main menu. Typical choices include Mediterranean fish soup, wood pigeon & bacon salad, fillet of sea bass in a tempura batter, honey-glazed ham hock, fragrant green Thai chicken curry and rib-eye or fillet steak. Generously filled sandwiches add

to the lunchtime choice, and a snack menu is available Monday to Saturday lunchtimes. The

Greyhound is also a splendid place to spend a few days relaxing, enjoying the pleasant surroundings or exploring the many attractions in the area. Six superbly appointed bedrooms, all with en suite facilities, three on the ground floor, are located across the courtyard in the converted old coach house.

471

159 KEMPS COUNTRY HOUSE HOTEL

East Stoke, nr Wareham,
Dorset BH20 6AL
☎ 0845 862 0315 Fax: 0845 862 0316
e-mail: info@kempscountryhouse.co.uk
⊕ www.kempshotel.com

'Stay in Luxury'

That's the motto, and that's what guests can look forward to at **Kemps Country House Hotel**, which stands by the A352 halfway between Wareham and Wool. Starting life as a Victorian rectory, it underwent a complete refurbishment before opening to the public in its current guise at the beginning of 2008 with an ETB Five-Star grading. No expense was spared in ensuring that every detail is just right, and the management and staff make great efforts to guarantee that guests enjoy the finest of modern-day necessities as well as providing the ultimate in bedroom comfort.

All the rooms have air-conditioning, super-size king beds, flat-screen television, wi-fi access, tea/coffee-making facilities, mineral water, power showers and heated towel rails. Executive and family rooms additionally have sofa beds and underfloor bathroom heating. Some rooms are adapted for disabled guests and all can be booked on a Bed & Breakfast or Dinner, Bed & Breakfast basis.

Breakfast is served from 7.30 to 9.30 in the week and from 8 to 10 Saturday and Sunday. Kemps is a lovely place to stay at any time of the year: in summer sipping an aperitif on the garden terrace while contemplating the world, in winter keeping snug by the roaring log fire in the lounge. The Restaurant and the Conservatory dining area are benchmarks for sophisticated dining. The table d'hôte and à la carte menus are based on the very finest ingredients including local farm produce and locally sourced fish and shellfish. The fine food is complemented by well-chosen wines, and attentive, professional service set the seal on a memorable meal in the most elegant and civilised surroundings.

Three excellent golf courses are within a few minutes' drive, and fishing, sailing, water skiing, windsurfing, riding and clay target shooting can all be arranged locally. Kemps is the nearest hotel to the Monkey World Ape Rescue Centre at Longthorns, Wareham, with 150 rescued and endangered apes and monkeys, and the Tank Museum at Bovington, with 150 armoured vehicles on display. Guests can follow the Hardy Trails and learn all about Lawrence of Arabia, and other easily accessible attractions include National Trust houses and gardens, Lulworth Castle, the Purbeck Hills and the Jurassic Coast World heritage Site.

53 Dorchester Road, Maiden Newton,
Dorset DT2 0BD
☎ 01300 320600
e-mail: inquire@chalkandcheese.org.uk
🌐 www.chalkandcheese.org.uk

When landlord and landlady Gail and Dave arrived at the **Chalk & Cheese** in the autumn of 2007 they set about putting it back on the map. And they are succeeding admirably in that task, making it once again the hub of the local community. The former coaching inn and smithy, with parts dating back to 1780, stands in the village of Maiden Newton, off the A356 a short drive northwest of Dorchester. Greene King IPA and two rotating guests head the list of drinks served in the bar, and the kitchen produces a good variety of pub favourites to please meat-eaters, fish-eaters and vegetarians. Saturday is curry night and Sunday lunch brings traditional roasts. On the social side, the pub hosts monthly pool and darts competitions

and a quiz that starts at 9 o'clock every other Sunday. Families are always made welcome – there's a family games room – and the pub has plenty of outside seating on the patio and in the paved beer garden. With all the qualities that make the traditional English such a valued institution, this fine old pub is always a delight to visit. Cash, cheques and most major cards accepted.

163 THE GILESGATE MOOR HOTEL

Teesdale Terrace, Gilesgate, Durham,
Co Durham DH1 2RN
☎ 0191 386 6453
e-mail: gilesgatemoorhotel@hotmail.com

Gilesgate Moor, once a separate village, is now virtually a suburb of Durham, on the northeastern edge of the city close to the A690 that runs up to Junction 62 of the A1(M), which is only minutes away, and on to Sunderland. The eponymous **Gilesgate Moor Hotel** has been providing hospitality for more than 100 years, and that long tradition is now being carried on by Graham and Wendy Blackmore, who took over the tenancy in the autumn of 2007. Funds from the owning Marston's Brewery have been made available for a revamp of the premises, a carefully planned refurbishment programme that has enabled the hotel to be updated while preserving the best of the period character.

The carpeted bar is in traditional style, with a feature fireplace surrounded by gleaming brass ornaments, and drinks are served here from 2pm to midnight Monday to Thursday and from midday to midnight Friday, Saturday and Sunday. Live music gets the place buzzing on the second Saturday of the month, and Sunday brings a quiz and a bingo session. The hotel also has a golfing society that meets regularly.

The Gilesgate Moor offers practical, good-value overnight accommodation in modernised bedrooms that cater for singles, couples and families; three of the rooms have en suite facilities and all are double-glazed and centrally heated, with television and complimentary beverage tray. The room rates are very reasonable, making the hotel a good choice for anyone working in the area or for tourists looking for budget accommodation while discovering the many historic attractions of the city. A cooked breakfast is included in the tariff, and the bar serves a section of sandwiches and light snacks – the plan is to extend the food side of the business. Home-cooked evening meals are available for guests on request.. It's an easy walk or short ride from the hotel to the heart of Durham, where the magnificent Cathedral, third only to Canterbury and York in ecclesiastical significance, the Castle, the University and the Museums are among the attractions that no visitor should miss.

A footnote for collectors of bizarre facts: a famous figure who occasionally hung out at the Gilesgate Moor Hotel was Albert Pierrepoint, who stayed here while plying his trade as Public Executioner at Durham Jail. It is recorded that he participated in six hangings at the jail, most of them as assistant to his uncle.

162 STONEBRIDGE INN

Nevilles Cross, Durham,
Co Durham DH1 3RX
☎ 0191 386 9591
e-mail: stonebridgeinn@aol.com

The **Stonebridge Inn** stands by the A690 Crook road on the western outskirts of Durham, no more than a mile from the city centre. Dating from the 1860s, it is one of Durham's best-loved pubs and a great place to meet old chums and make new friends. The bar has a delightfully traditional look, with beams, old oak floorboards, an open fire and well-spaced tables – pictures of classic film stars on the walls provide an interesting talking point. Outside is a pleasant little patio that's a popular spot in the summer months. Three real ales are usually on tap, typically Black Sheep, Marston's Pedigree and Old Speckled Hen. The pub has a fine reputation for its home-cooked food, combining quality with value for money and excellent service. The menus cater for a wide range of tastes and appetites, and the daily fresh fish specials are among the favourite dishes. Monday is steak night. As well as becoming increasingly a destination restaurant, the inn is also a popular, well-liked local with a hardworking, go-ahead host in Graham Baldridge. Pool and darts are played in a part of the bar away from the counter, Thursday sees a well-attended quiz and Friday is acoustic music night.

165 THE PUNCH BOWL

Craghead, Co Durham DH9 6EF
☎ 01207 232917

Glaswegian Robert Darroch and his wife have breathed new life into the **Punch Bowl**, which stands in the village of Craghead, on the B6313 three miles west of Chester-le-Street. It dates from the late 1800s, and the welcoming ambience created by the hosts and the loyal regulars is enhanced by a major refurbishment programme recently

completed by the owning Vaux Brewery. The pub is open all day, seven days a week, for drinks, and traditional pub snacks and dishes include a popular Sunday carvery that operates from 12 to 4. The Punch Bowl also provides a well-priced overnight stop for visitors exploring the region or working in the vicinity, with three B&B rooms with shared facilities. This well-kept pub is very much at the heart of the local community, with a Thursday night quiz, karaoke on Friday and Sunday and live bands every other Saturday.

Commercial Street, Cornsay Colliery,
Co Durham DH7 9BN
☎ 0191 373 4224
🌐 www.theroyaloak.co.uk

Long-serving hosts Sonyia and Ian Truby have created a very special atmosphere at the **Royal Oak** – warm and welcoming, with everyone who passes through the door treated like an old friend.

The inn, which was built in 1871, stands at the end of a row of terraced houses at the edge of the Pennine foothills. It sets the standards for the typical Durham pit village pub – rustic, down to earth, lived-in and convivial – and Sonyia is a real star: she seems to be everywhere at once, and locals throng to enjoy the special atmosphere she and Ian have created.

The interior has an unpretentious, homely appeal, with patterned tablecloths and curtains, old leather seats and walls and window ledges adorned with assorted knick-knacks and trinkets. It has a separate pool room, and tables are set out at the front in the summer. A good range of drinks is served in the bar, and the food served in the cosy restaurant offers good honest flavours at good honest prices. Among the favourite orders you might find a tasty dish of cod and prawns, chicken stuffed with apple and stilton and served with a creamy sauce and wild Cornsey rabbit pie – and you can't get more local than that! Some regulars turn up to enjoy a portion of real chips.

For guests wanting somewhere warm and friendly to stay the Royal Oak has five modern en suite bedrooms of various sizes. The pub was built, like the rest of the village, on empty fields and woodland in the 19th century; it is the most prominent building on the main street (B6301). The colliery after which the village is named once employed over 700 men; it closed in 1953. Cornsay Colliery is one of several small villages in the vicinity: others are Quebec, Esk Winning and Tow Law. The pub has a car park for patrons. All major credit cards are accepted.

476

166 THE RED LION

Milbanke Close, Ouston,
nr Chester-le-Street, Co Durham DH2 1JH
☎ 0191 410 4697

Food is big business at the **Red Lion**, a late-19th century roadside inn located a short drive from the A1(M) north of Chester-le-Street. Sandwiches, salad bowls and jacket potatoes are among the snackier items on chef-patron Paul Taylor-Burrell's menus, while main dishes run from classics such as

cod with mushy peas, liver & onions and roast chicken to more exotic options like Japanese-style prawns with a sweet chilli dip or poached salmon with a ginger and lemon dressing. Smaller portions are available of most of the main courses – a typical thoughtful touch from a host who puts his customers first. A good selection of drinks is served in the busy bar, which is open from noon to midnight seven days a week. Wednesday is quiz night, when the pool table is free to all-comers.

167 THE BEACONSFIELD

105 Galgate, Barnard Castle,
Co Durham DI12 8ES
☎ 01833 637194

The **Beaconsfield** makes a big, bold statement on the main A67 towards the top end of town. And the promise of the handsome exterior is matched by the generous welcome afforded by Kathryn Quinn, a lovely Irish lady who looks after her customers like old friends. Dating from the early years of the 19th century and originally the local manor house, it is now a busy, popular pub with lots of dark wood in the traditionally styled bar and lounge. Elegant yet homely, it's a super place

to meet for a drink – Black Sheep and Adnam's Bitter are the regular cask ales – and it's even better to take time to enjoy Kathryn's wholesome home cooking. Flavours are very much to the fore in her dishes, which include pub favourites like all-day breakfast, fish & chips, casseroles and steak & kidney pie. Desserts are equally and temptingly traditional: sticky toffee pudding, jam roly poly, hot chocolate fudge cake. The Beaconsfield is open from midday to 11pm Sunday to Wednesday and from midday to midnight Thursday to Saturday. The inn hosts a quiz every second Wednesday, when all are welcome to put their knowledge and memories to the test.

477

168 THE ANCIENT UNICORN

Main Street, Bowes, nr Barnard Castle,
Co Durham DL12 9HL
☎ 01833 628321
e-mail: ancient.unicorn@virgin.net
🌐 www.ancient-unicorn.com

The **Ancient Unicorn** is a real pub-lover's pub, a 16th century stone building with enormous character and everything a proper pub should be. When Joanne Foster took over in the summer of 2006 she brought a wealth of experience in the licensed trade, adding the finishing touches of knowledge and outstanding hospitality to the pub's other assets.

The three-storey building is impressive in its own right, and the expectations created by the exterior are fully realised in the public rooms, where 2 feet-thick walls, beams and a huge fire create an irresistible ambience for locals, walkers, hikers, families and tourists. Black Sheep and Fullers London Pride are the resident cask ales, but before the urge to sample the beer the pub serves morning coffee from 10 o'clock in the morning. The

main menu, served lunchtime and evening, highlights prime local produce in dishes such as deep-fried Cotherstone cheese fritters; warm salad of black pudding with mushrooms and a poached egg; Cumberland sausage; and slow-roasted Teesdale lamb shank. This is wonderful walking country, and the Ancient Unicorn offers a very comfortable, civilised base with four immaculate en suite bedrooms – including a family room – in a courtyard-style annexe.

170 FIR TREE COUNTRY HOTEL

The Grove, Fir Tree, nr Crook,
Co Durham DL15 8DD
☎ 01324 762161

Fir Tree Country Hotel, located on the main A68 Darlington-Corbridge road, is the perfect stopping-off point for the motorist and tourist, whether pausing for

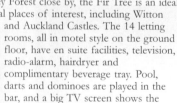

refreshment or enjoying an overnight or longer stay in the motel-style accommodation. The hotel, which takes its name from the village in which it stands, is run in fine style by Anne and Angus Downie, who have been in the hospitality business for many years. It is thanks to their experience and natural bonhomie that the hotel is one of the most popular for miles around, and the atmosphere in the public rooms is invariably warm and welcoming. A full range of drinks is served in the comfortable bar and lounge, and appetites small and large are catered for with bar menus and a wide-ranging à la carte menu served in Groves Bistro, from Thai fishcakes to cod Mornay, hunter's chicken, escalope of pork and juicy steaks. On the edge of Weardale, with Hamsterley Forest close by, the Fir Tree is an ideal base for a walking holiday or for discovering the many local places of interest, including Witton

and Auckland Castles. The 14 letting rooms, all in motel style on the ground floor, have en suite facilities, television, radio-alarm, hairdryer and complimentary beverage tray. Pool, darts and dominoes are played in the bar, and a big TV screen shows the major sporting events.

Middlestone Village, nr Bishops Auckland,
Co Durham DL14 8AB
☎ 01388 810904

Hosts Tony and Jane's watchword that the customer comes first has made the **Ship Inn** one of the most popular pubs in the region, and a notable local landmark that dates from 1729. Standing by the roadside in the village of Middlestone, northwest of Bishops Auckland, the Ship sets the standard in the area for the quality of its hospitality, food and drink. Connoisseurs of real ale are in their element here, with six cask-conditioned ales to choose from and up to 20 (plus a wider selection of ciders and wines) during the spring and late-autumn beer festivals that are such an attraction.

The Ship has won many awards for its beers, including CAMRA Pub of the Year several times, North East Pub of the Year, North East Regional Pub of the Year and runner-up in the National Pub of the Year awards. Food also brings

the crowds from all round the region to this lovely old pub. Traditional dishes, combining good honest flavours with excellent value for money they keep the prices very low and the portions very high!), run from pork & leek or Mediterranean sausages to crispy battered cod, scampi, spaghetti Bolognese, chilli con carne, lasagne, chicken à la king, Greek moussaka, steaks, home-made braised braised steak & ale pie topped with a puff pastry lid and the super Sunday roasts. For something a little more exotic, how about Jamaican pork (cooked in coconut milk with bananas, finished with baby spinach and celeriac, or creamy chicken tandoori?

Desserts such as strawberry jam pudding or passion fruit and vanilla ice cream in a passion fruit sorbet keep the enjoyment level high to the end.

The interior of the pub is warm and cosy, and a bonus when the sun shines is a rooftop patio with spectacular views over the Tees Valley to the Cleveland Hills. On the social side, Thursday is quiz night, and league darts and dominoes are played on Monday evenings. Pub hours are 4 to 11 Monday to Thursday, 12 to 11 Friday and Saturday and 12to 10.30 on Sunday. Food is served from 4 to 9 Monday to Thursday, 12 to 9 Friday, and 12 to 2 & 6 to 9 Saturday and Sunday. A large function room is available for parties and other celebrations, and a cosy snug caters for smaller groups. Monday sees darts and dominoes league matches, and Thursday is quiz night.

Self-catering accommodation for up to 6 guests is available in the old chapel opposite the pub, fully modernised, with a huge lounge, well-fitted kitchen, garden and patio.

479

171 THE CALBURY ARMS

Piercebridge, nr Darlington,
Co Durham DL2 3SJ
☎ 01325 374286

In the village of Piercebridge, west of Darlington by the A67 and B6275, the **Calbury Arms** is a proper pub-lover's pub, with big open fires, handsome furnishings, a pleasant beer garden, well-kept ales and a wide selection of food. Christine Morrison was on the staff here for many years before taking up the number one position in 2007, and with her husband Mike she is restoring its status as one of the finest pubs in the region. Greene King IPA, Theakston's Best and a guest ale are on tap to quench thirsts, and Mike's food can be enjoyed every lunchtime and evening. People come from miles around to tuck into his hearty steak & ale pie, but that's only one of the stars on his extensive menu, made even more extensive

by the daily chalkboard specials; vegetarians will be delighted with dishes

like mushroom stroganoff or baked butternut squash, spinach, walnut & parmesan filo tartlet with an orange and cranberry sauce. As well as being a great place for a drink and a meal, the Calbury Arms is also the social heart of the village. It hosts a quiz every other Monday, karaoke evenings one Saturday a month and a games night with pool, darts and dominoes every Friday.

172 CAFÉ 1618

16/18 Market Place, Middleton-in-Teesdale,
Co Durham DL12 0QG
☎ 01833 640300
e-mail: quality@cafe1618.com
⊕ www.cafe1618.com

Honest food, honestly cooked makes **Café 1618** one of the most popular and likeable eating places in the region, a lovely, friendly place to pause for refreshment in a beautiful, untamed part of the world. Jon Dunn in the kitchen and Bev Major front of house make an excellent team, and their lovely intimate licensed restaurant in the market place keeps the customers happy with home-made cakes and scones for morning coffee and afternoon tea, lunches both light and substantial and Aga-cooked evening meals offering both traditional English and some of European or Oriental inspiration. In the right weather this is available in the 'secret' beer garden, lovely! The Café is closed Monday and Tuesday in winter; in season it's open all day, every day. The town and the surrounding area are well worth taking time to explore, and Café 1618 provides a quiet, comfortable base for walkers and sightseers in two en suite bedrooms and a self-

contained one-up, one-down cottage in the garden. Middleton-in Teesdale, the Capital of Upper Teesdale, is a small town in a dramatically beautiful setting where several B roads meet ten miles northwest of Barnard Castle. It's a centre for some wonderful walks, one of them being the Pennine Way, which to the west of the town takes in the spectacular scenery of the River Tees and the thrilling power of the High Force and Low Force waterfalls.

Mickleton, nr Barnard Castle,
Co Durham DL12 0JZ
☎ 01833 640381

The **Rose & Crown** is the beating heart of the village of Mickleton, which lies in beautiful, rugged and unspoilt countryside on the B6281 northwest of Barnard Castle between Romaldkirk and Middleton-in-Teesdale. This handsome greystone inn, which dates from 1870, is a great base for a sporting, walking or touring holiday, and the three guest bedrooms all have en suite showers, television and tea/coffee tray.

The inn is the first venture into the licensed trade for Martin and Alexandra Clarkson, a lovely couple with a young family. The enthusiasm they bring to the job permeates the whole place, creating a particularly relaxed and happy atmosphere that makes it a delight to visit the inn, whether it's for a drink, a snack, a meal or an overnight or longer stay. Real ales from the Black Sheep and Cumbrian Breweries are on tap to quench fresh-air thirsts in the lively public bar, and the menus in the bar and smartly modernised restaurant are also geared to satisfy appetites generated by walks in the wild, spectacular countryside. The style is traditional English, and

the dishes, served every lunchtime and evening, run the gamut from snacks and light bites to main dishes that use the best seasonal local produce: lamb's liver & onions, venison casserole, seafood florentine and sirloin steak. The Sunday roasts always bring a good crowd, and there's always a choice for vegetarians.

The great outdoors beckons all around, and there are endless opportunities for undertaking anything from a gentle stroll to a serious hike. Mickleton is small farming community in the valley

beside the RiverTees with a population of about 350. It's an ideal place to start a walk and Beckstone Wath, a footbridge over the Tees, connects to various footpaths that have become a popular route for walkers. The Pennine Way runs nearby, cutting up from Yorkshire through County Durham and continuing through Upper Teesdale and on to Cumbria and Northumberland. At the back of the inn is a caravan park that also affords easy access to footpaths, as well as to canoeing on the Tees. Tuesday is poker night at the Rose & Crown and Wednesday sees a popular quiz. The pub is open from midday every day in season, otherwise from 5pm and all day at the weekend. Mickleton and its neighbours are well worth exploring: the Bowlees Visitor Centre, the four cares of beautiful gardens at Eggleston hall, the Church of St Romald at Romaldkirk, and the majestic High Force and Low Force waterfalls.

481

The Street, Hatfield Peverel,
nr Chelmsford, Essex CM3 2ET
☎ 01245 380205

The **William Boosey** has for a very long time been a familiar landmark in the village of Hatfield Peverel, on the B1137 northeast of Chelmsford and just a few short moments from junction 20 of the A12. Named after its first landlord, who was at the helm more than 300 years ago, this Shepherd Neame public house has been smartly modernised while retaining some original features like the gnarled old black beams in the convivial bar. It's a first pub venture for Paul and Judith, who came here in the spring of 2008. They have lost no time in enhancing its appeal as a popular place for locals to meet for a chat and a drink, and it's also a pleasant spot for motorists to take a break on a journey along the busy A12. Kent's Best is one of the regular cask ales served in the bar, which is open all day from 10 in the

morning (11 on Sunday) to 11 in the evening. There's a good selection of other drinks including non-alcoholic options for drivers. Food is also available throughout the day. The menu offers a selection of freshly prepared, cooked to order classic pub dishes that include traditional Sunday roasts served from midday to 4 o'clock. Every Thursday evening the pub goes Italian with a variety of popular Italian dishes. The William Boosey has a beer garden and ample off-road car parking space.

North Street, Tolleshunt D'Arcy,
Essex CM9 8TF
☎ 01621 860262

'The first thing that greets many who arrive in Tolleshunt D'Arcy is the maypole, but when hospitality and good food and drink are at the top of the wish list most visitors dance along to the **Queens Head** public house. The only pub in the village – there were once four – this is a real pub-lover's pub with all the traditional qualities of the quintessential English country hostelry and an excellent, experienced landlord and landlady, Terry and Maria Gaskin. The premises date back to 1725, and in the eyecatching public areas oak beams, flagstones, painted panelling, open fires and good-quality country furnishings paint an invitingly traditional scene that recent refurbishment has only enhanced.

The Green King Brewery in Bury St Edmunds supplies the two resident cask ales – IPA and Abbot – that are joined by two regularly changing brews. The bar is open from 11 in the morning to midnight seven days a week. The Queens

Head is very much food driven, and in the three separate dining areas the products of the talented kitchen team can be enjoyed from 11.30 to 2.30 and from 6 to 9, and all day on Saturday and Sunday. The menu of starters and 'lite bites' offers sandwiches and baguettes, ploughman's platters, prawn cocktail, garlicky tiger prawns, chicken liver pâté, potato skins and beef, chicken and vegetarian burgers. The full menu provides an excellent variety of dishes to please all palates, and the specials board widens the options still further with some super fish dishes – scampi, trout, battered cod or cod fillet glazed with olive oil and herbs, served on a bed of Mediterranean roasted vegetables. Tuscan vegetable and brie tart is one of several vegetarian dishes usually available. The Queens Head has a pleasant lawned garden with picnic benches under parasols and a well-stocked bird aviary.

The village takes its name from the D'Arcy family. Their moated manor house still stands, and memorials to the family can be seen in the parish Church of St Nicholas. A noted resident of the village was the writer Margery Allingham; a blue plaque is fixed outside her home D'Arcy House in South Street. Tolleshunt D'Arcy stands at the junction of the B1023 and B1026 northeast of Maldon. This part of Essex is very much tourist territory, with Maldon, Tiptree, Goldhanger, the extraordinary Layer Marney Tower and the Blackwater Estuary all nearby.

176 THE THREE BOTTLES

Leather Lane, Great Yeldham,
Essex CO9 4HY
☎ 01787 237122

In an area well served by country pubs , The **Three Bottles** is one of the very best. It stands in the Village of Great Yeldham, north of Sible Headingham on the A1017 Halstead to Haverhill road. Tenants Jim and Elaine Foster bring a wealth of experience to this fine old inn, parts of which date back to the late 18th century. The carpeted bar with handsome feature fireplace, shining brass and sparkling glass the gives the interior a traditional feel, creating warmth, ambience for good conversation over a quite drink. Outside, a newly erected gazebo on the patio gives shade as you look out onto a well kept garden area, there are picnic benches in this secluded garden a real boon on sunny days or a balmy evening.

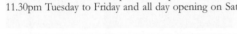

Courage Best heads the list of traditional ales, complimented by three other guest ales - these are changed with regularity; also a fine selection of lagers, sprits, wines, soft drinks and bottled drinks are available.

Food is limited to nibbles and Sunday lunch at this moment. Jim and Elaine have just introduced food on a Sunday and it has proved to be runaway success. Traditional Sunday Lunch is a set meal at £7.95 which consists of main course (a selection of three meats) and dessert. They do not take bookings and the advice is to come early to have sunday dinner "*Like Mum use to make*". It is served between noon and 4pm.

The Three Bottles is open from 6pm on a Monday, lunchtime 12.00-2.30 and evening 6.00-11.30pm Tuesday to Friday and all day opening on Saturday and Sunday.

177 THE CROSS KEYS

The Street, White Notley, nr Witham,
Essex CM8 1RQ
☎ 01376 583297
e-mail: scottreader32@hotmail.co.uk

The **Cross Keys** is a quaint little inn dating from the 1730s, standing on a corner site in White Notley, which is located on a minor road between Braintree and Witham. The Grade II listed building is charmingly traditional, with chunky black beams in the lounge and public bars. This Greene King pub has hardworking, enthusiastic hosts in Scott and Nicola Reader, who took over at the beginning of 2008. They have enhanced its status as a much-loved place for locals to meet, and they have an equally warm welcome for visitors from further afield or motorists taking a very worthwhile short detour from the busy A12 or A131. It's also only an easy drive from the newly opened Great Leighs racecourse, so it could well become a favourite place for racegoers to celebrate or drown their sorrows. Greene King IPA is the resident real ale, accompanied by two guest ales and a full range of other drinks. Good

honest pub food is served lunchtime and evening, and the steak & Guinness pie is always a popular choice. All are welcome to pit their wits against the local teams at the pub quiz held every other Wednesday, and the pub hosts an evening of live music once a month.

178 THE BUTCHERS ARMS

North End, nr Great Dunmow,
Essex CM6 3PJ
☎ 01245 237481

The **Butchers Arms** is a splendid 16th century roadside inn situated at North End, on the A130 about three miles south of Great Dunmow. It has excellent hosts in John and Brenda Powell and their son Mark, who is the chef. It's a big local favourite, a popular place that's open all day from 11 o'clock (from midday on Sunday). Colourful hanging baskets adorn the frontage in spring and summer, and the bar has an inviting, traditional look with beams, polished furniture, an old piano and a cast-iron stove in the brick hearth. Greene King IPA, Old Speckled Hen and two regularly changing guests provide a good choice for real ale fans, and Mark satisfies appetites large and small with an interesting selection of dishes. The menus

and daily specials span pub favourites (ploughman's

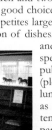

lunches, omelettes, fish & chips, pies and basket meals) as well as some less familiar dishes. There's always a particularly tempting selection of fish main courses, which might include pan-roasted Pollock with a sun-dried tomato dressing or roasted mackerel as well as battered cod and haddock and classic skate with burnt butter, capers and black pepper.

180 THE CROSS INN

Star Lane, Avening,
Gloucestershire GL8 8NT
☎ 08444 123100   Fax: 08444 123101
e-mail: info@crossinnavening.co.uk
🌐 www.crossinnavening.co.uk

The **Cross Inn** occupies a prominent corner site in the village of Avening, surrounded by picturesque Cotswolds countryside three miles north of Tetbury. To this pleasant part of the world Glyn and Claire Crosthwaite came with their children Jade and Jordan in July 2007 and set about restoring the inn to its former status as the hub of village life.

Otter Ale and two guest cask ales are on tap to quench thirsts in the smartly refurbished bar or out in the garden, and Glyn, a talented chef with 20 years' experience, is building a fine reputation in the area for his excellent cooking. His evolving menu is full of interest, mixing traditional and less familiar dishes. Beer-battered cod, shepherd's pie and rib-eye steaks are perennial favourites, while more unusual choices might include deep-fried tomato risotto with mozzarella, confit of pork terrine with glazed apple, seared sea bass, and sweet & sour vegetable tart.

Families with children are always made very welcome and there are toys and colouring books to keep the little ones busy and amused. The skittle alley is popular with the locals and there's also good support for the fortnightly quiz, the proceeds going to the local school. The inn is closed on Mondays except bank Holidays, otherwise open all day every day. Food times are 12 to 2.30 Tuesday to Friday, 12 to 4 Sunday and 6 to 10 Tuesday to Saturday.

485

179 THE RAILWAY INN

London Road, Fairford,
Gloucestershire GL7 4AR
☎ 01285 712284
e-mail: info@railwayinnfairford.co.uk
🌐 www.railwayinnfairford.co.uk

The name of Fairford will be familiar to anyone with an interest in the history of aviation, but it's another from of transport that gives its name to a haven of good food and hospitality. The **Railway Inn** is a handsome property standing on the A417 London Road close to the centre of Fairford.

It dates from the middle of the 19th century and has friendly, hardworking hosts in Catharine and Stephen. They took over here in August 2007 and undertook an immediate major refurbishment programme, re-opening in September of that year. At the front of the pub is a stone-paved garden terrace which is south facing and on a sunny day is always warm and inviting. The flagstoned bar, open all day every day, has been smartly redecorated and furnished in neat contemporary style, providing a very pleasant spot for meeting friends for a chat and a drink. Timothy Taylor Landlord, Wadworth's 6X and two regularly changing guests offer a good choice for real ale enthusiasts and there's a full range of other drinks.

Local producers and suppliers are used as much as possible for the dishes that are served daily from 12 to 3 at lunchtime and from 6 to 9 in the evening. Both sessions see beer-battered cod, salmon fish cakes, steaks, steak & ale pie, a curry and always vegetarian main courses like goat's cheese, onion and thyme tart. There's an excellent children's menu, and desserts such as warm chocolate tart or lemon posset with home-made shortcake make a delicious finale. Lunchtime also brings sandwiches, panini and snacky main courses, while the evening menu offers more 'restauranty' dishes like confit of duck with red onion marmalade or seared venison steak on red cabbage with a port and redcurrant sauce.

Fairford is a welcoming little town in the valley of the River Coln. It's well worth taking time to look at the superb Church of St Mary, renowned for its medieval stained glass depicting Old and New Testament scenes. RAF Fairford, south of town, has one of the longest runways in Europe. B52s made regular visits in the first Gulf War and during the invasion of Iraq, and it was also used for air trials for Concorde. The whole area really buzzes during the Royal International Air Tattoo, one of the largest of its kind. The date for 2008 is July 12 and 13.

181 THE SHIP INN

Brimscombe, nr Stroud,
Gloucestershire GL5 2QN
☎ 01453 884388 Fax: 01453 887688

The **Ship** is a popular public house and restaurant close to Brimscombe Port and Canal Basin. Chris and Dave Collins took the helm in 1996, since when they have made many friends not just among the local community but also with visitors from outside the area who come when passing this way. Exposed stone is a feature in the bar and lounge, where real ale connoisseurs can choose from four brews, typically Marston's Pedigree, Bass gem, Fuller's London Pride and Bob from the Wickwar Brewery.

The chef sets great store by fresh seasonal produce, using top producers and suppliers for meat, poultry and other raw materials. Starters like smoked haddock & spring onion fishcakes or crispy-coated brie and camembert precede main courses that include fish pie, steaks, pasta, curries, liver & bacon, five ways with chicken and always plenty of vegetarian dishes.

The bar is open every lunchtime and evening, and food is served at lunchtime from 12 to 2.30 and in the evening (not Sunday) from 6 to 9.30. Booking is advisable for Friday and Saturday dinner and Sunday lunch. Brimscombe lies off the A419 a short drive south of Stroud, and Nailsworth, Chalford and Minchinhampton are all nearby.

183 THE WHITE HORSE INN

Church Road, Soudley, Forest of Dean,
Gloucestershire GL14 2UA
☎ 01594 825968
e-mail: r.warford@sky.com

In their handsome 130-year-old pub in the Forest of Dean, Janet and Richard Warford offer a high standard of food and drink in the most convivial of surroundings. They were looking for a change of career from teaching when they took over the **White Horse** and they've quickly passed all the tests in how to run a country pub. They have built up a loyal following among the local community, and day by day they are attracting visitors from outside the area. Butcombe Bitter is a popular choice among the well-kept ales served in the bar or outside in the picturesque front garden. Janet is an excellent cook, making fine use of top-quality local produce in her wholesome, tasty dishes. Sandwiches, rolls and jacket potatoes cater for those with less time to spare – the special sandwich with hot silverside of beef (onions optional) is a great favourite. Whitebait, scampi, battered cod, breaded plaice and smoked haddock & spring onion provide a traditional choice for fish-eaters, while meat-eaters might go for a curry, braised lamb shank, fishcakes stuffed

chicken breast or steak and kidney pudding. There's also an exceptional choice for vegetarians – home-made lasagne, lentil moussaka, bean & cashew nut patties and quiche. The bar is open from 7pm Monday to Friday, all day Saturday, Sunday lunch and all Sunday in summer. Food is served Saturday and Sunday lunchtime, Friday evenings and summer Saturday evenings. The White Horse also has an en suite room for B&B guests. Cash/cheque only.

487

182 THE EDGEMOOR INN

Edge, nr Stroud,
Gloucestershire GL6 6ND
☎ 01452 813576
e-mail: info@edgemoor-inn.com
🌐 www.edgemoor-inn.com

The **Edgemoor Inn** stands in the village of Edge, midway along the Cotswold Way that runs from Chipping Norton in the north to Bath in the south, most of the route following the Cotswold escarpment. Resident owners Chris and Jill Bayes have a genuinely warm welcome for all who visit their 250-year-old stone inn, whether they be first-timers or familiar faces.

Real ale connoisseurs are in for a treat with some interesting local brews, typically including Old Spot from the Ulley Brewery, Bob from Wickwar and Bow Bells from Whtittingtons. The food at the Edgemoor Inn is also well worth more than a little detour, and at peak times it's best to book to be sure of a table at the time you want. Contemplating the menu poses a problem, but a pleasant one, as everything on the daily changing menu is worth trying. Each day proposes an excellent choice of dishes that cater for a wide variety of tastes and appetites. For fish-eaters: scampi; plaice; sea bass with a lemon & herb crumb; grilled salmon with prawns and Boursin; fillet of halibut with a Welsh rarebit crust or an orange butter sauce. For meat-eaters: loin of lamb with bubble & squeak and a port wine sauce; gammon steak; home-made steak pie; Elizabethan pork casserole. For vegetarians: nut loaf with a tomato and pesto sauce; broccoli & stilton quiche; roasted vegetable, mozzarella & basil roulade. It's all good, fresh and wholesome, with local raw materials used as much as possible, and this splendid fare is served every lunchtime and every evening except Sunday evening in winter, when the inn is closed. The continuing success of this outstanding place is shown with the creation in May 2008 of a large dining room extension with 70 additional covers and lovely Cotswold views.

There are equally delightful views of the Painswick Valley and the surrounding countryside from the paved terrace – an asset that's in great demand when the sun shines or on warm summer evenings. Families with children are very welcome, and the inn accepts the major credit cards. Edge has two picturesque village greens and a mid-Victorian church with an ornate spire. To the west of the village lies Scottsquarr Common, a Site of Special Scientific Interest that is home to an abundance of wild flowers and butterflies.

184 THE BAILEY INN

Bailey Hill, Yorkley, Forest of Dean,
Gloucestershire GL15 4RP
☎ 01594 562670
e-mail: thebaileyinn@hotmail.com
🌐 www.freeweb.com/baileyinn

The **Bailey Inn** is a handsome Victorian building in the village of Yorkley, in the heart of the Forest of Dean between the A48 and B4234 north of Lydney. It's a first pub venture for Val and Gary Brown, who since taking over in November 2007 have stamped their talents and personalities on the place.

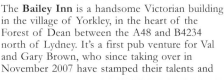

They have long been advocates of healthy eating, and the kitchen makes extensive use of organic and free-range meats and other top-quality local produce. They both cook, and their seasonal menus provide a fine choice of wholesome dishes served lunchtime and evening Tuesday to Saturday and from 1 to 3 for the organic Sunday lunch. Typical dishes run from Welsh rarebit with stilton and walnuts to meatballs in a special tomato sauce,

beef or lamb burgers, nachos with a salsa sauce and organic rump steak. To finish, perhaps organic carrot cake or double chocolate brownie. There's a separate menu of pizzas with very interesting or unusual toppings. Morning coffee and cakes are served from 10 on Tuesday and Thursday.

The bar is open lunchtime and evening and all day at the weekend. Closed Mondays except Bank Holidays. Families with children and dogs are welcome, and the inn has a beer garden and terrace commanding fine views of the Forest.

185 GLOUCESTERSHIRE AND WARWICKSHIRE RAILWAY

The Railway Station, Toddington,
Gloucestershire GL54 5DT
☎ 01242 621405

The railway offers a 20-mile round trip between Toddington and Cheltenham Race Course through some of the most spectacular scenery in the Cotswolds.

As you leave Toddington, once a major fruit distribution centre the train passes the workshops where the steam and diesel locomotives are maintained and restored. The journey then takes you past the village of Didbrook and the site of Hayles Abbey Halt, which served the nearby Abbey (English Heritage). Good views of the Cotswolds can be seen from both sides of the train, before arriving at Winchcombe station, which is actually at Greet, about a mile from the town.

The station building at Winchcombe once stood at Monmouth Troy and was painstakingly dismantled, moved and rebuilt by volunteers. This is also the headquarters of the carriage and wagon department. Shortly after leaving Winchcombe the train enters Greet tunnel which, at 693 yards, is the second longest on a preserved railway.

As the line approaches Cheltenham Race Course, views of Cleeve Hill (the highest point of the Cotswolds) open up. The original and unique Swindon-built pre-fabricated station building, reached by a ramp, is perched high above the track at road level. The station once again fulfils its original purpose – bringing race-goers for important meetings such as the Cheltenham Gold Cup.

Cold Aston, nr Cheltenham,
Gloucestershire GL54 3BN
☎ 01451 821459
e-mail: info@theploughcoldaston.com
🌐 www.theploughcoldaston.com

The **Plough** is a picture-postcard pub in the quiet village of Cold Aston, which lies a couple of miles southwest of Bourton-on-the-Water off the A429 or A436. Owners Philip and Annette Mason-Gordon are totally service orientated having spent 40 years in the hospitality industry; which accounts for the pub's popularity both with the local community and with visitors from outside the area.

Toby has been a chef at The Plough for 10 years, and anyone who has sampled his food will soon be back for more. His varied and imaginative menu changes regularly to reflect the very best of seasonal produce, most of it sourced from within the region. A typical meal might start with chicken liver and foie gras parfait coated in a thyme & black truffle butter or scallops served on cauliflower purée. The main course could be Donnington beer-battered cod, a mixed plate of Gloucester Old Spot meats or breast of chicken with creamy leeks, bacon and thyme. Those in the know

definitely leave room for one of the scrumptious desserts. Traditional roasts are added to the Sunday menu. The food is complemented by a well-chosen wine list, and other drinks include three real ales, usually from local breweries. The Plough is closed on Mondays but is otherwise open every lunchtime and evening, and food is served from 12 to 2 and from 6 to 10. Families with children are welcome, and the Plough accepts the major credit cards.

187 THE HAWBRIDGE INN

Hawbridge, nr Tirley,
Gloucestershire GL19 4HJ
☎ 01452 780316 Fax: 01452 780896
e-mail: relax@hawbridgeinn.co.uk
🌐 www.hawbridgeinn.co.uk

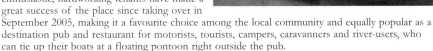

There's no mistaking the warmth of the welcome extended by Ian and Kelly at the **Hawbridge Inn**, which enjoys a superb location alongside the River Severn, by the B4213 southeast of Tewkesbury. The enthusiastic, hardworking tenants have made a great success of the place since taking over in September 2005, making it a favourite choice among the local community and equally popular as a destination pub and restaurant for motorists, tourists, campers, caravanners and river-users, who can tie up their boats at a floating pontoon right outside the pub.

This traditional waterside pub has a roomy, comfortable bar with beams and exposed stone walls, a restaurant stretching along the riverfront and outside seating both at the front and on a decked area at the rear. Wadworth's 6X, Henry's IPA and a changing guest provide a choice for real ale drinkers, and the bar stocks a full range of other draught and bottle beers, lagers, ciders, wines, spirits and non-alcoholic drinks. Ian and Kelly both cook, using locally sourced meat, poultry and vegetables for their dishes. The menus propose a wide variety of mainly tried-and-tested pub favourites, with baguettes, panini, jacket potatoes, spicy chicken wings, burgers and basket meals for satisfying snacks and main dishes from scampi, cod & chips and fish pie to gammon, sirloin and rump steaks, faggots, Cajun chicken, chilli con carne, mushroom stroganoff and Mediterranean vegetable risotto.

The River Severn is semi-tidal here because spring tides rise above the height of the weir above Gloucester and create a mini-bore that travels up the river as far as Tewkesbury Lock. The inn is a great place to visit at any time of the year but is particularly delightful in the summer, when it makes an unbeatable setting for a party, a wedding celebration or a barbecue.

The Hawbridge Inn has an adjacent field that's available from Easter to the end of October for tents, caravans and motor homes, with toilets, showers and eight electric hook-ups. The river is not the only attraction in the area – others include the Saxon Church of St Mary and Odda's Chapel at Deerhurst, the 14th century tithe barn at Ashlehurst and the area medieval set of bee hives at Hartpury. The inn is open all day every day in summer, with late hours (2am) on Friday and Saturday.

Malswick, nr Newent,
Gloucestershire GL18 1HE
☎ 01531 821061
⊕ www.travellersrest-malswick.co.uk

Malswick is a pleasant spot a mile or so south of Newent on the B4215 that runs down to the A40 to Gloucester. This rural location is a very agreeable place to pause on a journey, so the **Travellers Rest** is particularly well named. It started life in the early years of the 19th century, when it was a coaching inn called the Malswick Arms.

Behind the attractive pink-washed frontage the bar and dining areas have been smartly updated, creating an inviting ambience for relaxing over a drink, a snack or a leisurely meal. Leaseholders Jodie and Donovan, who took the reins in August 2007, are young, enthusiastic and very friendly; this is their first venture together into the licensed trade, but both have plenty of experience in the catering and hospitality business and their efforts are already bringing their rewards. They have really put the old place back on the map, and the reputation they have gained is spreading far beyond the local community. There's always a real ale on tap, accompanied by a good choice of keg bitters and lagers and a selection of wines available by the bottle and by two sizes of glass. The bar is open all day every day of the week except Sunday evenings in winter, and food is served from 12 to 3 and 6 to 9, Sunday 12 to 3 only.

The philosophy behind the cooking is to provide a menu of simple dishes using the finest - locally sourced where possible - raw ingredients freshly prepared. The lunchtime 'Travelling Light' menu runs from baguettes, ploughman's, stuffed garlic mushrooms and prawn cocktail to ham, egg & chips, salmon fish cakes, cannelloni, lasagne and cod or chicken goujons. The goujons can be ordered in smaller portions for children, with an ice cream included in the price. The evening menu adds more substantial main courses such as cod in beer batter, steaks, the day's pie and chicken roulade filled with black pudding, wrapped in bacon and served on a bed of spinach. The specials board adds further to the choice and Sunday brings traditional roasts with fish and vegetarian options.

Families with children are always welcome, and the inn accepts the major credit cards. The location, the expertise of the hosts and the amenities make the Travellers rest an excellent venue for a special occasion. The marquee in the garden is a permanent feature used for weddings, corporate events, local farmers market, summer jazz festivales etc.

189 THE WHITE HORSE

South Hill, Droxford, Hampshire SO32 3PB
☎ 01489 877490

A former coaching inn, **The White Horse** started in business during the 15th century. Inside it is a labyrinth of small cosy rooms providing a Restaurant, Main Bar, Snug, Family Room and Public Bar complete with pool table and darts board. Most of the year there are log fires providing a cosy warm glow in three of the bars, which makes the Pub popular with chilled walkers. The original stable blocks form a square, flower filled patio that is a super sun trap. The cellar is comprehensive with IPA as the regular real ale and 2 rotating guest ales, a comprehensive wine list and all wines can be bought by the glass.

The menu is predominately Indian, the Chefs were born in India and are devoted to authentic home cooking. Fish Amritsari, Onion Bhajias, home made Samosas some of the starters. Main courses are all the old favourites and vegetarians are very well catered for. Kebabs from the Tandoori oven a speciality. The menu also includes classic English dishes, Beer Battered Cod, Whitebait, Scampi, Braised Beef, Pork or Lamb Shank, a wide variety of Sandwiches and very special naan bread wraps. The White Horse is open from 11am to 11pm everyday of the year, with excellent food available at all times, major credit cards accepted, pets and children welcome, off road parking. Well worth a visit.

190 THE BLUE BELL INN

South Street, Emsworth,
Hampshire PO10 7EG
☎ 01243 373394
⊕ www.bluebellinnemsworth.co.uk

The Blue Bell Inn in Emsworth, is the former favourite haunt of the local fishermen. Only yards from the Quay, it's the perfect spot for a drink or a bite to eat after a walk around the Harbour watching the fishing boats unload their catch. A family owned pub, the Blue Bell is run by Thomas Babb and open all day. Parts of the building date back to the 17th century and the interior décor is very traditional. It's a popular venue for people who wish to enjoy great home cooked food prepared by chef Thomas Giles Babb (Gilo) son of the owner. "Cooking is an art," he says, "masterpieces take time!"

On offer are a wide variety of dishes including fresh fish which is the Blue Bell's specialty! Just try the oven-baked whole sea bream! Also available are homemade pies, fresh baguettes, baked jacket potatoes and monthly specials. Steak dishes are popular with the Aberdeen Angus meats supplied by the local butcher. To accompany your food, there's a choice of cask ales with Old Speckled Hen as the permanent brew on tap. The Blue Bell is open from 11am to 11pm, every day.

191 THE TRAVELLERS REST

Church Road, Newtown, nr Wickham,
Hampshire PO17 6LO
☎ 01329 833263

Located in the heart of the scenic Hampshire countryside, far from busy traffic routes, **The Travellers Rest** is a traditional 18th century country inn with a friendly atmosphere and real open fires. Mine hosts, Carol and Vince, who took over here in early 2007, offer a superb value-for-money menu every lunchtime and evening. Among the varied choices are the "Best Hand-Made Pies in Hampshire!" To accompany your meal, there's an excellent selection of well-kept real ales, including London Pride and Charlie Wells. During the summer months and fine weather, there's a large beer garden for customers to enjoy - ideal for bringing the whole family to relax in the open air. It

provides the ideal venue in which to celebrate any special occasions. Entertainment can be arranged if you wish. The inn is open from 11am to 11pm, daily; all major credit cards are accepted. To the rear of the pub is a large caravan and camping site.

192 THE WATERLOO ARMS

Pikes Hill, Lyndhurst,
Hampshire SO43 7AS
☎ 02380 282113
e-mail: mrage327@aol.com
⊕ www.waterlooarmsnewforest.co.uk

In the heart of the New Forest, just off the A337 on the northern edge of Lyndhurst, the **Waterloo Arms** is a great place to relax and enjoy a drink and a meal. Michael and Michelle Rogers, who took over the lease in the autumn of 2007, are enhancing its status as a real pub-lover's pub, and behind the 17th century thatch-roofed exterior the bar has an inviting, traditional appeal, with lots of ceiling beams and a grand feature fireplace. The locally brewed Ringwood Best is the resident real ale, accompanied by two guests, usually including Sharps Doom Bar. In the elegant restaurant, diners can savour a wide selection of home-cooked food, including popular fish specials and seasonal game.

Typical choices run from chicken liver pâté, potted crab and filo-wrapped port-soaked brie to Thai green curry, liver & bacon, cottage pie and fruit & nut roast with mozzarella & onion gravy. From the grill come chicken, lamb and juicy steaks served plain or with a choice of sauces – peppercorn, stilton, garlic & herbs, whisky and sweet chilli. Traditional roasts are served all day on Sunday. The inn, which is open from 11am to 11pm every day, has a pleasant garden and a large car park.

494

193 BUCKLER'S HARD

Bucklers Hard, Beaulieu, Brockenhurst,
Hampshire SO42 7XB
☎ 01590 616203

On the banks of the Beaulieu River, in the heart of the New Forest, you will find the picturesque village of Buckler's Hard. With a beautiful setting, Riverside Walk and River Cruises to enjoy, Buckler's Hard is one of the most attractive and unusual villages in England. Yet there is also much to see and do in this unique village where time has almost stood still since the days when wooden ships were built here for Nelson's fleet.

The Buckler's Hard Story reflects the history of the village, from its origins as a port for importing sugar cane from the West Indies, through its shipbuilding history covering the construction of more than 50 naval and merchant vessels that were built here. Displays include models of the ships that were built for Lord Nelson, featuring his favourite, HMS Agamemnon, and other items of memorabilia. Historic cottage displays portray life at Buckler's Hard in1793 and residents of the time gossip about local matters in the re-constructed Village Inn. Recent history of the village is portrayed through the River's role in the D-Day landings during World War II.

At the bottom of the Village street take a cruise on the tranquil Beaulieu River in 'Swiftsure' which runs between April and October. A lively commentary bringing the history of the Beaulieu River to life and some magnificent scenery makes for a lively and memorable trip, not to be missed. The delightful Riverside Walk takes you through woodland to the village of Beaulieu.

194 LOUNGES OF LYMINGTON

122 High Street, Lymington,
Hampshire SO41 9AQ
☎ 01590 671122
e-mail: enquiries@loungesoflymington.co.uk
🌐 www.loungesoflymington.co.uk

Welcomes don't come friendlier than the one that awaits visitors to **Lounges of Lymington**, which since 2003 has been owned and run by Mark and Alison Chandler. Mark, who has lived in Lymington for more than 25 years, knows many of his customers personally, and Alison has made just as many friends with her sweet and savoury delights.

Everything is fresh and wholesome, from panini and baguettes with generous fillings like mozzarella with roasted peppers, soups, jacket potatoes, breakfasts and salads to the cakes and pastries and the delicious cream teas. The interior is roomy, comfortable and inviting, with oak beams and solid wood or flagged floors, and the ambience generated by Mark and Alison adds to the pleasure of a visit. To accompany the food there's a good choice of teas, coffees, cold drinks and milk shakes. Lounges of Lymington is open from 9 to 5 Monday to Saturday and from 10 to 4 on Sunday.

Everything on the menu can be ordered to take away, and people in a hurry can call ahead with their order. Lounges also offers an outside catering service and a range of buffets to suit a variety of occasions.

195 THE FOREST HEATH HOTEL

Station Road, Sway, New Forest,
Hampshire SO41 6BA
☎ 01590 682287
e-mail: enquiries@forestheathhotel.co.uk
🌐 www.forestheathhotel.co.uk

The **Forest Heath Hotel** is located near the railway station in Sway, an upmarket village standing off the A337 three miles north of Lymington. The sturdy redbrick building dates from 1889, and behind the handsome façade the busy public bar and the lounge are delightful spots for relaxing with friends or enjoying a chat with the regulars. Outside is a pleasant garden with a children's play area. The locally brewed Ringwood Best is the resident real ale, accompanied by rotating guests, and the bars are open all day, seven days a week. In the bright, airy restaurant, food is served from midday to 2.30, covering a good choice of mainly tried-and-tested favourites:

baguettes, jacket potatoes, burgers, chilli, curries, ham & eggs, bangers & mash, beer-battered or grilled fish, steaks, steak & ale pie and a giant Yorkshire pudding filled with pork & leek sausages and gravy. Desserts are equally traditional – spotted dick, treacle sponge, blackberry & apple crumble. For guests taking a break in this attractive part of the world, tenant Michael Hoyles has four comfortably appointed en suite bedrooms. The village and the surrounding area are the setting for Captain Marryatt's much-loved *Children of the New Forest*.

196 THE BEAULIEU ROAD INN

Beaulieu Road, Brockenhurst,
Hampshire SO42 7YQ
☎ 02380 292342

Tenants Dominic and Jacqui Whelan and their friendly, helpful staff have a warm welcome for all who pass through the door of the **Beaulieu Road Inn**. The inn, which is leased from the adjoining Beaulieu Hotel, was converted from the hotel's stables. It enjoys a lovely setting in the heart of the New Forest, northwest of Beaulieu on the B3056 Lyndhurst road. Dominic worked here before taking over the lease in 2005, and he and Jacqui know personally many of their customers. The public and lounge bars, kept cosy by open fires in the cooler months, are convivial spots for relaxing with a glass of real ale – four are usually on tap, typically Ringwood Best and Old Thumper, Fullers London Pride and Courage Directors. The bars are open from 11 to 3 and from 6 to 11, all day Saturday and Sunday and all day every day in the summer. Dominic makes excellent use of local

produce in many of his dishes: among his signature dishes are New Forest mushrooms on toast or in stroganoff, steak & ale pie cooked in Old Thumper ale, beer-battered haddock, Thai green curry, seasonal game and barramundi, crayfish and spring onion fishcakes. Steak and seafood nights are popular events throughout the summer months. The inn has a large garden with a children's play area.

197 COACH & HORSES

Oxford Road, Sutton Scotney,
Hampshire SO21 3JH
☎ 01962 760279
Fax: 01962 760738
e-mail: linstevecoach@aol.com

A charming traditional village inn, the **Coach & Horses** has a history going back to at least 1762. A lease has been found giving that date. An interesting feature of the property is the thatched barn in the car park which was used by the Fire Brigade as the village fire station from 1939 to 1972. It was unique as it was the only thatched fire station in the country. The main building itself was extensively refurbished in 2004 but owners Lin Toomer and Steve Mehers went to great lengths to preserve original features such as the remains of a bread oven in a cupboard in the main bar. Just to the left, the exposed bricks were used as a sharpener by local darts players. And Lin and Steve were delighted

to find the original fireplace which had been hidden for many years. Today, the

Coach & Horses is well-known for the quality of the food on offer. Chefs Kathryn and Dean's menu contains old favourites such as steaks, sausage & mash, and fish and chips, along with less familiar dishes such as Sweet Chilli Salmon or a vegetarian Greek Salad. The inn also offers B&B accommodation in 3 comfortable rooms, all with en suite facilities.

198 THE HALFMOON & SPREAD EAGLE

Winchester Road, Micheldever,
nr Winchester, Hampshire SO21 3DG
☎ 01962 774339 Fax: 01962 774339
e-mail: halfmoonspreadeagle@hotmail.co.uk
⊕ www.thehalfmoonspreadeagle.webden.co.uk

Tenants Debbie, Sam and John cater for a wide cross-section of patrons and interests at the **Halfmoon & Spread Eagle**, which lies in the village of Micheldever, off the A33 north of Winchester and not far from Junction 9 of the M3.

Their pub is a great favourite with walkers, cyclists, motorists and tourists, and a good range of real ales, ciders, lagers and wines is served in the bar – a convivial spot with a solid oak floor, beams, brasses and country memorabilia. Outside, there's a beer garden and children's play area overlooking the old village cricket pitch and a new heated area with tables and chairs for diners and smokers. In the bar or restaurant, romantically lit at night, chef Jason Lawes uses local produce to excellent effect for his menus, which include both traditional English and speciality Indian dishes. Food

is served daily from 12 to 2 and 6 to 9.

Families are welcome, and well-behaved dogs are allowed in the bar area as well as outside. The pub is at the heart of village social life, with a regular programme of events from live music and karaoke to quizzes, bingo and poker. It also fields darts and pool teams in the local Winchester leagues.

199 THE HURSTBOURNE INN

Hurstbourne Priors, nr Whitchurch,
Hampshire RG28 7SE
☎ 01256 892000
e-mail: enquiries@thehurstbourne.com
🌐 www.thehurstbourne.com

The **Hurstbourne Inn** is a charming late-19th century building standing in the village of Hurstbourne Priors, west of Whitchurch at the point where the B3400 and B3408 meet. Maureen Kavanagh has run pubs in Hampshire for 30 years, and since taking over in 2005, she, Adrian and her exceptional staff have made the inn one of the best-loved in the region, a perfect place to relax and unwind in the beautiful Hampshire countryside. The cosy bar-lounge is a great spot to meet friends over a glass of beer, and visitors should not miss the opportunity to enjoy an outstanding meal. The dishes are all cooked to order and many are just that little bit

different, as shown by spinach, ricotta & toasted pine nut ravioli with a roast tomato & basil sauce; breaded camembert with plum compote; and roast rump of lamb with rosemary polenta & oyster mushrooms. Children are welcome at lunchtime and by prior arrangement for dinner. Midway along the lovely Test Valley, the inn is an ideal base for a walking or touring holiday, or for fishing on the Test and Bourne rivers. The three en suite bedrooms are quiet and comfortable, and a super breakfast starts the day.

200 THE GEORGE INN

St Mary Bourne, Hampshire SP11 6BG
☎ 01264 738340

The **George** is a Hall & Woodhouse pub in the village of St Mary Bourne, between Andover and Whitchurch, off the B3048 that links the main A303 and A343 roads. Extensively refurbished inside and out, it is in the care of Rich and Sue Jepson, who came here with their young family in the summer of 2007. The promise of the exterior, with its ornamental brickwork and porticoed entrance, is amply fulfilled within, where patrons can relax in the comfortable bar with a big open fire, half panelling and pictures of local scenes. Hall & Woodhouse and Badger Tanglefoot are the usual real ales, and bar and restaurant menus provide plenty of choice for a wide range of tastes and appetites. From the former come sandwiches, baked potatoes, burgers, all-day breakfasts, lasagne, chicken curry, battered cod and hearty pies – fish, cottage, steak, chicken & mushroom. Typical dishes on the restaurant menu run from a plate of smoked salmon and prawns to citrus-steamed salmon, beef stroganoff and T-bone steak. Weekly specials add to the choice, and senior citizens can enjoy a bargain lunch from Monday to Friday. The bar is open from midday every day; bar meals are served from 12 to 2.30 Monday to Thursday and from 5 to 8 on Saturday; the restaurant is open Thursday to Saturday evenings and Sunday carvery lunch.

201 THE CROWN

Romsey Road, Kings Somborne,
Stockbridge, Hampshire SO20 6PW
☎ 01794 388360
e-mail: minterevans@minterevans.plus.com

A former coaching inn dating back to the 17th century, **The Crown** looks very inviting with its thatched roof and sheltered garden. It was extensively refurbished both inside and out to a very high standard in early 2008 and now offers a very pleasant setting for a relaxed drink or meal. Food is available every day from a menu that contains traditional English pub fare supplemented by seasonal specials. On Sundays, a roast is added to the regular menu. Cask ales on tap include Abbot Ale, Greene King IPA and Ringwood Best. On Tuesday evenings the Crown hosts a quiz and curry night. The pub is popular with walkers on the Clarendon Way which passes through the village. During the summer

months the Crown is open from noon until 11 pm every day with food available from noon until 3pm

and 6.30pm until 9.30pm (except Sunday evenings). During the winter the pub is closed during the weekday afternoons from 3.30pm until 5.30pm. The team at the Crown look forward to welcoming you.

202 THE WHITE LION

Wilton Lane, Ross-on-Wye,
Herefordshire HR9 6AQ
☎ 01989 562785
🌐 www.whitelionross.co.uk

Since taking over as tenants in 2004, Jacqui Newman and her partner have made a roaring success of the **White Lion**. They have built up excellent local support, and visitors to Ross are delighted not just by the hospitality but also by the fascinating history of the inn. It was built in 1650 as a police station and retains many original features – the upstairs restaurant still has bars at its windows from

the days when it was the police cells. A huge open fire keeps things cosy in winter, while in summer the garden running down to the River Wye is a major plus. A rotating choice of cask ales can be enjoyed on their own or to accompany a selection of good honest pub favourites, including popular Sunday roasts. The White Lion also offers Bed & Breakfast accommodation in three en suite rooms, one with a four-poster bed. The pub is open from noon seven days a week.

Hoarwithy, Herefordshire HR2 6QH
☎ 01432 840900

The **New Harp Inn** attracts a very diverse clientele, including walkers, cyclists, canoeists and tourists as well as families, muddy boots and dogs. Starting life as a pair of cottages in the mid-19th century, it has been a pub since the 1880s and is really thriving under hosts Andrew and Fleur Cooper. They have created a splendidly relaxed, informal atmosphere, with drinkers and diners mingling merrily in the convivial bar. The choice for beer drinkers is truly amazing, with local cask ales, draught Belgian and German brews and around 80 bottled beers. They also keep real ciders and a good selection of wines, including 10 available by the glass. Fresh seasonal produce,

much of it local, is the basis of the food served here. Tuesday is fish night, and the summer barbecues are always popular. The pub has a lovely garden with a little brook running through it and a decked patio surrounded by exotic plants. Andrew and Fleur enjoy hosting events, which include themed dinners, comedy nights and beer festivals.

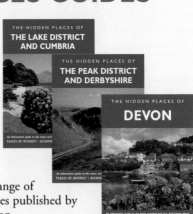

HIDDEN PLACES GUIDES

Explore Britain and Ireland with *Hidden Places* guides - a fascinating series of national and local travel guides.

Packed with easy to read information on hundreds of places of interest as well as places to stay, eat and drink.

Available from both high street and internet booksellers

For more information on the full range of *Hidden Places* guides and other titles published by Travel Publishing visit our website on

www.travelpublishing.co.uk
or ask for our leaflet by phoning **01752 276660** or
emailing **info@travelpublishing.co.uk**

THE HIDDEN PLACES OF
**THE LAKE DISTRICT
AND CUMBRIA**

THE HIDDEN PLACES OF
**THE PEAK DISTRICT
AND DERBYSHIRE**

THE HIDDEN PLACES OF
DEVON

Church Lane, Ledbury,
Herefordshire HR8 1DL
☎ 01531 632250
🌐 www.powledbury.com

In a quaint cobbled alley by the parish church, the **Prince of Wales**, much of which dates from the 1570s, is the very essence of an English tavern, with a landlord who treats his customers like old friends. Russell Smith, with the help of his equally affable parents, continues to enhance the inn's reputation for hospitality, welcoming locals and visitors into the warm, convivial surroundings. Behind the much-photographed black-and-white exterior, made colourful in spring and summer by baskets of flowers, the look in the public rooms is charmingly traditional, with low beams, red-tiled floors and lots of dark oak.

The Prince of Wales certainly knows its beers, and connoisseurs will appreciate not just the variety on offer but the information about each. Regular varieties include Banks's Bitter, Sharp's Doom Bar from Rock in Cornwall and the Reverend James from the brewery of SA Brain of Cardiff. There's also a choice of ciders, and a perry from Westons. Russell also keeps a selection of a dozen or more imported bottled beers and lagers, including Samichlaus, as strong as a full-bodied wine.

Lunchtime brings a choice of well-priced pub fare, including sandwiches, toasties, ploughman's platters, jacket potatoes, scampi, faggots, haddock, lasagne, chilli con carne and giant Yorkshire pudding filled with roast beef. Wednesday is folk music night at this splendid inn, with local and guest musicians getting together to make music. The Prince of Wales is open from 11 to 11 seven days a week.

4 Bridge Street, Bishops Frome,
Worcestershire WR6 5BP
☎ 01885 490234

Local residents, tourists, holidaymakers and business people are all equally welcome at **The Chase Inn**, a popular stopping place amid the maze of lovely little villages between Hereford and Leominster. Dominating the village of Bishops Frome on its prominent corner site, the building dates from 1830, and extensive refurbishment and modernisation undertaken by hosts Richard and

Helen Baker has enhanced the amenities while preserving the best period features. Outside, a newly created decked area is an added attraction in the warmer months.

Three cask ales, including Burton Bitter and Marston's Pedigree, have earned the pub a Cask Marque award, and Richard's cooking has also won wide acclaim. His menu of wholesome 'pub grub' spans sandwiches, hot baguettes, jacket potatoes, burgers, steaks, bangers & mash, scampi, fish & chips, cottage pie, spaghetti Bolognese, mushroom & nut tagliatelle and daily roasts. Richard will do his best to prepare a special request for something not on the menu, and the pub is unusual in offering a takeaway service.

The guest accommodation comprises seven comfortably appointed bedrooms – three doubles, two twins, 1 single and a family room – five of them with en suite facilities. The day starts with a full English breakfast, and packed lunches can be provided.

The Chase, is open from 12 to 11 (to 10.30 on Sunday) and food is served all day until 9 o'clock. St Mary's Church in the village, notable in particular for its massive 700-year-old font, is well worth a visit, as is the nearby Hop Pocket Craft centre with working kilns and a gift shop.

206 THE ROYAL LODGE HOTEL

Symonds Yat East, nr Ross-on-Wye,
Herefordshire HR9 6JL
☎ 01600 890238
e-mail: info@royallodgesymondsyat.co.uk

The **Royal Lodge**, built in 1876 as a hunting lodge, has been a hotel since 1920, offering today's visitors top-class food and accommodation in a glorious setting off the A40 seven miles below Ross-on-Wye. New management have changed the name (it was formerly the Royal Hotel) and carried out a room-by-room refurbishment programme that has enhanced its reputation as a marvellous place for a drink, a meal or a holiday. On the banks of the river Wye in a designated Area of Outstanding Natural Beauty, the hotel has 21 very well-appointed en suite bedrooms, almost every one enjoying a view of the river. Guests can relax, unwind and savour the scenery, take a riverside stroll or a river cruise, get out the fishing rod, admire the scenery from a helicopter or enjoy a spot of birdwatching in the Wye Valley

or the nearby Forest of Dean. A host of more energetic activities is available almost on the doorstep, most of which the hotel can help guests to arrange: canoeing (the hotel owns the nearby canoe centre), kayaking, abseiling, caving, horseriding, cycling, quad biking, 4-wheel driving, go-karting, clay pigeon shooting, paintballing.

The Royal Lodge is open to residents and non-residents for food, prepared and cooked by a team of talented chefs, many with international experience. Local produce, including superb beef and lamb, features prominently on menus that combine English classics with European and more exotic options. Typical dishes include grilled sardines with salsa verde, Cajun blackened salmon, cod in Wye Valley beer batter, ratatouille-stuffed peppers, minted lamb cutlets, steaks and the always popular Sunday lunch, which offer a choice of two roasts, ham, and fish and vegetarian alternatives. The excellent food is complemented by a selection of good-value, high-quality wines from around the world. Lunch is served from 12.30 to 2.30, dinner from 6.30 to 9, with bar drinks and tea and coffee available all day.

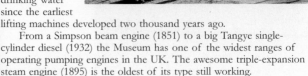
207 WATERWORKS MUSEUM

Broomy Hill, Hereford,
Herefordshire HR4 0JS
☎ 01432 344062
e-mail: info@waterworksmuseum.org.uk
🌐 www.waterworksmuseum.org.uk

Water is the most precious substance on earth. Learn at the Museum why every drop is important and have fun at the same time. The Museum tells the story of drinking water since the earliest lifting machines developed two thousand years ago.

From a Simpson beam engine (1851) to a big Tangye single-cylinder diesel (1932) the Museum has one of the widest ranges of operating pumping engines in the UK. The awesome triple-expansion steam engine (1895) is the oldest of its type still working.

Hereford's Victorian water-pumping station and other historic buildings stand in attractive grounds. The modern visitor Centre sets the scene and provides light refreshment.

The Waterworks Museum – Hereford has been included in the European Route of Industrial Heritage (ERIH.) The Route is a network of the most important industrial heritage sites in Europe.

208 THE PRIORY HOTEL

Priory Lane, Stretton Sugwas,
Herefordshire HR4 7AR
Tel: 01432 760264
e-mail: info@hotelpriory.co.uk
www.hotelpriory.co.uk

The Priory Hotel is a former rectory dating back to the 17th century with later additions in mid-Victorian times, today it is a comfortable and charming country house hotel. It is set within three acres of beautiful grounds and hidden in the Herefordshire countryside but just three miles from the City of Hereford. The family run country house hotel is a home from home where there's time to relax and be waited on without fuss or hurry by the friendly yet attentive staff.

The hotel boasts 8 en-suite bedrooms which include several with four poster beds all having been refurbished to a high standard offering every comfort. There is also a lounge bar, sitting room, restaurant and function / ballroom. The décor is traditional with a hint of contemporary throughout, boasting original sanded floorboards, sash windows, open fires and a depth of character you would expect from a former rectory. The new Hathway Restaurant (opened in Easter 2008) will serve first-class food in a warm, friendly ambience, using home-grown and locally sourced produce and complemented by wines from around the world. The Priory can be hired for exclusive use or for a reception, and personal packages can be planned and priced to suit a variety of budgets. The main function suite can seat up to 80 guests in comfort, and larger numbers can be accommodated in a marquee in the grounds.

The Priory Hotel offers superb holiday and corporate accommodation, restaurant open to non-residents, private dinner parties, weddings and many other special occasions catered for.

If you are looking for a romantic setting to celebrate your special day then The Priory Hotel offers you just that. With the fine food and luxurious accommodation your guests will be delighted too.

The Priory Hotel is the perfect base for browsing around the Herefordshire countryside. In an area of quiet country roads and leafy lanes, wild flowers, birds, animals and river life are in abundance. It is also cider country – with so many apple orchards, springtime is blossom time and autumn sees the orchards red with ripe fruit. There are various Pick Your Own fruit farms dotted around. The house is also very close to the Wye Valley walk and the River Wye.

The owners Chris Rowbotham and his wife have many years experience in the hospitality and catering business and look forward to welcoming guests whether it's a visit for a special occassion or just a break from a busy schedule.

505

Stoke Lacy, nr Bromyard,
Herefordshire HR6 4HY
☎ 01885 490658

On the A465 4 miles south of Bromyard, the **Plough** is a much-loved village local and a popular venue for meetings and functions. It has the warm, cosy atmosphere of a traditional old-world inn with

beamed ceilings, an open log fire and an assortment of gleaming brass. Diners can choose between a value-for-money bar menu and an à la carte menu served in the restaurant. Options range from sandwiches and baguettes to bar classics (Lasagne, fish pie, steak & ale pie) and restaurant choices typified by succulent steaks, roast salmon with garlic mash and dill sauce, pork tenderloin with a Camembert sauce and wild mushroom & red onion tart. The pub

stands next to the Wye Valley Brewery and carries all their brews, in addition to other draught and bottled beers and a selection of wines. The function room is an ideal venue for parties, weddings and other special occasions, with room for 60 seated or 150 buffet-style. The Plough is open lunchtime and evening for food and drink Tuesday to Sunday.

Bromyard Downs, Norton,
Herefordshire HR7 4QP
☎ 01885 482585
e-mail: info@royaloakbromyard.com
🌐 www.royaloakbromyard.com

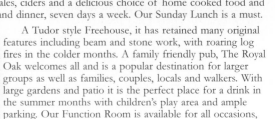

The Royal Oak stands in around 260 acres of beautiful public Downs on the edge of the historic market town of Bromyard amid the Herefordshire countryside.

Starting out as a 17th century Drovers Inn, these days you can be sure of a friendly welcome with a choice of local cask ales, ciders and a delicious choice of home cooked food and pub food favourites served at lunch and dinner, seven days a week. Our Sunday Lunch is a must.

A Tudor style Freehouse, it has retained many original features including beam and stone work, with roaring log fires in the colder months. A family friendly pub, The Royal Oak welcomes all and is a popular destination for larger groups as well as families, couples, locals and walkers. With large gardens and patio it is the perfect place for a drink in the summer months with children's play area and ample parking. Our Function Room is available for all occasions, including wedding receptions for up to 150. Coach parties are also welcome by arrangement.

We look forward to seeing you.

211 LINTON BROOK FARM

Bringsty, nr Bromyard,
Herefordshire WR6 5TR
☎ 01885 488875 Fax: 01885 488875

The glorious setting, with spectacular views from every room, enhance the pleasure of a stay at **Linton Brook Farm**. Sheila and Roger Steeds have three rooms for Bed & Breakfast guests in their tastefully renovated farmhouse, which combines home comforts with the romance and history of a 400-year-old building on a site that is known to have been inhabited as early as 1285. Two roomy doubles with en suite facilities and a smaller twin with a private bathroom provide comfort and peace in the most civilised surroundings, and all have central heating, television and hot beverage tray. Guests have the use of a sitting room with a television and woodburning stove,

and breakfast featuring local produce. Food is served in a superb dining room with a log fire and an enormous single beam. Evening

meals are available by arrangement. Guests are free to roam in the garden and the 68 acres of grassland, farmland, dells and orchard, beyond which there are wonderful walks over Bromyard Downs, the Brockhampton National trust estate and Bringsty Common. The hosts can supply a packed lunch to take on a day's walking. The farm lies on the B4220 Malvern Road half a mile south of the main A44.

212 THE CROWN

Longtown, Herefordshire H12 0LT
☎ 01873 860217
e-mail: info@crowninnlongtown.co.uk
⊕ www.crowninnlongtown.co.uk

Sheila Watkins, equally adept in the kitchen or behind the bar, welcomes locals, walkers, cyclists and tourists from both sides of the

border into the **Crown**, a 250-year-old former cider house

tucked away in glorious countryside. Behind the gleaming white frontage, with the original door still in place, the cosy bar and immaculate restaurant are nicely decorated and comfortably furnished, while outside is a pleasant beer garden for taking the summer sun. Spitfire and Butty Bach from the Wye Valley Brewery are the regular real ales, and the à la carte menu and daily and weekly specials tempt with an excellent selection of home-cooked dishes that include fresh fish, meat pies, curries and pasta. For guests taking a break in this lovely part of the world the Crown has two en suite family rooms, while for budget accommodation a bunkhouse sleeping up to six was opened in March 2008.

213 THE HOLLYBUSH INN

Hay-on-Wye, Herefordshire HR3 5PS
☎ 01497 847371
e-mail: hollybushcamping@btconnect.com

Barbara, Ian and their team run the **Hollybush Inn** with boundless energy and ambition and a welcome that would be hard to beat anywhere. Built as a roadhouse in 1746 and standing on the

Brecon road out of Hay-on-Wye, it has all the qualities of a traditional country inn – excellent hospitality throughout long opening hours, well-kept ales, wholesome, value-for-money food using prime local produce – and much more besides. Five rooms are available for B&B guests, and the 20 acres around the inn include a riverside caravan and camping site. Canoes can be hired at the inn, and the owners are developing the grounds on environmentally aware lines,

with planting of trees from local seeds, extensive recycling and

plans to make the whole site self-sustainable. Other amenities include wireless internet access at the inn, a shop selling camping/caravan essentials and – due on stream in 2008 – a public laundry.

215 SAVERYS LICENSED CAFÉ

20 Broad Street, Leominster,
Herefordshire HR6 8BS
☎ 01568 611051
e-mail: saverys@googlemail.com

Nick and Jenny Westington run **Saverys**, a friendly licensed café which they have quickly made a great local favourite. Bang in the town centre, with two rooms and a retail counter for takeaway, Saverys is open 7 days a week from 9 to 5 (10.30 to 4 on Sunday) for a good selection of snacks and meals. Breakfast offers full English or individual items, replaced at 11.30 by main dishes such as omelettes, cod in

batter, home-made lasagne, escalope of lemon chicken and smoked haddock & spring onion fishcakes. Freshly prepared sandwiches, baguettes and panini come with a variety of generous fillings/toppings like roast loin of pork with sage & onion stuffing, BLT, cheddar cheese with caramelised onion chutney and prawns with Marie Rose sauce; baked items include Danish pastries, scones and croissants. Blackboards list daily specials and desserts such as pear & almond tart. Saverys serves a good choice of hot and cold drinks and also, with meals, beer, cider, wines by glass or bottle and even champagne for those special occasions.

508

Lion Street, Hay-on-Wye,
Herefordshire HR3 5AD
☎ 01497 820841

Hands-on proprietor Dolan Lancaster-Leighton has assembled a first-class team at the **Olde Black Lion**, for many centuries a landmark on one of the historic streets of Hay-on-Wye. That team includes a terrific chef, and in the pretty dining room overlooking the garden terrace diners can feast on a superb variety of dishes featuring the pick of British produce, including locally reared meats (some organic), fish arriving fresh from Cornwall, and herbs and seasonal vegetables from the garden. The chef and his team combine skill and imagination at a high level on menus that are always full of interest: Bodega ham & poached pear on ginger-dressed salad leaves; creamy wild mushroom and fennel vol-au-vent; loin of halibut, roasted and served on buttered spinach and ceps; Moroccan lamb, apricot and fig compote with couscous; classic fish pie, beef Wellington and herb-crusted rack of lamb. The outstanding food is complemented by an extensive wine list and a range of local ales that includes their own Black Lion Brew from the Wye Valley Brewery.

The Olde Black Lion is not just a great place for a meal, it's also a delightful place to stay, and the quality en suite bedrooms offer abundant comfort and all the expected modern facilities – and the famous Black Lion Teddy Bears.

The main part of this distinguished inn dates from the 17th century, but some parts are considerably older, and original timber beams ooze historic charm and atmosphere. It stands close to what was known as the Lion Gate, one of the original entrances to the old walled town, it is rumoured that Oliver Cromwell stayed here while the Roundheads were besieging Hay Castle, at the time a loyal stronghold.

Book-lovers are in their element at Hay, which is renowned throughout the world for its second-hand book shops. It also offers an amazing variety of outdoor activities, including fishing and canoeing on the River Wye, pony trekking through the hills and walking on the Wye Valley and Offa's Dyke Paths.

509

216 THE LAMB

Stoke Prior, nr Leominster,
Herefordshire HR6 0NB
☎ 01568 760308
e-mail: patlambinn@aol.com

Chris Smith the landlord together with his wife Pat and other members of his family all lend a hand in running the **Lamb**, a family-friendly pub located off the A49 south of Leominster. Built 400 years ago and for long the focal point of the community, the pub is delightfully traditional in its appeal, with slate floors, oak beams and wonderful open log fire

and soft sofas to sink into. All this provides a perfect ambience in which to enjoy a drink and a chat, or to enjoy a meal from a menu of pub classics, including

excellent steaks, a hearty steak & ale pie and daily specials. Families are always welcome, and there's a children's play area in the garden. The inn also holds a quiz night on the first sunday of every month. The Lamb is open from 12 to 3 and from 6.30 seven days a week. There is a car park for customers and credit cards are accepted for payment.

218 YE OLDE OAK INN

Wigmore, Herefordshire HR6 9UJ
☎ 01568 770247

Ye Olde Oak Inn occupies a prominent corner site at the top of the village of Wigmore, just off the A4110 Hereford-Leintwardine road. Visitors to this excellent 300-year-old free house can expect a friendly greeting from hosts Penny and Geoff, savouring the convivial surroundings of the cosy little bar to enjoy a chat and a glass or two of real ale – Wye Valley Bitter is a local favourite.

Home-made meat and fish pies are popular choices on the menu of classic pub dishes served in the country-style conservatory restaurant. Sunday lunch brings a choice of roasts – it's guaranteed to bring in a good crowd, so booking is recommended to be sure of a table.

The inn is open lunchtime and evening and all day on Saturday, with food available every session except Sunday evening. Visitors to the inn should take time to look at the imposing ruins of Wigmore Castle, which was built in the 11th century and protected the village and the surrounding area until the Civil War.

510

217 LOWE FARM

Pembridge, nr Leominster,
Herefordshire HR6 9JD
☎ 01544 388395
e-mail: Williams_family@lineone.net
🌐 www.bedandbreakfastlowefarm.co.uk

Juliet Williams, who has travelled to Japan lecturing on public relations, business and banking matters, runs a very special B&B establishment with her husband Clive. **Lowe Farm**, set in 200 acres of picturesque rolling countryside just outside Pembridge, has been in the family as a working farm since 1939, and for the last ten years they have been offering exceptional Bed & Breakfast accommodation throughout the year.

The Grade II listed farmhouse has five en suite bedrooms – a single, two twins and two doubles – that provide an ideal base for tourists, walkers, cyclists and lovers of the great outdoors.

Guests have the use of a beautifully furnished lounge, a garden room and a lovely peaceful garden, and the day starts with a superb breakfast (served until 10 o'clock) featuring eggs from the farm's hens and meat from local farms, including Marston Court and Oakchurch Farm. The same top-quality produce is the basis of an outstanding set evening meal that guests can book in advance.

The guest list at Lowe Farm is truly international, and the exceptional standards of accommodation, service and cooking bring many repeat visits and many prestigious awards. Among the latter are the English Tourist Council's 4 Diamonds and the Gold Award Winner for B&B of the Year at the Heart of England Excellence Awards for 2006/07

The farm is located less than two miles west of Pembridge, signposted on the A44 Kington road at Marston. Pembridge has many attractions for the visitor, including the 16th century Market Hall and the 14th century church with its marvellous timber belfry and much more.

511

219 PAPILLON RESTAURANT AT THE WOODHALL ARMS

High Road, Stapleton, nr Hertford,
Hertfordshire SG14 3NW
☎ 01992 535123
e-mail: papillonwoodhall@aol.com
⊕ www.papillonwoodhallarms.co.uk

The **Papillon Restaurant at the Woodhall Arms** is located on High Road in Stapleford, a short drive from Hertford on the A119. It is a place to seek out and once found added to your top restaurants for the area. Dating from the middle of the 19th Century, it has been run since 1998 in fine style by the chef and owner.

The main restaurant and conservatory provide abundant space and comfort to enjoy top-class cooking. Prime fresh fish from Billingsgate is the basis for many of the favourite dishes including the Rendezvous, five fish simply grilled to include Sea Bass, Salmon and Swordfish. Other seafood options include Moules Meuniere, Smoked Salmon and Lobster Terrine and Dover Sole.If you prefer they have an extensive range of meat dishes, one favourite is Honey Roast Duckling. They also have Roast Saddle of Lamb and Steak Diane amongst a vast

range to choose from. A full menu can be found on their website. Special celebration menu's can be ordered for all kind of occasions, from Wedding Receptions, Anniversaries or just a get together with some friends.

They also have an extensive bar menu, which includes Lite Bite, Traditional Favourites and Baguettes.

They can also offer 12 ensuite bedrooms at very competitive prices and a convenient base for both business and leisure visitors.

221 ROBIN HOOD & LITTLE JOHN

Tonwell, nr Hertford,
Hertfordshire SG12 0HN
☎ 01920 463352
e-mail: julian405523@aol.com

The **Robin Hood & Little John** is a cosy, immaculate 17th century inn standing in the quiet village of Tonwell, just yards off the A602 in pleasant walking country. Run since 1990 by Julian & Sheila

Harding, the inn provides comfortable, practical accommodation for business or leisure visitors. Five of the rooms have en suite facilities, while the other three share a bathroom. Inter-connecting rooms are available, and one room has access for disabled guests. A light buffet Continental breakfast is available in the lounge. Lunch and dinner are served in the bar or dining room, where home-cooked local produce is the basis of an extensive choice of English dishes that include a hearty steak & kidney pie and a two-course traditional Sunday lunch. The main menus are

supplemented by daily specials. The fully licensed bar stocks a good selection of real ales, usually Greene King IPA with regularly changing guest brews. Food is served from 12 to 2.30 and 6.30 to 9.30 (Saturday and Sunday 12 to 3 and 7 to 9.30). Tonwell is a village of some 300 inhabitants, its skyline dominated by a futuristic 1960s concrete water tower. Ware is 2 miles away, Hertford 3, Stevenage 7. From the A1(M) take the A602 at Junction 7; from the M25, take the A10 at Junction 25 then the A602 at the Ware by-pass.

High Cross, nr Ware,
Hertfordshire SG11 1AA
☎ 01920 462996

Chef-proprietor Miki Jordan and Jacqui Thorne front of house make an excellent team at the **White Horse**, which stands in the village of High Cross just north of Ware by the Great Cambridge Road (A10). The premises were originally two cottages, built about 400 years ago; they were converted to a public house a century later and registered as such in 1713, since when the successive landlords have been dispensing hospitality and fine ales to all who pass through the door.

They first served food here in the 1970s, and that side of the business is thriving as a destination restaurant under the current tenants. Behind the lovely black-and-white frontage, made even lovelier in spring and summer by colourful hanging baskets, the interior of the pub has been totally refurbished, and the beams, the rafters, the country chairs set at polished tables, the brasses and the open fires create a warm, inviting atmosphere for meeting friends and enjoying a drink. Outside is a walled patio area with garden furniture and patio heaters, and beyond the car park is a grassed area where children can have a good time on the swings and slide.

The A10 ensures easy access north and south, making the White Horse a great place to pause on a journey or – even better – to take time to enjoy a leisurely meal. Miki is a terrific cook, with invaluable assistance from Pete, and their specials include steak & ale or steak & stilton pie, chicken & mushroom pie, braised shoulder of lamb with a mild minty gravy, and chicken William (stuffed with stilton, wrapped in bacon). Five bean, celery & coriander chilli and roasted vegetable and ricotta cannelloni are typical vegetarian dishes, and in addition to the traditional menu the White Horse has a feature unique in the area. Introduced in 2006, the Black Rock Grill provides a healthy, fun, interactive dining experience in which diners choose their main ingredient (steak, lamb, duck breast, butterflied chicken breast, tuna, tiger prawns, swordfish), cut into bit-sized pieces and cook it to their liking of 'doneness' on high-temperature rocks that seal in the natural flavours, juices and nutrients. Food is served from 12 to 3 and 6 to 9.30 (Sunday 12 to 6).

By the end of 2008 Miki and Jacqui will bring 12 en suite bedrooms, all en suite, in an adjacent building.

Epping Green, nr Hertford,
Hertfordshire SG13 8NB
☎ 01707 875959
e-mail: squirrell15@googlemail.com

The **Beehive** is a popular, cosy country pub located in the village of Epping Green, on a minor road three miles north of Cuffley. This late-18th century inn is well worth seeking out, whether it's to enjoy a drink or to relax over a home-cooked meal. The host is Martin Squirrell, who took over here at the beginning of 2008 after a spell as steward of a Bristol golf club. His parents had run the pub for a number of years, and Martin is continuing the tradition of hospitality that has made it a great favourite down the years with the local community as well as providing a particularly pleasant break for ramblers, motorists, business people and tourists. Hanging baskets and window boxes adorn the frontage in spring and summer, and inside it's traditional to the core, with black beams, an open fire and dozens of ornamental brasses in the inviting public areas.

Food is an integral part of the Beehive's success, and the seasonally changing menus provide a tempting combination of traditional dishes and less familiar options. Fresh fish delivered daily from Billingsgate is one of the reasons why the pub has become such a popular eating place. Battered cod, haddock and skate are always at the top of the list of favourites, and haddock also comes pan-fried or oak-smoked served with a poached egg. Other seafood choices might be pan-fried almond & lemon pollock, crab & mango salad and a classic scallops with bacon. There's plenty for meat-

eaters, including Cumberland sausage, burgers, barbecued chicken wings, beef and gammon steaks, shoulder of lamb and a super steak, mushroom and ale pudding. Caramelised pear, stilton and walnut stack and penne pasta with roasted vegetables and basil cream show that vegetarians are not forgotten. Sandwiches and jacket potatoes provide satisfying snacks for those with smaller appetites or less time to spare. A good choice of drinks, headed by Adnams Bitter and Greene King IPA, can be enjoyed with a meal, in the bar or outside in the garden looking out over the Essex countryside.

Martin's next project is to bring guest accommodation on stream. When that happens, the Beehive will be a comfortable, practical and very civilised base for both leisure and business travellers. Hertford, Hatfield, Ware, Welwyn Garden City and Hoddesdon are all with easy reach, and Lea Valley Park and Broxbourne Woods provide excellent opportunities for ramblers and nature-lovers.

223 THE WYNDHAM HOTEL

1 Church Road Marina, Douglas,
Isle of Man IM1 2HQ
☎ 01624 676913
e-mail: calvertronnie@manx.net

The **Wyndham Hotel** offers practical, comfortable accommodation just a few yards from the promenade and an easy walk from Douglas town centre. Owned and run by Ronnie and Tony Calvert (Ronnie is also a tax consultant), it has 17 bedrooms, five with en suite facilities, that are available for short or long stay letting at all times of the year. Dating from 1846, the hotel occupies one of a large number of terraced houses that were built at a time when the Isle of Man was becoming a popular place to reside or to visit. The tariff is on a Bed & Breakfast basis, but an evening meal is available with a little notice. There's a full on-licence for residents, and the hotel has plenty of off-road parking. The Wyndham is a very pleasant and convenient base for a business visit or for discovering all that Douglas has to offer – a

favourite introduction for the tourist is a leisurely ride along the promenade on the Douglas Bay Horse Tramway. It's also an ideal start point for a tour of the Island, which has a wealth of scenic, historic and sporting attractions to enjoy. Cash and cheque only.

224 THE WELBECK HOTEL

Mona Drive, off Central Promenade,
Douglas, Isle of Man IM2 4LF
☎ 01624 675663   Fax: 01624 661545
e-mail: mail@welbeckhotel.com
⊕ www.welbeckhotel.com

Michael and Irene are at the head of the family who have owned and run the **Welbeck Hotel** for well over 30 years, and the reputation for hospitality they have built up over the years is second to none. Up the hill just off the main promenade, the location is fairly quiet but at the same time convenient for all that Douglas has to offer. The main accommodation comprises 27 en suite rooms, some with sea views, all with en suite facilities, central heating, safe, fridge, digital TV, modem points, direct-dial telephone, iron, trouser press and hot beverage tray. The Welbeck also has seven excellent self-catering apartments – six one-bedroom, one two-bedroom – with bathroom, lounge-diner and partitioned kitchen area. Guests in these apartments have full use of the hotel's amenities, which include a small multi-gym with steam room and

shower. In the Conservatory Restaurant, open to residents and non-residents, the chefs prepare a fine selection of dishes of worldwide inspiration, from Manx kipper pâté and queenie scallops to Chinese-style spare ribs. The Welbeck boasts a wonderful bar where guests can relax and enjoy a refreshment or two. The owners and staff are ready with advice on all the Island's places of interest and can arrange booking for golf and riding.

225 JAKS

43 Loch Promenade, Douglas,
Isle of Man IM1 2LZ
☎ 01624 663786 Fax: 01624 677859
e-mail: andy@jakspub.com
⊕ www.jakspub.com

Built in Victorian times as a hotel, **Jaks** is now one of the Island's most popular and liveliest pub-restaurants, as well as one of the friendliest. On a huge corner site in the heart of the town's life, both day and night, it attracts a very broad-based clientele, from among both Manx residents and the many thousands who visit the island each year.

Customers can enjoy a wide range of drinks in the open-plan ground-floor public bar; the bar stocks one of the largest selections of draught beers on the Island, a doubles bar operates every day. Traditional pub dishes are served here, including vegetarian and fish dishes and Jaks classics like the 'greasy spoon' plate of sausage, egg, chips and beans. Steps lead down to the stylishly, recently refurbished restaurant with full table service, where the main menu offers more familiar favourites as well as more unusual options such as Cajun chicken sizzler, King Prawn sweet & Sour, Mixed Grill, Cumberland Sausage. Sunday lunch, served from 12 to 5, adds three roasts to classics like cod & chips and sirloin

and rump steaks. Scrumptious desserts like spotted dick or apple pie round things off in style. Children are always welcome, and can choose from their own menu.

Jaks is not just a place for good food and drink, it's also one of the most sociable spots on the Island. Live bands perform every Friday and Saturday and it's definitely the number one place for football fans, with 14 plasma and 2 big screens ensuring that no big game is missed. All the major attractions of Douglas are close at hand, including the Manx Museum and the Great Union Camera. Visitors can take a tram ride along the promenade, a steam train to Port Erin or an electric tram to Ramsey. And when they return to Douglas, they can be sure that the staff at Jaks will be ready and willing to provide the hospitality and good cheer that have made this such a popular place.

226 DUNCANS DINER & COFFEE SHOP

Michael Street, Peel, Isle of Man IM5 1HB
☎ 01624 844405

Michael Street is a narrow, winding street in the heart of Peel, and among the various shops and other outlets is **Duncans Diner & Coffee Shop**.

Open throughout the day from Monday to Saturday, it's run by Heather and Brian Horne, who have made it one of the most popular eating places on the whole island.

Warm, friendly and delightfully unpretentious, Duncans serves a good choice of generously plated dishes, with fish & chips and lasagne up among the favourites. Besides the main menu there's an 'everyday pensioners special' and a children's menu for the under-12s. Peel, traditionally the centre of the Manx fishing industry, has plenty to offer the visitor, including a newly opened museum, a historic sandstone castle, a picturesque harbour and a sandy beach. And after a stroll round town, guests can rely on Heather and Brian to provide excellent refreshment at their excellent diner.

227 THE WATERSIDE

72a High Street, Cowes,
Isle of Wight PO31 7RE
☎ 01983 293269

Cowes is the renowned home of the Royal Yacht Squadron, and Cowes Week is a rendezvous for sailors from all over the world. The nautical influence is very strong at any time of the year, and every aspect of the **Waterside** is in keeping with that influence. Host Keith Lumm welcomes all aboard his sociable pub, which stands on the

waterfront on the main street of Cowes. His distinctive inn has a definite maritime look and feel, with sea blue décor and assorted nautical touches. Patrons can splice the mainbrace all day, seven days a week, and if it's not with a tot of rum it might well be with a glass of Fuller's London Pride or one of the two guest cask ales. On the food side, hearty portions of snacks and more substantial dishes are available every day. The choice ranges from baguettes, jacket potatoes and salads to

breaded goat's cheese with sun-dried tomatoes, crab cakes with a sweet chilli sauce, fish & chips, chilli, steak & ale pie, curries, burgers and gammon and beef steaks. Smaller portions of most main courses can be ordered for under-14s. This most friendly and welcoming of pubs is the perfect spot for refreshment after a stroll round Cowes, and just the place for a landlubber to think of things nautical while staying safe on dry land.

517

228 THE OCTOPUS' GARDEN CAFÉ

63 High Street, Cowes,
Isle of Wight PO31 7RL
☎ 01983 291188
⊕ www.octopusgarden.co.uk

Beatlemania is alive and well at the **Octopus' Garden Café** on the main street of Cowes. It was founded in 1999 as a place where the original owner could share his vast collection of Beatles memorabilia with the public, to let them chill with him to the music and enjoy good food and drink. That philosophy is continued by current owner Chris Sanders, also a big fan of the Beatles, who welcomes locals, **Day Tripper's**, holidaymakers and especially families – children have their own dishes and drinks and an indoor play area. The kitchen provides dishes for everyone, and the excellent food is complemented by cheerful, on-the-ball service. The choice runs from sandwiches, toasties and omelettes to spaghetti

bolognese, chilli, curries, cottage pie, cakes and puddings, with hot and cold beverages to accompany. And if it's been a **Hard Day's Night**, you're guaranteed to say **I Feel Fine** after tucking into one of the café's super breakfasts. Once sampled, visitors can't wait to **Get Back** to this amazing place, which is unbeatable for its combination of vibrant setting, great music, great food and great company.

229 THE BELMORE GUEST HOUSE

101 Station Avenue, Sandown,
Isle of Wight PO36 8HD
☎ 01983 404189
e-mail: belmorebandb@aol.com
⊕ www.thebelmore.co.uk

The **Belmore** is a friendly, family-run 4-Star guest house in a fine location a short walk from the Blue Flag beach. It's a perfect place for a quiet break but is also close to all that the Island's premier holiday resort has to offer. Jim Izzard,

formerly pastor to the Fishermen's Mission, and his wife Alison came here in 2006 and in a short time have lost no time in establishing Belmore as one of the most relaxing and civilised small hotels on the Island. They believe that after working hard all year their guests deserve the best, and that philosophy is reflected in the spotless surroundings, the high standards of comfort and service and the feeling of warmth and welcome that is evident as soon as guests walk through the door. The eight tastefully decorated and furnished guest bedrooms – single, double, twin and family – all

have en suite facilities, complimentary beverage tray, iron and ironing board. One room has a four-poster bed, and one room is on the ground floor, making it suitable for less mobile guests. The care and thought that the owners put into running this excellent little guest house naturally extends to the breakfasts, a good wholesome meal based on Island produce that sets guests up for the day.

230 THE SANDHILL

6 Hill Street, Sandown,
Isle of Wight PO36 9DB
☎ 01983 403635 Fax: 01983 403695
e-mail: sandhillsandown@aol.com
🌐 www.sandhill-hotel.co.uk

The **Sandhill** is located in a quiet, pleasant residential area of Sandown, with all the town's amenities within easy reach and the safe, sandy beach just ten minutes' walk away. Kathy Hutchins, Stacey Martin and Steve Pointon and their friendly, helpful staff welcome guests of all ages into a particularly warm, relaxing ambience, and the success of their approach is shown by the large number of repeat bookings. The 16 en suite bedrooms provide excellent accommodation for visitors to the Island and for people working here. All the rooms have TV, direct-dial telephone with free wi-fi internet access and tea/coffee-making facilities. Some of the rooms are on the ground floor, making them suitable for less mobile guests. There's a good choice for breakfast, and the hotel has full

bar facilities. Day rooms also include a picture-windowed sun lounge and a TV lounge with DVDs, videos, books and games. The restaurant is open for breakfast and dinner, and the bar also has its own menu. There are choices for children, and special dietary arrangements can be made with a little notice. The hotel has its own car park. The owners and staff have worked well together to make the Sandhill one of the most pleasant and civilised places to stay on the whole Island.

231 THE FOUNTAIN

2 Carter Square, Sandown,
Isle of Wight PO36 8BP
☎ 01983 401492

The **Fountain** is a busy, popular pub standing in Carter Square, adjacent to the Red Jet ferry terminal. It's easy to spot with its redbrick, red-roofed frontage, canopied entrance and brown-and-white timbered-effect to the upper storey. When Phil Harris took over the tenancy in the summer of 2007 he brought a lifetime's experience in the licensed trade, and the complete interior refit he oversaw has greatly enhanced its appeal. Three regularly changing real ales are on tap in the cheerful bar, which is open from 11 o'clock every day of the week. Simple, down-to-earth pub grub is prepared in the newly re-equipped kitchen. Families with children are welcome, and the pub has some outside seating and a little children's play area. On the social side, Friday night at the Fountain sees a live

music session and all are invited to join in the regular Sunday quiz. The bar has Sky TV for the big sports events, a pool table and games (Trivial Pursuit) machines. Sandown is the Island's leading holiday resort, with plenty to see and do, Blue Flag beach, a traditional pier and abundant leisure and sporting facilities. And after a stroll round town, Phil and his staff are ready to welcome you into the Fountain with smiles and genuine hospitality.

232 DRIFTWOOD BEACH BAR

Culver Parade, Sandown, Isle of Wight
☎ 01983 404004
e-mail: info@driftwoodbeachbar.com
⊕ www.driftwoodbeachbar.com

'Life's a Beach.......with a Bar'

'The Bar on the Beach'

'The Hottest Place to be in the Summer'

Just a few ways to describe **Driftwood Beach Bar**, a destination pub/restaurant that offers the very best in hospitality and the true atmosphere of the Isle of Wight. Its founder Sean Ware modelled it on places he saw in Spain and the Caribbean. The name varies: in Spain they're Chiringuitos, in the USA and the Caribbean Beach Bars, in Mexico Palapas, in France Clubs, in Greece Tavernas. But they all have the same aims – to provide their clientele with food and drink for a long (hard) day on the beach, to be the social focus of the beach and its mood-setter.

Even if the sun has gone missing and the sea doesn't look too inviting, no one should leave Sandown without a visit to this splendid place, which is open long hours for food, drink and fun, from a wake-up breakfast to a leisurely lunch, tropical cocktails and a romantic dinner. Drinks

include beers from around the world- – Tiger from Singapore, San Miguel from Spain, Coors from the USA, Red Stripe from Jamaica, Sol from Mexico. Among the favourite cocktails are Key West Cooler, Mai Tai, Hurricane, Blue Hawaiian and banana, strawberry or pineapple daiquiris. You'll also find draught lager, bitter and Guinness, wines and champagne by glass or bottle and a vast range of spirits both familiar and obscure.

Breakfast is served until 11, and the menus cast their net very wide. Salads, jacket potatoes and burgers provide satisfying light meals; seafood fans can enjoy shell-on prawns, moules marinière, fish & chips, scampi and seafood tagliatelle, with crab and lobster when available; and the best British beef produces the rump, sirloin, rib-eye, fillet and T-bone steaks. Top of the range is a mighty 24oz rump steak – the reward for cleaning the plate unaided is a free pint of Coors! Other choices include lasagne, chilli, spaghetti bolognese, tuna pasta bake and roast vegetable tagliatelle. Sandwiches, baguettes and panini are available until 5 o'clock, to eat in or take away, when the main menu takes over until last orders at 9.30

233 MELBOURNE ARDENLEA HOTEL

4-6 Queen Road, Shanklin,
Isle of Wight PO37 6AP
☎ 01983 862283 Fax: 01983 862865
e-mail: melbourneardenlea@janzenhotels.co.uk
⊕ www.melbourneardenlea.co.uk

Families on holiday will find no better base on the Island than the **Melbourne Ardenlea Hotel**, where Yanika Oxley and her staff provide a high standard of service, comfort and hospitality. The hotel, which stands in a quiet road a short distance from the beach and Shanklin Old Village, is open all year round for short breaks and longer stays. The 54 bedrooms, all with en suite facilities, TV, radio, phone and beverage tray, include singles, doubles, twins and family rooms. Most are served by a lift. The accommodation for families is particularly versatile, with various combinations possible of bunk beds, separate children's rooms and interconnecting rooms. Cots and high chairs are available, and children's dishes can be ordered in the elegant dining room, where breakfast and a daily changing evening meal are served. The restaurant is open to non-residents as well as residents, and the hotel has full bar facility. A valuable asset of the hotel is

a leisure centre, open all year round, with an indoor swimming pool, spa bath and sauna. The lounge can double as a meeting room and hosts entertainment evenings six days a week in season.

234 THE ORCHARDCROFT HOTEL

Victoria Avenue, Shanklin,
Isle of Wight PO37 6LT
☎ 01983 862133
e-mail: admin@orchardcroft.co.uk
⊕ www.orchardcroft.co.uk

The **Orchard Croft Hotel** is a well-presented, comfortable, family-friendly small hotel with excellent management and cheerful, obliging staff. It stands in its own grounds a short walk from the Old Village, Shanklin Chine and all the delights of Sandown's quieter neighbour. Cris Quirk, a well-established hotelier and Chairman of the Shanklin Hoteliers Association, owns and runs this excellent hotel, where guests are assured of the best in hospitality and value for money; the number of return visits is testimony to this approach to hotel-keeping. The guest accommodation, available throughout the year, consists of 16 well-appointed bedrooms, some on the ground floor, all with en suite facilities, TV and tea/coffee tray. The hotel's outstanding amenities include a 10-metre indoor swimming

pool, Jacuzzi, sauna and games room with pool, darts and table football. Families with children are made very welcome, and the hotel has indoor and outdoor play areas. Cots, high chairs, bottle warmers and baby monitors are available. Rooms can be booked on a Bed & Breakfast or Dinner, Bed & Breakfast basis, and the bar is open all day for food and drink.

521

235 CLAREMONT GUEST HOUSE

4 Eastmount Road, Shanklin,
Isle of Wight PO37 6DN
☎ 01983 862083
e-mail: claremont@dsl.pipex.com
🌐 www.southernuk.com/claremont.htm

Avril and Dennis Holland offer high standards of comfort, service and cuisine at **Claremont Guest House**. It occupies a prime location in Shanklin, the quieter neighbour of Sandown, in the same sweeping bay. The accommodation comprises five centrally heated en suite bedrooms, all with TV, radio-alarm clock, complimentary beverage tray and hairdryer. A full English breakfast gets the day off to a good start, and guests on the optional Dinner, Bed & Breakfast tariff look forward to an excellent four-course evening meal. The guest house has ample private parking and is open all year round. Families with children are very welcome. Claremont is conveniently located a three-minute walk from the lift that takes passengers down from the clifftop to the seafront. The railway and bus/coach stations, the beach and all the shops and amenities

of the town are within easy reach on foot, as are the Old Village and Shanklin's major tourist attraction, the Chine. This extraordinary, mysterious and romantic 300 feet wooded ravine is full of surprises, with waterfalls, an abundance of rare flora, a Heritage Centre and a Royal Marines memorial.

237 THE WORLD'S END

Holyrood Street, Newport,
Isle of Wight PO30 5AU
☎ 01983 821082 Fax: 01983 524151
e-mail: dancroln@aol.com

There's no more sociable spot to take a break from shopping, sightseeing or the office than the **World's End**, which stands just north of Newport's High Street and seconds from the A3054 that cuts through the northern part of the Island all the way from Freshwater to Ryde. Len and Laura Bancroft are the most affable of hosts who like nothing more than to see the smiles on the faces of their loyal band of regulars – they also love their trips to Ireland. Behind its shopfront-like entrance this is a real pub-lover's pub – 'lively and long' in the words of the landlord, a down-to-earth, lived-in place to meet and get down to some serious chatting over a glass or two of ale – or to take on the locals at bar billiards. The drinks list is headed

by Courage Best and regularly changing guest ales. The bar is invariably cosy and convivial, and when the sun shines part of the scene shifts to the beer garden and partly-sheltered patio. This is essentially a drinker's pub, but lunchtime quaffing can be accompanied by a short selection of simple pub grub that fits the bill perfectly.

Main Road, Brighstone,
Isle of Wight PO30 4AH
☎ 01983 740226

Dating from 1750 but since much altered and extended, the **Three Bishops** is located in the village of Brighstone, one of the prettiest places on the Island. When it first became a public house it was called The New Inn, but in 1973 its name was changed to honour the three rectors of Brighstone who went on to be appointed bishops – a great achievement for a small community. When Chris and Helen Hessey took over here in 2006 the place was something of a local secret, secluded as it is in a rural part of the Island away from the main tourist destinations. They have overseen a major programme of refurbishment that has enhanced its appeal while retaining a good deal of its traditional character. It's a secret no longer, and it's not just the locals who enjoy the warmth and hospitality but also the many tourists who venture away from the Island's busy resorts to explore all its many places of scenic and historic interest.

The public areas are very roomy and comfortable, with welcoming fires, lots of pine and period photographs and pictures. The main bar leads off to a games room, and when the sun shines the huge beer garden, with picnic sets and a children's play area, really comes into its own. The pub also has a capacious car park. Real ale connoisseurs will be in their element at the Three Bishops, with a regularly changing selection of up to eight brews at any one time. The bar is open for drinks from midday to 10.30 (to 11 at the weekend) and food is served seven days a week from midday to 9 o'clock. Everything is prepared and cooked on the premises, with Island produce used as much as possible. Sandwiches are made to order, and other light dishes include mushroom bruschetta, local crab & prawn salad, nachos, jacket potatoes and ploughman's platters with cheese, ham or seafood. Other popular choices include burgers (beef, chicken or vegetarian), salmon & broccoli fishcakes, fish & chips, spaghetti Bolognese, liver & bacon, chilli con carne, curries, steaks, the pie of the day and a very satisfying steak, ale & mushroom suet pudding. The wine list includes four available by the glass.

Brighstone is a very attractive spot with a National Trust shop and a little museum depicting village life down the years. There's also splendid walking hereabouts, and Chris, Helen and their staff are always ready to deal with thirsts and appetites generated by a spell in the bracing Island air.

523

238 THE WHITE LION

Main Road, Arreton,
Isle of Wight PO30 3AA
☎ 01983 528479
e-mail: chrisandkatie@hotmail.co.uk

Dating back some 200 years – the licensing records go back to 1820 – the **White Lion** was once a staging post in the Valley of Arreton, nestling at the foot of the downs that dominate the landscape from the west at Brading to the east at Newport. Behind the attractive black-and-white frontage, the public rooms are in inviting traditional style, with beams and open fires and a warm, friendly ambience. The pub has a cheerful, hardworking host in Katie Cole, who came here in 2000 and has built up a loyal local following with her excellent brand of hospitality. Food is a major part of the pub's business, and Katie and her chef are kept busy preparing a good choice of well-sourced, wholesome

dishes. The menus offer something for everyone, and a blackboard proposes daily specials such as tuna steak with a Provençal sauce, chicken & leek suet pudding and pork medallions with a wholegrain mustard sauce. Wednesday is curry night. Four cask ales are on tap, usually Fullers London Pride, Timothy Taylor Landlord and one guests. St George's Church in Arreton is one of two Saxon churches on the Island. Arreton Ghost Walk passes by the White Lion, which is reputed to have a ghost. The staff call him George who has been seen on occasions!

239 LITTLE SPAN FARM

Rew Lane, nr Wroxall,
Isle of Wight PO38 3AU
☎ 01983 852419
e-mail: info@spanfarm.co.uk
🖳 www.spanfarm.co.uk

Little Span Farm is a working arable and stock farm in a designated Area of Outstanding Natural Beauty on the southwestern side of Wroxall. In this lovely peaceful setting Felicity Corry offers a choice of accommodation for Bed & Breakfast and self-catering guests. The Farmhouse is a fine 17th century stone building with two double bedrooms with en suite bathrooms and a double/twin with en suite shower. All have TV/video-player, beverage tray and hairdryer. The other B&B property is Harvester Cottage, located behind the farmhouse, with a king-size double-bedded room, bunk beds, a shower room and similar amenities to the farmhouse. A full English breakfast is served in the dining room in the farmhouse. Children are welcome, and cots and high chairs are available. For self-catering guests the Brewhouse has a double bed, bunk

beds, a sofa bed and an open-plan kitchen/living room. The Stable is an 18th century stone barn recently converted to provide comfortable 'upside down' accommodation with a roomy farmhouse kitchen, an open-plan beamed living/dining area and a first-floor sun deck. It also has its own small enclosed garden. Both these properties have spiral staircases linking the living and sleeping areas. Guests are free to roam round the farm, and children can help with feeding during the lambing season.

240 THE SUN INN

Sunhill, Calbourne,
Isle of Wight PO30 4JA
☎ 01983 531231
e-mail: thesuninniow@btconnect.com

The Sun is a cosy, homely little village pub brimful of charm and character. Built in the 18th century, it was rebuilt in classic style, with a Tudor look, after a fire in the early 19th century. Sisters Kate and Sandra, who took over the lease in 2006, have put a great deal of effort and enthusiasm into raising its profile, and their reward is a growing local following. It's a real pub-lover's pub, and the real ales - usually two, always including a local brew – are among the best kept on the Island. Home cooking also excels, and the sisters are committed to doing their best to put the food on the plate at prices that won't dent the appetite. Local produce is to the fore in classic pub fare that includes soup, sandwiches and jacket potatoes. Main meals on offer include home made pies, curries and daily roasts. Vegetarian, vegan and gluten free dishes are always available. Families are very welcome, and the pub has a beer garden. It also has ample off-road parking. The pub, which lies towards the west of the Island between Freshwater and Newport, is open from 11 to 11, with possible seasonal variations.

242 THE PEPPERBOX INN

Fairbourne Heath, nr Ulcombe,
Kent ME17 1LP
☎ 01622 842558
e-mail: thepepperbox@hotmail.co.uk

Leafy lanes lead from the A24 (Headcorn) and the A20 (Harrietsham) to the tiny hamlet of Fairbourne Heath and the **Pepperbox Inn**. Fairbourne Heath (you won't find it on most road atlases) stands a couple of miles northeast of Ulcombe just off the unnumbered road that links the villages of Kingswood and Platts Heath. The is lovely old Shepherd Neame pub is in the excellent care of Sarah and Geoff Pemble, with wags and purrs from the family pets. It's been in the family for 50 years and the current incumbents took over from Sarah's parents in 1986. The bar is in classic old-world style, with a feature fireplace, hop-hung beams, copper pans and kettles and inviting chairs and sofas. Outside, the hilltop terrace commands lovely views across the fields to distant hills. Shepherd Neame Masterbrew and Spitfire are the resident real ales served every session except Sunday evening, when the pub is closed, and food, based as far as possible on Kentish produce, is available from midday to 2 (to 3 on Sunday) and from 7 to 9.45.

the main menu tempts with interesting, beautifully prepared dishes like Maryland crab cakes with tarragon butter, chargrilled peppered lamb fillet with beetroot, crème fraîche & mint dressing, garganelli pasta with a wild mushroom & Madeira sauce and fillet, sirloin and rib-eye steaks with a piri piri, blue cheese & cream or peppercorn, brandy & cream sauce. A second menu of classic pub dishes is available Monday to Thursday lunchtime and evening and Friday and Saturday lunchtimes. Pepperbox is the name of an early form of revolver with a number of barrels.

241 THE GEORGE & NEW TERRITORIES RESTAURANT

76 London Road, Teynham,
nr Sittingbourne, Kent ME9 9QH
☎ 01795 521280
e-mail: gomm236@btinternet.com

The **George Inn & New Territories Restaurant** are located in the village of Teynham, which lies on the A2 three miles west of Faversham. At the heart of the Garden of England, this is an area known for its fruit trees, and it was in Teynham that England's first cherry tree was planted. A writer in the 16th century wrote of Teynham as 'the cherry garden and apple orchard of Kent', and fruit trees can still be seen in every direction.

Another English treasure is the traditional country pub, and Teynham also boasts one of these. The George Inn & New Territories Restaurant are premises with a difference, a good old-fashioned English country pub and an adjoining high-quality Chinese restaurant. Owners Peter and Oi-Lin are experienced restaurateurs who had previously run a restaurant in Minster for ten years. When they came here in November 2006 there was plenty to do – and they set about doing it with gusto. They kept the public bar but one side was completely refurbished, redecorated and turned into a very smart modern restaurant.

The George, which has carried that name since 1767, is open all day, seven days a week, for a full range of drinks, including Fullers London Pride. The bar also serves some light, tasty Chinese dishes at lunchtime, along with £1 'Snack Attack' items like satay chicken, curry trigon and mini-pancake rolls. For the full taste of traditional Peking and Cantonese cuisine, the New Territories Restaurant is the place to head for. Oi-Lin is a very talented chef, and her menus offer a very wide and extensive choice (130+) of dishes. The menu is divided into appetisers, soup, duck, sizzling dishes, seafood, poultry, beef, pork, curry, bean curd, vegetable, rice & noodles, and desserts. And if 130 items aren't enough, diners are free to ask the staff about any other favourite exotic dish! The menu also lists a number of set meals, including a Seafood Special Feast with crab, Dover sole, prawn balls and squid. The restaurant is open lunchtime and evening (from 5) Tuesday to Sunday.

For a really enjoyable East-meets-West experience, it's well worth taking a break from a journey on the A2 to enjoy a drink in the George (non-alcoholic of course for the driver) and a top-notch Chinese meal – but it's better still to make a special journey, to plan ahead and to book on Friday and Saturday evenings. A full takeaway service is also available.

243 THE BEACON

Tea Garden Lane, Rusthall,
nr Tunbridge Wells, Kent TN3 9JH
☎ 01892 524252 Fax: 01892 534288
e-mail: beaconhotel@btopenworld.com
⊕ www.the-beacon.co.uk

From its position on a sandstone outcrop, the **Beacon Bar & Restaurant** enjoys truly memorable views from the terrace. The house, built in 1895 for a Lieutenant to the City of London to the highest standards of craftsmanship, which can still be seen in the handsome fireplaces, ceilings,

oak panelling and stained glass in the restaurant. John and Di Cullen, who took over the Beacon in 1992, completely redesigned and redecorated the premises while retaining all the period features. The cooking is the top attraction here, and Head Chef James Horn and his team are dedicated to using the freshest ingredients available and locally reared/grown produce whenever possible. His menu ranges from lunchtime sandwiches and 'tried & tested favourites' (lasagne, haddock in Harveys Ale batter, steak, kidney & mushroom pie) to dishes that display a combination of

skill and innovation at a high level. Examples include duck breast cured in mulled wine with sour apricot marmalade; seared fillets of sea bass with glazed tiger prawns and a lemon & mustard dressing; and braised boneless lamb shank with crispy bacon, glazed dates and a potato & chestnut purée. The bar is open all day for a full range of drinks, including three real ales. The Beacon is also an excellent base for both business and leisure visitors with three comfortable en suite bedrooms available all year round.

244 BARNFIELD OAST

Mount Pleasant, Lamberhurst, Kent TN3 8LY
☎ 01892 890346 Fax: 01892 891246
e-mail: info@barnfieldoast.co.uk
⊕ www.barnfieldoast.co.uk

Oast houses – distinctively shaped kilns for the drying of hops – were once an integral part of Kent's working life. They are still a familiar and picturesque sight, most of them finding a new lease of life in a variety of roles.

One of the most distinguished of these is **Barnfield Oast**, set in 18 acres of farmland reached down a quiet country lane just outside Lamberhurst. The Oast House, along with its neighbours Oast Cottage and Orchard Cottage, have been imaginatively converted to provide a relaxing self-catering holiday with lovely views and the guarantee of peace and

tranquillity. Oast Cottage sleeps from 4 to 6, Orchard Cottage 6 and the Oast House 8. All are spacious, comfortable and extremely well equipped, with full central heating, en suite facilities, fridge-freezer, cooker, microwave, washing machine and tumble dryer, digital TV, DVD, radio & CD player and wireless broadband. The owners welcome families with children, and cots, high chairs and stairgates can be provided.

There's no more pleasant place to relax and unwind, to enjoy a gentle stroll in the lovely Kentish countryside or to discover the many attractions of the Garden of England.

The Down, Lamberhurst, Kent TN3 8EU
☎ 01892 890170
🌐 www.theswan.org

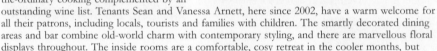

The **Swan at the Vineyard** is located five miles from Tunbridge Wells on the edge of Lamberhurst Vineyard overlooking the vines and the Down conservation area of Lamberhurst.

Voted among the top eating pubs in the UK and attracting local, national and international acclaim, this outstanding 14th century property – originally three thatched cottages – has earned an enviable reputation for both traditional and innovative, out-of-the-ordinary cooking complemented by an outstanding wine list. Tenants Sean and Vanessa Arnett, here since 2002, have a warm welcome for all their patrons, including locals, tourists and families with children. The smartly decorated dining areas and bar combine old-world charm with contemporary styling, and there are marvellous floral displays throughout. The inside rooms are a comfortable, cosy retreat in the cooler months, but during the summer the rear terrace, with views over the vineyard, provides a wonderful venue for enjoying a meal in the fresh air of the Kentish countryside.

The menus cater for a wide range of tastes and appetites, and everything from a light snack to a three-course meal receives commendable care in sourcing, preparation, cooking and presentation. The main menu offers plenty of choice for both familiar pub dishes and dishes from the modern British repertoire: cheddar or gammon ploughman's, line-caught sea bass with saffron & wild mushroom risotto, steak burger, coq au vin, fish pie with salmon & smoked cod, Gressingham dick breast caramelised in acacia honey and balsamic vinegar. Desserts could include dark chocolate tart, banoffee pie and apple & blackberry crumble. Starters/nibbles offer chicken liver parfait with pear chutney, salad of duck confit and some super sandwiches with fillings like roast sirloin with horseradish, bacon & brie melt with cranberry jelly and sunblush tomato with goat's cheese. Food times are 12 to 2.30 and 6 to 9, with extended hours on Sundays, when booking is recommended.

The Swan is closed on Sunday evenings in winter. Lamberhurst wines feature on the interesting list, and two or three real ales are served in the bar.

The village of Lamberhurst, on the main A21 between Tunbridge Wells and Hastings, definitely rewards a leisurely stroll. The gardens at Owl House and Scotney Castle are other local attractions, but for a combination of fine food and picturesque surroundings there's nothing to beat the Swan at the Vineyard.

247 THE CROWN @ OTFORD

10 High Street, Otford, Kent TN14 5PQ
☎ 01959 522847
e-mail: fengiescatering@aol.com
🌐 www.crownpubandrestaurant.co.uk

The village of Otford, off the A225 three miles north of Sevenoaks, has a long and interesting history that goes back beyond Roman times. King Offa of Mercia fought a battle here that brought Kent under his control; Henry VIII stopped here on his way to his encounter with king Farnçois I of France at the Field of the Cloth of Gold; Archbishops of Canterbury had a palace here. And one of them, Thomas à Becket, is reputed to have miraculously created the well that bears his name.

The Heritage Centre is just the place to find out more about this interesting village, and the **Crown @ Otford** is just the place to pause for refreshment. Mark and Fiona Fenge, who took over the pub in the summer of 2007, have made this the hub of village life, equally popular with the local community and with visitors from outside the area. Built in the 16th century as two cottages, and later an ale house and a coaching inn with its own smithy, has considerable old-world charm, with ceiling and wall timbers and open fires in inglenook hearths. Outside is a safe rear garden. The bar is open all day for drinks, including regularly changing real ales – some 60 different brews in the Mark and Fiona's first six months. The bar also stocks a good selection of other draught and bottled beers, lagers, wines, spirits and soft drinks.

Food is also a major part of the Crown's business, and the locally sourced traditional dishes with a modern twist have a strong following in the area. Sandwiches, panini, Welsh rarebit, nachos, jacket potatoes and salads provide excellent lighter/quicker meals, while main dishes might include omelettes, scampi, breaded plaice, Lincolnshire sausages & mash, pan-fried butterfly salmon, chicken kebabs, loin of pork with a creamy mushroom sauce and tortelloni ricotta pasta with a tomato & basil sauce. An excellent children's menu is available from Monday to Saturday, and Sunday lunch includes a choice of small, medium or large roasts. Children under 12 get a free ice cream with their meal. Food is served lunchtime Monday and Tuesday, lunchtime and evening Wednesday, Thursday and Friday, from 11 to 3 and 6 to 9 on Saturday (when there is no music) and from 12.30 to 5 on Sunday. From May to September The Crown @ Otford opens at 11 each day.

The Crown hosts regular entertainment evenings and top football and rugby matches are shown on Sky TV.

246 THE BISHOPS OAK

Shipbourne Road, Tonbridge,
Kent TN10 3NG
☎ 01732 356748
e-mail: alan.barron@btconnect.com

When Alan and
Sandra Barron
took over the lease
in the summer of
2006, the **Bishops
Oak** needed a
good 'shake-up'.
And that's exactly
what the 1960s pub on the A227 north of
Tonbridge got, and the local community came
flocking back. The location also makes it a
good place to break a journey, and locals and
motorists get together in the bar to enjoy
good conversation and a full range of drinks
throughout the day. Sandwiches and bar
snacks are always available, and a popular,
value-for-money Sunday lunch is served
between 12.30 and 3. Families with children
are welcome, and the pub has seats out at the
front and in the beer garden, and ample car
parking space. Cash only.

248 THE BRICKLAYERS ARMS

39 Chevening Road, Chipstead,
nr Sevenoaks, Kent TN13 2RZ
☎ 01732 743424
⊕ www.the-bricklayers-arms.co.uk

Andy and Jane welcome visitors to the
Bricklayers Arms, a super pub located a
mile from Sevenoaks, just moments from the
A21, A25 and M25. The bar is open
lunchtime
and
evening,
and freshly
prepared
food is
served
every
session
except

Sunday evening. The choice spans doorstop
sandwiches, jacket potatoes, classic pub main
courses and home-made puddings 'just like
mother used to make'. The excellent food is
complemented by a long list of wines from a
round the world, with many available by the
glass.

249 YE MAYDES RESTAURANT

High Street, Biddenden, Kent TN27 8AL
☎ 01580 291306 Fax: 01580 292064

Ye Maydes, a superb timber-framed building on
Biddenden's High Street, is a splendid restaurant
that offers a memorable dining experience. The
setting is intimate, romantic and instantly relaxing, and the rich colours, the open fire, the dark
beams and the carefully chosen furniture create an ambience of elegance and luxury. Owner Sheila
Daniels, here since 1973, and her talented chef Julie set great store by the very best local Kentish
produce. The meat comes from the village butcher and
the surrounding area is a bountiful source of fruit and
vegetables, beers, wines and ciders. The monthly à la
carte and daily changing special menu are filled with
tempting dishes typified by smoked mackerel mousse,
wine-poached fillet of sea bass, pork with an apple &
cider sauce and chicken with creamed stilton & spinach.
Throughout the summer patrons can enjoy this fine
food in the lush, secluded garden behind the restaurant.

The restaurant is
open lunchtime
and evening
Wednesday to
Saturday, and for
lunch on the first Sunday of the month. Ye Maydes is a
popular venue for special events such as wedding receptions,
birthday parties and anniversaries. They have a music licence
and are able to book singers and musicians. They also hold
Murder Mystery evenings, which are very popular and great
fun.

251 THE CHEQUERS INN

Ashford Road, High Halden,
Kent TN26 3LP
☎ 01233 850218 Fax: 01233 850762
🌐 www.chequershighhalden.co.uk

The **Chequers** is a traditional country pub in the village of High Halden, on the A28 three miles northeast of Tenterden. It dates back many centuries and was once an important coaching stop with three stables (these still stand). Behind the handsome frontage with a sign depicting chequers players the inn is full of rustic charm.

The Village Bar is a lively local, with pool and darts, and there's a second, relaxing lounge bar. The Chequers has even had a book written about it, with tales of village life and of the wizards, giants and smugglers who frequented the pub. The giants and the smugglers have long since gone, and so have the wizards, but leaseholders Lynne and Jenny are certainly doing a wizard job in running this splendid old place.

It's their first venture together in the licensed trade and one that they clearly relish. They have given the pub a fresh lease of life and their hard work, enthusiasm and warmth have won many friends.

It's a great favourite with the local community and also a popular place to take a break on a journey along the busy A28, which runs all the way from Hastings to Margate, by way of Tenterden, Ashford and Canterbury. Greene King IPA is

the resident real ale served in the bar, which is open lunchtime and evening and all day Friday, Saturday and Sunday.

Food plays an important part in the success of the Chequers, locally sourced as far as possible and freshly prepared to order. Typical starters on the restaurant menu include queen scallops and crispy bacon with a honey & mustard dressing, and baked cup mushrooms stuffed with spinach, brie and walnuts. An excellent meal might continue with wild mushroom & asparagus tahlatelle, smoked mackerel with leek mash, herb-crusted rack of lamb or a juicy sirloin or fillet steak served plain or with a diane, peppercorn or stilton sauce. The bar menu offers salads and sandwiches, jacket potatoes and a dozen or so main courses, including homemade fish cakes, cider-battered cod, steak & stilton pie and honey-glazed ham with eggs & chips. Children have their own short menu, and smaller portions of some items off the bar menu are available.

531

250 THE KING WILLIAM IV

The Street, Benenden, Kent TN17 4DJ
☎ 01580 240636
e-mail: kingwilliamIV@btconnect.com

The attractive village of Benenden, strung out along a ridge three miles southwest of Cranbrook, is best known for its girls' school and its cricketing tradition. But for lovers of the traditional English inn the **King William IV** is the main attraction. Built in the 16th century, it was originally a chapel, a resting place for Canterbury pilgrims, and later became a haunt of the notorious Hawkhurst gangs of smugglers. Since April 2008 the inn has been in the care of the father-and-son team of Ian and Matt McKirgan. It's their first venture together and already they have made it a popular destination not just for local residents but for the many tourists and motorists who pass this way. The strongest magnet is Matt's outstanding food, which is served from midday to 2 and from 6.30 to 9.30, Sunday 12 to 3 only. He sources his ingredients almost exclusively from Kent and Sussex, including fish freshly landed at Rye. His menu changes on a day-to-day basis according to what's best

and freshest, but among dishes that have become early favourites are sea bass fillets grilled and served with a cream & white wine sauce, and steaks, fully traceable, from locally slaughtered and butchered Kentish herds. Sunday sees traditional roasts, with fish and vegetarian options. Drinks served in the bar include Spitfire and Masterbrew from the owning Shepherd Neame Brewery. Families are very welcome and the climbing frame in the garden is guaranteed to keep the little ones busy and happy.

253 THE GRIFFINS HEAD

Chillenden, nr Canterbury, Kent CT3 1PS
☎ 01304 840325 Fax: 01304 842190
🌐 www.chillenden.co.uk

The **Griffins Head** has long been part of everyday life in the small, secluded village of Chillenden, which lies eight miles southeast of Canterbury on minor roads off the A256, A257 or B2046. Built in 1286 as a farmhouse, it was granted a full licence in 1766 at the dawn of coaching days, when it became an important stop on the Canterbury-Deal run. Jerry and Karen Copestake have been at the helm of this beautiful half-timbered building for a quarter of a century, regaling their patrons with their first-class hospitality. In the superb old-world interior or out in the equally delightful gardens up to five real ales, including Spitfire and Masterbrew from the owning Shepherd Neame Brewery, can be enjoyed, and delicious food is served from midday to 2 and from 7 to 9.30, with the menu changing every session. The blackboard list typically runs from broccoli & stilton

soup and smoked duck breast with red onion marmalade to pepper-sauced steaks, chicken & leek pie, butterfish (Arctic sea bass) baked in lemon butter, and roasted vegetable, chick pea & lentil bake. Lunchtime snacks include ham, egg & chips, scampi, tempura prawns & spring rolls and cottage pie. Summer Sunday lunch brings a popular barbecue, weather permitting. The bar is open all day Monday to Saturday and lunchtime on Sunday; the pub is closed on Sunday evening. When in Chillenden, have a look at the famous old windmill.

252 THE SWAN INN

1 Swan Street, Wiittersham,
Kent TN30 7PH
☎ 01797 270913
e-mail: info@swan-wittersham.co.uk
🌐 www.swan-wittersham.co.uk

The village of Wittersham stand high above the Rother Levels on the B2082 four miles south of Tenterden. At the heart of village life is the **Swan**, a homely 17th century inn with cracking hosts in Ray and Angie Pratt. They have lived in the village for more than 40 years and since taking over here in 1992 they have made their inn one of the most popular in the region, a place to meet or make friends over a chat and a drink in the bar, which is open all day, seven days a week. And it's the real ale that has helped to put this lovely old pub on the map.

Seven brews, usually including Harveys Sussex Best and Goachers Fine Light, are on tap to quench thirsts and lubricate conversation. They also keep six real ciders and a perry. The numbers increase greatly during the three annual festivals: seasonal winter ales in February, cider and perry in May and beer and cider, along with a hog roast, in August. In their time here Ray and Angie reckon they have featured more than 2,000 different brews, many of them award-winners.

The food side of the business is also important and professional chefs produce a fine variety of dishes to enjoy in the bar or in the very impressive newly created restaurant. Locally sourced ingredients are the basis of the cooked-to-order dishes served from 12 to 3 and 6 to 9, all day on Saturday and from 12 to 4 and 7 to 9 on Sunday. Many of the dishes on the bar and restaurant menus are pub classics such as beer-battered cod, the homemade pie of the day, home-cooked ham and sirloin and gammon steaks. Others look to Europe (plum tomatoes and buffalo mozzarella with rocket salad and pesto dressing; stuffed chicken breast with dolcelatte and herbs served with parma ham and olive mash), while some venture into other continents: tempura squid with a Thai sweet chilli dipping sauce; Southern fried chicken; Thai green chicken curry; duck spring rolls with hoisin sauce.

Wittersham, at the heart of the Isle of Oxney, is a pleasant place for a stroll, and local attractions include the National Trust's Smallhythe Place, the Royal Military Canal (a wonderful habitat for a variety of wildlife) and the Kent & East Sussex Railway. And after the sightseeing's done, it's good to know that Ray and Angie and their staff are ready to satisfy fresh-air thirsts and appetites.

Canterbury Road, Wingmore, Elham,
Canterbury, Kent CT4 6LP
☎ 01227 831463
⊕ www.palmtreeinn.co.uk

There can be few pubs in the county that have such an interesting tale to tell as the **Palm Tree Inn**. The Smugglers Bar dates back to 1725, when the building was known as the White House. A Folkestone man who owned the pub went to sea with Captain Cook to exotic far-flung islands and when he returned renamed the pub the Palm Tree. At the beginning of the 18th century a gang of smugglers and pirates maintained a reign of terror in the area. The vicar of nearby Aldington was at one time the gang's leader and they hid their contraband liquor and tobacco in the crypt of his church. When a member of the gang killed the vicar they had to find a new place to stash their stolen goods and for several years they used the Palm Tree. That explains the pub's pirate theme: the Jolly Roger flies outside the pub, and on a tropical beach life-size pirates stand among the palms. There are more of them in the bar, along with beautiful log fires, pipes, brass ornaments, hops, Toby jugs and a unique crystal garden for soothing weary travellers.

Carole and Ewart Wanstall and their family are the welcoming hosts; they no longer serve food, but for six evenings a week and Sunday lunchtime visitors can enjoy the unique surroundings, the convivial ambience and real ales kept in tip-top condition. Families with children and dogs (and sea dogs?) are always welcome, and the inn is a popular venue for private parties. The inn is set within the beautiful and largely unspoilt Elham Valley. The magnificent scenery of fields and forests attracts walkers and lovers of the great outdoors from all over the UK and beyond, and after a day in the bracing Kentish air there's nothing to beat a glass or two in jovial company at the Palm Tree.

The Jolly Roger that flies outside accompanies the Union Jack and the French tricolour, a nod to how close the inn is to our neighbours across the Channel.

The Channel Tunnel terminal is only 15 minutes' away, the ports of Dover and Folkestone 15 to 20 minutes and Canterbury 10 minutes. The Palm tree is an easy drive from the M20, via the A20, or the M2/A2 (leave at the Barham/Kingston exit). The Palm tree has a picturesque five-acre site for campers and caravanners with showers, toilets and electric hook-ups.

Horns Lane, Goosnargh, nr Preston,
Lancashire PR3 3FJ
☎ 01772 856230 Fax: 01772 864299
e-mail: info@hornsinn.co.uk
⊕ www.yehornsinn.co.uk

Owners Mark and Denise Woods, managers Louise and Paul and chef James run one of the finest pubs in Lancashire, standing at a crossroads on the B5269 a short drive from J32 of the M6. **Ye Horns Inn** is signposted from Goosnargh village, about two miles towards Chipping in a scenic setting below Beacon Fell. This wonderful traditional country inn first opened its doors in 1782, and today's visitors will be instantly won over by the combination of the charm and atmosphere of yesteryear and the comforts of the 21st century.

Behind the black-and-white mock-Tudor façade, original beams, open fires, and luxurious carpets and curtains create the most warm and welcoming ambience, and this is one of the very few inns where patrons can actually sit within and behind the bar serving area. Two cask ales are

regularly rotated, and the bar also stocks a fine selection of wines and malt whiskies. Local produce is the basis of the good wholesome food prepared by a busy team in the kitchen and served from 12 to 2 and 7 to 9, till 9.30 on Saturday and from 12 to 2.30 on Sunday (no food Monday Lunch). Dishes based on the renowned Goosnargh duck and chicken are always in demand, and other options might include smoked haddock & leek fish cakes, baked ham, hot potted shrimps, grilled trout, salmon hollandaise, steaks, steak & ale pie and a tasty vegetarian dish of peppers stuffed with rice, mushrooms & tomatoes, topped with cheese. A blackboard acknowledges top local producers and suppliers of meat, game, poultry, fish and shellfish, fruit and vegetables, dairy and bread.

In an adjacent building, six superb bedrooms – four doubles and two twins – have en suite bathrooms, tea/coffee makers, trouser presses and hairdryers. Three are located on the ground floor. A full English or Continental breakfast starts the day. The inn also has a caravan park with electric hook-ups for five vans or tents. The foothills of the Pennines provide superb walking combined with glorious views, and the inn can arrange golf and fishing (coarse and fly) in season. Visitors should find time to visit nearby Chingle Hall, one of the most haunted houses in Britain, and it's a short drive to Preston, the newest city in the county, with a wealth of shops, museums, galleries and other distinguished public buildings.

535

256 OLDE DUNCOMBE HOUSE

Garstang Road (A6), Bilsborrow,
nr Preston, Lancashire PR3 0RE
☎ 01995 640336 Fax: 01995 640336
e-mail: oldedunc@aol.com
🌐 www.party-boats.co.uk

Olde Duncombe House stands on the main A6 (four miles north of J32 of the M6 or 8 miles south of J33) in the village of Bilsborrow, which was originally known as Duncombe Village. The Bolton family have chalked up a quarter of a century at this fine old inn, and Jayne, Alec and their son Dan continue to tempt back old friends and win new fans with their excellent hospitality. The inn is thought to date back to the 16th century, and the story goes that some of Bonnie Prince Charlie's men slept in the barn that's attached to the main building and now houses the lounge and the bedrooms. The nine en suite bedrooms, each with its own charm and character, all have television, telephone, mini-bar, hot drinks tray and hairdryer.

Children are welcome, and three of the rooms are located on the ground floor. The house has ample off-road parking, and other services include delivering the daily newspapers and early morning calls. The tariff includes a hearty English breakfast served at a time to suit the guest – on a tray in bed if required. The accommodation is available throughout the year, and the hotel accepts all the major credit cards.

The house is close to many towns and tourist attractions: Beacon fell Country Park is four miles away, as is the market town of Garstang. It's seven miles to Preston, 14 to Blackpool, 15 to Lancaster with its ancient Castle. The Bolton family have a second string to their bow. The house stands alongside the Lancaster Canal, and Alec and Dan run the *Jungle Queen*, a magnificent 65 feet canal barge that's an ideal venue for a floating party or other special occasion. Catering for up to 45 passengers, this superb boat offers everything for the most discerning of partygoers. Amenities include a well-stocked licensed bar, a cosy all-weather heating system, the latest entertainment facilities and an extensive buffet menu. The owners make it easy for people hiring the barge to personalise their requirements, offering a wide range of possibilities regarding length, direction, stop-offs, food and entertainment. The Lancaster Canal is the longest lock-free canal in Europe – it's plain sailing to Preston Dock (14 miles) or Lancaster (30 miles).

33 Bonds Lane, Garstang,
Lancashire PR3 1ZB
☎ 01995 602387

Quality rises to the top in every aspect of the **Church Inn**, where familiar faces and first-timers are equally assured of the very best in hospitality. Kelly Wilkins, her family and staff do their jobs with the watchword that the customer always comes first, and their diligence and enthusiasm have built up a large and loyal band of regular patrons. The inn, which started life as a coaching inn in the middle of the 18th century, is located a short walk from the centre of Garstang, in Bonds Lane (B6430), formerly the main road through the town.

The Church Inn is a great place to meet for a drink (Theakstons Mild is a regular) and a chat in the comfortable bar – bar hours are lunchtime and evening Monday to Thursday and all day at the weekend. But it's an even better place to take time to enjoy the excellent food that comes from the kitchen lunchtime and evening every day of the week. Toasties, sandwiches and jacket potatoes cater for those with less time to spare, while the main dishes include pub classics like Cumberland sausage, chilli, lasagne, steak & ale pie, battered cod, rib-eye and gammon steaks, lamb Henry and the day's curry. Always popular are the giant Yorkshire puddings filled with chilli, lamb, beef or sausages with onion gravy. And how nice it is to see Morecambe Bay shrimps on the menu – a treat at any time. Typical of the consideration for

their customers is the 'small appetite menu' that proposes daintier portions of the most popular dishes.

Another splendid aspect of this outstanding inn is the recently completed one-acre garden, developed from the original two acres of grounds that included a bowling green. This lovely new area has tables and chairs, a covered smoking area, flowers, shrubs and fruit trees. All in all, the Church Inn is definitely worth a special trip and an excellent place to pause on a journey while discovering the local places of interest.

Garstang itself is an ancient, attractive town with a market that dates back to the time of Edward II. It still takes place every Thursday in the central square. The history of the town and the surrounding area is told in the Discovery Centre.

258 THE ORIGINAL FARMERS ARMS ⫚ ⊢

Eccleston, Chorley, Lancashire PR7 5QS
☎ 01257 451594 Fax: 01257 453329
e-mail: barnewton@btinternet.com

Barry and Shirley, here for more than 20 years, their daughter Tiffany and son Elliott make the **Original Farmers Arms** truly a family affair. Their well-known and well-loved 18th century coaching inn stands in the village of Eccleston, on the B5250, off the main A581 a short drive west of Chorley. The décor is nothing if not original, with big colourful murals, quotations on the walls, plates, clocks, brasses and prints under the low beams in the rustically furnished bar. A minimum of three real ales are kept in tip-top condition to be enjoyed throughout the day, seven days a week, heading a long list of other beers and lagers, wines, spirits and soft drinks. Food is served from midday to 10pm every day in the bar or in the 75-cover dining area. Six chefs are kept busy preparing brilliant dishes you probably won't find

anywhere else: sea bass with tiger prawns, scallops, mussels, tomato, chilli, pernod sauce; venison steak, pan-fried with a venison sausage in a damson & port sauce; ostrich steak with mushrooms, onion rings and a pepper sauce. Monday is quiz night with a light buffet and on Friday customers can tuck into free bacon sandwiches after 10pm. The inn also offers comfortable accommodation in 4 quality guest rooms – two doubles and two twins.

259 THE WHITE LION ⫚

117 Mossy Lea Road, Wrightington,
Wigan WN6 9RE
☎ 01257 425977
e-mail: mattandelliefurzeman@hotmail.co.uk

The **White Lion** is a charming hostelry at the centre of the village of Wrightington, on the B5250 a mile or so from J27. It was originally two cottages and a smithy, and behind the neat brick and stone exterior is a wealth of old-world character and atmosphere. Small-paned windows, black-and-white Tudor features (it was until recently called the Tudor Inn), open brickwork, old beams, well-chosen pictures on yellow-painted walls, burnished copper and brass, a snug corner with comfortable sofas, and a dining area with neatly laid tables and an elaborate chandelier paint a charming, traditional scene. Outside, the pub has an attractive beer garden and a large car park. It was refurbished to a high standard by tenants Matt and Ellie Furzeman, who since it re-opened have made it a popular spot with locals and visitors alike.

The inn is open all day for drinks, and top-quality cooking produces a wide range of dishes, from

warm chicken & bacon salad and deep-fried camembert to meatballs with a Bolognese sauce, steaks, steak & ale pie, fish & chips, fishcakes, burgers, Sunday roasts and home-made pizzas cooked in the stone-based oven. The pizzas come small, medium and large and include some unusual varieties like seafood with anchovies, prawns and tuna, or Bollywood with chicken tikka, green chillies, red onion and mixed peppers. Tuesday is quiz night, and there's a poker session on the first Wednesday of the month.

260 THE CUMBERLAND ARMS

39/41 Chapel Green Road, Hindley,
Wigan WN2 3LL
☎ 01942 255117

In the heart of Hindley, a couple of miles east of Wigan, the **Cumberland Arms** is an equally popular destination with the local community, tourists, business people and the considerable passing trade. It's open all day, seven days a week for drinks, which include a good range of draught real ales (John Smith's Smooth, Worthington, Caffreys) as well as real ales in bottles, lagers, wines, spirits and non-alcoholic drinks.

This splendid free house, which dates from 1879, is thriving under tenants Dorian and Alicia, who took it over in October 2006. Dorian is the talented chef, kept busy producing a good choice of pub classics for the printed menu and specials board. Cod & chips, burgers (including a veggie version), big breakfasts and basket meals are among the most popular dishes, along with the traditional Sunday roasts. Food is served from 12 to 3 and in the early evening, but is available all day during the school holidays. Besides the public bar, the pub has a games room and a family room, and the beer garden is a popular spot in the summer. As well as being a great place for a drink and a meal, the Cumberland Arms is very much at the social heart of the town.

Friday and Saturday nights bring DJs and karaoke sessions, an organist performs on Sunday, on Tuesday afternoons the locals play bingo, cards and dominoes, with hot and cold snacks and hot drinks to keep them going and from 10 o'clock on Sunday morning the Breakfast Club offers a full English breakfast – with or without a pint.

The pub's coat of arms is worth taking time to examine with its many references to the county: the flowers represent the Grass of Parnassus that grows on the marsh uplands; the pick and crook commemorate the local activities of mining and rearing sheep; the curlew is a common sight in the county; the bull is in the coat of arms of the well-known Dacre family; the roebuck is traditional to the county; and the masoned base represents Hadrian's Wall.

Halsall Square, Great Eccleston,
Lancashire PR3 0YE
☎ 01995 670738
e-mail: hardiegordon@aol.com
🌐 www.thefarmersgteccleston.com

Great Eccleston is a quiet, traditional agricultural community standing on the banks of the River Wyre. It was once known as Little London, perhaps because of the large number of inns it had in days gone by. The place really bustles on Wednesdays, when an open-air market on the charming village

square brings visitors from many miles around. Unlike many markets that can trace their history back many centuries, Great Eccleston's market started as recently as 1974 after a long campaign by the parish council.

On Wednesdays and any other day of the week the **Farmers Arms** is open all day with a friendly greeting from Gordon and Janet, real ales, real food and real fires. The pub dates back in part to the 17th century, starting life as a farmhouse on an old drovers' road; later it became a simple ale house and was first licensed in

the early 19th century. Gordon and Janet have really turned the old place round, bringing back the locals and welcoming a growing band of new patrons from inside the community and the surrounding towns and villages. Unicorn is the favourite cask ale, and draught Carling Extra Cold is another popular tipple. Beams abound in the bar, where the main feature is a vast brick fireplace adorned with horse brasses, copper platters and other ornaments. Janet is a super cook, and her delicious dishes can be enjoyed from 12 to 3 and 5 to 10 Tuesday to Sunday and Bank Holiday Mondays. Classic starters like pâté, prawn cocktail and garlic mushrooms precede generously served main courses including battered fish, BBQ chicken with cheese, steak & onion pie, steaks, lamb Henry, Lancashire hot pot, lasagne and chicken curry. Alternatives include all-day breakfast and burgers, with sandwiches and toasties for quicker or lighter options. The evening choice is added to by pizzas with a variety of interesting toppings such as Hawaiian (ham & pineapple) or Border Patrol (Mexican chicken, pepperoni, spicy beef & jalapeño peppers); and by kebabs – doner, kofte, lamb or chicken shish, in small or large sizes. Thursday is curry night and traditional roasts are the centrepiece of Sunday lunch.

Great Eccleston is a pleasant place for a stroll and another is its neighbour St Michael's-on-Wyre, where the church has a superb mural discovered as recently as 1956 during repair work in the sanctuary.

Whalley Road, Balderstone, nr Blackburn,
Lancashire BB2 7LE
☎ 01254 812222
e-mail: info@themyerscough.com
⊕ www.themyerscough.com

Built as a private residence in the late-18th century, the **Myerscough** was later an inn with a smithy attached and is now one of the busiest and best-loved hostelries in the region. It stands in the village of Balderstone on the A59 Clitheroe road from J31 of the M6 (the inn lies on the left, opposite the BAE Systems establishment). Set on the edge of the Ribble Valley this country inn offers comfortable, relaxed surroundings along with very friendly owners and staff. Since arriving

here in November 2005, licensees Adam, Alex and Tom have enhanced its long-established reputation for fine food and hospitality. The inn is equally popular as the lively hub of the community, a welcome break for motorists, tourists and business people, and as a comfortable, convenient base for an overnight stay or longer break.

There is a large beer garden where you can enjoy the sun with a drink or even try one of the in house picnic lunches available throughout the summer months. The menu offers a variety of home cooked foods such as lamb rump steak with root vegetables, roasted cod fillet in seafood sauce, traditional fish 'n' chips and of course the 'Babbies Head' steak pudding. Combine this with 2 letting ensuite bedrooms and a selection of the finest Robinsons Cask Ales, you will find the perfect destination house.

Business and leisure visitors looking for a place to stay will find an ideal base at the Myerscough, and the three guest rooms – two doubles and a twin, all with en suite shower, television, trouser press and beverage tray – are available throughout the year. The location and the amenities make the inn a popular choice for club meetings and small conferences. High life cards welcomed.

263 THE DOG INN

King Street, Whalley, nr Clitheroe,
Lancashire BB7 9SP
☎ 01254 823009
Fax: 01254 824090

In one of Lancashire's most attractive villages, the **Dog Inn** is a sturdy corner-site building of local stone, with tall, white-painted chimneys and white-painted door and window surrounds. Inside, long-serving tenants Norman and Christine Atty have created a particularly warm and inviting ambience in which to enjoy an all-day selection of six real ales from national, regional and small local breweries. They have built up a large and loyal following with their special brand of hospitality, the genuine smiles, the ales and the wholesome lunchtime food. The choice spans sandwiches, tortilla wraps, omelettes, salads, filo prawns and all-time favourites like scampi, Cumberland sausages, grilled gammon and cheese & onion or steak & kidney pie. Evening meals are available by prior

arrangement. Families with children are welcome at the inn, which has a pleasant, secluded patio garden. There's also a covered area where smokers can indulge. Whalley is well worth taking time to explore, with a 14th century abbey, the ancient parish Church of St Mary and the famous 48-arched Whalley Viaduct, built in 1850 to carry the Blackburn to Clitheroe railway line across the broad valley of the River Calder.

265 THE PENDLE INN

Barley, nr Burnley, Lancashire BB12 9JX
☎ 01282 614808 Fax: 01282 695242
🌐 www.pendleinn.co.uk

'Deep in the Heart of Witch Country'

The **Pendle Inn** is an outstanding country hostelry owned and personally run by the farming Lowcock family – Joanne, David and daughter Laura – with Keiron at the helm in the kitchen.

Purpose-built in the 1930s, it stands on the Pendle Way Walk, and there's no better place for a pint and a snack, a meal, an overnight break or longer stay while discovering the mysteries of Witch Country. The inn is open all day, seven days a week, for drinks, which include three cask ales – Pride of Pendle, Thwaites Original and a changing local brew. Good English is the order of the day, with pork and lamb from their own farm and everything sourced in Lancashire. The main menu is served from 12 to 9 (Sunday to 8) and a snackier bar menu is available from 12 to 6. Beautifully appointed guest accommodation is contained in modern stone-built cottages fully equipped for a self-catering

or Bed & Breakfast stay. The Pendle Inn, superb in every department, enjoys a scenic location on an unnumbered road between the A59 (through Downham) and the A682 (leave at Blacko). It can also be reached from the south – turn off the A6068 at Fence.

Mitton, nr Clitheroe, Lancashire BB7 9PQ
☎ 01254 826223
e-mail: simon@aspinallarms.co.uk
🌐 www.aspinallarms.co.uk

The Forster family – Simon and his parents
Eileen and Bill – have built up a great
following at the **Aspinall Arms**, which enjoys
a picturesque village setting on the B6246
southwest of Clitheroe and close to the River
Ribble. This family-friendly country inn dates
from the 17th century, when it was built at a
crossing point on the river. It was originally
the home of the ferryman, and the old
boathouse was incorporated into the present

structure. When it first became an inn, it was appropriately
called the Mitton Boat.

Simon is a very talented and experienced chef, and his
menus bring lovers of good food from many miles around.
Local suppliers of meat and vegetables are the basis of many
of his dishes, which include hearty pies (plate meat; steak,
mushroom & real ale), steaks, piri piri chicken, lamb Henry
(with mint and redcurrant gravy), haddock in real ale batter, and
spinach & feta pancake. A popular order to share is the Tex
Mex platter of hot mozzarella melt, jalapeño peppers, chilli
mushrooms, potato wedges and spicy onion rings, with accompanying salad and dips. Many of the
main courses are available in smaller portions for younger or more modest appetites. Food is
served lunchtime and evening Monday to Friday and all day Saturday and Sunday.

Regularly changing real ales include brews from the Copper Dragon Brewery in Skipton and
others from local breweries such as Bowland and Phoenix.

There's plenty of history in and around Mitton, including All Hallows Church, thought to date
back as far as the 13th century. The well-preserved Whalley Abbey, the last to be built in
Lancashire, is just three miles away. Also in Whalley are the even older parish church and the
imposing 48-arched viaduct built in 1850 to carry the Blackburn-Clitheroe railway across the broad
River Calder.

And for anyone exploring the region the Aspinall Arms has six rooms for Bed & Breakfast,
three of them en suite, one available as a holiday let. The inn has a lovely enclosed garden with
views of the river and a wooden play area where children can romp in safety. Barbecues are held in
the garden in the summer months. The inn hosts live music evenings twice a month, usually on a
Friday or Saturday, and an acoustic night on the second Thursday of each month.

543

266 THE WHITE BULL

Church Street, Ribchester, nr Preston,
Lancashire PR3 3XP
☎ 01254 878303
e-mail: enquiries@whitebullrib.co.uk
🌐 www.thebullrib.co.uk

With its handsome stone façade and pillared entrance, the **White Bull** has long been a familiar landmark in the ancient village of Ribchester. The Roman Museum is a very popular tourist attraction, and with Chris Bell at the helm this distinguished old inn is also pulling in the crowds. Food is definitely the star of the show, bringing patrons from an ever-widening area as the news spreads. Professional chef Chris sets great store by the best seasonal ingredients, and the promise of his mouthwatering menus is more than fulfilled by results on the plate. Typical triumphs include Bury black pudding fritters, salmon & cod fishcakes, roast Goosnargh

chicken with chestnut stuffing & thyme gravy, shank of fell-bred Cumbrian lamb and smoked haddock & leek bake served with Lancashire cheese mash and a tomato & shallot salad. Apple crumble or toasted oatmeal parfait with Bushmills whisky prunes makes a fine end to a memorable meal, and the outstanding food is complemented by a well-chosen, helpfully annotated wine list. The White Bull also hits the target for guests staying overnight with three upstairs en suite bedrooms. The pub is open from 6 o'clock on Monday, otherwise all day, every day, including Bank Holiday Mondays. Food times are 12 to 2.30 and 6 to 9.30 Tuesday to Saturday, 12 to 8 Sunday.

267 THE COBBLED CORNER

2 Club Lane, Chipping, Lancashire PR3 2QH
☎ 01995 61551
e-mail: mail@cobbledcorner.co.uk

A delightful name for a delightful café. The **Cobbled Corner** is located in the village of Chipping in the Forest of Bowland, and is a popular place with walkers, cyclists and tourists as well as locals from the village and surrounding area. The café, which is owned and run by Kathryn Bailey, is open from

10 o'clock to 5 every day for a splendid choice of home-made pastries, snacks and meals. On the savoury side are sandwiches, panini, breakfast things, soups, omelettes and pies (meat & potato, cheese & onion, steak & ale) while those with a sweeter tooth can tuck into superb cakes, sponges, scones, slices and fruit pies and crumbles. Beer and wine available with meals.

268 THE SUN INN

Windy Street, Chipping, Forest of Bowland,
Lancashire PR3 2GD
☎ 01995 61206

The **Sun Inn** stands across the road from the parish church in the picturesque village of Chipping, north of Longridge in the Forest of Bowland. It's a first pub venture for Stephen and Jannine, who have breathed fresh life into the old place and are winning new friends day by day. The bar is inviting and very traditional, with plenty of rustic seating, wood panelling and an assortment of bottles, plates and period photographs – and positively no sign of the barmaid said to haunt the place. The bar is open all day, every day for drinks – Boddingtons is the resident among the four real ales always available – and excellent food is served from 12 to 2 weekdays, 12 to 4 weekends and into the evening in summer. Typical dishes run from

sandwiches and jacket potatoes to pea & ham soup, burgers, hearty pasties and pies (cheese

& onion, meat & potatoes, steak & kidney) and giant Yorkshire pudding filled with sausage, mash & gravy or (on Sunday) roast beef with the traditional trimmings. The Sun fields a pool team in the local league and every Friday hosts a DJ or karaoke evening.

270 THE GRANGE COURTYARD GUEST ACCOMMODATION

Forrest Street, Shepshed,
Leicestershire LE12 9DA
☎ 01509 600189
e-mail:
linda.laurence@thegranarycourtyard.co.uk

Linda Lawrence draws a good mix of clients from all over the United Kingdom to the **Grange Courtyard**. Tucked away quietly in one of Shepshed's many side streets, with its own secure parking, the guest accommodation consists of 20 well-appointed, immaculately

kept annexe cottage rooms, each with its own name and each with its own distinctive appeal. All have en suite and self-catering facilities, and for Bed & Breakfast guests the morning meal can be served in the bedrooms or in the main house. Also in the house is an excellent residents' lounge

with inviting sofas and armchairs where guests can relax and plan the day's activities. The Grange, which is open all year round, is a good base for both leisure and business visitors and also a convenient stopover for motorists travelling along the M1, A6 and A42, all of them a short drive away. Shepshed, which stands on the A512 4 miles west of Loughborough, was once an important centre of the frame-knitting industry, and still offers factory shopping for knitwear and general clothing. Around the medieval market place are some of the thatched cottages used by the framework knitters in the 19th century.

269 THE ROSE & CROWN

Thurnby, nr Leicestershire,
Leicestershire LE7 9PJ
☎ 0116 241 9075

Mick and Kate Trower have been the landlord and landlady at the **Rose & Crown** since October 2006, attracting a wide cross-section of patrons from all over the region. Families (with their dogs and kids), walkers, tourists, business people and shoppers looking for a break from the hustle and bustle of Leicester......all are welcome at this friendliest of pubs, which stands in the village of Thurnby, easy to find off the A47 three miles from the city centre.

Hanging baskets add splashes of colour to the thatch-roofed exterior, and inside all is smartly traditional, with extensive wood panelling, lovely old fireplaces and comfortable lounge areas in both bars; at the back is a split-level terrace affording splendid views of the rolling countryside.

Mick, who is a New Zealander by birth, keeps an excellent cellar, with five cask ales, other draught and bottle beers, lagers, ciders, spirits and a fine selection of wines from Old and New Worlds. The bar is open for drinks from 11.30 to 3 and 5 to 11 Monday to Thursday and all day Friday, Saturday and Sunday. Mick and Kate are travelled in distant lands (and seas – they're both keen scuba-divers) and their travels and their local roots are reflected in the variety of dishes on the menu. Popular dishes include steak & ale pie, traditional beer-battered cod, steaks, seafood risotto and seafood specials such as monkfish. Another favourite is the kiwi burger served with beetroot and salad leaves. The main list is supplemented by daily specials, super Sunday roasts and regular themed food evenings.

The pub fields pool and skittles teams (it has its own skittle alley) and hosts a monthly quiz and occasional live music and karaoke evenings. Though close to the busy city of Leicester, the pub stands in excellent walking country, with several marked trails through the fields, and Mick and Kate are ready to cater for fresh-air thirsts from 11.30 to 3 and 5 to 11 Monday to Thursday and all day Friday, Saturday and Sunday. Food is served lunchtime and evening Monday to Friday, all day Saturday and from 12 to 4 on Sunday.

271 | THE CROFT GUEST HOUSE

19-21 Hallcroft, Shepshed,
Leicestershire LE12 9AN
☎ 01509 505657 Fax: 01509 651491
e-mail: js@croftguesthouse.demon.co.uk
🌐 www.croftguesthouse.demon.co.uk

Since 2003, Janet Soni has been taking excellent care of guests at the **Croft Guest House**, a friendly home from home in the Leicestershire market town of Shepshed. Janet ploughs everything back into the B&B, and her efforts have succeeded in providing really excellent accommodation at very reasonable prices. Her redbrick house with green-painted door and window surrounds has nine guest bedrooms, five of them with en suite facilities, with a very well priced year-round tariff that appeals to both leisure and business visitors, and it's a particularly practical and convenient base for anyone working in the vicinity. A generous breakfast starts the day, and Janet can provide an evening meal with a little notice. The house has good

secure parking, and the town-centre location puts the Croft in easy reach of shops, pubs and restaurants. Shepshed, which lies on the A512 four miles west of Loughborough, was once a centre of the hosiery industry, and some of the thatched cottages used by framework knitters still stand round the medieval market place. Loughborough is a place of many attractions, and the Croft is also a popular base for a day at Donington motor racing circuit.

VISIT THE TRAVEL PUBLISHING WEBSITE

Looking for:

- *Places to Visit?*
- *Places to Stay?*
- *Places to Eat & Drink?*
- *Places to Shop?*

Then why not visit the Travel Publishing website...

- Informative pages on places to visit, stay, eat, drink and shop throughout the British Isles.

- Detailed information on Travel Publishing's wide range of national and regional travel guides.

www.travelpublishing.co.uk

289 Main Street, Stanton Under Bardon,
Leicestershire, LE67 9TQ
☎ 01530 242460

The warmest of welcomes awaits visitors to the **Old Thatched Inn**, along with good food, wine and beer. The distinctively shaped white-painted building with a steeply raked thatched roof is a familiar landmark on the main street of Stanton-under-Bardon, off the A50/A511 Leicester-Coalville road and just minutes from J22 of the M1. it stands on the edge of the village, with open fields nearby, and appeals equally to the local community and to the considerable passing trade. The most loyal guest, but one who contributes to noting the coffers, is the resident ghost George, who keeps himself to himself upstairs.

Janet Lowe and Wallace Hastings took over the pub in June 2007 and have overseen a major transformation which has breathed new life into the pub. Inside, the public areas are bright and spacious, with lots of beams and two dining areas, one with a wood floor, the other carpeted. Marston's Pedigree is the resident cask ale, and there's a good choice of other draught or bottled beers, wines, spirits, liqueurs and non-alcoholic drinks. The menus have been revamped along with the premises, and a team of chefs are kept busy producing dishes to please all tastes and appetites, using fresh seasonal and local ingredients whenever possible. Among the favourite dishes are steak pie, beef Wellington and the regularly changing fish and seafood specials. Food is served from 12 to 3 Monday to Saturday and from 6 to 9 Tuesday to Saturday, with a Sunday carvery from 12 to 4; no food Sunday or Monday evenings however, tasty stonebaked pizzas are always available to eat in or takeaway. The regulars enjoy a game of pool, and all-comers are invited to put their brains to the test at the Wednesday quiz. Live music weekends take place each month along with a variety of entertainment. The pub is open from 12 noon to 3pm at lunchtime and from 6pm to 1am in the evening, and all day from noon to 1am Saturday and Sunday.

The area round Stanton-under-Bardon has plenty to see and do, including walking in Charnwood Forest, the Snibston Discovery Park at Coalville and Beacon Hill Country Park, one of the highest points in the county. And the busy city of Leicester is a short drive away (A50 or M1 (J21a).

273 THE CROWN

Main Street, Asfordby, nr Melton Mowbray,
Leicestershire LE14 3SA
☎ 01664 812175

When Robin and Christine Winter took over the tenancy of the **Crown** in 2006 they brought many years of experience in the licensed trade. Hardworking, warm and friendly, they have built up tremendous local support and are always happy to welcome new faces, whether they be singles, couples, families, business people, leisure visitors – even coach parties.

Their redbrick free house, which started in the 18th century as a coaching inn, has a long, narrow interior that includes a public bar with a sturdy undulating stone serving area and a feature of stone steps leading down to the original cellar doors (spot the Crown motifs), a lounge area with exposed brick and comfortable banquettes, and a smart conservatory-style restaurant with neatly set tables. The locals enjoy a game of pool, and a big TV screen shows the top sporting events. Tables are set outside in the summer months. Two rotating cask ales head the list of drinks,

and good honest home cooking at kind prices takes care of appetites large and small. Robin and Christine both cook, and their constantly changing menus combine tried-and-tested favourites like Aberdeen Angus burgers, steaks, fish & chips and the popular Sunday roasts with daily specials such as broccoli & stilton soup, a trio of breaded cheeses (goat's cheese, brie and gorgonzola) with a sweet chilli dip, lightly battered breast of chicken with lemon sauce noodles, chow mein sauce and prawn crackers, and crispy aromatic duck with pancakes, hoisin sauce, shredded vegetables and spring onions. The Crown is open Monday to Thursday evenings, lunchtime and evening Friday and all day from midday Saturday and Sunday. It stands on the main street of Asfordby, off the A6006 two miles west of Melton Mowbray near the River Wreake. There are possible plans to convert the old stable block on one side of the main building to letting bedrooms. That would add a valuable string to the Crown's bow and provide a very agreeable base for touring the region. There are pleasant walks in and around the village and its neighbours, including Grimston with its lovely green, old stocks beneath a chestnut tree and the Church of St John the Evangelist. Melton Mowbray has long been a gourmet's delight, famous for its hand-raised pork pies, Melton hunt cake and Stilton and Red Leicestershire cheeses.

Bolton Lane, Hose,
Leicestershire, LE14 4JE
☎ 01949 860424

Local history relates that Queen Victoria once stopped to admire the famous chestnut tree at Hose, but nowadays it's not a tree but a rose that attracts most visitors to this quiet village tucked

away down country lanes near the Grantham Canal in the picturesque Vale of Belvoir, off the A606 northwest of Melton Mowbray (leave at Nether Broughton). The **Rose at Hose** dates back to 1728, since when it has seen many changes, including a recent change of management. An extensive and expansive refurbishment programme was completed at the end of 2007, resulting in a fine example of the new breed of pub that reaches far beyond the traditional role of a village inn while remaining very much the hub of the local community with a terrific, friendly atmosphere. Four rotating brews will please real ale connoisseurs, with premium lagers also among the best-sellers, and local produce, some of it

organic, is the basis of many of the home-cooked dishes that are served every day. Familiar favourites feature strongly, with classics such as scampi, chunky cod with chips and mushy peas, lasagne, lamb chops in minted gravy, sirloin steak and steak & ale pie. Other choices might be duck breast with a plum and strawberry sauce or chicken breast in a Long Clawston stilton and white wine sauce. This cheese takes its name from the neighbouring village of Long Clawston, one of several cheese-making centres in the region. The main courses are framed by soup, a classic prawn cocktail or melon & parma ham, and freshly made sweets and puddings that the waitress will tell you all about. Pub hours are 5 to 11.30 Monday; 12 to 2 and 5 to 11.30 Tuesday, Wednesday and Thursday; and all day Friday, Saturday and Sunday. Food is served lunchtime and evening Tuesday to Saturday and Sunday 12-3.30pm.

Everyone is welcome at the Rose, including families with kids and dogs, and this hospitable inn is well equipped to handle medium-size wedding parties and other special occasions; a beautiful marquee is available to hire. The inn has a pleasant landscaped courtyard and a cosy outdoor smoking area with fires, cushions and blankets. On the social side, the Rose hosts regular weekend live music nights – as well as poker evenings and themed parties.

275 THE ROYAL HORSESHOES

4 Melton Road, Waltham-on-the-Wolds,
nr Melton Mowbray,
Leicestershire LE14 4AJ
☎ 01664 464289
e-mail: theroy.noble@btconnect.com

The **Royal Horseshoes** started life as a coaching inn in the 1600s, serving travellers on their journey south from Melton Mowbray. In 1843 Queen Victoria, who had been visiting the Duke and Duchess of Rutland at Belvoir Castle, was returning home when one of her horses lost a shoe, so while the local farrier shod her horse she rested at the Horseshoes Inn. So pleased was she at the hospitality she received that she later granted a Royal Charter to the inn.

In the 1950s and 1960s the inn acquired the nickname of Gin Palace, and to this day it stocks a wide variety of gins. Alan and Audrey Noble are a busy couple who have established a very well-run, popular pub, warm and welcoming, with period décor and furnishings and a welcome for friends old and new.

The inn stands in the lovely rural village of Waltham-on-the-Wolds, on the main A607 between Melton Mowbray and Grantham. The bar, lounge, restaurant and walled garden are all very pleasant places to linger awhile, and the inn has a large car park and electric hook-ups for touring caravans. Three cask ales are the favourite thirst-quenchers, and the quality and variety of the food served here brings patrons from many miles around. Many of the dishes on the main menu can be ordered as starters or main courses, including Thai fishcakes with chilli sauce, garlic or stilton mushrooms and tempura prawns. Standard main courses run from steak & Guinness pie and honey-roast ham to chicken in a maple syrup and korma cream sauce, traditional liver & bacon, steaks, haddock in beer batter and always a

good choice for vegetarians. Wednesday is fish night, Thursday is steak night, and the Sunday lunch menu includes a choice of three roasts. Daily specials such as ham & mushroom pie or braised lamb shank increase the choice still further, and a lite bite lunchtime menu caters for those with smaller appetites or less time to spare.

The Royal Horseshoes is also an excellent base for exploring the region, and the guest accommodation comprises four comfortable en suite rooms in a separate block by the main building.

551

21 Lutterworth Road, Walcote,
Leicestershire LE17 4JW
☎ 01455 553338
e-mail: thetaverninn@dsl.pipex.com

If ever there was a natural front-of-house man, it has to be Mario Vegas, host at the **Tavern Inn**, whose friendly, outgoing nature has made his inn one of the most popular in the whole region. Traditional pub values and a dash of Continental flair are a magnet not just for the locals and regularly returning patrons from further afield but also for motorists looking to take a break from a journey on the nearby M1 – the pub has excellent parking facilities off the busy A4304 that runs through the village of Walcote.

Visitors have only to step inside the bar to feel instantly that this splendid place is second to none when it comes to hospitality, and anyone who visits for the first time will be eager for more of the same. Theakstons Best is on tap to take care of thirsts, along with two guest ales and a full range of other draught and bottled beers, lagers, wines, spirits – and of course soft drinks for

drivers. Home and overseas mingle happily on the wide-ranging menus in the bar or conservatory-style restaurant, which start with sandwiches and work up through classics such as steak & kidney pie, specialities from Mario's native Portugal (tuna steak with a wine sauce, pork with cockles) and once in a while even some Asian-inspired dishes. Monday is speciality steak night, roasts are featured on Tuesdays, with curries taking centre stage on Wednesdays.

The pub is open from 11am to midnight Monday to Friday, and from 8am to midnight Saturday and Sunday. Food is served all day until 9:30pm, with breakfast served on Saturday and Sunday from 8am to 11.30am, when the main menu takes over. On Monday the pub hosts poker tournaments in the NUTS Poker League, and brains are given an airing in the Thursday night quiz.

Bed & Breakfast is available at Little Lodge next door (contact Tom on 01455 550949 or visit www.little-lodge.co.uk). These rooms provide a quiet, convenient base for travellers, for business people and for tourists exploring the local places of interest – among these are Lutterworth Museum and Stanford Hall, a distinguished country house set in meadows by the River Avon. The Tavern, which is open all day, seven days a week, stands on the Lutterworth side of Walcote, less than a mile from J20 of the M1.

277 THE RISING SUN

Gedney Drove End,
Lincolnshire PE12 9PQ

The spectacular Church of St Mary at Gedney, the Peter Scott Nature Walk, King John's Lost Jewels Trail and the wide open spaces of the marshes of the Wash – these and other attractions bring

visitors from near and far to this quiet part of South Lincolnshire. All this open-air activity can produce quite a thirst and appetite, and the **Rising Sun** is open lunchtime and evening and all day in summer to satisfy those needs. The compact redbrick building, its door and window surrounds painted bright white, has a cosy, welcoming bar with low black beams and an open fire – a convivial spot for enjoying a drink and something to eat. Good honest pub grub includes

burgers, fish specials, steaks and mixed grill, and host Bernard Collins, who came here in 2006 after 20 years running a hotel in Lancashire, can organise outside bars for local events; he also has two caravans that are available for long lets. The Rising Sun is located at Gedney Drove End, one of six settlements called Gedney, on the B1359 and a short drive from the main A17 (leave at Long Sutton).

278 THE BLUE COW INN

High Street, South Witham,
Lincolnshire NG33 5QB
☎ 01572 768432
e-mail: enquiries@bluecowinn.co.uk
🌐 www.bluecowinn.co.uk

On the main street of South Witham, the 13th century **Blue Cow Inn** serves a bull's eye on several targets. Warm hospitality is assured by well-established innkeeper Simon Crathorn, and the bars, with their stone walls, beams and open log fire, are a delightfully traditional setting for enjoying a drink and a chat – and perhaps a game of cribbage or dominoes. The

inn has its own tiny brewery next door, a four-barrel brewplant producing Blue Cow Best and Wobbler Ale only for in-house drinking. Decent food at sensible prices is another plus, and for anyone looking to stay awhile, on business or at leisure, the inn has six well-priced en suite bedrooms. The Blue Cow, which has a beer garden and plentiful off-road parking, is open from midday seven days a week. South Witham stands just moments from the A1 about halfway between Stamford and Grantham.

279 THE JOLLY BREWER

Foundry Road, Stamford,
Lincolnshire PE9 2PP
☎ 01780 755141
e-mail: thejollybrewer@aol.com

Dean and Jill are the welcoming hosts at the **Jolly Brewer**, a substantial town pub dating from the early 18th century. The interior is particularly inviting, with a lively, friendly atmosphere created by the hosts and by the mixed clientele that comes from all walks of life. The locals like a game of pool or a turn

on the pushpenny board (is that shove ha'penny hit by inflation?), or to chat about the world at large over a glass or two – Black Sheep Brewery provides one of the regular cask ales. The Jolly Brewer is also a good place for a snack or a meal, and the blackboard lists the day's choice of old favourites. Open from noon to midnight seven days a week, the pub stands on the corner of Foundry Road and the A6121. The other end of Foundry Road meets the A606 Empingham road, so access to the pub is easy from any direction.

280 THE HARE 'N' HOUNDS

Main Street, Greatford, nr Stamford,
Lincolnshire PE9 4QA
☎ 01778 560332
⊕ www.hareandhoundsgreatford.com

The Hare 'N' Hounds is a long-established landmark on the main street of Greatford, easily reached off the A15 north of Market Deeping or the A16 east of Stamford. Andrew and Gemma Dixey took over the reins in the autumn of 2007, and the combination of warm hospitality, the well-kept ales (Elgoods Cambridge and Charles Wells Bombardier), the good range of wines and Andrew's home-cooked country-style cooking brings patrons from the local community, the surrounding villages and the nearby towns. The food has rapidly become a major attraction, and among the favourite dishes are Lincolnshire pork and mushroom pancakes with a stilton sauce, beef and ale casserole with fried onion mash and cheddar, the Sunday roasts and a fish of the day such as herb-crusted cod with hand-cut chips and

a fresh tomato sauce. The public areas are in traditional style (an open fire warms the bar), and the beer garden is a popular spot for families in the summer. The pub also has a Camping and Caravan Club certified site with four pitches. Pub hours are Monday evening (but no food) and lunchtime and evening every other day, for both food and drink. The Hare 'N' Hounds hosts a quiz on the 2nd Tuesday of the month.

281 THE WILLOUGHBY ARMS

Little Bytham, nr Stamford,
Lincolnshire NG33 4RA
☎ 01780 410276
🌐 www.willoughbyarms.co.uk

Kip and Lynda Hulme brought many years' experience in the hospitality business when they took over the **Willoughby Arms** in 2007. The building dates from 1853, when it was built as Lord Willoughby's private railway station, and the interior is delightfully traditional, with solid wood floors and open fires – and excellent views from most of the windows. Outside, the inn has a large pleasant beer garden and ample off-road parking. A Batemans brew and five guests provide plenty of choice for real ale enthusiasts, and that choice is considerably increased during the quarterly beer festivals hosted here. No one who visits the Willoughby Arms leaves hungry, and a typical day might bring Thai fishcakes with a chilli dip, fish & chips, chicken jalfrezi, ham & eggs, scampi, steaks, steak and kidney pie, lincolnshire sausage and mash and four-cheese pasta. The food is complemented by a well-annotated wine list, with most available by two sizes of glass as well as by bottle. The bar is open all day, every day, and food is served from 12 to 2 and 6 to 9 Monday to Saturday, 12 to 4 Sunday. The inn also offers superior guest accommodation in three well-appointed bedrooms – a single, a double and a family room. Little Bytham stands on the River Glen, off the B1176 north of Stamford. Visitors on a famous day in 1938 might have seen the steam locomotive *Mallard* hurtling past on its way to achieving a world record speed of 126 mph.

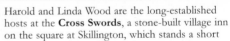

282 THE CROSS SWORDS INN — AA 3 STAR

The Square, Skillington,
Lincolnshire NG33 5HB
☎ 01476 861132
e-mail: harold@thecross-swordsinn.co.uk
🌐 www.thecross-swordsinn.co.uk

Harold and Linda Wood are the long-established hosts at the **Cross Swords**, a stone-built village inn on the square at Skillington, which stands a short drive from the A1 a few miles south of Grantham (leave at Stoke Rochford). It dates from the early 19th century, and the bar is full of character . A blackboard announces the day's selection of traditional home-cooked dishes, from sandwiches and snacks to country dishes and a full à la carte menu. An established country inn, with loyal support from the local community and also attracting passing trade from tourists and motorists, the Cross Swords has recently extended its appeal with the creation of three bedrooms (twins or doubles) for Bed & Breakfast guests. Lavishly furnished, with ultra-modern en suite facilities and all the expected up-to-date amenities, Fishwell, Cringle and Newton Cottage provide a very comfortable, civilised base. Among the nearby places of interest are the National Trust-owned manor at Woolsthorpe-by-Colsterworth where Isaac Newton was born, and near to Burghley House and other stately homes. The inn has a rear patio and plenty of off-road parking. Please email or telephone for tariffs.

283 THE ST VINCENT ARMS

Main Street, Norton Disney,
Lincolnshire LN6 9JU
☎ 01522 789987

The **St Vincent Arms** is a traditional
Lincolnshire village inn with a fine reputation
for its locally sourced home-cooked food. It
stands north-east of Newark-on-Trent in the
village of Norton Disney (Walt's ancestors
came from here) off the A46 Newark-Lincoln
road. It's easy to spot with its striking yellow-
painted frontage, and inside all is period charm,
with oak beams, wooden floors and open fires.

Outside is a pleasant garden dominated by
a huge oak tree. The food choice covers an exceptional range
headed by tried and tested favourites such as banger & mash,
lasagne, cottage pie, prawn cocktail, steaks and steak &
Guinness pie. Less traditional but equally appealing are
seafood fettuccine (starter or main), hot 'n' spicy prawns,
chicken breast in a bacon & brie sauce and pepper &
mushroom stroganoff. Host Gavin Holt is a wine expert, so
there's always a good choice of wines to complement the
food.

The pub is open from 7 Monday and Tuesday, lunchtime
and evening Wednesday to Saturday and all day on Sunday. Food is served lunchtime and evening
Wednesday to Saturday and from 12 to 7 on Sunday.

284 THE RED LION

62 High Street, Caythorpe, nr Grantham,
Lincolnshire NG32 3DN
☎ 01400 272632
e-mail: johncork@btconnect.com
🌐 www.redlioncaythorpe.org.uk

The **Red Lion** stands off the A607 on the
main street of Caythorpe, north of Grantham
and south of the junction with the A17
Sleaford-Newark road. John Cork, who took
over here in 2005, once worked for Everards
Brewery and knows his trade and his
customers very well. He has built up a loyal
local following among those who appreciate

the classic qualities of the quintessential English pub. This
splendid example dates from the 1650s, and sympathetic
updating has spoiled none of its traditional appeal. Everards
Tiger Ale and Adnams Bitter are the resident cask ales, and
home cooking makes excellent use of local produce for dishes
that include some well-loved Lincolnshire recipes. Popular
choices include fish & chips, burgers made with Lincoln Red
Beef and a not-to-be-missed steak & ale suet pudding. Bar
hours are 12 to 2.30 and 6 to 11 (all day Sunday); food is
served from 12 to 2 (to 3 on Sunday) and 6 to 9 (to 9.30 at the
weekend).

37 Upgate, Louth, Lincolnshire LN11 9HD
☎ 01507 609595
e-mail: melanies.restau@btconnect.com

Aileen and Steve Legg sold their house to launch this new venture in the autumn of 2007. Steve is a well-established and very talented chef, but **Melanie's** (named after the Leggs' daughter) is his first independent enterprise after working in corporate catering for many years. Everything, from the bread to the ice cream, is made on the premises by Steve, whose reputation is spreading throughout the region. He creates his dishes using the finest ingredients the Lincolnshire Wolds have to offer, and the quotation from Escoffier printed on the menu reflects the well-justified confidence Steve has in his abilities:

" Everything is relative but there is a standard which must not be deviated from, especially with reference to the basic culinary preparations."

Steve upholds and far exceeds that precept in the super dishes with which he regales his patrons. Dishes taken from a typical menu include spicy pork terrine with apple chutney; goat's cheese hash brown on a roasted beet salad; poached fillet of turbot with a champagne butter sauce, sautéed leeks and vanilla mash; sirloin and fillet steaks; breast of free-range chicken in a white wine mushroom sauce with fondant potatoes and glazed vegetables, roast best end of lamb with green lemon sauce, sautéd courgettes and a potatoe cake (see picture right) and pear and almond tart with chocolate ice cream. The outstanding food is complemented by impeccable service and an interesting wine list with informative notes. Melanie's is open for dinner Tuesday to Saturday and for lunch (a simpler menu) Monday to Friday.

286 THE NEWMARKET INN & HURDLES BISTRO

Junction of Church Street and Newmarket,
Louth, Lincolnshire LN11 9EG
☎ 01507 605146

Nigel and Victoria Hopper are the owners at the **Newmarket Inn**, where traditional and contemporary elements combine happily in the two little bars and separate restaurant. Adnams Bitter is the resident real ale, and the inn scores with a great choice of cuisine.

Lunch in the bar offers classics like fish & chips with mushy peas, scampi and gammon & pineapple, as well as baguettes and jacket potatoes and the Sunday roasts (choice of two joints). **Hurdles Bistro** is open from 7 to 9 Wednesday to Saturday for a tempting menu typified by warm bacon & parmesan salad, steaks plain and sauced, baked salmon now served on crushed tumeric potatoes. Fish & chips can be ordered to take away from 6 o'clock Wednesday to Saturday. Fridays and Saturdays are Fish and Steak night.

Pub hours are 5pm to 12 Monday and Tuesday, 12 to 3 and 5 to 12 Wednesday, Thursday and Friday, 12 to 12 on Saturday and 12 to 3 and 7 to 12 on Sunday. Sunday is quiz night.

287 YE OLDE WHYTE SWANNE

45 Eastgate, Louth,
Lincolnshire LN11 9NP
☎ 01507 601312

Ye Olde Whyte Swanne is the first solo venture for Wendy Woolnough, who has been making many new friends at her town-centre pub. A well-known landmark on one of Louth's most historic streets, the inn started life as a coaching inn with its own stables – a sign above the door is marked 1612. The interior is delightfully 'old-world', with handsome varnished wood panelling, low beams, quarry-tiled floors and a winter fire blazing a welcome in the brick hearth. Two cask ales are among the favourite

refreshments, and the kitchen provides a selection of great-value pub grub. As well as being a convivial place for locals to meet, Ye Olde Whyte Swanne has six well-priced guest bedrooms (two with en suite facilities) for anyone working in the area or for visitors to this historic market town.

Main Street, Donnington-on-Bain,
Lincolnshire LN11 9TG
☎ 01507 343640
e-mail: mike@blackhorse-donnington.co.uk
⊕ www.blackhorse-donnington.co.uk

Mike Wilson and his parents are the affable
hosts at the **Black Horse**, a fine old inn
nestling in the heart of the Wolds. It is one
of Lincolnshire's historic pubs & restaurants
on the Viking Way walk. Close to Cadwell
Park motorbike and motor car racing track.
(Cadwell Park is on the A153, between Louth
and Horncastle). The Black Horse is also
within easy reach of Market Rasen horse
racing, Horncastle, Lincoln and it's historic
Christmas Market.

The 17th century inn, and the bars are
rich in old-world charm, with beams, leaded windows and a huge brick fireplace. Food is an
important part of the inn's business, with home-cooked dishes catering for a wide range of tastes
and appetites. 'Good Old British Dishes' include steak & ale pie, home-cooked ham, Lincolnshire
sausages & mash, minted lamb shank and
a large Yorkshire pudding filled with local
Lincolnshire Red beef in a rich ale gravy.
From the grill come rump, sirloin, fillet
and gammon steaks. 'Selected Dishes
from Around the World' are represented
by the likes of lasagne and chicken
enchiladas, and seafood-lovers can enjoy
scampi, succulent salmon fillets with
asparagus tips and a watercress sauce or
deep-fried beer-battered haddock.
Vegetarians will find a good choice of
main courses, and the excellent food is
complemented by a well-chosen wine list
with succinct descriptions. Donnington-
on-Bain itself boasts an interesting 13th
century church and a grand old water
mill, and much of the surrounding
countryside is a designated Area of Outstanding Natural Beauty. For guests touring this beautiful
part of the world the Black Horse has eight smartly appointed en suite bedrooms in a separate
block with an AA 3 Diamond rating. Each bedroom has its own tea and coffee making facilities,
TV and traditional full English breakfast included in the tariff.

290 THE HAYWAIN MOTEL & RESTAURANT

Ulceby Cross, Alford,
Lincolnshire LN13 0EY
☎ 01507 462786
e-mail: haywainmotel@hotmail.co.uk

New owners Simon and Jane have assembled an enthusiastic team at the **Haywain Motel & Restaurant**, which stands on a busy roundabout on the A16 at Ulceby Cross. Starting life as a coaching inn in 1801, the two-storey redbrick building has been modernised and refurbished to provide modern comfort and up-to-date facilities for today's visitors.

Motorists travelling along the busy A16 trunk road that runs through Lincolnshire will find a warm welcome, whether they've come for a quick drink, a snack or a meal, or a stay in the motel-style accommodation. Good wholesome dishes, well-priced and generously served, are available in the restaurant every lunchtime and evening, and the carvery is a popular feature.

The 18 en suite bedrooms provide an ideal base for motorists on the move, for anyone with business in the area or for tourists looking for accommodation that is both economical and practical.

The A16 offers easy access north and south, and for tourists the hotel is close to a number of places of interest. Notable among these are the flourishing little town of Alford, often describes as Lincolnshire's craft centre, with its handsome medieval church, the largest manor house in England and the splendid five-sailed windmill, the Claythorpe Water Mill and the Wildlife Gardens at Aby; and the village of Willoughby, birthplace of Captain John Smith, founder of what became the state of Virginia and forever linked with the romantic tale of the Red Indian Princess Pocohontas.

The Haywain also functions admirably as a local place to meet, and the public and lounge bars, where Theakstons is the resident cask ales, are open from 11 to 3 and from 5 in the evening every day. The Haywain also has a function room and a meeting room that are available for parties, special occasions and small business groups.

On the last Monday of each month the South Lincolnshire Magic Club meets here, so patrons could be in for a surprise or two! There is free hotspot wifi available.

289 THE BLACK SWAN GUEST HOUSE

21 High Street, Marton, nr Gainsborough,
Lincolnshire DN21 5AH
☎ 01427 718878
e-mail: info@blackswanguesthouse.co.uk
⊕ www.blackswanguesthouse.co.uk

John and Judy Patrick and their son Graham put out the welcome mat at the **Black Swan**, which stands on the main street of Marton, five miles south of Gainsborough at the crossroads of the A156 and A1500. The premises, now Grade II listed, started life in the 18th century as a coaching inn, with an existing cellar where it is said that Oliver Cromwell rested during the Battle of Gainsborough in 1643. The property has been refurbished to a very high standard using many of the original materials, and the main house and cottage provide very comfortable guest accommodation that attracts business travellers and tourists from near and far. The ten rooms - a single, four twins, four doubles and a family room – all have en suite

facilities, TV and tea/coffee tray, and wireless broadband is available. Top of the range is the spacious premier room with a four-poster bed and sofa. A splendid breakfast starts the day, with locally sourced ingredients where possible and an exceptional choice of leaf and fruit teas. Guests have the use of a comfortable lounge where they can enjoy a drink, and the house has plenty of safe off-road parking.

291 ELM LODGE

Downham Grove, Wymondham,
Norfolk NR18 0SN
☎ 01953 607501
e-mail: elm.lodge@btinternet.com
⊕ www.smoothhound.co.uk/hotels/elmlodge

Elm Lodge is a lovely redbrick house set peacefully in two acres of garden and woods. Built in 1986 entirely from old materials, it is the home of Peter and Marion Bryce, who since 1998 have been sharing their unique property with Bed & Breakfast guests. The accommodation comprises three quiet rooms with private bathrooms, and features throughout the house include old beams, pantile floors and lots of interesting antiques. An excellent breakfast includes top-quality local bacon and sausages and eggs from their own hens. All groups are catered for, including wedding guests at nearby

Wymondham Abbey and people with business in Norwich who prefer the peace of the countryside. No credit cards.

283 THE CROWN INN

Pulham Market, Norfolk IP21 4TA
☎ 01379 676652
e-mail: blore76@hotmail.com

The **Crown** is a 400-year-old thatched inn overlooking the green in the village of Pulham Market, just off the A140

Norwich road a few miles north of Diss. Owner and manager welcome all who pass through the door into a traditional setting of beams, wooden floors and open fires – singles, couples, dog owners, families, walkers, cyclists, motorists, tourists and always good local support. Hanging baskets adorn the exterior in spring and summer, and the inn has a lovely little garden. A full range of drinks is served in the bar, and the daytime bar menu gives way to fine dining in the evening.

292 AMANDINES CAFÉ RESTAURANT

Norfolk House Courtyard, St Nicholas
Street, Diss, Norfolk IP22 4LB
☎ 01379 640449
e-mail: amandines@btinternet.com

Amandines Café Restaurant has enjoyed its charming courtyard setting in the market town of Diss, on the Norfolk Suffolk border for around 20 years. Currently run by Sue and her team, this unique restaurant promises you a warm welcome and great home cooked vegetarian food. Behind the attractive redbrick front, with large windows, climbing jasmine and roses, Amandines has a comfortable and interesting interior, and the ambience is friendly and relaxed. A wonderful internal glass covered courtyard is open all year, heated by the sun and a traditional wood burning stove.

Once comfortably settled, you can enjoy the café's range of tasty home cooked hot and cold lunchtime specials, fresh made soups, and scrumptious desserts. Amandines offers a full range of classic and specialist teas, the finest Italian coffee and hot chocolates, and an extensive range of alcoholic and non alcoholic refreshing drinks, fresh made milkshakes and smoothies. Be tempted by the fabulous home baked cakes and pastries! And if you enjoy a special diet - perhaps Vegan, diary free or gluten free, there are meals and tasty treats for you too.

Amandines is fully licensed, and open Tuesday to Saturday, from 10am until 4pm. On Special Saturday nights you can enjoy a relaxed three course home cooked meal, and great live music – jazz, folk, blues, flamenco.

Situated on the northern bank of the River Waveney, Diss is a handsome old market town that deserves time to explore its hidden treasures at leisure. And when the time comes for lunch and refreshment, you can be sure of a friendly welcome for the whole family at Amandines.

294 THE LANTERN RESTAURANT

26 High Street, Sheringham,
Norfolk NR26 8JR
☎ 01263 822780

Easy to spot with its black-and white frontage and outsize name boards, the **Lantern** is a warm and friendly little restaurant on the High Street of the popular seaside resort of Sheringham. In the eating area, with a small collection of sailing memorabilia, owner Peter Goman caters for all ages, sweet and savoury palates and a wide range of tastes, for meat-eaters, fish-eaters and vegetarians, with a good selection of cold snacks, main dishes and afternoon teas. Everything is prepared and cooked on the premises, and the restaurant is open from 11.30 to 4 in the winter and until about 8 o'clock during the peak season.

295 THE KINGS ARMS

28 The Green, Shouldham, nr King's Lynn,
Norfolk PE33 0BY
☎ 01366 347819
e-mail: sallykingsarms@yahoo.co.uk

A warm and friendly welcome awaits visitors of all ages – including families with children and dogs – to the **Kings Arms**, a delightful free house and country dining room on the green at Shouldham, which lies in peaceful Norfolk countryside just off the A134 Thetford to King's Lynn road. Behind the whitewashed, red-tiled exterior the traditional bar and dining area offer a selection of real ales and an extensive menu that caters for all tastes and appetites. The inn has a large patio and rear garden and plenty of off-road parking.

296 THE GLOBE INN

The Buttlands, Wells-next-the-Sea,
Norfolk NR23 1EU
☎ 01328 710206 Fax: 01328 713249
⊕ www.globeatwells.co.uk

The **Globe Inn**, which is in the portfolio of
the Holkham Estate, is a lovely place to relax
and unwind, whether it's for a drink, a snack,
a full meal or an overnight or longer stay. It
has a warm, welcoming bar, a comfortable
restaurant and a sunny courtyard for summer
eating and drinking. The bar is open from 11
to 11 (Sunday 12 to 10.30) and food is
served every lunchtime and evening. The menu takes advantage of the bounty of the local land and
sea, and small portions of many dishes are available for young diners. The picturesque harbour, the
narrow streets and the ancient houses are well worth taking time to explore, and the Globe is an
ideal base for touring the town and the surrounding area or for a traditional family seaside holiday.

The inn has seven light, airy guest bedrooms – five doubles and
two twins, with children's beds available. Several rooms have
views over the Green, and the beach is just a few minutes' walk
away. The local attractions include two charming little railways,
one running along the quay, the other following the old Great
eastern Railway to Little Walsingham. Also nearby is the majestic
Holkham Hall, a treasure house of artistic and architectural
history, with superb gardens and a Bygones Museum.

297 THE MALTSTERS COUNTRY INN

The Green, Badby, nr Daventry,
Northamptonshire NN11 3AF
☎ 01327 702905

The Maltsters is a fine 17th century country inn
standing on the green in the village of Badby,
which lies close to the River Nene on the A361 a
short drive south of Daventry. It's the first pub for
tenants Christine and Nick Ainsworth, who took over here at the beginning of 2008. The pub is
very much at the heart of village life, appealing to the local
community as an ideal place to meet for a drink or a meal.
The main public area is a long beamed room with a roaring
winter fire at each end, a convivial spot for meeting friends
over a glass of cask ale – Banks's, Marston's pedigree and
rotating guests. Lunchtime and evening appetites are
satisfied by good honest food at very kind prices: a
pleasant meal might start with prawn cocktail or chargrilled
vegetable terrine, continue with steak pie or sole stuffed
with smoked haddock and end with apple pie or jam roly

poly. The Maltsters is
also a great place for a
stopover or as a base
for touring a part of the world with many places of scenic and
historic interest. The four comfortable en suite bedrooms are
looking very smart after recent refurbishment, and the pub has
a nice garden and ample off-road parking. The pub has a
thriving social side, with darts, skittles, sports TV and regular
live music and karaoke nights.

298 THE SARACEN'S HEAD

Little Brington, nr Northampton,
Northamptonshire NN7 4HS
☎ 01604 770640

The **Saracen's Head** is a quintessential English inn that dates from the middle of the 19th century. It stands in the village of Little Brington, easily reached from J16 of the M1 (first right off the A45 Daventry road) and also signposted from the A428. Run by the Evans family – Duncan, Sarah and Tom – the inn is brimful of character, with flagstoned or solid wood floors, beams, alcoves, books and old prints – even a genuine red telephone box; outside are a neat patio and garden that are popular spots in the summer months. Greene King IPA, Timothy Taylor

Landlord and a guest provide a choice for real ale drinkers, and the kitchen produces a fine variety of food, from soup and sandwiches to a regularly changing choice of modern English dishes. Seafood fans might choose mussels with garlic, bacon and cream or sea bass with chilli, garlic, ginger & lime, while meat-eaters could opt for rib-eye steak, stuffed breast of lamb or pheasant breast with chestnuts and sherry-glazed turnips. There's always a choice for vegetarians, and a fine meal might end with traditional apple pie or a selection of sorbets. Althorp House and Holdenby House are close by, and for visitors to these and other local places of interest the Saracen's Head has four comfortable en suite bedrooms. The inn is open lunchtime and evening and all day Friday, Saturday and Sunday.

300 THE RED LION & TRUCK STOP

Weedon Road (A45), Heyford,
M1J16, Northamptonshire
☎ 01604 831914

Two enterprises in one location: a popular local and a truckers' café, located on the Weedon Road (A45) near J16 of the M1 and also close to the A5. Ali Sadrudin is building a very busy and popular stopping place for truck drivers or anyone wanting a refreshment break from a journey on the surrounding motorway and trunk road network. Simple dishes, hearty and filling, are listed on chalkboard menus. The long choice includes just about anything you would expect to find on a classic pub menu: bangers & mash, Cornish pasty, liver and sausages with onion gravy, steak & kidney pudding, steak & stout pie, mixed grill, pork chops, lamb steaks, roast chicken, spaghetti bolognese, chilli con carne, battered cod, burgers, scampi, 10oz rump

steak.......all guaranteed to provide fuel for the next journey – the chefs guarantee that nobody leaves here hungry.
There's enormous parking space with 24hr CCTV and the café is open from 7am till late into the evening, with the bar open until 11. The pub, quite quaint and traditional, is open only from the early evening (4 to 11, to 10 on Sunday). From the M!, leave at J16 and head on the A45 Northampton road; the Red Lion is 300 yards along this road.

Nether Heyford,
Northamptonshire NN7 3LL
☎ 01327 340164

Although it is sandwiched between the A5, A45 and the M1, the village of Nether Heyford is a pleasant, peaceful place. It has one of the biggest village greens in the country, but what brings many visitors is one of the most delightful pubs anywhere, the sort of pub for which the words, eclectic, eccentric and quirky might have been invented and one that restores faith in the time-honoured but increasingly threatened ideal of the quintessentially English country pub.

When Peter Yates and Alan Ford took over in the summer of 2006 they inherited a pub that was, and is, very, very different. The **Olde Sun Inn** is an 18th century golden-stone pub with a steeply-tiled roof and small-paned windows. But it's what's behind the porticoed entrance and heavy wooden door that makes this place one in a million. A merry jumble of bric-a-brac, bygones and memorabilia fills just about every spare inch of the little linked rooms: one fireplace flanked by a grotto of brass animals, old advertising signs, horse tackle and farm implements, cigarette cards, colourful relief plates, railway memorabilia......Even without the fascinating curiosities this would be a very inviting place with its friendly hosts and staff and the traditional look

of beams and low ceilings, wooden dividing panels, rugs on parquet floors, tiles or flagstones, a bog log fire and properly pubby furniture. On the left is a games room with skittles, darts, cribbage, dominoes and sports TV, while outside, the pub has a pleasant lawned garden with a children's play area and a front terrace with picnic sets and old farm machines.

The Olde Sun is, of course, essentially a much-loved local, serving the local community and the surrounding area with an excellent selection of food and drink. Four cask ales are on tap, typically Ruddles Best, Marston's Pedigree, a Banks's brew and a guest. The philosophy behind the food is to keep it simple and good, and the bar snack menu spans hot bites (jacket potatoes, panini, ham, egg & chips), soup, sandwiches, home-made steak pie and lemon peppered haddock. This remarkable pub is open lunchtime and evening Monday to Thursday and all day Friday, Saturday and Sunday.

301 THE KNIGHTLEY ARMS

49 High Street, Yelvertoft,
Northamptonshire NN6 6LF
☎ 01788 822401
e-mail: knightleyarms@aol.com

The **Knightley Arms** stands on the long main street of Yelvertoft, which runs down to Bridge 19 on the Leicester Line of the Grand Union

Canal. Boaters on the canal and walkers along the towpath join the locals and other visitors to the village to enjoy the excellent hospitality extended by Neil and Kim Crocker and Keiran Hallam – and a waggy welcome from Blue the Weimeraner. The inn dates from the 18th century, with later alterations and additions, and the bar has a particularly inviting, lived-in feel with a big log fire and shelves filled with books. Outside is a beer garden with a barbecue. The bar keeps a good choice of traditional cask ales, typically including Greene King IPA,

Fullers London pride, St Austell Tribute and Dent Kamikaze, and a wide selection of other beers, lagers, cider, wines, spirits and soft drinks. Produce from local butchers, farmers and suppliers is the basis of the snacks, light bites and meals freshly prepared by Neil and his helpers on the premises. The menu tempts with tried-and-tested favourites from ham, egg & chips to spaghetti carbonara, chilli con carne, gammon and beef steaks, lamb shanks, salmon and roast chicken. The hosts hold popular themed food nights and can organise functions and outside events. Yelvertoft stands in open countryside a short drive from J18 of the M1, by way of the A428.

302 THE OLD HOUSE

East End, Scaldwell, nr Northampton,
Northamptonshire NN6 9LB
☎ 01604 880359
⊕ www.the-oldhouse.co.uk

For many years Margaret Vinton has been opening her comfortable family home to Bed & Breakfast guests. The **Old House** is a delightful stone cottage located in the village of Scaldwell, in lovely countryside just off the main A508 Northampton to Market Harborough road. Sensitively renovated,

with period charm and character intact, it has three guest bedrooms – one en-suite double/family room, one en-suite twin and a single room with a private bathroom, all have television and tea-coffee-making facilities. Guests can look forward to an excellent breakfast that includes seasonal fruit and vegetables from the garden. Adjoining the Old House is the Old Barn, a 300-year-old building converted into spacious, self-contained, self-catering accommodation.

Downstairs is a kitchen area with gas cooker, fridge, washing machine and microwave, and a shower room. Upstairs, the open-plan room provides comfortable family occupation complete with TV, video-player and hi-fi; the Old Barn has a quiet, beautiful garden. The Old House and the Old Barn both provide an ideal base for touring an area with a wealth of scenic, historic and sporting attractions. The third family property is Casa Elceto, a restored farmhouse in a glorious setting among the rolling hills of Umbria.

303 THE RISING SUN

**Mill Road, Wellingborough,
Northamptonshire NN8 1PF
☎ 01933 276478**

Sally Brown, a hardworking landlady with a young family, makes it a real pleasure to visit the **Rising Sun**, which stands in the centre of town in an area bounded by the A5128, the B572 and the B573.

The pub takes its name from the Rising Sun well, one of the five ancient wells that gave Wellingborough its name and which appear on the town's municipal coat of arms. Behind the bright yellow exterior there's a cosy little public bar, a delightfully snug lounge and a pool room, while outside is a heated patio with tables and chairs. Three resident brews and rotating guest provide plenty of choice for real ale connoisseurs, and the menu of good honest pub food, from hot and cold sandwiches, burgers, jacket potatoes and all-day

breakfasts to the popular Sunday roasts and special lunchtime deals for

senior citizens. Wellingborough has plenty to interest the visitor, including the magnificent Church of St Mary, the 17th century Croyland Abbey, now a heritage centre, and the lovely Millennium Rose Garden at Swanspool Gardens. And when the sightseeing's done and thirst and appetite take over, Sally and her staff are ready with a friendly greeting and refreshment throughout the day and evening.

304 THE STAGS HEAD

**High Street, Earls Barton,
Northamptonshire NN6 0JG
☎ 01604 810520**

Five miles northeast of Northampton off the A45, Earls Barton has a great treasure in the shape of the Church of All Saints with its impressive Anglo-Saxon tower, its black oak Jacobean pulpit and its 15th century chancel screen adorned with thousands of dazzling butterflies. But for anyone looking for refreshment and hospitality, the **Stags Head** is another treasure – the social heartbeat of the village and a great favourite with the local community and a ready welcome for visitors from outside the area.

Since the summer of 2007 Ashley Wainwright has been the young, go-ahead tenant of this Charles Wells pub, which dates from the early 1800s and has been updated while preserving a certain period appeal. It has public and lounge bars, a games room, a good garden and a huge car park. Four cask ales, typically Charles Wells IPA and Bombardier, Youngs and Adnams Broadside,

are on tap to quench thirsts; Friday sees a happy hour that runs from 4 to 7, with all drinks at a bargain price. Lunchtime appetites are satisfied by a variety of simple pub dishes.

On the sporting/social side the pub fields skittles and cribbage teams in the local pub leagues, and the third Monday of the month brings a live music evening.

305 EAT 'N' ENJOY COFFEE SHOP

4 Eaton Walk, Rushden,
Northamptonshire NN10 9SH
☎ 01933 316516
e-mail: cazzie.k@btinternet.com

Eat 'n' Enjoy: the perfect name for a delightful, cosy coffee shop, a little diamond tucked away behind and between industrial buildings and a supermarket in the centre of Rushden. Since 2002, Carolyn Knight has run this small independent business, which aims to 'cater for many different likes, desires, cravings, allergies and intolerances'. The ingredients are GM-free, and if it says 'homemade' on the menu then homemade it certainly is! Every year since 2003 the coffee shop has won the Northamptonshire Heartbeat Award for healthy eating, an accolade of which Carolyn is justifiably proud.

Served from 8 to 3.30 Monday to Saturday, the menu proposes an excellent selection of freshly prepared snacks and meals to satisfy appetites large and small and palates

both savoury and sweet. Among the extensive choice are soup, sandwiches, jacket potatoes, omelettes, salads, full English or individual breakfast items, the day's pie and super desserts listed on their own chalkboard: sherry trifle, lemon meringue pie, jam sponge, treacle sponge, hot chocolate fudge cake – all delicious and very hard to resist. To drink, coffees, teas, hot chocolate, juices, fizzy drinks, still, sparkling or flavoured water, milk and milkshakes. Unlicensed; cash only.

306 THE GRIFFINS HEAD

28 Wilby Road, Mears Ashby,
Northamptonshire NN6 0DX
☎ 01604 812945 Fax: 01604 811802
e-mail: info@thegriffin.flyer.co.uk

The **Griffins Head** is a much-loved local public house in the village of Mears Ashby, which stands off the A4500 a short drive west of Wellingborough. It's a joint venture into the licensed trade for Lynette Ray and Peter Stubbins, and their mid-19th century inn offers everything that a village inn should offer: a warm greeting for both familiar faces and new faces, a convivial atmosphere, well-kept ales and a good choice of food. Behind the big, bold frontage the bar successfully mixes traditional and contemporary elements, and a big open fire and comfortable leather seats make a cosy setting for enjoying a glass or two of real ale – four are always on tap, typically Black Sheep, Adnams Bitter and two regularly rotating guests. The menus provide an

admirable choice of dishes on lists that include 'old favourites' and 'something new'. Among the former might be beef in ale pie, cod & chips, liver & bacon, scampi, chicken curry and steaks, while something new might be chicken Wellington, beef goulash or five-bean chilli casserole. Light bites (sandwiches, jacket potatoes, burgers, things with chips) cater for smaller appetites or those with little time to spare. The pub is open from 11 to 2.30 and from 5 Monday to Friday and all day Saturday and Sunday. All are welcome at the quiz held on the last Sunday of each month, and live music evenings.

307 THE ROYAL OAK

1 Chapel Lane, Blisworth,
Northamptonshire NN7 3BU
☎ 01604 858372
e-mail: babe4dave@aol.com

Built in the 17th century and once a circuit jail house, the **Royal Oak** now captures a more willing band of visitors with outstanding hospitality orchestrated by affable leaseholder Angelique Elliott. It stands at the junction of minor roads off the A43 Northampton-Towcester road in the centre of Blisworth, a village of Tudor and Jacobean

houses, with a church that dates back to the 13th century. Inside the pub, open fires keep things cosy in the bar-lounge, a convivial spot for meeting or making friends over a glass of real ale served at the panelled bar counter. The garden at the back is a popular alternative in the summer months. Angelique keeps her customers happy with a selection of good honest pub favourites such as cottage pie, steak & kidney pie and the popular Sunday roasts. The Royal Oak hosts monthly live music evenings and a quiz every other Wednesday. Blisworth is known far and wide for the Blisworth Tunnel on the Grand Union Canal. Almost two miles long – the longest in the UK – it runs down to Stoke Bruerne, where a museum tells the fascinating story of the canal and the tunnel.

308 THE DOLPHIN CAFÉ

175 Watling Street West, Towcester,
Northamptonshire NN12 6BX
☎ 01327 350808
⊕ www.thebestof.co.uk/towcester

Towcester is a busy little town with interesting shops, a fine church and a popular National Hunt racecourse. When a break is needed from shopping and sightseeing, many people head for the **Dolphin Café**.

Behind its double-fronted exterior it's a great place to relax and unwind, perhaps to read a paper or magazine or just sit back in the café or out in the patio/garden and revel in the warm, friendly atmosphere created by Cate and her daughter Phoebe Casey, while enjoying a snack, a pastry or a light meal. Cakes and pastries are baked fresh each morning, sandwiches are made to order throughout the day, breakfast is served until 11.30 and all day on

Sunday, and hot lunches and snacks being served

all day with pizza and pasta on the evening menu. There's a good choice of teas and the excellent Illy coffee, along with beer and wines by he glass. Most of the drinks and food items can be ordered to take away.

The café is open from 9am to 9pm Mon-Fri, Saturday 9 to 4, Sunday 10 to 3. Children are welcome until 7 o'clock. Please check our website for bank holiday opening times.

569

309 THE BUTCHERS ARMS

10 High Street,
Greens Norton, Towcester,
Northamptonshire NN12 8BA
☎ 01327 350488

The **Butchers Arms** is a traditional village inn standing at the top end of Greens Norton's main street. Built in 1939 to replace an earlier stone building that was burnt down, it has a strong local following and a great deal of potential, and Sarah Jones, who took over the reins at the end of 2007, is the perfect person to realise that potential. This is the sixth public house she has managed, so her knowledge of the licensed trade is second to none. Behind the bay-windowed frontage the bar is a convivial spot for meeting or making friends and enjoying a glass of cask ale – Courage tribute, Timothy Taylor Landlord, Fullers London Pride, Hook Norton Best and regularly changing guests provide plenty of choice. The bar is open from 12 to 3 and 5 to 11 Monday to Thursday and all day Friday, Saturday and

Sunday. The pub is also a popular place for a meal, with good honest cuisine and daily specials. Monday is curry night. The pub has a pool table, and on Sunday afternoons it hosts a live music session. Greens Norton, which stands off the busy A5 a mile northwest of Towcester, is at the southern end of the 12-mile Knightley Way, one of a number of mapped walking routes in the county. While in the village it's worth taking time to look at the parish church, which has Saxon stonework and a fine Norman font.

11 Market Place, Brackley,
Northamptonshire NN13 7AB
☎ 01280 702228 Fax: 01280 701647
e-mail: info@redliononthesquare.co.uk
🌐 www.redliononthesquare.co.uk

The **Red Lion** is an unmissable landmark on the market square in Brackley, a small, busy market town with a lot of charm and a good deal of history. The town was founded by a man called Bracca, who made a ley (clearing) here and in one go founded the town and the obvious name for it. If he were alive today he would no doubt head straight for this handsome old pub, which for centuries has been one of the focal points of the town. It certainly existed in 1772, when it was recorded as housing the inaugural meeting of a friendly society – the articles and the rule books are still in the owner's possession.

The current incumbent is Nigel Wiles, the second generation to run what is undoubtedly the best pub in Brackley. Nigel has an excellent team working for him, and a recent total refurbishment has enhanced the already strong appeal both for the people of Brackley and the surrounding area and with the legion of visitors who come here throughout the year, whether for business or pleasure. Behind the distinctive frontage in stone and slate this outstanding pub in the ownership of the Charles Wells Brewery takes the eye with bright contemporary colours, smart new tables and comfortable leather seats, but at the same time it manages to retain a good deal of period charm and atmosphere.

The bars are open from 11 in the morning to 11 at night for a wide selection of drinks. Charles Wells Bomardier and Eagle IPA, Youngs Special and Courage Directors are the resident real ales, and the cellar keeps a good choice of wines from the Old and New Worlds. Nigel is gradually building up the food side, winning a new band of regulars with food that is all locally sourced, all traditional and all freshly prepared and cooked on the premises. The choice runs from sandwiches to steaks by way of pasta, pies, fish dishes and roasts. Thursday is steak night, Friday brings roast pork. Food is served from 12 to 2 at lunchtime and

from 6.30 to 9 (not Friday or Saturday) in the evening. The Red Lion is not just a place for its varied clientele to drop into for a drink or a meal, it's also a very convenient base for anyone visiting the town, whether for business or leisure purposes.

Three bedrooms with shared facilities are open for Bed & Breakfast guests all year round. Brackley was once served by not one but two railway companies, the London Notrh Western and the Great Central, with stations at opposite ends of town. The railways have long since gone, but access to the town is easy by road. There's plenty to see in and around Brackley: Stowe is 5 miles away, Silverstone 6, Aynho Park 5 and Towcester 9.

311 THE GEORGE

High Street, Ashley,
Northamptonshire LE16 8HF
☎ 01858 565642
e-mail: enquire@thegeorgeatashley.co.uk
🌐 www.thegeorgeatashley.co.uk

The **George** is a traditional village inn on the main street of Ashley, off the A427 between Market Harborough and Corby. Since the spring of 2006 this handsome redbrick pub in the Welland Valley has been in the tender care of Donna and Cliff Garley, who, with their grown-up children Benjamin and Helen, have created a particularly cosy and welcoming ambience in the busy little bar and lounge. The George was built in 1746 as a coaching inn on the old Leicester road; now Grade II listed, it has changed little in appearance down the years, and the long tradition of hospitality remains alive and well under the new incumbents. Greene King IPA, Adnams Bitter, Youngs Bitter and regularly changing guests offer a splendid choice for real ale connoisseurs, heading a long list of drinks for all tastes.

Food is also an important part of the George's business, served every lunchtime and every evening except Sunday. The lunchtime choice includes sandwiches, salad bowls, ploughman's platters, omelettes and daily specials, and a 1-, 2- or 3-course Bistro 60+ menu is available Tuesday to Saturday. The evening brings classics such as scampi, cod & chips, herby salmon fillet, liver & bacon, braised lamb shank and steak & Guinness pie. If a table is booked for dinner in the cosy restaurant, it's booked for the whole evening, allowing diners to really relax and enjoy the food and the ambience to the full. The inn is open lunchtime and evening seven days a week. The George has recently added another string to its bow with the bringing on stream of six superior bedrooms in the converted old coach house. All have en suite facilities and a combination of original and contemporary features in keeping with the age and status of the inn.

The Welland Valley is a great place for walking amid lovely scenery, and the George is close to many places of interest, including the towns of Corby and Market Harborough, William the Conqueror's Rockingham Castle and East Carlton Countryside Park comprising 100 acres of parkland with nature trails and a steel-making heritage centre with craft workshops and a forge. Whether your visit to the George is for a quick drink, a snack, a leisurely meal or an overnight stay or longer break you can be sure of the friendliest reception and diligent attention from the

High Street, Cottingham,
Leicestershire LE16 8TL
☎ 01536 772038

The **Spread Eagle** was built in 1963 on a centuries-old hostelry. It stands on the main street of Cottingham of the A6003 close to Corby, Rockingham Castle and the popular Rockingham Raceway.

This handsome, well-maintained inn is in the expert care of Sam and Stella Perkins, a hardworking couple who combine a delightfully relaxed style and great enthusiasm with a thoroughly professional approach to the job. The inn has a comfortable bar warmed by an open fire in a brick hearth, an attractive dining area and a pleasant beer garden. Greene King IPA and Spitfire are the resident real ales, and the pub also stocks an excellent selection of wines. Food is very much the star turn here, and chefs Dariusz Swiecki and Arran McKenzie prepare a wide variety of dishes to order, using the best and freshest ingredients available, locally sourced wherever possible. The lunchtime menu offers snacks and very well-priced 2- or 3-course menus with classic main courses like fish & chips, ham & eggs, steak & ale pie, sausages & mash, breast of chicken and nut roast. The chefs really flex their culinary muscles for a contemporary main menu that's full of interest and imagination, and results on the plate fully justify the exciting descriptions: sweet pea & wild mushroom cappuccino served with a candied bacon biscuit; ham hock terrine with beetroot orange chutney and focaccia crisps; herb-crusted salmon topped with a prawn sauce; and chargrilled loin of pork with mesquite sauce, wild mushroom risotto and potato wedges. From the steakhouse come rump, sirloin and rib-eye steaks with optional pepper, Diane or stilton sauce, mixed grill and gammon steak served with white wine caramelised peaches. Sunday brings a popular carvery available from 12 to 4. The wine list is well chosen and well annotated, with a helpful taste guide. Pub hours are 11.30 to 3 and 5.30 to midnight Monday to Thursday and all through the day and evening Friday, Saturday and Sunday.

Sam is very keen on his music, so the Monday and Saturday live music sessions are always occasions to look forward to. Brains are put to the test on Thursdays, when the pub hosts a quiz evening. The ironstone village of Cottingham, which stands on the old Roman road to Leicester, provides fine views over the Welland valley. Its main public building is the 13th century parish church.

2 Bridge Street, Geddington,
Northamptonshire NN14 1AD
☎ 01536 742386 Fax: 01536 742386
🌐 www.star-inn-geddington.com

In the centre of Geddington, just moments from the main A43, the **Star** is an inn of very wide appeal – for locals enjoying a trip to their favourite pub, for workers, shoppers and business people dropping in for lunch, and for visitors to Geddington, home of the best-preserved of the Eleanor Crosses, taking a break from sightseeing. For more than 200 years this handsome stone-built, slate-roofed inn has been a welcoming sight in the heart of this historic town, and a favourite refreshment stop, first as the Swan, then as the Black Swan and latterly as the Star Inn.

Ali, Angela and Jean have a genuinely warm welcome for all their patrons, who since taking over the reins in 2002 have this a real pub-lover's pub, a convivial place where locals and visitors meet and chat in the cosy ambience of the traditionally appointed public and lounge bars. The Star is truly a happy hunting ground for those who like their real ale. The bar keeps a superb selection of brews from small local breweries: Beijing Black from the Pot Bellied Brewery; Barnwell Bitter from Digfield Ales;

Wot's Occurring from Great Oakley; Best Bitter from Nobby's Brewery; Black Pearl from Milestone. All these and other highly individualistic ales are kept in tip-top condition, earning the pub the accolade of CAMRA's Northamptonshire Summer Pub of the Year for 2006. Food-lovers are equally well catered for at the Star. Ali has been a chef for more than 25 years, and his printed

menus and specials board satisfy a wide range of tastes and appetites. Traditional dishes like garlic mushrooms, the pie of the week, roast duck and steaks are the choice of many, while the more adventurous peruse the Tex-Mex section for spicy delights like chicken or beef fajitas, rack of ribs in a tangy BBQ sauce or nachos with salsa piccante, chilli beef, cheese, sour cream, jalapeño peppers and olives. Fish-eaters will also fine plenty of choice (halibut steak with pink peppercorn sauce, sizzling swordfish, ocean pie) and vegetarians always have a choice of at least four main courses.

Paintings in a variety of media by professional artists are displayed in the pub's gallery area, with exhibitions changing every two months, an annual grand review at the turn of the year and all the artwork for sale. A charity quiz, with bargain food specials, is held every other Tuesday, and the pub holds a popular themed food night on the last Thursday of the month.

574

314 MRS MIGGINS COFFEE HOUSE

St Mary's Wynd, Hexham,
Northumberland NE46 1LW
☎ 01434 605808

Ashleigh Hutton is the owner and chef at **Mrs Miggins**, a delightful little café standing opposite Hexham Abbey. Converted from a granary and named after a character in *Blackadder*, the café is open from 9.30 to 5 Monday to Saturday for a selection of wholesome home-cooked fare, including soups, sandwiches, home baked scones, baked potatoes, salads and pasta. An excellent choice of teas and coffees accompanies the food.

315 THE QUEENS ARMS HOTEL

Main Street, Acomb, nr Hexham,
Northumberland NE46 4PL
☎ 01434 602176

For almost 200 years the **Queens Arms Hotel** has been a notable landmark on the main street of Acomb, a pleasant village located a short drive from the main A69 between Hexham and Hadrian's Wall.

Jeffrey and Janice Keen took over the tenancy in the spring of 2007 and oversaw a major facelift to the premises completed at the end of that year. Two rotating guest ales head the choice of drinks served in the bar, and hearty no-frills cooking by Janice offers pies, curries and other classics such as liver & bacon or mince with dumplings. Popular with the local community, the Queens Arms also provides a friendly refreshment stop for walkers and sightseers, and a comfortable holiday base in five cosy bedrooms. The pub has a pool room and a function room and hosts occasional karaoke evenings.

316 THE RAILWAY INN

Fourstones, Hexham,
Northumberland NE47 5DY
☎ 01434 674711
e-mail: therailwayinn@hotmail.co.uk

Walkers, fishermen, locals, families and visitors to nearby Hadrian's Wall are all welcome at the **Railway Inn**, which is located in the village of Fourstones, on the River South Tyne a few miles north of Hexham. Dating back as far as 1771, the stonebuilt village inn has emerged looking splendid after a major refurbishment by Jennings Brewery. The bar, lounge and two separate dining areas enhance the warm, welcoming atmosphere created by experienced publicans Lynn and David Meldrum. Food is a major part of the business here, and the chefs offer a great deal more than is usually found on pub menus. Typical choices include Derwentwater Duck – baked with hedgerow fruits and scented with damson gin; carpaccio of peppered beef; fish mixed grill served on a bed of chargrilled vegetables; and

Fourstones Fowl – chicken supreme filled with pancetta and shallots with a bacon, cream & mushroom sauce. Pub favourites like steaks and Sunday roasts will appeal to more conventional palates, and classic French cuisine is represented by the likes of steak Diane and tournedos Rossini. Senior citizens enjoy a special lunchtime deal on Wednesdays, and a takeaway service is available.

317 THE KINGS HEAD

Market Place, Allendale,
Northumberland NE47 9BD
☎ 01434 683681

Host Peter Wood, who worked for many years with the Scottish & Newcastle Brewery, lives beside the **Kings Head** and was very pleased to take the reins when the tenancy became available. Overlooking the Market Place in the old mining town of Allendale, this fine stone-built coaching inn dates back to 1767, and many of the best period features have been retained in a far-reaching refurbishment programme that started at the end of 2007. In the spacious bar/lounge, warmed in winter by a blazing fire, three cask ales – typically Marstons Pedigree, Banks's Original and Jennings Cumberland – are on tap, while whisky connoisseurs could sample a different malt every day for more than two months. This is great walking country, and fresh-air appetites are satisfied with a good choice of hearty, wholesome food. Among the favourite orders are home-cooked honey-roast ham, lasagne and chicken curry, along with tempting specials such as salmon & king prawn

pie. For guests enjoying a break in this pleasant part of the world the Kings Head has five neat, well-appointed bedrooms for Bed & Breakfast, four with en suite facilities, the other with a private bathroom. Allendale stands on the River East Allen against a backdrop of heathery moorland. It was once an important centre of the North Pennine lead-mining industry, but it has another claim to fame: a sundial in the churchyard records the fact that the village lies exactly halfway between Beachy Head in Sussex to Cape Wrath in the north of Scotland. The Kings Head is open all day for drinks and from midday to 8 or 9 for food.

318 THE BAY HORSE INN

West Woodburn, Kielder,
Northumberland NE48 2RX
☎ 01434 270218
⊕ www.bayhorseinn.org

The **Bay Horse Inn** is a late-18th century mellow sandstone hostelry standing in the heart of the Cheviot Hills, by a stone bridge on the main A68. Hilda Wright, who was first associated with the inn 20 years ago, is an admirable host and her immaculate inn is a delightful place to pause for a drink, to relax over a leisurely meal or to enjoy a break in a picturesque setting. Food is very much the

star here, with prime local produce taking centre stage for the home-cooked dishes on the wide-ranging menus. Among the perennial favourites are beer-battered haddock, lasagne, chilli con carne, mince with dumplings, lamb chops, chicken tikka masala and specials featuring seafood caught off the nearby Northumberland coast. The five cottage-style guest bedrooms, each with its own individual character, have en suite facilities, TV and hot drinks tray; they provide an ideal base for tourists, cyclists and walkers – the Pennine Way passes close by. The Bay Horse hosts occasional live music nights and a quiz every other Thursday.

320 THE HADRIAN HOTEL

Wark, nr Hexham,
Northumberland NE44 4EE
☎ 01434 681232
e-mail: david.lindsay13@btinternet.com
⊕ www.hadrianhotel.com

Tourists, walkers and lovers of the countryside will find an excellent refreshment stop or holiday base at the **Hadrian Hotel**, which stands off the A69, four miles from Hexham at the gateway to the Northumberland National Park and Hadrian's Wall

country. Behind the substantial, part creeper-covered stone façade, the public bar, lounge and restaurant are appealingly traditional, with open fires and period-style pictures and ornaments. Jennings Cumberland Ale is the resident cask ale, and a fine choice of food is served all day in the main bar and lunchtime and evening in the restaurant. When the sun shines, the large garden is a popular alternative. The six guest bedrooms – four en suite, some with four-posters – provide ample space and comfort, offering an ideal base for discovering the many attractions and activities that are almost on the doorstep. Notable among the sights is Hadrian's Wall: some of

the best sections of this World Heritage Site are close to the hotel. The hotel is also a popular place for locals to meet and socialise, with a pool table, dominoes, gaming machines and a big-screen TV for top sporting events.

319 BATTLESTEADS

Wark, nr Hexham,
Northumberland NE48 3LS
☎ 01434 230209 Fax: 01434 230039
e-mail: info@battlesteads.com
⊕ www.battlesteads.com

Battlesteads is a country inn and restaurant owned and run by Richard and Dee Slade. It was built as a traditional Northumberland farmhouse in 1747, and in summer the frontage is adorned by colourful hanging baskets and plantings. Inside, the scene is set by low beamed ceilings in the bar and lounge areas and a real fire in an old-fashioned hearth. Furnishings include leather settees and low tables in the lounge and high-backed leather chairs in the restaurant. Cream-painted walls are hung with antique prints of the countryside and country pursuits. At the back are a large conservatory and a hidden walled garden with a kitchen garden for

herbs and salad leaves. Richard is currently Regional Chairman of the British Institute of Innkeeping and previously ran a French-European restaurant and an award-winning town pub-restaurant. Dee is an award-winning dessert chef and chocolatier. Richard is a keen supporter of cask ales, and among the brews regularly appearing are the local Wylam Gold and Durham Magus, and Black Sheep Ale and Special. He also keeps an excellent cellar, with a well-chosen selection of more than 20 wines. Chef Eddie Shilton's style is modern British and international, with a strong reliance on local produce: oak-smoked duck, chicken and salmon from the Bywell Smokery, Cumbrian beef, Northumberland lamb and seasonal game, and seafood from North Shields Fish Quay. Lunch is served from 12 to 3, dinner from 6.30 to 9.30, and booking is recommended at peak times, as the restaurant is popular with diners from all over the region. The hosts have a warm welcome for all their visitors, who include walkers, cyclists, golfers, anglers and tourists, as well as loyal locals, and for those looking for a comfortable, civilised base. Battlesteads has 17 en suite bedrooms with TV with Freeview and DVD, broadband access, beverage tray, hairdryer and ironing facilities; the four rooms on the ground floor have wheelchair access and walk-in shower. Wark is situated in rural North Tynedale, a secluded dale to the north of Hadrian's Wall and close to Kielder Forest and Kielder Water.

321 RIVERDALE HALL COUNTRY HOUSE HOTEL

Bellingham, nr Hexham,
Northumberland NE48 2JT
☎ 01434 220254 Fax: 01434 220457
e-mail: reservations@riverdalehallhotel.co.uk
⊕ www.riverdalehallhotel.co.uk

Guests return year after year to enjoy the excellent hospitality dispensed for 30 years by John and Iben Cocker at **Riverdale Hall Hotel**. Built in 1868 for a railway developer, this handsome mansion stands on the eastern edge of the Northumberland National Park, on the road from Hadrian's Wall to

Kielder Forest. Since the 1970s no Tynedale hotel has received more accolades than this outstanding hotel, where the extensive leisure and sporting facilities include a swimming pool, sauna, cricket pitch and fishing for salmon and trout. The guest accommodation comprises 31 superbly appointed bedrooms, all with en

suite facilities, TV, telephone and hot drinks tray. Some are suitable for families, some have four-posters, and ground-floor rooms in the Museum Wing are ideal for less mobile guests. The high standards set by the accommodation and the amenities are matched in the kitchen, where Iben, ably assisted by Stuart Taylor and Tony Johnston, produce meals to remember using seasonal local ingredients of the highest quality: Northumberland lamb, Kielder venison, locally-reared game birds and fish from the hotel's own stretch of river. The Hall is a popular venue for functions, conferences and weddings for parties of up to 160.

323 THE OAK INN

Causey Park Bridge, Morpeth,
Northumberland NE61 3EL
☎ 01670 787388

Glaswegian Duncan MacKenzie has settled in well south of the border at the **Oak Inn**, the only pub on the A1 for many miles in either direction. The pub derives its clientele from locals, families

(children and dogs welcome) and a steady stream of motorists taking a break from a journey along the busy main road linking England and Scotland. Behind the relatively unassuming façade the bar, lounge and conservatory-style restaurant are warm and inviting, and when the summer comes the beer garden with its children's play area is of special appeal to families. Duncan and their staff dispense hospitality in good measure, along with Caledonian Deuchars ales and a

choice of home cooking that embraces sandwiches, snacks and full meals. Beer-battered cod, seafood platter, pies and Sunday roasts are among the most popular orders, and the choice is expanded by daily specials such as spicy tomato soup and lamb stew with parsley dumplings. To finish, perhaps lime & ginger cheesecake or a delectable honey & brandy gateau. The Oak is open all day, seven days a week.

Main Street, Corbridge, nr Hexham,
Northumberland NE45 5LA
☎ 01434 632119

The **Angel Inn** and the **Angel Radcliffe** are two facing properties, both recently superbly refurbished, the former with guest rooms and a restaurant, the latter for Bed & Breakfast only.

Corporate clients and leisure visitors will find everything they need for a comfortable stay at the **Angel Inn**. Dating from the early 1700s, and one of Northumberland's first coaching inns, it has been transformed in contemporary style, with careful attention to every aspect of the décor and furnishings. Real ales, wines and fine malts are served in the bar and the warm, well-lit lounge, and daily menus prepared by a team of

talented chefs will delight the diner in the impressive banqueting hall-style restaurant. All dishes feature freshly cooked local ingredients where possible. Weather permitting you may also dine or enjoy a glass of wine on our popular Terrace. The Inn has six bedrooms all with en-suite, T.V's, tea and coffee making facilities and free wifi access.

The Angel's owner John Gibson recently bought and refurbished the **Angel Radcliffe**, a boutique-style hotel on the other side of the road. Designed not as an overspill but to complement the Angel, the Angel Radcliffe has nine stunning rooms, all totally and elegantly refurbished and all commanding views, some of the River Tyne. Both Angels are open throughout the year.

324 THE ODDFELLOWS ARMS

Narrowgate, Alnwick,
Northumberland NE66 1JN
☎ 01665 605363

Standing in Narrowgate, right opposite the imposing Alnwick Castle, the **Oddfellows Arms** is a friendly, down-to-earth late-18th century pub where local residents and the many visitors to this impressive town are greeted with equal warmth by Jo and Graeme Helliwell. The welcome is reinforced by much tail-wagging from Millie and Truffle, the two lovely Newfoundlands, and wise looks from Barney the Owl. Flowers in baskets and troughs add splashes of colour to the bright white exterior, and in the convivial bar rotating cask

ales are on tap to quench thirsts. The food options run from sandwiches and snacks to burgers, chilli, steaks, lasagne, fish & chips, Cumberland sausage, steak & ale pie, chicken with BBQ sauce and the up-and-coming classic Thai fish cakes with a sweet chilli dip. Alnwick and the surrounding attractions of coast and countryside need plenty of time to explore, and the Oddfellows Arms provides an ideal base with its three pleasantly appointed en suite bedrooms. The pub hosts a popular quiz every other Wednesday.

325 THE HOPE & ANCHOR

Northumberland Street, Alnwick,
Northumberland NE66 2PA
☎ 01665 820363
e-mail: info@hopeandanchorholidays.co.uk
🌐 www.hopeandanchorholidays.co.uk

Two beautiful Dalmatian dogs join Barbara and John in welcoming visitors to the **Hope & Anchor**. Locals all year round and the whole world in season create a cheerful, convivial atmosphere in the bar and lounge, where Barbara's choice of warm colours adds to the pleasure of enjoying a chat and a glass of cask ale – perhaps Black Sheep or Farne Island. Another major contributor to the pub's popularity is chef Andrew Hudson, whose menus run from sandwiches in ciabatta bread to

three-course meals. Some dishes are pub classics – beer-battered cod, lasagne, steaks, Sunday's super roast beef, sticky toffee pudding – while others show Andrew's creative side, typified by pork and chicken pâté, poached salmon with sweet potato slices and a prawn & cucumber sauce, and grilled pork loin steak in a plum jus with a sage & onion medley mash. For anyone exploring the delights of Alnwick and the region's countryside and coast, the inn is an excellent place to drop anchor, with eight warm, stylish and well-fitted rooms for B&B.

Rennington, nr Alnwick,
Northumberland NE66 3AX
☎ 01665 577275
🌐 www.masonsarms.net

The **Masons Arms** is a handsome country inn with a fine restaurant and high-quality guest accommodation. It stands in the heart of England's beautiful Border Country at Stamford, on the B1340 Seahouses road four miles northeast of

Alnwick. Much expanded since its origins 200 years ago, it now comprises the original stone building, a converted blacksmiths forge next door and a new accommodation block at the rear. Bob and Alison Culverwell, here since 2004, are the busy, energetic hosts who take excellent care of guests old and new, and the beamed bar is a warm, convivial spot for making friends over a cask ale from a local brewery or a malt whisky. The whole place has been thoughtfully modernised while preserving the best traditional elements, and the bar features sturdy wooden chairs set at equally sturdy tables, plush bar stools, period pictures and photographs and gleaming brass ornaments. All are welcome to test their brainpower at Friday night's quiz. In the spacious dining rooms cooked-to-order meals, including fish, steaks and game, make excellent use of the best seasonal produce, most of it local.

The accommodation at the Masons Arms comprises 17 bedrooms, all with en suite bath/shower rooms, central heating, beverage tray, hairdryer and ironing facilities. Four rooms, including two for families, are in the converted stable block. Six 'Superior' rooms, two with sitting rooms, are

in the annexe. Those on the first floor open onto balconies, while the ground-floor rooms access a secluded patio garden. There are also 6 individually appointed rooms, retaining many original features in the recently converted blacksmiths forge.

The beautiful gardens at Howick Hall and the dramatic ruins of Dunstanburgh Castle are among the sights to see in the area, and the whole vicinity provides lovely walks in glorious countryside or on the coastal path. This outstanding hostelry is open from noon every day and food is served every lunchtime and evening.

327 THE RAILWAY HOTEL

Bridge Street, Rothbury,
Northumberland NE65 7SE
☎ 01669 620221
🌐 www.railwayhotelrothbury.co.uk

Locals, families, walkers and visitors from all walks of life make tracks for the **Railway Hotel**, a substantial sandstone hostelry on a corner site off the main street of Rothbury. The bars, lounge and dining areas are in traditional style, and hosts Lewis and Anne are on hand to dispense hospitality and a selection of cask ales, including some from the Caledonian Deuchars Brewery. It's a great place for anyone who appreciates honest, generously

served English food: mushrooms stuffed with black pudding and Stilton; scampi; fish pie; cottage pie; traditional Northumbrian beef stovies; Sunday roasts; steaks and grills from the top local Butterknowes Farm. With its four good-size en suite bedrooms, the Railway Hotel is a comfortable and convenient base for exploring the valley

of the River Coquet, with delightful walks along the valley or through the nearby woodland. Pool is played in the public bar, and the pub hosts a live music evening on the third Saturday of the month. The pub is open from noon to 11pm every day.

328 HOWICK SCAR FARMHOUSE

Craster, nr Alnwick,
Northumberland NE66 3SU
☎ 01665 576665
e-mail: stay@howickscar.co.uk
🌐 www.howickscar.co.uk

Farmer's wife Celia Curry has for many years welcomed B&B guests to her sturdy stone farmhouse at the heart of a 250-acre mixed farm. On the Coast & Castles Cycling Route, halfway between Craster and Howick, it has two guest bedrooms, available between April and October, with washbasin, radio-alarm, hairdryer, beverage tray and access to a bathroom with separate shower. A full cooked breakfast, with their own farm eggs and, when available, the famous Craster kippers, starts the day, and guests can watch TV or plan their day in the lounge. The area has much to offer the visitor, including glorious sandy beaches, wonderful walks and cycle rides, gardens and castles, golf courses and bird reserves.

583

329 BAMBURGH CASTLE

Bamburgh, Northumberland NE69 7DF
☎ 01668 214515 Fax: 01668 214060
e-mail: bamburghcastle@aol.com
🌐 www.bamburghcastle.com

Standing on a rocky outcrop overlooking miles of beautiful sandy beach, **Bamburgh Castle** dominates the Northumbrian landscape. The castle became the passion of the 1st Baron Armstrong who, in the 1890's, began its renovation and refurbishment. This love of Bamburgh was passed down through the family to the late Lord Armstrong, who personally oversaw the completion of his ancestor's dream.

Today Bamburgh Castle is still the home of the Armstrong family, and visitors are able to enjoy what has been described as the finest castle in all England. The public tour includes the magnificent King's Hall, the Cross Hall, reception rooms, the Bakehouse and Victorian Scullery, as

well as the Armoury and Dungeon. Throughout, these rooms contain a wide range of fine china, porcelain and glassware, together with paintings, furniture, tapestries, arms and armour.

The Armstrong Museum, occupying the former Laundry Building, is dedicated to the life and work of the first Lord Armstrong. An inventive engineer, shipbuilder and industrialist, he left a great legacy to the modern age and Tyneside in particular.

The castle is open daily from mid March to the end of October, between 11am and 5pm, and teas and light refreshments are available from The Clock Tower.

330 CARA HOUSE

44 Castlegate, Berwick-upon-Tweed,
Northumberland TD15 1JT
☎ 01289 302749
🌐 www.carahouse.co.uk

Since 2004 Pamela Thompson has been offering Bed & Breakfast accommodation at **Cara House**, which is located through an archway towards the top end of town a short walk from the town centre and the railway

station. Pamela, whose husband David skippers a fishing boat, welcomes guests from near and far into the warm, comfortable surroundings of the 18th century family home, where three excellent en suite bedrooms are available all year round. The rooms are spacious and well-appointed, spotless, warm and cosy, with TV, radio-alarm clock and hot drinks tray; one is a family suite, another has a handsome brass double bed. Guests have the use of a

cosy lounge, and the house has private off-road parking and secure storage for bicycles. Cara House is a friendly, unpretentious base for exploring historic Berwick-upon-Tweed, the Scottish Borders and North Northumberland. Berwick is one of England's most beguiling towns, with a long and fascinating history. It deserves a leisurely stay to discover all its attractions, and you couldn't find a more pleasant place to start than Cara House.

331 MEADOW HOUSE INN

North Road, Berwick-upon-Tweed,
Northumberland TD15 1UR
☎ 01289 304173

The Hearn family, at the helm 25 years, ensure that standards stay high at the **Meadow House Inn**, which stands in pleasant, well-tended grounds at the northern end of the Berwick-upon-Tweed bypass only five minutes from the town centre. Close to the Scottish border, it is the most northerly pub in England, which explains why it's sometimes called 'The First and Last'. The A1 runs close by, making it a convenient refreshment stop for motorists and tourists as well as being a very busy and popular local meeting place.

David Hearn, who recently took over the reins from his father, has worked in some top restaurants and is also a wine expert, so it is not surprising that the pub has acquired a fine reputation as a place to seek out for a meal. The chefs are kept busy preparing anything from a quick snack to a four-course meal, and the constantly changing menu of pub classics is supplemented by daily specials, OAP lunchtime specials and an Early Bird menu available between 5.30 and 7.

Even without the vast range of drinks (cask ales, wines, 30+ malt whiskies, dozens of liqueurs and cocktails) and the buzz and chat among the relaxed band of regulars, the busy bar would be a talking point in its own right for its unique collection of musical instruments and accessories. These include acoustic guitars, bass guitars, fiddles, a saxophone, even a sitar – and if you ask nicely you might even get to play one! There are no steps into the pub and the public rooms are all on one level, allowing easy access for wheelchairs.

332 THE BLACK LION

Main Road, Radcliffe-on-Trent,
Nottinghamshire NG12 2FD
☎ 0115 933 2138
e-mail:
black.lion.public.house@unicombox.co.uk

Coach driver Deborah Badcock changed many of her passengers into pub-lovers when she changed the steering wheel for the reins at the **Black Lion**. This big, bold landmark pub is easy to spot in the busy village of Radcliffe-on-Trent, just off the A52 east of Nottingham. Behind its stone and brick frontage, with a black-and-white upper storey, there's plenty of elbow and sitting room in the public bar and traditional lounge/dining area, where six cask ales, including Greene King IPA, Charles Wells Bombardier and Courage Directors, provide a fine choice for real ales fans. That choice rises to at least 30 and up to 50 to sample in the marquees during the late-May beer festival. Hungry patrons are also well catered for, with a wide range of snacks and meals that run from filled cobs and baguettes, burgers,

jacket potatoes and salads to omelettes, chilli (meat or veggie), lasagne (ditto), beer battered cod, steak & ale pie, chilli nachos, big breakfasts and rump, sirloin and gammon steaks. The Sunday roasts come in three sizes – child, small and large – and a fine meal ends with a great selection of naughty desserts. Apart from the annual beer festival, the pub, which is open from 11.30 every day, hosts many events throughout the year.

333 THE WHITE LION

Nottingham Road, Bingham,
Nottinghamshire NG13 8AT
☎ 01949 875541

Bingham, which lies by the A52, just beyond to the junction with the A46 and a few miles east of Nottingham, is the unofficial capital of the Vale of Belvoir, a medieval market town with a fine 13th century church. All Saints Church may be the spiritual heart of the town but the social heart is the **White Lion**, a fine old pub on a corner site at a busy crossroads near the town centre. Hands-on leaseholder Sue Boardman has built up an excellent rapport with her regular customers, and first-timers are greeted with equally genuine

smiles. In the roomy public bar and cosy lounge this Theakstons pub serves a full range of drinks from 11am to 11pm, and down-to-earth pub food is available lunchtime and evening Monday to Saturday. Monday is bingo night, Tuesday punters can play free pool, Friday sees a live music session, Sunday is quiz night and offers free choices on the juke box. The bar also has a big-screen TV for the major sports events. When the weather is kind, the tables and chairs set out on the patio come into their own

334 THE GREAT NORTHERN

134 Derby Road, Langley Mill,
Nottinghamshire NG16 4AA
☎ 01773 713834

A family friendly pub with friendly family owners. That's the **Great Northern**, and its appeal extends to a wide cross-section of the public, from locals to children with families, motorists, tourists, real ale lovers and music lovers – and many patrons tick more than one of those boxes. Dating from 1781, this landmark pub is well known all over Nottinghamshire and Derbyshire. It enjoys a pleasant canalside location at Langley Mill, just off the A610 west of Nottingham and northeast of Derby, and the garden by the water is a

real boon in the summer months. Inside, there's a specious public bar open all day every day, two dining areas and a pool room. Greene King IPA and Morland Bitter are the regular real ales, accompanied by two guest ales, and honest, down-to-earth food runs from freshly baked cobs, panini, pizza slices and jacket potatoes to scampi, cod & chips, seafood pasta, chicken tikka masala, chicken pie and steak & Guinness pie. Wednesday and Sunday see popular quiz evenings, Thursday is karaoke night, Friday it's disco or karaoke and Saturday brings a live music session.

335 THE GRANGE HOTEL

73 London Road, Newark,
Nottinghamshire NG24 1RZ
☎ 01636 703399 Fax: 01636 702328
e-mail: info@grangenewark.co.uk
🌐 www.grangenewark.co.uk

With its redbrick late-Victorian façade, the **Grange Hotel** is a familiar landmark in a quiet residential area opposite the Polish war memorial, on the edge of Newark's vibrant town centre. But secluded from view to passers-by is one of the hotels' hidden attractions, a unique garden with lawns, paved and cobble pathways, wooden tables and chairs, a floodlit patio with heaters, a gazebo and old-fashioned street lamps. With this and other assets, owner-managers Sandra and Tom Carr have firmly established the Grange as the top hotel in Newark and the surrounding area, and one that has gained recognition and acclaim at national as well as local level.

The guest accommodation comprises 19 tastefully appointed bedrooms – singles, doubles, twins, Executive rooms, four-posters and a triple room for families, all with superb, newly designed bathrooms en suite. The Grange is also a fine place for a meal, with extensive à la carte menus served in Cutlers Restaurant and the more informal Potters

Bar. There's lots to see and do in and around Newark, ranging from the Castle and the Church of St Mary Magdalene to the Air Museum, and there's no finer base for tourists than the Grange.

336 THE FULL MOON

Main Street, Morton, nr Newark,
Nottinghamshire NG25 0UT
☎ 01636 830251
⊕ www.thefullmoonmorton.co.uk

The **Full Moon** enjoys a secluded setting not far from the River Trent in a village off the A612 southeast of Southwell. The redbrick, red-tiled façade is adorned in spring and summer with flowers in tubs and window boxes, and the back there's a rear terrace and a lawn with a children's play area. Inside, open fires, beams, inviting lounge seats and country furniture in the dining area set a traditional scene, and Rebecca and William White make sure that the atmosphere is always friendly and relaxed. Real ale drinkers are in for a real treat at this mid-18th century inn, with Black Sheep, Harvest Pale, Batemans XB, Charles Wells

Bombardier and Greene King IPA among the regulars brews on tap. Rebecca makes sure that diners will also go home happy, and her excellent dishes offer 'big flavours and no frills', relying on excellent raw materials and treating them with the respect they deserve. Typical dishes on her always tempting menu might include scallops with black pudding and a mustard dressing, haddock fresh from Grimsby, Chicken, ham & apricot pie, Gonalstons Farm Shop's onion marmalade sausages, liver & bacon shepherds pie with cauliflower cheese and roast vegetables & goat's cheese salad. Lunchtime also brings sandwiches and light snacks.

337 THE QUEEN'S HOTEL

High Street, East Markham,
Nottinghamshire NG22 0RE
☎ 01777 870288

One of the many assets of the **Queen's Hotel** is its long-serving landlord and landlady Chris and Barbara Russon. They took over here in 1990, ever since when they have been welcoming locals and seasonal visitors with their excellent brand of hospitality. Behind its white-painted exterior with huge name boards and summer hanging baskets, the hotel (not a hotel in spite of its name) is spotless and very comfortable, with plenty of inviting seats in which to enjoy a chat and a glass of real ale. The bar is open from 2pm on Monday and from midday every other day, and food is served from 12 to 9.30 Tuesday to Saturday and from 12 to 6 on Sunday. The menu and specials board offer an extensive choice that runs from pub

favourites like homemade cottage pie, steak & kidney pie, lasagne and crispy-battered cod and haddock to sirloin and gammon steaks, lamb chops à l'orange, peppered pork, chilli con carne and always a good choice of curries. There's always a good selection of vegetarian main courses (broccoli & brie rösti, stilton & vegetable crumble, five bean chilli) and traditional desserts like spotted dick, jam roly poly and treacle sponge. East Markham lies off the A1 by the junction with the A57.

338 BRECKS COTTAGE

Green Lane, Moorhouse, nr Newark,
Nottinghamshire NG23 6LZ
☎ 01636 822445
e-mail: bandb@breckscottage.co.uk
🌐 www.breckscottage.co.uk

Susan Thomas welcomes Bed & Breakfast guests into her home in the village of Moorhouse. **Brecks Cottage** is an attractive 350-year-old redbrick building with a red-tiled roof, set in a pleasant garden, and Susan sets the highest standards of traditional hospitality while providing up-to-date amenities in surroundings that are more peaceful and more personal than a hotel. The accommodation comprises five pretty bedrooms – Pink, Peach, Primrose, Lilac and Mint, all with en suite facilities, TV with DVD and freeview and broadband internet access. Susan offers a very good choice for breakfasts, making sure that guests are ready for a day exploring a very interesting and scenically attractive part of the world. Moorhouse, in Robin Hood country close to the border with Lincolnshire, lies at the junctions of minor roads off the A1 – leave at Tuxford or Carlton-on-Trent. This is excellent walking country, and attractions within an easy drive include Egmanton Church with the Shrine of Our Lady of Egmanton, Laxton, with its medieval open field farming system, the Queen's Dovecote Inn and the Museum of Dolls and Bygone Childhood in the village of Cromwell. Newark and Retford are also close by.

339 THE JOHN BARLEYCORN

Manor Road, Goring-on-Thames,
Oxfordshire RG8 9DP
☎ 01491 872304
e-mail: enquiries@thejohnbarleycornpub.co.uk
🌐 www.thejohnbarleycornpub.co.uk

Gordon Reilly and Ruth Lloyd realised a long-held ambition to run a pub when they acquired the **John Barleycorn**. Built as three cottages in the 17th century, it is first recorded as a pub in 1810 and was later used to house workmen building the London-Bristol railway. It now attracts a wide cross-section of patrons, who come from near and far to savour the hospitality, the well-kept ales, the well-chosen wines and the home cooking, or to enjoy a break in the superbly fitted new bedrooms. Hanging baskets adorn the exterior, while inside there are real fires and plenty of comfortable seating in the convivial public bar, the snug and the restaurant. Food is an important part of the pub's business, with a choice that runs from lunchtime snacks and light

meals to Thai fish cakes, mushroom & stilton melt, sweet chilli pan-fried salmon and classics such as sirloin or gammon steak, toad in the hole, steak & kidney pie, battered cod and a super Sunday roast. Close to the River Thames, the pub is an ideal base for a walking, boating or touring holiday.

Banbury Road, Tackley,
Oxfordshire OX5 3EP
☎ 01869 331328 Fax: 01869 331686
e-mail: enquiries@sturdyscastle.com
🌐 www.sturdyscastle.com

Family proprietors have established a long tradition of hospitality at **Sturdy's Castle**, a country inn and restaurant that lies just east of Woodstock on the A4260 Oxford to Banbury road at the Tackley turn. They provide the highest standards in all its aspects, as a traditional bar, a destination restaurant and an ideal base for the business traveller or for exploring the many sights and places of interest in Oxford and the Oxfordshire countryside. The pub's sign explains its name. It depicts a Mr Sturdy and Mr Castle engaged in fisticuffs next to the pub and a gibbet. The outcome of the fight is not known, but it would be nice to think that they shook hands and repaired to the pub for a drink.

The inn is open all day, every day of the week, and food and drink are served throughout the day in the traditionally appointed bar and the 80-cover restaurant. The lunchtime and à la carte menus provide plenty of choice for all tastes and appetites. They stick mainly to familiar pub favourites, from scampi and fish & chips to curries, big breakfasts, lasagne, steak & Guinness pie, roast chicken with stuffing & gravy and gammon, sirloin, T-bone and fillet steaks. Other choices might include trout with almonds & lemon, Southern fried chicken and pork belly ribs herbs or a BBQ dip. The specials board extends the choice still further with dishes like haggis with neeps & tatties or meat loaf with a red wine and peppercorn sauce. Traditional sweets like treacle pudding or apple pie round things off in style, and the food is complemented by wines by bottle or glass. Sandwiches, baguettes and jacket potatoes cater for snackers or those with less time to spare, and children can choose from their own special menu. The large beer garden, part-paved, part-lawned, is a pleasant spot to enjoy a drink (Hook Norton Cask is the regular real ale) or a meal on a sunny summer's day or a balmy summer evening.

The separate accommodation block has 20 nicely appointed en suite bedrooms with TV, telephone and complimentary beverage tray. Ten are on the ground floor, two are suitable for disabled guests and four can sleep families of up to four. Interconnecting rooms are available. The inn has a function room with its own skittle alley, a perfect venue for a business meeting or private celebration. Woodstock and Blenheim Palace are nearby, and the city of Oxford is less than ten miles away.

High Street, Whitchurch-on-Thames,
Oxfordshire RG8 7DB
☎ 0118 984 2161
e-mail: info@theferryboat.eu
⊕ www.theferryboat.eu

A warm welcome awaits visitors to the **Ferry Boat Inn**, which stands on the main street of Whitchurch-on-Thames, just off the A329 Reading to Goring road. Hosts David (who cooks), Jesse (who runs the busy bar) and their team make their patrons feel instantly at ease, and the bar is a particularly pleasant spot for enjoying traditional ale or a glass of wine and a chat, and in the 30-cover dining area regularly changing menus provide plenty to satisfy all palates and appetites. The choice includes pub classics as well as European favourites (confit of duck) and more exotic options (Asian-style sea bass). Room should definitely be left for delectable desserts such as nectarine tart or banana tarte tatin. Fair Trade coffee can be enjoyed with Danish fresh pastries from 11 o'clock, and baguettes and sandwiches provide quicker

alternatives to the main menu at lunchtime. The pub is closed on Mondays except Bank Holidays. For guests staying overnight the pub has three cosy cottage-style rooms that provide an excellent base for exploring the area – among the local places of interest are the National Trust's Basildon Park, Beale Park, home to an abundance of wildlife and unusual farm animals; and the Elizabethan Mapledurham House with its notable literary connections.

92 East Street, Fritwell,
Oxfordshire OX27 7QF
☎ 01869 346738
e-mail: enquiries@thekingsheadfritwell.co.uk
⊕ www.thekingsheadfritwell.co.uk

North Oxfordshire's favourite steak house is a super country inn located in the rural village of Fritwell, signposted off the A43 (via the B4100) and only a short drive from Junction 10 of the M40. Gregor Stevenson took over the **Kings Head** in 2002, and he has made it a big favourite with both the local residents and with visitors from all over the region. Succulent steaks, supplied by a top local butcher, are the speciality, but there's plenty of other choice, including some vegetarian dishes. Food is served lunchtime and evening Tuesday to Saturday and Sunday lunchtime.

HIDDEN PLACES GUIDES

Explore Britain and Ireland with *Hidden Places* guides - a fascinating series of national and local travel guides.

Packed with easy to read information on hundreds of places of interest as well as places to stay, eat and drink.

Available from both high street and internet booksellers

For more information on the full range of *Hidden Places* guides and other titles published by Travel Publishing visit our website on

www.travelpublishing.co.uk or ask for our leaflet by phoning **01752 276660** or emailing **info@travelpublishing.co.uk**

Woodleys, Woodstock,
Oxfordshire OX20 1HT
☎ 01993 811460 Fax: 01993 810165
e-mail: sales@dukeofmarlborough.co.uk
🌐 www.dukeofmarlborough.co.uk

Standing by the A44 Oxford to Stratford road two miles north of Woodstock, the **Duke of Marlborough** is an 18th century coaching inn with abundant charm and character. Tenants Derek and Jan Allan, who came here in 1999, have made this one of the most successful dining pubs in the whole county, offering an impressively high standard of hospitality, comfort, service and cuisine.

The menus put a premium on the very best seasonal produce, including locally reared beef and fresh seafood specialities. Sirloin, rib-eye and fillet steaks are served plain or with a choice of sauces, and cod, salmon, halibut, swordfish and marlin are accompanied by a sweet chilli or coriander & lime dressing, lemon butter or tarragon butter. There's always a good choice for vegetarians – brie and roasted peppers in a filo pastry parcel, mushroom ravioli – and a children's menu that treats children as little grown-ups. Sandwiches and classic bar snacks provide quicker or lighter bites. The bar, with dark oak, chintz and a log-burning stove, is a convivial spot for a drink, with Adnams Bitter and Hook Norton Old Hookey on tap and a fine selection of wines to enjoy on their own or to accompany a meal. The beer garden comes into its own in the summer months, either for a drink or a meal.

The Duke of Marlborough is also a superb place for a short break or a longer stay. Four-Star Graded accommodation comprises 13 en suite rooms, all beautifully decorated and furnished, with television, telephone and hospitality tray. Seven of the rooms are on the ground floor, one is fully equipped for disabled guests and there are three Executive rooms. Guests can stay on a Room Only, Bed & Breakfast or Dinner, Bed & Breakfast basis.

The inn takes its name from the great military commander who led his troops to victory over the French in 1704 at Blenheim, on the north bank of the Danube, in the War of the Spanish Succession. A grateful Queen Anne granted him an estate at Woodstcok and £100,000 of public funds to build a palace. The (now rather different) Blenheim Palace is just one of many visitor attractions in the vicinity of the inn. On the southern edge of the Blenheim Estate is the village of Bladon, where in 1965 Sir Winston Churchill, a descendant of the Duke, was buried in a simple grave after a state funeral.

592

Banbury Road, Swerford, nr Chipping
Norton, Oxfordshire OX7 4AP
☎ 01608 683212 Fax: 01608 683105
e-mail: admin@masons-arms.com
🌐 www.masons-arms.com

A short drive from the A361 a few miles
north of Chipping Norton brings visitors to
the village of Swerford and the **Masons
Arms**. This is the domain of Bill and
Charmaine Leadbeater, who took over this
classic stone-built roadside inn in 2003 after
spending a year looking around Oxford and
the Cotswolds for the right place.

In subsequent years they have made this one of the very best destination dining pubs in the
region, and one that has attracted acclaim locally and nationally, including an AA Rosette and a Bib
Gourmand from Michelin. Regulars in the know and first-timers (many of them regulars-to-be)
flock here to enjoy the hospitality and the superb cooking. Bill has been in the catering and
hospitality business for nearly 30 years, mostly as a chef, and his experience with such masters as
Gordon Ramsay and Marco Pierre White, as well as a four-year spell in France, have given him a
thorough understanding of ingredients and a mastery of technique. He seeks the best seasonal
produce, locally sourced as far as possible, for menus that really do cater for all tastes and appetites,
from a light snack to a three-course meal. The meat is rare-breed and fully traceable, the poultry
free-range, the fish delivered daily, and Bill and his team make everything on the premises,
including bread, terrines, pies, pasties, pastries and desserts.

Bill puts a modern, personal touch on both familiar and old-fashioned cuts of meat such as
shin of beef, pig's cheek, belly of pork and ox tongue – witness confit of lamb shoulder with a
mixed bean stew; slow-cooked clod of Shorthorn
beef with potato gnocchi and carrots roasted with
honey & cumin; and home-cured ox tongue with
egg mayonnaise, gherkins and ox jelly. Seafood
lovers are equally well catered for with superb
dishes like brochette of queenie scallops and
chorizo with a salad of mache and papaya,
polenta-fried hake fillet or seared fillet of red
gurnard served with a Caesar salad. Vegetarians
are by no means overlooked, and it would be folly
to leave the table without sampling one of the
delicious desserts.

345 THE SAYE & SELE ARMS

Main Road, Broughton, nr Banbury,
Oxfordshire OX15 5ED
☎ 01295 263348
e-mail: mail@sayeandselearms.co.uk
🌐 www.sayeandselearms.co.uk

A truly warm welcome from chef-proprietor Danny, his wife Liz and their staff awaits visitors to the **Saye & Sele Arms**. Their immaculate pub is located on the B4035 in the village of Broughton, three miles into the countryside from Banbury Cross, and is very handy for visitors to Broughton Castle.

Food is very much the driving force here, while the locals enjoy a fine selection of Cask Marque approved real ales; Adnams is the resident ale, with three ever-changing guests such as London Pride or Brakespear Bitter. The cosy restaurant and bar, with exposed stone walls and an open fire, have beams decked with over 200 colourful water jugs and horse brasses. The extensive menu, based on established and reliable local suppliers, has something for everyone, including those with special dietary needs. Danny's famous 'proper pies' are always on the menu, and other popular choices range from ham, egg

& chips to steaks from prime Oxfordshire herds. And Danny's home-made desserts – souffléd bread & butter pudding, lemon & almond roulade, chocolate cheesecake with dark chocolate ice cream – are definitely not to be missed.

All the wines have been personally tried and tested for customer appeal by the chef! In the summer the mature garden creates an ideal spot for outside dining on the lawn or patio. Food is served every session except Sunday evening. Bookings are advisable.

346 THE WHITE SWAN

Pretty Bush Lane, Wigginton,
Oxfordshire OX15 4LE
☎ 01608 737322

The **White Swan** is a fine old pub in excellent walking country off the A361 between Banbury and Chipping Norton.

Tenants Joe and Joanne take very good care of their patrons, quenching thirsts with Hook Norton ales

and satisfying appetites with an across-the-board selection of hearty home-cooked dishes. The choice includes steak pies, curries, ham & eggs, lasagne, fish & chips, casseroles and Sunday roasts. The bar is closed on Monday lunchtime except Bank Holidays, otherwise it's open lunchtime and evening and all day at the weekend. Food times are 12 to 2.30 and 6 to 9.

Fulbrook Hill, Fulbrook, nr Burford,
Oxfordshire OX18 4BH
☎ 01993 823275
e-mail:
info@thecarpentersarmsfulbrook.co.uk
🌐 www.thecarpentersarmsfulbrook.co.uk

Lovers of fine cuisine come from near and far to the village of Fulbrook and the **Carpenters Arms**. Paul Griffith and his wife Mandy are the leaseholders at this outstanding inn, which lies on the A361 just across the River Windrush from the historic town of Burford. Paul, one-time chef to the Saudi royal family and a number of celebrities, has successfully transferred his talents to the less formal, more intimate atmosphere of a country inn, and the thousands of diners who eat here every week are testimony to his skills.

Paul and Mandy oversaw a stylish, extensive refurbishment of the rooms, which include a cosy bar and a conservatory-style restaurant looking out over the garden. There are seats for 65 inside and for a further 36 in the outside areas, which are floodlit at night and include a lovely floor-lit decked area. A blackboard lists the day's dishes, which are based on the best and freshest of what the local markets and producers can supply. Fish and seafood are among Paul's specialities, with fish landed overnight in Newlyn, Looe and Brixham and rushed to his kitchen. Typical fishy dishes include sea bass fillets with artichokes and asparagus, caramelised scallops served in the shell with garlic butter and lemon sole with brown shrimps, basil and pine nut butter. Meat-eaters are also in for a treat with dishes ranging from pressed rabbit terrine to bacon chops with free-range eggs & fat chips; crispy Old Spot pork belly with black pudding mash, beans and a mustard sauce; rib-eye steak with an exemplary béarnaise sauce and skinny fries; and haunch of venison with dauphinoise potatoes and salsa verde. It's always best to book (and essential at the weekend) to be sure of a table at the time you want.

The pub is closed on Mondays except on Bank Holiday weekends. A swell as being one of the area's top destination restaurants the Carpenters Arms is also a much-loved local, with well-kept Greene king ales on tap in the bar. The local community is lucky indeed to have such a gem of a place on their doorstep, and it's a gem that they are sharing with a growing number of food-lovers from many miles around and with motorists and tourists discovering the delights of Burford and other places.

595

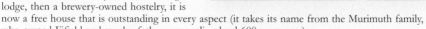

Stow Road, Fifield, nr Stow-on-the-Wold,
Oxfordshire OX7 6HR
☎ 01993 831652
e-mail: billandmo@merrymouthinn.co.uk
🌐 www.merrymouthinn.co.uk

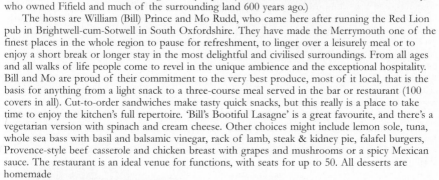

The **Merrymouth Inn** enjoys a glorious
setting in rolling countryside by the A424
four miles north of Burford and five miles
south of Stow-on-the-Wold. It started life in
the 13th century, when it was almost certainly
a travellers' hospice for pilgrims to the nearby
Cistercian Bruern Abbey. Later a hunting
lodge, then a brewery-owned hostelry, it is
now a free house that is outstanding in every aspect (it takes its name from the Murimuth family,
who owned Fifield and much of the surrounding land 600 years ago.)

The hosts are William (Bill) Prince and Mo Rudd, who came here after running the Red Lion
pub in Brightwell-cum-Sotwell in South Oxfordshire. They have made the Merrymouth one of the
finest places in the whole region to pause for refreshment, to linger over a leisurely meal or to
enjoy a short break or longer stay in the most delightful and civilised surroundings. From all ages
and all walks of life people come to revel in the unique ambience and the exceptional hospitality.
Bill and Mo are proud of their commitment to the very best produce, most of it local, that is the
basis for anything from a light snack to a three-course meal served in the bar or restaurant (100
covers in all). Cut-to-order sandwiches make tasty quick snacks, but this really is a place to take
time to enjoy the kitchen's full repertoire. 'Bill's Bootiful Lasagne' is a great favourite, and there's a
vegetarian version with spinach and cream cheese. Other choices might include lemon sole, tuna,
whole sea bass with basil and balsamic vinegar, rack of lamb, steak & kidney pie, falafel burgers,
Provence-style beef casserole and chicken breast with grapes and mushrooms or a spicy Mexican
sauce. The restaurant is an ideal venue for functions, with seats for up to 50. All desserts are
homemade

The accommodation at the inn comprises nine
superbly appointed en suite bedrooms in the converted
stables, with their own entrance and a guarantee of
peace and privacy. A super breakfast includes top-quality
sausages from the local butcher (they also appear in a
red wine gravy on the main menu).

The Merrymouth is the perfect base for exploring a
part of the world that is rich in wonderful scenery and
has some of the prettiest towns and villages in the
whole land.

349 THE GRAINSTORE BREWERY

Station Approach, Oakham,
Rutland LE15 6RE
☎ 01572 770065
e-mail: grainstorebry@aol.com
🌐 www.grainstorebrewery.com

'The Largest Brewery in the Smallest County'

Situated off the A606 next to Oakham railway station, a three-storey Victorian granary has been converted into a traditional tower brewery. In the **Grainstore Brewery**, experienced brewers use the finest-quality ingredients and traditional methods to produce a range of beers that have found wide acclaim and the Royal seal of approval. The finest variety of beers for every season range from Cooking (3.6ABV), a smooth-flavoured golden bitter, and Rutland Panther (3.4ABV), a dark mild whose chocolate and fruity flavours complement its roasted long bitter finish, to Rutland

Beast (5.3ABV – November to March), 'dark earthy brown in colour, its fantastic flavours blend together to produce a mind-blowing great beer, a real drinker's ale', and Winter Nip (7.5ABV – October to March), a smooth and warming true barley wine. All the ingredients are the very best. Malt made from Maris Otter barley is supplied ready made by the maltster, and once in the brewery the first of several stages starts with the mashing of the crushed malt (grist) with water. Raw materials start at the top of the tower and the finished beer comes out at the bottom, all through the force of gravity. All the beers can be

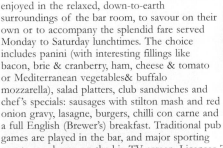

enjoyed in the relaxed, down-to-earth surroundings of the bar room, to savour on their own or to accompany the splendid fare served Monday to Saturday lunchtimes. The choice includes panini (with interesting fillings like bacon, brie & cranberry, ham, cheese & tomato or Mediterranean vegetables & buffalo mozzarella), salad platters, club sandwiches and chef's specials: sausages with stilton mash and red onion gravy, lasagne, burgers, chilli con carne and a full English (Brewer's) breakfast. Traditional pub games are played in the bar, and major sporting events are shown on the big TV screen. Licensee Tony Davis can arrange brewery tours, and the beers can be taken away in 4-pint jugs or 18/36-pint polypins. Outside bars are available for special events.

Tony is also the licensee at the **Old Plough** at nearby Braunston-in-Rutland, offering food, drink and accommodation. Tel: 01572 7221714.

597

350 NICK'S RESTAURANT WITH ROOMS

Lord Nelson House, 11 Market Place,
Oakham, Rutland LE15 6DT
☎ 01572 723199 Fax: 01572 723199
e-mail: simon@nicksrestaurant.co.uk
⊕ www.nicksrestaurant.co.uk

The chief magnet on Oakham for those who appreciate top-notch cooking is **Nick's Restaurant**, part of the Lord Nelson House Hotel on a corner of the market square. Owners Simon and Kasia McEnery have taken the Restaurant with Rooms concept to a new level for the region, offering an unbeatable combination of superb cooking, abundant comfort and impeccable service. Behind the bow-windowed, slate-roofed exterior all is style and elegance, with well-spaced tables in the dining area and a lovely old-fashioned lounge. The daily changing menu presents diners with the pleasant problem of what to order, when everything is so tempting. Head chef Dameon Clarke and his talented team combine technique and innovation at the highest level in complex dishes such as crab and tarragon

risotto with brown crab ice cream; four ways with foie gras (ballotine, tortellini, mousse and roasted); confit of pork belly with poached langoustines, apple and carrot salad, spiced carrot purée and red wine jus; and pan-fried venison with beetroot dauphinoise, smoke garlic, beetroot purée and chocolate jus. Canapés start the meal and delectable desserts round it off setting the seal on a memorable dining experience. Dinner is served Tuesday to Saturday, and lunchtime (Tuesday to Sunday) brings simpler choices such as sandwiches, salads, omelettes and cod in batter. Nick's Restaurant with rooms has recently been awarded 2 AA rosettes for the food and 4 AA stars for the bedrooms.

351 THE VAULTS

Market Place, Uppingham,
Rutland LE15 9QH
☎ 01572 823259
e-mail: kasparskrauja@hotmail.com
⊕ www.rutnet.co.uk/vaults

Small in size but big in interest, the county of Rutland has two delightful market towns, Oakham and Uppingham. The latter, the major community in the south part of the county, has a wealth of visitor attractions, including bookshops and an art gallery. But for many visitors the place to head for first is **The Vaults**, standing on a corner of the market place and virtually attached to the neighbouring church. New landlord Kaspars Krauja, originally from Latvia, is continuing the inn's long tradition of hospitality, and the bar, with its traditional décor, slate floors and oak beams, is a favourite spot for enjoying a chat over a glass of cask ale – perhaps Marstons Pedigree, Greene King IPA or Theakstons Bitter. The bar is open all day, and The Vaults is also an excellent place for a meal. The menus are full of interest, with bar snacks and meals and a full à la carte that mixes classic pub dishes with less familiar options like grille black pudding with stilton, pot-roast game specials and ratatouille-stuffed grille peppers. The place is

particularly busy at lunchtime, when baguettes with generous hot and cold fillings and giant haddock with all the trimmings are among the favourite orders. The Vaults is an ideal base for exploring the area, and the three twin-bedded rooms and a family room all have en suite facilities, TV and beverage tray.

Corve Street, Ludlow,
Shropshire SY8 1DU
☎ 01584 873555

With more than 500 listed buildings and a wealth of history, Ludlow is a great place to explore, and when the walking's done and thirsts and appetites arrive the **Unicorn** is one of the best places to head for. Behind the attractive black-and-white exterior just off the main street, the pub has a spacious bar, a gallery kitchen bar and the oak room for live music on Firdays, pub games or private parties. The Unicorn is equally popular with the towns folk, who go there for the hospitality provided by experienced proprietor Graham Moore, the real ales and the good food produced by his team with a menu built around seasonally available local produce ranging from

nibbles and light bites to traditional farm house fare offering the best

of the regions produce with daily variations. A traditional English breakfast is served from 11.00am to 2.15pm, with the full menu available from 12.oo noon to 2.15pm and 6pm to 9.15pm. The bars are open from 11am to 11:30pm - 7 days a week. Why not call in for a Sunday Roast - a speciality of the House. They look forward to giving you a warm welcome.

353 THE BARON OF BEEF

Bucknell, nr Knighton,
Shropshire SY7 0AH
☎ 01547 530549
e-mail: info@baron-of-beef.co.uk
🌐 www.baron-of-beef.co.uk

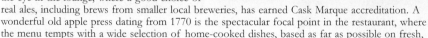

Proprietors Debra and Phil Wright run the **Baron of Beef**, a fine country pub and campsite in the heart of the beautiful Shropshire countryside – it lies just off the A4113 at Bucknell, six miles east of Knighton. Shropshire's best-kept secret (the owners' words!) will not be a secret for long, as patrons come from many miles around to savour the welcome, the hospitality and the excellent food. Interesting bric-a-brac takes the eye in the lounge, where a good choice of real ales, including brews from smaller local breweries, has earned Cask Marque accreditation. A wonderful old apple press dating from 1770 is the spectacular focal point in the restaurant, where the menu tempts with a wide selection of home-cooked dishes, based as far as possible on fresh, seasonal local produce. Typical dishes run from mushrooms in stilton sauce and classic prawn cocktail to crispy-battered cod, salmon with lemon & herb butter, beef & ale pie, sirloin steak, lasagne, supreme of chicken stuffed with garlic mushrooms and wrapped in bacon, and Mexican bean chilli with rice and tortilla chips. All the starters can be ordered in larger snack sizes. Daily specials and a children's menu add to the choice and well-chosen wines accompany the excellent food. A first-floor room is a popular venue for private parties, functions and other special occasions. It can seat up to 70 for banquets, and a buffet menu is also available. There is also a large pretty beer garden and a caravan/camping site adjoining the pub that has electric hook-ups and access to the pub's toilets. The Area of Outstanding Natural Beauty in which the pub stands is wonderful walking country, and the owners have compiled a selection of walks of varying length and difficulty that start from the pub. The area also offers an extensive range of cycling paths, from country lanes to championship-standard mountain bike tracks. Horse riding is also popular, and the large paddock behind the pub can be used to accommodate horses while their owners enjoy a relaxing lunch. Pub hours are 12 to 3 and 6.30 to 11 (open all day Saturday, Sunday and Bank Holidays). Food is served every lunchtime and evening.

Church Street, Bishops Castle,
Shropshire SY9 5AA
☎ 01588 630144

In the ten years since taking over the **Six Bells**, Nev and Sue Richards have built up a large and loyal band of regular patrons. Nev, a jovial, larger-than-life character, is the ale expert, with his own micro-brewery on the premises, while Sue cooks and does just about everything else.

Their handsome mid-17th century inn stands on a corner site at the bottom of Church Street, which runs into the main street of Bishops Castle. A big stone fireplace is the focal point in the bar, where drinkers and diners mingle to create a really relaxed, cheerful atmosphere. It also features bare boards, benches set round plain wooden tables, darts and board games. Next to it is a much smaller but equally inviting and unpretentious lounge bar.

Big Nev's (3.8 abv) is the locals' favourite brew, and others from the micro-brewery include Goldings BB (4.0), Cloud Nine (4.2) and DA (4.6). Sue's menu of home-cooked dishes, which changes every day, runs from hearty sandwiches and baguettes to lunchtime light bites, steaks, quiches, steak & ale and fish pies, and some super puddings.

The Six Bells is friendly, buzzy and generally very busy, particularly at the weekend. It's open Monday evening, both sessions Tuesday to Friday and all day on Saturday. Bishops Castle, which stands amid the great natural beauty of the border country, is well worth taking time to explore. Little remains of the castle built in the 12th century for the Bishops of Hereford, and the most interesting and picturesque of the old buildings still standing is the House on Crutches Museum. When the walking's done in this pleasant little town Nev, Sue and their staff are ready to satisfy thirsts and appetites in their outstandingly friendly old pub.

355 ROCKE COTTAGE TEAROOMS

Clungunford, nr Craven Arms,
Shropshire SY7 0RX
☎ 01588 660631

Owner Karin Clarke invites visitors to **Rocke Cottage Tearooms** to step back in time and enjoy the quintessential experience of taking tea within the old-world charm of an English setting.

Soft music from the 1920's and 1930's creates just the right note, Karin chooses the pick of the local produce in preparing light lunches, chef's specials and homemade cakes served from 10 o'clock to 5pm Wednesday to Sunday and also on Bank Holidays. Typifying the delights on offer are a ploughman's with Shropshire blue, the days homemade quiche,

specials such as creamy trout and lime pate, also our strawberry cream teas and our unique bread and butter pudding. Visitors can take a stroll in the pretty gardens, which has a stream and a tree house. A cosy self-catering cottage is also available.

356 THE ENGINE & TENDER

Broome, nr Craven Arms,
Shropshire SY7 0NT
☎ 01588 660275

Tina Burton and her family are continuing a long tradition of hospitality at the **Engine & Tender**, the social hub of one of the many villages clustered in picturesque countryside around Craven

Arms. Down to earth and with a genuinely welcoming feel, the pub has a homely bar with an open log burner and a rustic look, and two eating areas, one in conservatory style. There's also a separate games room and hosts regular disco, karaoke and theme nights. Bar snacks, a full à l carte and a children's menu provide plenty of eating choice, and senior citizens can take advantage of a special deal for Thursday lunch. Liquid refreshment includes several locally brewed real ales, among them Six Bells

from Bishops Castle and Engine Oil

produced specially for the pub. The Engine & Tender is open Wednesday, Thursday and Friday lunchtimes, Monday to Friday evenings and all day Saturday and Sunday. The pub has another string to its bow in the form of a camping/caravan park with space for up to 18 vans, shower and toilet block and electric hook-ups.

357 THE GREEN DRAGON INN

Little Stretton, nr Church Stretton,
Shropshire SY6 6RE
☎ 01694 722925 mob: 07813 792622

For almost ten years Gary Medlicott and his hardworking staff have been welcoming friends old and new to the **Green Dragon Inn**, which enjoys a lovely scenic setting in a village by the lower slopes of Long Mynd – Little Stretton lies on the B4371 just off the A49 2 miles south of Church Stretton. Behind a black-and-white frontage that's given splashes of spring and summer colour with flowers in tubs and baskets, the inn, which started life in the 17th century as a roadhouse, has a cosy L-shaped bar and adjoining restaurant. Gary is a true professional who really knows his ales, and he regales his patrons with a fine choice of real ales both from major breweries (Bass, Worthington) and smaller local breweries (the Wye Valley Brewery's Buttie Ben). Wholesome home cooking provides a wide variety of

familiar dishes, from

cod, haddock, scampi and fish pie to burgers, chilli con carne, curries, grills, roasts, chicken & ham pie, steak & ale pie, liver & onions and vegetable kiev. Sandwiches and light snacks are added to the menu at lunchtime, and the food is complemented by a dozen well-chosen wines. The ancient hills and moorland that make up Long Mynd are criss-crossed by paths, and walkers know that Gary and his team are ready and waiting to cater for fresh-air thirsts and appetites. Pub hours are 12 to 3.30 every day and 6 to 11 (Sunday 7 to 10.30).

358 THE RED LION

Holyhead Road, Wellington, nr Telford,
Shropshire TF1 2EW
☎ 01952 223937

After 25 years in the computer science industry Julian Goode changed careers and acquired the **Red Lion**. That was in 2003, and with his wife Sarah he has built up a strong following among local residents. Their pretty late-19th century roadside inn a mile from Wellington is immaculate outside and inside, where the neat, compact bar and stylish lounge provide the perfect setting for enjoying a glass of cask ale from local

breweries.

Two beers regularly featured are Quaff from Woods Brewery and Hop Twister from the Salopian Brewery. The inn also serves a choice of classic pub dishes, including a splendid steak & ale pie. The pub stands beside The Wrekin, one of the best-known landmarks in the whole country. Reaching up to some 1,300 feet, it is criss-crossed by a number of public footpaths and attracts thousands of visitors with the walks and the views. It's an ideal place to build up a thirst and appetite that Julian and Sarah are ready and willing to satisfy from noon seven days a week.

359 THE SWAN

Wharfage, Ironbridge, Shropshire
☎ 01952 432306
e-mail: theswanironbridge@hotmail.com
🌐 www.theswanironbridge.com

James Freeston is the all-action licensee of **The Swan**, a superb pub that's equally popular as a place to enjoy a drink, to relax over a meal or to spend a few nights in the well-appointed accommodation. This splendid late-18th century hostelry overlooking the river in Ironbridge, the heart of England's industrial heritage, has a large, comfortable bar and two separate dining areas. Charles Wells's Bombardier and Fuller's London Pride are on tap to quench thirsts, and the wide-ranging menus (last orders 10pm), with everything freshly prepared and cooked on the premises, cater.s for all tastes and appetites. Traditional palates will seek out pub classics such as beer-battered haddock, lasagne, steak & ale pie or a plain grill, while those looking for something a little bit different might choose

something like mini scallops & lime kebabs, seared tuna steak in a light lemon, tomato, garlic & coriander marinade, fillet steak wrapped in Parma ham and topped with blue cheese and chorizo, or honey squash & wild mushroom risotto. The 13 en suite bedrooms provide an ideal base for exploring the ten or so museums that tell the story of the region that gave birth to the English Industrial Revolution.

360 THE ACTON ARMS

Morville, nr Bridgnorth,
Shropshire WV16 4RJ
☎ 01746 714209 Fax: 01746 714102

The **Acton Arms** is located in the village of Morville, on the busy A458 a short drive northwest of Bridgnorth. This is a cosy, friendly country pub with all the traditional virtues – a warm welcome for all the family, friendly hosts and staff, a good choice of food and drink – that has served the local community and visitors to the locality for more than 200 years. Susan Simmons front of house and her husband at the stoves extend outstanding hospitality to all their patrons and they guarantee that nobody leaves thirsty or hungry – or anything less than determined to come back soon! His home-cooked dishes include all-time favourites such as omelettes and chilli con carne, salmon hollandaise and chicken korma, and some less familiar combinations like black pudding with a

mushroom salad and mustard dressing. Real ales from the Banks and Jennings Breweries head the list of drinks, and Banks ales feature in some of the dishes, including the beer in the beer-battered cod and the ale in the steak & ale pie. The new beer garden is a popular spot for families, with a new play area all enclosed and safe for children. Pool and darts are the favourite games at this splendid inn, which is open lunchtime and evening and all day on Saturday and Sunday.

361 THE COALBROOKDALE INN

Wellington Road, Coalbrookdale,
nr Ironbridge, Shropshire TF8 7DX
☎ 01952 433953
🌐 www.coalbrookdaleinn.co.uk

Danny and Dawn Wood make a great team at the **Coalbrookdale Inn**, which stands opposite the Museum of Iron and the historic Darby Furnace. A flight of stone steps leads into this handsome dark-brick hostelry, where the bar features heavy oak, tiled floors, a log fire, an amazing bottle beer collection, local pictures and prints and an assortment of interesting bric-a-brac. It began life in the 1830s, when it provided rest and refreshment for hundreds of iron-workers; it now attracts patrons from all walks of life, who come here to enjoy the unrivalled hospitality, the wonderful friendly atmosphere, the food and the outstanding selection of real ales and other draught and bottled beers.

The ever-changing variety (always at least half-a-dozen real ales) includes nationally known breweries like Adnams and Timothy Taylor and smaller, often local breweries such as Ossett, Salopian, Wye Valley and Slaters. The food, served every session except Sunday evening, covers an equally impressive range. With award-winning Dawn at the stoves, the kitchen produces a fine selection of generously served, good-value snacks and meals. Sandwiches come with interesting fillings like pear & dolcelatte, sweet chilli lamb or bacon, brie & mango, while hot dishes span Thai fish cakes, fiery stuffed jalapeño peppers, saffron-sauced salmon, sea bass with langoustines, pork tenderloin with a caramelised shallot & white wine sauce, and sizzling satay with prawns, chicken, beef or vegetables. The bar menu deals in classics such as burgers, fish & chips, faggots & mash, chicken curry and lasagne. Booking is advisable at the weekend to be sure of getting a table.

The inn also has three luxuriously appointed en suite bedrooms, recently refurbished and updated while preserving the best period elements. They are ideal for an overnight stay or as a base for discovering the many scenic and historic attractions that are almost on the doorstep. The Coalbrookdale Inn is open from 12 to 11 (to 10.30 on Sunday), and food is served from 12 to 5 and 6 to 9 (no food Sunday evening).

Real Ale, Real Food for Real People

362 FENNELLS

8 Market Place, Shifnal,
Shropshire TF11 9AZ
☎ 01952 463020

In a Tudor-style building on Shifnal's Market Place, **Fennells** attracts discerning diners with a seasonally changing menu of modern British and European dishes. Owner Richard Brooks creates a notably relaxed and welcoming ambience, and the quality of cooking ensures that the restaurant is always busy – booking is strongly recommended. His menu invariably makes interesting reading, and results on the plate never disappoint. Starters could include wild boar terrine with port, red onion marmalade and granary toast; grilled marinated Cornish sardines served on a tomato & basil salad; and twice-baked Newport Gold soufflé. Among the mains might be steamed sea bass with seasonal vegetables, a white wine sauce and noisette potatoes; breast of chicken cooked in a spicy

curry coconut sauce with basmati rice; and goat's cheese & wild mushroom tartlet. Room should definitely be left for a delectable sweet such as sticky toffee pudding with ice cream and hot butterscotch sauce or Toblerone chocolate fondue with strawberries, bananas and marshmallows. The excellent food is complemented by a well-chosen, sensibly priced selection of wines. Fennells is open from 7 to 9 Tuesday to Saturday evenings. Lunch by prior arrangement.

363 SHROPSHIRE REGIMENTAL MUSEUM

Castle Street, Shrewsbury, Shropshire
☎ 01743 358516 Fax: 01743 270023
e-mail: shropsrm@zoom.co.uk
ⓦ www.shropshireregimental.co.uk

Housed in Shrewsbury Castle the **Shropshire Regimental Museum** tells the proud story of the four Shropshire Regiments – King's Shropshire Light Infantry, Shropshire Yeomanry, Shropshire Royal Horse Artillery and 4th Battalion King's Shropshire Light Infantry TA. On display are the colours bearing hard-won battle honours, now beautifully restored and hung around the Great Hall, the splendid regimental silver and china, the exotic uniforms and badges, weapons ranging from sword to machine gun, and medals gained in campaigns around the world, including three Victoria Crosses. Copious exhibits trace the history of the regular

regiments as they helped to carve out and then garrison a world-wide empire, and of the territorial regiments at home ready for any crisis that might threaten the nation.

Of particular interest amongst the many treasures on display are the Standard of the Harford Dragoons, seized from the American Army outside Washington in 1814; the Croix de Guerre presented by the French nation to the 4th Territorial Battalion KSLI for their gallantry at the Battle of Bligny in 1918; and the baton of Grand Admiral Doenitz, Hitler's successor, taken in 1945. The last figure visitors see as they leave wears the uniform of the 5th Battalion The Light Infantry – today's volunteers and inheritors of the long tradition of service in Shropshire.

Montford Bridge, nr Shrewsbury,
Shropshire SY4 1EB
☎ 01743 850750
e-mail: mail@thewingfieldarms.com
🌐 www.thewingfieldarms.com

Known for a while as the Old Swan, this outstanding pub of great appeal to the whole family has now reverted to its earlier name of the **Wingfield Arms**. It stands in the picturesque village of Montford Bridge, on the B4380 just off the main A5 3 miles from Shrewsbury. Business partners and good friends Frank and Denise, Stephen and Julie have made enormous improvements at the

pub, parts of which date back some 400 years. Behind the mellow yellow-painted, part creeper-clad exterior the public areas feature beams and some interesting exposed brickwork, setting a welcoming, traditional note, and when the sun shines the terrace and beer garden, with a children's play area, come into their own. Three real ales are always available to quench fresh-air thirsts, and the various menus and daily specials tempt with a wide-ranging selection of home-cooked food. Chef Dai, a well-known personality in the region, has considerably enhanced the pub's reputation as a dining destination, and in the recently refurbished

Riverside Restaurant booking is recommended at peak times, particularly for the very popular Sunday carvery, available from 12 to 3. Everything on his menus is worth trying, and room should definitely be left for one (or more) of his super sweets. The pub can cater for all special occasions, from business lunches to birthdays, weddings and funerals.

The Wingfield Arms has an extensive site for caravans and motor homes (23 pitches), tents and trailer tents, with showers, toilets and hook-ups. This provides a super base for a walking holiday, or for exploring the local villages and the historic

town of Shrewsbury (the bus for Shrewsbury stops outside the pub). It also has fishing rights along a three-quarter-mile stretch of the River Severn, with salmon, roach and barbel among the expected catch. The four partners are always looking for ways to improve this already excellent place: recent developments include the opening of Sizzlers bistro-style family restaurant off the main bar and a coffee station, and plans for the near future include creating rooms for B&B guests.

Grindley Brook, Shropshire SY13 4QJ
☎ 01948 662723
e-mail: carolleonard@btconnect.com

The **Horse & Jockey** is a popular roadhouse built in 1828 and much altered and extended down the years. Big and bold inside and out, it stands on the main A41 Chester road a short drive northwest of Whitchurch. Tenants Carole Leonard and Keith Fahrenholz have transformed the old place since taking over the reins in 2005, breathing new life into the décor and furnishings and building an enviable reputation in the region for the quality of the service and cooking. Exposed brickwork is a feature in the public areas, along with beams and an assortment of pictures and prints, and there are seats outside for enjoying a drink in the sun. Food is an important part of the pub's business and brings many regular patrons from miles around. The menus offer excellent value for money and plenty of variety. Blackboards list the day's dishes, typified by home-made broccoli & stilton soup, spicy chicken bites, mushroom stroganoff and Cumberland sausage in a Yorkshire pudding nest. Room must be kept for the delectable

sweets, which have their own blackboard: lemon meringue pie, sticky toffee pudding, coffee & walnut gateau, caramel charlotte gateau, lemon & lime bavarois, rhubarb & raspberry frangipane, apple & blackberry pie. Children have the option of their own special menu, and senior citizens enjoy a special lunchtime deal during the week. Black Sheep and the Rev James are the regular real ales, backed up by a good choice of other draught and bottle beers, wines, spirits and soft drinks. At the back of the pub is a camping/caravan site. It provides an ideal base for exploring the area or for a walking holiday.

365 THE BURLTON INN ¶ ⊨

Burlton, nr Shrewsbury,
Shropshire SY4 5TB
☎ 01939 270284 Fax: 01939 270647
e-mail: burltoninn@yahoo.co.uk

Diners who appreciate good food, good service and superior accommodation will find both in abundance at the **Burlton Inn**, which has earned a reputation for its hospitality and cuisine that extends far beyond the locality. With racehorse-owner Robert Lester at the helm, this outstanding hostelry, which started life as a roadhouse in 1830, has been refurbished in truly eyecatching style. Pristine outside, with hanging baskets adding splashes of colour to the black-and-white frontage, it's equally immaculate within, with slate floors, bleached wooden beams, open fires in winter, gleaming brasses, sporting prints and plenty of comfortable chairs. Three real ales, including Robinson's Unicorn, are always available in the bar, and the talented team in the kitchen have earned many accolades, including Shropshire Dining Pub of the Year 2007. They pride themselves on

serving the freshest fish in the county, a claim justified when diners tuck into superb dishes like whole lemon sole with a lemon & dill butter, or halibut bourguignon – grilled, served on wilted spinach with a red wine, bacon and mushroom sauce. Meat-eaters are equally well treated with the likes of chicken breast stuffed with herb mascarpone, wrapped in bacon and served on green beans with a watercress sauce and there's always a choice for vegetarians. Business and leisure guests will find peace, quiet and comfort in the six superior en suite bedrooms.

368 THE RED LION ¶ ⊨

Bailey Head, Oswestry,
Shropshire SY11 1PZ
☎ 01691 656077

Frank cooks and Angela does just about everything else at the **Red Lion**, which stands on the busy town square in the centre of Oswestry. They have really transformed the 200-year-old inn both inside and out: repainted throughout, new carpets, new tables and chairs, a newly created Mediterranean garden in addition to the existing beer garden and courtyard area. Local produce, including the superb Black Welsh beef, is the basis of the enticing menu of prepared-to-order dishes, which run from jumbo cod in a crispy batter to chilli con carne, grilled chicken in a bap, sausages with onion gravy and extra-mature rump steak. Daily specials such as braised lamb shank, BBQ pork ribs and seafood pasta add to the choice, and most main courses are

served with super home-made chips. Sandwiches,

toasties and jacket potatoes provide quicker/lighter alternatives at lunchtime. For guests staying in the town (business and leisure visitors are equally welcome) the Red Lion has five comfortably appointed en suite rooms. Paintings on display in the public areas and bedrooms include works by the Llandudno-based artist Marjorie Roberts. Pub hours are 11am to 11pm seven days a week.

Welsh Walls, Oswestry,
Shropshire SY11 1AW
☎ 01691 670970 Fax: 01691 653870
e-mail: info@the-walls.co.uk
🌐 www.the-walls.co.uk

Geoffrey and Kate Bottoms have made **The Walls** the top place on Oswestry for food and entertainment. The setting is the first thing to impress, with spacious dining areas in a former school building at the top of the town. This outstanding venue is richly and traditionally comfortable, roomy and relaxing, a place to have fun as well as enjoying high-quality food and drink.

The chefs use leading local suppliers for the freshest produce to create the very best dishes on the various menus – à la carte, fixed price and less formal paper blackboard menu. Much-loved classics share the menus with elaborate or more exotic dishes such as twice-baked cheese & thyme soufflé, smoked fish terrine, sole with a prawn & butter sauce, seared spicy beef fillet thinly sliced and dressed with garlic, sesame oil and soy sauce, crispy duck and pheasant & beef stroganoff. The Sunday lunch carvery offers a choice of five roasts, with fish and vegetarian alternatives. This superb food is complemented by a magnificent, global wine list that includes the Gosset range of champagnes.

The Walls is the perfect choice for almost any occasion, from dinner for two to family celebrations and corporate get-togethers. It's an ideal choice for wedding celebrations and hosts frequent theme nights and jazz and cabaret nights that often feature big-name performers. If you're thinking of throwing a party for that someone special,. this is definitely the place to look into. With 3 mouth-watering set menus to choose from and a varied list of delicious desserts there is definitely something to suit everyone. The Walls also offers flexible facilities for meetings and conferences: basic audio and visual aids are available on site, and most other audio-visual requirements can be met with a little notice. Friendly, helpful staff put the seal on the pleasure of a visit to this marvellous place, which is open from 10.30am till late Monday to Saturday and lunchtime only (last orders 2.30) on Sunday.

369 THE PENRHOS ARMS

Station Road, Whittington,
Shropshire SY11 4DA
☎ 01691 679977
⊕ www.penrhosarms.co.uk

Starting life in the 17th century as a coaching inn and once owned by Lord Harlech, the **Penrhos Arms** is situated on the A495 Whitchurch road three miles east of Oswestry. When Mark and Amanda Stevenson arrived here in early 2006 they took over a tired pub, and they have made a splendid job of reviving its fortunes and creating a particularly warm and convivial ambience. Banks Original and rotating guests are on tap to quench thirsts in the cosy little bar, and food is served in the restaurant whenever the pub is open. Amanda cooks everything from scratch on menus that span the classics, from scampi, cod and Old English fish pie to chilli, cottage pie (topped with parmesan mash), chicken tikka, liver & onions, lasagne and the popular Penrhos Footer – a

foot-long hot dog. Sandwiches, toasties and jacket potatoes are among the snackier items. Pool, darts and dominoes are played here, and Friday night brings a live music session. The pub has a large lawned beer garden with a play area and an aviary. Beyond the garden is a camping/caravan site with washing/toilet facilities and electric hook-ups. Pub hours are Monday and Tuesday evenings and all day (noon to midnight) Wednesday to Sunday.

370 THE BLACK HORSE INN

Maesbrook, Oswestry,
Shropshire SY10 8QG
☎ 01691 682472 Fax: 01691 683811
e-mail: enquiries@blackhorse-
maesbrook.co.uk
⊕ www.blackhorse-maesbrook.co.uk

The **Black Horse Inn** is a popular pub and restaurant run in fine style by enthusiastic hosts Steve and Ann Parr. It stands a stone's throw from the Welsh border in the village of Maesbrook, on the B4398 between Knockin and Llanymynech. Very much the social hub of the village, it's a great place for locals to meet, and visitors from both sides of the border are also assured of the warmest of welcomes. The old-world interior features wooden beams, sturdy old pub tables and chairs and real fires – just the right ambience for enjoying a chat and a glass or two of cask ale. Ann is a super cook, using mostly local ingredients in excellent dishes such as poached salmon hollandaise, grilled plaice, Old English fish pie, steaks, roast duck with a chunky orange sauce, beef or vegetable lasagne, and chicken or vegetable tikka masala. The lunchtime choice includes old favourites like macaroni cheese and steak & kidney pudding.

371 THE BULL INN

Hardway, Brewham, nr Bruton,
Somerset BA10 0LN
☎ 01749 812200 Fax: 01749 812200
e-mail: martinwsmith007@hotmail.co.uk
🌐 www.thebullinnbrewham.co.uk

The **Bull** is a white-painted traditional country inn located off the B3081 Bruton to Wincanton road at the sign for Stourhead and King Alfred's Tower. The hamlet of Hardway lies in the parish of Brewham, which is why the pub is sometimes called the Bull Inn at Brewham. It first saw the light of day in 1650, when it was established as a point for horses and passengers to draw breath before tackling the steep climb up King Settle Hill (past King Alfred's Tower) and beyond. There are few more popular places for locals to meet, but the reputation that the Bull has gained has spread throughout the Southwest – and further afield.

Experienced hosts Ann and Martin Smith escaped from the bustle of London in search of a quieter, less hectic life, but they certainly work hard for their patrons – and many of those have themselves travelled from London with just the same idea in mind. There's plenty of space in

the bar to enjoy a drink – two or three real ales are headed by Butcombe Bitter – and there are more tables and chairs in the lovely lawned garden and seats and a barbecue in the rose garden across the road.

Three chefs are kept busy preparing and cooking an exciting range of dishes served in the 36-cover restaurant, the bar or the garden every lunchtime and evening (the pub is closed on Sunday evenings in winter). Fresh local produce is to the fore, much of it very local indeed, coming from Brewham, Charlton Musgrave, Godminster and Redlynch. Showing the variety are pork and herb terrine; fillet of black bream with a chilli and ginger dressing; kangaroo, buffalo, beef and gammon steaks; pan-fried scallops with crispy bacon; steak & mushroom pie; blue crab & smoked salmon timbale; haddock & leek fishcakes; game pie (pigeon and pheasant); chicken & cashew nut curry; beer-battered fish & chips; chicken & chorizo pasta and bacon, brie & red onion tartlet. And it would be a grave error to leave the table without sampling one of Ann's delectable desserts. Special occasion evenings celebrate red-letter days such as St George's Day, and in summer live music events are held in the garden.

Ilton, nr Ilminster, Somerset TA19 9EY
☎ 01460 52164
e-mail: eryl-ellis@hotmail.com

The **Wyndham Arms** is a free house situated in the village of Ilton, off the A303 or A358 a short drive north of Ilminster. The oldest parts of the premises date back as far as the 15th century, and subsequent additions and alterations have not detracted at all from the traditional appeal. With a cosy fire in winter in the oak-beamed bar and a spacious beer garden for sunny days and balmy evenings, it's a delightful place to visit at any time of the year.

The hospitality extended by the owners Eryl and Theresa Ellis and their son Thomas is second to none, making the Wyndham Arms the sort of pub that once found will become a place to return to at every opportunity. They came here in the spring of 2007, and by their hard work and enthusiasm they have brought the locals back on board and, as the good news spreads, have created a growing following from outside the area. Butcombe Bitter is the resident real ale served in the bar, along with regularly changing guest ales from local breweries, real ciders and a full range of other drinks.

All aspects of the product that is the Wyndham Arms are outstanding and that naturally includes the food. Seeking out the very best seasonal local produce, the talented team in the

kitchen produce a splendid variety of dishes that cater for a wide spectrum of tastes and appetites. For those with not much time to spare a sandwich, a baguette or a jacket potato will provide a tasty, satisfying snack, but a much better plan is to allow time to relax over a top-class meal. Macaroni cheese is a dish seen all too rarely on menus, but the one they do here is excellent. Other choices run from omelettes and burgers to chilli con carne, cottage pie, moussaka, rump or sirloin steak, braised lamb shank and always some super seafood dishes – maybe a creamy fish & leek pie or sea bass fillet cooked simply with lemon and garlic to bring out the fine flavour. For Sunday lunch it's roasts only, and booking is advisable for this meal and for dinner on Friday and Saturday. Food is served from 12 to 2 and 6.30 to 9 (not Tuesday lunch or Sunday evening). The inn is closed at lunchtime on Tuesday but is otherwise open for drinks every lunchtime and evening, with extended hours in the summer season. Families with children are always made welcome, and the inn has ample off-road parking.

Silver Street, South Petherton,
Somerset TA13 5AN
☎ 01460 240382
e-mail: stevewheatsheaf@btopenworld.com
🌐 www.thewheatsheafontheweb.co.uk

The **Wheatsheaf** is the ideal spot to break a journey on the A303, and once found it's the sort of place people want to return to time and time again. This down-to-earth little sandstone pub stands in the village of South Petherton, just seconds from that busy main road, between Ilminster and Ilchester.

Since 1995 the Wheatsheaf has been in the care of Steve Wainwright, who has made it one of the most sociable and likable pubs in the whole region. It's definitely the perfect place to bring an appetite, and the hardworking professional chef and his assistants produce a wide variety of dishes that patrons can enjoy midday right through to 9 o'clock every day of the week. Pub classics like scampi, cod, chilli con carne and pies always go down a treat, and from the grill come steaks – 8oz or 16oz rump with all the trimmings, gammon, burgers and chicken with a barbecue sauce. The specials board lists daily offerings such as lamb rogan josh or Irish stew. Wednesday is steak & a pint evening, Sunday brings traditional roasts, and there's always a good choice for vegetarians with the likes of mushroom carbonara or red onion & goat's cheese tart. Baguettes, burgers and jacket potatoes cater for smaller appetites or those with less time to spare, and many of the dishes can be ordered to take away.

The bar is a really chatty, sociable place to enjoy a drink, and there are also outside options: picnic benches are set out at the front and to the rear is an enclosed beer garden where Steve has built a superb sheltered wooden den for drinking, dining and darts. The Wheatsheaf is a pub for all the family, and toys and games area available to keep the little ones happy while their parents are enjoying Steve's outstanding hospitality. No pub in the area – maybe in the county, maybe even in the West Country – has a more thriving sporting side.

The Wheatsheaf fields football, cricket, darts, pool and skittles teams and holds regular pool, darts and skittles knock-out competitions. It also has a motorcycle club, a hot rod club, a traditional music club, a carnival club, a Friday club and a breakfast club.....all of which means that whatever the time, whatever the season, there's always something interesting going on at this terrific little pub.

Kingsbury Episcopi, Somerest TA12 6AT
☎ 01935 823239
🌐 www.wyndhamarms.com

The **Wyndham Arms**, which started life as a farmhouse in the 16th century, is a traditional country pub in the village of Kingsbury Episcopi, a short drive from Martock off the A303 or B3168 – it's also accessible from the A372 and the B3165. When it became a pub it took its name from the then Lord of the manor and the sign still bears his crest and motto 'Au Bon Droit'. Proprietor Rob Rigby, a fellow of the British Institute of Innkeeping, has a wealth of experience in the licensed trade, and this is the fifth pub that he has run.

Behind the handsome stone frontage adorned with shrubs, plants and creeper, flagstones and a log fire set the traditional tone in the bar, while outside the pub has a large beer garden and a superb covered area which Rob has created. This latest feature has attracted local and national coverage and Rob is rightly proud of this latest addition to the pub's amenities, which confirms its status as one of the most widely recommended in the region for hospitality and amenity as well as well-kept ales and excellent food. The raw materials that go into the kitchen are sourced from the area as far as possible, including absolutely outstanding locally raised and butchered rump and ribeye steaks that are always a popular order here. Other British classics include home-baked ham, steak & ale pie, Somerset faggots, 8oz burgers with Somerset cheddar, lasagne and salmon with a hollandaise sauce. The choice continues with such temptations as creamy stilton mushrooms, Somerset brie wedges wrapped in Serrano ham, caramelised

duck breast with honey & five-spice, venison steak and red Thai vegetable curry. The fishy specials board offers further delights in the shape of whitebait, trout, cod, plaice or sautéed grey mullet with lemon thyme. Lunch brings the lighter options of sandwiches, baguettes and jacket potatoes, with traditional roast and vegetarian options on Sunday.

The bar is open lunchtime and evening and all day on Saturday and Sunday and food is served from 12 to 2 and 7 to 9 (Sunday 12 to 4). Booking is always advisable. There's lots for the visitor to see in the area, including the Gertrude Jekyll garden at Barrington Court and the 'Home of English Cottage Gardening' at Lambrook Manor. But for anyone who admires the traditional qualities of the English country inn the Wyndham Arms must be at the top of the list.

375 THE LAMB & LION

The Green, Hambridge,
Somerset TA10 0AT
☎ 01460 281355

The **Lamb & Lion** is a superb country inn in a picturesque location at Hambridge, on the B3168 that runs between the A378 (Curry Rivel) and the busy A303 near Ilminster. With parts dating back as far as the 16th century, it's delightfully traditional, with warming winter fires, oak beams and a really friendly ambience created by tenants Kevin and Tracie Biswell. And when the sun shines the picnic benches in the beer garden or on the village green come into their own.

The bar, with two rotating guest ales on tap and a good selection of other quality ales, lagers and wines, is open lunchtime and evening, all day at the weekend and all day every day from Easter to the end of the summer. In the cosy restaurant an excellent range of home-style cooking is served from 11 to 3 and 6 to

9.30. The choice spans sandwiches, baguettes and baked potatoes, snacks like burgers, ham, egg & chips, nachos (starter or main), cottage pie, chilli con carne, chicken & ham pie, steaks and, for vegetarians, broccoli & cauliflower cheese, mushroom & ale pie and Mediterranean vegetable Wellington. Desserts include home-made apple or rhubarb crumble.

Booking is advisable on Friday and Saturday evenings and for the traditional Sunday roasts

376 THE STRODE ARMS

West Cranmore, nr Shepton Mallet,
Somerset BA4 4QJ
☎ 01749 880450
e-mail:
thestrodearmscranmore@hotmail.co.uk
🖥 www.fromeonline.co.uk/thestrodearms

Opposite the village pond and close to the headquarters station of the steam-hauled East Somerset Railway, the **Strode Arms** is a charming, picturesque inn with an abundance of period character. Tenants Tim and Ann-Marie Gould have built up an enviable reputation for a combination of warm

hospitality, excellent food and wines at this lovely old Wadsworth inn. Country furnishings in the linked rooms of this former farmhouse provide a comfortable ambience for enjoying a drink, and when the sun shines the tables and chairs on the front terrace and back garden really come into their own. Wadsworth's 6X, Henry's IPA and Bishops Tipple are the usual resident cask ales, and the bar and restaurant menus offer an unusually varied choice for lunchers and

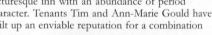

diners. A typical bar menu runs from baguettes and ploughman's to pork & leek sausages, Wiltshire ham with eggs & fries, heart pies and tandoori chicken served with saffron mash and a spiced

onion relish. The restaurant menu is equally diverse, as shown by Thai-style crab balls, oriental pan-fried salmon, pasta, steaks, guinea fowl with a creamy herb sauce and venison medallions with sun-dried tomato pesto, oregano mash and a chianti sauce. The pub is open for food and drink every session except Sunday lunchtime.

Prestleigh, nr Shepton Mallet,
Somerset BA4 4NL
☎ 01749 830179
e-mail: theinn@prestleigh.com
🌐 www.prestleighinn.co.uk

Standing by the A37 a short drive south of Shepton Mallet, the **Prestleigh Inn** overlooks the open spaces of the Bath & Wells Showground. It's a super country inn and much more: it's also a popular destination restaurant and a comfortable, practical Bed & Breakfast base.

The vision of the Walker family – Paul, Linda and their son Simon – was to create a fine pub for Prestleigh and the surrounding community as well as visitors and exhibitors at the Mid-Somerset Show, the Royal Bath & Wells Show and other events held at various times throughout the year at this venue a stone's throw from the inn. Paul has been in the licensed/catering trade for 35 years and he has put that experience to excellent use here. The family have certainly succeeded in their aims, and the transformation began with an extensive refurbishment programme that included the bar, the restaurant and the bedrooms.

The bar is open from 11 in the morning to 11 in the evening (to midnight Friday and Saturday) for drinks, which include two rotating cask ales, almost always from local breweries. Food is also available throughout the day, and in the 42-cover beamed dining area with modern pine furniture all the food is locally sourced, freshly prepared and where possible cooked to order. A popular starter for two to share is a generous combo of onion rings, potato chunks, garlic bread, breaded mushrooms and spicy chicken wings, served with three dips and a salad garnish. Classic main courses run from scampi, beer-battered cod and home-made fish pie to home-made lasagne (meat or vegetable), gammon and rump steaks, liver & bacon and a perky chicken & bacon salad bowl. The choice is broadened by daily specials such as seafood lasagne, baked trout fillet and chicken chasseur. Breakfast is served in the restaurant from 7 to 10.30, and the inn can offer a range of buffets to suit different occasions and different dietary requirements.

The accommodation at Prestleigh comprises five rooms in a variety of sizes, three with en suite facilities. Besides the agricultural shows (the 2008 date for the Mid-Somerset Show is Sunday 17th August) the area has plenty to offer the visitor, including the pleasant little town of Shepton Mallet, the vineyard at Pilton Manor, two superb old tithe barns and the steam-hauled East Somerset Railway base at Cranmore Station.

378 THE PILGRIMS AT LOVINGTON ‖ ⊨

Lovington, Somerset BA7 7PT
☎ 01963 240600
e-mail: jools@thepilgrimsatlovington.co.uk
🌐 www.thepilgrimsatlovington.co.uk

'The Pub That Thinks It's a Restaurant – With Rooms'

That's how hosts Sally and Jools Mitchinson describe the **Pilgrims at Lovington**, their outstanding hostelry off the B3153 a short drive east of the A37 (leave at Lydford on Fosse). Their guiding principle is that their patrons are here to enjoy themselves, an approach that has made their pub one of the most popular in the whole region. Secluded and civilised, it has a really delightful bar with flagstones, a mix of furniture, prints, books and china. It provides an unbeatable

ambience in which to meet or make friends over a chat and a glass of real ale – one of the choices might be Champflower Ale brewed in a neighbouring village.

A meal here is an occasion to savour, a delight from beginning to end. The seasonally changing menus proposed by Jools and his talented team make mouthwatering reading, and results on the plate never disappoint. Lovers of classic pub food could go for the fish cakes, beer-battered cod, sausages and mash or a succulent steak, with some luscious ice cream to finish. But there's much, more on offer, from smoked eel with bacon, and fish soup ('the soup that thinks it's a stew') to duck leg confit served on a bed of lentils, braised blade of beef and whole grilled lemon sole. The menu gives due credit to the top local suppliers and producers – the meat from local farms, the wet fish direct from Bridport, the smoked products from Brown & Forrest, the locally grown vegetables and salads, the bread made from locally milled organic flour. The food is served from 12 to 3 (last orders 2) Wednesday to Sunday and from 7 to 11 (last orders 9) Tuesday to Sunday. The table is guaranteed for the evening, and bookings are taken for half-hourly intervals. They take a very grown-up approach to young diners, offering not a specials kids' menu but smaller portions of most main courses at a smaller price for smaller appetites – an approach that they are sure better engenders a love and appreciation of good food in children.

The accommodation at the Pilgrims achieves the same high standards as every other aspect of this truly outstanding place. Each of the five king-size guest rooms has its own individual charm and all have superb bathrooms en suite. One room is adapted for disabled guests.

379 THE TRAVELLERS REST

Stone, East Pennard, Shepton Mallet,
Somerset BA4 6RY
☎ 01749 860069
e-mail: inewman@btinternet.com

The **Travellers Rest** is a traditional country pub standing in the village of Stone, which lies by the A37 (Fosse Way) a few miles south of Shepton Mallet. Built in 1790 as a coaching inn, it has excellent tenants in Ian and Sally Newman, whose warmth and enthusiasm are winning a loyal local following and also appeals to a growing number of visitors to the area. They both cook, and their menu of pub classics includes faggots in a succulent onion gravy, cauliflower cheese, steak & kidney pudding and a warming winter stew with dumplings. Baguettes, jacket potatoes and salads provide lighter/quicker alternatives. The food is complemented by a short, well-chosen list of wines available by bottle or glass. Families with children are very welcome, and the inn has a very pleasant

garden and ample car parking space. For guests

looking for somewhere to stay in the area this aptly named pub has two en suite rooms offering excellent Bed & Breakfast accommodation. It's a very convenient base for visitors and exhibitors at the wide variety of shows held at the Bath & West Showground, and for tourists exploring the local scenic and historic attractions.

380 THE WHITE HART INN

Corfe, nr Taunton, Somerset TA3 7BU
☎ 01823 421388

The **White Hart** is a cosy, likable village inn situated in Corfe, on the B3170 south of Taunton. Formerly a farm, with the oldest parts dating back to the 17th century, it has a comfortable lounge and a well-stocked bar serving local real ales, and a good range of other draught and bottled beers, lagers, wines and spirits. The tenants are Sue and Kev Pearson, and Sue's cooking has earned the

White Hart a loyal following among the local community and the surrounding area. The bar menu offers soup, jacket potatoes, ploughman's lunches and an interesting selection of baguettes – hot,

with chicken, bacon & mushrooms; cold, with brie, grapes and cranberry sauce. The restaurant menu tempts with steaks, battered cod, steak, kidney & ale pie, lamb shank and five-bean chilli. Home-made desserts round off a meal in style. Sunday lunch brings traditional roasts with several other options. The pub is closed Tuesday lunchtime, otherwise open lunchtime and evening and all day on Saturday. Food times are 12 to 2 and 7 to 9 every day except Tuesday. It's best to book at the weekend. Families with children (and their dogs) are very welcome, and the inn has a capacious patrons' car park.

381 THE WHITE HORSE INN

Regent Street, Bradford-on-Tone,
nr Taunton, Somerset TA4 1HF
☎ 01823 461239
e-mail: donnamccann31@btinternet.com
🌐 www.whitehorseinnbradford.co.uk

The **White Horse** is a handsome old inn in a quiet village, a magnet for lovers of good food and drink and the cherished qualities of the traditional English country pub. Locals, walkers, motorists and tourists meet in the bar to enjoy a drink – Cotleigh Tawny and

Sharp's Doom Bar are the resident real ales, always kept in tip-top condition that has earned CAMRA accreditation. Donna and Philip McCann have also built up a strong following for the food that's prepared and cooked to order every lunchtime and evening. Dishes based on fish fresh from Brixham are always popular, and for meat-eaters the half-shoulder of Cornish lamb with an orange, cranberry and port jus is a signature dish. The wide-ranging printed menus are supplemented by a daily changing list of chalkboard specials such as Cajun spiced chicken sizzler served with a timbale of Basmati rice, medallions of Somerset pork with a

wholegrain mustard and honey sauce, or fillet of sea bass served with parsley mash and a creamy mushroom sauce. Pub classics are the lunchtime favourites, and a two-course special lunch is available Monday to Saturday. The White Horse has a function room, a skittle alley, a pétanque pitch and outside seating on the lawn and on a sheltered paved patio. Bradford-on-Tone lies just north of the A38 between Taunton and Wellington and only five minutes from J26 of the M5.

382 THE FARMERS ARMS

Combe Florey, nr Taunton,
Somerset TA4 3HZ
☎ 01823 432267
e-mail: patvincent@hotmail.co.uk
🌐 www.farmersarmsatcombeflorey.co.uk

Margaret and Pat are the mother-and-daughter team who own and run the **Farmers Arms**, a marvellous thatched 16th century inn that oozes charm and character. It lies on the A358 seven miles above Taunton, on the edge of the Quantocks alongside the

privately-owned West Somerset Railway. There are no gaming machines, no pool table and no juke box in the bar – just winter log fires and good conversation lubricated by a glass of real ale: Exmoor Ale and Gold, HSD and Cotleigh Tawny are the regular brews. The owners' award-winning chef makes fine use of local produce in his good, honest, cooked-to-order dishes. The meat and vegetables are supplied by local family-run businesses in Taunton and Bishops Lydeard. Typical choices on his always interesting

menus include smoked chicken & cranberry parcels; salmon steak

baked with a crust of sun-dried tomatoes, olives and parmesan cheese; crispy roast duck with a plum & ginger sauce; and chargrilled steaks with all the traditional accompaniments. The bar is open all day, and food is served from midday to 2.30 and from 7 to 9, and booking is recommended on Friday and Saturday evenings and Sunday lunchtime. Families with children are welcome, and the inn accepts the major credit cards

383 THE BOAT & ANCHOR

Huntworth, nr Bridgwater,
Somerset TA7 0AQ
☎ 01278 662473 Fax: 01278 662542
🌐 www.infoattheboatandanchor.co.uk

The **Boat & Anchor** is a traditional West Country hostelry in a beautiful location alongside the picturesque Taunton-Bridgwater Canal. It's very much at the social heart of the little village of Huntworth, just seconds from J24 of the M5.

The setting and the views are a real delight, and the inn – recently refurbished and extended – is an ideal spot to pause for refreshment on a journey to or from Devon and Cornwall. The welcome from owner Michael

Rodosthenous and his staff is invariably warm and friendly, and the bar is a convivial spot for enjoying a chat and a drink – real ales (Butcombe Bitter is the regular) are among a fine range of draught and bottle beers, lagers, wines, spirits and soft drinks served lunchtime and evening and all day in the summer months. The dishes listed on the big chalkboard offer an excellent choice for carnivores, meat-eaters and vegetarians, with baguettes, ploughman's platters and jacket potatoes for light lunchtime choices and steaks, seafood specials and sizzling dishes among the favourites on the main list.

The Boat & Anchor also provides a very pleasant base for discovering all the scenic, historic and sporting attractions that Somerset has to offer. The 11 en suite bedrooms are available throughout the year. The inn has a self-contained function suite with a private bar and the staff can cater for a wide variety of special occasions.

The Olive Mill (formerly The Toby - see below) at nearby Chilton Polden is in the same ownership.

384 THE OLIVE MILL

Chilton Polden, nr Bridgewater
Somerset TA7 9AH
☎ 01278 722202

The **Olive Mill** (formerly called The Toby) is a purpose-built modern pub with a restaurant and road house-style accommodation. It stands by the A39 Glastonbury road east of Bridgwater, five miles from J25 of the M5. The look is smartly contemporary, the amenities state-of-the-art, the service efficient and friendly. Food is a major part of the business, with the talented chefs in friendly rivalry with their equally gifted counterparts at the Boat & Anchor. The style here is Mediterranean, with several Greek-inspired dishes among the first-rate choice. The location is delightful, commanding lovely views to the rear of the rolling Somerset countryside. The Olive Mill also offers accommodation. The seven spotless en suite bedrooms combine superb comfort with practicality; one of the rooms is on the ground floor, specially adapted for disabled guests, and the bar and restaurant are also accessible to wheelchair users.

385 THE KNOWLE INN

Bath Road, Bawdrip, nr Bridgwater,
Somerset TA7 8PN
☎ 01278 683330
e-mail: peter@matthews3.wanadoo.co.uk
🌐 www.knowleinn.co.uk

On the A39 east of Bridgwater and a short drive from J23 of the M5 towards Glastonbury, the **Knowle Inn** has excellent hosts in Peter Matthews, front of house, and his wife Christina, the queen of the kitchens. The inn started life in the 16th century, and the

tenants have put their personal stamp on the place, enhancing the appeal of the quaint public bar, the side lounge and the elegant restaurant. One of the most striking features is a big copper-topped hearth on a huge stone wall topped with an ancient brass-adorned beam. Patrons come from a wide catchment area to enjoy the hospitality, the well-kept ales and above all the food. The bar is open all day for drinks, which include Otter Ale and two other locally brewed real ales that have earned a Cask Marque accreditation. Christina's cooking

can be enjoyed from 11 to 3 and 6 to 9 (no food winter Sunday evenings). Everything is well worth trying, but for many diners the fish is the star of the show, typically including gurnard, John Dory, sea bass, cod and tiger prawns, all from a top supplier in Plymouth. Steak & ale pie, mutton pie and curries are other popular dishes, and sandwiches and jacket potatoes provide lighter/quicker options. The hosts offer a takeaway service for most dishes. The Knowle Inn has a terrace and a sheltered patio that's a great place to sup in the summer shade and a retreat for smokers. Families are welcome, and the pub accepts the major credit cards.

Wrantage, nr Taunton, Somerset TA3 6DF
☎ 01823 480210
e-mail: info@thecanalinn.net
🌐 www.thecanalinn.net

If there was ever a canal here, there's no sign of it now, but the **Canal Inn** is easy to spot in the village of Wrantage. The white-painted building, which dates back to the 17th century, lies on the A378 Langport road close to the junction with the A358 a few miles east of Taunton and only four miles from J25 of the M5. When Sandi and Nigel Brooks took over this traditional free house in September 2007 it was their first venture together into the licensed trade, but they have lost no time in turning the old place round; they have restored it to its rightful place as the hub of the local community and are attracting new faces from the surrounding area and beyond.

Good food, good beer and a good, friendly atmosphere make a winning combination, and the hosts have a genuinely warm greeting for all who pass through the door into the flagstoned bar – villagers, families with their children and their dogs, bikers, motorists and holidaymakers. Otter Ale and St Austell Tribute are the resident real ales, accompanied by a regularly changing guest, and the

first weekend in July sees the pub's annual Beer Festival when up to 20 real ales and real ciders can be sampled. The bar also stocks a good variety of Belgian beers. The hosts have the services of a talented chef who sets great store by locally sourced or locally produced raw materials. The 'pub grub' menu offers a good variety of English favourites to cater for appetites large and small. Baguettes and jacket potatoes make satisfying snacks, while main courses include beef lasagne, cottage pie and steak & ale pie. Seafood fans might go for beer-battered cod, scampi, Thai prawns with a sweet chilli dip or smoked haddock & leek fishcakes. Game pie is an eagerly awaited seasonal special, and for the truly ravenous the mighty 28oz mixed grill consists of steak, pork chop, lamb chop, gammon, sausage, kidney, liver, mushrooms, onion rings, egg and chips.

The pub is open for drinks every lunchtime and evening and all day Saturday and Sunday, also all day Friday and Bank Holidays in summer. Booking is recommended at the weekend. The Canal Inn has a lawned beer garden with picnic benches and an area where children can romp. The pub has ample off-road parking and a site for caravans and camping is available with notice – ring for details.

387 THE ANCHOR INN

Exebridge, Dulverton,
Somerset TA22 9AZ
☎ 01398 323433 Fax: 01398 324621
e-mail: exmooranchorinn@hotmail.co.uk
⊕ www.exmooranchorinn.co.uk

The **Anchor** is a picturesque inn that enjoys a scenic setting in the village of Exebridge, alongside the River Exe, which marks the border between Somerset and Devon. The country border signs are outside the inn, which stands on the B3222 a short drive south of Dulverton. The promise of the immaculate cream-painted exterior is amply fulfilled inside, where the bar features a wealth of panelling.

John and Roberta, who took over the lease in May 2007, have been in the licensed trade for more than 30 years, and with their experienced chef Dan – recent winner of a Taste of the West Award – they have made this a great favourite with the local community and with the many walkers, motorists and holidaymakers who pass this way. The bar is open all day for drinks, which include Wadworth's 6X, Greene King IPA and a regularly changing guest real ale. Dan seeks out

the very best West Country produce for his always interesting menus, served from midday to 3 and from 6 to 9. Starters might include smoked trout pâté, marinated king prawns with chilli and coriander, and chicken & wild mushroom terrine. Typical main courses run from scampi and sea bass with lemon butter to honey-roast ham with egg & chips, sautéed liver with smoked bacon and steak, ale & mushroom pie. One of the most popular dishes of the day is based on the excellent local Staple Cross lamb. Lunchtime also brings baguettes, ciabattas and jacket potatoes, spicy Cajun chicken wraps and a big breakfast, and the dinner menu also includes chargrilled steaks. Children have a 'proper' menu of lasagne, mixed grill and baked-to-order pizzas. Sunday lunch sees carvery roasts with vegetarian and salad alternatives. This super inn is not just a fine destination restaurant, it's also a great place to drop anchor when touring this lovely part of the world.

Six upstairs bedrooms – five doubles and a family room – are available all year for Bed & Breakfast guests. It's a popular place for a fishing holiday, as the inn has rights on a threequarters of a mile stretch of the Exe. Exebridge is at the very southern tip of Exmoor National Park in great walking country. The headquarters of the main visitor centre of the Park are located in the pretty little town of Dulverton, a short drive north.

388 THE GREYHOUND INN

Burston, nr Sandon, Stafford,
Staffordshire ST18 0DR
☎ 01889 508263

Generations of the Jordan family have run the **Greyhound Inn** for more than 50 years, and the current hosts are keeping it at the top of the tree for good ales, good food and excellent service. This wonderful, traditional country inn stands in the beautiful village of Burston, just yards off the A51 southeast of Stone, and its reputation brings patrons from all over Staffordshire, Cheshire and beyond.
A fine selection of beers, lagers, wines, spirits, liqueurs and soft drinks is served every session and all day on Sunday, and the quality cuisine is available from 11.30 to 2.30 and from 6 to 10 Monday to Saturday and from 12 to 10 on Sunday. The food choice is truly impressive, from English favourites (chicken liver pâté, prawn cocktail, beer-battered haddock, salads, roasts, steak & ale

pie, chargrilled steaks) to chicken tikka masala, moussaka and broccoli & brie rösti. To finish, perhaps

sherry trifle, treacle sponge or a homley apple pie. Children are very welcome, and the pub has a pleasant beer garden. A caravan site at the back has space for up to five vans. In the neighbouring village of Sandon stands historic Sandon Hall, with a fascinating little museum and 400 acres of lovely parkland.

389 THE STAR INN

Copmere End, Eccleshall,
Staffordshire ST21 6EW
☎ 01785 850279
⊕ www.thestarinn-eccleshall.co.uk

The **Star Inn** is the beating heart of the tiny, picturesque village of Copmere End, located a sho3rt drive west of Eccleshall, off the A519 or B5026. Experienced licensees Elaine and Simon Wood took over in the summer of 2007 and have already boosted its reputation as a fine place to drink and dine. Four real ales are on tap to sip in the bar or out in the superb grounds, which include a beautiful lake that's hidden when the trees and bushes are in bloom. The printed menu and specials board propose an excellent selection of home-cooked classic English pub food: typical main courses are gammon (with the time-honoured accompaniment of a fried or pineapple), poached salmon hollandaise, Cumberland

sausages, spaghetti Bolognese, beef & Guinness pie and sirloin steak garnished with tomatoes and onion rings. This top-quality food is served every session except Sunday evening and Monday. The pub is closed Sunday evenings in winter, otherwise open lunchtime and evening and all day Saturday and Sunday in the summer. Copmere End is a short drive from Eccleshall, where the Castle is typical of the best features of the William & Mary period. Both the house and the gardens are well worth a visit.

625

Macclesfield Road, Rushton Spencer,
Cheshire SK11 0SE
☎ 01260 226219
e-mail: dining@theroyaloakrushton.co.uk
🌐 www.theroyaloakrushton.com

The **Royal Oak** is a splendid pub in the village of Rushton Spencer, by the A523 Leek-Macclesfield road on the Staffordshire border. It started life in the early 18th century as a coaching inn with stables, but the years took their toll and when Colin and Donna took over the reins in 2006 they found it in urgent need of an injection of enthusiasm, expertise and money. Together, they've given the old place a new lease of life and were careful to ensure that the changes they oversaw were in keeping with the delightful rural surroundings. Open lunchtime and evening and all day on Saturday and Sunday, it keeps up to four real ales, always in tip-top condition – regular brews include Banks's Bitter and Marston's Pedigree. The tenants are lucky to have the services of an excellent chef who produces a fine selection of dishes served from 11.30 to 2.30 and from 6.30 to 9.30 (all day at the weekend). The menu is extensive, offering best quality home-cooked food with something for everyone. The choice is updated seasonally, but a good selection of fish dishes, vegetarian option and grills, as well as traditional favorites such as freshly battered cod are always available. One of the more popular choices is the variety of homemade sausages, with flavours ranging from the classic Lincolnshire, to the more unusual 'Spicy Thai' style. A traditional Sunday lunch menu is

available alongside the offerings, and on Thursday evenings a selection of curries dominate the specials boards. If you have a smaller appetite then sandwiches, jacket potatoes and bar snacks are served until 6:00pm. Special promotions run Monday - Wednesday evenings and take away fish and chips are available during food service times. You can enjoy your visit in the relaxed comfort of the oak-floored lounge area, in the fireside luxury offered by the dining room, or even in the covered heated patio area. Booking is advisable at peak times, especially on the last Thursday of the month when the fun quiz night guarantees a full house. Log on to the website for up to date menus and promotions.

391 THE CROSS INN

Caulden Lowe, nr Waterhouses, Leek,
Staffordshire ST10 3EX
☎ 01538 308338 Fax: 01538 308338

Well-kept ales, super food, quality accommodation, a caravan and camping park – all this and more brings the crowds to the **Cross Inn**, which stands in delightful rural surroundings by the main A52 between Ashbourne and Stoke-on-Trent. Craig Barlow is the young, eager and ambitious landlord, and his enthusiasm has been a major factor contributing to the success of the pub, which is just two miles from the boundary of the Peak District National Park. It is also only three miles from Alton Towers, one of the most visited family attractions in the whole country.

There's plenty of room in the bar to meet friends and enjoy a drink, and when the sun shines the tables and chairs out on the patio come into their own. Charles Wells Bombardier and Marston's Pedigree are the regular real ales. The conservatory restaurant is equally roomy, and the printed menu and specials board provide abundant choice for lunchers and diners. The chef uses fresh seasonable produce from Staffordshire as much as possible in his dishes, and among the favourite selections are lasagne, moussaka, battered cod and breaded plaice, lamb's liver & onions, steaks and pasta with a choice of tasty sauces. Vegetarians are catered for with main courses such as parsnip & leek bake or broccoli & cream cheese bake. Snackier items are also available, including sandwiches, salads, jacket potatoes and burgers. Food is served from 6 to 9 on Monday (the pub is closed Monday lunchtime) from 12 to 3 and 6 to 9 Tuesday to Thursday and all day Friday, Saturday and Sunday.

Comfortable guest accommodation at the Cross comprises three double rooms and three family rooms, all with en suite facilities and all but one on the ground floor. In addition, five static caravans sleeping up to 6 or 8 are available for self-catering between March and November. The pub also has a site for touring caravans (22 pitches) and tents (40) with a toilet block, showers and a laundry room.

The exciting attractions of Alton Towers brings many visitors here, but this is also an area of great scenic beauty, with a number of marked walks and trails in the vicinity, beautiful walks along the Manifold and Dove rivers and an 8-mile walk (the Hamps-Manifold Track) on a level tarred surface.

627

Froghall, Staffordshire ST10 2HA
☎ 01538 754782
🌐 www.cantrirobe@aol.com

The brother and sister team of Bob and Christine took over here in July 2006 to continue a fine tradition of hospitality at the **Railway Inn**. You'll find no warmer welcome anywhere than at this late-19th century inn, which stands in the village of Froghall, on the A52. It is directly opposite Kingsley & Froghall railway station on the privately owned Churnet Valley preserved railway. The Calder canal also runs through the village, and the world-famous attraction of Alton Towers is close by.

The pub's handsome interior boasts some interesting railway memorabilia, and outside is a lovely beer garden with picnic tables and a wealth of greenery – a delightful spot when summer is in full swing. Four real ales headed by Charles Wells bombardier are on tap to quench thirsts, and there's a good choice of other draught and bottled beers and lagers, stout, cider, wines, spirits and non-alcoholic drinks.

In the bright, roomy and relaxing dining area, Christine regales lovers of good food with some really excellent dishes based on the best seasonal produce the local markets have to offer. The blackboard entices with dishes such as brie and cranberry filo parcels or Chinese-style chicken skewers to start; mains like diced pork in a cider & apple sauce, herby lamb casserole with dumplings or mixed bean tikka masala; and, to finish, bilberry cheesecake, lemon brûlée or fresh fruit waffle basket. The pub is open all day for drinks, and Christine's cooking is served from 12 to 2 and 6 to 9, and all day on Sunday.

This fine inn also boasts five handsome, comfortable en suite guest bedrooms. Two have four-poster beds and one is a family room sleeping up to six. The rooms are available throughout the year. The tariff includes an excellent breakfast that provides the perfect start to a day's walking or sightseeing in the area, which offers plenty in the way of sights and attractions.

Alton Towers provides a great day out for the whole family, and another major attraction is Hawksmoor Nature and Bird Sanctuary in 300 acres of the Churnet Valley. Kingsley & Froghall Station, in the imposing style of the North Staffordshire Railway, gives access to the Churnet valley Railway, which runs steam-hauled trains or DMUs on a 10-mile return journey. The Railway's headquarters are in Chaddleton.

393 THE ROYAL OAK HOTEL

69 High Street, Cheadle, nr Stoke-on-Trent,
Staffordshire ST10 1AN
☎ 01538 753116 Fax: 01538 753116
e-mail: adelpegg@royalhotel1734.co.uk
🌐 www.royalhotel1734.co.uk

The **Royal Oak Hotel** is an imposing late-18th century former coaching inn centrally located in Cheadle, at the spot where the A521 meets the A522. Easy to spot with its redbrick façade

and white-painted window surrounds, it has excellent hosts in Dave and Adele Pegg and their son Craig. They took the reins in the spring of 2007 and have quickly made it a very popular place not just with the local community but also with tourists and the considerable passing trade, as well a good stopover for nearby Alton Towers. The bar is open all day, every day, for drinks (Courage Director is the resident cask ale) and food is served every lunchtime and evening; the food hours are

sometimes more restricted out of season. The main menu of familiar favourites is supplemented by Thai dishes on Wednesday to Saturday evenings; Sunday lunch is a well-patronised carvery. The accommodation at the Royal Oak comprises ten excellent en suite rooms of various sizes, including a bridal suite; the basic tariff is room only, but breakfast is available on request. No one should leave Cheadle without visiting the wonderful Roman Catholic Church of St Giles, the Gothic Revival masterpiece of A W N Pugin, who also designed the Houses of Parliament.

394 THE HUNTSMAN

The Green, Cheadle,
Staffordshire ST10 1XS
☎ 01538 753448

The **Huntsman** is a former coaching inn and stables dating back in part to the middle of the 18th century. It stands half a mile outside Cheadle (take the A521 road towards Forsbrook) and has enthusiastic tenants in David Wardle and his daughter Sarah. They arrived in October 2007, bringing experience in the trade to this, their first venture as licensees, and they have lost no time in enhancing the inn's reputation as a place to seek out for a drink, a snack or a meal. It's open all day, every day of the week, for drinks (Marston's

Pedigree is the resident real ale) and bar food is served between 12 and 6 Monday to Saturday and from 12 to 4 on Sunday. The choice runs from freshly baked baguettes with interesting fillings like bacon with melted cheese or roast beef, fried onions & gravy to burgers, pizzas and basket meals, with chocolate fudge cake or caramel & apple pie among the desserts. Sunday lunch is a carvery with three roasts with all the traditional trimmings. On the social side, the Huntsman hosts live music evenings on Saturday and live music followed by a quiz on Sunday evenings.

College Road, Denstone,
Staffordshire ST14 5HR
☎ 01889 590847 Fax: 01889 591092
e-mail: clarencetavern@btconnect.com

The **Tavern** is an early-17th century village inn with a large and loyal following among the local community. Owner Chris Podmore has been in the licensed trade for more than 20 years and since 2003 he has been welcoming familiar faces and new friends with fine hospitality, cask ales kept in tip-top condition and delicious food that caters for both traditional and more adventurous palates.

Antiques add to the charm of the bar, where Marston's pedigree and Burton Best and a regularly changing guest ale head the list of drinks. The lunchtime and evening menus provide an exceptional choice of home-cooked dishes, with 90% of the produce sourced locally, and their own butcher supplying the prime locally farmed meat. The steak is matured for a minimum of 17 days, giving it the most wonderful flavour. Fillet and sirloin steak are grilled to succulent perfection

and served either plain or with a choice of creamy pepper or a classic Diane sauce. The chef's fish of the day and curry of the day are always in demand, and other top choices include salmon & red pepper fish cake, gammon steak, the famous steak & stilton pie and – a vegetarian treat – leek & parsnip bake with chips or five-bean chilli with rice. From the classical repertoire come duck with a port & orange sauce and beef bourguignon, while local produce and recipes are highlighted in a black pudding and bacon galette with a warm apple compote.

This terrific pub (once called the Railway Tavern) is closed Monday lunchtimes, but is otherwise open every lunchtime and evening. Food is served Tuesday to Saturday from 12 to 2 and 7 to 9, and Sunday 12 to 2 for the two-sitting carvery (booking recommended). Children are welcome, and the Tavern has a pleasant patio area and a huge rear garden. All the major credit cards are accepted.

Denstone is located off the B5032 northwest of Rocester on the way to Cheadle and very close to Alton Towers. This is fine walking country, and Chris and his staff are always happy to cope with fresh-air thirsts and appetites.

396 MANOR HOUSE FARM & KEEPERS COTTAGE

Prestwood, Denstone, nr Uttoxeter,
Staffordshire ST14 5DD
☎ 01889 590415 Fax: 01335 342198
e-mail: cm_ball @yahoo.co.uk
🌐 www.4posteraccom.com

Chris and Margaret Ball offer outstanding Bed & Breakfast and self-catering accommodation in serene, scenic surroundings. Their listed Jacobean farmhouse stands at the heart of the 170-acre **Manor House Farm**, which lies at the confluence of the valleys of the Dove and Churnet rivers. The four bedrooms, all with four-poster or half-tester beds, enjoy beautiful views over the terraced garden or the dramatic Weaver Hills. Tea and coffee making facilities and televisions are available in all rooms. A full English or Continental breakfast is served in the handsome oak-panelled dining room, and guests can relax and plan their days in the cosy sitting room.

The large gardens are also lovely places to relax and unwind and listen to the songs of the varied birdlife. Part of the farm, which has been in Chris's family for 200 years (he was born here), is still worked, and the owners breed the very rare Irish Moiled cattle, which can be seen grazing in the grounds.

Next to the farmhouse, **Keepers Cottage** offers something quite unique in self-catering accommodation, an antidote to double glazing, DIY furniture and chipboard doors. It delights guests with the period charm of exposed stone walls, oak panelling, oak and pine doors and antique furniture while providing a range of modern appliances that today's guests would expect in accommodation of this quality. It has an

entrance hall, a comfortable kitchen/dining/living room and two bedrooms. The master room has oak panelling and a magnificent four-poster bed and an adjacent shower/WC room, and a little twisting staircase leads up to the second bedroom, a twin/double with an en suite bathroom. The garden offers space to relax or set up a barbecue, and guests in both properties can enjoy a game of tennis or croquet. Short breaks are available in the low season.

The farm is an ideal centre for exploring the beautiful, tranquil valleys of the Dove, the Churnet and the Manifold rivers, or enjoying a day out at Alton Towers (2 miles away) or visiting the several stately homes in the area, including Shugborough Hall, Haddon hall and Chatsworth. Also close by are the historic market towns of Ashbourne and Uttoxeter. Manor House is also a good base for golf, swimming, cycling and pony trekking, as well as walking or rambling in the quiet country lanes and fields.

The tiny community of Prestwood, which lies close to the B5032 a mile from Denstone, is not marked on all road maps. Note that it is NOT the Prestwood near Stourbridge.

397 CASTRO'S RESTAURANT & LOUNGE

11 Cheadle Road, Cheddleton, nr Leek,
Staffordshire ST13 7HN
☎ 01538 361500
e-mail: james@castros-restaurant.co.uk
e-mail: enquiries@castros-restaurant.co.uk
🌐 www.castros-restaurant.co.uk

**'A taste of Latin America that's
closer than you think.'**

Authentic Latin American cuisine brings
diners from all over the region to **Castro's
Restaurant & Lounge**. This smart, spacious
modern restaurant sits right by the Cauldon
Canal in the pleasant village of Cheddleton,
on the A520 south of Leek.

The energy and enthusiasm of Jamie, Nikki and Thom, the quality of the food and the high
standard of service have made it *the* place to eat in the area: it's the coolest eating place for miles
around (smart, stylish, fashionable) and also the hottest (busy, buzzy, and the dishes really deliver a
kick). Behind the eyecatching redbrick exterior the restaurant is brightly contemporary, with tiled
floor, exposed brick and pine tables and chairs. Large windows look out onto the canal, and a drink
or a meal can be enjoyed outside on warm summer days.

Fresh, locally sourced produce is given the Latin American treatment by talented chefs Jamie
and Thom, along with the imported spices and other ingredients that impart the authentic flavours.
You'll find all the Mexican favourites on the main menu, including fiery Cajun chicken enchilada,
chimichanga (chicken, steak, pork or vegetables) and fajitas (chimichanga options plus king
prawns). Onions and peppers are involved in all these dishes, and the chefs will make the dishes as
mild or as fiery as you like. Other dishes – everything is well worth trying – include fish specials,
coconut & chilli chicken, tequila & orange pork, and steaks served plain from the grill or with a
choice of peppercorn, mushroom & brandy, mustard & paprika or hot & spicy sauces. The choice
is further expanded by a specials board that reflects what's best and freshest in season. Lunchtime
also brings the option of traditional pub dishes like steak & ale pie, scampi, lasagne or baked
potatoes with a variety of fillings. Lunches are served from 12 to 3 Tuesday to Friday and evening
meals from 6pm till late Tuesday to Saturday.

This place is so popular that whatever the proposed time of a visit it's best to book to be sure
of a table, and essential on Saturday evening. Service is friendly, speedy and efficient, and the prices
offer outstanding value for money. And if you're not eating, you're still welcome to drop in for a
coffee, a beer or a glass of wine.

Top Station Road, Mow Cop,
nr Stoke-on-Trent, Staffordshire ST7 3NP
☎ 01782 514211
☎ www.cheshireview.co.uk

It would be hard to find a more appropriate name for the **Cheshire View**, which stands high up in the village of Mow Cop, half in Staffordshire, half in Cheshire, and reached off the A234 or A527 between Newcastle-under-Lyne/Stoke and Engleton. The views over the two counties are truly astounding, and walkers, ramblers, cyclists and tourists join the locals in enjoying the outstanding country inn hospitality dispensed by Josie Bedson and her staff. Dating back some 320 years, and once called the Railway Inn, it has been smartly updated without losing any of its traditional appeal.

Three real ales – Marston's Burton Bitter and Pedigree and a regularly changing guest – are waiting to satisfy fresh-air thirsts, which are quickly generated among visitors to this lovely part of the world. Josie and a helper produce a good selection of wholesome dishes that include all the English pub classics and the Sunday lunchtime roasts; booking is recommended in season, especially for groups. Food is served from 12 to 3 and 6 to 9. Sunday lunchtime brings only the roasts, reverting to the main menu in the

evening. Karaoke gets the place buzzing every other Saturday, and the pub hosts an acoustic evening on one Thursday a month; it also has a pool table.

The Cheshire View is open in December and January from 4 o'clock Monday to Thursday and lunchtime and evening at the weekend, otherwise from midday and all day in the summer. Cash only – there's an ATM on the premises.

They hope to have accommodation available soon, which will make the pub an ideal base for walking, cycling and discovering all the many attractions of the region. Mow Cop, which stands 1,100 feet above sea level, has two well-known landmarks, one made by man, the other the result of man's activities. The Castle was built in 1754 and was acquired by the National Trust in 1926. The Old Man of Mow is an isolated pillar of limestone left behind from the centuries of mining carried on here until well into the last century.

399 THE RAILWAY TAVERN

The Common, Mellis, nr Eye,
Suffolk IP23 8DU
☎ 01379 783416

Built in 1840 as a station hotel, **The Railway Tavern** is a handsome landmark in the village of Mellis, which spreads around the largest common in Suffolk, located near Eye, southwest of Diss, between the A140 towards Needham Market and A143 towards Bury.

The interior is comfortable and relaxing with its leather sofas and warm atmosphere it is the ideal place to relax. Food is served all day from 12 noon until 9 pm except Monday when it is served from 5.30 pm until 9 pm. The menu comprises of freshly baked baguettes, oven baked potatoes and excellent hot meals or salads, everything freshly cooked using the best fresh, and whenever possible, local ingredients. Sunday lunch is very popular due to its very high quality and reasonable price. There are three to four real ales to choose from. The Railway Tavern has three lovely, clean and bright letting rooms in an annex building. The Railway Tavern is a warm welcoming pub and you can be sure you will greeted with a smile and served great quality food and drink by landlord Bob Caddy and landlady Pamela Roper. Opening hours are Mon 5.30 pm - 11.00 pm, Tuesday to Friday 12 noon to 11.00 pm and Sunday 12 noon to 10.30 pm.

400 THE FOX

Station Road, Elmswell, Suffolk IP30 9HD
☎ 01359 244594

The **Fox** is a popular pub by the level crossing in Elmswell, a village of some 3,000 souls lying just moments from the A14 (J47) between Bury St Edmunds and Stowmarket.

When Joy and Nigel Bailey took over the pub at the beginning of 2008 they quickly made their mark, and if the locals have anything to do with it they are definitely here to stay. In the busy bar they gather to put the world to rights over a glass of Greene King ale, perhaps IPA, Abbot or Mild, or something else from the extensive choice. The printed menus and specials board provide plenty of freshly prepared dishes by their head chef Craig, from lunchtime sandwiches to homemade curries, gammon and beef steaks, liver & bacon, fisherman's platter, lasagne, linguine and goat's cheese & spring onion tartlet. All the main courses are available as children's portions, so they might have room for a treacle tart or banana split. Pub hours are 12 noon to 3pm and 5pm to 11pm (12 noon to 12pm Friday and Saturday).

A notable landmark in Elmswell is the Church of St John with its massive flint spire. It stands at the entrance to the village and is clearly visible from the A14 and from the railway – yes, the station is still open, with trains stopping on a regular service between Cambridge and Ipswich.

401 THE PEACOCK INN

**Chelsworth, nr Lavenham,
Suffolk IP7 7HU
☎ 01449 740758**

The **Peacock Inn** enjoys a fine location in the picture-postcard village of Chelsworth, an unspoilt gem in the valley of the River Brett. The listed 14th century building has a delightful rustic bar with beams, copper and brass ornaments and a roaring winter fire in a big brick hearth.

Outside is a lovely garden with glorious views to the river. In this attractive setting Helen and Andrew greet locals, walkers, ramblers, cyclists, motorists, tourists and families with dogs – they have a dog of their own and are happy to welcome well-behaved visiting dogs. Adnams Broadside and Bitter, and Woodforde's Wherry are the regular real ales, and in the separate restaurant, recently refurbished by the owning brewery, Andrew's cooking is a magnet for food-lovers from a wide area.

Using what's best and freshest from the top local sources, he puts his individual stamp on dishes like confit of duck (with an orange, apricot and port sauce), breast of chicken (with a Thai green curry sauce, baby pineapple and lychees) and pan-fried fillets of sea bass (with a Disaronno and almond sauce, asparagus and balsamic vinegar). The starters are equally interesting, and light meals include whitebait, scampi, steamed mussels and braised Suffolk sausages with mash & onion gravy.

402 THE GLOBE

**10 Callis Street, Clare, nr Sudbury,
Suffolk CO10 8PX
☎ 01787 277551**

The **Globe** is a handsome 16th century inn on the corner of a busy street in the delightful old wool town of Clare. The outside is decked with colourful tubs and hanging baskets in spring and summer, and in the bar and lounge the scene is invitingly traditional, with heavy doors, sturdy beams and log fires.

Caroline Byers worked at the bar before talking over as the landlady of this Greene King pub, so she knows her customers well. The locals love her and love the place, which is also a favourite with many of the tourists who come to explore this marvellous little town. Abbot and IPA are the cask ales from the owning brewery, heading a full range of drinks. The bar is open lunchtime and evening and all day at the weekend in season, and food is served from 12 to 2.15 and from 6 to 9, Sunday from 12 to 4. The menu proposes a fine variety of pub classics, typified by traditional fish &

chips (cod, haddock and plaice), meat or vegetable lasagne, ham, egg & chips, steaks, chicken & ham pie and steak & kidney suet pudding. Smaller portions can be provided on request for young diners.

Monday is curry night, Tuesday is steak night, it's cribbage on Wednesday, the ladies throw darts on Thursday, and major sports events are shown on Sky TV.

635

403 THE GREYHOUND

2 Ipswich Road, Claydon, Suffolk IP6 0AR
☎ 01473 830262

Bubbly landlady Michelle Morgan is the major contributor to the popularity of the **Greyhound**, the social hub of the village of Claydon. She loves the locals and they love her, and between them they ensure that the atmosphere in invariably warm and convivial, whatever the weather, whatever the time of year. Behind the pink-washed façade with its steeply raked tiled roof the bar is a cosy spot for enjoying good conversation and a glass or two of Adnams Bitter or Greene King IPA. Michelle's excellent and loyal cook prepares a selection of pub fare for Monday to Friday lunchtimes. Her choices include sandwiches, burgers, liver & bacon and hearty stews that are enjoyed by all comers and especially by the older, more traditional brigade. OAP lunches are available on Tuesdays and Thursdays.

The clientele tends to drop a generation in the evening and at the weekend, when the pub shows its sporty side and the regulars get together to swap tales of their latest heroics on the football field, the pool table or the oche. The pub fields teams for all three sports in the local leagues. Sky is available via large plasma TV's and there is entertainment on the 1st and 3rd Saturdays of the month

404 THE MOON & MUSHROOM

High Street, Swilland, nr Ipswich, Suffolk IP6 9LR
☎ 01473 785320
⊕ www.moonandmushroom.co.uk

The **Moon & Mushroom** is a fine country inn with bags of character and a top landlady in Nikki Gavin from Co Cork, who took over here in 2005. The village of Swilland is signposted off the B1078 Needham Market to Wickham Market road, and off the B1077 that runs north from Ipswich. It started as an ale house in the 16th century and has retained a great deal of its period charm.

Beyond the archway of vines and creepers the bar has a wonderful country pub décor with slate floors, a winter log fire in a brick hearth, old furniture and cushioned stools. Outside are little terraces with a small beautiful rose garden with heaters and a colourful array of roses, vines and shrubs. In this homely, inviting setting patrons can enjoy a variety of real ales from East Anglia drawn straight from the barrel. The choice changes regularly, with appearances made by Nethergate's Umbel, Crouch Vale's Brewers gold, Buffy's hop Leaf, Suffolk County, Norwich Brewery's Little Terrier and Woodforde's Wherry. Widely acclaimed for its ales, the Moon & Mushroom also brings lovers of good food from all over the region. Accolades include winning the Evening Star's Best Country/Village pub two years running. The menu is not long, but everything is well worth trying, prepared and cooked to order from excellent ingredients, sourced locally as far as possible. The pub hosts many community events often fund raising for local charities. There are always plenty of things to do and sights to see in the region, but there's only one Moon & Mushroom, and it should come at the top of every visitor's list.

73 Cumberland Street, Woodbridge,
Suffolk IP12 4AG
☎ 01934 384627
⊕ www.thecherrytreepub.co.uk

A landmark for visitors entering the town from Ipswich, the **Cherry Tree** is a flagship pub in the historic town of Woodbridge, equally popular as a place for locals to meet and chat and a refreshment stop or base for tourists.

The Grade II listed building, a blaze of colour in spring and summer with flower tubs and hanging baskets, is in the excellent acre of Sheila and Geoff Ford, who have been making friends ever since 2001 with their fine hospitality and the quality of the beer, food and accommodation. Cooking starts with breakfast, served from 7.30 to 10.30 (9 to 11 at the weekend), with the main menu coming on stream at midday and continuing right through to 9 in the evening. The choice of pub favourites runs from sandwiches, wraps, jacket potatoes and omelettes to scampi, cod, haddock and salmon,

sausages & mash, lasagne, curry, beef & ale pie and beef and gammon steaks. A range of Adnams and other real ales is served in the bar, increased to about eight during the annual Beer Festival held in May/June.

The guest bedrooms, in a converted Suffolk barn overlooking the garden, are named after Adnams brews: Broadside sleeps up to 4, Explorer is a double and Regatta is a twin with wheel chair access. All have TV with DVD and VCR and broadband access. The family-friendly Cherry Tree has a children's play area in the secluded garden.

HIDDEN PLACES GUIDES

Explore Britain and Ireland with *Hidden Places* guides - a fascinating series of national and local travel guides.

Packed with easy to read information on hundreds of places of interest as well as places to stay, eat and drink.

Available from both high street and internet booksellers

For more information on the full range of *Hidden Places* guides and other titles published by Travel Publishing visit our website on

www.travelpublishing.co.uk
or ask for our leaflet by phoning **01752 276660** or
emailing **info@travelpublishing.co.uk**

Shottisham, nr Woodbridge,
Suffolk IP12 3HD
☎ 01394 411617
e-mail: Frankie.new@tiscali.co.uk

Tom Fox, king of the stoves, and Frankie New at the bar make a winning team at the **Sorrel Horse**, a listed 16th century building in the centre of Shottisham. The pink-washed frontage is topped with a thatched roof that is beautifully sculpted round the dormer windows. Inside, the inn is no less delightful, with an open wood-burner in a great brick heath to keep out the North Sea chill.

This traditional setting is the perfect spot to meet the locals for a chat and a glass of beer – perhaps Adnams Bitter or Greene King IPA. Tom's cooking is a major attraction here, and in the neat, cosy little restaurant he regales his customers with a splendid choice of dishes prepared from the pick of local ingredients and freshly cooked to order. The lunch and bar menus propose filled crusty rolls and ciabattas, Suffolk farmhouse sausages, baked potatoes, three-egg omelettes, home-made burgers and Yorkshire pudding filled with chicken, leeks and stilton. From the main (evening) menu come devilled whitebait, beer-battered cod, poached salmon, Suffolk ham hock & parsley terrine, confit of Gressingham duck leg, peppered steak & mushroom pie, chargrilled steaks and baked field mushrooms topped with aubergine Bolognese, brie and basil pesto.

On the social side, the Sorrel Horse hosts quiz and bingo nights on alternate Wednesday evenings, both for charity. The inn is open for food and drink lunchtime and evening but is closed all Sunday evenings and Mondays out of season.

Shottisham is set in open countryside on the B1083 running south east from Woodbridge on the way to Bawdsey, the mouth of the River Deben and the ferry that crosses the river to Felixstowe. It's very much on the tourist trail, and the Sorrel Horse is a popular place for walkers, ramblers, cyclists, motorists and lovers of the great outdoors to pause for refreshment. And if they should happen to arrive on horseback they will discover that the inn has a stable block by the main building.

Mill Road, Buxhall, Suffolk IP14 3DW
☎ 01449 736521
⊕ www.thebuxhallcrown.co.uk

*'People come from miles around on a
gastronomic pilgrimage to dine at the
tables of the Crown'.*

That's just one of many accolades from local
and national food guides and publications
earned by the **Buxhall Crown**. This fine
timber-framed country pub dates from the
early 18th century and started life as a
coaching inn; it's now a fully paid-up member
of the Quintessential Country Inn Club, a
stunning little pub that once found will
become a place to put at the top of the list when returning to the area.

The lovely, cosy public bar, with a smartly panelled serving area and a huge open fire, serves
Greene King IPA, two guest ales and a full range of other drinks lunchtime and evening Tuesday
to Saturday and lunchtime on Sunday (closed Mondays). The tradition of excellent hospitality is
being carried on in fine style by Wayne Felgate, who brought a wealth of experience when he took
over here in the spring of 2008.

The food is all locally sourced, prepared and cooked on the premises, and anyone who
appreciates good food will find that the menus pose quite a problem – it's all very tempting, and
results on the plate never disappoint. The menu is seasonal and changes on a regular basis.
Traditionalists will be delighted with scampi, deep-fried haddock, sausages with onion gravy, steak &
mushroom pie or a succulent steak with all the usual accompaniments, while those looking for
something a little bit different might go for warm

smoked chicken Caesar salad, prawn soup with ciabatta
croûtons, smoked salmon with rösti, salad leaves and
horseradish yoghurt or Moroccan lamb with herby
couscous. Everything on the wine list is available by the
bottle or two sizes of glass. On warm days or balmy
evenings the enclosed paved patio is a popular addition
to the amenities of this outstanding place.

From the A14, take the B1115, turn right by
Great Finborough Post Office, left at the Buxhall
village sign, second right into Mill Road, right at the
T-junction and there you are. It's not very tricky the
first time and no problem at all for the next visit!

408 PAINSHILL PARK

Portsmouth Road, Cobham,
Surrey KT11 1JE
☎ 01932 868113 Fax: 01932 868001
e-mail: info@painshill.co.uk
🌐 www.painshill.co.uk

This once barren heathland was transformed by the celebrated plantsman and designer, the Hon Charles Hamilton, into one of Europe's finest 18th Century landscape gardens. **Painshill** was one of the earliest 'naturalistic' gardens ever created, Hamilton conjured up a mysterious and magical place in which to wander- the equivalent of a 20th century theme park - where fashionable society could wander through a landscape theatre, moving from scene to scene. Staged around a huge serpentine lake with surprises at every turn. A Gothic Temple, Chinese Bridge, Ruined Abbey, a Grotto, Turkish Tent, Gothic Tower and the most magnificent waterwheel all disappear and reappear as the walk proceeds.

But Hamilton eventually ran out of money and to discharge his debts sold the estate in 1773. Since then it has been in the possession of many owners but was eventually fragmented and sold off in lots in 1948 and the gardens, which had been well-maintained for nigh on two centuries, were allowed to deteriorate. By 1981 they lay derelict and overgrown and it seemed that what had been a national treasure would be lost for all time. However Elmbridge Borough Council, conscious of the importance of Painshill, purchased 158 acres and formed the Painshill Park Trust with a view to restoring the gardens and opening them to the public. The subsequent ongoing restoration has been one of the great success stories of garden conservation. Most of the principal features of the garden are open for viewing and the restored planting schemes are steadily maturing. The restoration has been a slow process. It's not simply a matter of clearing undergrowth and repairing features. Lots

of detailed and painstaking research is required. Archaeological excavation, documentary research and the identification and dating of trees, tree stumps and historic paths. From this, detailed plans and maps are created to show what the estate would have looked like in the 18th century and all the later stages to the present day.

Now there are a variety of walks which allow visitors to explore Hamilton's idyll. The historic circuit is a signposted two-mile long route that an 18th century visitor would have followed to view all the attractions of the garden. A shorter path round the lake passes delights such as the ruined abbey, boat house and crosses the Chinese bridge. A vineyard flourished at Painshill from 1740 to 1812. This has been replanted with Pinot noir, Chardonnay and Seyval blanc grapes and once again wine is being produced at Painshill. Painshill is not allowed to call their sparkling white wine champagne but when Charles Hamilton was making wine here in the 18th century the French ambassador of the day, mistook Hamilton's product for the champagne of his native land. In a tribute to the man who made it all possible, the Painshill trust have named the new visitor centre restaurant Hamilton's. It's open from early morning serving breakfasts, coffee, light lunches and splendid afternoon teas. The shop is a cornucopia for present and souvenir buyers containing everything from trugs and dibbers to umbrellas, food, china, books, honey and beeswax candles and, of course, Painshill wine. Open March to October Tuesday to Sunday and Bank Holidays 10.30am - 6.00pm; November - February: Wednesday to Sunday and Bank Holidays 11.00am - 4.00pm. Closed Christmas Day.

409 THE CROWN

The Street, Capel, Surrey RH5 5JY
☎ 01306 711130
e-mail: thecrowncapel@btconnect.com
🌐 www.thecrowncapel.com

In the village of Capel, off the A24 south of Dorking, the **Crown** is a 400-year-old traditional country inn with a cheerful little public bar, a back lounge bar and a separate restaurant. Hosts Robert and Vivienne Long are committed to making it a place for everyone, with a friendly, welcoming ambience throughout the long opening hours, great food, superb real ales and wines. The locals, including a big overspill from London, love the pub, and it's also a good place to break a journey on the busy A24. Youngs Bitter, Fullers London Pride, Spitfire and a guest provide a good choice for real ale drinkers, and food is served from 12 to 3 and 6 to 9.30 (Sunday 12 to 4, no evening food). The lunch & bites menu runs from sandwiches and ploughmans to chorizo & sauté potatoes in a sweet chilli sauce,

koftas, burgers, bangers, lasagne, homemade steak & kidney pie and steak or chicken in a tortilla wrap. Main courses on the evening menu include more pub classics and others, such as moules & frites, teriyaki salmon and mushroom stroganoff. The pub has a games area with popular dart board, and a jam session takes place every other Monday.

410 THE SALEHURST HALT

Salehurst, nr Robertsbridge,
East Sussex TN32 5PH
☎ 01580 880620
🌐 www.salehursthalt.co.uk

The Salehurst Halt is a popular redbrick free house and restaurant by the church in a village signposted from the Robertsbridge bypass on the A21 Tunbridge Wells to Battle road. Owners and business partners Gail and Karen, ex-teachers and hardworking members of the church, took over the inn when closure threatened in the spring of 2006. A petition was organised and with support from the church and the villagers they have given the inn a new lease of life, popular both among the local residents and by a growing passing trade. The bar is in fine traditional style, with beams and a long panelled serving area. Outside, there's a charming back garden with terraces and lovely views. Two or three real ales, usually including Harveys Sussex Best Bitter, are on tap, and food, all freshly prepared to order, is served every

session except Sunday evening and Monday. The owners are passionate about the provenance of their ingredients, supporting local, farmers, producers and brewers and ensuring that full justice is done to the raw materials. The bar at Salehurst Halt is closed on Monday except Bank Holidays, but is otherwise open lunchtime, evening and all day at the weekend.

**37 Mount Street, Battle,
East Sussex TN33 0EG
☎ 01424 772317
e-mail: jozef6@mac.com
⊕ www.yeoldekingshead.org**

The historic settlement of Battle, on the A260 six miles northwest of Hastings, is renowned as the site of the momentous battle that took place in 1066 between the armies of Harold, the Saxon King of England, and William, Duke of Normandy. The Abbey that William built after the Battle is still a magnificent sight, and visitors can learn all about the Battle in a fascinating exhibition.

And when thoughts turn from feud to food and battles to bottles, it's just a few steps from the Abbey to the **Kings Head** in Mount Street. Battle's favourite pub, previously called Ye Olde Kings Head, has excellent leaseholders in Joe and Helen Rytlewski, who are proud of the pub's reputation for outstanding hospitality, honest British pub food, decent wine and excellent cask-conditioned ales. They are also justifiably proud of the wonderful flower displays that adorn the front in the summer months and which have won many awards. Real fires keep things cosy in even the coolest times, and at any time of the year the bars are cheerful and convivial, with good conversation and a full range of liquid refreshment.

The bars are open all day, every day of the week, and two or three real ales, including Harveys Sussex Best, are on tap. Helen is a super cook, and locals and the many visitors who come to Battle throughout the year can look forward to a splendid meal served in comfortable, relaxed surroundings. Helen and her helpers seek out the best seasonal produce for an across-the-board menu that is available from 12 to 2.30 and 6.30 to 9.30 Monday to Saturday and from 12 to 8.30 on Sunday. Classic starters include soup of the day, whitebait, deep-fried brie and prawn cocktail,

and main courses run from lamb & mint sausages to wine-poached salmon with hollandaise sauce, fish cakes, Alaskan pollock, chilli-glazed boneless duckling, lamb shank in mint gravy, home-made lasagne and home-made steak, kidney & Guinness pie. A number of items on the menu are available in child's portions (with a free ice cream) and at lower prices for senior citizens.

Wednesday is steak night, followed by a quiz, and on Thursday Irish folk bands perform.

This most sociable of pubs hosts a wide variety of events, and the back room can be hired for a private party.

412 THE CHEQUERS INN

Lower Lake, Battle, East Sussex TN33 0AT
☎ 01424 772088 Fax: 01424 772088
e-mail: thechequersinn@hotmail.com
⊕ www.chequersinn.eu

The **Chequers** is a cosy, family-friendly inn located a short walk from the centre of Battle. The oldest part dates back to the  13th century and it is reputed that it once had a tunnel leading to the Abbey. Derek and Julie Miller, here since 2005, have won many friends with their warm, genuine hospitality, CAMRA award-winning ales and home-cooked food. The bar is open all day, seven days a week, and locally sourced food for a variety of tastes and appetites is served from 10.30 to 12 (brunch), 12 to 3 and 5 to 10, all day on Sunday. Booking is recommended at the weekend and for the curry (Thursday) and steak(Friday) nights. The Chequers has a heated sheltered patio, a beer garden and a large car park.

414 THE WHITE HART

High Street, Wadhurst,
East Sussex TN5 6AP
☎ 01892 782878

The small town of Wadhurst lies on the B2099, between the A21 and the A267. The **White Hart** is a distinctive landmark on the High Street, redbrick below, a black-and-white timbered look above, with a first-floor balcony and a steeply raked grey-tiled roof. It was John and Annette Morriss's local before they took over the lease, since when they have had the locals and visitors to the town flocking here to enjoy their hospitality. The bar of this  Greene King pub, with beams and an open fire, is open all day for drinks, which typically include Greene King IPA, Old Speckled Hen and Ruddles County real ales; on summer days and warm evenings the secluded rear courtyard is a real asset.

Lunchtime (12 to 2.30) sees a good choice of home-cooked food, including salads and snacks, macaroni cheese, fish & chips, Cumberland sausages & mash, 'Harty' burgers, haddock crumble, 'all-day' breakfast and steak/chicken & ham pies. Booking is recommended for the Sunday carvery and for the Friday evening themed food nights. Big sporting events are shown on Sky TV, and all are welcome at Wednesday's weekly jamming session

413 THE QUEEN'S HEAD

The Green, Sedlescombe, nr Battle,
East Sussex TN33 0QA
☎ 01424 870228 Fax: 01424 870228
e-mail: grant.burberry@btinternet.com

On the B2244 east of Battle and north of Hastings, Sedlescombe was once a flourishing iron founding settlement. That industry is long since gone, and it's now a pleasant, picturesque and peaceful village stretched along a sloping green. One of the landmark buildings on the green is the **Queen's Head**, a handsome redbrick building with the oldest parts dating back to the 15th century.

The leaseholders are Grant and Jan Burberry, who came here in the spring of 2007 after running other enterprises in the county for ten years. They have enhanced its role as a much-loved village local, and with the main A21 Hastings to Tunbridge Wells road just moments away, it also provides a very pleasant and convenient refreshment stop for motorists, cyclists and tourists. The fully stocked bar is open all day, every day of the week for a full range of beers, lagers, wines, spirits and non-alcoholic drinks. The four real ales, always kept in tip-top condition, usually include Harveys Sussex best and Tanglefoot. The bar is a delightful spot to enjoy a drink and a chat at any time of the year, but in summer the scene shifts to the outstanding beer garden, where barbecues are a popular regular event.

Excellent food can also be enjoyed in the bar, the garden or the comfortable 60-cover restaurant. One of the favourite dishes is Sussex Smokie – smoked haddock and prawns in a cheese sauce – as either starter or main course. Other fishy dishes include scampi, fish cakes with a mustard sauce, beer-battered cod and fish pie in parsley sauce. There's an equally good choice for meat-eaters – minted lamb steak, Hungarian goulash, lasagne, chilli con carne, homemade burgers, steak 'n' ale pie and steaks served with all the trimmings and a choice of pepper, mushroom or stilton sauce. Tiger prawns, chicken and beef teriyaki are popular 'sizzlers' and there are always three vegetarian dishes and plenty of salad platters. Monday is fish & chip night – eat in or take away – and Wednesday evening brings a selection of curries. Food times are 12 to 2.30 and 6 to 9 Monday to Friday (with sandwiches available in between), 12 to 9.30 on Saturday and 12 to 5 on Sunday, when roasts are added to the menu. Lighter lunch alternatives include sandwiches, baguettes, ploughman's platters, jacket potatoes and ham, eggs & chips.

415 THE WHITE DOG INN

Village Street, Ewhurst Green,
East Sussex TN32 5TD
☎ 01580 830264

The **White Dog** is a cheerful, friendly and delightfully unpretentious 17th century pub/restaurant in the village of Ewhurst Green, in an area fringed by the A28, A268, B2165 and B2244.

Bill and Jacqui Tipples, with 35 years' experience in the trade, manageress Danni, head chef Alex and second chef his brother William took over here in March 2008 and their talents and professionalism are ensuring that the White Dog is already becoming a popular choice for a drink, a snack, a meal or an overnight or longer stay. Three real ales, usually including Harveys Bitter and Masterbrew, are served in the bar, which is open lunchtime and evening and all day at the weekend from May to the end of October. Tables in the garden take full advantage of the attractive country setting. The brothers' dishes, served lunchtime and evening, cover a particularly interesting that takes in snacks and light dishes, pub classics and excellent dishes more usually seen

on top restaurant menus, such as fillets of sea bass, Rye Bay scallops pan-fried with garlic butter and pancetta, and warm seared fillet of beef marinated in green chillies, spring onions and soy sauce. All the puddings are homemade, so it would be a grave error to leave the table without sampling a baked raspberry & sherry trifle, black cherry cheesecake or roasted plum & vanilla crumble. Three super en suite B&B rooms, one suitable for families, are available all year. Local attractions include Bodiam Castle, the magnificent Great Dixter Hall and the delightful steam-hauled Kent & East Sussex Railway.

416 THE CINQUE PORTS INN

Rye, East Sussex TN31 7AN
☎ 01797 222319
e-mail: enquiries@cinqueportsinn.co.uk
🌐 www.cinqueportsinn.co.uk

The **Cinque Ports Inn** is one of the most welcoming as well as one of the most aptly named hostelries in the old and picturesque town of Rye. Previously known as the Railway Inn, it has been run since 2006 by Neil and Jana Sheppard, who

came with many years' experience in the hotel and allied industries. They both cook, and the kitchen starts up at 10 o'clock (11 on Sunday) for a good breakfast choice. The main menu includes old favourites like beer-battered cod, curries and steak & kidney pudding as well as Jana's authentic beef goulash – always popular – and the Cinque Ports deep-fried seafood platter with cod goujons, breaded lobster pieces, calamari, whitebait and prawn rolls. Roasts are added on Sundays. For lighter snacks, panini and jacket potatoes are available to eat in

or take away. No food Sunday evenings or all day Monday. In

the bar or out in the beer garden/patio – part-lawned, part paved, part covered – patrons can enjoy a full range of drinks, including three real ales, typically Masterbrew, Bishops Finger and a guest. The inn also offers a very pleasant base for exploring historic Rye and the surrounding area. Three en suite rooms, two doubles and a family room, are available throughout the year.

The Green, Newick, East Sussex BN8 4LA
☎ 01825 722055
e-mail: bull.inn@hotmail.co.uk
⊕ www.bullinn.org

The **Bull Inn** has been offering hospitality for 500 years. In the early 16th century it was a stopping place for pilgrims travelling from Winchester to Canterbury. It stands in the village of Newick, on the A272 between Haywards Heath and Uckfield, and on the Green at Newick is an old signpost showing the distance between the two Cathedrals. (Also on the Green is an unusual long-handles pump installed to mark Queen Victoria's Diamond Jubilee in 1897.)

The Bull, whose name relates to a Papal Bull or edict, now offers a superb combination of historic country pub, destination restaurant and luxury hotel. Tenant Cinzia Cirignano, a lovely Italian lady, has a natural empathy with her customers, and with her partner and staff welcomes young and old from all walks of life to meet and enjoy first-class hospitality and quality in all departments. As a place to meet for a chat and a drink, it has a convivial main bar with beams and inglenook fireplaces. The real ales, typically including Spitfire and Kents Best, are among the best kept in the region. Bar hours are 11 to 3 and 6 to 11, all day Saturday and from 12 to 4 and 6.30 to 10.30 on Sunday. Happy Hour, with special prices for lagers and spirits, operates from 6 to 9 on Tuesday and Thursday. Patrons can play pool or watch major sporting events on two big screens in the adjacent snug bar. As a restaurant, it also holds its own with the best in the area, with extensive menus spanning light snacks and full à la carte meals. Among the popular choices are calamari with an aioli dip, moules marienière or provençale, Spitfire-battered cod, lasagne, rack of lamb, steaks and always some interesting vegetarian dishes such as roasted aubergine boats with green beans, saffron & smoked cheddar risotto and roasted pine nuts. Classic desserts like bread & butter pudding or apple crumble round off a meal in style. Head chefs Alex and Kristian will create a menu tailor-made for a function, party or reception.

As a hotel, the original barn has been converted to provide modern comfort and amenity in a traditional setting. The Pilgrims Rest comprises eight charming rooms with open beams and full en suite facilities. They are named after pilgrims in Chaucer's *Canterbury Tales* and each has its own mural depicting scenes from the tales, hand-painted by Jane Churchill.

417 THE SUSSEX OAK

Church Street, Warnham,
West Sussex RH12 3QW
☎ 01403 265028 Fax: 01403 265128
e-mail: sussexoakwarnham@aol.com

The **Sussex Oak** is a gem of a country inn, a wonderful 16th century hostelry in the pleasant village of Warnham, just off the A24 Horsham to Dorking road. Peter and Angela Nottage are terrific hosts and they and their staff have the warmest of welcomes for locals, cyclists, ramblers, tourists and anyone who appreciates the qualities of a classic English pub. The bar areas are delightfully traditional, with log fires in inglenook hearths, flagstone or wooden floors, beams, timbers and a variety of tables and chairs. It's open all day, seven days a week, for a full range of drinks, including at least four real ales and a selection of wines by the glass. Food is a major part of the Sussex Oak's business, with a particularly busy lunchtime trade (no food Sunday or Monday evenings). Peter's menu spans a fine range of British and European dishes, from pâté, red onion & blue cheese tartlet and chargrilled mackerel fillet to steak, ale & mushroom pie, grilled salmon hollandaise, chargrilled steak and tagliatelle carbonara. There's a children's menu, and many of the adult dishes can be ordered in smaller portions. The hosts can organise private functions, and a field at the back is available for hire. Picnic benches are set out in the garden and there's ample off-road parking.

419 DUDDLESWELL TEA ROOMS

Fairwarp, Ashdown Forest,
East Sussex TN22 3BH
☎ 01825 712126

A tea room has existed in this lovely location since 1935. **Duddleswell Tea Rooms** opens from 10am to 5pm from Thursday to Monday. Homemade scones, cakes and cream teas are served throughout the day, with several variations on the Welsh rarebit theme added from 10am to 2.30pm and lunchtime specials of home-cooked ham and ploughman's platters. There are seats for 38 inside and as many again outside in this pretty Ashdown Forest setting.

HIDDEN PLACES GUIDES

Explore Britain and Ireland with *Hidden Places* guides - a fascinating series of national and local travel guides.

Packed with easy to read information on hundreds of places of interest as well as places to stay, eat and drink.

Available from both high street and internet booksellers

For more information on the full range of *Hidden Places* guides and other titles published by Travel Publishing visit our website on

www.travelpublishing.co.uk
or ask for our leaflet by phoning
01752 276660 or emailing
info@travelpublishing.co.uk

Five Ash Down, nr Uckfield,
East Sussex TN22 3AN
☎ 01825 732191

The **Pig & Butcher** is a very distinctive gables redbrick building located in the village of Five Ash Down, a mile north of Uckfield where the A26 meets the A272. Until recently called the Firemans Arms, it has an excellent tenant in Lyn Funnell, who has the valuable assistance of manageress Lorna, who worked here previously as the cook. These two friendly, energetic ladies have really put the place back on the map, and the locals are flocking back to enjoy their hospitality, the food and the drinks. The inn is also growing in popularity as a place for motorists and visitors to the area to pause for refreshment or to relax over a leisurely meal.

This super place is open all day, every day, from 9 o'clock in the morning until late in the evening. Harveys Sussex Best is the permanent real ale, and in the two bars there's also a good selection of other draught and bottled beers, lagers and draught and cask ciders. Food is a major and growing part of the business. Breakfasts and brunches range from bacon butties and peppery huevos rancheros to the full works – Butcher's Blow-Out, with two of everything. The summer menu takes a trip round the UK, Europe and beyond, with anything from garlic mushrooms, tapas-

for-two and gazpacho andaluz to fish & chips, Harveys beef pie of the day, rib-eye steak, coq au vin, spaghetti with a variety of sauces and Massaman curry with roasted spices, potatoes, cauliflower, tomatoes and peas with coconut cream. The inn also offers what must surely be the longest and most interesting list of sandwiches and baguettes. The inn has a bar menu and a take-away service until 11pm. Orders 'to go' can be taken over the phone.

Live groups and bands accompany some lunches and dinners, usually on Friday or Saturday. The hospitality, the food and the drink are good reasons to visit the Pig & Butcher, and there could soon be another. They hope soon to have Bed & Breakfast accommodation available (phone for progress), when the inn will become a very pleasant base for a break away from the bustle of city life. Local attractions include the Wealden towns of Uckfield and Crowborough, the popular Bluebell Railway and the ancient Ashdown Forest, a place of recreation and a designated Area of Outstanding Natural Beauty, a Site of Special Scientific Interest and a Special Protection Area for birds.

Uckfield Road (A26), nr Ringmer,
East Sussex BN8 5RX
☎ 01273 812040
e-mail: matt@cockpub.co.uk
🌐 www.cockpub.co.uk

The **Cock Inn** enjoys a superb location on the A26 between Lewes and Uckfield. The 16th century former coaching inn has retained many handsome original features, including oak beams, flagstone floors and a log fire in an inglenook hearth. Outside, there's a small terrace to the front and a huge garden and patio at the side with trees, shrubs and flowers that commands lovely views across the open fields to the South Downs. The pub takes its name not from a rooster but a horse: a cock horse was a spare horse kept ready at the foot of a hill to help with a heavy load on the uphill haul.

Today's visitors will find all the assistance they need along with excellent hospitality dispensed by the Ridley family, Ian and Val and their children Matt, Nick and Caroline. The whole family takes great pride in the professional way they run this splendid old inn, an approach that extends far beyond the welcoming smiles to the top-notch food and drink. The bar is open Monday to Saturday 11am-3pm and 6pm-11.30pm; Sunday 11am - 11.30pm for drinks, which usually include a selection of real ales from Harvey's Brewery

– Best, Old and Mild – and London Pride from Fuller's, as well as a hand-pulled cider and a good choice of wines to enjoy on their own or to accompany a meal.

Matt is one of the chefs and whether you choose to eat inside (there is seating for 72 diners - 36 of which are in the air-conditioned restaurant) or out in the garden, lovers of good food are in for a real treat. Matt and his colleagues seek out the best local produce and everything is freshly cooked to order. The menu offers an exceptional choice that's made even wider by the specials board. All the pub classics are there, from garlic mushrooms, chicken liver pâté and prawn cocktail to scampi, battered cod, home-cooked ham and steak pie or pudding. The steaks are Scotch Premier and, along with most of the other meat, are supplied by top butchers, Lew Howard & Son, of Ringmer. Daily specials might include vegetarian quiches, whole fresh brill, Thai-style mussels, pan-fried duck breast with warm cherries and Moroccan-style lamb tagine. Some dishes are so popular that they make the move from the board to the regular menu: local venison sausages with mash & onion gravy; Val's Purse – sirloin steak stuffed with stilton and served with a cream & mushroom sauce. Home-made sweets like apple pie, treacle tart and rhubarb crumble set the seal on a meal to remember. Food is available Monday to Friday 12 noon - 2.15pm and 6pm - 9.30pm; Saturday 12 noon - 2.30pm and 6pm - 9.30pm; Sunday 12 noon - 9.30pm. Reservations are recommended, especially for the week-ends.

422 THE GARDEN ROOM CAFÉ GALLERY

14 Station Street, Lewes,
East Sussex BN7 2DA
☎ 01273 478636

The **Garden Room Café Gallery** is a real
gem standing near the station in the county
town of East Sussex. It also has a gem of an
owner in Cynthia Parrott, a lady, now in her
80th year, who didn't feel like quiet
retirement and took up the challenge of
creating this super tea room and making it
such a success not just with the local
community but with the many visitors who
come to Lewes throughout the year. The
home-made cakes are a treat definitely not to
be

missed, and on the savoury side the daily choice might include
soups, jacket potatoes, nut loaf with apricot sauce, spinach &
mushroom pie, chicken, ham & mushroom pie, buttered leek &
potato bake and a super fish pie with Pollock, king prawns and
sweetcorn. There are seats for 30 inside and a further 20 in the
garden, a lovely spot with a paved area, shrubs and bushes and
green garden furniture. The Garden Room is open from 10 to 5
Monday to Saturday and by arrangement at other times for
private parties. No credit cards

423 THE FORESTERS ARMS

6 South Street, East Hoathley,
East Sussex BN8 6DS
☎ 01825 840208
e-mail: forestersarms1@aol.com

The **Foresters Arms** stands by the church in
the village of East Hoathley, signposted off
the A22
Hailsham to
Uckfield road.
It has splendid
hosts in Rachel
and Steve, and
in the linked
bar areas or at
picnic sets at

the front patrons can enjoy a full range of
drinks including up to three real ales. They
have also built up a good reputation for the
food served at the inn, which includes a light
bar menu, a main menu mixing pub classics
and less familiar dishes, and a breakfast menu
served from 10 to 12 on Sunday. No food
Monday lunchtime. Families with children
and dogs are always welcome, and the inn
accepts the major credit cards.

424 THE BLACK LION

Lewes Road, Halland,
East Sussex BN8 6PN
Tel: 01825 840304   Fax: 01825 840940
e-mail: info@theblacklion-halland.co.uk

The **Black Lion** is an attractive tile-hung inn
standing in the village of Halland, on a
roundabout at the junction of the A22 and
the B2192. Leaseholders John and Mandy
Davies, son Sean and daughter Grace make
this a real family affair, and since their arrival
here in the spring of 2005 they have been steadily growing the business. The bar is open from
midday to 11 every day of the week, and food is served from 12 to 2.30 and 6.30 to 9 and all day
on Sunday. Mandy's dishes attract a loyal band of regulars from all around the region, and booking
is strongly recommended to be sure of getting a table at the time you want. Typical dishes on her
tempting menus range from mussels in a creamy garlic sauce and breaded brie with cranberry jelly

to burgers, fish & chips, steaks, lamb shanks, curries, pasta, rack of
ribs and nut roasts. Sandwiches, baguettes, jacket potatoes and salads
are available at lunchtime for smaller appetites or for those with less
time to spare. The inn is a very pleasant and comfortable base for a
break, with five en suite double/twin rooms and two singles that
share a bathroom. Among the many nearby attractions is Bentley
House and motor Museum, a splendid Palladian mansion with art
treasures, wonderful formal gardens and a superb collection of
vintage and historic motor cars and motorcycles.

425 THE BLACK HORSE

Byworth, nr Petworth,
West Sussex GU28 0HL
☎ 01798 342424
website: www.theblackhorsebyworth.com

Pub lovers flock from all over the county to enjoy
the excellent hospitality offered at the **Black
Horse**, a charming old country pub on the A283
Pulborough road a mile east of Petworth. When
Jeff Paddock took over the reins in the autumn of
2007 he brought a wealth of experience in the licensed
trade, and his expertise and affable character are rewarded
with a growing band of regulars from within and outside
the local community.

The main bar, in classic style with pew seating, bare
floorboards, scrubbed wooden tables, an open fire and
period pictures and photographs, is a convivial spot for
enjoying good conversation and a glass of well-kept ale.
In summer, the scene shifts to the attractive garden with

tables and chairs on
grassy terraces,
shrubs, flowers and
views across the

valley. In the back dining room or in the upstairs restaurant a
fine range of food is served. Starters like smooth duck pâté,
moules marinière or baby Dover sole could precede sausages &
mash, seared mackerel fillet with saffron rice, veal escalope
with linguini and wild mushroom sauce or chargrilled fillet
steak. Roasts are added to the Sunday choice, and the inn has
an excellent 'grown-up' children's menu.

426 THE THATCHED HOUSE

Limmer Lane, Felpham, Bognor Regis,
West Sussex PO22 7EJ
☎ 01243 865953
e-mail: thatchedhouse@safe.mail.net

The artist and poet William Blake came to Felpham in 1800 to undertake some engraving work for a local gentleman. In Blake's Road still stands Blake's Cottage, where he wrote; '*Away to sweet Felpham for Heaven is there*' and *Jerusalem*. Felpham, on the coast east of Bognor Regis, is still a charming place and the **Thatched House** is a delightful spot to pause for refreshment or to enjoy a break. Built in 1778, it is believed to be the oldest pub in the village, with traditional décor, a pleasant ambience and an excellent host in Jim Driscoll. Fullers London Pride and a superbly kept Guinness are among the favourite tipples, and bar and restaurant menus provide a great choice for hungry patrons. From the former come classics like omelettes, ham & eggs, liver & bacon and steak & ale

pie, while a meal from the Saturday evening à la carte menu might include baked avocado and crab mornay, skate with capers and black butter, chicken breast with bacon, cheese & a barbecue sauce or a succulent steak, with summer pudding or white chocolate cheesecake to finish. Two quiet en suite bedrooms provide a comfortable base for ramblers, cyclists, holidaymakers or people working in the area.

427 THE COACH & HORSES

Compton, nr Chichester,
West Sussex PO18 9HA
☎ 02392 631228
e-mail: coachandhorses@sky.com

The **Coach & Horses** is a 17th century pub in a peaceful village of brick and flint buildings under the steep slope of Telegraph Hill, on the B2146 south of Petersfield and David and Christiane, established here for more than 20 years, welcome everyone from locals and ramblers to tourists, families and coach parties. The interior is everything a traditional country pub should be, with an open fire in the roomy front bar, pine shutters and panelling in the Village Bar, a restored pitched-pine block floor and a mix of sturdy old tables and chairs. Real ale fans are in for a treat with a choice of five brews, typically Harveys Best Bitter, Fullers ESB, Dark Star Hophead plus their range of mild and seasonal beers. This is also

a good place to bring an appetite. David's chalkboard menu offers plenty of choice, from baguettes with a variety of generous fillings to crackling pork belly, warm salad of pigeon breast and bacon, daily fish specials, chicken & mushroom pie, large rib-eye steaks, vegetarian main courses and tempting homemade desserts. There are tables and chairs by the square at the front of the inn – an attractive asset when the sun shines.

428 RUSSONS RESTAURANT

8 Church Street, Stratford-upon-Avon,
Warwickshire CV37 6HB
☎ 01789 268822
🌐 www.russonsrestaurant.co.uk

Two cheerful rooms in a Grade II listed
building are an inviting setting for enjoying a
fine meal from an excellent seasonal menu,
with service to
match. There's
always a good
choice for meat-
eaters and
vegetarians as well
as an exceptional
selection of daily

seafood specials typified by battered fish &
chips, grilled smoked haddock, Cajun-inspired
swordfish, garlicky grilled king prawns and
plaice topped with mango and banana. This
popular family run restaurant, which lies just
south of the town centre, is open for lunch
from 11.30 to 2 and for dinner (including
lighter pre-theatre suppers) from 5.15 to 9.
Closed Sunday evening and all day Monday.

430 LARKRISE COTTAGE

Upper Billesley, nr Stratford-upon-Avon,
Warwickshire CV37 9RA
☎ 01789 268618
🌐 www.larkrisecottage.co.uk

Alan and Jenny Bailey have made a lovely old
gamekeeper's cottage available for Bed &
Breakfast guests. The location of **Larkrise
Cottage** is both beautiful and tranquil, with a
pretty garden and
superb views over
the Avon Valley and
the rolling Cotswold
hills. It's also just
three miles from the
centre of Stratford,
making it an ideal
stopover for the

theatre, for walkers, cyclists and tourists
exploring the local places of interest – Mary
Arden's house is a 15-minute walk away. The
accommodation at the cottage comprises a
double room and a twin room, both with
private bathroom, television and beverage
tray, and the excellent breakfast that starts the
day includes eggs from the owners' own free-
range hens.

429 THE OLD THATCH TAVERN

23 Greenhill Street, Stratford-upon-Avon,
Warwickshire CV37 6LE
☎ 01789 295216

New management (Sandie Coleman took over
in 2007), new staff and a new chef are
bringing the good times back to the **Old
Thatch Tavern**, which stands close to the
town centre by
the Rother Street
Market Cross, the
Civic Hall and the
Teddy Bear
Museum. First
licensed in 1623,
the oldest and
only thatched pub

in Stratford has enormous period appeal, with
lovely open fires, rustic furniture and well-
chosen pictures. The cooking is fittingly
traditional, with classics like fish & chips,
cottage pie, liver with bacon & onions, faggots,
beef hotpot and the day's roast. Three real ales
are on tap in the bar – typically Flowers IPA,
Shepherd Neame Spitfire and UBU from the
Warwickshire Purity Brewery – and there's a
good selection of house wines.

653

431 FOLLY FARM COTTAGE

Back Street, Ilmington,
Warwickshire CV36 4LJ
☎ 01608 682425
🌐 www.follyfarm.co.uk

Folly Farm offers luxurious Bed & Breakfast and self-catering accommodation in pleasant and peaceful rural surroundings. The farm stands at the foot of the Campden Hills, part of the Cotswolds Area of Outstanding Natural Beauty, providing an ideal base for walking, cycling or visiting the nearby villages and towns. The cottage, once a stable for the now long-gone village farm, was sympathetically restored and extended by owners Bruce and Pam McFarlane to create a large country cottage offering superb accommodation that combines the charm of the old with the comfort and

amenities of the new. Rose, Honeysuckle and Lavender Suites are decorated to match their names; the first two have king-size four-poster beds and en suite bathrooms with corner whirlpool bath and shower, while Lavender has a Victorian-style half-tester bed. All overlook the large sunny garden. A full English breakfast (with options) is served in the lovely dining room. The self-catering accommodation consists of two suites, each with a king-size pine four-poster, en suite double whirlpool bath, television and video in the bedroom and lounge, a fully-equipped kitchenette and a private garden or patio.

432 THE FOX & GOOSE COUNTRY INN

Armscote, nr Stratford-upon-Avon,
Warwickshire CV37 8DD
☎ 01608 682293
e-mail: mail@foxandgoose.co.uk
🌐 www.foxandgoose.co.uk

What started life several centuries ago as a pair of cottages with a blacksmith's forge is now a fine country inn of wide appeal – as a popular local, as a destination restaurant and as a comfortable hotel. The **Fox & Goose Country inn**, in the excellent care of the Royal family, lies in beautiful Warwickshire countryside six miles south of Stratford-upon-Avon off the A3400 Shipston-on-Stour road. Sensitively refurbished with due respect to its age, it has a cosily traditional bar with red-painted walls and inviting cushions on pew seats, and an equally appealing restaurant with cream-coloured walls. Outside is a lovely garden with lawns, benches and tables and chairs under vines in a decked area. 12 rotated ales, come mainly from regional breweries, and the bar keeps a good selection of wines. Bar and restaurant menus provide a good choice of wholesome,

generously served dishes prepared by a talented team at the stoves. The daily changing choice might include red onion and feta-stuffed mushrooms, sea bass fillets, beef stir-fry and a super beef and butcombe ale pie. The inn is an ideal base for both business and leisure visitors, and the bedrooms are stylish, comfortable and superbly appointed. The Inn also has open log fires and free internet access. They're also highly individual, even quirky, as each is named and themed after a character in the board game Cluedo. The Fox & Goose is open lunchtime and evening and all day in the summer.

433 THE PEACOCK

Oxhill, nr Stratford-upon-Avon,
Warwickshire CV35 0QU
☎ 01295 688060

The **Peacock** is a 16th century village inn
tastefully updated and run in fine style by
friends Yvonne Hamlett and Pam Farrell.
Yvonne is a professional caterer who relished
the challenge
of providing
top-class
home-cooked
food to her
patrons, who
can enjoy her
classic English
cooking with
some imaginative touches either in the slate-
floored bar or in the 30-cover dining room.
Fish fresh from Brixham is always popular
among the daily specials. Oxhill is a pretty
Cotswold-stone village just off the A422
Stratford-Banbury road. Its 12th century
Church of St Laurence is well worth a look,
and the site of the Battle of Edgehill (1642)
is another local attraction.

HIDDEN PLACES GUIDES

Explore Britain and Ireland with
Hidden Places guides - a fascinating
series of national and local travel
guides.

Packed with easy to read information
on hundreds of places of interest as
well as places to stay, eat and drink.

Available from both high street and
internet booksellers

For more information on the full range
of *Hidden Places* guides and other
titles published by Travel Publishing
visit our website on

www.travelpublishing.co.uk
or ask for our leaflet by phoning
01752 276660   or emailing
info@travelpublishing.co.uk

434 THE ROSE & CROWN

Church Lane, Ratley, nr Stratford-upon-
Avon, Warwickshire OX15 6DS
☎ 01295 678148
e-mail: k.marple@btinternet.co.uk
🌐 www.roseandcrownratley.co.uk

In the quiet, unspoilt village of Ratley, the **Rose &
Crown** is a charming old golden stone inn with a
steeply-raked roof and distinctive tall chimneys. It's
run in the friendliest of ways by Mary Houguez
and her partner
Ken Marples,
who always have a warm and genuine welcome for anyone who
passes through the door –and that includes families with children
and dogs. Inside, there's a wonderful old-world feel assisted by a
real fire in the vast stone hearth and a wood-burning stove in
another area. A patio with tables and chairs is a lovely spot to
enjoy a drink and something to eat on a summer's day. Five real
ales, typically including Winter Warmer, Charles Wells Eagle IPA
and Bombardier, St Austell Tribute and Greene King Abbot Ale,
provide a super choice for real ale connoisseurs, and various

menus cater for a wide range of tastes and appetites. Patrons come
from miles around to enjoy a meal here, so it's wise to book, especially
at the weekend. Food is served from 12 to 2.30 and from 7 to 9 (no
food Sunday evening or Monday (the pub is closed Monday
lunchtime). Ratley lies just a few miles north of Banbury off the A422
Stratford road. This is excellent walking country, with circular walks
of various lengths that take in the local scenery and sights, including
the Edgehill Battle site (1642). Another much-visited local attraction is
the National Herb Centre at Warmington.

435 THE GOLDEN CROSS COUNTRY INN & DINING HOUSE

Wixford Road, Ardens Grafton,
nr Stratford-upon-Avon,
Warwickshire B50 4LG
☎ 01789 772420

The **Golden Cross** is a charming stone-built country inn and restaurant in an attractive country setting among open fields, reached off the B439 a short drive west of Stratford-upon-Avon. Thanks to the hard work and enthusiasm of owners Steve and Pat Wainwright, the inn, immaculate after a top-to-toe refurbishment programme, is firmly established as one of the most appealing and inviting inns in the area, and one of the very best for a drink and a meal. The tastefully updated

public rooms are particularly warm and welcoming, and in the sunnier months the garden provides a very pleasant outdoor alternative. Four real ales, usually a Charles Wells brew and some from local breweries, are on tap to quench thirsts, and excellent wines can be enjoyed on their own or to accompany a bar snack or a meal. Everything on the menus is freshly prepared and cooked on the premises, and the chefs use as much local produce as possible. Blackboard menus make mouthwatering reading, and results on the plate never disappoint. Fish brought fresh from Brixham is always a popular order, and other choices might include home-cured beetroot and vodka-cured gravid lax, slow-braised lamb shank, the Sunday roasts and a delicious lemon tart with fruit compote. Food and drink are served lunchtime and evening and all day at the weekend. The owners also have the Stag at Red Hill (qv), four miles west of Stratford.

436 THE STAG AT RED HILL

Alcester Road, Red Hill, nr Stratford-upon-
Avon, Warwickshire B49 6NQ
☎ 01789 764634 Fax: 01789 764431
e-mail: info@thestagatredhill.co.uk
⊕ www.thestagatredhill.co.uk

In the same ownership as the Golden Cross at Ardens Grafton (qv), the **Stag at Red Hill** stands in attractive grounds on the A435 four miles west of Stratford-upon-Avon. The lovely location, with views south to the Cotswolds and the Vale of Avon,

makes it a delightful place to visit, whether it's for a drink, a snack, a meal or an overnight or longer break. The building itself, which dates from the 16th century, is full of charm and character; it once served as a courthouse and jail for Stratford assizes, and some of the original cell doors and windows are still in place. Today's visitors are only too happy to be detained to enjoy the outstanding hospitality extended by Steve and Pat Wainwright and their staff. The

bar is a perfect spot for a drink and a chat, and super food is served lunchtime and evening.

The menus are full of interest, as shown by a typical list that offers River Exe mussels marinière, pancetta-wrapped monkfish, lamb & red wine casserole with spring onion mash & rosemary dumplings, and wild mushroom, spinach & Roquefort filo tart. The guest accommodation comprises ten quiet, comfortable rooms, seven with en suite shower, three with bath and shower.

437 THE VINEYARD COUNTRY PUB & RESTAURANT

Abbot's Salford, Warwickshire WR11 8UT
☎ 01386 870217
⊕ www.vineyardinn.co.uk

The **Vineyard** is a superb country pub and restaurant that's the vibrant heartbeat of Abbot's Salford, which lies just moments from the A46 between Evesham and Bidford-on-Avon. Terry Maleary and his team have created a particularly warm and friendly atmosphere in which everyone is made to feel welcome, and the bar, with its stone floors and open log fires, is an inviting, traditional setting for enjoying a variety of cask ales and ciders, draught and bottled beers, lagers and fine wines. The bar is open all day, seven days a week, and a wide variety of excellent food, freshly prepared and cooked by Terry, is served lunchtime and evening and all day at the weekend in the roomy high-beamed restaurant. As well as the regular menu, there's a separate theme for

every day of the week: a typical week might include comfort food on Monday, steak on Tuesday, quiz and paella on Wednesday, surf 'n' turf on Friday and a Sunday carvery. The Vineyard has full disabled access, a beer garden and sheltered patio, a children's play area and a large car park. It also has a site for caravans and camper vans. As experienced caterers, Terry and his staff are happy to help in organising wedding, birthday and other social occasions.

438 THE COTTAGE OF CONTENT

Barton, nr Bidford-on-Avon,
Warwickshire B50 4NP
☎ 01789 772279
e-mail: cofc@btinternet.com

The **Cottage of Content** – the perfect name for a great place to wine, dine and make merry. This most sociable of spots stands near the River Avon in the pretty little of Barton. Richard Armstrong team have a warm welcome for one and all, and in the delightful surroundings visitors can enjoy a fine selection of real ales and wines to enjoy on their own or to accompany anything from a lunchtime bar snack to a wide-ranging main menu of superb English dishes freshly prepared and cooked to order by Richard and his team. The Cottage of Content is open lunchtime and evening and all day at the weekend and in the summer months. At the back of the cottage are pitches for 27 caravans available from March to October.

439 THE PLOUGH INN

Tower Hill, Bidford-on-Avon,
Warwickshure B50 4DZ
☎ 01789 778782

With its cream-painted frontage and brown-painted timbers, the **Plough Inn** is easy to spot on the B439 on the edge of Bidford-on-Avon, eight miles west of Stratford. Dating back to the 18th century, it has been completely renovated by Enterprise Inns, and in Jezz Walker it has a host who really knows his trade. The comfortable bar, with settees and benches in bay windows, is a pleasant spot to enjoy a drink, and at the back is a games room with pool and darts. A good choice of food, from panini to pizza and home-made pies, is served lunchtime seven days a week and every evening except Sunday, and Jezz organises regular steak and curry nights.

657

440 THE ARROW MILL

Arrow, nr Alcester, Warwickshire B49 5NL
☎ 01789 762419 Fax: 01789 765170
e-mail: enquiries@arrowmill.co.uk
⊕ www.arrowmill.com

For 20 years the Woodhams family have been dispensing hospitality, real ales, traditional food and a good choice of wines at the **Arrow Mill**. Their handsome redbrick hotel enjoys an attractive riverside setting opposite Ragley Hall, and just a mile south of the Roman town of Alcester. Its appearance has changed little since its days as a working flour mill, and beyond the ivy-clad porch the inn has abundant traditional appeal, with oak beams and log fires. The hotel has 18 en suite bedrooms, each with its own individual appeal, all with en suite bathrooms, television, direct-dial phone and tea/coffee-making facilities. The Millstream Restaurant has earned a far-reaching reputation for culinary excellence, and

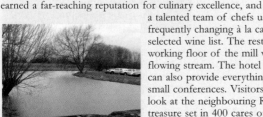

a talented team of chefs use the best market-fresh produce for a frequently changing à la carte menu complemented by a carefully selected wine list. The restaurant incorporates the original working floor of the mill with its mill still turning, driven by the flowing stream. The hotel caters well for private functions and can also provide everything needed for business meetings and small conferences. Visitors to the Arrow Mill should take time to look at the neighbouring Ragley Hall, a genuine 17th century treasure set in 400 cares of parkland and gardens landscaped by Capability Brown.

411 ROBBIES OF WARWICK

74 Smith Street, Warwick,
Warwickshire CV34 4HU
☎ 01926 400470
e-mail: brian@robbiesofwarwick.co.uk
⊕ www.robbiesofwarwick.co.uk

Owner Brian Mallett puts his long experience in catering to fine use in **Robbies of Warwick**, his top-class restaurant located halfway between the Castle and St Johns in the old part of town. A short, imaginative, modern British menu is served

from 6 to 11.30, with lunch available by arrangement. Typical dishes include seared tuna steak, guinea fowl stuffed with black pudding & winter berries, braised pork belly and lobster Thermidor. The outstanding food is complemented by a well-chosen wine list featuring wines from Italy and Lebanon. Booking is recommended, particularly at the weekend.

442 KENILWORTH CASTLE

Castle Green, Kenilworth,
Warwickshire CV8 1NE
☎ 01926 852078
⊕ www.english-heritage.org.uk

Explore the Medieval Living Village within the castle walls as it would been in the Middle Ages. Watch the potter, shoemaker, blacksmith and rat catcher at work, Wander through the stalls and houses to the sounds of medieval music or relax in the village tavern with some real ale!

443 THE THREE HORSESHOES INN

Spring Hill, Bubbenhall, nr Coventry,
Warwickshire CV8 8BD
☎ 02476 302108
🖳 www.threehorseshoesinn.co.uk

The **Three Horseshoes** is situated in an
attractive village between Coventry and
Leamington Spa.
Bridget and Richard
are excellent hosts,
and their pub is a
very pleasant place
to pause for
refreshment. Three
traditional ales are

on tap to be enjoyed in the bar or out on the
terrace overlooking the village green. The bar
and the surrounding area are also good spots
to relax over a meal from a menu that
includes traditional English food in addition
to Anglo-Indian and Italian options. Seven
spacious en suite bedrooms, one adapted for
guests with mobility difficulties, provide a
quiet base for both business and leisure
visitors. Although Coventry Airport is close
by there is no airport noise thus ensuring a
good nights sleep.

444 THE CROSS KEYS

16 High Street, Great Bedwyn,
nr Marlborough, Wiltshire SN8 3NU
☎ 01672 870678
🖳 www.thekeys.com

Bruce and Sue welcome one and all to their
cheerful, comfortable village pub on the main street
of Great Bedwyn. Open from 12 to 3 and 6 to 11
and all day on Sunday, the **Cross Keys** is an
excellent choice for a meal, with a menu that offers
something for everyone. Favourites range from fish
cakes (salmon & crab, smoked haddock &
spring onions), to lasagne, battered cod with home-
made chips, crusty pies (steak & kidney, creamy
chicken), rack of BBQ pork ribs, chicken fajitas and
rump steak with all the traditional trimmings. There's
always a good choice of vegetarian main courses, with
baguettes and jacket potatoes for quicker meals. Steps
lead up to a pretty garden where tables and chairs are
set out in the summer. The Cross Keys is also a good

base for
exploring the
region, and the
three bedrooms,
including a family
room, are quiet

and comfortable. In Great Bedwyn itself the 11th century
Church of St Mary the Virgin is well worth a visit, as is the
Lloyds Stone Museum, a monument to the skills of the
English stonemason. Among the many nearby attractions are
the Kennet & Avon Canal and Savernake Forest.

445 THE FOXHAM INN

Foxham, nr Chippenham,
Wiltshire SN15 4NQ
☎ 01249 740665
e-mail: info@thefoxhaminn.co.uk
⊕ www.thefoxhaminn.co.uk

Privately owned by Neil and Sarah Cooper, the **Foxham Inn** is a place to seek out for its outstanding food. The owners are proud to use as much local produce as possible in dishes that combine classic technique with a generous measure of creativity. Lamb comes from their neighbours at Avon Farm, pork from Carpenters Farm 2 miles away and eggs from their own chickens. Many of the vegetables, fruit and herbs come from their own kitchen garden, and they cure their own bacon and smoke their own ham, venison and sea trout. The cheeseboard features the products of Bath Soft Cheese. Desserts (all homemade of course) include some super ice creams to enjoy on their own or in delicious dishes such as

champagne and raspberry jelly (vanilla ice cream) or Irish whiskey steamed pudding (Guinness ice cream). The inn serves two real ales and a weekly changing guest, and they stock an extensive range of wines, including ten by the glass) from Heritage Wines. The inn also offers a takeaway menu that includes fish & chips and a selection of curries.

44647 THE OLIVER CROMWELL

71 St Edith's Marsh, Bromham,
Wiltshire SN15 2DF
☎ 01380 850293
e-mail: carol_massey@live.co.uk

The **Oliver Cromwell** is a former coaching inn standing on the A342 Devizes to Chippenham road. Flower troughs adorn the cream-painted frontage, while inside all is delightfully traditional, with exposed stone walls, black beams, old implements and armoury and a massive stone hearth topped with a portrait of Cromwell. Carol Massey, who took over the tenancy in May 2007, has a warm welcome for friends old and new of all ages, and she has enhanced the pub's popularity as a place to seek out for a drink and a meal. Wadworth's 6X and

Sharp's Doom Bar are the regular real ales, and home-cooked food includes classics such as fish & chips and bangers & mash. The pub is very much the social hub of the local community; it has a function room with its own bar and a skittle alley in the old stable. If you're at a loose end on a Sunday, the Oliver Cromwell also serves a wholesome sunday lunch. The pub's large garden affords a distant view of Roundway Hill, scene of a violent Civil War battle in 1643 won by the Royalists under Maurice, brother of Prince Rupert.

447 THE CROWN INN

Chandler's Lane, Bishop's Canning,
nr Devizes, Wiltshire SN10 2JZ
☎ 01380 860218
e-mail: thecrown@bishopscanning.com

The **Crown Inn** is a top-of-the-range hostelry standing on Crown Land in the shadow of the Church of St Mary in the picturesque village of Bishop's Canning, just off the A361 four miles northeast of Devizes. Local lady Tanya Wynyard, and chef

Claire run the place in seriously professional style but with a light-hearted touch typified by a note on the menu – 'families, muddy boots and dogs with well-behaved owners are all most welcome'. Claire ensures that as much as possible of what goes into her kitchen comes from local growers and suppliers, and her menu, supplemented by blackboard specials, runs from devilled whitebait and prawn purses with a sweet chilli dip to lasagne (meat or vegetarian), battered cod, steak & ale pie and various chicken options curry, chasseur, sweet &

sour.). Lunchtime brings sandwiches, jacket potatoes, omelettes, a big breakfast and ham, egg & chips, and a popular carvery operates on Wednesday and Sunday. The Crown has ample off-road parking and a spacious beer garden with a children's play area. The pub is open all day Saturday and Sunday, lunchtime food is served from 12 until 2pm (to 3 on Sunday) evening food is served from 7pm until 9pm and extended to 9:30pm on Fridays and Saturdays.

448 THE LAMB INN

The Green, Urchfont, nr Devizes,
Wiltshire SN10 4QU
☎ 01380 848848
e-mail: elliott620@btinternet.com

In the picturesque village of Urchfont, 4 miles south of Devizes, the **Lamb** is a traditional country inn with parts going back as far as the 15th century. The redbrick

façade, part pink-washed and topped with a steeply raked thatched roof, hides an equally appealing interior, with a mix of traditional and contemporary décor and furnishings in the carpeted bar and dining area. John and Julie Elliott welcome visitors into a comfortable, relaxed ambience for enjoying a drink or a meal. Wadworth 6X and Henry's IPA are the resident real ales, and the printed menu and specials board provide a good choice of dishes that use locally

sourced ingredients whenever possible. The options span baguettes, salads and all-time favourites such as liver and bacon, battered cod, ham, egg & chips, steak & kidney pie and cottage pie, as well as the modern offering like chilli crab cakes. The Lamb has a good beer garden and ample off-road parking. Pub hours are 6 to 11 Monday, 12 to 3 & 6 to 11 Tuesday to Saturday and 12 to 11 Sunday. Traditional sunday roast is served from 12 - 6.

449 THE ROSE & CROWN

108 High Street, Worton, nr Devizes,
Wiltshire SN10 5SE
☎ 01380 724202
e-mail: theroseandcrown07@btconnect.com
⊕ www.theroseandcrown-worton.org.uk

Matt and Jean Bungay are the affable landlord and landlady at the **Rose & Crown** at Worton, which lies off the A360 (leave at Potterne) southwest of Devizes. They serve a good selection of real ales in the bar, which has the traditional look of low ceilings, sturdy wooden beams and a log fire in an inglenook fireplace. The hosts have made their pub not just a pleasant place to meet for a drink and good conversation, but a destination restaurant serving an across-the-board range of home-cooked snacks and meals. Bar snacks, including burgers and nachos, are available from 12 to 2 and from 6 to 9, and lunchtime also brings a light menu of sandwiches, jacket potatoes, basket meals and salads. The kitchen really comes into its own in the evening, when the menu combines tried-and-tested favourites with less familiar options. Deep-fried camembert, ham, egg & chips, rack

of ribs with a barbecue sauce and a mighty mixed grill are among the more familiar dishes, while the chef puts an individual stamp on dishes rarely seen on pub menus: roast pepper & mushroom couscous, halibut green curry, tamarind chicken, belly pork with a cider sauce, seared scallops with a white wine reduction and mushrooms with ginger, chilli and egg noodles. The pub has a dual-purpose skittle alley and function room, and outside is a patio/garden area and a large car park.

450 STOURHEAD HOUSE AND GARDENS

Stourhead Estate Office, Stourton,
Warminster, Wiltshire BA12 6QD
☎ 01747 841152
⊕ www.nationaltrust.org.uk

Often referred to as 'Paradise', lying in secluded privacy in its own valley, Stourhead is one of the finest landscape gardens in the world.

Stourhead's 18th century garden was created by Henry Hoare II. Inspired by the views of Italy captured by artists in paint, he decided to create a landscape garden with temples and Gothic ruins that would bring art to life. Sitting majestically above the garden and surrounded by delightful lawns and parkland is Stourhead

House: a fine Palladian mansion built by Colen Campbell, home to a unique collection of Chippendale furniture, magnificent paintings and an exquisite Regency library.

The House and Garden are at the heart of a 1,072 hectare (2,650 acre) estate. Enjoy strolling through the woodland, open countryside, and chalk downs on a range of way-marked walks. King Alfred's Tower, is a 2.5 mile walk from the garden. A 49 metre (160ft) triangular red brick folly, it commands magnificent views across Wiltshire, Somerset and Dorset.

451 THE CROSS KEYS INN

Upper Chute, Andover,
Hampshire SP11 9ER
☎ 01264 730295
e-mail: crosskeysinn@upperchute.com
⊞ www.upperchute.com

The village of Upper Chute stands in attractive countryside on the Hampshire-Wiltshire border, off the A342 seven miles northwest of Andover. There are two landmarks in the village: one is the parish church of St Nicholas, the other is the

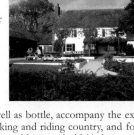

Cross Keys Inn. Go-ahead tenants George and Sonia Humphrey run this delightful place, which is equally appealing to the local community and to visitors from outside the area. The inn has earned Cask Marque recognition for its well-kept cask ales, which usually include three Fullers brews – LP, Discovery and Butser – as well as regularly changing guests. In the elegant restaurant chef Peter Bull's blackboard menu proposes a good choice of home-cooked dishes. There's usually a curry on the menu, as well as specials such as

marinated tuna steak. A good selection of wines, with many available by glass as well as bottle, accompany the excellent food. This is wonderful walking and riding country, and four en suite bedrooms in the converted barn and old kitchen provide a very quiet, civilised base for exploring the area. The inn has two loose boxes for guests who bring their horses for a riding holiday. Locals who arrive on horseback can tie up outside, where the hosts have provided a water trough.

452 THE EXPRESS INN

71 Quest Hills Road, Malvern,
Worcestershire WR14 1RN
☎ 01684 574777
e-mail: warnerlynette@hotmail.com

The **Express Inn** started life in the 1760s as a coaching inn, and for the local community it has long been a familiar landmark on its substantial corner site in a largely residential area in the angle of the B4503 and the A449 Ledbury to Worcester

road a little way above Malvern Link railway station. Express may be its name, but no one who discovers this friendly pub should be in a hurry to leave; it's open from noon to midnight seven days a week. At the beginning of 2008 the only food to be offered was a Sunday carvery operating from 12 to 3, but hardworking tenants Lynette and John, who took over here in 2005, hope soon to expand the food side of the business. They like to keep things simple, a principle that has been

rewarded with a strong and loyal local following. The tidy bar is a pleasant spot to put the world to rights over a glass of Marston's Bitter, and when the sun shines the scene could shift to the patio/beer garden. The pub hosts a disco/karaoke night once a month on a Friday, and a folk night once every two months on a Thursday.

663

453 THE COTFORD HOTEL & L'AMUSE BOUCHE RESTAURANT ★★★ ◎ ⊨ ¶

51 Graham Road, Malvern,
Worcestershire WR14 2HU
☎ 01684 572427 Fax: 01684 572952
e-mail: reservations@cotfordhotel.co.uk
⊕ www.cotfordhotel.co.uk

The **Cotford Hotel & L'Amuse Bouche Restaurant** is a 3 star establishment which offers outstanding accommodation and food in a lovely setting at the foot of the Malvern Hills. Since arriving here in the spring of 2007, Chris and Barbara Morgan have invested considerable time and resources into improving and updating the hotel's look and facilities. Built in 1851 in Gothic style for the Bishop of Worcester, it stands in mature landscaped gardens a few minutes' walk from the town centre yet with the feel of being miles from anywhere.

The tranquil setting, just off the A449 Worcester road, is just one of many attractions at this splendid place, where the owners and staff devote their energies into ensuring that their guests enjoy their stay to the full. The guest accommodation comprises 15 superb rooms, each with its own very individual charm and character. Top of the range are the grand Bishop's Room and the Garden Room in the coach house with its own private terrace. All are beautifully decorated and furnished, and all are equipped with satellite TV, high-speed internet access and tea/coffee facilities.

The tariff includes a full English breakfast, and special breaks with dinner, bed and breakfast for 2 nights or more. Guests can enjoy a game of croquet or take afternoon tea in the garden, chat over a glass of wine in the bar, relax in the piano lounge or take the air in the Malvern Hills. Chris has cooked in some of the world's top hotels, and a meal in L'Amuse Bouche restaurant is an experience to savour. Lovers of good food will appreciate his uniquely creative style that provides a taste of French gastronomy using the very best of the wonderful English produce that he seeks out. Typical dishes include young leaf spinach and Chardonnay soup, tian of organic pork and duckling rillettes, baked salmon fillet with a delicate lobster velouté, and flash-roasted rack of Ledbury lamb with a cordon of mint chiffonade and rosemary infusion. The restaurant has been awarded an AA rosette and is open to non-residents. It is also an ideal choice for pre-theatre suppers and small conferences.

454 THE THREE KINGS

Hanley Castle, Worcestershire WR8 0BL
☎ 01684 597686

Local lady Sue Roberts – she was born here – welcomes visitors of all ages to the **Three Kings**, which has the timeless charm and traditional appeal of a much-loved country inn. The building dates back to the early 16th century, and some original beams can still be seen in the only public room, the homely, cosy and down-to-earth Nell's Lounge Bar. It's a great place for connoisseurs of real ales, with varieties from the Hobson and Butcombe Breweries supplemented by three ever-changing guests (upwards of 400 different brews in a year!). For those with a taste for whisky the inn keeps an impressive selection of malts. Food is limited to a choice of hot and cold snacks, including popular toasties. The pub fields a

quiz team and hosts live music sessions on

Sunday nights. Opening hours are 12 to 3 and 7 to 11 seven days a week. The Three Kings stands just off the B4211 Upton-Malvern road at Hanley Castle. The village takes its name from the castle, which was originally a hunting lodge for King John. Except for the moat, the castle is long gone, but the village still has a number of attractions for the visitor, including picturesque cottages, a 16th century school and the brick-and-stone Church of St Mary.

455 THE ROYAL OAK

Broadwas-on-Teme,
Worcestershire WR6 5NE
☎ 01886 821353 Fax: 01886 821954
🌐 www.oakatbroadwas.co.uk

Food is the star of the show at the **Royal Oak**, a 19th century redbrick roadhouse in the village of Broadwas-on-Teme, on the A44 Bromyard-Leominster road and just ten minutes' drive from the centre of Worcester and 15 from J7 of the M5. The pub is a superb conversion of old barns, and the bars and lounge areas and the high-raftered restaurant areas are smart, stylish and absolutely immaculate. During the day there are excellent snacks, sandwiches, panini, jacket potatoes, ploughman's platters and traditional pub fare to choose from, while in the evening diners compose their own meals by selecting their main ingredient from the two extensive cool displays and telling the chefs how they want it cooked and what they want to accompany it. The choice

includes a wide variety of prime

steaks, gammon, lamb chops, up to 10 sorts of fish (to be grilled, fried, poached or steamed) and rotisserie chicken, duck and shoulder of lamb. There's also a do-it-yourself salad bar. The Royal oak is also a popular village local with a choice of bars and a wide selection of cask ales, bottled and draught beers, lagers, cider and wine. Bar times are 11 to 3 and 6 to 11, all day Saturday and Sunday; food times 12 to 2.30 and 6 to 9.30, all day Saturday and Sunday.

665

456 YE OLDE RED HORSE

Vine Street, Evesham,
Worcestershire WR11 4RE
☎ 01386 442784

Alwyn Sullivan was the manager here before taking over the lease in 2007, so she knows her customers – and they know her. One of the oldest hostelries in the Vale of Evesham, **Ye Olde Red Horse** attracts a wide cross-section of patrons from all walks of life – locals, families with their children and dogs, business people and visitors touring this lovely part of the world. Flowers in hanging baskets add splashes of colour to the black-and-white frontage, while inside all is

delightfully traditional, with roaring log fires keeping the cold at bay. The resident real ale comes from the Bass brewery, with popular guests including Mitchells brews, Cheddar Valley and Hobgoblin. The inn is an excellent place for a meal, with home-made pies and juicy steaks among the favourite dishes; Wednesday is steak night, with a 2 for 1 bargain deal. For those short of time or appetite there's a selection of snacks and quick bites. Major sporting events are shown on the big TV screen, and the pub hosts regular quizzes and occasional live music evenings. Five excellent bedrooms (four en suite, the other with its own private

bathroom), provide a very comfortable, civilised base for visitors. Evesham, which stands on a loop of the River Avon, is a pleasant, bustling market town at the centre of the Vale of Evesham. The town has a wealth of interesting buildings, including the Almonry Heritage Centre, the neighbouring churches of All Saints and St Lawrence and the magnificent bell tower of the long-ruined abbey. The Spring Blossom Trail is another attraction, a circular driving trail that takes in the sights and smells of the countryside in spring. This splendid old inn is open from 10am to 11pm (from 12 on Sunday) and food is served lunchtime and evening.

457 THE FLEECE INN

The Cross, Bretforton, nr Evesham,
Worcestershire WR11 7JE
☎ 01386 831173
e-mail: Nigel@thefleeceinn.co.uk
⊕ www.thefleeceinn.co.uk

The Fleece is a quintessential English country inn, originally a farmhouse, first licensed in 1848 and now in the care of the National Trust. Nigel Smith is an exceptional landlord, a man who knows his ales, his food and his customers, and he has made The Fleece a must for anyone who appreciates proper ale and decent food. Behind the lovely half-timbered frontage this outstanding hostelry is full of old-world charm and atmosphere, with small-paned lattice windows, low black-beamed ceilings, stone walls, sturdy old furniture and log fires in large open hearths. At the rear is an equally inviting beer garden.

Nigel offers a choice of some half-dozen real ales, including Hook Norton Best and Hooky, Pigs Ear from the Uley Brewery and regularly rotating guests. Two hand-pumped local ciders are also available. Cooking at the Fleece combines traditional and contemporary elements, with plenty of choice for both tastes. Sandwiches, either cold (tuna mayonnaise & cucumber, ham with vine tomatoes and/or Tewkesbury mustard) or hot (chicken,

mozzarella and red pesto; bacon, cranberry & brie) make excellent and filling snacks, along with the tasty and very moreish Gloucester potatoes: chips in a bowl served with melted Double Gloucestershire cheese and crispy bacon. Other choices run from chicken, walnut & stilton salad to scampi and the fish of the day, sausages and chive mash with red wine gravy and red onion marmalade; traditional local faggots; 100% beef burgers; steak, vegetable & ale casserole; spicy chilli; slow-roasted belly of pork and properly matured steaks (an evening speciality).

The Fleece can cater for barbecues and hog roasts on patrons' premises, weddings, parties and functions; it can provide an outside bar and has a barn for hire. A room in the oldest (15th century) part of the building is available for B&B guests. The Fleece is host to an asparagus festival, complete with auctions, at the end of May each year, and a special menu based on the wonderful Evesham Vale asparagus is offered in its short season. The Fleece, which is located in the attractive village of Bretforton, just east of Evesham, is open lunchtime and evening, all day Saturday and Sunday and all day every day during the summer months.

667

Alcester Road, Radford,
Worcestershire WR7 4LR
☎ 01386 792207

The **Wheelbarrow Castle** has been the social hub of the tiny village of Radford and the surrounding communities since the late-18th century. Recently refurbished in smartly contemporary style, it still retains the traditional appeal of a much-loved country inn, a real pub-lover's pub with an excellent host in Adrian Reidy. A Galway man, he worked here for a long time before taking over at the beginning of 2008 and really putting it, and Radford, back on the map (figuratively, but not quite literally, as Radford is not shown on all the large-scale road atlases – it is best reached by turning south off the A422 road between Inkberrow and Kington). Once found, this is a place to return to time and again for the warm, friendly ambience, the sociability and the good food and drink.

There's plenty of comfortable seating in the long beamed bar, where Timothy Taylor Landlord and a brew from the Wye Valley Brewery will satisfy the thirsts of real-ale connoisseurs, supported by a full range of other draught and bottled beers, lagers, wines, spirits and soft drinks. When the weather is warm, the sheltered terrace and garden really come into their own. In the bar or in the

elegant restaurant patrons can enjoy an exceptional variety of food. Typical choices run from Thai fish cakes and a home-made mushroom & garlic terrine to sea bass with parsley butter, roasted duck leg confit, succulent steaks and chicken breast stuffed with bacon, served with a cheddar cream sauce. For smaller appetites or anyone with less time to sit back and relax, a light menu proposes baguettes and medium servings of old favourites like scampi, lasagne, fish & chips or beef & mushroom pie. Vegetarians will always find plenty of choice, and the enjoyment level stays high to the end with scrumptious desserts like chocolate & orange bread & butter pudding, lemon meringue pie or strawberry & champagne sorbet. A lunchtime carvery operates every lunchtime, and in the evening a three-course table d'hote menu is an alternative to the à la carte choice.

Adrian and his staff host regular themed food nights (fish & chips on Friday) and are dab hands at organising parties and other celebrations. Tuesday brings an early-evening happy hour, Friday and Saturday are disco nights and Sunday sees a session music evening. This most likeable of pubs, with an affable landlord, cheerful staff and convivial company, is open from 11 in the morning till 11 at night Monday to Thursday and until 1am at the weekend.

459 BROMSGROVE MUSEUM

Bromsgrove, Worcestershire
☎ 01527 831809

Much of the earlier history of Bromsgrove can be seen at **Bromsgrove Museum**, which contains exhibits of the glass, salt and nail industries, and of the Bromsgrove Guild. It also contains an attractive range of shop windows, which feature costumes, toys, cameras and much more. The building is the former Coach House of Davenal House, built in 1780. On the front of the Museum the wrought iron balcony that originally adorned the stationmasters house at Bromsgrove can be seen. It is said that, in 1848, Stephenson, the great engineer, stood on it. The Museum is open Monday to Saturday, 10.30am - 12.30pm and 1.00pm - 4.30pm. Free admittance.

Looking for:

- *Places to Visit?*
- *Places to Stay?*
- *Places to Eat & Drink?*
- *Places to Shop?*

460 THE LENCHFORD INN

Shrawley, Worcestershire WR6 6TB
☎ 01905 620229 Fax: 01905 621125
e-mail: info@lenchfordinn.plus.com
⊕ www.thelenchfordinn.co.uk

The **Lenchford Inn** is a Georgian building with modern extensions, located on the banks of the River Severn, in a small village between Stourport and Worcester. The four partners in the enterprise, David & Marie Taylor and Ian & Wendy Hadley, welcome a wide cross-section of the public, from locals, walkers and boaters to bikers, fishermen, motorists and coach parties.

The interior of the pub, including a bar, lounge, dining area and games room, was smartly redecorated at the beginning of 2008, and outside is a pleasant garden and a decked area overlooking the river. The inn has 120 feet of moorings and a very large car park. The owners offer an extensive choice of draught beers and a wide variety of lagers, cider, wines and spirits. A bar/snack menu is available every day except Sunday, along with an à la carte menu. The inn is open from 11am to midnight, and food is served from 12 to 3 and 6 to 9 weekdays and all day Saturday. Sunday lunch is a traditional carvery operating from 12 to 4 and additionally from 6 to 9 in the summer. There's also a carvery on summer Wednesday evenings.

The Lenchford has nine en suite letting rooms, all with lovely river views, and a large function room. It holds a civil ceremony licence.

669

461 THE TALBOT HOTEL ⊨ ¶

Newnham Bridge, Tenbury Wells,
Worcestershire WR15 8JF
☎ 01584 781355 Fax: 01584 781186
e-mail: sue@thetalbothotel.co.uk
⊕ www.thetalbothotel.co.uk

Guests have only to walk through the door to feel the warmth of the welcome provided by Sue and Michael James at the **Talbot Hotel**. Standing amid the lovely scenery

of the Teme Valley, this fine example of Victorian architecture is equally distinguished outside and inside, where the beautiful rooms range from a traditional public bar to a modern, airy lounge and three restaurants in different styles. Upstairs are five en suite guest rooms with TV, WIFI, radio-alarm clock, hairdryer, beverage tray with Fair Trade tea and coffee and views of the countryside and the hotel's stretch of the river.

Guests have the choice of a very varied breakfast menu, and allergies and special preferences can be catered for with a little notice. The hotel, which has plenty of well-lit parking space, stands at the junction of the A456 Birmingham-Leominster road and the A443 Worcester-Tenbury Wells road. The hotel is open for delicious food and local ales everyday exept Monday Lunchtime.

462 THE GREAT WESTERN INN ¶

Manchester Road, Marsden, Huddersfield,
West Yorkshire HD7 6NL
☎ 01484 844315
e-mail: enquiries@greatwesterninn.co.uk
⊕ www.greatwesterninn.co.uk

Alex and Rachel guarantee the warmest of welcomes for visitors to the **Great Western Inn**, an outstanding country pub in an outstanding country location. It stands on the A62 a mile southwest of Marsden, surrounded by thousands of acres of moorland looking over and towards Wessenden and Saddleworth Moors. In this superb setting Alex and Rachel have made their early Victorian coaching inn a magnet for those who appreciate the qualities of a classic English pub. One of those qualities is good wholesome food generously served, and Rachel's menus offer just that, with tried-and-tested favourites like scampi, lasagne, spaghetti bolognese, pies, curries, lamb Henry and Friday's fish specials guaranteed to leave diners happy and satisfied. No one is forgotten at the Great Western, and the main menu is supplemented by

menus for children and the over-60s An Early Bird menu (5 to 7.30 Tuesday to Friday) adds further to the eating options. At least three cask ales are on tap in the bar, typically Black Sheep and Timothy Taylor's Best and Golden Best, along with a real cider and a full range of other beers, lagers, wines and spirits. The pub is closed on Mondays except Bank Holidays, otherwise open lunchtime and evening and all day on Saturday and Sunday.

670

Netherton Moor Road, Netherton,
Huddersfield West Yorkshire HD4 7LE
☎ 01484 668949
Fax: 01484 668940
🌐 www.hinchliffes.com/restaurant

The **Old Farmhouse** stands in the grounds of the widely acclaimed Hinchliffe Farm Shop, a short walk from the centre of Netherton. It's a licensed tea room by day and a licensed restaurant in the evening and both are far removed from the eating outlets that sometimes attach themselves to farms and farm shops. Louise and Richard run this outstanding two-in-one enterprise for owner Simon Hirst, and they and their staff produce 'food that soothes' for their definitely soothed customers, many of whom make regular trips from many miles away.

The tea room, open from 9 to 5 (Sunday 10 to 4), serves a wide selection of savoury and sweet snacks and meals that make use of as much local produce as possible, including beef and eggs from our own farms. A range of sausages is produced on the farm, and the bacon is cured on the premises. Cakes, pastries, scones and biscuits can be enjoyed with morning coffee or afternoon tea (or indeed throughout opening hours) and the lunch menu offers sandwiches, salads and daily hot specials. The sandwiches are not just ordinary sandwiches, they are satisfying meals in themselves: Hinchliffe sausage with melted brie and home-made sticky red onion; grilled goat's cheese with sun-blush tomatoes, thick pesto and olives; farmhouse beef burger with bacon, smoked applewood cheese, pickles & hand-cut chips and the mighty speciality pan-fried rump steak with blue stilton, sticky onions, port wine sauce & chips.

Daily lunch specials might include fish & chips with Timothy Taylor beer batter, garlicky king prawns, sausage casserole with mixed beans, tomatoes & rosemary, and Hinchliffe's speciality Aberdeen Angus roast beef with Yorkshire pudding, roast potatoes and onion gravy. A brunch menu proposes a choice of breakfast items and a full breakfast from 9 to noon Tuesday to Saturday and from 10 to noon on Sunday. In the restaurant, the Early Bird menu (5.30 to 7.30 Friday & Saturday) and the dinner menu (last orders 9) offer similar wholesome, hearty fare, and more – corned beef hash with fried egg & sticky gravy; seared wood pigeon breast with beetroot, reggiano & walnut salad; soubise of halibut, salmon & prawns with creamed garlic, saffron spinach & puff pastry; pork belly roasted for 24 hours with crackling, black pudding, savoy cabbage, mashed potatoes & port sauce. Desserts attain the same level of desirability, making the likes of Tate & Lyle syrup sponge with thick custard or the day's crème brûlée very hard to resist.

671

463 THE CASK & SPINDLE

112 Abbey Road, Shepley, Huddersfield,
West Yorkshire HD8 8EL
☎ 01484 602950
e-mail: bestfood@ntworld.com

Since coming here in the summer of 2003,
Margaret and Graham have made the **Cask &
Spindle** a magnet for lovers of good food.
The homemade
steak pie always
goes down a treat,
and other choices
run from
sandwiches and
salads to duck
spring rolls,
salmon dishes,

gammon and beef steaks, roasts and lasagne.
Age has no place in the Cask & Spindle, with
a children's menu and senior citizens' specials
as well as the main menu and the Sunday
roasts. Food is served lunchtime and evening
Tuesday to Saturday and all day on Sunday;
closed Monday. The bar stocks three real ales
– Marston's Pedigree and two guests. Full
disabled access.

HIDDEN PLACES GUIDES

Explore Britain and Ireland with
Hidden Places guides - a fascinating
series of national and local travel
guides.

Packed with easy to read information
on hundreds of places of interest as
well as places to stay, eat and drink.

Available from both high street and
internet booksellers

For more information on the full range
of *Hidden Places* guides and other
titles published by Travel Publishing
visit our website on

www.travelpublishing.co.uk
or ask for our leaflet by phoning
01752 276660 or emailing
info@travelpublishing.co.uk

465 WUTHERING HEIGHTS

26 Main Street, Stanbury, nr Haworth,
West Yorkshire BD22 0HB
☎ 01535 643322
e-mail: info@thewutheringheights.co.uk
🌐 www.thewutheringheights.co.uk

The **Wuthering Heights** is an outstanding village
inn located on the main street of Stanbury, a short
drive from Haworth. Built as an ale house in the
early 18th century, it has been run since the end of
2006 by
Nicola and
Darren, who have enhanced its appeal as a favourite
refreshment point for walkers, cyclists, tourists and locals
alike. It is ideally situated for those exploring the beautiful
surrounding countryside and the Brontë connection (Top
Withins and Ponden Hall, which are locations in the novel
'Wuthering Heights' are both in walking distance). The inn is
open all day, seven days a week. Nicola and Darren pride
themselves on their warm welcome and the quality of their
three cask ales. Lunches
are served daily with the
menu based on the best
of traditional British pub food with many locally sourced
ingredients. Don't miss out on their famous Ploughman's lunch
with local pork pie, ham and Wensleydale cheese. As a hub of
the community there are regular folk nights and a weekly quiz.
WiFi internet is available to customers at no charge. An open
fire is currently being reinstated in the bar. Future plans include
evening meals and accommodation. This is a dog friendly pub.

466 THE GREYHOUND

82 Main Street, Riccall,
North Yorkshire YO19 6TE
☎ 01757 249101

The **Greyhound** is a well-maintained, welcoming pub standing in the village of Riccall, four miles north of Selby a short drive from the main A19. The pub is a first venture in their own premises for Stephen and Sue Bell, who took over at the end of 2007. The atmosphere in the bar is always warm and friendly, with locals and visitors from outside the area getting together to enjoy a drink and a chat. The bar is open all day, every day, for drinks, which include four cask ales, typically Tetley's Bitter, John Smith's Cask, Black Sheep and a guest that changes twice a week. Stephen is a talented chef with almost 30 years' experience, and he attracts lovers of good food with his wholesome home cooking. An across-the-board menu spans hot and cold sandwiches and hot roast baguettes to pub favourites like 8oz beef burgers, scampi,

lasagne (meat/vegetarian), steak & ale pie, chicken korma, chilli con carne and the Friday fish specials. Food is served from 12 to 3 Tuesday to Saturday, 5 to 8 Tuesday to Friday and 12 to 3 for the super Sunday carvery, for which booking is recommended. Stephen and Sue hope to have accommodation available (phone for details), which will make the Greyhound an excellent base for a walking or sightseeing holiday. The pub has a beer garden, a patio and ample off-road parking.

467 THE PERCY ARMS

89 High Street, Airmyn, nr Goole, East
Yorkshire DN14 8LD
☎ 01405 764408
e-mail:
enquiries@thepercyarmsairmyn.co.uk
🌐 www.thepercyarmsairmyn.co.uk

The mood is always bright and cheerful at the **Percy Arms**, but leaseholders Liz and Simon are also very serious about food. This true hidden gem is located across the road from the River Aire in the rural village of Airmyn, on a minor road a mile or so north off the A614 and a short drive from J36 of the M62. The building dates back to 1782 and was originally called the Beverley Arms before its name was changed to honour a local Lord of the Manor. A John Smith brew, Black Sheep and two weekly rotating guests will keep cask ale enthusiasts happy, and the bar also stocks a good range of other draught and bottled beers, ciders, wines, malt whiskies and soft drinks. Fresh seasonal ingredients are the

basis of the dishes that make up the menu, which ranges from chicken liver parfait and Caesar salad to battered haddock, poached salmon, chicken & bacon pie, steak & kidney pudding, curries and fillet steak Rossini. Weekday lunchtime brings lighter options (baguettes, wraps, burgers, jacket potatoes) and a senior citizens menu. Booking is recommended for all meals. All are invited to take on the local brains in the Tuesday quiz, and the inn hosts regular fun days and summer barbecues. Families with children and dogs are welcome, and beyond the conservatory the inn has a pleasant garden with lawns, shrubs and flower beds.

673

468 THE KINGS HEAD

Main Street, Pollington,
East Yorkshire DN14 0DN
☎ 01405 861507

Dating from the late-18th century, when it started life as a coaching inn, the **Kings Head** is a substantial and familiar landmark on the main street of

Pollington. This peaceful village stands a mile or so off the A645 between Junctions 34 and 35 of the M62 and close to the Aire & Calder Navigation Canal. Tony and Tracey took over the lease at the end of 2006, since when they have been welcoming all the old regulars and making many new friends day by day. In the smart, traditional public areas, with comfortable seating and Regency-stripe wallpaper, patrons enjoy a fine selection of drinks, including cask ales from Tetley and Daleside and two guest ales. The pub is open for drinks from 5.30 Monday to Friday and from midday on Saturday and

Sunday, and for food from 5.30 to 8.30 Monday to Friday, from 12 to 8.30 on Saturday and from 12 to 3 on Sunday. Tracey is a super cook, satisfying a wide range of tastes and appetites with anything from sandwiches, burgers and salads to golden crispy haddock, cod cakes, spicy chicken kebabs and juicy steaks. Additionally, Saturday brunch (11 to 1) brings butties and a full breakfast. The pub has five wheelchair-friendly en suite chalet-style rooms let on a room only or Bed & Breakfast basis. It also has a camping site (a caravan park is planned), stabling for horses and a dog room, a beer garden and a children's play area.

469 THE NEW GLOBE INN

Yorkersgate, Malton,
North Yorkshire YO17 7AA
☎ 01653 692395

The year 2008 marks the 200th anniversary of the **New Globe Inn**, originally a coaching inn and now a friendly family-run pub with accommodation. Situated in the heart of

Malton, on the edge of the North Yorkshire Moors, it's run in fine style by Rob and Shelley, who welcome old friends and new in to the inviting surroundings of the bar. Cameron's Strong Arm is the resident real ale, with two regularly changing guests, and Rob and Shelley prepare a choice of pub favourites at lunchtime Tuesday to Sunday. Three guest rooms are available all year for B&B guests looking for a quiet place to stay while touring this beautiful part of the world. The pub has a paved patio area and its own car park – a very useful asset in busy Malton.

470 THE HIDDEN MONKEY TEA ROOMS

34 Market Place, Malton,
North Yorkshire YO17 7LW
☎ 01653 694982
⊕ www.hiddenmonkeytearooms.co.uk

The appetising aroma of home cooking wafts visitors inside the **Hidden Monkey Tea Rooms**, located in a hard-to-miss blue-painted building on a corner of Malton's market place. Since 2004 owner Helen Knapp has been inviting customers into her warm and cosy tea rooms with an excellent selection of wholesome snacks and meals, both savoury and sweet, the great majority freshly prepared and cooked on the premises from locally sourced ingredients. On the savoury side there are soups, jacket potatoes, hot and cold sandwiches, snacks on toast, all-day breakfasts, omelettes, lasagne and super pies – such as cottage pies, with a fluffy topping of mashed potatoes and cheese; steak & mushroom; chicken, ham & leek. Equally delicious sweet things include a wonderful array of cakes on

display on the dresser and tempting desserts like sticky

toffee pudding or fruit crumbles and pies. To drink, coffee, Yorkshire Tea, speciality and herbal teas, hot chocolate, juices, fizzy drinks and milkshakes. This charming place, an ideal refreshment stop for locals, workers, shoppers and tourists discovering the many attractions of Malton, is open from 9 to 5 Monday to Saturday. The bright front area looks straight out on to the market place and there's a second area and upstairs seating – 60 covers in all.

471 THE CROSS KEYS

Thixendale, nr Malton,
North Yorkshire YO17 9TG
☎ 01377 288272
⊕ www.thixendale.org.uk

What started life in the 18th century as a farmhouse is now the **Cross Keys**, a delightful one-roomed pub that enjoys a scenic setting in the heart of the Yorkshire Wolds. Long-established hosts Paddy,

Steve and Mary run this delightful award-winning gem, offering a warm, cosy ambience, real ales and wholesome bar meals prepared as far as possible from local ingredients and served lunchtime and evening. Paddy and Mary cook a varied selection of dishes that include burgers, omelettes, chilli con carne, steak & Guinness pie, pasties and vegetarian specials like a tasty chestnut casserole. Jennings and Tetley real ales are served in the bar, where a log fire burns in a huge brick hearth. When the sun shines, picnic

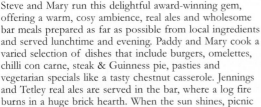

benches on the hedge-fringed lawn come into their own. This is glorious walking

country: the Wolds Way passes through the village, and established walks in the vicinity include one that takes in the deserted village of Wherram Percy. For guests taking a break in these superb surroundings the Cross Keys has three en suite rooms for B&B – a double and two twins – in the refurbished old stable block. Thixendale is located a short drive north of the A166 York-Driffield road (leave at Fridaythorpe).

472 THE SCHOOL HOUSE INN

Low Marishes, nr Malton,
North Yorkshire YO17 6RJ
☎ 01653 668247
e-mail: matrichardson@hotmail.co.uk
🌐 www.schoolhouseinn.co.uk

The **School House Inn** is a true hidden gem, a place to seek out, to enjoy and to return to time and time again. It lies along a single-track lane just off the A169 Malton to Pickering road in the little village of Low Marishes. In this peaceful,

picturesque setting a young Yorkshire couple Matt and Sarah Richardson have quickly made their mark since becoming the heads of the School House in the summer of 2007, Matt and his staff in the kitchen and Sarah and her helpers doing a great job front of house. It's very popular locally, and the reputation they have established for fine food, ale and hospitality has reached out to visitors from further afield day by day. The games room, stylishly contemporary décor and furnishings, a bright modern conservatory and an up-to-date kitchen producing a tempting

range of dishes from around the world show that the inn moves with the times; but it is still essentially a traditional village inn, with stone flag floors, log fires crackling in the hearth, an old-fashioned welcome and charm and character in abundance.

Outside is a pleasant garden with a pets corner to delight young and old alike. Matt has been a chef for more than 10 years, Sarah a restaurant manager for 12, and they put that joint experience to excellent use. Local produce is used whenever possible, and all the dishes are prepared and cooked on the premises. Lunchtime (12 to 2) brings lighter options like soup, sandwiches, pies and scampi, while the full menu provides an exceptional choice that caters for all tastes. Typical dishes run from French onion soup, gravadlax and seafood risotto to steaks, free-range chicken breast with honey & thyme, herb-crusted salmon fillet and braised oxtail served on a perky horseradish mash. To finish, perhaps apple & cherry pie, chocolate & caramel cheesecake or passion fruit & raspberry brûlée. Sunday lunch brings a choice of traditional roasts with a vegetarian option.

Black Sheep and a range of draught keg ales provide a choice for beer-drinkers, and an interesting wine list with informative notes features mainly New World wines. The School House is closed on Sunday evening, also all day Monday except in peak season.

The School House Inn's kitchen larder sells jams, chutneys, homemade quiches, pâtés, desserts and afternoon teas. Something for all the family!

473 THE STAR COUNTRY INN

Main Street, Weaverthorpe, nr Malton,
North Yorkshire YO17 8EY
☎ 01944 738273
e-mail: starinn.malton@btconnect.com

The **Star** enjoys a scenic country location in the village of Weaverthorpe, in the heart of the Yorkshire Wolds. January 2008 saw a change at the top, with business partners Benji and Eddie at the helm. Benji was more or less born into the trade and Eddie is a chef with many years' experience, and between them they have already made many new friends at their late-18th century country inn. The bar is open all day, seven days a week, for drinks, with John Smith's Smooth a popular choice. Eddie keeps his customers happy with his excellent home cooking, served lunchtime and evening in the bar or dining area. The menu of popular favourites is

supplemented by tempting daily specials such as smoked haddock & herb risotto, grilled Whitby turbot with caper butter, or pan-fried loin of venison with cabbage, bacon and a bitter chocolate sauce. This is fine walking country, and for guests taking a break in these quiet, picturesque surroundings the Star has five upstairs en suite bedrooms up to family size. The village of Weaverthorpe lies east of Malton and north of Driffield and can be reached from the A64 Malton-Scarborough road (leave at Sherburn), from the B1249 up from Driffield (turn left at Langtoft) or from the B1253 at Sledmere.

474 THE WHITE HORSE INN

High Street, Bempton, nr Bridlington,
East Yorkshire YO15 1HB
☎ 01262 850266

Tourists and birdwatchers flock from near and far to see the renowned 400 feet Bempton Cliffs, home to huge colonies of seabirds, and after a spell in the bracing sea air visitors in the know head for the **White Horse Inn**.

Standing on the main street of the coastal village of Bempton, on the B1229 5 miles north of Bridlington, it's the first venture together in their business for Steven and Jayne Greenway, who welcome all who pass through the door with smiles, hospitality and a good choice of food and drink. Four real ales head the list of drinks served in the bright, comfortable bar, which is open lunchtime and evening, all day Thursday to Sunday and all day every day in the summer months. The menus cater for a wide range of tastes and appetites, from 'something light' (soup, sandwiches, panini, chips with dips) to 'something more', with pub classics like beer-battered haddock, lasagne, chicken & ham pie, steak & ale pie, gammon and Yorkshire pudding filled with sausage & mash. Food is served at lunchtime and also early evening Thursday to Saturday in season.

The pub has a recently created outdoor (and partly covered) terrace. No credit cards.

475 THE NEW CROWN HOTEL

158 Quay Road, Bridlington,
East Yorkshire YO16 4LB
☎ 01262 401874
Fax: 01262 403474

The **New Crown Hotel** is a handsome and substantial three-storey building in a prominent position in Bridlington, a short stroll from the shops and the seashore. Business partners John & Judith and Tony & Bev have been here since April 2006. It's their first venture together into this type of business, but through their hard work and enthusiasm they have made great strides in putting the place back on the map. Well supported on the pub side by the local community, it's also becoming a popular choice with tourists and visitors to the town. The bar is open all day, seven days a week, for drinks – John Smith's Cask and Smooth are among the favourites – and excellent food is served from 10 to 2 and 5 to 7 Tuesday to Saturday and from 12 to 3 on Sunday. Food options include a slap-up breakfast, sandwiches, jacket potatoes, salads, chilli, chicken curry, lasagne, quiche, steak pie, shepherd's pie and chicken & mushroom pie – all homemade, tasty and satisfying. Bookings are welcome at all times and essential for the Sunday roast lunch, when there's a choice of roast joints. On the

accommodation side, the New Crown has nine letting bedrooms with shared bathrooms; all have a washbasin, TV and hot drinks are available and two of the rooms are family-size. The tariff includes a hearty breakfast. All are welcome at the Thursday quiz and the Saturday evening live entertainment.

477 THE TROUT INN

Wansford, nr Driffield,
East Yorkshire YO25 8NX
☎ 01377 254204

Keith and Marie Robinson are the long-established tenants at the **Trout Inn**, a former farmhouse with comfortable, roomy public areas and many attractive Victorian features. The bar stocks a good selection of keg beers,  and bar and restaurant menus offer an excellent choice of good wholesome home cooking, from classics like their tasty game soup, lasagne, steak & kidney pie, scampi, goujons of plaice to evening specialities such as fillet steak medallions with a red wine sauce or roast duckling. Food is served Tuesday to Sunday lunchtime and Wednesday to Saturday evening. The Trout is close on Mondays. Wansford lies on the B1249 three miles southeast of Driffield.

476 THE OLD STAR INN & RESTAURANT

Church Street, Kilham, nr Driffield,
East Yorkshire YO25 4RG
☎ 01262 420619
e-mail: oldstarkilham@hotmail.com

The **Old Star** is a super country inn and restaurant located in the quiet, picturesque village of Kilham, which lies northeast of Driffield off the A614 or B1249. Rightly describing itself as 'the Wold famous' Old Star, this outstanding inn has excellent, friendly and highly professional leaseholders in Lauren and Helen, who brought many years' experience in the catering trade when they took over the reins at the beginning of 2007. In the short time since then they have delighted the local community and made many new friends with their own special brand of hospitality, allied to the very highest standards of food, drink and service. Behind the whitewashed exterior, with tiled roof and shuttered windows, the public areas are immaculate, with beams, open fires, half-panelling and paintings by a local artist.

There are always four real ales available: John Smiths the resident alongside Theakstons Best or Black Sheep Best Bitter. Two other pumps rotate regularly using northern micro-breweries. The choice increases to more than a dozen during the Beer Festival held over a weekend in Autumn – ring for exact times and details. The bar is open from 6 to 11.30 on Monday, 5 to 11.30 on Tuesday, 12 to 2.30 and 5 to 11.30 Wednesday to Saturday and 12 to 10.30 on Sunday.

The hosts believe in 'proper' home-cooked food, never sacrificing quality for profit. They pride themselves on using only the best seasonal ingredients from local suppliers, and everything is freshly prepared and cooked to order. Lauren produces a mouthwatering selection of dishes that really do provide something for everyone. Starters range from mini-croissants stuffed with creamy garlic mushrooms to fish goujons and chicken liver, garlic and tomato pâté with balsamic onion relish. From the list of main courses come Rack of Burdass Lamb with parsnip mash & minted jus, haddock on a bed of parsley mash with wholegrain mustard sauce, Scott's rib-eye steak with all the traditional trimmings, the Sunday roasts and vegetarian options decided on the day. The menu changes regularly so theres always something different to try and the early bird menu (available at lunchtimes & tea time) changes quarterly. Steak and ale pie is always a favourite! Even the sandwiches are several cuts above the average: roast beef dipped in gravy, tuna with lemon & black pepper mayonnaise. Desserts like bread & butter pudding, crème brûlée, apple crumble or chocolate brownie make the perfect finale to a memorable meal. Food is served Monday to Friday evenings, lunchtime and evening Friday and Saturday and from 12 to 6 on Sunday.

679

478 ARABIAN HORSE

Main Street North, Aberford,
Leeds LS25 3AA
☎ 0113 281 3312

Quality is the keynote at the **Arabian Horse**, making it a winner not just with the local community but with lovers of good food and good hospitality from many miles around. The pub is equally handsome from the outside and within, where a huge open fire in the beautifully restored 18th century fireplace keeps things cosy even in the coldest months. Sarah and Andy Ridgeon, who took over the reins in September 2007, have really breathed new life into the inn, with the warmth of the welcome and the excellence of Sarah's cooking. Her menu offers both light bites (nachos, chips, chicken strips with a mayonnaise dip) and more hearty familiar favourites as well a choice of vegetarian main courses available . The pub is closed

Monday lunchtime except on Bank Holidays, otherwise open every session and all day Friday, Saturday, Sunday and Bank Holidays. Food times are 12 to 2 Tuesday to Friday and 12 to 3 Sunday, and booking is advisable for all meals. The Arabian Horse stands in the village of Aberford, five miles east of Leeds, and easily reached from the M1 (J47), A1 (J45), A64 or B1217. Cash only.

480 THE RIVIERA

West Cliff, Whitby,
North Yorkshire YO21 3EL
☎ 01947 602533
e-mail: info@rivierawhitby.com
🌐 www.rivierawhitby.com

When experienced hotelier Richard Ward bought the **Riviera** in August 2007 he set about a complete refurbishment, adding high standards of décor and comfort to the outstanding location in the heart of historic Whitby. The imposing building, which dates from 1847, is open all year for Bed & Breakfast, and the 15 en suite rooms, some with sea views, offer a choice of accommodation from singles to family rooms.

An excellent cooked breakfast is served in the smartly appointed dining room. Children are welcome, and the hotel accepts the major credit cards.

Malton Road, Pickering,
North Yorkshire YO18 8EA
☎ 01751 475258

The **Black Bull Inn** is located by the main A169 a mile south of Pickering on the road to Malton. Parts of it date back as far as the late-17th century, and the bar is in appropriately traditional style, with a handsome wood-panelled serving counter, a fire in a huge stone hearth and some well-chosen pictures.

The inn has first-class tenants in Paul and Sadie Worthington; Paul was the manager here from 2003 until the spring of 2007, when he and Sadie took over the lease. Paul has been in the catering business since 1979 and in the licensed trade since 1993 – and always in Yorkshire, so he really knows what his customers want and they respond by returning time and again to enjoy the super hospitality on offer. The inn is open for drinks lunchtime and evening in the winter and all day in the summer months. Two or three real ales are always available, with Black Sheep and John Smith's Cask the regulars.

As well as being an excellent host, hardworking Paul also hits the bull's eye in the kitchen, where he and his team prepare a splendid variety of dishes for the printed menu and the constantly

changing specials board. Served at lunchtime from 12 to 2.30 and in the evening from 6 to 9, the dishes – all the meat and vegetables are sourced locally – span all the pub classics, from breaded mushrooms with garlic mayo, deep-fried brie with a sweet chilli dip and prawn cocktail to lasagne, steak pie, battered haddock, gammon steak, pork chops and rump or sirloin steak served plain or with a choice of pepper, Dijon mustard or chasseur sauce.

The inn is not just a great stopover for refreshment, it's also a convenient and practical base for both leisure and business guests. Five rooms in chalet style, offering B&B or self-catering accommodation, are available throughout the year; one room is wheelchair-accessible, and one is big enough for a family to share.

Pickering, the largest of the four market towns in Ryedale, is well worth taking time to explore. Exhibitions in the castle ruins show the lives of the castle and the surrounding royal forest, and the Church of St Peter and St Paul has some fine 15th century murals. Pickering is also the northern terminus of the popular North York Moors Heritage Railway, and the station has been restored to how it was in 1937.

681

New Quay Road, Whitby,
North Yorkshire YO21 1DH
☎ 01947 603937
e-mail: stationinn@btconnect.com
🌐 www.beerintheevening.com

Cask ales, fine wines, morning coffee, home-cooked lunches, afternoon tea and regular live entertainment – all this and more awaits visitors to the **Station Inn**, which stands in the heart of historic Whitby overlooking the harbour and Captain Cook's ship *Endeavour*. The inn was built as a cellar pub towards the end of the 19th century, and was rebuilt in today's incarnation in 1937. Until recently known as the Tap & Spile, it enjoys a delightful setting among the shops and restaurants on the New Quay side of the town.

Leaseholders Colin and Andrew brought many years' experience in the licensed trade when they became the 'station-masters' at the beginning of 2007, and they have reinforced and enhanced the inn's popularity with both the citizens of Whitby and with the many visitors who come to the town throughout the year. The inn is open from 10 o'clock in the morning seven days a week.

The Station is one of the best places in the whole region for real ale connoisseurs, with eight well-kept brews on tap. A board in the bar lists the day's choices (complete with ABVs), which might include Whitby's Black Dog Abbey Ale, Copper Dragon Best and Challenger IPA, Courage Directors, Timothy Taylor Golden Best, Daleside Blonde, Theakston's Black Bull and Jennings Cumberland Ale. There's also a real cider, and a separate board lists the day's special wine selection. These can be enjoyed by themselves or to accompany a lunchtime snack or meal – the fish dishes and the hearty steak pies and casseroles are among the favourites.

On the social side, Wednesday and Friday bring live music sessions, a folk group performs on Sunday and brains are clicked into gear for the Thursday evening quiz. Children are welcome at the Station until 8 o'clock in the evening. Cash only. Visitors to this attractive and historic town will find plenty of interest, including the Abbey ruins high up on a cliff, and the Captain Cook memorial Museum. The town is also known for its jet and for the Dracula connection – it was here, according to Bram Stoker's novel, that the Count came ashore in the form of a wolf. And when the tour of the town is over it's good to know that Colin, Andrew and their staff are ready, willing and eager to provide abundant hospitality and welcome refreshment.

482 THE CAPTAIN COOK INN

60 Staithes Lane, Staithes,
North Yorkshire TS13 5AD
☎ 01947 840200
🌐 www.thecaptaincookinn.co.uk

On top of a bank above the fishing village of Staithes, the **Captain Cook Inn** is a great place for a drink, a meal, an overnight stay or a longer break. Built in Victorian times as a railway hotel, it now offers outstanding hospitality to the local community and to the many tourists who flock to the area throughout the year.

For more than 15 years the inn has been run by real ale devotee Trevor Readman and his family – wife Betty, son Neil and daughter Sharon. An ever-changing selection of real ales is always available – typically Banks's Bitter, John Smith's Magnet, Rudgate Viking (brewed on a disused WW2 airfield near York) and at least two guests, and also a real cider. Food is also an important part of the inn's business, served every lunchtime and evening. Pub classics, from fish & chips and scampi to chilli con carne, lasagne (meat/vegetable), pies and curries, make up the main menu, which is supplemented by more unusual dishes such as buffalo, wild boar and venison. All the meat and vegetables are sourced locally, and all the pastry is made on the premises. This is deservedly a very popular place, and booking is advisable for any meal in the summer months.

The inn hosts regular music evenings and several special annual events. In April a Beer and Jazz Festival has an English Heritage theme, and in late July/early August a Beer Festival with a nautical theme is part of the local Lifeboat Fete, with up to 30 real ales to sample. A Hallowe'en/Guy Fawkes Beer & Burger Festival also offers many real ales – call or look at the website for details and times of these popular events.

Tourists and holidaymakers are very welcome at the inn, which has four well-appointed en suite bedrooms – a double, a twin and two family rooms. Easter 2008 saw the additional facility of a holiday cottage for up to six guests created from the old stables at the rear of the premises. The inn is a very friendly base learning all about the Captain Cook connection, for exploring the coast and for enjoying the scenic grandeur of the North York Moors National Park. The inn can provide packed lunches for guests setting out on a day's sightseeing. Staithes is still a working fishing port, and family attractions include a sandy beach and a long rocky shoreline pitted with little rock pools.

483 ESTBEK HOUSE

East Row, Sandsend, nr Whitby,
North Yorkshire YO21 3SU
☎ 01947 893424 Fax: 01947 893625
e-mail: reservations@estbekhouse.co.uk
🌐 www.estbekhouse.co.uk

A few steps from the shore on the edge of the North Yorkshire moors, **Estbek House** is well known throughout Yorkshire and far beyond for outstanding food, service and accommodation. With the Cleveland Way in front and the National Park boundary to the rear, the Georgian house enjoys a glorious setting in one of England's prettiest villages, a short drive or a pleasant walk up from Whitby. Hands-on owners David Cross and Tim Lawrence have made Estbek one of the finest restaurants with rooms in the whole county, and repeat visits attest to its excellence in all aspects of what if offers.

The guest accommodation is top-class, comprising three double-bedded rooms and a twin, all with flat-screen television, CD/DVD player, alarm clock and hairdryer. The food is truly exceptional, with chef James and his hardworking team combining traditional skill and technique with contemporary flair and imagination at the highest level and putting their individual stamp on every dish. The Fresh Wild Fish section is one of the kitchen's specialities. Fillets of cod, halibut and seabass are pan-seared and served with a squeeze of lemon and a sprinkling of black pepper accompanied by a choice of sauces: roasted vine tomato & fresh basil, lemon cream, Sauvignon Blanc cream and seafood (brown shrimps, crayfish & lobster). Alternatively, the fish can be baked, or steamed with Sauvignon Blanc and fresh herbs. Other options on a menu that tempts at every turn include pan-seared rack of local lamb served with wilted rocket and a pan juice reduction; medallions of fillet steak with a mushroom and red onion sauce served in a bubble & squeeze basket; spiced duck breast, and always a vegetarian main course such as sweetcorn fritters with goat's cheese and a hint of chilli with grilled asparagus and a red pepper sauce. The dessert list makes equally mouthwatering reading: plum soup with stem ginger ice cream; old English rhubarb trifle; baby figs preserved in rum and white wine served cold with vanilla pod ice cream. Each dessert has a suggested wine taster to accompany. An alternative to a dessert is a superb selection of English – mainly Yorkshire – cheeses, including a goat's cheese made in the nearby village of Littlebeck. They're as passionate at Estbek about wine as about food, and the outstanding wine list includes quality wines by the glass and several rarities, including Australian wines seldom seen outside Australia. The house was built around 1750 for the manager of the local alum works that once dominated the coastline, producing a substance that was once more valuable than gold.

484 THE WORLD OF JAMES HERRIOTT

23 Kirkgate, Thirsk,
North Yorkshire YO7 1PL
☎ 01845 524234 Fax: 01845 525333
e-mail: wojhemails@hambleton.gov.uk
🌐 www.worldofjamesherriott.org

Celebrating the world's best-known vet, **The World of James Herriott** opened in the spring of 1999, since when it has welcomed more than 400,000 visitors. The setting is Skeldale House, now a Grade II listed building, where James Herriott lived

and worked. The house has been lovingly restored to how it was in the 1940s and 1950s, with many original pieces of furniture donated by the author's family. Beyond the famous red door, visitors enter the dining room, which doubled as the practice office. Then on to the cosy family room where the vet's favourite music – Bing Crosby – plays. Further down the corridor is the dispensary where he made up the prescriptions

and the little surgery where he would treat domestic animals. Skeldale houses the only veterinary science museum in the country and a new interactive surgery and farm. The World of James Herriott moves with the times with audio tapes escorting visitors round the house and a short film of the vet's life story narrated by Christopher Timothy. The garden has also been taken back in time, and other attractions include studio sets from *All Creatures Great and Small*, some 70s cameras and

equipment and the original Austin Seven tourer AJO 71. This fascinating, family-friendly place is open throughout the year.

HERRIOT
Museum I Attraction I Historic Site
www.worldofjamesherriot.org

VISIT THE TRAVEL PUBLISHING WEBSITE

Looking for:

- *Places to Visit?*
- *Places to Stay?*
- *Places to Eat & Drink?*
- *Places to Shop?*

Then why not visit the Travel Publishing website...

- Informative pages on places to visit, stay, eat, drink and shop throughout the British Isles.

- Detailed information on Travel Publishing's wide range of national and regional travel guides.

www.travelpublishing.co.uk

485 THE ROEBUCK INN

Bagby, nr Thirsk, North Yorkshire YO7 2PF
☎ 01845 597315
e-mail: nicholas@roebuckinn-bagby.co.uk
e-mail: paul@roebuckinn-bagby.co.uk
🌐 www.roebuckinn-bagby.co.uk

The **Roebuck** is a top-quality country inn located in the village of Bagby, a mile or so off the A170 or A19 a short drive from Thirsk. When business partners Nicholas Stanley and Paul Taylor (headed by son Stephen Stanley and Niki Warren) took over the Roebuck Inn in September 2007 they kept the front bar open but closed the rear section and totally redesigned and refurbished it, creating a first-class restaurant in the process. They've lost no time in putting the place firmly back on the map, and the inn's reputation for fine dining is spreading day by day. The locals love it, and as the word spreads patrons are travelling from many miles away – and coming back for more!

Professional chef Helen Green heads a talented team in the kitchen producing outstanding food for lunch, dinner, à la carte, table d'hôte, Sunday and children's menus changing quarterly. The choice really does offer something for everyone, from lunchtime sandwiches and hot baguettes to evergreen pub classics (beer-battered cod, liver & bacon, steak & ale pie) and the kitchen's individualistic take on the classics – roasted pepper with roast vegetables and local Fine Fettle cheese; roast Gressingham duck with a marmalade gravy; ham with a cider & apple sauce; chicken liver & cranberry pâté; red mullet with a lemon & rosemary sauce; spicy apple crumble; and chocolate & brandy cream roulade. The children's menu treats youngsters as gourmets-to-be, with

not a turkey twizzler in sight. The kitchen relies heavily on top local ingredients, and the menu gives due credit to Yorkshire-based suppliers of meat and poultry, fish and seafood, vegetables and cheese. Fine food deserves fine wines, and at the Roebuck a well-chosen list features both Old and New World wines. The bar stocks three or four real ales, with Black Sheep and John Smith resident and rotating guests from other Yorkshire breweries.

The Cleveland Way passes close by and the Hambledon Hills are visible from the inn. One of the area's most famous landmarks is the White Horse, near Kilburn, created in 1857 and inspired by the pre-historic hill-carving at Uffingham in Berkshire. Kilburn is where Robert 'Mouseman' Thompson made his unique pieces of furniture and where two of his grandsons carry on the work. Bagby Village has it's own furniture maker in Graham Duncalf who is part of the Thirsk Furniture Trail with his trade mark being a swan. When the walking and the sightseeing are done, it's good to know outstanding hospitality awaits at the Roebuck, which is open Monday evening, lunchtime and evening on other days and all day at the weekend in the summer months. Food is served lunchtime and evening Tuesday to Sunday.

Carlton Miniott, nr Thirsk,
North Yorkshire YO7 4NJ
☎ 01845 522150
🌐 www.thedogandgun.co.uk

The genuinely warm welcome, the friendly atmosphere, the well-kept beer and the home-cooked food all contribute to the popularity of the **Dog & Gun**. Originally a row of three terraced houses, it stands on the A61 two miles west of Thirsk in Carlton Miniott, a village and civil parish in the Hambleton district of North Yorkshire, population about 1,000. Oak beams, log burner and abundant traditional comfort make the bar a cosy, convivial spot for meeting the locals and putting the world to rights over a glass of real ale – five are usually available, all from Northern breweries, and that number increases to more than 20 during the beer festivals hosted by the pub in February and October.

The inn has a little decking area at the front and a lovely beer garden at the back, and there's ample off-road parking. Nigel and Dawn Pattinson, who took over the lease of this Enterprise Inns free house in June 2007, brought ten years' related experience and have lost no time in applying that experience and their hard work and enthusiasm – and the assistance of excellent staff – in putting the Dog & Gun firmly back on the map.

Food is an important part of the business, drawing patrons from many miles around, and Nigel and his chef are kept busy producing super food to be enjoyed in the 45-cover conservatory-style restaurant or in the bar (35 covers). For many regulars the home-made pies are the stars of the show, and a separate board lists the daily versions, typically steak & guinness, steak & kidney, chicken & leek and game with red wine and brandy. Other popular choices include cod and scampi from Whitby, fish cakes, burgers, a range of masham sausages and mash, steaks, salmon with lemon mayonnaise and that new pub classic chicken tikka masala. A tasty option for two sharing is nacho grande – tortilla chips with melted cheese, salsa, guacamole and sour cream. Children are welcome, and smaller portions of most dishes are available.

The pub is open lunchtime and evening and all day Saturday and Sunday; closed on Mondays from November to Easter. Food is served from 12 to 2 and from 6 (5.30 Saturday) to 9, and it's always best to book to be sure of a table at your preferred time. All are welcome to pit their wits against the locals in the Sunday quiz, which starts at 9 o'clock. The Dog & Gun has an area for caravans and camper vans to stay overnight – ring for details.

487 THE CARPENTERS ARMS

Felixkirk, nr Thirsk,
North Yorkshire YO7 2DP
☎ 01845 537369
Fax: 01845 537889
🌐 www.carpentersarmsfelixkirk.co.uk

The **Carpenters Arms** is the social heartbeat of the little village of Felixkirk, which stands on the edge of the moors and Hambleton Hills off the A170 east of Thirsk. The scenic setting is a major asset, so too the unbeatable hospitality extended to everyone who passes through the door by genuinely friendly tenants Karen Bumby and her mother Linda. The old-world bar and lounge consist of several cosy areas around the bar counter (part of which is made from huge beer casks), dark beams and joists, comfortable seats round check-clothed tables, well-chosen pictures and ancient carpentry tools set an invitingly traditional scene, with Japanese fans by the stone fireplace adding an exotic touch.

It's a lovely spot to relax, unwind, sit down with a drink and enjoy a chat, perhaps to explain why the good thing failed to oblige at Thirsk races, or to celebrate when it did. The Carpenters has an enviable reputation as a first-class destination restaurant, recognised by an award of Yorkshire Life's North Yorkshire Dining Pub of the Year.

In the beautifully appointed dining room a very talented team in the kitchen – Gary Dunn, Jamie Ballantyne and Phil Martin – produce a selection of dishes for the bistro menu (served Tuesday to Saturday lunchtimes) and the restaurant menu (Wednesday to Saturday evenings and Sunday lunch). Quality is the keynote throughout – the beef is hung for a minimum of 21 days – and all the dishes are individually prepared and cooked to order. From the bistro menu come fisherman's pie, 8oz homemade steak burgers, and Indonesian chicken curry. Typical dishes on the restaurant menu run from Panfried duck liver salad bacon and duck egg, baked queenie scallops, whole baked seabass with orange and ginger & spring onions, Panfried calves liver, bacon mash with port wine sauce. The fine food is complemented by an extensive wine list.

Booking is not always essential, but reservations are recommended at peak times to be sure of getting a table at the time you want.

This outstanding inn is open from 11.30 to 3 and 6.30 to 11 Tuesday to Saturday and from 12 to 3 on Sunday; closed Sunday evening, all Monday and the first week in February. Food is served 12 midday - 2pm & 6.30pm - 9pm.

488 WOODY'S AT THE BLACK SWAN

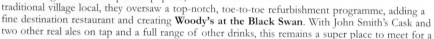

Thornton-le-Moor, nr Northallerton,
North Yorkshire DL7 9DN
☎ 01609 774117
e-mail: woodys@thornton-le-moor.co.uk
🌐 www.thorntonlemoor.co.uk

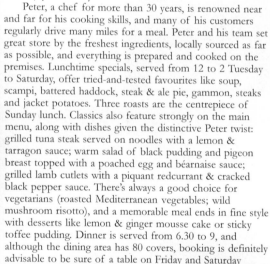

Having found considerable acclaim and success in a restaurant in Northallerton, Peter and Angela Wood transferred their skills in 2004 to nearby Thornton-le-Moor, located just off the A168 Northallerton to Thirsk road. Taking as their start point a popular, traditional village local, they oversaw a top-notch, toe-to-toe refurbishment programme, adding a fine destination restaurant and creating **Woody's at the Black Swan**. With John Smith's Cask and two other real ales on tap and a full range of other drinks, this remains a super place to meet for a

drink and a chat, but those in the know take time to relax and enjoy a leisurely lunch or dinner.

Peter, a chef for more than 30 years, is renowned near and far for his cooking skills, and many of his customers regularly drive many miles for a meal. Peter and his team set great store by the freshest ingredients, locally sourced as far as possible, and everything is prepared and cooked on the premises. Lunchtime specials, served from 12 to 2 Tuesday to Saturday, offer tried-and-tested favourites like soup, scampi, battered haddock, steak & ale pie, gammon, steaks and jacket potatoes. Three roasts are the centrepiece of Sunday lunch. Classics also feature strongly on the main menu, along with dishes given the distinctive Peter twist: grilled tuna steak served on noodles with a lemon & tarragon sauce; warm salad of black pudding and pigeon breast topped with a poached egg and béarnaise sauce; grilled lamb cutlets with a piquant redcurrant & cracked black pepper sauce. There's always a good choice for vegetarians (roasted Mediterranean vegetables; wild mushroom risotto), and a memorable meal ends in fine style with desserts like lemon & ginger mousse cake or sticky toffee pudding. Dinner is served from 6.30 to 9, and although the dining area has 80 covers, booking is definitely advisable to be sure of a table on Friday and Saturday evenings as well as Sunday lunch. Children are welcome, and they can even choose from their own menu.

Picnic tables on a paved outside area are popular in the summer months, and the inn has plenty of off-road parking.

Woody's at the Black Swan has recently added yet another string to its bow with the creation of four quality guest bedrooms with superb décor and furnishings, outstanding bathrooms and modern amenities like flat-screen TV. At the rear of the pub is a certified caravan site with some electric hook-ups.

489 THE WHEATSHEAF INN

Main Street, Borrowby, nr Thirsk,
North Yorkshire YO7 4QP
☎ 01845 537274
🌐 www.borrowbypub.co.uk

Emily and Tony are the leaseholders at the **Wheatsheaf Inn**, which stands on the main street of the village of Borrowby, off the A19 north of Thirsk. This impressive, secluded gem of an inn started life in 1695 as an ale house, and for as long as it has had a name that name has been the Wheatsheaf. Emily was born into the licensed trade, but this is their first joint venture into the business, and they are happy to be at the helm of an inn that's full of warmth, charm and character. The bar has a classic traditional look assisted by stone walls, slabstone floors, half-panelling, pictures and brass and china ornaments. Three or four real ales are always available – usually including brews from Tetley and Daleside – kept in tip-top condition that have earned the inn Cask Marque recognition. Chef Steven Sharp is enhancing the inn's reputation as a dining destination with a menu that makes excellent use of prime seasonal ingredients including as much local produce as possible. Skill and imagination combine in dishes like seared scallops with slow-braised featherblade of Dales beef with hollandaise sauce, pan-fried halibut with asparagus, roasted new potatoes and intense herb oil, and roast rack of Dales lamb with a wild mushroom fricassee. Darts and dominoes are the favourite pub games, and all are welcome to pit their wits against the locals in the monthly quiz.

490 THE OLD ROYAL GEORGE

Morton-upon-Swale, nr Northallerton,
North Yorkshire DL7 9QS
☎ 01609 780254

On the A684 Bedale-Northallerton road and just five miles from the A1 (M), the **Old Royal George** is an ideal refreshment stop for motorists and tourists. In the comfortably traditional bar and lounge (beams, brasses, banquettes, a ship's wheel) – the Baty family – Neil, Shirley and son Jamie – dispense amiable hospitality and a good choice of drinks, including real ales from the Black Sheep and Jennings Breweries. For lunches (12 to 2, not Monday) and diners (5 to 9) Jamie makes fine use of local produce for his home-cooked dishes: steak pies and curries, with sandwiches and light bites for those in a hurry. The pub takes its name from the splendid old sailing ship depicted on the pub's sign.

491 LASTINGHAM GRANGE COUNTRY HOUSE HOTEL

Lastingham, nr York,
North Yorkshire YO62 6TH
☎ 01751 417345/417402
Fax: 01751 417358
e-mail: reservations@lastinghamgrange.com
⊕ www.lastinghamgrange.com

In the heart of the North York Moors National Park, **Lastingham Grange** is the perfect centre for touring the Moors and Dales. It also provides an ideal base for enjoying a walking or sporting holiday, with golf, riding and fishing all available nearby. Built as a farmhouse in the 17th century, it was converted into today's fine country house in the 1920s and has been a hotel since 1946. It stands round a courtyard in ten peaceful acres of grounds that include a beautiful rose garden. Long-established owners the Wood family are the most charming and welcoming of hosts, and guests will feel instantly at ease in the relaxing home-from-home ambience, with courteous personal service a watchword. The 12 excellent centrally heated bedrooms have en suite bathrooms, television, telephone, wi-fi, hairdryer, trouser press, beverage tray and baby listening. Accommodation is free for children under 12 sharing their parents' room, special meals are available for children and the hotel has an adventure playground. The tariff (B&B or Dinner, B&B) includes morning coffee, afternoon tea and newspapers. Light lunches and picnic lunches can be supplied. Lastingham Grange has a first-class restaurant, licensed for residents and non-residents and serving a fine choice of classic dishes complemented by well-chosen wines.

492 THE BLACKSMITHS ARMS

Lastingham, nr York,
North Yorkshire YO62 6TL
☎ 01751 417247 Fax: 01751 417247
e-mail:
pete.hils@blacksmithslastingham.co.uk
⊕ www.blacksmithslastingham.co.uk

The **Blacksmiths Arms** stands in the village of Lastingham, at the foot of the North York Moors, signposted off the A170 west of Pickering. Lying by the ancient village church at a point where three roads meet, the neat stone inn is run in great style by Peter and Hilary Trafford, who welcome visitors with genuine warmth, good food and drink and comfortable, stylish accommodation. Three cask ales – Theakstons Best, a local guest and a national guest – are on tap in the cosy, old-fashioned bar, which features an old cast-iron oven, log fire, beams, tankards, brass and copper ornaments and local-interest pictures. Hilary and the chef produce a fine selection of dishes served lunchtime and evening in the bar and

restaurant. Lunchtime

favourites include hot toasted panini, beer-battered cod and steak & ale pie, while a typical selection from the evening menu might include stuffed mushrooms, salmon fillet with a chive & prawn sauce and beef in a giant Yorkshire pudding. The en suite accommodation, including a splendid four-poster room, is available all year round apart from the first two weeks in November, offering a comfortable base for a walking, fishing or sporting holiday or for discovering the many scenic and historic delights of the region.

493 THE COACH HOUSE INN

Rosedale Abbey, nr Pickering,
North Yorkshire YO18 8SD
☎ 01751 417208
e-mail: info@coachhouseinn.co.uk
🌐 www.coachhouseinn.co.uk

The welcome from hosts Howard and Daphne Hebron is always warm and friendly at the **Coach House Inn**, which was built as a garage 100 years ago and has been an inn for nearly 30 years. Black Sheep and Mars Magic from the nearby Wold Top Brewery are the regular

cask ales, and lunchtime and evenings bring a fine variety of home-cooked dishes accompanied by well-chosen wines. Lunchtime choices might include sandwiches, speciality burgers and tasty delights like hot ham & mustard potato cakes or lager-battered chicken, while the dinner menu runs from the always popular Desperate Dan steak pie to ham & eggs, braised lamb steak, curries, traditional fish & chips and roast salmon stuffed with salsa verde. The pub is very much at the heart of the community, staging regular charity quizzes and live entertainment evenings. The hosts are experts in organising functions and parties and can also provide outside bars, marquees and live music or discos. Rosedale Abbey, which stands nine miles northwest of Pickering off the A170, is the largest settlement in Rosedale, the charming steep-sided valley of the River Severn. A good way to build up a thirst before a visit to the Coach House is to take a walk on the moors to Ralph Cross, erected in medieval times as a guide for travellers.

494 THE GREYHOUND INN

Hackforth, nr Bedale,
North Yorkshire DL8 1PB
☎ 01748 811415

The **Greyhound Inn** started life as a farmhouse 300 years ago, later becoming an ale house, then a coaching inn, and now a public house with real ales, excellent food and neat, spacious overnight accommodation. Paul and Paula Milsom, who had previously owned and run a B&B farmhouse in Normandy, took over the Greyhound in 2007 and set about realising once again its full potential. The proximity of the A1 (leave at Catterick or Leeming Bar) makes it an excellent refreshment stop for motorists, who mingle happily with the locals and tourists to create a very sociable ambience in the traditionally appointed bar. Four real ales include the Yorkshire brews of Black Sheep and Theakstons (both brewed in Masham) and local meat and game feature on a good choice of home cooking served lunchtime and evening. For guests taking a break in this pleasant part of the world the Greyhound has three well-appointed en suite bedrooms let on a Bed & Breakfast basis. The setting is peaceful and attractive, and there are many opportunities for enjoying the scenic surroundings, for walking in the Dales, for game and coarse fishing and for a wide range of other outdoor activities. Catterick races and the Wensleydale Railway are also nearby.

Main Street, Rainton, nr Thirsk,
North Yorkshire YO7 3PH
☎ 01845 577284

Five miles southwest of Thirsk and a similar distance northeast of Ripon, the **Lamb Inn** at Rainton is easily reached from J49 of the A1 (M), the A61 and the A168. Whatever direction you're coming from, you'll find a super village inn with affable, go-ahead hosts in Steven and Bev Bannister, who took over here in December 2007 after six years in the licensed trade, mainly in West Yorkshire.

The inn dates in part from the late-18th century and the interior is full of period charm and character, with old beams and a real fire to warm you up on cold days. Once again the social hub of Rainton, a village with a pretty green and a maypole, the Lamb is open lunchtime and evening and all day on Friday, Saturday and Sunday, and all day every day in the summer. Tetleys, Black Sheep and two guests make up the real ale list, supported by a full range of other drinks. The news is spreading rapidly about the quality of the cooking, and the printed menu and the specials board make excellent use of the best seasonal produce, including locally reared meat and poultry and fish from Whitby. The steak & ale pie is proving to be one of the most popular dishes, and cheesecake is just one of several delicious desserts.

Children are welcome, and the Lamb has a large beer garden and plenty of off-road parking.

496 DALEGARTH AND THE GHYLL HOLIDAY COTTAGES

Buckden, nr Skipton,
North Yorkshire BD23 5JU
☎ 01756 760877 Fax: 01756 760877
e-mail: info@dalegarth.co.uk
🌐 www.dalegarth.co.uk

Dalgarth and the Ghyll Country Holiday Cottages provide a charming base for a break in the heart of the picturesque Yorkshire Dales National Park. This unique cluster of cottages was designed and built by David and Susan Lusted, who have managed this enterprise for more than 25 years. **Dalgarth** comprises ten handsome cottages in their own private cul-de-sac in the landscaped grounds of an extensive old walled kitchen garden, bounded on one side by the stream known as Buckden Beck. All these cottages are centrally heated having a double and a twin bedroom, bathroom, fully fitted kitchen including a

dishwasher and freezer, a spacious lounge-dining area with a three-piece suite, a dining suite and a double sofa bed that allows them to sleep up to six guests in great comfort. Seven of the cottages (Type A) have a sauna room attached to the downstairs bathroom and an en suite bathroom for the upstairs bedroom. The south-facing first-floor lounge has sliding picture windows leading on to a balcony that commands glorious views over the River Wharfe and the fells beyond. To the rear of Dalgarth are an indoor heated swimming pool, a combined mini-gym and games room, a laundry room and a roomy furnished patio. Two hundred yards away, at the foot of Buckden Ghyll, **The Ghyll** comprises three cottages designed to sleep up to 4 (Dipper and Swallow) or 6 (Heron).

All are furnished and decorated to the highest standard, with special consideration for guests with mobility difficulties. Each has a level main entrance, and a door and ramp lead from the south-facing lounge on to a patio with superb views. Car parking is adjacent to a loggia that gives access to a comfortable lounge-dining room and on to a superbly appointed kitchen and also to a double bedroom with en suite bathroom. The cottages provide the perfect base for a walking

holiday or a tour of the Dales; Buckden, which marks the beginning of Wharfedale proper, offers a wide variety of walks, from riverside strolls along the Dales Way to the challenge of the 2,300 feet Buckden Pike. Guests at the cottages are full of praise for the setting, the comfort and the amenities; one guest writes that 'it's like staying in the Garden of Eden when you're in town all year'; another: 'whatever time of year you come here, there's always somewhere new to walk or visit, and the scenery changes week by week'.

TRAVEL PUBLISHING ORDER FORM

To order any of our publications just fill in the payment details below and complete the order form. For orders of less than 4 copies please add £1.00 per book for postage and packing. Orders over 4 copies are P & P free.

Name:

Address:

Tel no:

Please Complete Either:

I enclose a cheque for £ _____ made payable to Travel Publishing Ltd
Or:

Card No: Expiry Date:

Signature:

Please either send, telephone, fax or e-mail your order to:
Travel Publishing Ltd, 64-66 Ebrington Street, Plymouth, Devon PL4 9AQ
Tel: 01752 276660   Fax: 01752 276699   e-mail: info@travelpublishing.co.uk

	Price	Quantity		Price	Quantity
HIDDEN PLACES REGIONAL TITLES			**COUNTRY PUBS AND INNS**		
Cornwall	£8.99	....	Cornwall	£5.99	....
Devon	£8.99	....	Devon	£7.99	....
Dorset, Hants			Sussex	£5.99	....
& Isle of Wight	£8.99	....	Wales	£8.99	....
East Anglia	£8.99	....	Yorkshire	£7.99	....
Lake District & Cumbria	£8.99	....	**COUNTRY LIVING RURAL GUIDES**		
Northumberland & Durham	£8.99	....			
Peak District and Derbyshire	£8.99	....	East Anglia	£10.99	....
Yorkshire	£8.99	....	Heart of England	£10.99	....
HIDDEN PLACES NATIONAL TITLES			Ireland	£11.99	
			North East	£10.99	
England	£11.99	....	North West	£10.99	....
Ireland	£11.99	....	Scotland	£11.99	....
Scotland	£11.99	....	South of England	£10.99	
Wales	£11.99	....	South East of England	£10.99	....
OTHER TITLES			Wales	£11.99	
			West Country	£10.99	....
Off the Motorway	£11.99	....	**TOTAL QUANTITY:**		
Garden Centres & Nurseries	£11.99	....			
			POST & PACKING:		
			TOTAL VALUE:		

READER REACTION FORM

The *Travel Publishing* research team would like to receive reader's comments on any visitor attractions or places reviewed in the book and also recommendations for suitable entries to be included in the next edition. This will help ensure that the *Country Living series of Guides* continues to provide its readers with useful information on the more interesting, unusual or unique features of each attraction or place ensuring that their visit to the local area is an enjoyable and stimulating experience. To provide your comments or recommendations would you please complete the forms below and overleaf as indicated and send to:

The Research Department, Travel Publishing Ltd,
64-66 Ebrington Street, Plymouth, Devon PL4 9AQ

Your Name:

Your Address:

Your Telephone Number:

Please tick as appropriate:

Comments ☐   Recommendation ☐

Name of Establishment:

Address:

Telephone Number:

Name of Contact:

READER REACTION FORM

COMMENT OR REASON FOR RECOMMENDATION:

....

....

....

....

....

....

....

....

....

....

....

....

....

....

....

....

....

....

READER REACTION FORM

The *Travel Publishing* research team would like to receive reader's comments on any visitor attractions or places reviewed in the book and also recommendations for suitable entries to be included in the next edition. This will help ensure that the *Country Living series of Guides* continues to provide its readers with useful information on the more interesting, unusual or unique features of each attraction or place ensuring that their visit to the local area is an enjoyable and stimulating experience. To provide your comments or recommendations would you please complete the forms below and overleaf as indicated and send to:

The Research Department, Travel Publishing Ltd,
64-66 Ebrington Street, Plymouth, Devon PL4 9AQ

Your Name:

Your Address:

Your Telephone Number:

Please tick as appropriate:

Comments ☐   Recommendation ☐

Name of Establishment:

Address:

Telephone Number:

Name of Contact:

READER REACTION FORM

COMMENT OR REASON FOR RECOMMENDATION:

....
....
....
....
....
....
....
....
....
....
....
....
....
....
....
....
....
....
....

READER REACTION FORM

The *Travel Publishing* research team would like to receive reader's comments on any visitor attractions or places reviewed in the book and also recommendations for suitable entries to be included in the next edition. This will help ensure that the *Country Living series of Guides* continues to provide its readers with useful information on the more interesting, unusual or unique features of each attraction or place ensuring that their visit to the local area is an enjoyable and stimulating experience. To provide your comments or recommendations would you please complete the forms below and overleaf as indicated and send to:

**The Research Department, Travel Publishing Ltd,
64-66 Ebrington Street, Plymouth, Devon PL4 9AQ**

Your Name:

Your Address:

Your Telephone Number:

Please tick as appropriate:

Comments ☐   Recommendation ☐

Name of Establishment:

Address:

Telephone Number:

Name of Contact:

READER REACTION FORM

COMMENT OR REASON FOR RECOMMENDATION:

....
....
....
....
....
....
....
....
....
....
....
....
....
....
....
....
....
....
....

READER REACTION FORM

The *Travel Publishing* research team would like to receive reader's comments on any visitor attractions or places reviewed in the book and also recommendations for suitable entries to be included in the next edition. This will help ensure that the *Country Living series of Guides* continues to provide its readers with useful information on the more interesting, unusual or unique features of each attraction or place ensuring that their visit to the local area is an enjoyable and stimulating experience. To provide your comments or recommendations would you please complete the forms below and overleaf as indicated and send to:

The Research Department, Travel Publishing Ltd,
64-66 Ebrington Street, Plymouth, Devon PL4 9AQ

Your Name:

Your Address:

Your Telephone Number:

Please tick as appropriate:

Comments ☐   Recommendation ☐

Name of Establishment:

Address:

Telephone Number:

Name of Contact:

READER REACTION FORM

COMMENT OR REASON FOR RECOMMENDATION:

Towns, Villages and Places of Interest

713

Index of Advertisers

FOOD AND DRINK

INDEX OF ADVERTISERS